Londonderry
LONDONDERRY
ANTRIM

**NORTHERN IRELAND**

TYRONE

BELFAST

DOWN

ARMAGH

MONAGHAN

CAVAN

Dundalk

LOUTH

**MIDLANDS**

EATH

MEATH

**DUBLIN**

KILDARE

WICKLOW

AOIS

CARLOW

**SOUTHEAST IRELAND**

KILKENNY

WEXFORD

Waterford

Wexford

**NORTH**
*Pages 246–277*

**NORTH OF THE LIFFEY**
*Pages 82–91*

DUBLIN CITY CENTRE

NORTH OF THE LIFFEY

LIFFEY

SOUTHWEST DUBLIN

SOUTHEAST DUBLIN

**SOUTHWEST DUBLIN**
*Pages 70–81*

**SOUTHEAST DUBLIN**
*Pages 54–69*

**THE MIDLANDS**
*Pages 228–245*

**SOUTHEAST IRELAND**
*Pages 116–143*

# EYEWITNESS TRAVEL GUIDES

# IRELAND

# EYEWITNESS TRAVEL GUIDES
# IRELAND

*Main Contributors:*
## LISA GERARD-SHARP AND TIM PERRY

**DORLING KINDERSLEY**
LONDON • NEW YORK • MUNICH
MELBOURNE • DELHI

**www.dk.com**

LONDON, NEW YORK,
MELBOURNE, MUNICH AND DELHI
www.dk.com

PROJECT EDITOR Ferdie McDonald
ART EDITOR Lisa Kosky
EDITORS Maggie Crowley, Simon Farbrother, Emily Hatchwell,
Seán O'Connell, Jane Simmonds
DESIGNERS Joy FitzSimmons, Jaki Grosvenor,
Katie Peacock, Jan Richter
RESEARCHERS John Breslin, Andrea Holmes
PICTURE RESEARCHERS Sue Mennell, Christine Rista
DTP DESIGNERS Samantha Borland, Adam Moore

CONTRIBUTORS
Una Carlin, Polly Phillimore, Susan Poole, Martin Walters

PHOTOGRAPHERS
Joe Cornish, Tim Daly, Alan Williams

ILLUSTRATORS
Draughtsman Maps, Maltings Partnership, Robbie Polley

Reproduced by Colourscan, Singapore
Printed and bound by L. Rex Printing Company, China

First published in Great Britain in 1995
by Dorling Kindersley Limited
80 Strand, London WC2R 0RL
**Reprinted with revisions 1996 (twice), 1997, 1999,
2000, 2001, 2002, 2003**

Copyright 1995, 2003 © Dorling Kindersley Limited, London
A Penguin Company

A CIP CATALOGUE RECORD IS AVAILABLE FROM THE BRITISH LIBRARY.
ISBN 1 4053 0205 4

---

**The information in this Dorling Kindersley Travel Guide
is checked annually.**
Every effort has been made to ensure that this book is as up-to-date
as possible at the time of going to press. Some details, however,
such as telephone numbers, opening hours, prices, gallery hanging
arrangements and travel information, are liable to change. The
publishers cannot accept responsibility for any consequences arising
from the use of this book, nor for any material on third-party
websites, and cannot guarantee that any website address in this
book will be a suitable source of travel information. We value the
views and suggestions of our readers highly. Please write to:
Publisher, DK Eyewitness Travel Guides,
Dorling Kindersley, 80 Strand, London, Great Britain WC2R 0RL.

---

# CONTENTS

## HOW TO USE
## THIS GUIDE *6*

An evangelical symbol from the
*Book of Kells (see p62)*

## INTRODUCING
## IRELAND

### PUTTING IRELAND
### ON THE MAP *10*

### A PORTRAIT OF
### IRELAND *12*

### THE HISTORY OF
### IRELAND *28*

### IRELAND THROUGH
### THE YEAR *46*

## DUBLIN AREA
## BY AREA

### DUBLIN
### AT A GLANCE *52*

Georgian doorway in Fitzwilliam
Square, Dublin *(see p67)*

SOUTHEAST DUBLIN 54

SOUTHWEST DUBLIN 70

NORTH OF THE LIFFEY 82

FURTHER AFIELD 92

ENTERTAINMENT IN DUBLIN 102

DUBLIN STREET FINDER 108

**IRELAND REGION BY REGION**

Lighthouse at Spanish Point near Mizen Head *(see p159)*

## TRAVELLERS' NEEDS

WHERE TO STAY 280

RESTAURANTS, CAFÉS AND PUBS 302

SHOPPING IN IRELAND 322

ENTERTAINMENT IN IRELAND 328

## SURVIVAL GUIDE

PRACTICAL INFORMATION 338

TRAVEL INFORMATION 350

GENERAL INDEX 362

ROAD MAP INSIDE BACK COVER

Detail of the Chorus Gate at Powerscourt *(see pp126–7)*

Façade of a pub in Dingle *(see p149)*

IRELAND AT A GLANCE 114

SOUTHEAST IRELAND 116

CORK AND KERRY 144

THE LOWER SHANNON 172

THE WEST OF IRELAND 192

NORTHWEST IRELAND 212

THE MIDLANDS 228

NORTHERN IRELAND 246

Bunratty Castle in County Clare *(see pp184–5)*

# HOW TO USE THIS GUIDE

THIS GUIDE helps you to get the most from your visit to Ireland. It provides both expert recommendations and detailed practical information. *Introducing Ireland* maps the country and sets it in its historical and cultural context. The seven regional chapters, plus *Dublin Area* by *Area*, contain descriptions of all the important sights, with maps, pictures and illustrations. Restaurant and hotel recommendations can be found in *Travellers' Needs*. The *Survival Guide* has tips on everything from the telephone system to transport both in the Republic and in Northern Ireland.

## DUBLIN AREA BY AREA

Central Dublin is divided into three sightseeing areas. Each has its own chapter, which opens with a list of the sights described. A fourth chapter, *Further Afield*, covers the suburbs and County Dublin. Sights are numbered and plotted on an *Area Map*. The descriptions of each sight follow the map's numerical order, making sights easy to locate within the chapter.

**Sights at a Glance** lists the chapter's sights by category: Churches, Museums and Galleries, Historic Buildings, Parks and Gardens.

**2 Street-by-Street Map**
*This gives a bird's-eye view of the key area in each chapter.*

**A suggested route** for a walk is shown in red.

**All pages** relating to Dublin have red thumb tabs.

**A locator map** shows where you are in relation to other areas of the city centre.

**1 Area Map**
*For easy reference, the sights are numbered and located on a map. Sights in the city centre are also shown on the* Dublin Street Finder *on pages 110–11.*

**Stars** indicate the sights that no visitor should miss.

**3 Detailed information**
*The sights in Dublin are described individually with addresses, telephone numbers and information on opening hours and admission charges.*

**Story boxes** highlight noteworthy features of the sights.

### 1 Introduction
*The landscape, history and character of each region is described here, showing how the area has developed over the centuries and what it offers to the visitor today.*

**IRELAND REGION BY REGION**
Apart from Dublin, Ireland has been divided into seven regions, each of which has a separate chapter. The most interesting towns and places to visit in each area have been numbered on a *Pictorial Map*.

**Each region** of Ireland can be quickly identified by its colour coding, shown on the inside front cover.

### 2 Pictorial Map
*This shows the road network and gives an illustrated overview of the whole region. All interesting places to visit are numbered and there are also useful tips on getting around the region by car and train.*

**Getting Around** gives tips on travel within the region.

### 3 Detailed information
*All the important towns and other places to visit are described individually. They are listed in order, following the numbering on the Pictorial Map. Within each town or city, there is detailed information on important buildings and other sights.*

**The Visitors' Checklist** provides all the practical information you will need to plan your visit for all the top sights.

### 4 Ireland's top sights
*These are given two or more full pages. Historic buildings are dissected to reveal their interiors. The most interesting towns or city centres are shown in a bird's-eye view, with sights picked out and described.*

# INTRODUCING
# IRELAND

PUTTING IRELAND ON THE MAP 10-11
A PORTRAIT OF IRELAND 12-27
THE HISTORY OF IRELAND 28-45
IRELAND THROUGH THE YEAR 46-49

# Putting Ireland on the Map

THE ISLAND OF IRELAND covers an area of 84,430 sq km (32,598 sq miles). Lying in the Atlantic Ocean to the northwest of mainland Europe, it is separated from Great Britain by the Irish Sea. The Republic of Ireland takes up 85 per cent of the island with a population of 3.5 million. Northern Ireland, part of the United Kingdom, has 1.5 million people. Dublin is the capital of the Republic and has good international communications.

EUROPE

NORWAY

SWEDEN

DENMARK

NORTHERN IRELAND

REPUBLIC OF IRELAND

UNITED KINGDOM

NETHERLANDS

GERMANY

BELGIUM

LUXEMBOURG

CZECH REPUBLIC

FRANCE

SWITZERLAND   AUSTRIA

SPAIN

ITALY

### Europe

*Most visitors to Ireland come through Dublin, either by air or on the ferry to Dun Laoghaire or Dublin Port. The main ferry routes are from Wales, Scotland and France. There are also international flights to Shannon, Belfast and Cork airports. Many European flights are routed via Great Britain, but flight times are generally only around an hour on from British airports.*

0 kilometres                 100

0 miles              50

## KEY

✈  Airport

⛴  Ferry port

⛴  Fast ferry port

▬  Motorway

▬  Major road

—  Railway line

Londonderry (Derry)

Donegal

N O

I R

Lower Lough Erne

Enniskillen   A4

Sligo   N16   Upper Lough Erne

Knock

R E P U B L I

I R E L A N

Athlone

Galway

Lough Mask

Lough Corrib

Lough Allen

Lough Ree

Shannon

Lough Derg

Shannon   Limerick   Kilker

Cashel

Suir

Tralee

Blackwater

Killarney

Lee   Cork

Bantry

Roscoff

**GREATER DUBLIN**

Swords
Malahide
N1
N3
Finglas
Dublin Airport
N2
Royal Canal
M50
Glasnevin
Liffey N4
Marino
Howth
Lucan
Kilmainham
Dublin
Grand Canal
Clondalkin
Ballsbridge
Dublin Bay
Rathmines
M50
Blackrock
N81
0 km        5
Dundrum
N11
Dun Laoghaire
0 miles       5

**Greater Dublin**
*Nearly one third of the Republic's population
lives in Dublin. Nevertheless the city is relatively
uncongested and access to the centre from the
ports and airport is easy outside the rush hour.*

Islay
SCOTLAND
Arran
Glasgow
A83
A82
Troon
A77
Campbeltown
North Channel
Ballycastle
Coleraine
A37
A6
A2
A26
A29
A36
Cairnryan
A75
Larne
Stranraer
'HERN
Lough Neagh
AND
M10
Belfast
M1
A1
A2
'magh
A4
A3
Newry
A2
Isle of Man
ENGLAND
A595
Douglas
A65
N2
Dundalk
Heysham
OF
M6
Fleetwood
Irish Sea
M62
Manchester
Liverpool
Boyne
M3
M1
Mostyn
M62
DUBLIN
M56
N7
Dun Laoghaire
Holyhead
A5
A55
M6
M7
N9
Liffey
N11
A5
Carlow
A487
A470
M54
N80
Staney
N11
Cherbourg
WALES
M50
N25
Wexford
'aterford
Rosslare
A487
Fishguard
St George's Channel
A40
A477
M4
M5
Roscoff/Cherbourg
Pembroke
Swansea
M4
CARDIFF
Bristol
Bristol Channel
M5

# A PORTRAIT OF IRELAND

*M*ANY VISITORS *see Ireland as a lush green island, full of thatched cottages, pubs, music, wit and poetry. Like all stereotypes, this image of the country has a basis in truth and the tourist industry helps sustain it. The political and economic reality is, of course, rather less ideal, but the relaxed good humour of the people still makes Ireland a most welcoming place to visit.*

Ireland, at least for the time being, is a divided island. History and religion created two hostile communities in North and South. The IRA ceasefire of 1997 and the subsequent Good Friday Agreement brought new hope, however. John Hume of the SDLP and David Trimble of the Ulster Unionist Party were jointly awarded the Nobel prize for peace for their work in the peace process, and the inaugural meeting of the Northern Ireland Assembly took place on 1 July 1998.

Ireland has had more than its fair share of wars and disasters, culminating in the Great Famine of 1845–8, since when poverty and emigration

**Cathleen ni Houlihan, personification of Ireland**

have been part of the Irish way of life. More people of Irish descent live in the USA than in Ireland itself. Suffering and martyrdom in the cause of independence also play an important part in the Irish consciousness. The heroine of WB Yeats's play *Cathleen ni Houlihan* inspires young men to lay down their lives for Ireland. Her image appeared on the first bank note issued by the newly created Irish Free State in 1922.

Yet, the Irish retain their easy-going attitude to life, with a young, highly educated population working hard to make its way in today's European Union. In the Republic, 40 per cent of the population is aged under 25.

Façade of Trinity College, Dublin, the Republic's most prestigious university

◁ Thatching a traditional cottage in Adare, County Limerick

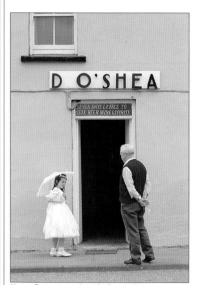
Young first communicant in County Kerry

Despite its high birth rate, rural Ireland is sparsely populated. The Industrial Revolution of the 19th century barely touched the South and for much of the 20th century the Republic seemed an old-fashioned place, poorer than almost all its fellow members of the European Union.

### ECONOMIC DEVELOPMENT

In recent years, tax breaks and low inflation have attracted more foreign investment to the Republic and many multinationals, especially computing and chemical companies, have subsidiaries here. Ireland joined the single European currency on 1 January 1999, and the Republic's economy continues to grow while unemployment is falling. Another important industry is tourism. The South receives over 3 million visitors a year and visitors to the North are now steadily increasing.

Traditionally, Northern Ireland had far more industry than the South, but during the 25 years of the Troubles, old heavy

**Traditional Irish dancing**

industries, such as ship-building, declined and new investors were scared away. However, the election of members to the new Northern Ireland Assembly in June 1998 ushered in a new political and economic era for the North. For both parts of Ireland, geography is still a barrier to prosperity. Located on the periphery of Europe, the island is isolated from its main markets and thus saddled with high transport costs. Fortunately, subsidies from the EU have helped improve the infrastructure in the Republic.

### RELIGION AND POLITICS

The influence of Catholicism is strong. In the Republic, the Church runs most schools, along with some hospitals and social services. Irish Catholicism runs the gamut from missionary zeal to simple piety. According to some

Pavement artist on O'Connell Street, Dublin

estimates, over 90 per cent of the population goes to Mass. Religion plays an important role in the politics of the Republic and moral conservatism is evident in attitudes to divorce, contraception, abortion and homosexuality.

The election of liberal lawyer Mary Robinson as President in 1990, the first woman to hold the post, was seen as a sign of more enlightened times by many people, an attitude reinforced by the election of Mary McAleese as her successor in 1998. A new political climate has favoured the quiet spread of feminism

Traditional farming: a field of haystacks overlooking Clew Bay, County Mayo

and challenged the old paternalism of Irish politics, not only in social issues but also in helping break down the clannish cronyism of the traditional parties Fianna Fáil and Fine Gael.

### LANGUAGE AND CULTURE

Ireland was a Gaelic-speaking nation until the 16th century, since when the language has declined. Today, however, the Republic is officially bilingual. Knowledge of Irish is a requirement for university entrance and a career in the public sector, although only 11 per cent of the population speaks Gaelic fluently.

Irish culture, on the other hand, is in no danger of being eroded. The people have a genuine love of old folk legends and epic poetry and songs. Festivals, whether dedicated to St Patrick or James Joyce, pubs or oysters, salmon or sailing, are an important part of community life. Music is a national passion – from the rock of U2 and the Cranberries to the folk music of Clannad, the Chieftains and Mary Black.

Connemara pony show

Another national passion is horse racing. Ireland's breeders and trainers are masters of their trade and enjoy astonishing international success for such a small country. Other sports are followed with equal intensity, as witnessed during the 1994 football World Cup. Drinking also plays an important part in Irish culture: social life centres on the pub and the "crack" (convivial chat) to be enjoyed there. When the Republic introduced stricter drink-driving laws in 1994, many rural publicans said traditional Irish society would collapse. Given the attachment to Guinness, gossip and music, this is extremely unlikely.

Matt Molloy's pub in Westport, County Mayo

# The Landscape and Wildlife of Ireland

THE LANDSCAPE is one of the Ireland's greatest attractions. It varies from bogs and lakes in the central lowlands to mountains and rocky islands in the west. Between these two extremes, the island has abundant lush, green pastureland, the result of plentiful rainfall, but little natural woodland.

**Corncrake**

Parts of the far west, where the land is farmed by traditional methods, are havens for threatened wildlife, including the corncrake, which needs undisturbed hay fields in which to nest.

## THE FAUNA OF IRELAND

Many animals (including snakes) did not make it to Ireland before the Irish Sea rose after the Ice Age.

**Natterjack toad**

Other surprising absentees are the mole, weasel and common toad (the natterjack, however, can be seen). The wood mouse is the only small native rodent, but the once common red squirrel has now been virtually taken over by the grey.

## ROCKY COASTS

The Dingle Peninsula (see pp150–51) is part of a series of rocky promontories and inlets created when sea levels rose at the end of the Ice Age. Cliffs and islands offer many sites for sea birds, with some enormous colonies, such as the gannets of Little Skellig (pp156–7). The chough

**Chough**

still breeds on cliffs in the extreme west. Elsewhere in Europe, this rare species of crow is declining in numbers.

*Thrift grows in cushion-like clumps, producing its papery pink flowerheads from spring right through to autumn.*

*Sea campion is a low-growing plant. Its large white flowers brighten up many a cliff top and seaside shingle bank.*

## LAKES, RIVERS AND WETLANDS

This watery landscape around Lough Oughter is typical of the lakelands of the River Erne (pp262–3). Rainfall is high throughout the year, which results in many wetlands,

**Great crested grebe**

especially along the Shannon (pp176–7) and the Erne. The elegant great crested grebe breeds mainly on the larger lakes in the north.

*Water lobelia grows in the shallows of stony lakes. Its leaves remain below the water, while the pale lilac flowers are borne on leafless stems above the surface.*

*Fleabane, once used to repel fleas, thrives in wet meadows and marshes. It has yellow flowers like dandelions.*

**Grey seals** *are a common sight in the waters off the Atlantic coast, feeding on fish and occasionally on sea birds.*

**Otters** *are more likely to be seen in the shallow seas off rocky coasts than in rivers and lakes, though they live in both habitats.*

**Pine martens***, though mainly nocturnal, may be spotted in daytime during the summer.*

**Red deer** *have been introduced into many areas, notably the hills of Connemara.*

## MOUNTAIN AND BLANKET BOG

## PASTURELAND

As well as the raised bogs of the central lowlands *(p244)*, much of Ireland's mountainous ground, particularly in the west, is covered by blanket bog such as that seen here in Connemara *(pp198–201)*. On drier upland sites this grades into heather moor and poor grassland. The wheatear, which inhabits rocky scree and heathland, is a restless bird with an unmistakeable white rump. It flits about, dipping and bobbing in pursuit of flies.

**Wheatear**

Rolling pastureland with grazing livestock, as seen here in the foot-hills of the Wicklow Mountains *(pp130–31)*, is a very common sight throughout Ireland. The traditional farming methods employed in many parts of the island (particularly in the west) are of great benefit to wildlife. Rooks, for example, which feed on worms and insect larvae found in pasture, are very common.

**Rook**

**Bog myrtle** *is an aromatic shrub, locally common in Ireland's bogs. Its leaves can be used to flavour drinks.*

**Meadow vetchling** *uses its tendrils to clamber up grasses and other plants. It has clusters of pretty pale yellow flowers.*

**Bogbean***, a plant found in fens and wet bogland, has attractive white flowers splashed with pink. Its leaves were once used as a cure for boils.*

**Marsh thistle** *is a common flower of wet meadows and damp woodland. It is a tall species with small, purple flowerheads.*

# Architecture in Ireland

**Window of an Irish cottage**

IRELAND'S TURBULENT HISTORY has done incalculable damage to its architectural heritage. Cromwell's forces, in particular, destroyed scores of castles, monasteries and towns in their three-year campaign against the Irish in the mid-17th century. However, many fascinating buildings and sites remain, with Iron Age forts being the earliest surviving settlements. Christianity in Ireland gave rise to mon-asteries, churches and round towers; conflict between Anglo-Norman barons and Irish chieftains created castles and tower houses. The later landlord class built luxurious country mansions, while their labourers had to make do with basic, one-roomed cottages.

### LOCATOR MAP

- ☐ Iron Age forts
- ☐ Round towers
- ☐ Tower houses
- ☐ Georgian country houses

## IRON AGE FORT

*Ring forts* (raths) were Iron Age farmsteads enclosed by an earth bank, a timber fence and a ditch to protect against cattle-raiders. Inside, people lived in huts with a souterrain (underground passage) for storage and refuge. Some were in use as late as the 17th century, but all you can usually see today are low circular mounds. In the west, stone was used for cahers (stone ring forts) and promontory forts (semi-circular forts built on cliff tops using the sea as a natural defence).

**Thatched hut**

**Entrance**     **Souterrain**

## ROUND TOWER

**Lookout window**  **Conical roof**

*Round towers*, often over 30m (100 ft) tall, were built between the 10th and 12th centuries on monastic sites. They were bell towers, used as places of refuge and to store valuable manuscripts. The entrance, which could be as high as 4 m (13 ft) above ground, was reached by a ladder that was hauled up from the inside. Other moveable ladders connected the tower's wooden floors.

**Wooden floor**

**Moveable ladder**

## TOWER HOUSE

**Machicolation**

**Outer wall around bawn**

**Spiral staircase**

*Tower houses* were small castles or fortified residences built between the 15th and 17th centuries. The tall square house was often surrounded by a stone wall forming a bawn (enclosure), used for defence and as a cattle pen. Machicolations (projecting parapets from which to drop missiles) were sited at the top of the house.

## COTTAGE

*One-roomed cottages*, thatched or slate-roofed, are still a common feature of the Irish landscape. Built of local stone with small windows to retain heat, the cottages were inhabited by farm workers or smallholders.

**Bog-oak timbers**     **Thatched, clay-lined chimney**

**Clay floor**

## IRON AGE FORTS

①  Staigue Fort *p156*
②  Dún Aonghasa *p206*
③  Craggaunowen *p182*
④  Grianán of Ailigh *pp218–19*
⑤  Hill of Tara *p240*

## ROUND TOWERS

⑥  Kilmacduagh *p204*
⑦  Ardmore *p137*
⑧  Clonmacnoise *pp242–3*
⑨  Devenish Island *p263*
⑩  Kilkenny *pp136*
⑪  Glendalough *pp132–3*

## TOWER HOUSES

⑫  Aughnanure Castle *p201*
⑬  Thoor Ballylee *pp204–5*
⑭  Knappogue Castle *p181*
⑮  Blarney Castle *p163*
⑯  Donegal Castle *p222*

## GEORGIAN COUNTRY HOUSES

⑰  Strokestown Park House *pp210–11*
⑱  Castle Coole *p264*
⑲  Emo Court *p245*
⑳  Russborough House *pp124–5*
㉑  Castletown House *pp122–3*

**The well-preserved round tower at Ardmore**

## GEORGIAN COUNTRY HOUSE

Wing containing family rooms · Doric pillar · Balustrade · Pediment · Main house containing formal rooms · Blind colonnade · Portico · Ionic pillar

*Between the 1720s and 1800, prosperous landlords commissioned palatial country mansions in the Palladian and Neo-Classical styles popular in England over that period. Castle Coole (above) has a Palladian layout, with the main house in the centre and a colonnade on either side leading to a small pavilion. The Neo-Classical influence can be seen in the unadorned façade and the Doric columns of the colonnades. Noted architects of Irish country houses include Richard Castle (1690–1751) and James Wyatt (1746–1813).*

## STUCCO

Stucco (decorative relief plasterwork), popular in the 18th century, is found in many Georgian country houses as well as town houses and public buildings. The Italian Francini brothers were particularly sought after for their intricate stuccowork (notably at Castletown and Russborough) as was Irish craftsman Michael Stapleton (Trinity College, Dublin and Dublin Writers Museum).

**Trompe l'oeil detail at Emo Court**

**Ceiling at Dublin Writers Museum**

**Stucco portrait at Castletown House**

**Stuccowork at Russborough House**

## OTHER TERMS USED IN THIS GUIDE

**Beehive hut:** Circular stone building with a domed roof created by corbelling (laying a series of stones so that each projects beyond the one below).

**Cashel:** Stone ring fort.

**Crannog:** Defensive, partly artificial island on a lake. Huts were often built on crannogs (*see p31*).

**Curtain wall:** Outer wall of a castle, usually incorporating towers at intervals.

**Hiberno-Romanesque:** Style of church architecture with rounded arches highly decorated with geometric designs and human and animal forms. Also called Irish-Romanesque.

**Motte and bailey:** Raised mound (motte) topped with a wooden tower, surrounded by a heavily fenced space (bailey). Built by the Normans in the 12th century, they were quickly erected in time of battle.

**Tympanum:** Decorated space over a door or window.

# Literary Ireland

**F**OR A LAND the size of Ireland to have produced four Nobel prizewinners in Shaw, Yeats, Beckett and Séamus Heaney is a considerable feat. Yet it is not easy to speak of an "Irish literary tradition" as the concept embraces rural and urban experiences, Protestant and Catholic traditions and the Gaelic and English languages. Irish fiction today, as in the past, is characterized by a sense of community and history, a love of storytelling and a zest for language.

**A first edition of *Ulysses***

WB Yeats – Ireland's most famous poet

The Blasket Islands, which provided inspiration for several writers

## GAELIC LITERATURE

**I**RISH LITERATURE proclaims itself the oldest vernacular literature in Western Europe, dating back to early monastic times when Celtic folklore and sagas such as the epics of Cuchulainn *(see p24)* were written down for the first time. The disappearance of Gaelic literature followed the demise, in the 17th century, of the Irish aristocracy for whom it was written. Gaelic literature has had several revivals. Peig Sayers is famous for her accounts of the harsh life on the Blasket Islands *(see p150)* in the early 20th century.

## ANGLO-IRISH LITERATURE

**T**HE COLLAPSE of Gaelic culture and the Protestant Ascendancy led to English being the dominant language. Most literature was based around the privileged classes.

An early Anglo-Irish writer was satirist Jonathan Swift *(see p80)*, author of *Gulliver's Travels*, who was born in Dublin in 1667 of English parents. Anglo-Irish literature was strong in drama, the entertainment of the cultured classes, and owed little to Irish settings or sensibilities. By the 1700s, Ireland was producing an inordinate number of leading playwrights, many of whom were more at home in London. These included Oliver Goldsmith, remembered for his comedy *She Stoops to Conquer*, and Richard Brinsley Sheridan, whose plays include *The School for Scandal*. Near the end of the century, Maria Edgeworth set a precedent with novels such as *Castle Rackrent*, based on the class divide in Irish society.

**Novelist Maria Edgeworth**

The 19th century saw an exodus to England of Irish playwrights, including Oscar Wilde, who entered Oxford University in 1874 and later became the darling of London society with plays such as *The Importance of Being Earnest*. George Bernard Shaw *(see p98)*, writer of *St Joan* and *Pygmalion*, also made London his home. This dramatist, critic, socialist and pacifist continued to write until well into the 20th century.

Playwright George Bernard Shaw

## 20TH-CENTURY WRITERS

**I**N 1898, WB Yeats and Lady Gregory founded Dublin's Abbey Theatre *(see p86)*. Its opening, in 1904, heralded the Irish Revival, which focused on national and local themes. Playwright John Millington Synge drew inspiration from a love of the Aran Islands and Irish folklore, but the "immoral language" of his *Playboy of the Western World* caused a riot when first performed at the Abbey Theatre. Along with contemporaries, like Sean O'Casey and WB Yeats, Synge influenced subsequent generations of Irish writers, including novelist Seán O'Faolain, humorous writer and columnist Flann O'Brien, and hard-drinking, quarrelsome playwright Brendan Behan. The literary revival also produced many notable poets in the mid-20th century such as the gifted Patrick Kavanagh and Belfast-born Louis MacNeice, often considered to be one of the finest poets of his generation.

The writer Brendan Behan enjoying the company in a Dublin pub

Caricature of protesters at Dublin's Abbey Theatre in 1907

## THREE LITERARY GIANTS

FROM the mass of talent to emerge in Irish literature, three figures stand out as visionaries in their fields. WB Yeats *(see p225)* spent half his life outside Ireland but is forever linked to its rural west. A writer of wistful, melancholic poetry, he was at the forefront of the Irish Revival, helping forge a new national cultural identity. James Joyce *(see p88)* was another trailblazer of Irish literature – his complex narrative and stream of consciousness techniques influenced the development of the modern novel. *Ulysses* describes a day in the life of Joyce's beloved Dublin and shaped the work of generations of writers. Bloomsday, which is named after one of the novel's characters, Leopold Bloom, is still celebrated annually in the city. The last of the three literary giants, novelist and playwright Samuel Beckett *(see p60)*, was another of Dublin's sons, though he later emigrated to France. His themes of alienation, despair, and the futility of human existence pervade his best-known plays, *Waiting for Godot* and *Endgame*.

The poet Patrick Kavanagh celebrating Bloomsday

## CONTEMPORARY WRITERS

IRELAND's proud literary tradition is today upheld by a stream of talented writers from both North and South. Among the finest are Cork-born William Trevor, regarded as a master of the short story, and Brian Moore, whose stories of personal and political disillusionment are often based in his native Belfast. Similarly, Dubliner Roddy Doyle mines his working-class origins in novels such as *The Snapper* and *Paddy Clarke Ha Ha Ha*. Other established Irish writers are Brian Friel and Edna O'Brien. Out of Ireland's contemporary poets, the Ulster-born writers Séamus Heaney and Derek Mahon are considered among the most outstanding.

## IRELAND IN THE MOVIES

Ireland has long been fertile ground for the world's film makers, and its people have been the subjects of major films, notably *The Crying Game* (1992), *In the Name of the Father* (1994) and *Michael Collins* (1996). Another popular film was *The Commitments* (1991). Filmed on location in and around Dublin with an all-Irish cast, it was based on a novel by Roddy Doyle. More recently, parts of Co Wexford doubled as the beach heads of Normandy in Steven Spielberg's World War II epic *Saving Private Ryan* (1997).

Cast of *The Commitments*, written by Roddy Doyle

# The Music of Ireland

IRELAND IS THE ONLY COUNTRY in the world to have a musical instrument – the harp – as its national emblem. In this land, famous for its love of music, modern forms such as country-and-western and rock flourish, but it is traditional music that captures the essence of the country. Whether you are listening to Gaelic love songs that date back to medieval times or 17th- and 18th-century folk songs with their English and Scottish influences, the music is unmistakeably Irish. Dance is an equally important aspect of Irish traditional music, and some of the most popular airs are derived from centuries-old reels, jigs and hornpipes. Nowadays these are mainly performed at *fleadhs* (festivals) and *ceilís* (dances).

***Turlough O'Carolan*** *(1670– 1738) is the most famous Irish harper. The blind musician travelled the country playing his songs to both the rich and poor. Many of O'Carolan's melodies, such as* The Lamentation of Owen O'Neill, *still survive.*

**An Irish jig**

**Piano accordion**

**The *bodhrán*** is a hand-held goatskin drum that is usually played with a small stick. It is particularly effective when accompanying the flute.

**Flute**

**Two-row button accordion**

***John F McCormack*** *(1884–1945) was an Irish tenor who toured America to great acclaim during the early part of this century. His best-loved recordings were arias by Mozart. Another popular tenor was Derry-born Josef Locke. A singer of popular ballads in the 1940s and '50s, he was the subject of the 1992 film,* Hear My Song.

## THE CURRENT MUSIC SCENE

Ireland today is a melting pot of musical styles. The resurgence of Irish traditional music has produced many highly-respected musicians, such as the pipe-players Liam Ó Floin and Paddy Keenan from Dublin. Groups like the Chieftains and the Fureys have gained world-wide fame by melding old with new. Ireland is also firmly placed on the rock'n'roll map, thanks to bands such as Them in the 1960s and Thin Lizzy a decade later. The most famous rock band to come out of Ireland is Dublin's U2 who, in the 1980s, became one of the world's most popular groups. More recently, the series of albums entitled *A Woman's Heart* has been a showcase for talents such as Mary Black and Sinéad O'Connor, and bands like The Cranberries and Boyzone have conquered the world stage.

**Mary Black**

**Bono of U2**

***Traditional Irish dancing*** *is currently enjoying renewed popularity. From the 17th century the social focus in rural areas was the village dance held every Sunday. From these gatherings, Irish dancing became popular.*

## LIVE TRADITIONAL MUSIC

Wherever you go in Ireland, you won't be far from a pub with live music. For the Irish traditional musician, there are few set rules – the improvisational nature of the music means that no two performances of any piece are ever likely to be the same.

**Violins**, or fiddles, can either be tucked under the chin or held against the upper arm, shoulder or chest.

***Irish folk songs***, *such as this one about the 1916 Easter Rising, tend to have a patriotic theme. But some of the most powerful songs have been written not just about the national struggle, but also on hardship, emigration and the longing for the homeland.*

## TRADITIONAL INSTRUMENTS

There is no set line-up in traditional Irish bands. The fiddle is probably the most common instrument used. Like the music, some instruments have Celtic origins – the uillean pipes are related to the bagpipes played in Scotland and Brittany today.

***The melodeon*** *is a basic version of the button accordion. Both these instruments are better suited to Irish music than the piano accordion.*

***The uillean pipes*** *are similar to bagpipes and are generally considered to be one of the main instruments in Irish traditional music.*

***The harp*** *has been played in Ireland since the 10th century. In recent years, there has been a keen revival of harp playing in Irish traditional music.*

***The banjo*** *comes from the Deep South of the US and adds a new dimension to the sound of traditional bands.*

**Tin whistle**

**Flute**

***The flute and tin whistle*** *are among the most common instruments used in traditional Irish music. The latter is often called the penny whistle.*

***The violin*** *is called a fiddle by most musicians. The style of playing and sound produced varies from region to region.*

# Ireland's Celtic Heritage

Stone carving on Boa Island

IRELAND'S RICH TRADITION of storytelling embraces a folk heritage that abounds with myths and superstitions. Some stories have been in written form since the 8th century, but most originated over 2,000 years ago when druids passed on stories orally from one generation to the next. Like the Gaelic language itself, many of Ireland's legends have links with those of ancient Celtic races throughout Europe. As well as the heroic deeds and fearless warriors of mythology, Irish folklore is also rich in tales of fairies, leprechauns, banshees and other supernatural beings.

**The formidable Queen Maeve of Connaught**

**Part of the 2,300-year-old Gundestrup Cauldron unearthed in Denmark, which depicts Cuchulainn's triumph in the Cattle Raid of Cooley**

## CUCHULAINN

THE MOST FAMOUS warrior in Irish mythology is Cuchulainn. At the age of seven, going by the name of Setanta, he killed the savage hound of Culainn the Smith by slaying it with a hurling stick (one of the first times the sport of hurling is mentioned in folklore). Culainn was upset at the loss so Setanta volunteered to guard the house, earning himself the new name of Cuchulainn, meaning the hound of Culainn.

Before he went into battle, Cuchulainn swelled to magnificent proportions, turned different colours and one of his eyes grew huge. His greatest victory was in the "Cattle Raid of Cooley" when Queen Maeve of Connaught sent her troops to capture the coveted prize bull of Ulster. Cuchulainn learned of the plot and defeated them single-handedly. However, Queen Maeve took revenge on Cuchulainn by using sorcerers to lure him to his death. Today, in Dublin's GPO (see p87), a statue of Cuchulainn commemorates the heroes of the 1916 Easter Rising.

## FINN MACCOOL

THE WARRIOR Finn MacCool is the most famous leader of the Fianna, an elite band of troops chosen for their strength and valour and who defended Ireland from foreign forces. Finn was not only strong and bold but also possessed the powers of a seer, and could obtain great wisdom by putting his thumb in his mouth and sucking on it. When they were not at war, the Fianna spent their time hunting. Finn had a hound called Bran which stood almost as high as himself and is said to be the original ancestor of the breed known today as the Irish wolfhound. Many of the

## FAIRIES, LEPRECHAUNS AND BANSHEES

**The diminutive figure of the leprechaun**

The existence of spirits, and in particular the "little people", plays a large part in Irish folklore. Centuries ago, it was believed that fairies lived under mounds of earth, or "fairy raths", and that touching one of these tiny figures brought bad luck. The most famous of the "little people" is the leprechaun. Legend has it that if you caught one of these, he would lead you to a crock of gold, but take your eyes off him and he would vanish into thin air. The banshee was a female spirit whose wailing presence outside a house was said to signal the imminent death of someone within.

**A banshee with long flowing hair**

Fianna possessed supernatural powers and often ventured into the life beyond, known as the Otherworld. Among these was Finn's son Ossian who was not only a formidable warrior, like his father, but was also renowned as a wise and knowledgeable poet. Through time, Finn has come to be commonly portrayed as a giant. Legend has it that he constructed the Giant's Causeway in County Antrim *(see pp254–5).*

**A 19th-century engraving of Finn MacCool dressed for battle**

## THE CHILDREN OF LIR

ONE OF the saddest tales in Irish folklore involves King Lir, who so adored his four children that their stepmother was driven wild with jealousy. One day she took the children to a lake and cast a spell on them, turning them into white swans confined to the waters of Ireland for 900 years. However, as soon as she had done the deed, she became racked with guilt and bestowed upon them the gift of exquisite song. The

**The children of King Lir being turned into white swans**

end of the children's 900-year ordeal coincided with the coming of Christianity. The four children regained human form but were wizened and weak. They died soon afterwards, but not before being baptized. King Lir then decreed that no swan in Ireland should be killed – an act which is still illegal today.

## SAINT BRENDAN

BRENDAN THE NAVIGATOR, like many other 6th-century monks, travelled widely. It is known that although he lived in western Ireland he visited Wales, Scotland and France. It is likely, though, that his most famous journey is fictitious. This story tells of a shipload of monks who, after seven years of all kinds of strange encounters designed to test their faith, found the Land of Promise. It is essentially a Christian retelling of the common tales of the Celtic Otherworld. The Feast of St Brendan on 16 May is celebrated in Kerry by the climbing of Mount Brandon.

**Engraving showing St Brendan and his monks encountering a siren**

## ORIGINS OF IRISH PLACE NAMES

The names of many of Ireland's cities, towns and villages today are largely based on ancient Gaelic terms for prominent local landmarks, some of which no longer exist. Here are just a few elements of the place names the traveller may come across.

**The fort on the Rock of Cashel that gives the town its name**

**Ar, ard** – *high, height*
**Ass, ess** – *waterfall*
**A, ah, ath** – *ford*
**Bal, bally** – *town*
**Beg** – *small*
**Ben** – *peak, mountain*
**Carrick, carrig** – *rock*
**Cashel** – *stone fort*
**Crock, knock** – *hill*
**Curra, curragh** – *marsh*
**Darry, derry** – *oak tree*
**Dun** – *castle*
**Eden** – *hill brow*
**Innis, inch** – *island*
**Inver** – *river mouth*
**Isk, iska** – *water*
**Glas, glass** – *green*
**Glen, glyn** – *valley*
**Kil, kill** – *church*
**Lough** – *lake, sea inlet*
**Mona, mone** – *peat bog*
**Mor** – *great, large*
**Mullen, mullin** – *mill*
**Rath, raha** – *ring fort*
**Slieve** – *mountain*
**Toom** – *burial ground*
**Tul, tulagh** – *small hill*

**St Canice's Cathedral in Kilkenny (the town's name means "church of Canice")**

# The Sporting Year

Aʟʟ ᴍᴀᴊᴏʀ ɪɴᴛᴇʀɴᴀᴛɪᴏɴᴀʟ team sports are played in Ireland, but the most popular games are the two uniquely native ones of Gaelic football and hurling. Most of the big games, plus soccer and rugby internationals, are sold out well in advance. However, if you can't get a ticket you'll find plenty of company with whom to watch the event in pubs. Horse racing, with over 240 days of racing a year, attracts fanatical support. For those keen on participatory sports, there are also Ireland's famous fishing waters and golf courses *(see pp332–3).*

*The North West 200 is the fastest motorcycle race in the world over public roads – held near Portstewart(see p252).*

**Football Association of Ireland Cup – the Republic's football final**

**Round-Ireland Yacht Race – held every two years**

**Four-day national hunt racing festival at Punchestown**

*The Irish Grand National is a gruelling steeplechase run at Fairyhouse in County Meath.*

| January | February | March | April | May | June |
|---------|----------|-------|-------|-----|------|

**Irish Champion Hurdle, run at Leopardstown, County Dublin**

**The International Rally of the Lakes** is a prestigious car rally around the Lakes of Killarney *(see pp154–5).*

**Start of the salmon fishing season**

*The Six Nations Rugby Tournament, between Ireland, Scotland, Wales, England, France and Italy, runs until April. Ireland play their home games at Lansdowne Road, Dublin.*

### Kᴇʏ ᴛᴏ Sᴇᴀsᴏɴs

▬ Hurling
▬ Gaelic football
▬ Flat racing
▬ National Hunt racing
▬ Rugby
▬ Association football
▬ Salmon fishing
▬ Equestrianism

**Irish Football League Cup – Northern Ireland's final**

*The Irish Derby, Ireland's premier flat race, attracts many of Europe's best three-year-olds to the Curragh (see p121).*

*Cork Week* is a biennial regatta, organized by Royal Cork Yacht Club, where crews and boats of all classes meet and compete.

***The All-Ireland Football Final*** *is held at Croke Park in Dublin. The top two counties play for this Gaelic football championship. More people watch the game than any other event in Ireland.*

**Greyhound Derby, run at Shelbourne Park, Dublin**

***The Dublin Marathon*** *is Ireland's foremost marathon event. It attracts a huge field including top-class athletes from around the world.*

**Galway Race Week** is one of Ireland's premier festival meetings and a popular social event.

**Millstreet Indoor International showjumping event**

| uly | August | September | October | November | December |
|---|---|---|---|---|---|

***The Dublin Horse Show*** *is Ireland's premier horse show and a major event in the social calendar.*

**All-Ireland Hurling Final at Croke Park, Dublin**

***The Irish Open Golf Championship*** *is held at a different course each year and attracts a world-class field to courses such as Ballybunion in County Kerry.*

## THE GAELIC ATHLETIC ASSOCIATION

The GAA was founded in 1884 to promote indigenous Irish sport and discourage British influences – members were once forbidden from playing foreign games such as cricket. Today, despite heavy competition from soccer, the most popular sport in Ireland remains Gaelic football. However, the more intriguing GAA game is hurling – a fast and physical field sport played with sticks – which is said to have originated in ancient Celtic times. Both Gaelic football and hurling are played at parish and county level on a wholly amateur basis. The season ends with the All-Ireland finals, which draw large and passionate crowds to Dublin.

**Camogie, a version of hurling played by women**

# THE HISTORY OF IRELAND

IRELAND'S RELATIVE ISOLATION has cut it off from several of the major events of European history. Roman legions, for example, never invaded and the country's early history is shrouded in myths of warring Gods and heroic High Kings. Nevertheless, the bellicose Celtic tribes were quick to embrace Christianity after the arrival of St Patrick on the island in AD 432.

Until the Viking invasions of the 9th century, Ireland enjoyed an era of relative peace. Huge

**South Cross, Clonmacnoise**

monasteries like Clonmacnoise and Glendalough were founded, where scholarship and art flourished. The Vikings failed to gain control of the island, but in 1169 the Anglo-Normans did. Many Irish chiefs submitted to Henry II of England, who declared himself Lord of Ireland. He left in 1172, and his knights shared out large baronies between themselves.

Matters changed when Henry VIII broke with the Catholic church in 1532. Ireland became a battleground between native Irish Catholics and the forces of the English Crown. Where the Irish were defeated, their lands were confiscated and granted to Protestants from England and Scotland. England's conquest was completed with the victory of William of Orange over James II at the Battle of the Boyne in 1690. Repressive Penal Laws were put into place, but opposition to English rule continued.

The Famine of 1845 to 1848 was one of the bleakest periods in Irish history. Two million people died or emigrated, and many who stayed were evicted by English landlords. A campaign for Home Rule gathered strength, but it was 1920 before the Government of Ireland Act divided the island. The South became the Irish Free State, gaining full independence in 1937, while the North became part of the UK. For more than 25 years Northern Ireland has been a battle ground, with both Loyalist and Republican paramilitary groups waging bombing campaigns. In 1998, the Good Friday Agreement was signed, paving the way for a new Northern Ireland Assembly and hopes of peace.

Map of Ireland, printed in 1592, showing the four traditional provinces

◁ *The Feast of St Kevin amid the Ruins of Glendalough* by Joseph Peacock (1813)

# Prehistoric Ireland

UNTIL ABOUT 9,500 YEARS ago Ireland was uninhabited. The first people, who may have crossed by a land bridge from Scotland, were hunter-gatherers and left few traces of permanent settlement. The 4th millennium BC saw the arrival of Neolithic farmers and herdsmen who built stone field walls and

**Early Bronze Age stone axe-head**

monumental tombs such as Newgrange. Metalworking was brought from Europe around 2000 BC by the Bronze Age Beaker people, who also introduced new pottery skills. The Iron Age reached Ireland in the 3rd century BC along with the Celts, who migrated from Central Europe, via France and Britain, and soon established themselves as the dominant culture.

**IRELAND C. 8000 BC**

Former coastline

Present-day coastline

**The terminal discs** were worn on the shoulders.

**GLENINSHEEN GORGET**
Many remarkable pieces of gold jewellery were created in the late Bronze Age. This gold collar dates from about 700 BC. The Iron Age Celts produced similarly fine metalwork and ornaments.

**Dolmens or Portal Tombs**
*These striking megalithic tombs date from around 2000 BC. Legananny Dolmen in the Mountains of Mourne (see p276) is a fine example.*

**Three strands of ropework**

**Wooden Idol**
*This Iron Age fetish would have played a role in pagan fertility rites.*

**Celtic Stone Idol**
*This mysterious three-faced head was found in County Cavan. In Celtic religion the number three has always had a special significance.*

**Bronze Bridle Bit**
*Celtic chiefs rode into battle on two-horse chariots with beautifully decorated harnesses.*

## TIMELINE

**c. 7500 BC** First inhabitants of Ireland

*Extinct giant deer or "Irish Elk"*

**5000–3000** Ireland covered by dense woodland dominated by oak and elm

**2500** Building of Newgrange passage tomb *(see pp238–9)*

**1500** Major advances in metalworking, especially gold

| 8000 BC | 6000 | 4000 | 2000 | 1000 |
|---------|------|------|------|------|

**6000** Date of huts excavated at Mount Sandel, Co Londonderry; oldest known dwellings in Europe

**3700** Neolithic farmers reach Ireland; they clear woods to plant cereals

**2050** Beaker people (so-called for their delicate pottery vessels) reach Ireland at the beginning of Bronze Age

Pallisade (fence)

Thatched houses

Causeway to lake shore

### Reconstruction of a Crannog

*Originating in the Bronze Age, crannogs were artificial islands built in lakes. At first used for fishing, they soon developed into well-protected homesteads. Some remained in use up to the 17th century.*

**The raised bands** on the collar were created by *repoussé* work, pushed through from the back. The delicate rope motifs were added from the front with a knife.

**Bone Slip**
*(c. AD 50)*
*This may have been used for divination or for gambling.*

**Gold Boat**
*Part of a hoard of gold objects found at Broighter, County Londonderry, the boat (1st century AD) was made as a votive offering.*

### WHERE TO SEE PREHISTORIC IRELAND

Prehistoric sites range from individual tombs such as Newgrange, Browne's Hill Dolmen *(see p133)* or Ossian's Grave to whole settlements, as at Céide Fields *(p196)* and Lough Gur *(p186)*. The largest Stone Age cemetery is at Carrowmore *(p226)*. Good reconstructions of prehistoric structures can be seen at Craggaunowen *(p182)* and the Ulster History Park *(p261)*. The National Museum in Dublin *(pp64–5)* houses the finest collection of artifacts, including wonderful gold objects from the Bronze Age.

*Newgrange* (pp238–9) *is Ireland's finest restored Neolithic tomb. At the entrance lie huge spiral-patterned boulders.*

*Ossian's Grave is a court grave, the earliest kind of Neolithic tomb (p259). An open court stood before the burial mound.*

---

**600** First wave of Celtic invaders

**500** Intertribal warfare; chieftains vie for title of *Ard Ri* (High King)

**AD 80** Roman general Agricola considers invasion of Ireland from Britain

**367** Roman Britain attacked by Irish, Picts and Saxons

| 750 | 500 | 250 | AD 1 | AD 250 |
|---|---|---|---|---|

*Bronze goad decorated with birds*

**250** Second wave of Celts, who bring La Tène style of pottery

*Bronze sword hilt imported from southern France*

**c. 150** Greek geographer Ptolemy draws up map and account of Ireland

# Celtic Christianity

**Monk illuminating a manuscript**

CELTIC IRELAND was divided into as many as 100 chiefdoms, though these often owed allegiance to kings of larger provinces such as Munster or Connaught. At times, there was also a titular High King based at Tara *(see p240)*. Ireland became Christian in the 5th century AD, heralding a golden age of scholarship centred on the new monasteries, while missionaries such as St Columba travelled abroad. At the end of the 8th century, Celtic Ireland was shattered by the arrival of the Vikings.

**IRELAND IN 1000**

Viking settlements

Traditional Irish provinces

**Ogham Stone**
*The earliest Irish script, Ogham, dates from about AD 300. The notches correspond to Roman letters, like a form of Morse code.*

## CELTIC MONASTERY

Monasteries were large centres of population. This reconstruction shows Glendalough *(see pp132–3)* in about 1100. The tall round tower served as a lookout for Viking raiders.

Craftmen's dwellings

Refectory and kitchen

Round tower

Abbot's house

St Mary's Church

**The water-mill** was used for grinding wheat and barley.

**The Magnus Domus** was a large communal building used by the abbot and the monks.

St Kevin's Church

Dry-stone bridge

**A High Cross** marks the monastery boundary.

**Battle of Clontarf**
*After their defeat by the Irish High King, Brian Boru, in 1014, the Vikings began to integrate more fully with the native population. Brian Boru himself was killed in the battle.*

## TIMELINE

**430** Pope sends first Christian missionary, Palladius

**455** St Patrick founds church at Armagh

*St Patrick*

**563** St Columba (Colmcille), the first Irish missionary, founds monastery on Iona in the Hebrides

**664** Synod of Whitby decides that Irish Church should conform with Rome over date of Easter

| 400 | 500 | 600 | 700 |
|---|---|---|---|

**432** Start of St Patrick's mission to Ireland

**c. 550** Beginning of golden age of Celtic monasticism

**615** St Columbanus dies in Italy after founding many new monasteries on the Continent

**c. 690** *Book of Durrow* *(see p61)* completed

### Viking Raids and Settlements

*The first longships reached Ireland in 795. Though notorious for pillaging monasteries, the Vikings introduced new farming methods and coinage. They also founded walled cities such as Dublin, Waterford and Limerick.*

**Garryduff Gold Bird**
*Irish metalwork in the early Christian era was of very high quality. This gold ornament, possibly a wren, dates from around the 7th century AD.*

## WHERE TO SEE EARLY CHRISTIAN IRELAND

Important early monastic sites besides Glendalough include Clonmacnoise and Devenish Island. Churches from this period can also be seen at Gallarus (see p149), Clonfert (p205) and the Rock of Cashel (pp188–9), while High Crosses (p235) and round towers (p18) survive all over Ireland. Dublin's National Museum (pp64–5) has the best collection of ecclesiastical (and Viking) artifacts and Trinity College (pp60–62) houses the finest illuminated manuscripts.

***Devenish Island** has a fine 12th-century round tower and enjoys a peaceful setting on Lower Lough Erne (p263).*

**Cathedral**

**Gatehouse**

**Guesthouse and stables**

**Monks' dwellings and barns**

**St Kieran's Church** and other important churches were built of stone, but most buildings were wood.

### Clonmacnoise Crozier
*This 11th-century bishop's staff is decorated with an ornate silver casing. The style of the incised patterns shows Viking influence.*

***Clonmacnoise** (pp242–3) lies on the east bank of the Shannon. This Romanesque doorway is part of the ruined Nuns' Church.*

*Viking silver brooch*

**795** First Viking invasion of coastal monasteries

**807** Work starts on Kells monastery (see p233)

**841** A large Viking fleet spends the winter at Dublin

**967** Irish warriors sack Limerick and begin military campaign against Viking overlords

**1014** High King Brian Boru of Munster defeats joint army of Vikings and the King of Leinster at Clontarf

*Viking coin*

**999** Sitric Silkenbeard, the Viking king of Dublin, surrenders to Brian Boru

**1134** Cormac's Chapel is built at Cashel (see pp188–9)

**1166** Dermot McMurrough, King of Leinster, flees overseas

**1142** Ireland's first Cistercian house founded at Mellifont (see p237)

| 800 | 900 | 1000 | 1100 |

# Anglo-Norman Ireland

**IRELAND IN 1488**

▢ *Extent of the Pale*

ANGLO-NORMAN NOBLES, led by Richard de Clare (nicknamed Strongbow), were invited to Ireland by the King of Leinster in 1169. They took control of the major towns and Henry II of England proclaimed himself overlord of Ireland. In succeeding **13th-century gold brooch** centuries, however, English power declined and the Crown controlled just a small area around Dublin known as the Pale *(see p124)*. Many of the Anglo-Norman barons living outside the Pale opposed English rule just as strongly as did the native Irish clans.

**Marriage of Strongbow**
*The King of Leinster gave his daughter to Strongbow for helping him regain his lands. Daniel Maclise's painting (1854) emphasizes Anglo-Norman power over the Irish.*

**Norman Weapons**
*These bows and arrows, unearthed at Waterford, may be relics of Strongbow's assault on the city in 1170.*

## CARRICKFERGUS CASTLE
The first Anglo-Norman forts were wooden structures, but they soon started to build massive stone castles. Carrickfergus *(see p267)* was begun in the 1180s and by 1250 had acquired a keep and a gatehouse.

**The keep** contained a hall on the first floor and, above that, the lord's private apartments.

Guardroom

Storeroom

Stables

Bakery

## TIMELINE

*Dermot McMurrough, King of Leinster, who invited Strongbow to come to his aid*

**1172** Pope affirms King Henry II of England's lordship over Ireland

**1177** John de Courcy's forces invade Ulster

**1318** Bruce killed in battle

**1315** Scots invade Ireland; Edward Bruce crowned king

| 1200 | 1250 | 1300 |

**1169** Strongbow's Anglo-Normans arrive at invitation of exiled King of Leinster, Dermot McMurrough

**1224** Dominican order enters Ireland and constructs friaries

**1260** Powerful Irish chieftain Brian O'Neill killed at the Battle of Down

**1297** First Irish Parliament meets in Dublin

**Richard II's Fleet Returning to England in 1399**
*Richard made two trips to Ireland – in 1394 and 1399.
On the first he defeated Art McMurrough, King of Leinster,
and other Irish chiefs, but the second was inconclusive.*

## WHERE TO SEE ANGLO-NORMAN IRELAND

The strength of Norman fortifications is best seen in the castles at Carrickfergus, Limerick *(see p183)* and Trim *(p240)* and in Waterford's city walls. Gothic cathedrals that survive include Dublin's Christ Church *(pp78–9)* and St Patrick's *(pp80–81)* and St Canice's *(p136)* in Kilkenny. There are impressive ruins of medieval Cistercian abbeys at Jerpoint and Boyle *(p211).*

*Jerpoint Abbey (p137) has a
well-preserved 15th-century
cloister decorated with carvings
of curiously elongated figures.*

Kitchen

**The gatehouse**
was the last addition made in the 13th century. The two towers have arrow loops for longbowmen.

Drawbridge

Chapel

**Éamonn Burke**
*The 14th-century Lord
of Mayo was a typically
independent chieftain of
Anglo-Norman descent.*

**The Hall** was where the lord of the castle held public court and decided cases brought before him.

*Waterford's Anglo-Norman
city walls include this sturdy
watchtower (pp138–9).*

*Great Charter Roll
of Waterford (1372)
showing portraits
of the mayors of
four medieval cities*

**1394** King Richard II lands with army to reassert control; returns five years later but with inconclusive results

**1471** 8th Earl of Kildare made Lord Deputy of Ireland

**1496** Kildare regains Lord Deputy position

**1491** Kildare supports Perkin Warbeck, pretender to the English throne

| 1350 | 1400 | 1450 |
|---|---|---|

**1366** Statutes of Kilkenny forbid marriage between Anglo-Normans and Irish

**1348** The Black Death: one third of population killed in three years

*English forces (left)
confront Irish horse-
men on Richard II's
return expedition*

**1487** Kildare crowns Lambert Simnel, Edward VI in Dublin

**1494** Lord Deputy Edward Poynings forbids Irish Parliament to meet without royal consent

# Protestant Conquest

**Hugh O'Neill, Earl of Tyrone**

ENGLAND'S BREAK with the Catholic Church, the dissolution of the monasteries and Henry VIII's assumption of the title King of Ireland incensed both the old Anglo-Norman dynasties and resurgent Irish clans such as the O'Neills. Resistance to foreign rule was fierce and it took over 150 years of war to establish the English Protestant ascendancy. Tudor and Stuart monarchs adopted a policy of military persuasion, then Plantation. Oliver Cromwell was even more forceful. Irish hopes were raised when the Catholic James II ascended to the English throne, but he was deposed and fled to Ireland, where he was defeated by William of Orange (William III) in 1690.

**IRELAND IN 1625**

Main areas of Plantation in the reign of James I

**The first relief ship** to reach Londonderry was the *Phoenix*. For three months English ships had been prevented from sailing up the Foyle by a wooden barricade across the river.

**James II's army** on the east bank of the Foyle attack the ship.

**Battle of the Boyne**
*This tapestry, from the Bank of Ireland (see p58), shows William of Orange leading his troops against the army of James II in 1690. His victory is still celebrated by Orangemen in Northern Ireland.*

**Silken Thomas Fitzgerald**
*Silken Thomas, head of the powerful Kildares, renounced his allegiance to Henry VIII in 1534. He was hanged along with his five uncles in 1537.*

**The artist's depiction** of 17th-century weapons and uniforms is far from accurate.

## TIMELINE

**1541** Henry VIII declared King of Ireland by Irish Parliament

*Sir Thomas Lee, an officer in Elizabeth I's army, dressed in Irish fashion*

**1585** Ireland is mapped and divided into 32 counties

**1592** Trinity College, Dublin founded

*Henry VIII*

| 1500 | 1525 | 1550 | 1575 | 16 |
|------|------|------|------|-----|

**1534** Silken Thomas rebels against Henry VIII

**1504** 8th Earl of Kildare becomes master of Ireland after victory at Knocktoe

**1539** Henry VIII dissolves monasteries

**1557** Mary I orders first plantations in Offaly and Laois

**1582** Desmond rebellion in Munster

**1588** Spanish Armada wrecked off west coast

**The Siege of Drogheda**
*Between 1649 and 1652 Cromwell's army
avenged attacks on Protestant settlers with
ruthless efficiency. Here Cromwell himself
directs the gunners bombarding Drogheda.*

## PLANTATION IRELAND

James I realized that force alone could
not stabilize Ireland. The Plantation
programme uprooted the native Irish and
gave their land to Protestant settlers from
England and Scotland. London livery
companies organized many of the new
settlements. The policy created loyal
garrisons who supported the Crown.

***Bellaghy*** *in County Londonderry was
settled by the Vintners Company. This map
of the neatly planned town dates from 1622.*

**The Walls of Derry** have never been
breached by any attacker and many
of the original 17th-century gates and
bastions that withstood the siege of
1689 are still in place *(see pp250–51)*.

St George's
flag

Ship Quay

**Protestants** emerge
from the besieged city
to greet the English
relieving force and to
engage the enemy.

**Loftus Cup**
*Adam Loftus,
Chancellor of
Ireland, used his
position to enrich
his family. In 1593
he had the Great
Seal of Ireland
melted down and
made into this
silver-gilt cup.*

## THE RELIEF OF DERRY *(1689)*

Some 20,000 Protestants were besieged for 105 days in
Londonderry by James II's forces. Thousands died from
starvation, until relief finally came from English warships.
This 18th-century painting by William Sadler II gives a
rather fanciful picture of the ending of the siege.

**1607** Flight of the
Earls: old Irish
leaders flee to
the Continent;
Plantation of Ulster

**1632** Important Irish history,
*The Annals of the Four Masters*,
written by four Franciscan
friars from Donegal

*Protestant
apprentice boys
closing the gates
of Derry before
the siege of 1689*

**1690** William of Orange defeats
James II at Battle of the Boyne;
James's army surrenders the
following year in Limerick

| 1625 | 1650 | 1675 | 1700 |
|---|---|---|---|

**1603** Earl of Tyrone ends
nine years of war by signing
the Treaty of Mellifont

**1641** Armed rebellion in
Ulster opposes Plantation

**1649** Cromwell lands in
Dublin; razes Drogheda
and Wexford; Catholic
landowners transplanted
to far west

**1688** James II,
deposed Catholic
king of England,
flees to Ireland
and raises army

**1689** Siege of Derry

**1695** Penal code
severely reduces rights
of Roman Catholics

# Georgian Ireland

**IRELAND IN 1703**

Counties where Protestants owned over 75 per cent of land

**Lacquer cabinet in Castletown House**

THE PROTESTANT ASCENDANCY was a period of great prosperity for the landed gentry, who built grand country houses and furnished them luxuriously. Catholics, meanwhile, were denied even the right to buy land. Towards the end of the century, radicals, influenced by events in America and France, started to demand independence from the English Crown. Prime Minister Henry Grattan tried a parliamentary route; Wolfe Tone and the United Irishmen opted for armed insurrection. Both approaches ultimately failed.

**The Irish House of Commons**
*This painting shows Irish leader Henry Grattan addressing the house (see p58). The "Grattan Parliament" lasted from 1782 to 1800, but was then abolished by the Act of Union.*

**State Bedroom**

**The saloon**, the Casino's main room, was used for formal entertaining. It has a magnificent parquet floor.

**Stone lions by Edward Smyth (1749–1812)**

**The basement** contains the servants' hall, the kitchen, pantry and wine cellar.

**Surveyors**
*The 18th century saw work begin on ambitious projects such as the Grand Canal, new roads and Dublin's network of wide streets and squares.*

## TIMELINE

*Jonathan Swift (1667–1745)*

**1724** Swift attacks Ireland's penal code in *A Modest Proposal*

**1731** Royal Dublin Society founded to encourage agriculture, art and crafts

**1738** Death of Ireland's most famous harper, Turlough O'Carolan (see p22)

| 1710 | 1720 | 1730 | 1740 | 1750 |

**1713** Jonathan Swift appointed Dean of St Patrick's Cathedral (see p80)

**1731** First issue of the *Belfast Newsletter*, the world's oldest continually running newspaper

**1742** First performance of Handel's *Messiah* given in Dublin

**1751** Dublin's Rotunda Lying-In Hospital is first maternity hospital in the British Isles

**Linen Bleaching**
*Ulster's linen industry flourished thanks to the expertise of Huguenot weavers from France. The woven cloth was spread out in fields or on river banks to bleach it (see p260).*

**The Classical urns** on the roof conceal chimneys.

**The china closet** was originally designed as a bedroom.

**Irish Painting**
*Aristocratic patronage encouraged the development of an Irish school of painting. This picture, by an unknown artist, shows Leixlip Castle in an idealized rural setting.*

**The hall** ends in a semi-circular apse leading to the saloon.

**Entrance**

## MARINO CASINO
This frivolous summer house was built in the 1760s for the first Earl of Charlemont on his estate just north of Dublin *(see p98)*. Palladian architecture of this kind was popular among the Irish aristocracy, who followed 18th-century English fashions.

## WHERE TO SEE GEORGIAN IRELAND

Dublin preserves many fine Georgian terraces and public buildings such as the Custom House *(see p86)* and the Four Courts *(p91)*. Around Dublin, the grand houses at Castletown *(pp122–3)*, Russborough and Powerscourt *(pp126–7)* are fascinating reminders of the lifestyle of the gentry. Other 18th-century country seats open to the public include Emo Court, Westport House *(pp196–7)* and Castle Coole *(p264)*.

***Emo Court's** façade, with its plain Ionic portico, is by James Gandon, architect of many of Dublin's public buildings (p245).*

***Russborough House** (p124) was built in 1741 by Richard Castle. Elegant niches with Classical busts flank the grand fireplace in the entrance hall.*

Guinness Brewery Gate

**1782** Parliament gains greater degree of independence from Westminster

*The Irish Volunteers, a local militia which pressed Parliament for reform*

**1798** Rebellion of Wolfe Tone's United Irishmen quashed

| 1760 | 1770 | 1780 | 1790 |
|---|---|---|---|

*Custom House*

**1791** James Gandon's Custom House built in Dublin

**1759** Arthur Guinness buys the St James's Gate Brewery in Dublin

**1793** Limited emancipation for Irish Catholics

**1795** Orange Order formed by Ulster Protestants

# Famine and Emigration

T HE HISTORY of 19th-century Ireland is dominated by the Great Famine of 1845–8, which was caused by the total failure of the potato crop. Although Irish grain was still being exported to England, around one million people died from hunger or disease, with even more fleeing to North America. By 1900, the pre-famine population of eight million had fallen by half. Rural hardship fuelled a campaign for tenants' rights which evolved into demands for independence from Britain. Great strides towards "Home Rule" were made in Parliament by the charismatic politician, Charles Stuart Parnell.

**IRELAND IN 1851**

*Areas where population fell by over 25% during the Famine*

**The ships** that brought the Irish to America were over-crowded and fever-ridden, and known as "coffin ships".

### Daniel O'Connell
*Known as "The Liberator", O'Connell organized peaceful "monster rallies" of up to a million people in pursuit of Catholic emancipation. He was elected MP for Clare in 1828.*

**Castle Clinton** was used for processing new arrivals to New York prior to the con-struction of the huge depot on Ellis Island.

### The Boycotting of Landlords
*In 1880, troops guarded the crops of Captain Boycott, the first notable victim of a campaign to ostracize landlords guilty of evicting tenants. His name later passed into the English language.*

## TIMELINE

*Charles Bianconi's coach service, 1836*

**1815** First coach service begins in Ireland

**1817** Royal Canal is completed

**1838** Father Mathew founds temperance crusade – five million Irish take abstinence pledge and whiskey production is reduced by half

**1845** Start Great Famir which lasts four ye

| 1800 | 1810 | 1820 | 1830 | 1840 |
|------|------|------|------|------|

**1803** Uprising, led by Robert Emmet, is crushed after feared Napoleonic invasion of England fails to materialize

**1828** After a five-year campaign by Daniel O'Connell, Catholic Emancipation Act is passed, giving a limited number of Catholics the right to vote

**1800** Act of Union: Ireland legally becomes part of Britain

*Father Mathew*

**Eviction of Irish Farmers**
*In the late 1870s, agricultural prices plummeted. Starving tenant farmers fell into arrears and were mercilessly evicted. Their plight spawned the Land League, which lobbied successfully for reform.*

## THE IRISH ABROAD

One result of the Famine was the growth of a strong Irish community in the USA. From the lowest rung of American society, the immigrants rose up the social scale and became rich by Irish Catholic standards. They sent money to causes back home, and as a well-organized lobby group put pressure on the American government to influence British policies in Ireland. A more militant group, Clan na Gael, sent veterans of the American Civil War to fight in the Fenian risings of 1865 and 1867.

**New Yorkers** *stage a huge St Patrick's Day parade, 17 March 1870.*

**The Irish** were widely perceived as illiterate peasants in the USA and often met with a hostile reception.

## IMMIGRANTS ARRIVE IN NEW YORK

The Irish who survived the journey to America landed at Castle Garden in New York, seen here in a painting by Samuel Waugh (1855). Although mainly country people, most new arrivals settled in Manhattan, often enduring horrific living conditions.

**Charles Stuart Parnell**
*A campaigner for the Land League and Home Rule, Parnell saw his political career ruined in 1890, when he was cited as co-respondent in a divorce case.*

**1853** Dublin Exhibition is opened by Queen Victoria

*Dublin Exhibition*

**1877** Charles Stuart Parnell becomes leader of the new Home Rule Party

**1884** Founding of Gaelic Athletic Association, first group to promote Irish traditions

**1892** Second Home Rule Bill is defeated

| 1850 | 1860 | 1870 | 1880 | 1890 |
|------|------|------|------|------|

**1867** Irish-Americans return home to fight in a rising led by the Irish Republican Brotherhood, also known as the Fenians

**1848** Failure of the Young Ireland Uprising – a spontaneous response to insurrections elsewhere in Europe

**1879–82** Land War, led by Michael Davitt's Land League, campaigns for the reform of tenancy laws

**1881** Parnell is jailed in Kilmainham, Dublin

**1886** British PM Gladstone sponsors first Home Rule Bill but is defeated by Parliament

# War and Independence

**Irish Free State stamp of 1922**

PLANS FOR IRISH HOME RULE were shelved because of World War I; however, the abortive Easter Rising of 1916 inspired new support for the Republican cause. In 1919 an unofficial Irish Parliament was established and a war began against the "occupying" British forces. The Anglo-Irish Treaty of 1921 divided the island in two, granting independence to the Irish Free State, while Northern Ireland remained in the United Kingdom. There followed a civil war between pro-Treaty and anti-Treaty factions in the South.

**IRELAND IN 1922**

☐ *Northern Ireland*

☐ *Irish Free State*

**The Unionist Party**
*Leader of the campaign against Home Rule was Dublin barrister Edward Carson. In 1913 the Ulster Volunteer Force was formed to demand that six counties in Ulster remain part of the UK.*

**Sean J Heuston**

**Thomas McDonough**

**Major John McBride**

**The 1916 Service Medal**, issued to all who fought in the Easter Rising, depicts, on one side, the mythical Irish warrior Cuchulainn.

**William Pearse**

**Patrick Pearse**, a poet, read the Proclamation of the Republic from the steps of the GPO on Easter Monday.

**The Black and Tans**
*Named for their makeshift uniforms, these British troops – mostly demobbed World War I soldiers – carried out savage reprisals against the Irish in 1920–21.*

## TIMELINE

*The Titanic*

**1913** General strike in Dublin

**1912** Belfast-built *Titanic* sinks on her maiden voyage

**1918** Sinn Féin wins 73 seats at Westminster; Constance Markievicz elected first woman MP

**1916** Easter Rising quashed

**1919** First meeting of independe[nt] parliament (Dáil Éirea[nn])

| 1905 | 1910 | 1915 | 1920 |
|------|------|------|------|

**1905** Sinn Féin (We Ourselves) party founded

**1912** Edward Carson rallies Ulster Protestants; solemn covenant to defeat Home Rule signed by 471,414 people

**1920** Government of Ireland Act proposes partition of the island

**1904** Dublin's Abbey Theatre opens

*Despatch bag carried by Constance Markievicz during Easter Rising*

**1921** Anglo-Irish Treaty signed; de Valera resigns; southern Ireland plunged into civil wa[r]

**The General Post Office, Easter 1916**
*What was supposed to be a national uprising was confined to 2,500 armed insurgents in Dublin. They managed to hold the GPO and other public buildings for five days.*

**This Mauser rifle**, smuggled in from Germany in 1914, was used by rebels in the Rising.

### EAMON DE VALERA (1882–1975)

After escaping execution for his part in the Easter Rising, American-born de Valera went on to dominate Irish politics for almost 60 years. The opposition of his party, Sinn Fein, to the Anglo-Irish Treaty of 1921 plunged the new Irish Free State into civil war. After forming a new party, Fianna Fáil, he became Prime Minister *(Taioseach)* in 1932. De Valera remained in office until 1948, with further terms in the 1950s. Between 1959 and 1973 he was President of Ireland.

Tom Clarke

James Connolly

Joseph Plunkett

**Mementoes** of the Rising at Dublin's Kilmainham Gaol *(see p95)* include this crucifix made by a British soldier from rifle bullets.

**Election Poster**
*Cumann na nGaedheal, the pro-Treaty party in the Civil War, won the Free State's first general election in 1923. It merged with other parties in 1933 to form Fine Gael.*

### LEADERS OF THE 1916 RISING

This collage portrait shows 14 leaders of the Easter Rising, who were all court-martialled and shot at Kilmainham Gaol. The brutality of their executions (the badly injured James Connolly was tied to a chair before being shot) changed public opinion of the Rising and guaranteed their status as martyrs.

---

**1922** Irish Free State inaugurated; Michael Collins shot dead in ambush in Co Cork

*Michael Collins (1890–1922), hero of the War of Independence, became chairman of the Irish Free State and Commander-in-Chief of the Army*

**1932** Fianna Fáil sweep to victory in general election, and de Valera begins 16-year term as *Taioseach* (Prime Minister)

**1936** IRA proscribed by Free State Government

**1939** Éire declares neutrality during World War II

| 1925 | 1930 | 1935 |
|---|---|---|

**1923** WB Yeats wins Nobel prize for Literature

**1925** GB Shaw also receives Nobel prize

**1926** De Valera quits Sinn Féin; sets up Fianna Fáil (Soldiers of Destiny) party

**1929** Work started on River Shannon hydro-electric power scheme

**1933** Fine Gael (United Ireland) party formed to oppose Fianna Fáil

**1937** New constitution declares complete independence from Britain; country's name changes to Éire

# Modern Ireland

SINCE JOINING the European Economic Community (now called the European Union) in 1973, the Irish Republic has done much to modernize its traditional rural-based economy. There have been social changes too, and laws prohibiting abortion and divorce have slowly been relaxed. Meanwhile, Northern Ireland has lived through more than 25 years of bombings and shootings. But recent peace agreements have brought new hope to the province, especially since the inauguration in 1998 of the new Northern Ireland Assembly.

**Mary Robinson, Ireland's first woman President**

**1972** Bloody Sunday – British soldiers shoot dead 13 demonstrators in Derry. Northern Ireland Parliament is suspended and direct rule from Westminster imposed

**1970** Reverend Ian Paisley, a radical Protestant Unionist, wins the Bannside by-election

**1969** Violent clashes between the police and demonstrators in Belfast and Derry. British troops sent to restore order

**1956** IRA launches a terrorism campaign along the border with Northern Ireland which lasts until 1962

**1967** Northern Ireland Civil Rights Association is set up to fight discrimination against Catholics

| NORTHERN IRELAND | | | |
|---|---|---|---|
| 1945 | 1955 | | 1965 |
| REPUBLIC OF IRELAND | | | |

**1949** New government under John A Costello. Country changes name from Éire to Republic of Ireland and leaves British Commonwealth

**1955** Republic of Ireland joins United Nations. Irish troops have played an important role in UN peace-keeping missions around the world ever since

**1959** Eamon de Valera resigns as *Taoiseach* (Prime Minister) and is later elected President

**1969** Samuel Beckett, seen here rehearsing one of his own plays, is awarded the Nobel prize for literature, but does not go to Stockholm to receive it

**1963** John F Kennedy, the first American President of Irish Catholic descent, visits Ireland. He is pictured here with President Eamon de Valera

**1947** Statue of Queen Victoria is removed from the courtyard in front of the Irish Parliament in Dublin

**1973** Republic of Ireland joins the European Economic Community at same time as the UK. Membership has given the country access to much-needed development grants

~~4~~ Power-sharing experiment is ~~b~~ught down by a devastating ~~stri~~ke, organized by Protestant ~~wo~~rkers. Direct rule is reimposed

**1991** Peace talks instituted by Westminster between the main political parties of Northern Ireland (except Sinn Féin) and the British and Irish governments

**1985** Barry McGuigan beats the Panamanian, Eusebio Pedroza, for world featherweight boxing title

**1976** Organizers of the Ulster Peace Movement, Mairead Corrigan and Betty Williams, are awarded the Nobel Peace Prize in Oslo

**1986** Bitter Loyalist opposition follows the previous year's signing by the British and Irish governments of the Anglo-Irish Agreement

**1994** IRA and Protestant cease-fires. Gerry Adams, Sinn Féin leader, allowed to speak on British radio and television

**1995** For the first time in 25 years, there are no troops on daylight patrols in Northern Ireland

**1982** De Lorean car factory in Belfast closes just four years after £17 million investment by British government

**1987** IRA bomb explodes during Enniskillen's Remembrance Day parade, killing 11 people

**1998** The Good Friday Agreement sets out proposed framework for self-government in Northern Ireland

**1981** Hunger-striker Bobbie Sands dies in Maze Prison

**NORTHERN IRELAND**

| 1975 | 1985 | 1995 |
|------|------|------|

**REPUBLIC OF IRELAND**

**1988** Dublin's millennium is celebrated, boosting the city's image

**1991** Mary Robinson becomes first female President of the Republic, succeeded by Mary McAleese in 1998

**1992** In a referendum, 62 per cent of the Irish vote in favour of allowing pregnant women to seek an abortion abroad. A vote in favour of divorce follows in 1995

**1994** Republic of Ireland football team reaches quarterfinals of World Cup in the USA. Here, Ray Houghton is congratulated on scoring the winning goal against Italy

**1999** Ireland joins the single European currency on 1 January

**1979** Pope John Paul II visits Ireland and celebrates Mass in Dublin's Phoenix Park, in front of more than a million people

**1985** Irish pop singer Bob Geldof organizes Live Aid concerts in London and Philadelphia; £40 million is raised for African famine relief

**1987** Dubliner Steven Roche wins the Tour de France, Giro d'Italia and World Championship in one incredible season

# IRELAND THROUGH THE YEAR

POPULAR MONTHS for visiting Ireland are July and August, though whatever the season it's rarely crowded. June and September can be pleasant but never count on the weather, for Ireland's lush beauty is the product of a wet climate. Be aware that most tourist sights are open from Easter to September but have restricted opening hours or close in the low season. During spring and summer, festivals are held in

Ladies' Day at Dublin Horse Show

honour of everything from food to religion. A common thread is music, and few festivities are complete without musical accompaniment. Ireland is at its best when it has something to celebrate, so is an inspired choice for Christmas or New Year. Look out for the word *fleadh* (festival) on your travels but remember, too, that the Irish are a spontaneous people: festivities can spring from the air, or from a tune on a fiddle.

![Dublin's annual parade]

**Dublin's annual parade to celebrate St Patrick's Day (17 March)**

## SPRING

ST PATRICK'S DAY is often said to mark the beginning of the tourist season. Later, the spring bank holiday weekend in May, when accommodation is in short supply, is celebrated with music in most places. After the quiet winter months, festivals and events start to become more common.

### MARCH

**St Patrick's Day** *(17 Mar)*. Parades and pilgrimages held at Downpatrick, Armagh, Dublin, Cork, Limerick and many other places.
**Dublin Film Festival** *(One week in Mar or Apr)*. International film festival.
**Horse Ploughing Match and Heavy Horse Show**, Ballycastle *(17 Mar, see p258)*. The popular annual competition is more than 100 years old.

**A St Patrick's Day float advertising Guinness**

## APRIL

**Feis Ceoil**, Dublin *(end Mar or early Apr)*. A classical music festival held at many different venues throughout the city.
**Pan Celtic Festival**, Tralee *(mid-Apr, see p148)*. A lively celebration of Celtic culture, with music, dance and song.
**Cork Choral Festival** *(late Apr–May, see pp166–7)*.

## MAY

**Belfast Civic Festival and Lord Mayor's Show** *(mid-May, see pp268–71)*. Street parade with bands and floats.
**Royal Ulster Agriculture Society Show**, Belfast *(mid-May)*. A three-day show with diverse events ranging from sheep-shearing competitions to fashion shows.
**"A Taste of Baltimore" Shellfish Festival** *(end May, see p162)*.
**Fleadh Nua**, Ennis, *end May, see p181)*. Four days of traditional Irish music, songs and dance.

## SUMMER

FOR THE VISITOR, summer represents the height of the festive calendar. This is the busiest time of year for organized events, from music and arts festivals to lively local race meetings, summer schools and matchmaking festivals. Book accommodation if your plans include a popular festival.

**Beach races at Laytown (June)**

## JUNE

**Laytown Beach Races**, Co Meath *(late May or early June)*. Horse races on the sand.
**County Wicklow Garden Festival** *(all month)*. Held at private and public gardens around the county, including Powerscourt *(see pp126–7)*.
**National Country Fair**, Birr Castle Demesne, Co Offaly *(early June, see p245)*. One of Ireland's most popular country fairs.
**Women's Mini Marathon**, Dublin City *(early June)*.
**Bloomsday**, Dublin *(16 June)*. Lectures, pub talks, readings, dramatizations and walks to celebrate James Joyce's greatest novel, *Ulysses*.

AVERAGE DAILY HOURS OF SUNSHINE

Hours

Jan Feb Mar Apr May Jun Jul Aug Sep Oct Nov Dec

**Sunshine Chart**
*The chart gives figures for Dublin, though conditions are similar around the country. The Southeast enjoys more sunshine hours than any other part of Ireland, while Northern Ireland receives marginally fewer hours of sun than the Republic.*

**Scurlogstown Olympiad Celtic Festival**, Trim *(mid-Jun, see p240).* Traditional Irish music, dance, fair and selection of a festival queen.

**Music in Great Irish Houses** *(second and third weeks).* Classical music recitals in grand settings at various venues.
**Castle Ward Opera**, Strangford *(end Jun, see p276).* Opera festival in the grounds of 18th-century stately home.
**County Wexford Strawberry Fair**, Enniscorthy *(end Jun– early Jul, see p141).* Includes a craft fair, music, street theatre and, of course, strawberries.

### JULY

**Battle of the Boyne Day** *(12 Jul, see p236).* Members of the Orange Order march in towns across Northern Ireland to celebrate the Protestants' landmark victory over King James II's Catholic army in 1690.
**Galway Arts Festival** *(third & fourth weeks, see pp202–3).* Processions, concerts, street theatre, children's shows and many other events in the medieval city centre. Followed

Traditional sailing craft in the Cruinniú na mBad at Kinvarra (August)

immediately by Galway's popular five-day race meeting.
**Mary from Dungloe International Festival**, Dungloe *(last week, see p220).* Dancing, music and selection of "Mary", the beauty queen.
**Lughnasa Fair**, Carrickfergus Castle *(end Jul, see p267).* A popular medieval-style fair.
**Ballyshannon International Folk Festival** *(end Jul or early Aug, see p223).* Three days of traditional Irish music.
**O'Carolan Harp and Traditional Music Festival**, Keadue, Co Roscommon *(end Jul or early Aug).* Traditional music and dance celebrations.

### AUGUST

**Stradbally Steam-engine Rally**, Co Laois *(early Aug).* Many types of steam-engine join this rally.

Orangemen parading on
Battle of the Boyne Day

**Letterkenny Folk Festival**, Co Donegal *(early Aug, see p219).* A week of celebration.
**Dublin Horse Show** *(first or second week).* A premier showjumping competition and social event.
**Puck Fair**, Killorglin, Co Kerry *(mid-Aug, see p157).* A wild goat is crowned "king" at this two-day-long traditional festival.
**Blessing of the Sea** *(second or third Sunday).* Held in seaside towns all over Ireland.
**Oul' Lammas Fair**, Ballycastle *(mid-Aug, see p258).* A popular fair that is particularly famous for its edible seaweed.
**Kilkenny Arts Week** *(middle of the month, see pp134–6).* A major arts festival including poetry, film and crafts.
**Rose of Tralee Festival**, *(end Aug, see p148).* Bands, processions, dancing and selection of the "Rose".
**Cruinniú na mBad**, Kinvarra *(end Aug, see pp203–4).* Various types of traditional sailing craft take part in this "gathering of the boats".

Steam-engine at Stradbally Rally (August)

**AVERAGE MONTHLY RAINFALL**

MM
100
80
60
40
20
0
Jan Feb Mar Apr May Jun Jul Aug Sep Oct Nov Dec

Inches
4
3
2
1
0

**Rainfall Chart**
*Ireland is one of the wettest countries in Europe, with rainfall distributed evenly through the year – the figures displayed here are for Dublin. The West has the heaviest annual rainfall, while the Southeast receives marginally less rain than other regions.*

**Galway Oyster Festival (September)**

## Autumn

OYSTERS AND OPERA are the two big events in autumn. There are also festivals devoted to jazz, film and music. The October bank holiday weekend is celebrated with music in many towns; though it is low season, it can be difficult to find accommodation.

## September

**Heritage Week** (early Sep). Special events countrywide.
**All-Ireland Hurling Final**, Croke Park, Dublin (first or second Sunday, see p27).

**Lisdoonvarna Match-making Festival** (all month and first week of Oct, see p180). Singles gather for traditional music and dance.
**Waterford International Festival of Light Opera** (mid-Sep –early Oct, see p329). Musicals and operettas at the Theatre Royal.
**All-Ireland Football Final**, Croke Park, Dublin (3rd Sunday, see p27). Gaelic football final.
**Galway Oyster Festival** (end Sep, see pp202–3). Oyster tastings at different venues.

## October

**Octoberfest**, London-derry (all month, see pp250–51). Dance, poetry, film, comedy, theatre and music.
**Cork Film Festival** (early Oct, see pp166–7). Irish and international films.
**Kinsale Gourmet Festival** (early Oct, see pp164–5). Superb food is served in the

**All-Ireland Hurling at Croke Park, Dublin**

hotels, restaurants and pubs of Ireland's "Gourmet Capital".
**Ballinasloe Fair**, Co Galway (first week). One of Europe's oldest horse fairs, staged amid lively street entertainment.
**Dublin Theatre Festival** (first and second week). Features works by both Irish and foreign playwrights.
**Wexford Opera Festival** (last two weeks in Oct, see p329). A festival of lesser known operas.
**Hallowe'en (Sham-hana)** (31 Oct). An occasion celebrated all over the country.
**Cork Jazz Festival** (end Oct, see pp166–7). An extremely popular festival, with music all over the city.

**Horse and trap at Lisdoonvarna fair**

## November

**Sligo International Choral Festival** (early Nov, see p226). Choirs from around the world in concert and competition.
**Belfast Festival at Queen's**, Queen's University (end Oct to early Nov, see pp268–71). Arts festival featuring drama, ballet, cinema and all types of music from classical to jazz.
**Eigse Sliabh Rua**, Slieverue, Co Kilkenny (mid Nov). Festival of local history and music with special guests and interesting talks.

**Traditional horse fair at Ballinasloe in County Galway (October)**

## AVERAGE MONTHLY TEMPERATURE

**Temperature Chart**
*This chart gives the average minimum and maximum temperatures for the city of Dublin. Winter is mild throughout Ireland, except in the high mountain ranges, while the warmest summer temperatures are in the Southeast.*

## WINTER

ALTHOUGH a quiet time for festivals, there's a range of entertainment including musical and theatrical events. Christmas is the busiest social period and there are plenty of informal celebrations. There is also a wide choice of National Hunt race meetings *(see p26)*.

## DECEMBER

**Pantomime Season** *(Dec–Jan)*. Traditional pantomime performed at many theatres throughout Ireland.
**Leopardstown Races** *(26 Dec, see p121)*. The biggest meeting held on this traditional day for racing. There are other fixtures at Limerick and Down Royal.
**St Stephen's Day** *(26 Dec)*. Catholic boys traditionally dress up as Wren boys (chimney sweeps with blackened faces) and sing hymns to raise money for charitable causes.

**Young boys dressed up as Wren boys on St Stephen's Day**

## JANUARY

**Salmon and Sea Trout Season** *(1 Jan–end Sep)*. Start of the season for one of the most popular pastimes in Ireland.

## FEBRUARY

**Dublin Film Festival** *(end Feb–early Mar)*. International films at various venues.
**Belfast Music Festival** *(end Feb–mid-Mar)*. Young people take part in music (and speech and drama) competitions.
**Six Nations Rugby Tournament**, Lansdowne Road, Dublin *(varying Saturdays Feb–Apr, see p26)*.

**Glendalough** *(see pp132–3)* **in the snow**

# DUBLIN AREA BY AREA

DUBLIN AT A GLANCE 52–53
SOUTHEAST DUBLIN 54–69
SOUTHWEST DUBLIN 70–81
NORTH OF THE LIFFEY 82–91
FURTHER AFIELD 92–101
ENTERTAINMENT IN DUBLIN 102–107
DUBLIN STREET FINDER 108–111

# Dublin at a Glance

Iᴿᴇʟᴀɴᴅ'ꜱ ᴄᴀᴘɪᴛᴀʟ has a wealth of attractions, most
within walking distance of each other. For the
purpose of this guide, central Dublin has been
divided into three sections: *Southeast Dublin*, heart
of the modern city and home to the prestigious
Trinity College; *Southwest Dublin*, site of the old
city around Dublin Castle; and *North of the Liffey*,
the area around the imposing O'Connell Street. The
map references given for sights in the city refer to
the *Dublin Street Finder* on pages 110–111.

***Christ Church Cathedral***
*was built by Dublin's Anglo-
Norman conquerors between
1172 and 1220. It stands on
high ground above the River
Liffey. Much of the
cathedral's present
appearance is due
to restoration carried
out in the 1870s.
(See pp78–9.)*

**NORTH OF THE LIFFEY**
*Pages 82–91*

LIFFE

**SOUTHWEST
DUBLIN**
*Pages 70–81*

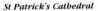

***Dublin Castle*** *stands in the heart of old
Dublin. St Patrick's Hall is part of the suite
of luxury State Apartments housed on the
upper floors on the south side of the castle.
Today, these rooms are used for functions of
national importance such as presidential
inaugurations. (See pp74–5.)*

***St Patrick's Cathedral***
*has a spectacular choir featuring
banners and stalls decorated with
the insignia of the Knights of St
Patrick. The cathedral also holds
Ireland's largest and most powerful
organ, as well as memorials to Dean
Jonathan Swift and prominent
Anglo-Irish families. (See pp80–81.)*

**O'Connell Street**, Dublin's main and busiest thoroughfare, has a fine mix of architectural styles and a grand central mall punctuated with statues of famous Irish citizens. Just off O'Connell Street, on Moore Street, is a colourful and lively market. (See pp86–7.)

**The Custom House**, a classic Georgian public building by James Gandon, was built between 1781 and 1791. The sculpted heads on the keystones are personifications of the rivers of Ireland; the one shown above represents the River Foyle. (See p86.)

**Trinity College** is home to the Old Library which contains priceless, illuminated manuscripts. These include the Book of Durrow which dates from the middle of the 7th century. (See pp60–62.)

SOUTHEAST
DUBLIN
Pages 54–69

0 metres        400
0 yards         400

**The National Gallery** was opened in 1864. Housed on two floors, the well-organized gallery holds an eclectic collection, particularly strong on Irish and Italian paintings. The gallery's most prized painting is its recent acquisition The Taking of Christ by Caravaggio. (See pp68–9.)

**The National Museum** has an impressive collection of artifacts dating from the Stone Age to the 20th century. The Ardagh Chalice (c. 800 AD) is one of the many Celtic Christian treasures on display. (See pp64–5.)

# SOUTHEAST DUBLIN

**D**ESPITE ITS location close to the old walled city, this part of Dublin remained virtually undeveloped until the founding of Trinity College in 1592. Even then, it was almost a hundred years before the ancient common land further south was enclosed to create St Stephen's Green, a spacious city park.

The mid-18th century saw the beginning of a construction boom in the area. During this time, magnificent public buildings such as the Old Library at Trinity College, Leinster House and the Bank of Ireland were built. However, the most conspicuous reminders of Georgian Dublin are the beautiful squares and terraces around

**Georgian doorknocker in Merrion Square**

Merrion Square. Many of these buildings still have their original features, including doorknockers, fanlights and wrought-iron balconies.

Today, Southeast Dublin is very much the tourist heart of the city: few visitors can resist the lively atmosphere and attractive shops of Grafton Street. The area is also home to much of Ireland's cultural heritage. The National Gallery has a good collection of Irish and European paintings while the National Museum has superb displays of Irish Bronze Age gold and early Christian treasures. Nearby, the fascinating Natural History Museum has preserved its wonderful Victorian interior.

## SIGHTS AT A GLANCE

**Museums, Libraries and Galleries**
*National Gallery pp68–9* **11**
National Library **8**
*National Museum pp64–5* **7**
Natural History Museum **10**
Royal Hibernian Academy **13**

**Historic Buildings**
Bank of Ireland **1**
Leinster House **9**
Mansion House **5**
*Trinity College pp60–61* **2**

**Historic Streets**
Fitzwilliam Square **14**
Grafton Street **3**
Merrion Square **12**

**Churches**
St Ann's Church **6**

**Parks and Gardens**
St Stephen's Green **4**

### KEY

- Street-by-Street map
  See pp56–7
- Railway station
- DART station
- Luas stop
- Parking
- Tourist information

0 metres 250
0 yards 250

◁ **Marble bust of Jonathan Swift in the Old Library, Trinity College**

# Street-by-Street: Southeast Dublin

T HE AREA AROUND COLLEGE GREEN, dominated by the
façades of the Bank of Ireland and Trinity College, is
very much the heart of Dublin. The alleys and malls
cutting across busy pedestrianized Grafton Street boast
many of Dublin's better shops, hotels and restaurants.
Just off Kildare Street are the Irish Parliament, the
National Library and the National Museum. To escape the
city bustle many head for sanctuary in St Stephen's
Green, which is overlooked by fine Georgian buildings.

To Dublin
Castle

COLLEGE GRE

SUFFOLK ST

GRAFTO

**Bank of Ireland**
*This grand Georgian
building was origi-
nally built as the
Irish Parliament* ❶

**Statue of Molly
Malone (1988)**

**Grafton Street**
*Bewley's Oriental Café is the social hub of
this busy pedestrian street, alive with
talented buskers and pavement artists* ❸

**St Ann's Church**
*The striking façade
of the 18th-century
church was
added in 1868.
The interior
features lovely
stained-glass
windows* ❻

GRAFTON STREET

DUKE ST

ANNE ST STH

**Mansion House**
*This has been the official
residence of Dublin's Lord
Mayor since 1715* ❺

DAWSON ST

**Fusiliers' Arch (1907)**

ST STEPHEN'S GREEN NO

★ **St Stephen's Green**
*The relaxing city park is surrounded by many
grand buildings. In summer, lunch-time
concerts attract tourists and workers alike* ❹

To O'Connell Bridge

★ **Trinity College**
*Pomodoro's sculpture,* Sphere within Sphere *(1982), adds a modern dimension to the grand buildings of the campus* ❷

**National Library**
*Saintly cherubs appear on the frieze around the library's magnificent old reading room, once a haunt of novelist James Joyce* ❽

★ **National Museum**
*The museum's collection of Irish antiquities includes a mysterious bronze object known as the Petrie Crown (2nd century AD)* ❼

**Leinster House**
*This grand house has been the home of the Irish Parliament since 1922* ❾

NASSAU STREET

FREDERICK STREET

MOLESWORTH STREET

KILDARE STREET

**The Shelbourne Hotel**, built in 1867, dominates the north side of St Stephen's Green. It is a popular spot with tourists and locals for afternoon tea.

0 metres     50
0 yards      50

**STAR SIGHTS**

★ Trinity College

★ National Museum

★ St Stephen's Green

**KEY**

− − Suggested route

🚉 Luas stop

ℹ️ Tourist information

Original chamber of the Irish House of Lords at the Bank of Ireland

## Bank of Ireland ❶

2 College Green. **Map** D3. 📞 *604 3837.* ⏲ *10am–4pm Tue–Fri.* ⚫ *Mon & public hols.* **House of Lords** 🎫 *10:30am, 11:30am & 1:45pm Tue or by appt.*

THE PRESTIGIOUS offices of the Bank of Ireland began life as the first purpose-built parliament house in Europe. The original central section was started by Irish architect Edward Lovett Pearce and completed in 1739 after his death. Sadly, Pearce's masterpiece, the great octagonal chamber of the House of Commons (*see p38*), was destroyed by fire in 1792. The House of Lords, however, remains gloriously intact. Attendants lead tours that point out the coffered ceiling and oak panelling. There are also huge tapestries of the *Battle of the Boyne* and the *Siege of Londonderry*, and a splendid 1,233-piece crystal chandelier dating from 1788.

The east portico was added by architect James Gandon in 1785. Further additions to the building were made around 1797.

After the dissolution of the Irish Parliament in 1800, the Bank of Ireland bought the building. The present structure was then completed in 1808 with the transformation of the former lobby of the House of Commons into a magnificent cash office and the addition of a curving screen wall and the Foster Place annexe.

At the front of the bank on College Green – common grazing land in the 17th century – is a statue (1879) by John Foley of Henry Grattan (*see p38*), the most formidable leader of the old parliament.

## Trinity College ❷

See pp60–61.

## Grafton Street ❸

**Map** D4.

THE SPINE OF DUBLIN'S most popular and stylish shopping district runs south from Trinity College to the glass St Stephen's Green Shopping Centre. At the junction with Nassau Street is a statue by Jean Rynhart of *Molly Malone* (1988), the celebrated street trader from the traditional song "Molly Malone". This busy pedestrianized strip, characterized by energetic buskers and talented street

Bronze statue of *Molly Malone* on Grafton Street

theatre artists, boasts Brown Thomas, one of Dublin's finest department stores (*see p325*). However, the street's most famous landmark is Bewley's Oriental Café at No. 78 (*see p306*). Although not the oldest branch of this 150-year-old Dublin institution, this is Bewley's most popular location. It stands on the site of Samuel Whyte's school, whose illustrious roll included Robert Emmet (*see p75*), leader of the 1803 Rebellion, and the Duke of Wellington.

Despite the removal of the old wooden pews, the café retains its Victorian ambience, especially in the James Joyce Room on the first floor.

## St Stephen's Green ❹

**Map** D5. ⏲ *daylight hours.* **Newman House** 85–86 St Stephen's Green. 📞 *706 7422.* ⏲ *Jun–Aug: noon–5pm Tue–Fri, 2–5pm Sat, 11am–2pm Sun (Sep–May: by appointment).* ⚫ *public hols.* 📷 🎫 *obligatory.*

Royal College of Surgeons, which overlooks St Stephen's Green

ORIGINALLY one of three ancient commons in the old city, St Stephen's Green was enclosed in 1664. The 9-ha (22-acre) green was laid out in its present form in 1880, using a grant given by Lord Ardilaun, a member of the Guinness family. Landscaped with flowerbeds, trees, a fountain and a lake, the green is dotted with memorials to eminent Dubliners, including Ardilaun himself. There is a bust of James Joyce (*see p88*), and a memorial by Henry Moore (1967) dedicated to WB Yeats (*see pp224–5*). At

**Dubliners relaxing by the lake in St Stephen's Green**

the Merrion Row corner stands a massive monument (1967) by Edward Delaney to 18th-century nationalist leader Wolfe Tone – it is known locally as "Tonehenge". The 1887 bandstand is still the focal point for free daytime concerts in summer.

The imposing Royal College of Surgeons stands on the west side. Built in 1806, it was commandeered by rebel troops under Countess Constance Markievicz in the 1916 Rising (see pp42–3) and its columns still bear the marks of bullets from the fighting.

The busiest side of the Green is the north, known during the 19th century as the Beaux' Walk and still home to several gentlemen's clubs. The most prominent building is the venerable Shelbourne Hotel (see p287). Dating back to 1867, its entrance is adorned by statues of Nubian princesses and attendant slaves. It is well worth popping in for a look at the chandeliered foyer and for afternoon tea in the Lord Mayor's Lounge.

Situated on the south side is Newman House, home of the Catholic University of Ireland (now part of University College). Opened in 1854, its first rector was English theologian John Henry Newman. Famous past pupils include Patrick Pearse, a leader of the 1916 Rising, former Taoiseach Eamon de Valera (see p43) and author James Joyce.

Tours reveal some of the best Georgian interior decor to survive in the city. The walls and ceilings of the Apollo Room and Saloon at No. 85 are festooned with intricate Baroque stuccowork (1739) by the Swiss brothers Paolo and Filippo Francini. The Bishops' Room at No. 86 is decorated with heavy 19th-century furniture.

The small University Church (1856) next door has a colourful, richly marbled Byzantine interior. Also on the south side of St Stephen's Green is Iveagh House, a town house once owned by the Guinness family and now the Department of Foreign Affairs.

## Mansion House ❺

Dawson St. **Map** E4. ⬤ *to the public.*

Set back from Dawson Street by a neat cobbled fore-court, the Mansion House is an attractive Queen Anne-style building. It was built in 1710 for the aristocrat Joshua Dawson, after whom the street is named. The Dublin Corporation bought it from him five years later as the official residence of the city's Lord Mayor. A grey stucco façade was added in Victorian times.

The Dáil Eireann (see p63), which adopted the Declaration of Independence, first met here on 21 January 1919. The Fado Restaurant (see p306) in the old supper room is in period style.

## St Ann's Church ❻

Dawson St. **Map** E4. ☎ 676 7727. ⬤ *10am–4pm Mon–Fri (also for Sun service, phone to check).*

Founded in 1707, St Ann's striking Romanesque façade was added in 1868. Inside are colourful stained-glass windows, dating from the mid-19th century. The church has a long tradition of charity work: in 1723 Lord Newton left a bequest to buy bread for the poor. The original shelf for the bread still stands next to the altar.

Famous past parishioners include Wolfe Tone (see p39), who was married here in 1785, Douglas Hyde (see p43) and Bram Stoker (1847–1912), author of *Dracula*.

**Detail of window depicting Faith, Hope and Charity, St Ann's Church**

# Trinity College ❷

**Trinity College coat of arms**

Trinity college was founded in 1592 by Queen Elizabeth I on the site of an Augustinian monastery. Originally a Protestant college, it only began to take Catholics in numbers after 1970, when the Catholic Church relaxed its opposition to their attending. Among Trinity's many famous students were playwrights Oliver Goldsmith and Samuel Beckett, and political writer Edmund Burke. The college's lawns and cobbled quads provide a pleasant haven in the heart of the city. The major attractions are the Old Library and the *Book of Kells*, housed in the Treasury.

**★ Campanile**
*The 30-m (98-ft) bell tower was built in 1853 by Sir Charles Lanyon, architect of Queen's University, Belfast (see p270).*

**Reclining Connected Forms (1969) by Henry Moore**

**Dining Hall (1761)**

**Chapel** *(1798)*
*This was the first university chapel in the Republic to accept all denominations. The painted window above the altar is from 1867.*

**Parliament Square**

**Statue of Edmund Burke (1868) by John Foley**

**Main entrance**

**Statue of Oliver Goldsmith (1864) by John Foley**

**Provost's House (c. 1760)**

## SAMUEL BECKETT (1906–89)

Nobel prizewinner Samuel Beckett was born at Foxrock, south of Dublin. In 1923 he entered Trinity, and later graduated with a first in modern languages and a gold medal. He was also a keen member of the college cricket team. Forsaking Ireland, Beckett moved to France in the early 1930s. Many of his major works such as *Waiting for Godot* (1951) were written first in French, and later translated, by Beckett, into English.

**Examination Hall**
*Completed in 1791 to a design by Sir William Chambers, the hall features a gilded oak chandelier and ornate ceilings by Michael Stapleton.*

**Library Square**
*The red-brick building (known as the Rubrics) on the east side of Library Square was built around 1700 and is the oldest surviving part of the college.*

**VISITORS' CHECKLIST**

College Green. **Map** D3. 608 1724. DART to Tara Street. 14, 15, 46 & many other routes. **Old Library and Treasury** 9:30am–5pm Mon–Sat, 9:30am (noon in winter)–4:30pm Sun & some public hols (last adm: 30 min before closing). 10 days at Christmas. by arrangement. **Chapel** by appt. **Douglas Hyde Gallery** for exhibitions only.

**Shop and entrance to Old Library**

**The Museum Building**, completed in 1857, is noted for its Venetian exterior, and its magnificent multicoloured hall and double-domed roof.

**New Square**

**Sphere within Sphere** (1982) was given to the college by its sculptor Arnaldo Pomodoro.

**Berkeley Library Building by Paul Koralek** (1967)

**Fellows' Square**

**Entrance from Nassau Street**

**The Douglas Hyde Gallery** was built in the 1970s to house temporary art exhibitions.

★ **Treasury**
*This detail is from the* Book of Durrow, *one of the other magnificent illuminated manuscripts housed in the Treasury along with the celebrated* Book of Kells *(see p62).*

★ **Old Library** (1732)
*The spectacular Long Room measures 64 m (210 ft) from end to end. It houses 200,000 antiquarian texts, marble busts of scholars and the oldest surviving harp in Ireland.*

**STAR FEATURES**

★ **Old Library**

★ **Treasury**

★ **Campanile**

# The Book of Kells

THE MOST RICHLY decorated of Ireland's medieval illuminated manuscripts, the *Book of Kells* may have been the work of monks from Iona, who fled to Kells *(see p233)* in AD 806 after a Viking raid. The book, which was moved to Trinity College *(see p60–61)* in the 17th century, contains the four gospels in Latin. The scribes who copied the texts also embellished their calligraphy with intricate interlacing spirals as well as human figures and animals. Some of the dyes used were imported from as far as the Middle East.

Pair of moths

Stylized angel

The Greek letter "X"

*The symbols* of the four evangelists are used as decoration throughout the book. The figure of the man symbolizes St Matthew.

**The letter** that looks like a "P" is a Greek "R".

The letter "I"

Interlacing motifs

Cat watching rats

*A full-page portrait* of St Matthew, shown standing barefoot in front of a throne, precedes the opening words of his gospel.

**Rats eating** bread could be a reference to sinners taking Holy Communion. The symbolism of the animals and people decorating the manuscript is often hard to interpret.

## MONOGRAM PAGE
This, the most elaborate page of the book, contains the first three words of St Matthew's account of the birth of Christ. The first word "XRI" is an abbreviation of "Christi".

*The text* is in a beautifully rounded Celtic script with brightly ornamented initial letters. Animal and human forms are often used to decorate the end of a line.

The magnificent domed Reading Room on the first floor of the National Library

## National Museum **❼**

See pp64–5.

## National Library **❽**

Kildare St. **Map** E4. **(** 603 0200.
**☐** 10am–9pm Mon–Wed, 10am–
5pm Thu & Fri, 10am–1pm Sat.
**●** public hols.

DESIGNED BY Sir Thomas Deane, the National Library was opened in 1890. It was built to house the collection of the Royal Dublin Society, which was formed in 1731 to promote the arts and sciences and improve conditions for the poor. The Library contains first editions of every major Irish writer and a copy of almost every book ever published in Ireland. The list of distinguished Irish writers is well known and all are represented here. There is a huge collection of old maps, papers, and manuscripts by such names as playwright George Bernard Shaw and politician and liberator, Daniel O'Connell (see p40).

The first-floor Reading Room (where Joyce sited the literary debate in *Ulysses*) has well-worn desks and green-shaded lamps. Simply ask an attendant for a visitor's pass. There is also a small genealogy exhibit; a more extensive display,

along with details on how to trace family trees, can be found at the Heraldic Museum in the Genealogical Office a few doors down at Nos. 2 and 3 Kildare Street.

## Leinster House **❾**

Kildare St. **Map** E4. **(** 618 3000.
**☐** to the public by appt only.
**☒** phone for details.

THIS STATELY MANSION houses the *Dáil* and the *Seanad* – the two chambers of the Irish Parliament. It was originally built for the Duke of Leinster in 1745. Designed by German-born architect Richard Castle, the Kildare Street façade resembles that of a large town house. However, the rear, looking on to Merrion Square, has the air of a country estate complete with sweeping lawns. The Royal Dublin Society bought the building in 1815. The government obtained a part of it in 1922 for parliamentary use and bought the entire building two years later.

To arrange a guided tour of the main rooms, including the *Seanad* chamber with its heavily ornamented ceiling, phone before you visit.

### THE IRISH PARLIAMENT

The Irish Free State, forerunner of the Republic of Ireland, was inaugurated in 1922 (see p42), although an unofficial Irish parliament, the *Dáil*, had already been in existence since 1919. Today, parliament is made up of two houses: the *Dáil* (House of Representatives) and the *Seanad Éireann* (Senate). The Prime Minister is the *Taoiseach* and the deputy, the *Tánaiste*. The *Dáil's* 166 representatives – *Teachta Dala*, known as TDs – are elected by proportional representation. The 60-strong *Seanad* is appointed by various individuals and authorities, including the *Taoiseach* and the University of Dublin.

Opening of the first parliament of the Irish Free State in 1922

# National Museum ●

THE NATIONAL MUSEUM OF IRELAND was built
in the 1880s to the design of Sir Thomas
Deane. Its splendid domed rotunda features
marble pillars and a zodiac mosaic floor.
The Treasury houses priceless items such as
the Broighter gold boat (see p31), while Ór –
Ireland's Gold, an exhibition on Ireland's
Bronze Age gold, has fine jewellery such as
the Gleninsheen Gorget (see pp30–31). Many
collections have now moved to the annexe
of the museum at Collins Barracks (see p90).

**Egyptian Mummy**
*This mummy of the lady Tentdinebu
is thought to date back to c.945–716
BC. Covered in brilliant colours, it is
part of the stunning
Egyptian collection.*

**★ Ór – Ireland's Gold**
*This is one of the most extensive
collections of Bronze Age gold in
Western Europe. This gold lunula
(c. 1800 BC) is one of many pieces
of fine jewellery in the exhibition.*

## KEY TO FLOORPLAN

- ☐ The Road to Independence
- ☐ Ór – Ireland's Gold
- ☐ The Treasury
- ☐ Prehistoric Ireland
- ☐ Medieval Ireland
- ☐ Viking Ireland
- ☐ Ancient Egypt
- ☐ Temporary exhibition space
- ■ Non-exhibition space

**Flag from 1916 Rising**
The Road to Independence
*exhibition covers historical
events between 1900 and
1921. This flag flew over
Dublin's GPO during the
Easter Rising* (see p87).

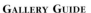

## GALLERY GUIDE
*The ground floor holds The Treasury, Ór – Ireland's
Gold exhibition, The Road to Independence and
the Prehistoric Ireland display. On the first floor is
the Medieval Ireland exhibition, which illustrates
many aspects of life in later medieval Ireland. Also
on the first floor are artifacts from Ancient Egypt
and from the Viking settlement of Dublin.*

**Main entrance**

**The domed
rotunda**, based
on the design of
the Altes Museum
in Berlin, makes
an impressive
entrance hall.

**The Treasury**
houses masterpieces
of Irish crafts such as
the Ardagh Chalice
(see p53).

**First floor**

**Temporary exhibition space** is located in the gallery of the second floor. Recent exhibitions have included *Viking Ships* and *Finds from Irish Wetlands.*

**VISITORS' CHECKLIST**

Kildare St. **Map** E4. **[** 677 7444.
**▢** *DART to Pearse Station.*
**▦** *10, 11, 13 and many other routes.* **◯** *10am–5pm Tue–Sat, 2–5pm Sun.* **●** *Good Fri & 25 Dec.* **◼ ◺** *ground floor only.*
**◻ ◻ ◻** **w** www.museum.ie

**Wooden Object**
*The Viking exhibition houses many items, including coins, pottery and swords, uncovered in the 1970s from the Viking settlement discovered beside the Liffey at Wood Quay (see p61).*

**★ Cross of Cong**
*Some 75 cm (30 inches) in height, this processional cross shows a high level of craftsmanship. Dating from 1123, its gilt-bronze plating is adorned with silver wire, crystals and enamelled studs.*

**Ground floor**

**Crucifixion Plaque**
*This plaque is one of the earliest depictions of the crucifixion found in Ireland. Dating from the late 7th century, it may have been decoration for a manuscript cover.*

**St Patrick's Bell**, made of bronze-coated iron, is housed in a beautiful 12th-century shrine *(see inset p3).*

**★ Tara Brooch**
*Found at Bettystown, County Meath, this ornate brooch dates from the 8th century AD. It is decorated on the front and rear with a filigree of gold wire entwined around settings of amber and enamel.*

**STAR EXHIBITS**

★ **Ór – Ireland's Gold**

★ **Cross of Cong**

★ **Tara Brooch**

## Natural History Museum 🔟

Merrion St. **Map** E4. 🕿 677 7444.
🕐 10am–5pm Tue–Sat, 2–5pm Sun.
⬤ Good Fri & Dec 25. 🚻 ground
floor only.

**K**NOWN AFFECTIONATELY as the "Dead Zoo", this museum is crammed with antique glass cabinets containing stuffed animals from around the world. The museum was opened to the public in 1857 with an inaugural lecture by Dr David Livingstone. The building has barely altered since Victorian times, and is now practically a museum piece itself.

The Irish room on the ground floor holds exhibits on Irish wildlife. Inside the front door are three huge skeletons of the extinct giant deer, better known as the "Irish elk". Also on this floor are shelves stacked with jars of bizarre creatures such as octopuses, leeches and worms preserved in embalming fluid.

The upper gallery houses the noted Blaschka Collection of glass models of marine life, and a display of buffalo and deer trophies. Suspended from the ceiling are the skeletons of a fin whale, found at Bantry Bay *(see p159)* in 1862, and a humpback whale, which was found stranded at Inishcrone in County Sligo in 1893.

**Lawn and front entrance of the Natural History Museum**

## National Gallery 1️⃣1️⃣

*See pp68–9.*

**Georgian town houses overlooking Merrion Square gardens**

## Merrion Square 1️⃣2️⃣

**Map** F4.

**M**ERRION SQUARE is one of Dublin's largest and grandest Georgian squares. Covering about 5 ha (12 acres), the square was laid out by John Ensor around 1762.

On the west side are the impressive façades of the Natural History Museum, the National Gallery and the front garden of Leinster House *(see p63)*. However, this august triumvirate does not compare with the lovely Georgian town houses on the other three sides of the square. Many have brightly painted doors with original features such as wrought-iron balconies, ornate doorknockers and fanlights. The oldest and finest houses are on the north side.

Many of the houses – now predominantly used as office space – have plaques detailing the rich and famous who once lived in them. These include Catholic emancipation leader Daniel O'Connell *(see p40)*, who lived at No. 58 and poet WB Yeats *(see pp224–5)*, who lived at No. 82. The playwright Oscar Wilde *(see p20)* spent his childhood at No. 1.

The attractive central park features colourful flower and shrub beds. In the 1840s it served a grim function as an emergency soup kitchen, feeding the hungry during the Great Famine *(see p211)*. On the northwest side of the park stands the restored Rutland Fountain. It was originally erected in 1791 for the sole use of Dublin's poor.

Just off the square, at No. 24 Merrion Street Upper, is the birthplace of the Duke of Wellington, who, when teased about his Irish background, said, "Being born in a stable does not make one a horse."

## Royal Hibernian Academy 1️⃣3️⃣

15 Ely Place. **Map** E5. 🕿 661 2558.
🕐 11am–5pm Tue, Wed, Fri & Sat, 11am–9pm Thu, 2–5pm Sun.
⬤ public & Christmas hols. 🚻

**T**HE ACADEMY is one of the largest exhibition spaces in the city. It puts on touring exhibitions and mounts shows of painting, sculpture and other work by Ireland's best young art and design students. This modern brick-and-plate-glass building does, however, look out of place at the end of Ely Place, an attractive Georgian cul-de-sac.

## Fitzwilliam Square 1️⃣4️⃣

**Map** E5. **No. 29 Fitzwilliam St Lower**
🕿 702 6165. 🕐 10am–5pm Tue–Sat, 2–5pm Sun. ⬤ 3 weeks at Christmas. 📷🚻

**D**ATING FROM 1825, this was one of the last Georgian squares to be laid out in central Dublin. Much smaller than Merrion Square, it is a popular location for medical practices.

In the 1960s, more than 20 town houses on Fitzwilliam Street Lower, a continuation of the east side of the square, were destroyed to make way for the headquarters of the Electricity Supply Board. The company has since tried to appease public indignation by renovating No. 29 as a Georgian showpiece home.

# Dublin's Georgian Terraces

THE 18TH CENTURY was Dublin's Age of Elegance, a time of relative prosperity when the Irish gentry, keen not to appear as the poor relations of Britain, set about remodelling Dublin into one of the most elegant cities in Europe. Terraced town houses were built, forming handsome new streets and squares. During the 19th century the city's wealth declined,

*Doorknocker, Merrion Square*

forcing some middle-class families to divide their homes into tenements. Many of Dublin's once grand streets slowly deteriorated. A century later the property boom of the 1960s threatened to rip out what was left of Georgian Dublin. Fortunately, much has survived and some of the city's finest architecture can be seen in Merrion Square and Fitzwilliam Square.

**The bedrooms** were usually on the second floor, while the upper floors contained the servants' quarters and children's rooms.

Playroom

Attic

*Wrought-iron balconies gave added prestige to the Georgian house. Those still in place today are mostly later Victorian additions.*

*Lavish stuccowork was an important way of showing an owner's wealth during the 18th century.*

**The drawing room** was always on the first floor. The high ceiling was decorated with the finest plasterwork.

**The dining room** was normally on the ground floor.

Architrave

**The kitchen** contained a huge cooking range which was fired by either coal or wood. The adjoining pantry was used to store the household's groceries.

*The doorway was usually crowned with a segmented fanlight. The principal decoration on the door itself was a heavy brass knocker.*

### GEORGIAN TERRACED HOUSE

While Georgian streetscapes may appear uniform, closer inspection reveals a diversity of styles in terms of details such as fanlights, architraves and balconies. The hallways usually had stone floors and, facing the hall door, a staircase rising to the upper floors. Many of the town houses did not have gardens – the railed-off parks in the centre of the squares were reserved for residents only and served as such.

# National Gallery ⑪

THIS PURPOSE-BUILT gallery was opened to the public in 1864. It houses many excellent exhibits, largely due to generous bequests, such as the Milltown collection of works of art from Russborough House *(see p124).* Playwright George Bernard Shaw was also a benefactor, leaving a third of his estate to the gallery. A new wing has been added to the gallery, which now has more than 700 works on display. Although the emphasis is on Irish landscape art and portraits, the major schools of European painting are well represented with works by Goya, El Greco, Vermeer, Titian and Monet.

**The Houseless Wanderer by John Foley**

## GALLERY GUIDE

*The main entrance is through the lofty Millennium Wing on Clare Street. Irish and British collections are housed on level 1, with the National Portrait Gallery on the mezzanine level. The European Schools are located in the original gallery building on level 2, with changing special exhibitions installed in the adjacent Millennium Wing.*

★ **Pierrot**
*This Cubist-style work, by Spanish-born artist Juan Gris is one of many variations he painted on the theme of Pierrot and Harlequin. This particular one dates from 1921.*

★ **For the Road**
*The Yeats Museum houses works by Jack B Yeats (1871–1957) and his family. This mysterious painting reflects the artist's obsession with the Sligo countryside.*

**The Shaw Room** is an elegant hall, lined with full-length portraits, dating from the 17th century onwards, and lit by magnificent Waterford Crystal chandeliers.

**Merrion Square entrance**

---

## STAR PAINTINGS

★ **The Taking of Christ by Caravaggio**

★ **Pierrot by Juan Gris**

★ **For the Road by Jack Yeats**

★ **The Taking of Christ**
*Rediscovered in a Dublin Jesuit house in 1990, this 1602 composition by Caravaggio has enhanced the gallery's reputation.*

**VISITORS' CHECKLIST**

Merrion Square West. **Map** E4.
661 5133. DART to Pearse.
5, 6, 7, 8, 44, 47, 48A.
9:30am–5:30pm Mon–Wed, Fri & Sat, 9:30am–8:30pm Thu, noon–5:30pm Sun. Good Fri, 24–26 Dec. for special exhibitions.
w www.nationalgallery.ie

**The Millennium Wing**, a new airy entrance court, has provided the gallery with space to showcase major travelling shows.

**Mezzanine level**

**Level 2**

**Judith with the Head of Holofernes**
*This monochrome image by Andrea Mantegna (c. 1431–1506) depicts the decapitation of an Assyrian chief.*

**Level 1**

**The Sick Call**
*Painted in a Pre-Raphaelite style by Matthew James Lawless, this 1863 canvas evokes the suffering of the Irish population in the years following the Famine.*

**Entrance level**

**Main entrance (Clare Street)**

**KEY TO FLOORPLAN**

- Irish School
- British School
- Portraiture
- European Sculpture and Decorative Arts
- Print Room
- Italian School
- French School
- Spanish School
- Northern European Schools
- Baroque
- Greek and Russian Schools
- Temporary exhibitions
- Non-exhibition space

# SOUTHWEST DUBLIN

THE AREA around Dublin Castle was first settled in prehistoric times, and it was from here that the city grew. Dublin gets its name from the dark pool *(Dubh Linn)* which formed at the confluence of the Liffey and the Poddle, a river which once ran through the site of Dublin Castle. It is now channelled underground and trickles out into the Liffey by Grattan Bridge. Archaeological excavations behind Wood Quay, on the banks of the Liffey, reveal that the Vikings established a trading settlement here around 841.

Following Strongbow's invasion of 1170, a medieval city began to emerge; the Anglo-Normans built strong defensive walls around the castle.

**Memorial to Turlough O'Carolan in St Patrick's Cathedral**

A small reconstructed section of these old city walls can be seen at St Audoen's Church. More conspicuous reminders of the Anglo-Normans are provided by the grand medieval Christ Church Cathedral and Ireland's largest church, St Patrick's Cathedral. When the city expanded to the north and east during the Georgian era, the narrow cobbled streets of Temple Bar became a quarter of skilled craftsmen and merchants. Today this area is considered to be the trendiest part of town, and is home to a variety of alternative shops and cafés. The Powerscourt Townhouse, an elegant 18th-century mansion, has been converted into one of the city's best shopping centres.

## SIGHTS AT A GLANCE

**Museums and Libraries**
Chester Beatty Library and Gallery of Oriental Art ❷
Dublinia ❽
Marsh's Library ⓬

**Historic Buildings**
City Hall ❸
*Dublin Castle pp74–5* ❶
Powerscourt Townhouse ❹
Tailors' Hall ❿

**Historic Streets**
Temple Bar ❺
Wood Quay ❻

**Churches**
*Christ Church Cathedral pp78–9* ❼
St Audoen's Church ❾
St Patrick's Cathedral ⓫
Whitefriar Street Carmelite Church ⓭

## KEY

Street-by-Street map See pp72–3

**P** Parking

0 metres 250
0 yards 250

◁ **Temple Bar, a centre for the arts and a popular meeting spot for young Dubliners**

# Street-by-Street: Southwest Dublin

**D**ESPITE ITS WEALTH of ancient buildings, such as Dublin Castle and Christ Church Cathedral, this part of Dublin lacks the sleek appeal of the neighbouring streets around Grafton Street. In recent years, however, redevelopment has helped to rejuvenate the area, especially around Temple Bar, where the attractive cobbled streets are lined with interesting shops, galleries and cafés.

**Sunlight Chambers** were built in 1900 for the Lever Brothers company. The delightful terracotta decoration on the façade advertises their main business of soap manufacturing.

**Wood Quay**
*This is where the Vikings established their first permanent settlement in Ireland around 841* **6**

★ **Christ Church Cathedral**
*Huge family monuments including that of the 19th Earl of Kildare can be found in Ireland's oldest cathedral, which also has a fascinating crypt* **7**

**St Werburgh's Church**
An ornate interior hides behind the somewhat drab exterior of this 18th-century church.

**Dublinia**
*Medieval Dublin is the subject of this interactive museum, located in the former Synod Hall of the Church of Ireland. It is linked to Christ Church by a bridge* **8**

**City Hall**
*Originally built as the Royal Exchange in 1779, the city's municipal headquarters is fronted by a huge Corinthian portico* **3**

★ **Dublin Castle**
*The Drawing Room, with its Waterford crystal chandelier, is part of a suite of luxurious rooms built in the 18th century for the Viceroys of Ireland* **1**

Ha'penny Bridge

O'Connell Bridge

Millennium Bridge

QUAY

TEMPLE BAR

FOWNES ST

CROWN ALLEY

TEMPLE LANE

EUSTACE STREET

DAME STREET

STH GT GEORGE'S ST

DAME CT

EXCHEQUER ST

WILLIAM ST SOUTH

DRURY ST

★ **Temple Bar**
*This arts and entertainments district occupies a maze of narrow, cobbled streets* ❺

**Central Bank of Ireland**

**LOCATOR MAP**
*See Dublin map pp110–11*

NORTH OF THE LIFFEY
SOUTHWEST DUBLIN
SOUTHEAST DUBLIN

**The Covered Market**
between Drury Street and South Great George's Street is a popular spot for buying second-hand clothes and antique jewellery.

**Powerscourt Townhouse**
*This shopping centre is one of the best places in Dublin to find fashion accessories and arts and crafts* ❹

**To Grafton Street**

**KEY**

– – – Suggested route

**The Long Hall** is a magnificent, old-fashioned, smoky pub. Behind the narrow room's long bar stands a bewildering array of antique clocks.

**Dublin Civic Museum**, set in the former City Assembly House, has a wide range of displays covering the history of Dublin from pre-Viking times until the 1960s.

0 metres 50
0 yards 50

**STAR SIGHTS**

★ **Dublin Castle**

★ **Temple Bar**

★ **Christ Church Cathedral**

# Dublin Castle ❶

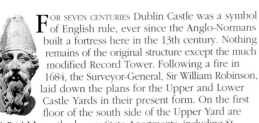

F OR SEVEN CENTURIES Dublin Castle was a symbol
of English rule, ever since the Anglo-Normans
built a fortress here in the 13th century. Nothing
remains of the original structure except the much
modified Record Tower. Following a fire in
1684, the Surveyor-General, Sir William Robinson,
laid down the plans for the Upper and Lower
Castle Yards in their present form. On the first
floor of the south side of the Upper Yard are
the luxury State Apartments, including St
Patrick's Hall. These rooms, with Killybegs
carpets and chandeliers of Waterford glass, served as
home to the British-appointed Viceroys of Ireland.

**St Patrick by Edward Smyth**

**Figure of Justice**
*Facing the Upper Yard
above the main entrance
from Cork Hill, this statue
roused much cynicism
among Dubliners, who
felt she was turning her
back on the city.*

**★ Throne Room**
*Built in 1740, this room
contains a throne said to
have been presented by
William of Orange after
his victory at the Battle of
the Boyne (see p236).*

**Bedford Tower (1761)**

**Entrance from Cork Hill**

**Portrait Gallery**

**Wedgwood Room**

**Entrance to State Apartments**

**Upper Yard**

**Bermingham Tower** dates from
the 13th century.
It was turned into
an elegant supper
room around 1740.

**Entrance to Upper Yard**

**Octagonal Tower (c. 1812)**

**Record Tower (1226)**

**★ St Patrick's Hall**
*This hall, with its banners of
the now defunct Knights of St
Patrick, has ceiling paintings
by Vincenzo Valdré (1778),
symbolizing the relationship
between Britain and Ireland.*

**The Chapel Royal** was
completed in 1814 by
Francis Johnston. The 100
heads on the exterior of this
Neo-Gothic church were
carved by Edward Smyth.

## ROBERT EMMET

Robert Emmet (1778–1803), leader of the abortive 1803 rebellion, is remembered as a heroic champion of Irish liberty. His plan was to capture Dublin Castle as a signal for the country to rise up against the Act of Union (see p40). Emmet was caught and publicly hanged, but the defiant, patriotic speech he made from the dock helped to inspire future generations of Irish freedom fighters.

Government offices

wer Yard

Dame Street

## STAR FEATURES

★ St Patrick's Hall

★ Throne Room

Manuscript (1874) from the Holy Koran written by calligrapher Ahmad Shaikh in Kashmir, Chester Beatty Library

# Chester Beatty Library and Gallery of Oriental Art ❷

Clock Tower Building, Dublin Castle. 407 0750. 10am–5pm Mon–Fri (Tue–Fri Oct–Apr), 11am–5pm Sat, 1pm–5pm Sun. Good Fri, 24–26 Dec & public holidays.

THIS COLLECTION of Oriental manuscripts and art was bequeathed to Ireland by the American mining magnate and art collector Sir Alfred Chester Beatty, who died in 1968. This generous act no doubt led to his selection as Ireland's first honorary citizen in 1957. During his lifetime, Beatty accumulated almost 300 copies of the Koran, representing the works of many master calligraphers. Among the other exhibits are 6,000-year-old Babylonian stone tablets, Greek papyri and biblical material written in Coptic, the original language of Egypt.

Treasures from the Far East include a collection of Chinese jade books – each leaf is made from thinly cut jade, engraved with Chinese characters which are then filled with gold. Burmese and Siamese art is represented by the collection of 18th- and 19th-century *Parabaiks*, books of folk tales with colourful illustrations on mulberry leaf paper. The Japanese collection includes paintings, woodblock prints and books and scrolls from the 16th to 18th centuries. The illustrations were painted

by Buddhist monks. One of the most beautiful manuscripts in the western European collection is the *Coëtivy Book of Hours*, an illuminated 15th–century French prayer book.

# City Hall ❸

Cork Hill, Dame St. **Map** C3. 672 2204. 10am–5:15pm Mon–Sat, 2pm–5pm Sun and public holidays. Good Fri, 24–26 Dec.

DESIGNED BY Thomas Cooley, this imposing Corinthian-style building was erected between 1769 and 1779 as the Royal Exchange. It was taken over by Dublin Corporation in 1852 as a meeting place for the city council – a role it keeps to this day.

The building has recently been restored to its original condition and a permanent exhibition on the city's history, Dublin City Hall - The Story of the Capital, is housed on the lower ground floor.

City Hall from Parliament Street

**Interior of Powerscourt Townhouse Shopping Centre**

# Powerscourt Townhouse ❹

South William St. **Map D4.** 679 4144. ☐ 10am–6pm Mon–Fri (8pm Thu), 9am–6pm Sat, noon–6pm Sun. See also **Shopping in Ireland** pp322–5.

COMPLETED IN 1774 by Robert Mack, this grand mansion was built as the city home of Viscount Powerscourt, who also had a country estate at Enniskerry (see pp126–7). Granite from the Powerscourt estate was used in its construction. Today the building houses one of Dublin's best shopping centres. Inside it still features the original grand mahogany staircase, and detailed plasterwork by Michael Stapleton.

The building became a drapery warehouse in the 1830s, and major restoration during the 1960s turned it into a centre of specialist galleries, antique shops, jewellery stalls, cafés and other shop units. The enclosed central courtyard, topped by a glass dome, is a popular meeting place with Dubliners. The centre can also be reached from Grafton Street down the narrow Johnson Court alley.

# Temple Bar ❺

**Map C3. Temple Bar Information** 671 5717 (24hr info line). See also **Entertainment in Dublin** p106. **Dublin's Viking Adventure** Essex Street West. 679 6040. ☐ Tue–Sat. 📷 obligatory. W www.templebar.ie

SOME OF DUBLIN'S best night spots, restaurants and unusual shops line these narrow, cobbled streets running between the Bank of Ireland (see p58) and Christ Church Cathedral. In the 18th century the area was home to many insalubrious characters – Fownes Street was noted for its brothels. It was also the birthplace of parliamentarian Henry Grattan (see p38). Skilled craftsmen and artisans, such as clockmakers and printers, lived and worked around Temple Bar until postwar industrialization led to a decline in the area's fortunes.

In the 1970s, the CIE (the national transport authority) bought up parcels of land in this area to build a major bus depot. Before building, the CIE rented out, on cheap leases, some of the old retail and warehouse premises to young artists and to record, clothing and book shops. The area developed an "alternative" identity and when redevelopment plans were scrapped the artists and retailers stayed on. Described by some cynics as the city's "officially designated arts zone", Temple Bar has prospered and today is an exciting place with bars, restaurants, shops and galleries. Stylish residential and commercial development is contributing further to the area's appeal.

Organizations based here include the Irish Film Centre, the experimental Project Arts Centre and the DESIGNyard, an applied arts centre showing and selling contemporary Irish jewellery and furniture. Also here is Dublin's Viking Adventure, a multimedia reconstruction of life in Dublin during the 9th century. The Children's Cultural Centre offers theatre, workshops and other children's entertainment.

**A pub in Temple Bar**

# Wood Quay ❻

**Map** B3.

NAMED AFTER the timber supports used to reclaim the land, excavations at Wood Quay have revealed the remains of one of the earliest Viking villages in Ireland (see p77). It is hoped that part of the excavated area will eventually be open to public view.

Adjacent to Wood Quay, artifacts including coins, pottery, swords and leatherwork, form part of Dublin's Viking Adventure, an entertaining multimedia tour complete with "stormy" ship voyage, recreated houses, authentic smells, and actors in period costume. More Viking artifacts can be seen at the Dublinia exhibition (see p77) and at the National Museum (see p64–5).

**Strolling through the streets of Temple Bar**

Former Synod Hall, now home to the Dublinia exhibition

## Christ Church Cathedral ❼

*See pp78–9.*

## Dublinia ❽

St Michael's Hill. **Map** B3. 679
4611. ☐ Apr–Sep: 10am–5pm daily;
Oct–Mar: 11am–4pm Mon–Sat,
10am–4:30pm Sun. ● 24–26 Dec &
public holidays. minimum charge
to enter Christ Church Cathedral via
bridge. W www.dublinia.ie

MANAGED BY the non-profit-making Medieval Trust, the Dublinia exhibition covers the formative period of Dublin's history from the arrival of the Anglo-Normans in 1170 to the closure of the monas-teries in the 1540s *(see p36)*. The exhibition is housed in the Neo-Gothic Synod Hall, which, up until 1983, was home to the ruling body of the Church of Ireland. The building and the hump-backed bridge linking it to Christ Church Cathedral date from the 1870s. Before Dublinia was established in 1993, the Synod Hall was briefly used as a nightclub.

The exhibition is entered via the basement where visitors walk through life-size reconstructions of the Medieval City. These depict major events in Dublin's history, such as the Black Death and the rebellion of Silken Thomas *(see p36)*. The ground floor houses a large scale model of Dublin in around 1500, a display of artifacts from the Wood Quay excavation, and reconstruc-tions including the inside of a late medieval merchant's kitchen. There are also infor-mation panels on the themes of trade, merchants and religion. A multi-screen presentation on Dublin's medieval history can be seen in the dark-wood panelled Great Hall on the first floor.

The 60-m (200-ft) high St Michael's Tower offers one of the best vantage points for views across the city.

## St Audoen's Church ❾

Cornmarket. **Map** B3. 677 0088.

Tower of St Audoen's Church

DESIGNATED a national monument and open for visitors in the summer months, St Audoen's is Dublin's earliest surviving medieval church. The 15th-century nave remains intact and the three bells date from 1423. The church stands in an attractive churchyard with well-maintained lawns and shrubs. To the rear, steps lead down to St Audoen's Arch, the only remaining gateway of the old city. Flanking the gate are restored sections of the 13th-century city walls.

Next door stands St Audoen's Roman Catholic Church, which was built in the 1840s. The two Pacific clam shells by the front door hold holy water. In the basement is an audiovisual presentation on pre-Viking Ireland.

---

### THE VIKINGS IN DUBLIN

Viking raiders arrived in Ireland in the late 8th century and founded Dublin in 841. They built a fort where the River Poddle met the Liffey at a black pool *(Dubh Linn)*, on the site of Dublin Castle. They also established a settlement along the banks of the Liffey at Wood Quay *(see p76)*. Much of their trade was based on silver, slaves and piracy.

Following their defeat by Brian Boru at the Battle of Clontarf in 1014 *(see p32)*, the Vikings integrated fully with the local Irish, adopting Christian beliefs. After Strongbow's Anglo-Norman invasion in 1170 *(see p34)*, the flourishing Hiberno-Viking trading community declined, and many were banished to a separate colony called Oxmanstown, just north of the river.

Artist's impression of a Viking ship in Dublin Bay

# Christ Church Cathedral ❼

**Arms on Lord Mayor's pew**

CHRIST CHURCH CATHEDRAL was established by the Hiberno-Norse king of Dublin, Sitric "Silkbeard", and the first bishop of Dublin, Dunan. It was rebuilt by the Anglo-Norman archbishop, John Cumin in 1186. It is the cathedral for the Church of Ireland (Anglican) diocese of Dublin and Glendalough. By the 19th century it was in a bad state of repair, but was completely remodelled by architect George Street in the 1870s. The vast 12th-century crypt has recently been restored.

**★ Medieval Lectern**
*This beautiful brass lectern was hand-wrought during the Middle Ages. It stands on the north side of the nave, in front of the pulpit. The matching lectern on the south side is Victorian.*

**The Lord Mayor's pew** is usually kept in the north aisle, but is moved to the front of the nave when used by Dublin's civic dignitaries. It features a carving of the city arms and a stand for the civic mace.

**Great Nave**
*The 25-m (68-ft) high nave has some fine early Gothic arches. On the north side, the original 13th-century wall leans out by as much as 50 cm (18 in) due to the weight of the roof.*

**Entrance**

**★ Strongbow Monument**
*The large effigy in chain armour is probably not Strongbow. However, his remains are buried in the cathedral and the curious half-figure may be part of his original tomb.*

**The bridge** to the Synod Hall was added when the cathedral was being rebuilt in the 1870s.

| STAR FEATURES |
| --- |
| ★ **Strongbow Monument** |
| ★ **Crypt** |
| ★ **Medieval Lectern** |

**Chapel of St Laud**
*The casket on the wall contains the heart of St Laurence O'Toole. The chapel features original medieval floor tiles.*

**VISITORS' CHECKLIST**

Christchurch Place. **Map** B3.
677 8099. 50, 66, 77 & many other routes. 10am–5pm daily (6pm in summer). 26 Dec. **Donation** 9:45 & 12:45pm Mon–Sat, 11am & 3:30pm Sun. W www.cccdublin.ie

**The Lady Chapel** is used to celebrate the daily Eucharist.

★ **Crypt**
*This decorated plate by Francis Garthorne is part of a collection presented to Christ Church Cathedral by King William III to mark his victory at the Battle of the Boyne in 1690.*

Stairs to crypt

Crypt

**The foundations** of the original Chapter House date back to the early 13th century.

**Romanesque Doorway**
*Leading to the south transept, this ornately carved doorway is one of the finest examples of 12th-century Irish stonework.*

**TIMELINE**

| | | | | |
|---|---|---|---|---|
| | **1240** Completion of stone cathedral | **1600** Shopkeepers rent crypt space | **1689** King James II of England worships in cathedral | **1983** Cathedral ceases using Synod Hall |
| **1038** Construction of original wooden Viking cathedral | | **1541** King Henry VIII alters constitution of cathedral | | |

| 1000 | 1200 | 1400 | 1600 | 1800 |
|---|---|---|---|---|

| | | | | |
|---|---|---|---|---|
| **1186** The first Anglo-Norman archbishop, John Cumin, begins work on the new cathedral. | *Meeting between Lambert Simnel and the Earl of Kildare (see p35)* | **1742** Choir participates in first performance of Handel's *Messiah*<br>**1487** Coronation of 10-year-old Lambert Simnel as King of England | | **1871** Major rebuilding of the cathedral begins, including Synod Hall and bridge |

## Tailors' Hall ⑩

Back Lane. **Map** B4. ⬤ *to the public.*

DUBLIN'S only surviving guildhall preserves a delightful corner of old Dublin in an otherwise busy redevelopment zone. Built in 1706, it stands behind a limestone arch in a quiet cobbled yard. The building is the oldest guildhall in Ireland and was used by various trade groups including hosiers, saddlers and barber-surgeons as well as tailors. It also hosted many political meetings – Wolfe Tone addressed a public United Irishmen rally here before the 1798 rebellion *(see p39)*. The building closed in the early 1960s due to neglect, but a successful appeal by Desmond Guinness saw the hall completely refurbished. It is now the home of *An Taisce* (the Irish National Trust).

**Façade of Tailors' Hall, home of the Irish National Trust**

**St Patrick's Cathedral with Minot's Tower and spire**

## St Patrick's Cathedral ⑪

St Patrick's Close. **Map** B4.
📞 475 4817. ◻ Mar–Oct:
9am–5pm Mon–Sat, 9am–5pm Sun;
Nov–Feb: 9am–5pm Mon–Sat,
9am–3pm Sun. Tours are not
admitted during services. ♿

IRELAND'S LARGEST CHURCH was founded beside a sacred well where St Patrick is said to have baptized converts around AD 450. A stone slab bearing a Celtic cross and covering the well was unearthed at the turn of the 20th century. It is now preserved in the west end of the cathedral's nave. The original building was just a wooden chapel and remained so until 1192 when Archbishop John Comyn rebuilt the cathedral in stone.

Over the centuries, St Patrick's came to be seen as the people's church, while the older Christ Church Cathedral *(see pp78–9)* nearby was more associated with the British establishment. In the mid-17th century, Huguenot refugees from France arrived in Dublin, and were given the Lady Chapel by the Dean and Chapter as their place of worship. The chapel was separated from the rest of the cathedral and used by the Huguenots until the late 18th century. Today St Patrick's Cathedral is the Protestant Church of Ireland's national cathedral.

Much of the present building dates back to work completed between 1254 and 1270. The cathedral suffered over the centuries from desecration, fire and neglect but, thanks to the generosity of Sir Benjamin Guinness, it underwent extensive restoration during the 1860s. The building is 91 m (300 ft) long; at the western end is a 43-m (141-ft) tower, restored by Archbishop Minot in 1370 and now known as Minot's Tower. The spire was added in the 18th century.

The interior is dotted with memorial busts, brasses and monuments. A leaflet available at the front desk helps identify and locate them. The largest, most colourful and elaborate tomb was dedicated to the Boyle family in the 17th century. Erected by Richard Boyle, Earl of Cork, in memory of his second wife Katherine, it is decorated with painted figures of his family,

### JONATHAN SWIFT (1667–1745)

Jonathan Swift was born in Dublin and educated at Trinity College *(see pp60–61)*. He left for England in 1689, but returned in 1694 when his political career failed. Back in Ireland he began a life in the church, becoming Dean of St Patrick's in 1713. In addition to his clerical duties, Swift was a prolific political commentator – his best-known work, *Gulliver's Travels*, contains a bitter satire on Anglo-Irish relations. Swift's personal life, particularly his friendship with two younger women, Ester Johnson, better known as Stella, and Hester Vanhomrigh, attracted criticism. In his final years, Swift suffered from Menière's disease – an illness of the ear which led many to believe him insane.

including his wife's parents. Other famous citizens remembered in the church include the harpist Turlough O'Carolan (1670–1738) and Douglas Hyde (1860–1949), the first President of Ireland.

Many visitors come to see the memorials associated with Jonathan Swift, the satirical writer and Dean of St Patrick's. In the north transept is "Swift's Corner", containing various memorabilia such as an altar table and a bookcase holding his death mask and various pamphlets. A self-penned epitaph can be found on the wall on the southwest side of the nave. A few steps away, two brass plates mark his grave and that of his beloved Stella, who died in 1728.

At the west end of the nave is an old door with a hole in it – a relic from a feud which took place between the Lords Kildare and Ormonde in 1492. The latter took refuge in the Chapter House, but a truce was soon made and a hole was cut in the door by Lord Kildare so that the two could shake hands in friendship.

## Marsh's Library ⑫

St Patrick's Close. **Map** B4.
📞 454 3511. 🕐 10am–1pm & 2–5pm Mon & Wed–Fri, 10:30am–1pm Sat. ⬤ Tue & Sun, 10 days at Christmas & public hols. ♿

THE OLDEST public library in Ireland was built in 1701 for Archbishop Narcissus Marsh, a Dean of St Patrick's Cathedral. It was designed by Sir William Robinson, architect of much of Dublin Castle (see pp74–5) and the Royal Hospital Kilmainham (see p95).

Inside, the bookcases are topped by a mitre and feature carved gables with lettering in gold leaf. To the rear of the library are wired alcoves (or "cages") where readers were locked in with rare books. The collection of books from the 16th, 17th and early 18th centuries includes irreplaceable volumes, such as Bishop Bedell's 1685 translation of the Old Testament into Irish. There is also a volume of Clarendon's History of the Rebellion, with anti-Scottish margin notes by Jonathan Swift.

**Statue of Virgin and Child in Whitefriar Street Carmelite Church**

## Whitefriar Street Carmelite Church ⑬

56 Aungier St. **Map** C4. 📞 475 8821. 🕐 8am–6:30pm Mon & Wed–Fri, 8am–9pm Tue, 8am–7pm Sat, 8am–7:30pm Sun.

DESIGNED by George Papworth, this Catholic church was built in 1827. It stands on the site of a 16th-century Carmelite priory of which nothing remains.

In contrast to the two Church of Ireland cathedrals, St Patrick's and Christ Church, which are usually full of tourists, this church is frequented by local worshippers. Every day they come to light candles to various saints, including St Valentine – the patron saint of lovers. His remains, previously buried in the cemetery of St Hippolytus in Rome, were offered to the church as a gift from Pope Gregory XVI in 1836. Today they rest beneath the commemorative statue of St Valentine, which stands in the northeast corner of the church beside the high altar.

Nearby is a Flemish oak statue of the Virgin and Child, dating from the late 15th or early 16th century. It may have belonged to St Mary's Abbey (see p91) and is believed to be the only wooden statue of its kind to escape destruction when Ireland's monasteries were sacked at the time of the Reformation (see p36).

**Carved monument (1632) to the Boyle family in St Patrick's Cathedral**

# NORTH OF THE LIFFEY

**D**UBLIN'S NORTHSIDE was the last part of the city to be developed during the 18th century. The city authorities envisioned an area of wide, leafy avenues, but the reality of today's heavy traffic has rather spoiled their original plans. Nonetheless, O'Connell Street, lined with fine statues and monuments, is an impressive thoroughfare. This is where Dubliners come to shop and some of the adjacent streets, particularly Moore Street, have a colourful parade of stalls and street vendors offering cut-price tobacco.

Some public buildings, such as James Gandon's glorious Custom House and majestic Four Courts, together with

**Statue of James Joyce on Earl Street North**

the historic General Post Office *(see p87)*, add grace to the area. The Rotunda Hospital, Europe's first purpose-built maternity hospital, is another fine building. Dublin's two most celebrated theatres, the Abbey and the Gate, act as a cultural magnet, as do the Dublin Writers Museum and the James Joyce Cultural Centre, two museums dedicated to writers who lived in the city.

Some of the city's finest Georgian streetscapes are found in the north of the city. Many have been neglected for decades, but thankfully some areas, most notably North Great George's Street, are undergoing restoration.

## SIGHTS AT A GLANCE

**Museums and Galleries**
Dublin Writers Museum **9**
Hugh Lane Municipal Gallery of Modern Art **10**
Old Jameson's Distillery **13**
James Joyce Cultural Centre **5**

**Historic Buildings**
Custom House **1**
Four Courts **15**
King's Inns **11**
Rotunda Hospital **7**

**Historic Streets and Bridges**
Ha'penny Bridge **17**
O'Connell Street **3**
Smithfield **12**

**Theatres**
Abbey Theatre **2**
Gate Theatre **6**

**Churches**
St Mary's Abbey **16**
St Mary's Pro-Cathedral **4**
St Michan's Church **14**

**Parks and Gardens**
Garden of Remembrance **8**

**KEY**

| | Street-by-Street map See pp84–5 |
| --- | --- |
| | Coach station |
| | Luas stop |
| P | Parking |
| i | Tourist information |

**0 metres** 250
**0 yards** 250

◁ **Portico of the Custom House, illuminated at night**

# Street-by-Street: Around O'Connell Street

Tʜʀᴏᴜɢʜᴏᴜᴛ ᴛʜᴇ Georgian era, O'Connell Street was very much the fashionable part of Dublin to live. However, the 1916 Easter Rising destroyed many of the fine buildings along the street,

**Detail of pavement mosaic, Moore Street**

including much of the General Post Office – only its original façade still stands. Today, this main thoroughfare is lined with shops and businesses. Other attractions nearby include St Mary's Pro-Cathedral and James Gandon's Custom House, overlooking the Liffey.

**James Joyce Cultural Centre**
*This well-restored Georgian town house contains a small Joyce museum* ❺

**Parnell Monument (1911)**

**Gate Theatre**
*Founded in 1928, the Gate is renowned for its productions of contemporary drama* ❻

**Rotunda Hospital**
*Housed in the Rotunda Hospital is a chapel built in the 1750s to the design of Richard Castle. It features lovely stained-glass windows, fluted columns, panelling and intricate iron balustrades* ❼

**Moore Street Market** is the busiest of the streets off O'Connell. Be prepared for the shrill cries of the stall holders offering an enormous variety of fresh fruit, vegetables and cut flowers.

**The Monument of Light,** an elegant stainless steel spire, rises to 120 m (394 ft).

**The General Post Office,** the grandest building on O'Connell Street, was the centre of the 1916 Rising.

**James Larkin Statue (1981)**

### Key

— Suggested route

🚊 Luas stop

ℹ Tourist information

0 metres    50

0 yards    50

### Star Sights

★ Custom House

★ O'Connell Street

NORTH OF THE LIFFEY

**St Mary's Pro-Cathedral**
*Built around 1825, this is Dublin's main place of worship for Catholics. The plaster relief above the altar in the sanctuary depicts* The Ascension **4**

**LOCATOR MAP**
*See Dublin map pp110–11*

**The statue of James Joyce** (1990), by Marjorie Fitzgibbon, commemorates one of Ireland's most famous novelists. Born in Dublin in 1882, he catalogued the people and streets of Dublin in *Dubliners* and in his most celebrated work, *Ulysses*.

**Abbey Theatre**
*Ireland's national theatre is known throughout the world for its productions by Irish playwrights, such as Sean O'Casey and JM Synge* **2**

**★ O'Connell Street**
*This monument to Daniel O'Connell by John Foley took 19 years to complete from the laying of its foundation stone in 1864* **3**

**Butt Bridge**

**CUSTOM HOUSE QUAY**

**★ Custom House**
*This grotesque head, by Edward Smyth, symbolizes the River Liffey. It is one of 14 carved keystones that adorn the building* **1**

**O'Connell Bridge**

**To Trinity College**

Illuminated façade of the Custom House reflected in the Liffey

# Custom House ❶

Custom House Quay. **Map** E2. **[**
888 2538. ◯ mid-Mar–Oct: 10am–
12.30pm Mon–Fri, 2pm–5pm Sat–Sun
& Bank Holidays; Nov–mid-Mar:
10am–12.30pm Wed–Fri, 2pm–5pm
Sun. ♿ on weekdays only.

THIS MAJESTIC BUILDING was
designed as the Custom
House by the English architect
James Gandon. However, just
nine years after its completion,
the 1800 Act of Union (see p40)
transferred the custom and
excise business to London,
rendering the building
practically obsolete. In 1921,
supporters of Sinn Fein celebrated their election victory
by setting light to what they
saw as a symbol of British
imperialism. The fire blazed
for five days causing extensive
damage. Reconstruction took
place in 1926, although further
deterioration meant that the
building was not completely
restored until 1991, when it reopened as government offices.
    The main façade is made up
of pavilions at each end with
a Doric portico in its centre.
The arms of Ireland crown the
two pavilions and a series of
14 allegorical heads, by Dublin
sculptor Edward Smyth, form
the keystones of arches and
entrances. These heads depict
Ireland's main rivers and the
Atlantic Ocean. Topping the
central copper dome is a
statue of Commerce, while the
north façade is decorated with
figures representing Europe,
Africa, America and Asia.
The best view of the building
is from the south of the Liffey
beyond Matt Talbot Bridge.

# Abbey Theatre ❷

Lower Abbey St. **Map** E2. **[** 878
7222. ◯ for performances only. **Box
office** ◯ 10:30am–7pm Mon–Sat. See
also **Entertainment in Dublin** p107.

Logo of the Abbey Theatre

FOUNDED in 1898 with WB
Yeats and Lady Gregory as
co-directors, the Abbey staged
its first play in 1904. The early
years of this much lauded
national theatre witnessed
works by WB Yeats, JM Synge
and Sean O'Casey. Many were
controversial: nationalist sensi-
tivities were severely tested in
1926 during the premiere of
O'Casey's The Plough and the
Stars when the flag of the Irish
Free State appeared on stage
in a scene which featured a
pub frequented by prostitutes.
    While presenting the work
of eminent foreign authors
from time to time, the prime
objective of the Abbey &
Peacock Theatres is to
provide a performance space
for Irish dramatic writing.
Some of the most acclaimed
performances have been Brian
Friel's Dancing at Lughnasa
and Translations, Partrick
Kavanagh's Tarry Flynn, Dion
Boucicault's The Colleen
Bawn and Hugh Leonard's
Love in the Title.

# O'Connell Street ❸

**Map** D1–D2.

O'CONNELL STREET is very
different from the original
plans of Irish aristocrat Luke
Gardiner. When he bought
the land in the mid-18th
century, Gardiner envisioned
a grand residential parade
with an elegant mall running
along its centre. Such plans
were short-lived. The construction of Carlisle (now
O'Connell) Bridge in 1790
transformed the street into the
city's main north-south route.
Also, several buildings were
destroyed during the 1916
Easter Rising and the Irish
Civil War. Since the 1960s

many of the old buildings have been replaced by the plate glass and neon of fast food joints, amusement arcades and chain stores.

A few venerable buildings remain, such as the General Post Office (1818), Gresham Hotel (1817), Clery's department store (1822) and the Royal Dublin Hotel, part of which occupies the street's only original town house.

A walk down the central mall is the most enjoyable way to see the street's mix of architectural styles and take a close look at the series of monuments lining the route. At the south end stands a massive monument to Daniel O'Connell *(see p40)*, unveiled in 1882. The street, which throughout the 19th century had been called Sackville Street, was renamed after O'Connell in 1922. Higher up, almost facing the General Post Office, is an animated statue of James Larkin (1867–1943), leader of the Dublin general strike in 1913. The next statue is of Father Theobald Mathew (1790–1856), founder of the Pioneer Total Abstinence

South end of O'Connell Street with monument to Daniel O'Connell

**Statue of James Larkin (1981) in O'Connell Street**

Movement. At the north end of the street is the obelisk-shaped monument to Charles Stewart Parnell (1846–91), who was leader of the Home Rule Party and known as the "uncrowned King of Ireland" *(see p41)*. A new addition to O'Connell Street is the Monument of Light, erected on the site where Nelson's column used to be. The monument is a stainless steel, conical spire which tapers from a 3-metre diameter base to a 10 cm pointed tip of optical glass at a height of 120 metres.

## St Mary's Pro-Cathedral ❹

Marlborough St. **Map** D2. 874 5441. 8:30am–6.30pm.

DEDICATED in 1825 before Catholic emancipation was fully effected *(see p40)*, St Mary's is Dublin's Catholic cathedral. Its backstreet site was the best the city's Anglo-Irish leaders would allow.

The façade is based on a Greek temple. Doric columns support a pediment with statues of St Mary, St Patrick and St Laurence O'Toole, 12th-century Archbishop of Dublin and patron saint of the city. Inside, one striking feature is the intricately carved high altar.

St Mary's has a great musical tradition and is home to the famous Palestrina Choir, with which the great tenor, John McCormack *(see p22)*, began his career in 1904. The choir can still be heard every Sunday morning at 11am.

---

### THE GENERAL POST OFFICE (GPO)

*Irish Life* magazine cover showing the 1916 Easter Rising

Built in 1818 halfway along O'Connell Street, the GPO became a symbol of the 1916 Irish Rising. Members of the Irish Volunteers and Irish Citizen Army seized the building on Easter Monday, and Patrick Pearse *(see p42)* read out the Proclamation of the Irish Republic from its steps. The rebels remained inside for a week, but shelling from the British eventually forced them out. At first, many Irish people viewed the Rising unfavourably. However, as WB Yeats wrote, matters "changed utterly" and a "terrible beauty was born" when, during the following weeks, 14 of the leaders were caught and shot at Kilmainham Gaol *(see p95)*. Inside the building is a sculpture of the mythical Irish warrior Cuchulainn *(see p24)*, dedicated to those who died for their part in the Easter Rising.

**Austere Neo-Classical interior of St Mary's Pro-Cathedral**

## James Joyce Cultural Centre ❺

35 North Great George's St. **Map** D1.
[ 878 8547. ◯ 9:30am– 5pm
Mon–Sat, 12:30–5pm Sun (11am–
5pm Jun–Aug). ● Good Fri &
23–27 Dec. 🎨 ✓

THIS AGREEABLE STOP on the
literary tourist trail is
primarily a meeting place for
Joyce enthusiasts, but is also
worth visiting for its Georgian
interior. The centre is in a
1784 town house which was
built for the Earl of Kenmare.
Michael Stapleton, one of the
greatest stuccodores of his
time, contributed to the plasterwork, of which the friezes are
particularly noteworthy.

The main literary display is
an absorbing set of biographies
of around 50 characters from
Joyce's novel Ulysses, who
were based on real Dublin
people. Professor Dennis J
Maginni, a peripheral character
in Ulysses, ran a dancing school
from this town house. Leopold
and Molly Bloom, the central
characters of Ulysses, lived a
short walk away at No. 7
Eccles Street. The centre also
organizes walking tours of
Joyce's Dublin, so a visit is a
must for all Joycean zealots.

At the top of the road, on
Great Denmark Street, is the
Jesuit-run Belvedere College
attended by Joyce between
1893 and 1898. He recalls his
unhappy schooldays there in
A Portrait of the Artist as a
Young Man. The college's
interior contains some of
Stapleton's best and most
colourful plasterwork (1785).

### JAMES JOYCE (1882–1941)

Born in Dublin, Joyce spent
most of his adult life in Europe.
He used the city of Dublin as
the setting for all his major
works including Dubliners,
A Portrait of the Artist as a
Young Man and Ulysses. Joyce
claimed that if the city was
ever destroyed it could be recreated through the pages of
Ulysses. However, the Irish
branded the book pornographic
and banned it until the 1960s.

## Gate Theatre ❻

1 Cavendish Row. **Map** D1.
◯ for performances only. **Box office**
[ 874 4045. ◯ 10am–7pm Mon–
Sat. See also **Entertainment in
Dublin** pp102–7.

**Entrance to the Gate Theatre**

RENOWNED FOR its staging of
contemporary international
drama in Dublin, the Gate
Theatre was founded in 1928
by Hilton Edwards and Mícheál
Mac Liammóir. The latter is
now best remembered for The

Importance of Being Oscar, his
long-running one-man show
about the writer Oscar Wilde
(see p20). An early success
was Denis Johnston's The
Old Lady Says No, so-called
because of the margin notes
made on one of his scripts by
Lady Gregory, founding director of the Abbey Theatre (see
p86). Although still noted for
staging new plays, the Gate's
current output often includes
classic Irish plays. Among the
young talent to get their first
break here were James Mason
and a teenaged Orson Welles.

## Rotunda Hospital ❼

Parnell Square West. **Map** D1.
[ 873 0700.

STANDING in the middle of
Parnell Square is Europe's
first purpose-built maternity
hospital. Founded in 1745 by
Dr Bartholomew Mosse, the
design of the hospital is similar
to that of Leinster House (see
p63). German-born architect,
Richard Castle, designed both.

At the east end of the hospital is the Rotunda, after
which the hospital is named.
It was built in 1764 by John
Ensor as Assembly Rooms to
host fundraising functions and
concerts. Franz Liszt gave a
concert here in 1843.

On the first floor is a chapel
featuring striking stained-glass
windows and exuberant
Rococo plasterwork and
ceiling (1755) by the stuccodore Bartholomew Cramillion.

Across the road from the
hospital is Conway's Pub.
Opened in 1745, it is a popular
retreat for expectant fathers.

**Stained-glass Venetian window (c. 1863) in Rotunda Hospital's chapel**

## Garden of Remembrance 8

Parnell Square. **Map** C1.
○ dawn–dusk daily.

A T THE NORTHERN END of
Parnell Square is a small,
peaceful park, dedicated to
the men and women who
have died in the pursuit of
Irish freedom. The Garden of
Remembrance marks the spot
where several leaders of the
1916 Easter Rising were held
overnight before being taken
to Kilmainham Gaol (see
p95), and was also where the
Irish Volunteers movement
was formed in 1913.

Designed by Daithí Hanly,
the garden was opened by
President Eamon de Valera
(see p43) in 1966, to mark the
50th anniversary of the
Easter Rising. In
the centre of the
garden's well-
kept lawns is a
cruciform pool.
A mosaic on
the floor of the
pool depicts
abandoned,
broken swords,
spears and shields,
symbolizing peace.
The focal point at
one end of the          *Children of Lir* in the
garden is a large    **Garden of Remembrance**
bronze sculpture
by Oisín Kelly (1971) of the
legendary *Children of Lir*, who
were changed into swans by
their stepmother (see p25).

**Gallery of Writers at Dublin Writers Museum**

## Dublin Writers Museum 9

18 Parnell Sq North. **Map** C1. 872
2077. ○ 10am–5pm Mon–Sat
(Jun–Aug: 10am–6pm), 11am–5pm
Sun & public hols. ● 25 & 26 Dec.

O PENED IN 1991, the museum
occupies a tasteful 18th-
century town house. There
are displays relating to Irish
literature in all its forms from
around the 10th century to
the present day. The
exhibits include paint-
ings, manuscripts, letters,
rare editions and
mementoes of many
of Ireland's finest
authors. There are a
number of temporary
exhibits and a sum-
ptuously decorated Gallery of
Writers upstairs. The museum
also hosts frequent poetry
readings and lectures. A good
café and a specialist book-
store, providing an out-of-
print search service, add to
the relaxed, friendly ambience.

## Hugh Lane Municipal Gallery of Modern Art 10

Charlemont House, Parnell Square
North. **Map** C1. 874 1903.
○ 9:30am–6pm Tue–Thu (Apr–Sep
8pm Thu), 9:30am–5pm Fri & Sat,
11am–5pm Sun. ● 23–25 Dec &
public hols. W www.hughlane.ie

A RT COLLECTOR Sir Hugh Lane
donated his collection of
Impressionist paintings to the
Dublin Corporation in 1905.
However, the failure to find a
suitable location for them
prompted Lane to begin the
process of transferring his gift
to the National Gallery in
London. The Corporation then
proposed Charlemont House
and Lane relented. However,
in 1915, before Lane's revised
will could be witnessed, he
died on board the torpedoed
liner *Lusitania (see p170).*
This led to a 50-year dispute
which has been resolved by
Dublin Corporation and the
National Gallery swapping the
collection every five years.

Besides the Lane bequest,
which includes paintings by
Degas, Courbet and Monet,
the gallery has an extensive
collection of modern Irish
paintings and a sculpture hall
with work by Rodin and
others. An exciting new
addition is a bequest by John
Edwards of the contents of
Francis Bacon's London studio.

*Beach Scene* (c. 1876) by Edgar Degas, Hugh Lane Municipal Gallery

Detail of wood carving (c. 1724) at St Michan's Church

# King's Inns ⓫

Henrietta St/Constitution Hill.
**Map** B1. ● *to the public.*

THIS CLASSICALLY proportioned public building was founded in 1795 as a place of residence and study for barristers. To build it, James Gandon chose to seal off the end of Henrietta Street, which at the time was one of Dublin's most fashionable addresses. Francis Johnston added the graceful cupola in 1816, and the building was finally completed in 1817. Inside is a fine Dining Hall, and the Registry of Deeds (formerly the Prerogative Court). The west façade has two doorways flanked by Classical caryatids carved by Edward Smyth. The male figure, with book and quill, represents the law.

Caryatid, King's Inns

Sadly, much of the area around Constitution Hill is less attractive than it was in Georgian times. However, the gardens, which are open to the public, are still pleasing.

# Smithfield ⓬

**Map** A2.

LAID OUT IN THE mid-17th century as a marketplace, Smithfield used to be one of Dublin's oldest residential areas. However, the two and a half acre space has received a £3.5 million makeover with

a well-designed pedestrian cobbled plaza. It is used as a venue for outdoor civic events and is lit by tall gas lighting masts. The traditional horse fair is still held here on the first Sunday of the month and is well worth seeing.

# Old Jameson's Distillery ⓭

Bow St. **Map** A2. ☏ 807 2355.
☐ 9am–5:30pm daily (last tour: 5:15pm). ● Good Friday, 25 & 26 Dec. ⓰ ⓰ ⓰ ⓰ ⓰

PROOF OF recent investment in the emerging Smithfield area is this large exhibition in a restored part of John Jameson's distillery, which produced whiskey from 1780 until 1971. A visit here starts with a video and further whiskey-related facts are then explained on a 20-minute tour. This takes you around displays set out as a working distillery, with different rooms devoted to the various stages of production.

The tour guides show how the Irish process differs from that of Scotch whisky: here the barley is dried with clean air, while in Scotland it is smoked over peat. The claim is that the Irish product is a smoother, less smoky tipple. After the tour, visitors can test this in the bar.

Sampling different brands at Old Jameson's Distillery

# St Michan's Church ⓮

Church St. **Map** B3. ☏ 872 4154.
☐ mid-Mar–Oct: 10am–12:45pm & 2–4:45pm Mon–Fri, 10am–12:45pm Sat; Nov–mid-Mar: 12:30–3:30pm Mon–Fri, 10am–12:45pm Sat. ⓰ ⓰

LARGELY REBUILT IN 1686 on the site of an 11th-century Hiberno-Viking church, the dull façade of St Michan's hides a more exciting interior. Deep in its vaults lie a number of bodies that have barely decomposed because of the dry atmosphere created by the church's magnesian limestone walls. Their wooden caskets, however, have cracked open, revealing the preserved bodies, complete with skin and strands of hair. Among those thought to have been mummified in this way are the brothers Henry and John Sheares, leaders of the 1798 rebellion (see p39), who were executed that year.

Other less gory attractions include the magnificent wood carving of fruits and violins and other instruments above the choir. There is also an organ (1724) on which Handel is said to have played. It is thought that the churchyard contains the unmarked grave of United Irishman Robert Emmet (see p75), leader of the abortive 1803 Rising.

# Four Courts ⓯

Inns Quay. **Map** B3. ☏ 872 5555.
☐ 10am–1pm, 2–4pm Mon–Fri (when courts in session).

COMPLETED IN 1796 by James Gandon, this majestic public building overlooks the River Liffey. It was virtually gutted 120 years later during the Irish Civil War (see pp42–3) when government forces bombarded anti-Treaty rebels into submission. The adjacent Public Records Office, with its irreplaceable collection of historical and legal documents dating back to the 12th century, was destroyed by fire.

By 1932, the main buildings were sympathetically restored using Gandon's original design. An imposing copper-covered lantern dome rises above the six-columned Corinthian portico, which is crowned with the figures of Moses, Justice and Mercy. This central section is flanked by two wings containing the four original courts: Common Pleas, Chancery, Exchequer and King's Bench. It is possible to walk into the central waiting hall under the grand dome; an information panel to the right of the entrance gives details of the building's history and functions.

## St Mary's Abbey ⑯

Meetinghouse Lane. **Map** C2.
[ 872 1490. ] mid-Jun–mid-Sep: 10am–5pm Wed & Sun.

FOUNDED BY Benedictines in 1139, but transferred to the Cistercian order just eight years later, this was one of the largest and most important monasteries in medieval Ireland. As well as controlling extensive estates, including whole villages, mills and fisheries, the abbey acted as state treasury and meeting place for the Council of Ireland. It was during a council meeting in St Mary's that "Silken Thomas" Fitzgerald (see p36) renounced his allegiance to Henry VIII and marched out to raise the short-lived rebellion of 1534. The monastery was dissolved in 1539 and during the 17th century the site served as a quarry. Stone from St Mary's was used in the construction of Essex Bridge (replaced by Grattan Bridge in 1874), just to the south of the abbey.

All that remains of the abbey today is the vaulted chamber of the Chapter House. This contains a historical display and a model of how the entire complex would have looked 800 years ago.

The Ha'penny Bridge looking from Temple Bar to Liffey Street

## Ha'penny Bridge ⑰

**Map** D3.

LINKING THE Temple Bar area (see p76) and Liffey Street, this high-arched cast-iron foot bridge is used by thousands of people every day. It was built by John Windsor, an ironworker from Shropshire, England. One of Dublin's most photographed sights, it was originally named the Wellington Bridge. It is now officially called the Liffey Bridge, but is also known as the Metal Bridge. Opened in 1816, the bridge got its better known nickname from the halfpenny toll that was levied on it up until 1919. A recent restoration, which included the installation of period lanterns, has made the bridge even more attractive.

James Gandon's Four Courts overlooking the River Liffey

# FURTHER AFIELD

THERE ARE many interesting sights just outside the city centre. The best part of a day can be spent exploring the western suburbs taking in the modern art museum housed in the splendid Royal Kilmainham Hospital and the eerie Kilmainham Gaol. Phoenix Park, Europe's largest city park, is a good place for a stroll and also has a zoo. Further north are the National Botanic Gardens, with over 20,000 plant species from around the world. Nearby is Marino Casino, one of Ireland's finest examples of Palladian architecture.

*Candelabra at Malahide Castle*

The magnificent coastline with its stunning views of Dublin Bay is easily reached by the DART rail network. It encompasses the towering promontory of Howth, while the highlights of the southern stretch are around Dalkey village and Killiney Bay. One of many Martello towers built as defences along this coast is known as the James Joyce Tower and houses a collection of Joyce memorabilia. To the northeast, a bit further from the city centre, is Malahide Castle, former home of the Talbot family.

## SIGHTS AT A GLANCE

**Museums and Galleries**
Collins Barracks **9**
Guinness Storehouse **4**
Irish Museum of Modern Art/
  Royal Hospital Kilmainham **3**
James Joyce Tower **13**

Kilmainham Gaol **2**
Shaw's Birthplace **6**
Waterways Visitors' Centre **8**

**Parks and Gardens**
National Botanic Gardens **5**
Phoenix Park **1**

**Historic Buildings**
Malahide Castle **10**
Marino Casino **7**

**Towns and Villages**
Dalkey **14**
Dun Laoghaire **12**
Howth **11**
Killiney **15**

### CENTRAL DUBLIN

GREATER DUBLIN AND ENVIRONS

0 kilometres 4
0 miles 2

**KEY**

Main sightseeing areas
Greater Dublin
Motorway
Major road
Minor road
Railway
Airport
Ferry port
Fast ferry port

15 km = 10 miles

◁ Martello tower at Howth Head

## Phoenix Park ❶

Park Gate, Conyngham Rd, Dublin 8.
🚌 *10, 25, 26, 37, 38, 39.* ⏰ *7am–11pm daily.* **Phoenix Park Visitor Centre** ☎ *677 0095.* ⏰ *Nov–mid March: 9:30am–4:30pm Sat & Sun only; Apr & May: 9:30am–5:30pm (mid to end Mar & Oct: 5pm) daily; Jun–Sep: 10am–6pm daily.* 🎟 🚻 ♿ *ground floor only.* **Zoo** ☎ *677 1425.* ⏰ *9:30am–6pm (4pm in winter) Mon–Sat, 10:30am–6pm (5pm in winter) Sun. Last admission 45 mins before closing.* 🎟 🚻 ♿
W *www.dublinzoo.ie*

J UST TO the west of the city centre, ringed by an 11-km (7-mile) wall, is Europe's largest enclosed city park. The name "Phoenix" is said to be a corruption of the Gaelic *Fionn Uisce*, or "clear water", referring to a spring near the **Phoenix Column**, crowned by a statue of the mythical bird. Phoenix Park originated in 1662, when the Duke of Ormonde turned the land into a deer park. In 1745 it was landscaped and opened to the public.

Near Park Gate is the lakeside **People's Garden** – the only part of the park which has been cultivated. A little further on are the **Zoological Gardens**, established in 1830, making them the third oldest zoo in the world. The zoo is renowned for the successful breeding of lions, including the one that appears at the beginning of MGM movies. The African Plains savannah houses the larger residents.

In addition to the Phoenix Column, the park has two other conspicuous monuments. The **Wellington Testimonial**, a 63-m (204-ft) obelisk, was begun in 1817 and completed in 1861. Its bronze bas-reliefs were made from captured French cannons. The 27-m (90-ft) steel **Papal**

**Pope John Paul II celebrating Mass in Phoenix Park in 1979**

**Cross** marks the spot where the pope celebrated Mass in front of one million people in 1979. Buildings within the park include two 18th-century houses: **Áras an Uachtaráin**, the Irish President's official residence, for which 525 tickets are issued every Saturday for a free guided tour, and **Deerfield**, home of the US Ambassador. **Ashtown Castle** is a restored 17th-century tower house, now home to the Phoenix Park Visitor Centre.

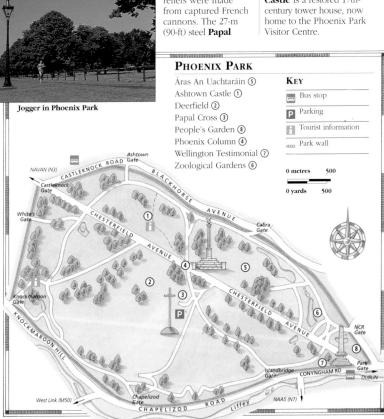

**Jogger in Phoenix Park**

### PHOENIX PARK

Áras An Uachtaráin ⑤
Ashtown Castle ①
Deerfield ②
Papal Cross ③
People's Garden ⑧
Phoenix Column ④
Wellington Testimonial ⑦
Zoological Gardens ⑥

**KEY**

🚌 Bus stop
P Parking
ℹ Tourist information
▦ Park wall

0 metres    500
0 yards     500

NAVAN (N3)
Ashtown Gate
CASTLEKNOCK ROAD
Castleknock Gate
BLACKHORSE AVENUE
White's Gate
CHESTERFIELD AVENUE
Cabra Gate
Knockmaroon Gate
CHESTERFIELD AVENUE
NCR Gate
KNOCKMAROON HILL
Islandbridge Gate
Park Gate
CONYNGHAM RD
DUBLIN
West Link (M50)
Chapelizod Gate
CHAPELIZOD ROAD
Liffey
NAAS (N7)

**Restored central hall at Kilmainham Gaol**

## Kilmainham Gaol ②

Inchicore Rd, Kilmainham, Dublin 8.
453 5984. 51B, 78A, 79.
Apr–Sep: 9:30am–6pm Sun–Fri;
Oct–Mar: 9:30am–5pm Mon–Fri,
10am–6pm Sun. Last adm 1 hr 15 min
before closing. 25 & 26 Dec.

Along tree-lined avenue runs
from the Royal Hospital
Kilmainham to the grim, grey
bulk of Kilmainham Gaol. The
building dates from 1789, but
was restored in the 1960s.
During its 130 years as a
prison, it housed many of
those involved in the fight for
Irish independence, including
Robert Emmet (see p75) and
Charles Stewart Parnell (p41).
The last prisoner held was
Eamon de Valera (p43), who
was released on 16 July, 1924.

Tours start in the chapel,
where Joseph Plunkett
married Grace Gifford just a
few hours before he faced the
firing squad for his part in the
1916 Rising (see pp42–3). The
tours end in the prison yard
where Plunkett's badly
wounded colleague James
Connolly, unable to stand up,
was strapped into a chair

before being shot. You also
pass the dank cells of those
involved in the 1798, 1803,
1848 and 1867 uprisings, as
well as the punishment cells
and hanging room. Exhibits
in the central hall include
personal momentoes of some
of the former inmates and
depictions of various events
which took place in the Gaol
until it closed in 1924.

Standing in the courtyard is
the *Asgard*, a ship used to
deliver arms from Germany
to the Nationalists in 1914.

## Irish Museum of Modern Art – Royal Hospital Kilmainham ③

Military Road, Kilmainham, Dublin 8.
612 9900. 68, 68A, 69, 78A,
79, 90, 123. **Irish Museum of
Modern Art** 10am–5:30pm
Tue–Sat, noon–5:30pm Sun & public
hols. Good Fri & 24–26 Dec.
W www.modernart.ie

Ireland's finest surviving 17th-
century building was laid out
in 1680, styled on Les Invalides
in Paris. It was built by Sir
William Robinson as a home
for 300 wounded soldiers – a
role it kept until 1927. When
it was completed, people were
so impressed by its Classical
symmetry that it was suggested it would be better used as
a campus for Trinity College.
The Baroque chapel has fine
carvings and intricate stained
glass. The plaster ceiling is a
replica of the original, which
fell in 1902. The hospital's
Formal Gardens, restored
using many of the 17th-
century designs, are now
open to the public.

In 1991, the hospital's former
residential quarters became the
Irish Museum of Modern Art.
The collection includes a
cross-section of Irish and
international modern and
contemporary art. Works are
displayed on a rotating basis
and include group and solo
shows, retrospectives and
special visiting exhibitions. A
recent addition is the separate,
multi-screen film theatre.

**The Royal Hospital Kilmainham**

**Drinking Guinness at a local pub**

## Guinness Storehouse ❹

St James's Gate, Dublin 8.
📞 408 4800. 🚌 78A, 51B, 123.
🕐 9:30am–5:00pm daily.
⬤ Good Fri, 24–26 Dec, 1 Jan.
♿ 📷 ♿ 🏠 ⓫ 🍴
🌐 www.guinnessstorehouse.com

THE GUINNESS STOREHOUSE is a new development based in St James's Gate Brewery, the original house of Guinness, now completely remodelled. This 1904 listed building covers nearly four acres of floor space over six floors built around a huge pint glass atrium. The first impression the visitor has is of walking into a large glass pint with light spilling down from above and the original lease signed by Arthur Guinness enshrined on the floor. The Ingredients section is next where visitors can touch, smell and feel the ingredients through interactive displays. The tour continues into an authentic Georgian anteroom to 'meet' Arthur Guinness and see him at work. The Brewing Process is a noisy, steamy and 'hoppy' area giving the impression of brewing all around with full explanantion of the process. The historical development of Guinness cooperage is accompanied by a live demonstration of the craft. Models and displays tell the story of Guinness transportation, the appeal of Guinness worldwide, and their popular advertising campaigns. The tour ends with a generous tasting of draught Guinness in the traditional Brewery Bar and the rooftop Gravity Bar.

# The Brewing of Guinness

**Label from a Guinness bottle**

GUINNESS IS A BLACK BEER, known as "stout", renowned for its distinctive malty flavour and smooth creamy head. From its humble beginnings over 200 years ago, the Guinness brewery site at St James's Gate now sprawls across 26 ha (65 acres). It is the largest brewery in Europe and exports beers to more than 120 countries throughout the world. Other famous brands owned by Guinness include Harp Lager and Smithwick's Ale.

**HOW GUINNESS IS MADE**
The four main ingredients used to brew Guinness are barley, hops, yeast and water which, contrary to popular belief, comes from the Wicklow Mountains rather than the River Liffey.

Barley

Flaked barley

Malted barley

Roasted barley

Grist mill

Grist

Masher

Water

Kieve

Sweet wort

Residual husks are removed

1 Irish barley is prepared in three ways – malted, flaked and roasted (to give the distinctive tint). These are all ground together in a grist mill to form a grist.

2 The grist is mixed together with hot water and mashed into a porridge-like consistency. The mixture is strained into a kieve, or mash tun, and left to stand for an hour. Here starches are turned into sugars, producing a dark, sweet wort.

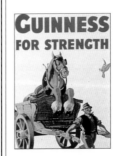

***Guinness advertising** has become almost as famous as the product itself. Since 1929, when the first advertisement announced that "Guinness is Good for You", poster and television advertising campaigns have employed many amusing images of both animals and people.*

## ARTHUR GUINNESS

**Arthur Guinness**

In December 1759, 34-year-old Arthur Guinness signed a 9,000-year lease at an annual rent of £45 to take over St James's Gate Brewery, which had lain vacant for almost ten years. At the time the brewing industry in Dublin was at a low ebb – the standard of ale was much criticized and in rural Ireland beer was virtually unknown, as whiskey, gin and poteen were the more favoured drinks. Furthermore, Irish beer was under threat from imports. Guinness started brewing ale, but was also aware of a black ale called porter, produced in London. This new beer was so called because of its popularity with porters at Billingsgate and Covent Garden markets. Guinness decided to stop making ales and develop his own recipe for porter (the word "stout" was not used until the 1920s). So successful was the switch that he made his first export shipment in 1769.

**Engraving (c. 1794) of a satisfied customer**

5 The liquid has now become a stout. The Guinness is matured and conditioned for up to ten days in tall storage tanks. It is then pumped into tankers or kegs to be sold throughout the world.

**Stainless steel kegs**

**Hops**

**Yeast**

**Kettle**

**Hopped wort**

**Stout**

**Centrifuge**

3 Hops, which provide the tangy taste in Guinness, are added to the wort in huge 20-tonne kettles. The ingredients are boiled to very high temperatures for about 90 minutes and then strained.

4 The hopped wort is cooled and the yeast is added. The mixture is passed to a fermenting vessel where some sugars are turned to alcohol. It is left to ferment for 48 hours and the yeast is removed by centrifuge.

**Draught and bottled Guinness**

*The Guinness brewery has relied heavily on water transport since its first export was shipped to England in 1769. The barges, which up until 1961 made the short trip with their cargo up the Liffey to Dublin Port, were a familiar sight on the river. Once at port, the stout would be loaded on to huge tanker ships for worldwide distribution.*

**Steel kettles used in modern-day brewing**

**Giant water lilies in the Lily House, National Botanic Gardens**

## National Botanic Gardens ❺

Botanic Ave, Glasnevin, Dublin 9.
**C** 837 4388. ▩ 13, 19, 19A, 134.
◯ Mar–Oct: 9am–6pm Mon–Sat,
11am–6pm Sun; Nov–Feb: 10am–
4:30pm Mon–Sat, 11am–4:30pm Sun.
● 25 Dec. ▨ ▦ ▨ ▨ on
request. **Glasnevin Cemetery** Finglas
Rd. **C** 830 1133. ▩ 40A, 40B from
Parnell Street. ◯ 8am–4:30pm daily.

O PENED in 1795, the National
Botanic Gardens are
Ireland's foremost centre of
botany and horticulture. They
still possess an old-world feel,
thanks to the beautiful cast-
iron Palm House and other
curvilinear glasshouses. These
were built between 1843 and
1869 by Richard Turner, the
architect who was also
responsible for the Palm House
at Kew Gardens, London, and
the glasshouses at Belfast's
Botanic Gardens (see p270).
  The 20-ha (49-acre) park
contains over 20,000 different
plant species. A particularly
attractive feature is the display
of colourful, old-fashioned
Victorian carpet bedding. There
are also rich collections of
cacti and orchids, a renowned
rose garden, and a 30-m (100-
ft) high redwood tree.

The gardens back on to the
huge Glasnevin or Prospect
Cemetery where many of
Ireland's political figures are
buried, including Charles
Stewart Parnell (see p41) and
Daniel O'Connell (see p40).

## Shaw's Birthplace ❻

33 Synge St, Dublin 8. **C** 475 0854.
▩ 16, 19, 122. ◯ May–Sep: 10am–
5pm Mon–Sat, 11am– 5pm Sun &
public hols. ▨ ▨

**Kitchen at Shaw's Birthplace**

P LAYWRIGHT and Nobel prizewinner George Bernard
Shaw was born in this house
on 26 July 1856. In 1876 he
followed his mother to London.
She had left four years earlier
with her daughters, fed up with
her husband's drinking habits.
It was in London that Shaw

met his wife Charlotte Payne-
Townsend. He stayed in England until his death in 1950.
  Inside the house visitors can
see the young Shaw's bedroom
and the kitchen where the
author remembered he drank
"much tea out of brown delft
left to 'draw' on the hob until
it was pure tannin". Although
there is little on Shaw's pro-
ductive years, the home gives
a fair idea of the lifestyle of a
Victorian middle-class family.

## Marino Casino ❼

Fairview Park, Dublin 3 (off Malahide
Rd. **C** 833 1618. ▩ 20A, 20B, 27,
42, 42C, 123. ◯ Feb–Mar &
Nov–Dec: noon–4pm (Apr: 5pm) Sat
& Sun only; Jun–Sep: 10am–6pm
(May & Oct: 5pm) daily. ▨ ▨
obligatory.

T HIS DELIGHTFUL little villa
(see pp38–9), built by Sir
William Chambers in the
1760s for Lord Charlemont,
now sits incongruously next
to a busy road and a housing
estate. Originally built
as a summer
house for the
Marino Estate, the
villa survives
although the main
house was pulled
down in 1921.
The Casino is
acknowledged
to be one of
the finest
examples of
Palladian
architecture        **Carved stone lion**
in Ireland.          **at Marino Casino**
Some
innovative features were used
in its construction, including
chimneys disguised as urns
and hollow columns that
accommodate drains. Outside,
four carved stone lions,
thought to be by English
sculptor Joseph Wilton, stand
guard at each of the corners.
  The building's squat, compact exterior conceals eight
rooms built on three floors
around a central staircase.
The ground floor comprises a
spacious hall and a saloon,
with beautiful silk hangings,
elaborate flooring and a coffered ceiling. On the first floor
is the ostentatious State Room.

# Waterways Visitors' Centre ❽

Grand Canal Quay, Dublin 2.
📞 677 7510. 🚌 2,3. 🕐 Jun–Sep: 9:30am–5:30pm daily; Oct–May: 12:30pm–5pm Wed–Sun (last adm 45 mins before closing). ⬤ 25 Dec. ♿ 📷 on request.

FIFTEEN MINUTES' WALK from Trinity College this building overlooks the Grand Canal Basin. Audiovisual displays and models illustrate Ireland's inland waterways and the wildlife found on and around them. One of the most interesting displays focuses on their construction: in the 18th century, canals were often called "navigations" and the men who built them were "navigators", a term shortened to "navvies".

## DUBLIN'S CANALS

The affluent Georgian era witnessed the building of the Grand and Royal canals linking Dublin with the River Shannon and the west coast. These two canals became the main arteries of trade and public transport in Ireland from the 1760s until the coming of the railways, which took much of the passenger business, almost a century later. However, the canals continued to carry freight until after World War II, finally closing to commercial traffic in 1960. Today the canals are well maintained and used mainly for pleasure-boating, cruising and fishing.

**Late 18th-century engraving of passenger ferry passing Harcourt Lock on the Grand Canal, taken from a painting by James Barralet**

**Stretch of the Grand Canal near Waterways Visitors' Centre**

# National Museum at Collins Barracks ❾

Benburb St, Dublin 7. 📞 677 7444. 🚌 25, 25A, 66, 67, 90. 🕐 10am–5pm Tue–Sat, 2–5pm Sun. ⬤ Good Fri, 25 Dec. 📷 ♿ 🚫

CLOSE TO Phoenix Park and just across the Liffey from the Guinness Brewery, stands the wonderful annexe of the National Museum (see pp64–5). Its setting in this historic building is an inspired move. The massive complex was commissioned by King William III in 1700, just ten years after victory at the Battle of the Boyne, and was the largest barracks in his domain, with living accommodation for over 5,000 people. It was in continuous use right up to the 1990s. Originally known as Dublin Barracks, the prefix was changed to "Royal" in 1803. After Irish independence the barracks was finally named for Michael Collins, the first commander-in-chief of the Irish Army.

The large central courtyard, measured at one hundred marching paces, is an object lesson in simplicity. In marked contrast to the grey institutional exterior, the museum's interior presents the exhibits in an innovative way that makes use of the latest technology.

Furniture, silver and scientific instrument collections form the bulk of items on show in the South Block. In the West Block, however, visitors get an insight into the history, work and development of the National Museum. The Out of Storage exhibit brings together a wide array of artefacts from around the world, with background information obtainable from banks of interactive multimedia computers. One of the highlights of the museum is the Curator's Choice section where 25 unusual exhibits – such as, for instance, an early hurling stick and ball – are displayed with a story line that explains their cultural significance.

There is also a large hall set aside for temporary displays. On-going expansion plans incorporate the entire barracks.

**An 18th-century, gilded wooden chair on display at Collins Barracks**

The oak-beamed Great Hall at Malahide Castle

## Malahide Castle 🔟

Malahide, Co Dublin. 🚉 and DART
from Connolly Station. 🚌 42 from
Beresford Place, near Busarus.
📞 846 2184. 🕐 Apr–Oct:
10am–5pm Mon–Sat, 11am–6pm
Sun & public hols; Nov–Mar: 10am–
5pm Mon–Sat, 11am–5pm Sun &
public hols. 🅿️ 🎫 obligatory.
**Fry Model Railway** 🕐 Apr–Sep:
10am–6pm Mon–Fri (5pm Sat),
2–6pm Sun & public hols; Oct–Mar:
2–5pm Sat, Sun & public hols. 🅿️ ♿
🌐 www.visitdublin.com

N EAR THE SEASIDE dormitory
town of Malahide stands
a huge castle set in 100 ha
(250 acres) of grounds. The
castle's core dates from the
14th century but later additions,
such as its rounded towers,
have given it a classic fairy-
tale appearance. The building
served  as a stately home for
the Talbot family until 1973.
They were staunch supporters
of James II: on the day of the
Battle of the Boyne in 1690
(see p236), 14 members of the
family breakfasted here; none
came back for supper.
   Guided tours take you round
the castle's collection of 18th-
century Irish furniture, the
oak-beamed Great Hall and
the impressively carved Oak

Room. Part of the Portrait
Collection, on loan from the
National Gallery (see pp68–9),
can be seen at the castle. It
includes portraits of the Talbot family and other figures
such as Wolfe Tone (see p39).
   In the old corn store is the
Fry Model Railway, started in
the 1920s by Cyril Fry, a local
railway engineer. The 240 sq m
(2,500 sq ft) exhibit contains
models of Irish trains, mini-
atures of stations, streets and
local landmarks such as the
River Liffey and Howth Head.

## Howth 🈡

Co Dublin. 🚉 DART. **Howth Castle
grounds** 🕐 8am–sunset daily.

T HE COMMERCIAL fishing town
of Howth marks the north-
ern limit of Dublin Bay.
Howth Head, a huge rocky
mass, has lovely views of the
bay. A footpath runs around
the tip of Howth Head, which
is known as the "Nose".
Nearby is Baily Lighthouse
(1814). Sadly, much of this
area – some of Ireland's prime
real estate – has suffered from
building development.
   To the west of the town is
Howth Castle, which dates
back to Norman times. Its
grounds are particularly
beautiful in May and June
when the rhododendrons and
azaleas are in full bloom.The
National Transport Museum in
the grounds is worth a visit
   Ireland's eye, an islet and
bird sanctuary where puffins
nest, can be reached by a
short boat trip from Howth.

## Dun Laoghaire 🈯

Co Dublin. 🚉 DART. **National
Maritime Museum of Ireland**
📞 280 0969. ⬤ Temporarily closed
for renovations. Telephone for up-to-
date information.

I RELAND'S MAJOR passenger
ferry port and yachting
centre, with its brightly
painted villas, parks and palm
trees, makes a surprising

Baily Lighthouse on the southeastern tip of Howth Head

**Yachts anchored in Dun Laoghaire harbour**

introduction to Ireland. On a good day it exudes a decidedly continental feel. Many visitors head straight out of Dun Laoghaire (pronounced Dunleary) but the town offers some magnificent walks around the harbour and to the lighthouse along the east pier. The villages of Sandycove and Dalkey can be reached via "The Metals" footpath which runs alongside the railway line.

Located in the 1837 Mariners' Church is the National Maritime Museum. Exhibits tell the story of Robert Halpin, who captained the ship that laid the first transatlantic telegraph cable in 1866. Also on display are a huge clockwork-driven lighthouse lens formerly used at Howth, and a longboat used by French officers during Wolfe Tone's unsuccessful invasion at Bantry in 1796 *(see pp160–61)*.

## James Joyce Tower ⓭

Sandycove, Co Dublin. 📞 280 9265. 🚉 *DART to Sandycove.* 🚌 59. 🕐 *10am–5pm Mon–Sat, 2–6pm Sun & public hols.* ⬤ *1–2pm weekdays.* 📷 ♿

Ⓢ TANDING on a rocky promontory above the village of Sandycove is this Martello tower. It is one of 15 defensive towers erected between Dublin and Bray in 1804 to withstand a threatened invasion by Napoleon. One

**Guitar at James Joyce Tower**

hundred years later James Joyce *(see p88)* stayed here for a week as the guest of Oliver St John Gogarty, poet and model for the *Ulysses* character Buck Mulligan. Gogarty rented the tower for a mere £8 per year. Inside the squat 12-m (40-ft) tower's granite walls is a small museum with some of Joyce's correspondence, personal belongings, such as his guitar, cigar case and walking stick, and his death mask. There are also photographs and first editions of his works, including a de luxe edition (1935) of *Ulysses* illustrated by Henri Matisse. The roof, originally a gun platform but later used as a sunbathing deck by Gogarty, affords marvellous views of Dublin Bay. Below the tower is Forty Foot Pool, tradition-ally an all-male nude bathing spot, but now open to all.

## Dalkey ⓮

Co Dublin. 🚉 *DART.*

Ⓓ ALKEY was once known as the "Town of Seven Castles", but only two of these now remain. They are both on the main street of this attractive village whose tight, winding roads and charming villas give it a Mediterranean feel.

A little way offshore is tiny Dalkey Island, a rocky bird sanctuary with a Martello tower and a medieval Benedictine church, both now in a poor state of repair. In summer the island can be reached by a boat ride from the town's Coliemore Harbour.

## Killiney ⓯

Co Dublin. 🚉 *DART to Dalkey or Killiney.*

Ⓢ OUTH OF DALKEY, the coastal road climbs uphill before tumbling down into the village of Killiney. The route offers one of the most scenic vistas on this stretch of the east coast, with views often compared to those across the Bay of Naples. Howth Head is clearly visible to the north, with Bray Head *(see p125)* and the foothills of the Wicklow Mountains *(see pp130–31)* to the south. There is another exhilarating view from the top of Killiney Hill Park, off Victoria Road – well worth tackling the short steep trail for. Down below is the popular pebbly beach, Killiney Strand.

**Shopfronts on the main street of Dalkey**

# ENTERTAINMENT IN DUBLIN

ALTHOUGH DUBLIN is well served by theatres, cinemas, nightclubs and rock venues, what sets the city apart from other European capitals is its pubs. Lively banter, impromptu music sessions and great Guinness are the essential ingredients for an enjoyable night in any one of dozens of atmospheric hostelries.

Olympia Theatre façade

One of the most popular entertainment districts is the rejuvenated Temple Bar area. Along this narrow network of cobbled streets you can find everything from traditional music in grand old pubs to the latest dance tracks in a postindustrial setting. The many pubs and venues around this area make the city centre south of the Liffey the place to be at night. The north side does, however, boast the two most illustrious theatres, the largest cinemas and the 7,000-seater Point Theatre, a converted 19th-century rail terminal beside the docks. It is now the venue for all major rock concerts and stage musicals as well as a number of classical music performances.

**Buskers playing near Grafton Street in southeast Dublin**

## ENTERTAINMENT LISTINGS

THE MAIN LISTINGS magazine, *In Dublin*, comes out every two weeks and is readily available from all newsagents. *Hot Press*, a national bimonthly newspaper that covers both rock and traditional music, has comprehensive listings for Dublin. The *Dublin Event Guide* is a free sheet available from pubs, cafés, restaurants and record shops. Also published every two weeks, it is particularly strong on music and nightclubs.

## BOOKING TICKETS

TICKETS FOR MANY EVENTS are available on the night, but it is usually safer to book in advance. All the major venues take credit card payment over the telephone. **Ticket Shop** accepts phone bookings by credit card only for many of the major shows and events in and around Dublin, while

HMV and Dublin Tourism (Suffolk Street) sell tickets for most of the top theatres and major rock gigs.

## THEATRE

ALTHOUGH DUBLIN has only a limited number of theatres, there is almost always something worth seeing and the productions are of a very high standard. Most of Dublin's theatres are closed on Sunday.

The most famous venue is Ireland's national theatre, the **Abbey** *(see p86)*, which concentrates on major new Irish productions as well as revivals of work by Irish playwrights such as Brendan Behan, Sean O'Casey, JM Synge and WB Yeats. The smaller Peacock Theatre downstairs covers more experimental works. Also on the north side is the **Gate Theatre** *(see p88)* founded in 1929 and noted for its interpretations of well-known international plays.

The main venue south of the Liffey, the **Gaiety Theatre**, stages a mainstream mix of plays, emphasizing the work of Irish playwrights. Some of the best fringe theatre and modern dance in Dublin can be seen at the **Project Arts Centre** in Temple Bar and the **City Arts Centre**, which sometimes has midnight performances. **Andrews Lane Theatre** provides a forum for new writers and directors. The **Olympia Theatre** has the feel of a Victorian music hall. It specializes in comedy and popular drama and occasionally stages rock and Irish music concerts.

Every October the **Dublin Theatre Festival** takes over all the venues in the city with mainstream, fringe, Irish and international plays.

**Record shop and ticket office in Crown Alley, Temple Bar**

Crowds enjoying the Temple Bar Blues Festival

## CLASSICAL MUSIC, OPERA AND DANCE

DUBLIN may not have the range of classical concerts of other European capitals, but it has a great venue in the **National Concert Hall**. In the 1980s, this 19th-century exhibition hall was completely redesigned and acoustically adapted, and is where the National Symphony Orchestra plays most Friday evenings. The National Concert Hall's programme also includes opera, chamber music, jazz, dance and some traditional music.

The **Hugh Lane Municipal Gallery of Modern Art** *(see p89)* has regular Sunday lunchtime concerts. Other classical venues include the **Royal Hospital Kilmainham** *(see p95)* and the **Royal Dublin Society (RDS)** main hall and showground. International opera is staged in the **Point Theatre**. The DGOS (Dublin Grand Opera Society) performs every April and November at the Gaiety Theatre.

## TRADITIONAL MUSIC AND DANCE

TO MANY IRISH PEOPLE the standard of music in a pub is just as important as the quality of the Guinness. Central Dublin has a host of pubs reverberating to the sound of bodhráns, fiddles and uilleann pipes. One of the most famous is **O'Donoghue's**, where the

The listings magazine *In Dublin*

legendary Dubliners started out in the early 1960s. **Cobblestones** and the **Auld Dubliner** are also renowned venues. Established acts play venues such as **Mother Redcap's Tavern**, which is a fun place occupying an old factory. **Jury's Hotel** and the **Castle Inn** stage Irish cabaret (May–October) featuring dancing, singing and music.

## ROCK, JAZZ, BLUES AND COUNTRY

DUBLIN has had a thriving rock scene ever since local band Thin Lizzy made it big in the early 1970s. U2's international success has acted as a further catalyst for local bands, and each night there's usually an interesting gig somewhere in the city. **Whelan's** and the **Baggot Inn** feature the best up-and-coming Irish bands

nightly. The upstairs room at the likeable **International Bar** caters mostly for acoustic acts and singer-songwriters, while **Break for the Border** is a popular nightclub that also features a wide variety of live bands. All the big names play at either the Point Theatre or, in summer, Smithfield and other stadia. The Olympia also attracts top performers with its more intimate setting. **The Temple Bar Music Centre** and **The Sugar Club** offer jazz, salsa, latin and blues throughout the year, with the **Heineken Green Energy Festival** a highlight in May. Country music enjoys a massive following in Ireland, and country acts play regularly at several Dublin pubs. Check local entertainment listings for details.

## NIGHTCLUBS

UNTIL A CLUSTER of new dance venues opened in the early 1990s, Dublin's club-life was fairly unremarkable. Nowadays the **POD** (Place of Dance) attracts visiting stars taking time out from their film shoots in the city. Another extremely trendy place is the **Kitchen**, downstairs in the (U2-owned) Clarence Hotel. **Ri-Rá** (Irish for uproar) is at the cutting edge of dance music, while **River Club** and **Lillie's Bordello** provide a more mainstream dance sound.

Most clubs close at 2am. For further action, head for clubs like **Buck Whaleys** on Leeson Street which stay open until 5am. Admission is free, but drinks prices are high.

A traditional Irish music session in O'Donoghue's

Traditional façade of Doheny and Nesbitt

## PUBS AND BARS

DUBLIN'S PUBS are a slice of living history. These are the places where some of the best-known scenes in Irish literature have been set, where rebellious politicians have met and where world-famous music acts have made their debuts. Today, as well as the memorabilia on the walls, it's the singing, dancing, talk and laughter that make a pub tour of Dublin an absolute must.

There are nearly 1,000 pubs inside the city limits. Among the best of the traditional bars are **Neary's**, popular with actors and featuring a gorgeous marble bar, the atmospheric **Long Hall** and the friendly **Stag's Head**, dating from 1770.

Cosy snugs – where drinkers could lock themselves away for private conversation – were an important feature of 19th-century bars. A few remain, notably at the tiny, journalists' haunt of **Doheny and Nesbitt** and the intimate **Kehoe's**.

The **Brazen Head** claims to be the city's oldest pub, dating back to 1198. The present pub, built in the 1750s, is lined with old photographs and dark wood panelling. Every pub prides itself on the quality of its Guinness, though most locals acknowledge that **Mulligan's**, founded in 1782, serves one of the best pints in the city.

The range extends beyond smoky pubs with nicotine-stained ceilings: the splendid decor of the **Shelbourne Bar**, in the Shelbourne Hotel, pulls in a sophisticated crowd. Good bars abound in the Trinity College and Temple Bar areas, including **The Norseman** and **Oliver St John Gogarty**.

## A LITERARY PUB CRAWL

PUBS with strong literary associations abound in Dublin, particularly around Grafton Street. **McDaid's**, an old pub with an Art Deco interior, still retains some of the Bohemian air from the time when famous writer-drinkers such as Patrick Kavanagh and Brendan Behan were regulars. **Davy Byrne's** has much plusher decor than when Leopold Bloom dropped in for a gorgonzola and mustard sandwich in *Ulysses*, but it is still well worth paying a visit. These and about six other pubs, once frequented by Ireland's most famous authors and play-wrights, are featured on the excellent **Dublin Literary**

**Pub Crawl**. This is by far the most entertaining way to get a real feel for the city's booze-fuelled literary heritage. The two-and-a-half-hour tours, which are led by actors, start with a beer in **The Duke**. Tours take place daily in summer, but are usually only at weekends in winter.

## CINEMA

DUBLIN'S CINEMAS had a boost in the 1990s with the success of Dublin-based films such as *My Left Foot* (1989). Huge growth in the country's movie production industry followed, and hits like *Dancing at Lughnasa* (1998) keep Ireland in the spotlight.

The **Irish Film Centre** opened its doors in 1992 and is a most welcome addition to the city's entertainment scene. Showing mostly independent and foreign films, along with a programme of lectures and seminars, it boasts two screens, as well as a bar and restaurant. Another cinema whose reper-toire is mostly art house is the **Screen**, close to Trinity College. The large first-run cinemas are all located on the north side. These usually offer tickets at reduced prices for their afternoon screenings and show late-night films at the week-end. The **Dublin Film Festival**, which is held over ten days between late February and early March, shows a varied selection of the latest inter-national and Irish releases.

**GUINNESS TIME**

A Guinness sign on the outside of a Dublin pub

Bustling interior of the Oliver St John Gogarty pub in Temple Bar

## DIRECTORY

### BOOKING AGENTS

**HMV**
18 Henry St. **Map** D2.
65 Grafton St. **Map** D4.

**Ticketmaster**
1890 925 100.
www.ticketmaster.ie

### THEATRE

**Abbey Theatre**
Abbey St Lower. **Map** E2.
878 7222.

**Andrews Lane Theatre**
9–11 St Andrew's Lane.
**Map** D3.
679 5720.

**City Arts Centre**
23–25 Moss St. **Map** E2.
677 0643.

**Dublin Theatre Festival**
44 Essex St. East. **Map** C3.
677 8439.

**Focus Theatre**
6 Pembroke Place.
**Map** E5.
676 3071.

**Gaiety Theatre**
King St South. **Map** D4.
677 1717.

**Gate Theatre**
Cavendish Row. **Map** D1.
874 4045.

**Olympia Theatre**
Dame St.
**Map** C3.
1890 925 130.

**Project Arts Centre**
39 East Essex St.
**Map** C3.
671 2321.

### CLASSICAL MUSIC, OPERA AND DANCE

**Hugh Lane Municipal Gallery of Modern Art**
Charlemont House, Parnell Sq North. **Map** C1.
874 1903.

**Irish Museum of Modern Art**
Kilmainham.
612 9900.

**National Concert Hall**
Earlsfort Terrace. **Map** D5.
475 1666.
www.nch.ie

**Point Theatre**
East Link Bridge, North Wall Quay. **Map** D1.
836 3633.
www.thepoint.ie

**Royal Dublin Society (RDS)**
Ballsbridge.
668 0866.
www.rds.ie

### TRADITIONAL MUSIC AND DANCE

**Auld Dubliner**
24–25 Temple Bar.
**Map** D3.
677 0527.

**Castle Inn**
5–7 Lord Edward St.
**Map** C3.
475 1122.

**Cobblestones**
77 King Street North.
**Map** A2.
872 1799.

**Jury's Hotel**
Pembroke Rd, Ballsbridge.
660 5000. May–Oct.

**Mother Redcap's Tavern**
Back Lane, Christchurch.
**Map** B4.
453 8306.

**O'Donoghue's**
15 Merrion Row.
**Map** E5. 660 7194.

### ROCK, JAZZ, BLUES AND COUNTRY

**Break for the Border**
Grafton Capital Hotel,
Lower Stephen Street.
**Map** D4. 478 0300.

**International Bar**
23 Wicklow Street.
**Map** D3. 677 9250.

**Temple Bar Music Centre**
Curved Street, Temple Bar.
**Map** E4. 670 9202.
www.tbmc.ie

**Whelan's**
25 Wexford St. **Map** C5.
478 0766.

### NIGHTCLUBS

**Buck Whaleys**
67 Lower Leeson St.
**Map** E5 676 1755.

**Kitchen**
6–8 Wellington Quay.
**Map** C3.
677 6635.

**Lillie's Bordello**
Adam Court, off Grafton St. **Map** D4.
679 9204.

**POD**
Harcourt St. **Map** D5.
478 0166.

**Ri-Rá**
11 South Great George's St. **Map** C3.
671 1220.

**River Club**
Merchants' Arch. **Map** D3.
677 2382.

**The Sugar Club**
8 Lower Leeson Street.
**Map** E5.
678 7188.

### PUBS AND BARS

**Brazen Head**
20 Bridge St Lower.
**Map** A3.
677 9549.

**Davy Byrne's**
21 Duke St. **Map** D4.
677 5217.

**Doheny and Nesbitt**
5 Lower Baggot St.
**Map** E5.
676 2945.

**Dublin Literary Pub Crawl**
37 Exchequer Street.
**Map** D3.
670 5602.

**The Duke**
9 Duke Street.
**Map** D4.
679 9553.

**Kehoe's**
9 South Anne St. **Map** D4.
677 8312.

**Long Hall**
51 South Great George's St. **Map** C4.
475 1590.

**McDaid's**
3 Harry St, off Grafton St.
**Map** D4. 679 4395.

**Mulligan's**
8 Poolbeg St. **Map** E3.
677 5582.

**Neary's**
1 Chatham St. **Map** D4.
677 8596.

**The Norseman**
29 East Essex St, Temple Bar. **Map** C3.
671 5135.

**The Octagon Bar**
The Clarence, 6–8 Wellington Quay.
**Map** C3. 671 5135.

**Oliver St John Gogarty**
58–59 Fleet St, Temple Bar.
**Map** D3. 671 1822.

**Queen's**
12 Castle St, Dalkey.
285 4569.

**Shelbourne Bar**
27 St Stephen's Green North. **Map** E4.
676 6471.

**Stag's Head**
1 Dame Court, off Dame Lane. **Map** D3.
679 3701.

**Toner's**
139 Lower Baggot St.
**Map** E5. 676 3090.

### CINEMA

**Dublin Film Festival**
1 Suffolk St. **Map** D3.
679 2937.

**Irish Film Centre**
6 Eustace St, Temple Bar.
**Map** C3. 679 5744.

**U.G.C. Cinemas**
Parnell St. **Map** C2.
872 8400.

**Screen**
D'Olier St. **Map** D3.
672 5500.

# Dublin's Best: Entertainment

IT'S EASY TO PACK a lot into a night out in Dublin. Most of the best nightspots are situated close to each other and, in the Temple Bar area alone, there are plenty of exciting haunts to try out. The city offers something to suit every taste and pocket: choose from world-class theatre, excellent concert venues, designer café-bars and lively or laid-back clubs hosting nights of traditional, country, jazz or rock music. Even when there is no specific event that appeals, you can simply enjoy Dublin's inexhaustible supply of great traditional pubs.

**Gate Theatre**
*The Gate puts on both foreign plays and Irish classics such as Sean O'Casey's* Juno and the Paycock. *(See p88.)*

**Stag's Head**
*This gorgeous Victorian pub has a long, mahogany bar and has retained its original mirrors and stained glass. Located down an out-of-the-way alley, this atmospheric pub is well worth seeking out. (See p105.)*

NORTH OF THE LIFFEY

SOUTHWEST DUBLIN

0 metres        500
0 yards         500

## THE TEMPLE BAR AREA

It will take more than a couple of evenings to explore fully all that these narrow streets have to offer. Many of Dublin's best mid-priced restaurants are here, while modern bars sit next to traditional pubs hosting fiddle sessions. There are also theatres and the Irish Film Centre. Later, clubs play music ranging from country to the latest dance sounds.

MILLENNIUM BRIDGE    HA'PENNY BRIDGE

LIFFEY

WELLINGTON QUAY

THE GARAGE BAR

PROJECT

BAD BOBS

ESSEX STREET EAST

SYCAMORE ST

MEETING HOUSE SQUARE

Irish Film Centre

TEMPLE LANE

CROW ST

FOWNNES STREET

CROWN ALLEY

TEMPLE BAR

THE AULD DUBLINER

THE BAD ASS CAFE

COPE STREET

OLYMPIA

DAME STREET

0 metres        100
0 yards         100

**Queuing for a concert in Temple Bar**

**Street theatre events** take place throughout the summer in Temple Bar. This actor is portraying George Bernard Shaw in a typical street performance.

**Abbey Theatre**
*Despite recurring financial problems, Ireland's prestigious national theatre still manages to stage compelling new drama, such as* Dancing at Lughnasa *by Brian Friel. (See p86.)*

**Point Theatre**
*Once a Victorian railway terminus, this is now the country's top live music arena. Major acts, including Van Morrison (above) and Luciano Pavarotti, have appeared here and it's also a popular venue for hit musicals. (See p105.)*

L I F F E Y

SOUTHEAST
DUBLIN

**McDaid's**
*Playwright Brendan Behan (see p21) downed many a pint in this pub, which dates from 1779. Though firmly on the tourist trail, McDaid's retains its bohemian charm, and bars upstairs and downstairs provide space for a leisurely drink. (See p105.)*

**National Concert Hall**
*The National Symphony Orchestra performs most Friday evenings. A combination of dance, chamber music and other performance arts makes up a full programme of events. From May to July, inexpensive Tuesday lunch-time concerts are held. (See p103.)*

# Street Finder Index

## KEY TO THE STREET FINDER

| | | |
|---|---|---|
| Major sight | Coach station | Church |
| Place of interest | Taxi rank | Post office |
| Railway station | Main car park | Railway line |
| DART station | Tourist information office | One-way street |
| Luas stop | Hospital with casualty unit | Pedestrian street |
| Main bus stop | Police station | |

0 metres     200
0 yards     200

1:11,500

## KEY TO STREET FINDER ABBREVIATIONS

| Ave | Avenue | E | East | Pde | Parade | Sth | South |
|---|---|---|---|---|---|---|---|
| Br | Bridge | La | Lane | Pl | Place | Tce | Terrace |
| Cl | Close | Lr | Lower | Rd | Road | Up | Upper |
| Ct | Court | Nth | North | St | Street/Saint | W | West |

**A**

| | |
|---|---|
| Abbey Street Lower | D2 |
| Abbey Street Middle | D2 |
| Abbey Street Old | E2 |
| Abbey Street Upper | C2 |
| Abbey Theatre | D2 |
| Adair Lane | D3 |
| Adelaide Hospital | C4 |
| Amiens Street | F1 |
| Anglesea Row | C2 |
| Anglesea Street | D3 |
| Anne Street North | B2 |
| Anne Street South | D4 |
| Anne's Lane | D4 |
| Ardee Row | A5 |
| Ardee Street | A5 |
| Arran Quay | A3 |
| Arran Street East | B2 |
| Asdill's Row | D3 |
| Ash Street | A4 |
| Aston Place | D3 |
| Aston Quay | D3 |
| Aungier Place | C5 |
| Aungier Street | C5 |

**B**

| | |
|---|---|
| Bachelors Walk | D3 |
| Back Lane | B4 |
| Baggot Court | F5 |
| Baggot Rath Place | E5 |
| Baggot Street Lower | F5 |
| Ball's Lane | B2 |
| Bank of Ireland | D3 |
| Bass Place | F4 |
| Beaver Street | F1 |
| Bedford Row | D3 |
| Bella Place | F1 |
| Bella Street | E1 |
| Bell's Lane | E5 |
| Benburb Street | A2 |
| Beresford Lane | E2 |
| Beresford Place | E2 |
| Beresford Street | B2 |
| Bewley's Oriental Café | D4 |
| Bishop Street | C5 |
| Blackhall Parade | A2 |
| Blackhall Place | A2 |
| Blackhall Street | A2 |
| Blackpitts | B5 |
| Bolton Street | C1 |
| Bonham Street | A3 |
| Borris Court | B3 |
| Bow Lane East | C4 |
| Bow Street | A2 |
| Boyne Street | F4 |
| Brabazon Row | A5 |
| Brabazon Street | A4 |
| Bracken's Lane | E3 |
| Braithwaite Street | A4 |
| Bride Road | B4 |
| Bride Street | C4 |

| | |
|---|---|
| Bride Street New | C5 |
| Bridge Street Lower | A3 |
| Bridge Street Upper | A3 |
| Bridgefoot Street | A3 |
| Britain Place | D1 |
| Brown Street North | A2 |
| Brown Street South | A5 |
| Brunswick Street North Lower | A2 |
| Buckingham Street Lower | F1 |
| Bull Alley Street | B4 |
| Burgh Quay | D3 |
| Busáras | E2 |
| Butt Bridge | E2 |
| Byrne's Lane | C2 |

**C**

| | |
|---|---|
| Camden Place | C5 |
| Camden Row | C5 |
| Camden Street Lower | C5 |
| Capel Street | C2 |
| Carman's Hall | A4 |
| Castle Market | D4 |
| Castle Steps | C3 |
| Castle Street | C3 |
| Cathal Brugha Street | D1 |
| Cathedral Lane | B5 |
| Cathedral Street | D2 |
| Cathedral View Court | B5 |
| Chamber Street | A5 |
| Chancery Lane | C4 |
| Chancery Place | B3 |
| Chancery Street | B3 |
| Chapel Lane | C2 |
| Charles Street West | B3 |
| Chatham Row | D4 |
| Chatham Street | D4 |
| Christ Church Cathedral | B3 |
| Christchurch Place | B4 |
| Church Avenue West | B2 |
| Church Lane South | C5 |
| Church Street | B3 |
| Church Street New | A2 |
| Church Street Upper | B2 |
| Church Terrace | B2 |
| City Hall | C3 |
| City Quay | F2 |
| Clanbrassil Street Lower | B5 |
| Clare Lane | E4 |
| Clare Street | E4 |
| Clarence Mangan Road | A5 |
| Clarendon Row | D4 |
| Clarendon Street | D4 |
| Clonmel Street | D5 |
| Coke Lane | A3 |
| Coleraine Street | B1 |
| College Green | D3 |
| College Lane | E3 |
| College Street | D3 |
| Commons Street | F2 |
| Connolly Station | F1 |

| | |
|---|---|
| Constitution Hill | B1 |
| Convent Close | F5 |
| Cook Street | B3 |
| Coombe Court | A4 |
| Cope Street | D3 |
| Copper Alley | C3 |
| Cork Hill | C3 |
| Cork Street | A5 |
| Corporation Street | E1 |
| Crane Lane | C3 |
| Creighton Street | F3 |
| Crown Alley | D3 |
| Cuckoo Lane | B2 |
| Cuffe Street | C5 |
| Cumberland Street North | D1 |
| Cumberland Street South | F4 |
| Custom House | E2 |
| Custom House Quay | E2 |

**D**

| | |
|---|---|
| D'Olier Street | D3 |
| Dame Lane | C3 |
| Dame Street | C3 |
| Dawson Lane | D4 |
| Dawson Street | D4 |
| Dean Street | B4 |
| Dean Swift Square | B4 |
| Denzille Lane | F4 |
| Diamond Park | E1 |
| Digges Street Upper | C5 |
| Dominick Lane | C1 |
| Dominick Place | C1 |
| Dominick Street Lower | C1 |
| Dominick Street Upper | B1 |
| Donore Road | A5 |
| Dorset Street Upper | C1 |
| Dowlings Court | F3 |
| Drury Street | D4 |
| Dublin Castle | C3 |
| Dublin Civic Museum | D4 |
| Dublin Writers Museum | C1 |
| Dublinia | B4 |
| Duke Lane | D4 |
| Duke Street | D4 |

**E**

| | |
|---|---|
| Earl Place | D2 |
| Earl Street North | D2 |
| Earl Street South | A4 |
| Earlsfort Terrace | D5 |
| Ebenezer Terrace | A5 |
| Eden Quay | D2 |
| Ellis Quay | A3 |
| Ely Place | E5 |
| Erne Place Lower | F3 |
| Erne Street Upper | F4 |
| Erne Terrace Front | F3 |
| Essex Quay | C3 |
| Essex Street East | C3 |
| Essex Street West | C3 |

| | |
|---|---|
| Eustace Street | C3 |
| Exchange Street Lower | C3 |
| Exchange Street Upper | C3 |
| Exchequer Street | D3 |

**F**

| | |
|---|---|
| Fade Street | C4 |
| Father Mathew Bridge | A3 |
| Father Mathew Square | B2 |
| Fenian Street | F4 |
| Fishamble Street | B3 |
| Fitzwilliam Lane | E5 |
| Fitzwilliam Square East | E5 |
| Fitzwilliam Square North | E5 |
| Fitzwilliam Square West | E5 |
| Fitzwilliam Street Lower | F5 |
| Fitzwilliam Street Upper | F5 |
| Fleet Street | D3 |
| Foley Street | E1 |
| Foster Place | D3 |
| Fountain Place | A2 |
| Four Courts | B3 |
| Fownes Street | D3 |
| Francis Street | B4 |
| Frederick Street South | E4 |
| Frenchman's Lane | E2 |
| Friary Avenue | A2 |
| Fumbally Lane | B5 |

**G**

| | |
|---|---|
| Garden Lane | A4 |
| Garden of Remembrance | C1 |
| Gardiner Street Lower | E1 |
| Gardiner Street Middle | D1 |
| Gate Theatre | D1 |
| General Post Office | D2 |
| Geoffrey Keating Road | A5 |
| George's Dock | F2 |
| George's Hill | B2 |
| George's Lane | A2 |
| George's Quay | E2 |
| Gloucester Diamond | E1 |
| Gloucester Place | E1 |
| Gloucester Street South | E3 |
| Glover's Alley | D4 |
| Golden Lane | C4 |
| Grafton Street | D4 |
| Granby Lane | C1 |
| Granby Place | C1 |
| Granby Row | C1 |
| Grangegorman Upper | A1 |
| Grant's Row | F4 |
| Grattan Bridge | C3 |
| Gray Street | A4 |
| Greek Street | B2 |
| Green Street | B2 |

## H

| | |
|---|---|
| Hagan's Court | F5 |
| Halston Street | B2 |
| Hammond Lane | A3 |
| Hammond Street | A5 |
| Hanbury Lane | A4 |
| Hanover Lane | B4 |
| Hanover Street | B4 |
| Hanover Street East | F3 |
| Ha'penny Bridge | D3 |
| Harbour Court | D2 |
| Harcourt Street | D5 |
| Hawkins Street | E3 |
| Haymarket | A2 |
| Hendrick Lane | A2 |
| Hendrick Street | A2 |
| Henrietta Lane | B1 |
| Henrietta Place | B2 |
| Henrietta Street | B1 |
| Henry Place | D2 |
| Henry Street | D2 |
| Herbert Lane | F5 |
| Herbert Street | F5 |
| Heytesbury Street | C5 |
| High Street | B3 |
| Hill Street | D1 |
| Hogan Place | F4 |
| Holles Place | F4 |
| Holles Row | F4 |
| Holles Street | F4 |
| Hugh Lane Municipal Gallery of Modern Art | C1 |
| Hume Street | E5 |

## I

| | |
|---|---|
| Inner Dock | F2 |
| Inns Quay | B3 |
| Irish Whiskey Corner | A2 |
| Island Street | A3 |
| Iveagh Gardens | D5 |

## J

| | |
|---|---|
| James Joyce Cultural Centre | D1 |
| James's Place | F5 |
| James's Place East | F5 |
| Jervis Lane Lower | C2 |
| Jervis Lane Upper | C2 |
| Jervis Street | C2 |
| John Street North | A3 |
| John Street South | A5 |
| John Dillon Street | B4 |
| John's Lane East | B3 |
| John's Lane West | A4 |
| Johnson Court | D4 |

## K

| | |
|---|---|
| Kevin Street Lower | C5 |
| Kevin Street Upper | B5 |
| Kildare Street | E4 |
| Killarney Street | F1 |
| King Street North | A2 |
| King Street South | D4 |
| King's Inns | B1 |
| King's Inns Park | B1 |
| King's Inns Street | C1 |
| Kirwan Street | A1 |

## L

| | |
|---|---|
| Lad Lane | F5 |
| Lamb Alley | B4 |
| Leeson Lane | E5 |
| Leeson Street Lower | E5 |
| Leinster House | E4 |
| Leinster Street South | E4 |
| Lemon Street | D4 |
| Liberty Lane | C5 |
| Liberty Park | E1 |
| Liffey Street Lower | D2 |
| Liffey Street Upper | C2 |
| Lincoln Place | E4 |
| Linenhall Parade | B1 |
| Linenhall Street | B2 |
| Linenhall Terrace | B1 |
| Lisburn Street | B2 |
| Little Britain Street | B2 |
| Little Green Street | B2 |
| Litton Lane | D2 |
| Loftus Lane | C2 |
| Lombard Street East | F3 |

| | |
|---|---|
| Long Lane | B5 |
| Longford Street Great | C4 |
| Longford Street Little | C4 |
| Lord Edward Street | C3 |
| Lotts | D2 |
| Luke Street | E3 |
| Lurgan Street | B2 |

## M

| | |
|---|---|
| Mabbot Lane | E1 |
| Madden Road | A5 |
| Magennis Place | F3 |
| Malpas Street | B5 |
| Mansion House | D4 |
| Mark Street | E3 |
| Mark's Alley West | B4 |
| Mark's Lane | F3 |
| Marlborough Street | D1 |
| Marshall Lane | A3 |
| Marsh's Library | B4 |
| Mary Street | C2 |
| Mary Street Little | B2 |
| Mary's Lane | B2 |
| Matt Talbot Memorial Bridge | E2 |
| May Lane | A2 |
| Mayor Street Lower | F2 |
| Meade's Terrace | F4 |
| Meath Hospital | B5 |
| Meath Place | A4 |
| Meath Street | A4 |
| Meetinghouse Lane | C2 |
| Mellowes Bridge | A3 |
| Memorial Road | E2 |
| Mercer Street Upper | C5 |
| Merchant's Quay | B3 |
| Merrion Row | E5 |
| Merrion Square | F4 |
| Merrion Square East | F5 |
| Merrion Square North | F4 |
| Merrion Square South | E4 |
| Merrion Square West | E4 |
| Merrion Street Lower | F4 |
| Merrion Street Upper | E5 |
| Michael's Terrace | A5 |
| Mill Street | A5 |
| Millennium Bridge | C3 |
| Molesworth Place | D4 |
| Molesworth Street | D4 |
| Montague Place | C5 |
| Montague Street | C5 |
| Moore Lane | D1 |
| Moore Street | D2 |
| Morning Star Avenue | A1 |
| Moss Street | E2 |
| Mount Street Lower | F4 |
| Mount Street Upper | F5 |
| Mountjoy Street | C1 |
| Mountjoy Street Middle | B1 |

## N

| | |
|---|---|
| Nassau Street | D3 |
| National Gallery | E4 |
| Natural History Museum | E4 |
| National Library | E4 |
| National Museum | E4 |
| New Row South | B5 |
| New Street North | B2 |
| New Street South | B5 |
| Newman House | D5 |
| Newmarket | A5 |
| Nicholas Street | B4 |
| North Great George's Street | D1 |
| North Wall Quay | F2 |

## O

| | |
|---|---|
| O'Carolan Road | A5 |
| O'Connell Bridge | D2 |
| O'Connell Street Lower | D2 |
| O'Connell Street Upper | D1 |
| O'Curry Avenue | A5 |
| O'Curry Road | A5 |
| O'Donovan Rossa Bridge | B3 |
| Oliver Bond Street | A3 |
| O'Rahilly Parade | D2 |
| Oriel Street Upper | F1 |
| Ormond Quay Lower | C3 |
| Ormond Quay Upper | B3 |

| | |
|---|---|
| Ormond Square | B3 |
| Ormond Street | A5 |
| Oscar Square | A5 |
| Oxmantown Lane | A2 |

## P

| | |
|---|---|
| Palmerston Place | B1 |
| Parliament Street | C3 |
| Parnell Place | D1 |
| Parnell Square East | D1 |
| Parnell Square West | C1 |
| Parnell Street | C2 |
| Patrick Street | B4 |
| Pearse Station | F3 |
| Pearse Street | E3 |
| Pembroke Lane | E5 |
| Pembroke Row | E5 |
| Pembroke Street Lower | E5 |
| Peter Row | C4 |
| Peter Street | C4 |
| Peterson's Court | F3 |
| Phibsborough Road | B1 |
| Phoenix Street North | A3 |
| Pimlico | A4 |
| Pleasants Street | C5 |
| Poolbeg Street | E3 |
| Poole Street | A4 |
| Powerscourt Townhouse | D4 |
| Prebend Street | B1 |
| Preston Street | F1 |
| Price's Lane | D3 |
| Prince's Street North | D2 |
| Prince's Street South | F3 |

## Q

| | |
|---|---|
| Queen Street | A2 |
| Quinn's Lane | E5 |

## R

| | |
|---|---|
| Railway Street | E1 |
| Rath Row | E3 |
| Redmond's Hill | C5 |
| Reginald Street | A4 |
| River Liffey | A3 |
| Ross Road | B4 |
| Rotunda Hospital | D1 |
| Royal Hibernian Academy | E5 |
| Rutland Place | D1 |
| Rutland Street Lower | E1 |
| Ryder's Row | C2 |

## S

| | |
|---|---|
| Sackville Place | D2 |
| St Andrew's Street | D3 |
| St Ann's Church | D4 |
| St Audoen's Church | B3 |
| St Augustine Street | A3 |
| St Cathedral Lane East | A4 |
| St Kevin's Avenue | B5 |
| St Mary's Abbey | C2 |
| St Mary's Pro-Cathedral | D1 |
| St Mary's Terrace | C1 |
| St Michael's Close | B3 |
| St Michael's Hill | B3 |
| St Michan's Church | A2 |
| St Michan's Street | B2 |
| St Paul Street | A2 |
| St Patrick's Cathedral | B4 |
| St Patrick's Close | B4 |
| St Patrick's Park | B4 |
| St Stephen's Green | D5 |
| St Stephen's Green East | E5 |
| St Stephen's Green North | D4 |
| St Stephen's Green South | D5 |
| St Stephen's Green West | D5 |
| St Thomas Road | A5 |
| St Werburgh's Church | D2 |
| Sampson's Lane | D2 |
| Sandwith Street Upper | F4 |
| Sandwith Street Lower | F3 |
| Schoolhouse Lane | E4 |
| Schoolhouse Lane West | B3 |
| Sean Mac Dermott Street Lower | E1 |
| Sean Mac Dermott Street Upper | D1 |

| | |
|---|---|
| Setanta Place | E4 |
| Seville Place | F1 |
| Seville Terrace | F1 |
| Shaw Street | E3 |
| Shelbourne Hotel | E4 |
| Sheriff Street Lower | F1 |
| Ship Street Great | C4 |
| Ship Street Little | C4 |
| Smithfield | A2 |
| South Great George's Street | C4 |
| Spring Garden Lane | E3 |
| Stable Lane | A3 |
| Stanhope Street | A1 |
| Stephen Street Lower | C4 |
| Stephen Street Upper | C4 |
| Stephen's Lane | F5 |
| Stephen's Place | F5 |
| Stirrup Lane | B2 |
| Stokes Place | D5 |
| Stoneybatter | A2 |
| Store Street | E2 |
| Strand Street Great | C3 |
| Strand Street Little | C3 |
| Strong's Court | D1 |
| Suffolk Street | D3 |
| Summerhill | E1 |
| Susan Terrace | A5 |
| Swift's Alley | A4 |
| Swift's Row | C3 |
| Sycamore Street | C3 |

## T

| | |
|---|---|
| Tailors' Hall | B4 |
| Talbot Place | E2 |
| Talbot Street | D2 |
| Tara Street | E3 |
| Tara Street Station | E3 |
| Temple Bar | C3 |
| Temple Cottages | B1 |
| Temple Lane North | D1 |
| Temple Lane South | C3 |
| The Coombe | A4 |
| Thomas Court | A4 |
| Thomas Court Lane | A4 |
| Thomas Davis Street South | B4 |
| Thomas Street West | A4 |
| Thomas's Lane | D1 |
| Townsend Street | E3 |
| Trinity College | E3 |
| Trinity Street | D3 |

## U

| | |
|---|---|
| Usher Street | A3 |
| Usher's Island | A3 |
| Usher's Quay | A3 |

## V

| | |
|---|---|
| Vicar Street | A4 |

## W

| | |
|---|---|
| Wards Hill | B5 |
| Watkins Buildings | A4 |
| Weaver's Square | A5 |
| Weaver's Street | A4 |
| Wellington Quay | C3 |
| Werburgh Street | C4 |
| Western Way | B1 |
| Westland Row | F4 |
| Westmoreland Street | D3 |
| Wexford Street | C5 |
| Whitefriar Place | C4 |
| Whitefriar Street | C4 |
| Whitefriar Street Carmelite Church | C4 |
| Wicklow Street | D3 |
| William Street South | D4 |
| William's Place South | B5 |
| William's Row | D2 |
| Windmill Lane | F3 |
| Windsor Place | E5 |
| Winetavern Street | B3 |
| Wolfe Tone Park | C2 |
| Wolfe Tone Street | C2 |
| Wood Quay | B3 |
| Wood Street | C4 |

## Y

| | |
|---|---|
| York Street | C4 |

D E F

1

2

3

4

5

HILL
NORTH GREAT GEORGE'S STREET
GARDINER STREET MIDDLE
TEMPLE LANE NTH
SUMMERHILL
BELLA STREET
RUTLAND PL
BELLA STREET
KILLARNEY STREET
SEVILLE PL
SEVILLE TERRACE

RUTLAND PLACE
James Joyce Cultural Centre
GLOUCESTER PLACE
GLOUCESTER
SEAN MAC DERMOTT STREET LOWER
BUCKINGHAM STREET
PRESTON ST

PARNELL
DIAMOND PARK
GLOUCESTER
DIAMOND PARK
RAILWAY
BEAVER STREET
AMIENS STREET
STREET

RUTLAND SQUARE EAST
Rotunda Hospital
CATHAL BRUGHA STREET
St Mary's Pro-Cathedral
SEAN MAC DERMOTT ST UP
CUMBERLAND STREET NORTH
BRITAIN
MARBORO LANE
CORPORATION STREET
LIBERTY PARK
Connolly
SHERIFF STREET LOWER
O'RIEL ST UP

O'CONNELL STREET UPPER
MARLBOROUGH STREET
EARL ST NTH
Tyrone House
TALBOT STREET LOWER
STORE STREET
TALBOT PLACE
Inner Dock

MOORE STREET
HENRY PL
EARL PLACE
Cathedral St
TALBOT STREET
BERESFORD LANE
FRENCH'S LANE
MARY'S LANE
STORE STREET
Busáras
MAYOR STREET LOWER
COMMONS STREET

NY STREET
General Post Office
SACKVILLE
PRINCE'S STREET NORTH
ABBEY STREET LOWER
Abbey Theatre
ABBEY STREET OLD
BERESFORD PL
Custom House
MEMORIAL RD
George's Dock

STREET MIDDLE
WILLIAMS ROW
LOTTS
LITTON LANE
HARBOUR ST
EDEN QUAY
CUSTOM HOUSE QUAY
NORTH WALL QUAY

BACHELORS WALK
Liffey
O'CONNELL BRIDGE
BURGH QUAY
HAWKINS STREET
GEORGE'S QUAY
Memorial Br
Matt Talbot
CITY QUAY
Liffey

ASTON QUAY
D'OLIER STREET
WESTMORELAND ST
POOLBEG STREET
MOSS STREET
Tara Street

FLEET STREET
ADAIR LANE
COLLEGE STREET
TARA STREET
LUKE STREET
RATH ROW
BRACKEN'S LANE
GLOUCESTER STREET SOUTH
PRINCE'S STREET SOUTH
DOWLING'S COURT
CREIGHTON STREET
WINDMILL LANE

ANGLESEA STREET
TEMPLE BAR
FOSTER PLACE
Bank of Ireland
COLLEGE GREEN
TOWNSEND STREET
MARK STREET
MARK'S LANE
LOMBARD STREET EAST
MAGENNIS PLACE
SANDWITH STREET LOWER
HANOVER STREET EAST
ERNE PL LR

TRINITY ST
ANDREW'S ST
SUFFOLK STREET
PEARSE STREET
COLLEGE LANE
PEARSE STREET
WESTLAND ROW
Pearse
ERNE TCE FRONT

WICKLOW ST
NASSAU STREET
Trinity College
LINCOLN PLACE
CUMBERLAND STREET SOUTH
FENIAN STREET
BOYNE STREET
BASS PLACE
SANDWITH ST UPPER
HOGAN PLACE

Powerscourt Townhouse
St Teresa's Church
DUKE STREET
DAWSON STREET
FREDERICK STREET SOUTH
SETANTA PLACE
Heraldic Museum
National Library
CLARE STREET
MERRION STREET LR
DENZILLE LANE

Dublin Civic Museum
Bewley's Oriental Café
LEMON STREET
ANNE STREET SOUTH
MOLESWORTH STREET
National Museum
National Gallery
CLARE LANE
MERRION SQUARE NORTH
HOLLES PLACE
HOLLES ROW

GRAFTON STREET
CHATHAM STREET
St Ann's Church
SCHOOLHOUSE LA
KILDARE STREET
Leinster House
Natural History Museum
MERRION SQUARE SOUTH
MERRION SQUARE
MOUNT ST LR

Mansion House
DAWSON STREET
Shelbourne Hotel
Government Buildings
FITZWILLIAM STREET
GRANT'S ROW

ST STEPHEN'S GREEN WEST
ST STEPHEN'S GREEN NORTH
National Museum
MERRION ROW
FITZWILLIAM STREET LR
STEPHEN'S PLACE
STEPHEN'S LA

College of Surgeons
ST STEPHEN'S GREEN
HUME STREET
ELY PLACE
BAGGOT STREET LOWER
MOUNT STREET UPPER
JAMES STREET EAST
JAMES'S PLACE

ST STEPHEN'S GREEN SOUTH
Newman House
Iveagh House
Royal Hibernian Academy
BELL'S LA
WINDSOR PLACE
PEMBROKE STREET UP
PEMBROKE LANE
BAGGOT STREET LOWER

IVEAGH GARDENS
EARLSFORT TCE
LEESON ST LR
LEESON LANE
QUINN'S LANE
FITZWILLIAM SQ W
FITZWILLIAM SQUARE NTH
FITZWILLIAM SQUARE
FITZWILLIAM ST UP
PEMBROKE ROW

D E F

# IRELAND REGION BY REGION

IRELAND AT A GLANCE 114-115
SOUTHEAST IRELAND 116-143
CORK AND KERRY 144-171
THE LOWER SHANNON 172-191
THE WEST OF IRELAND 192-211
NORTHWEST IRELAND 212-227
THE MIDLANDS 228-245
NORTHERN IRELAND 246-277

# Ireland at a Glance

THE LURE of Ireland's much-vaunted Atlantic shores, from the wild coastline of Cork and Kerry to the remote peninsulas of the Northwest, is strong. However, to neglect the interior would be to miss out on Ireland's equally characteristic landscapes of lush valleys, dark peatlands and unruffled loughs. Most regions are rich in historic sights: from world-famous Neolithic sites in the Midlands to imposing Norman castles in the North and Palladian mansions in the Southeast.

*Yeats Country is a charming part of County Sligo closely associated with WB Yeats. The poet was born here and is buried within sight of Ben Bulben's ridge. (See pp224–5.)*

NORTHWI
IRELANI
(See pp212

**THE WEST OF IRELAND**
*(See pp192–211)*

***Connemara National Park*** *in County Galway boasts stunning landscapes in which mountains and lakes are combined with a dramatic Atlantic coastline. The extensive blanket bogs and moorland are rich in wildlife and unusual plants. (See p200.)*

**Bunratty Castle**
***(See pp184–5)***

***The Rock of Cashel****, a fortified medieval abbey, perches on a limestone outcrop in the heart of County Tipperary. It boasts some of Ireland's finest Romanesque sculpture. (See pp188–9.)*

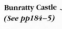

**THE LOWER SHANNON**
*(See pp172–91)*

**CORK AND KERRY**
*(See pp144–71)*

**Bantry House**
***(See pp160–61)***

***The Lakes of Killarney****, flanked by the lush, wooded slopes of some of the country's highest mountains, are the principal attraction in the southwest of Ireland. (See pp154–5.)*

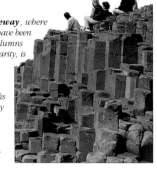

***The Giant's Causeway**, where ancient lava flows have been eroded to reveal columns of unnatural regularity, is Northern Ireland's most curious sight. According to local mythology, the rocks were placed here by a giant called Finn MacCool to enable him to walk across the sea to Scotland. (See pp254–5.)*

**NORTHERN IRELAND**
*(See pp246–77)*

***Mount Stewart House**, a 19th-century mansion, is most renowned for its magnificent gardens. These were created as recently as the 1920s, but a colourful array of exotic plants has thrived in the warm microclimate enjoyed in this part of County Down. (See pp274–5.)*

**Newgrange**
*(See pp238–9)*

**THE MIDLANDS**
*(See pp228–45)*

**SOUTHEAST IRELAND**
*(See pp116–43)*

***Powerscourt** is a large estate in superb countryside on the edge of the Wicklow Mountains. Its grounds rank among the last great formal gardens of Europe. Originally planted in the 1730s, they were restored and embellished in the 19th century. (See pp126–7.)*

0 kilometres     50

0 miles     25

***Kilkenny Castle** was for centuries the stronghold of the Butler dynasty, which controlled much of southeast Ireland in the Middle Ages. The vast Norman fortress was remodelled during the Victorian period and still dominates Kilkenny – one of the country's most historic and pleasant towns. (See pp134–6.)*

# SOUTHEAST IRELAND

KILDARE · WICKLOW · CARLOW · KILKENNY
WATERFORD · WEXFORD

BLESSED WITH *the warmest climate in Ireland, the Southeast has always presented an attractive prospect for settlers. Landscapes of gently rolling hills have been tamed by centuries of cultivation, with lush farmland, imposing medieval castles and great houses enhancing the region's atmosphere of prosperity.*

The Southeast's proximity to Britain meant that it was often the first port of call for foreign invaders. Viking raiders arrived here in the 9th century and founded some of Ireland's earliest towns, including Waterford and Wexford. They were followed in 1169 by the Anglo-Normans *(see pp34–5)*, who shaped the region's subsequent development.

Given its strategic importance, the Southeast was heavily protected, mostly by Anglo-Norman lords loyal to the English Crown. Remains of impressive castles attest to the power of the Fitzgeralds of Kildare and the Butlers of Kilkenny, who between them virtually controlled the Southeast throughout the Middle Ages. English influence was stronger here than in any other part of the island.

From the 18th century, wealthy Anglo-Irish families were drawn to what they saw as a stable zone, and felt confident enough to build fine mansions like the Palladian masterpieces of Russborough and Castletown. English rule was not universally accepted, however. The Wicklow Mountains became a popular refuge for opponents to the Crown, including the rebels who fled the town of Enniscorthy after a bloody battle during the uprising against the English in 1798 *(see p39)*.

This mountainous region is still the only real wilderness in the Southeast, in contrast to the flat grasslands that spread across Kildare to the west. To the east, sandy beaches stretch almost unbroken along the shore between Dublin and Rosslare in Wexford.

Traditional thatched cottages in Dunmore East, County Waterford

◁ Staircase hall with ornate 18th-century stuccowork in Castletown House, County Kildare

# Exploring Southeast Ireland

THE SOUTHEAST has something for everyone, from busy seaside resorts to quaint canalside villages, Norman abbeys and bird sanctuaries. The Wicklow Mountains, the location of several major sights such as the monastic complex of Glendalough and the magnificent gardens of Powerscourt, provide perfect touring and walking territory. Further south, the most scenic routes cut through the valleys of the Slaney, Barrow and Nore rivers, flanked by historic ports such as New Ross, from where you can explore local waterways by boat. Along the south coast, which is more varied than the region's eastern shore, beaches are interspersed with rocky headlands, and quiet coastal villages provide good alternative bases to the busy towns of Waterford and Wexford. Further inland, the best places to stay include Lismore and Kilkenny, which is one of the finest historic towns in Ireland.

Graiguenamanagh, on the Barrow north of New Ross

## SIGHTS AT A GLANCE

Ardmore ⑲
Avondale House ⑭
Bray ⑧
Browne's Hill Dolmen ⑮
Castletown House pp122–3 ①
Dunmore East ㉑
Enniscorthy ㉔
Glendalough ⑬
Hook Peninsula ㉒
Irish National Heritage Park ㉕
Jerpoint Abbey ⑰
Johnstown Castle ㉗
Kildare ⑤
Kilkenny pp134–6 ⑯
Killruddery House ⑨
Lismore ⑱
Monasterevin ④
Mount Usher Gardens ⑫
New Ross ㉓
Peatland World ③
Powerscourt pp126–7 ⑦
Robertstown ②
Rosslare ㉙

Russborough House ⑥
Saltee Islands ㉘
Waterford pp138–9 ⑳
Wexford ㉖
Wicklow Mountains ⑪

**Tours**
Military Road ⑩

**CASTLETOWN HOUSE** ①

② **ROBERTSTOWN**

R403

Grand Canal

N7 → Dublin

KILDARE

Liffey

M7

⑥ **RUSSBOROUGH HOUSE**

N81

R756

R759

⑦ **POWERSCOURT**

⑧ **BRAY**

⑨ **KILLRUDDERY HOUSE**

⑩ **MILITARY ROAD**

R761

A 19th-century winged horse at Powerscourt

⑪ M O U N T A I N S

W I C K L O W

⑬ **GLENDALOUGH**

**BALTINGLASS**

R755

R750

Avonmore

⑫ **MOUNT USHER GARDENS**

**WICKLOW**

N9

N81

**ARLOW**

⑮ **BROWNE'S HILL DOLMEN**

Slaney

R747

Avoca

W I C K L O W   W A Y

⑭ **AVONDALE HOUSE**

**ARKLOW**

N11

N80

Barrow

N11

● **GOREY**

**GETTING AROUND**

Routes N11, N9 and N7 fan out from Dublin, serving Wexford, Waterford and Kildare respectively. Rail lines follow a similar course: the eastern coastal towns are served by the Dublin–Rosslare railway, and there are good train services to Kildare and Kilkenny. You will need a car to explore the south coast; the Passage East–Ballyhack ferry is a useful shortcut between Waterford and Wexford.

**SEE ALSO**

• *Where to Stay* pp289–91

• *Restaurants, Cafés and Pubs* pp308–9 & 318–19

**KEY**

| | |
|---|---|
| ▨ | Motorway |
| ▨ | Major road |
| ▨ | Minor road |
| ▨ | Scenic route |
| ∿ | River |
| – – | Walk |
| ※ | Viewpoint |

R703

R702

R731

**AIGUENAMANAGH**

N30

⑭ **ENNISCORTHY**

**IRISH NATIONAL HERITAGE PARK**

● **NEW ROSS**    N25

㉕

㉖ **WEXFORD**

㉗ **JOHNSTOWN CASTLE**    N25

**ROSSLARE**

㉙

R733

R733

R736

R739

**ASSAGE AST**

**NMORE T**

**KILMORE QUAY**

**ROSSLARE HARBOUR**

㉒ **HOOK PENINSULA**

㉘ **SALTEE ISLANDS**

0 kilometres     15

0 miles     15

The seaside resort of Bray on the east coast

# Castletown House ❶

*See pp122–3.*

# Robertstown ❷

**Road map** D4. Co Kildare. 👥 240. 🚌

Ten locks west along the Grand Canal from Dublin, Robertstown is a characteristic 19th-century canalside village, with warehouses and cottages flanking the waterfront. Freight barges plied the route until about 1960, but pleasure boats have since replaced them. Visitors can take barge cruises from the quay and the Grand Canal Company's Hotel, built in 1801 for canal passengers, is now used for banquets.

Near Sallins, about 8 km (5 miles) east of Robertstown, the canal is carried over the River Liffey along the **Leinster Aqueduct**, an impressive structure built in 1783.

# Peatland World ❸

**Road map** D4. Lullymore, Co Kildare. 📞 045 860133. 🚌 🚌 to Newbridge. 🕐 Apr–Oct: 9am–6pm Mon–Fri, 2–6pm Sat & Sun; Nov–Mar: 9am–5pm Mon–Fri, weekends by appointment. 🎟 ♿ limited.

Anyone interested in the natural history of Irish bogs should visit Peatland World. Housed in an old farmhouse at Lullymore, 9 km (6 miles) northeast of Rathangan, Peatland World lies at the heart of the Bog of Allen, a vast expanse of raised bogland

The Grand Canal Company's Hotel in Robertstown

*(see p244)* that extends across the counties of Offaly, Laois and Kildare. An exhibition of flora, fauna and archaeological finds explores the history and ecology of the bog, while guided walks across the peatlands introduce visitors to the bog's delicate ecosystem.

Stacking peat for use as fuel

# Monasterevin ❹

**Road map** D4. Co Kildare. 👥 2,200. 🚌

This Georgian market town lies west of Kildare, where the Grand Canal crosses the River Barrow. Waterborne trade brought prosperity to Monasterevin in the 18th century, but the locks now see little traffic. However, you can still admire the aqueduct, which is a superb example of canal engineering.

**Moore Abbey**, next to the church, was built in the 18th century on the site of a monastic foundation, but the grand Gothic mansion owes much to Victorian remodelling. Once the ancestral seat of the Earls of Drogheda, in the 1920s Moore Abbey became the home of the celebrated tenor, John McCormack *(see p24)*. It is now a hospital.

# Kildare ❺

**Road map** D4. Co Kildare. 👥 4,200. 🚌 🚌 ℹ Market House (Jun–Sep: 045 522696). 🚌 Thu.

The charming and tidy town of Kildare is dominated by **St Brigid's Cathedral**, which commemorates the saint who founded a religious community on this site in 480. Unusually, monks and nuns lived there under the same roof, but this was not the only unorthodox practice associated with the community. Curious pagan rituals, including the burning of a perpetual fire, continued until the 16th century. The fire pit is visible in the grounds today. So too is a round tower, which was probably built in the 12th century and has

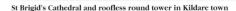

St Brigid's Cathedral and roofless round tower in Kildare town

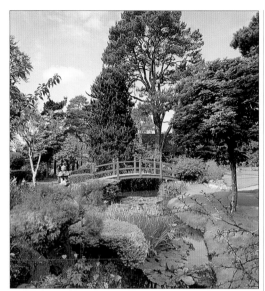
**Japanese Gardens at Tully near Kildare**

Irish life. Exhibits include the frail skeleton of Arkle, a famous champion steeple-chaser in the 1960s.

Sharing the same estate as the National Stud are the **Japanese Gardens** and **St Fiachra's Garden**. The Japanese Gardens were laid out in 1906–10 by Japanese landscape gardener Tassa Eida, with the help of his son Minoru and 40 assistants. The impressive array of trees and shrubs includes maple, bonsai, mulberry, magnolia, sacred bamboo and cherry. The gardens take the form of an allegorical journey through life, beginning with the Gate of Oblivion and leading to the Gateway of Eternity, a con-templative Zen rock garden.

St Fiachra's Garden covers four acres (1.6 ha) of wood-land, wetland, lakes and islands, and features a Waterford Crystal Garden within the monastic cells.

a Romanesque doorway. The cathedral was rebuilt in the Victorian era, but the restorers largely adhered to the original 13th-century design.

### St Brigid's Cathedral
Market Square. **045 521229.**
*May–Oct: daily.* **Donation.**

**ENVIRONS:** Kildare lies at the heart of racing country: the Curragh racecourse is nearby, stables are scattered all around and bloodstock sales take place at Kill, northeast of town.

The **National Stud** is a state-run bloodstock farm at Tully, just south of Kildare. It was founded in 1900 by an eccentric Anglo-Irish colonel called William Hall–Walker. He sold his foals on the basis of their astrological charts, and put skylights in the stables to allow the horses to be "touched" by sunlight or moonbeams. Hall–Walker received the title Lord Wavertree in reward for be-queathing the farm to the British Crown in 1915.

Visitors can explore the 400-ha (1,000-acre) grounds and watch the horses being exercised. Mares are generally kept in a separate paddock from the stallions. Breeding stallions wait in the covering shed: each one is expected to

cover 50 mares per season. There is a special foaling unit where the mare and foal can remain undisturbed for a few days after the birth.

The farm has its own forge and saddlery, and also a Horse Museum. Housed in an old stable block, this illustrates the importance of horses in

### National Stud and Japanese and St Fiachra's Gardens
Tully. **045 521617.** *mid-Feb–mid-Nov: 9:30am–6pm daily (last admisson 60 mins before closing).* National Stud only.

### HORSE RACING IN IRELAND

Ireland has a strong racing culture and, thanks to its non-elitist image, the sport is enjoyed by all. Much of the thoroughbred industry centres around the Curragh, a grassy plain in County Kildare stretching unfenced for more than 2,000 ha (5,000 acres). This area is home to many of the country's studs and training yards, and every morning horses are put through their paces on the gallops. Most of the major flat races, including the Irish Derby, take place at the Curragh racecourse just east of Kildare. Other fixtures are held at nearby Punchestown – most famously the steeplechase festival in April/May – and at Leopardstown, which also hosts major National Hunt races *(see pp26–7).*

**Finishing straight at the Curragh racecourse**

# Castletown House ❶

**B**UILT IN 1722–32 for William Conolly, Speaker of the Irish Parliament, the facade of Castletown was the work of Florentine architect, Alessandro Galilei and gave Ireland its first taste of Palladianism. The magnificent interiors date from the second half of the 18th century. They were commissioned by Lady Louisa Lennox, wife of William Conolly's great-nephew, Tom, who lived here from 1759. Castletown remained in the family until 1965, when it was taken over by the Irish Georgian Society. The state now owns the house and it is open to the public.

**Conolly crest on an armchair**

**★ Long Gallery**
*The heavy ceiling sections and friezes date from the 1720s and the walls were decorated in the Pompeian manner in the 1770s.*

**Red Drawing Room**
*The red damask covering the walls of this room is probably French and dates from the 19th century. This exquisite mahogany bureau was made for Lady Louisa in the 1760s.*

**Green Drawing Room**

**West wing with kitchen**

**The Dining Room**, with a compartmentalized ceiling, was designed by Isaac Ware.

**Boudoir Wall Paintings**
*The boudoir's decorative panels, moved here from the Long Gallery, were inspired by the Raphael Loggia in the Vatican.*

**VISITORS' CHECKLIST**

Road map D4. Celbridge,
Co Kildare. ☎ 01 6288252.
🚌 67, 67A from Dublin.
🕐 Easter Day–Sep: 10am– 6pm
Mon–Fri, 1–6pm Sat, Sun &
public hols; Oct: 10am–5pm
Mon–Fri, 1–5pm Sun & public
hols; Nov: 1–5pm Sun. ♿ 📷
🅿 📷 obligatory. **Concerts.**

★ **Print Room**
*In this, the only in tact 18th century print room in Ireland,
Lady Louisa  indulged her taste for Italian engravings. It was
fashionable at that time for ladies to paste prints directly on
to the wall and frame them with elaborate festoons.*

**The Boar Hunt, painted by
Paul de Vos (1596–1678)**

★ **Staircase Hall**
*This portrait of Lady
Louisa is part of the superb
Rococo stuccowork by the
Francini brothers which
decorates the staircase.*

**The east wing** originally
housed the stables.

**Entrance**

**The Entrance Hall** is an
austere Neo-Classical room.
Its most decorative feature is
the delicate carving on the
pilasters of the upper gallery.

**STAR FEATURES**

★ **Long Gallery**

★ **Print Room**

★ **Staircase Hall**

**CONOLLY'S FOLLY**

This folly, which lies just
beyond the grounds of
Castletown House, provides
the focus of the view from
the Long Gallery. Speaker
Conolly's widow, Katherine,
commissioned it in 1740
as a memorial to her late
husband, and to provide
employment after a harsh
winter. The unusual structure
of superimposed arches
crowned by an obelisk was
designed by Richard Castle,
architect of Russborough
House *(see p124).*

Saloon in Russborough House with original fireplace and stuccowork

# Russborough House ❻

**Road map** D4. Blessington, Co Wicklow. 045 865239. 65 from Dublin. May–Sep: 10:30–5:30pm daily; Apr & Oct: 10:30–5:30pm Sun & public hols.

THIS PALLADIAN MANSION, built in the 1740s for Joseph Leeson, Earl of Milltown, is one of Ireland's finest houses. Its architect, Richard Castle, also designed Powerscourt House (see pp126–7) and is credited with introducing the Palladian style to Ireland.

Unlike many grand estates in the Pale, Russborough has survived magnificently, both inside and out. The house claims the longest frontage in Ireland, with a façade adorned by heraldic lions and curved colonnades. The interior is even more impressive. Many rooms feature superb stucco decoration, which was done largely by the Italian Francini brothers, who also worked on Castletown House (see pp122–3). The best examples are found in the music room, saloon and library, which are embellished with exuberant foliage and cherubs. Around the main staircase, a riot of Rococo plasterwork

depicts a hunt, with hounds clasping garlands of flowers. The stucco mouldings in the drawing room were designed especially to enclose marine scenes by the French artist, Joseph Vernet (1714–89). The paintings were sold in 1926, but were tracked down more than 40 years afterwards and returned to the house.

Russborough has many other treasures, including finely worked fireplaces of Italian marble, imposing mahogany doorways and priceless collections of silver, porcelain and Gobelins tapestries.

Such riches aside, one of the principal reasons to visit Russborough is to see the **Beit Art Collection**, famous for its Flemish, Dutch and Spanish Old Master paintings. These include fine works by Gainsborough, Oudry and Belloto. Sir Alfred Beit, who bought the house in 1952, inherited the pictures from his uncle – also named Alfred Beit and co-founder of the de Beer diamond mining empire in South Africa. In 1974, several masterpieces were taken by the IRA, but they were later retrieved. Several pictures are still missing, following a second robbery in 1986. Only a selection of paintings is on view in the house at any one time, while

Vernet seascape in the drawing room

---

## THE HISTORY OF THE PALE

The term "Pale" refers to an area around Dublin which marked the limits of English influence from Norman to Tudor times. The frontier fluctuated, but at its largest the Pale stretched from Dundalk in County Louth to Waterford town. Gaelic chieftains outside the area could keep their lands provided they agreed to bring up their heirs within the Pale.

The Palesmen supported their rulers' interests and considered themselves the upholders of English values. This widened the gap between the Gaelic majority and the Anglo-Irish, a fore-taste of England's doomed involvement in the country. Long after its fortifications were dismantled, the idea of the Pale lived on as a state of mind. The expression "beyond the pale" survives as a definition of those outside the bounds of civilized society.

An 18th-century family enjoying the privileged lifestyle typical within the Pale

**Tourist road train on the beachfront esplanade at Bray**

others are on permanent loan to the National Gallery in Dublin (*see pp68–9*).

Russborough enjoys a fine position near the village of **Blessington**, with a good view across to the Wicklow Mountains. The house lies amid wooded parkland rather than elaborate flower gardens. As Alfred Beit said of Irish Palladianism, "Fine architecture standing in a green sward was considered enough."

**ENVIRONS:** The **Poulaphouca Reservoir**, which was formed by the damming of the River Liffey, extends south from Blessington. The placid lake is popular with watersports enthusiasts, while other visitors come simply to enjoy the lovely mountain views.

## Powerscourt ❼

*See pp126–7.*

## Bray ❽

**Road map** D4. Co Wicklow.
🏃 *33,000.* 🚉 *DART.* 🚌 ℹ️ *Old Court House, Main St (01 2867128).*

ONCE A REFINED Victorian resort, Bray is nowadays a brash holiday town, with amusement arcades and fish and chip shops lining the seafront. Its beach attracts large crowds in summer, including many young families. Anyone in search of peace and quiet can escape to nearby Bray Head, where there is scope for bracing cliffside walks. Bray also makes a good base from which to explore Powerscourt Gardens, the Wicklow Mountains and the delightful coastal villages of Killiney and Dalkey (*see p101*).

## Killruddery House and Gardens ❾

**Road map** D4. Bray, Co Wicklow.
📞 *01 286 2777.* 🕐 *May–Sep: 1pm–5pm daily.* 🎫 ♿ *limited.*

KILLRUDDERY HOUSE lies just to the south of Bray, in the shadow of Little Sugar Loaf Mountain. Built in 1651, it has been the family seat of the Earls of Meath ever since, although the original mansion was remodelled in an Elizabethan Revival style in the early 19th century. The house contains some good carving and stuccowork, but it is a rather faded stately home. The real charm of Killruddery lies in the 17th-century formal gardens, regarded as the finest French Classical gardens in the country. They were laid out in the 1680s by a French gardener named Bonet, who also worked at Versailles.

The gardens, planted with great precision, feature romantic parterres, a whole array of different hedges and many fine trees and shrubs, both native and foreign. The sylvan theatre, a small enclosure surrounded by a bay hedge, is the only known example of its kind in Ireland.

The Long Ponds, a pair of canals which extend 165 m (550 ft), were once used to stock fish. Beyond, a pool enclosed by two circular hedges leads to a Victorian arrangement of paths flanked by statues and hedges of yew, beech, lime and hornbeam.

**View across the Long Ponds to Killruddery House**

# Powerscourt ❼

T HE GARDENS AT POWERSCOURT are probably the finest in Ireland, both for their design and their dramatic setting at the foot of Great Sugar Loaf Mountain. The house and grounds were commissioned in the 1730s by Richard Wingfield, the 1st Viscount Powerscourt. New ornamental gardens were completed in 1858–75 by the 7th Viscount, who added gates, urns and statues collected during his travels in Europe. The house was gutted by an accidental fire in 1974, but the ground floor has been beautifully renovated and now accommodates an upmarket shopping centre with an excellent restaurant and café.

**Laocoon statue on upper terrace**

**Bamberg Gate**
*Made in Vienna in the 1770s, this gilded wrought-iron gate was brought to Powerscourt by the 7th Viscount from Bamberg Church in Bavaria.*

**The Walled Gardens** include a formal arrangement of clipped laurel trees but are also used for growing plants for Powerscourt's nursery.

**The Pets' Cemetery** contains the graves of Wingfield family dogs, cats and even horses and cattle.

**Statue of Laocoon**

**Dolphin Pond**
*This pool, designed as a fish pond in the 18th century, is enclosed by exotic conifers in a lovely secluded garden.*

## POWERSCOURT HOUSE

In 1974 a fire at the Palladian mansion at Powerscourt left the fine building a burnt-out shell. In recent years the Slazenger family, who now own the estate, have restored the ground floor and the ballroom upstairs, although much work remains to be done to the rest of the house. Originally built in 1731 on the site of a Norman castle, the house was designed by Richard Castle, who was also the architect of Russborough House (*see p124*).

**Powerscourt ablaze in 1974**

**★ The Perron**
*Leading down to Triton Lake is the Perron, a beautiful Italianate stairway added in 1874. Beside the lake, it is guarded by two statues of Pegasus – the mythical winged horse and emblem of the Wingfield family.*

**Pebble Mosaic**
*Many tonnes of pebbles were gathered from nearby Bray beach to build the Perron and to make this mosaic on the terrace.*

**The Italian Garden**
is laid out on terraces which were first cut into the steep hillside in the 1730s.

**The Pepper Pot Tower** was built in 1911.

**★ Triton Lake**
*Made for the first garden, the lake takes its name from its central fountain, which is modelled on a 17th-century work by Bernini in Rome.*

**★ Japanese Gardens**
*These enchanting Edwardian gardens, created out of bogland, contain Chinese conifers and bamboo trees.*

**STAR FEATURES**

★ The Perron

★ Japanese Gardens

★ Triton Lake

**Powerscourt Gardens with Great Sugar Loaf Mountain beyond**

# A Tour of the Military Road ⑩

THE BRITISH BUILT the Military Road through the heart of the Wicklow Mountains during a campaign to flush out Irish rebels after an uprising in 1798 *(see p141)*. Now known as the R115, this road takes you through the emptiest and most rugged landscapes of County Wicklow. Fine countryside, in which deer and other wildlife flourish, is characteristic of the whole of this tour.

**Rare red squirrel**

### Glencree ①
The former British barracks in Glencree are among several found along the Military Road.

### Powerscourt Waterfall ⑨
The River Dargle cascades 130 m (425 ft) over a granite escarpment to form Ireland's highest waterfall.

### Great Sugar Loaf ⑧
The granite cone of Great Sugar Loaf Mountain can be climbed in under an hour from the car park on its southern side.

### Sally Gap ②
This remote pass is surrounded by a vast expanse of blanket bog dotted with pools and streams.

### Lough Tay ⑦
Stark, rocky slopes plunge down to the dark waters of Lough Tay. Though it lies within a Guinness-owned estate, the lake is accessible to walkers.

### Glenmacnass ③
After Sally Gap, the road drops into a deep glen where a waterfall spills dramatically over rocks.

### Roundwood ⑥
The highest village in Ireland at 238 m (780 ft) above sea level, Roundwood enjoys a fine setting. Its main street is lined with pubs, cafés and craft shops.

### Glendalough ④
This ancient lakeside monastery *(see pp132–3)*, enclosed by wooded slopes, is the prime historical sight in the Wicklow Mountains.

**Map labels:** DUBLIN, Enniskerry, Powerscourt, Glencree, R115, R760, Dargle, R755, Lough Tay, R759, R755, Vartry Reservoir, Annamoe, Lough Dan, Glenmacnass, R756, Laragh, R755, Laghmore, Clara, RATHDRUM

## TIPS FOR DRIVERS

**Length:** 96 km (60 miles).
**Stopping-off points:** There are several pubs and cafés in Enniskerry (including Poppies, an old-fashioned tearoom), and also in Roundwood, but this area is better for picnics. There are several marked picnic spots south of Enniskerry. *(See also pp355–7.)*

0 kilometres      5

0 miles       3

## KEY

▬▬ Tour route

= = = Other roads

☆ Viewpoint

### Vale of Clara ⑤
This picturesque wooded valley follows the River Avonmore. It contains the tiny village of Clara, which consists of two houses, a church and a school.

# Wicklow Mountains ⑪

Road map D4. 🚌 to Rathdrum & Wicklow. 🚌 to Enniskerry, Wicklow, Glendalough, Rathdrum & Avoca. 🛈 Rialto House, Fitzwilliam Square, Wicklow (0404 69117).

STANDING AMID the rugged wilderness of the Wicklow Mountains, it can be hard to believe that Dublin is under an hour's drive away. The in-accessibility of the mountains meant that they once provided a safe hideout for opponents of English rule. When much of the Southeast was obedient to the English Crown, within an area known as the Pale *(see p124)*, warlords such as the O'Tooles held sway in the Wicklow Mountains. Rebels who took part in the 1798 uprising *(see p39)* sought refuge here too. One of their leaders, Michael Dwyer, remained at liberty in the hills around Sally Gap until 1803.

The building of the **Military Road**, started in 1800, made the area more accessible, but the mountains are still thinly populated. There is little traffic to disturb enjoyment of the exhilarating scenery of rock-strewn glens, lush forest and bogland where heather gives a purple sheen to the land. Turf-cutting is still a thriving cottage industry, and

**Bearnas na Diallaite**
**SALLY GAP**

↑ **Bealach Mileata**
**MILITARY ROAD** ✈

← **Gleann Life**
**LIFFEY VALLEY** ↗

↗ **Bealach Fheartire** →
**VARTRY DRIVE**

**Road sign in the Wicklow Mountains**

you often see peat stacked up by the road. Numerous walk-ing trails weave through these landscapes. Among them is the **Wicklow Way**, which extends 132 km (82 miles) from Marlay Park in Dublin to Clonegal in County Carlow. It is marked but not always easy to follow, so do not set out without a decent map. Although no peak exceeds 915 m (3,000 ft), the Wicklow Mountains can be dangerous in bad weather.

Hiking apart, there is plenty to see and do in this region. A good starting point for explor-ing the northern area is the picture-postcard estate village of **Enniskerry**. In summer, it is busy with tourists who come to visit the gardens at Powerscourt *(see pp126–7)*. From Laragh, to the south, you can reach Glendalough *(see pp132–3)* and the **Vale of Avoca**, where cherry trees are laden with blossom in the spring. The beauty of this gentle valley was captured in the poetry of Thomas Moore (1779–1852):

"There is not in the wide world a valley so sweet as that vale in whose bosom the bright waters meet" – a reference to the confluence of the Avonbeg and Avonmore rivers, the so-called **Meeting of the Waters** beyond Avondale House *(see p132)*. Nestled among wooded

**Mount Usher Gardens, on the banks of the River Vartry**

hills at the heart of the valley is the hamlet of Avoca, where the **Avoca Handweavers** produce colourful tweeds in the oldest hand-weaving mill in Ireland, in operation since 1723.

Further north, towards the coast near Ashford, the River Vartry rushes through the deep chasm of the **Devil's Glen**. On entering the valley, the river falls 30 m (100 ft) into a pool known as the Devil's Punchbowl. There are good walks around here, with fine views of the coast.

🏠 **Avoca Handweavers**
Avoca. 📞 0402 35105. ◯ daily. ● 25 & 26 Dec. 🛈 🚻

# Mount Usher Gardens ⑫

Road map D4. Ashford, Co Wicklow. 📞 0404 40205. 🚌 to Ashford. ◯ Mar–Oct: daily. 🎫 🛈 🚻 ♿ limited.

SET BESIDE the River Vartry just east of Ashford are the Mount Usher Gardens. They were designed in 1868 by a Dubliner, Edward Walpole, who imbued them with his strong sense of romanticism.

The gardens contain many rare shrubs and trees, from Chinese conifers and bamboos to Mexican pines and pampas grass. There is also a Maple Walk, which is glorious in autumn. The river provides the main focus of the Mount Usher Gardens, and amid the exotic vegetation you can glimpse herons on the weirs.

**Colourful moorland around Sally Gap in the Wicklow Mountains**

# Glendalough **⓭**

**Road map** D4. Co Wicklow. 🚌 *St Kevin's Bus from Dublin.* **Ruins** ⬜ *daily.* 🅿 *in summer.* **Visitors' Centre** ☎ *0404 45325/45352.* ⬜ *daily.* 🔴 *24–27 Dec.* 🈳 🅿 🏛

**View along the Upper Lake at Glendalough**

THE STEEP, WOODED slopes of Glendalough, the "valley of the two lakes", harbour one of Ireland's most atmospheric monastic sites. Established by St Kevin in the 6th century, the settlement was sacked time and again by the Vikings but nevertheless flourished for over 600 years. Decline set in only after English forces partially razed the site in 1398, though it functioned as a monastic centre until the Dissolution of the Monasteries in 1539 *(see p36)*. Pilgrims kept on coming to Glendalough even after that, particularly on St Kevin's feast day, 3 June, which was often a riotous event *(see p28)*.

The age of the buildings is uncertain, but most date from the 8th to 12th centuries. Many were restored during the 1870s.

**Remains of the Gatehouse, the original entrance to Glendalough**

The main group of ruins lies east of the Lower Lake, but the earliest buildings associated with St Kevin are by the Upper Lake. Here, where the scenery is much wilder, you are better able to enjoy the tranquillity of Glendalough and to escape the crowds which inevitably descend on the site. Try to arrive as early as possible in the day, particularly during the peak tourist season. You enter the monastery through the double stone arch of the **Gatehouse**, the only surviving example in Ireland of a gateway into a monastic enclosure.

A short walk leads to a graveyard with a **Round tower** in one corner. Reaching 33 m (110 ft) in height, this is one of the finest of its kind in the country. Its cap was rebuilt in the 1870s using stones found inside the tower. The roofless **Cathedral** nearby dates mainly from the 12th century and is

**St Kevin's Kitchen**

the valley's largest ruin. At the centre of the churchyard stands the tiny **Priest's House**, whose name derives from the fact that it was a burial place for local clergy. The worn carving of a robed figure above the door is possibly of St Kevin, flanked by two disciples. East of here, **St Kevin's Cross** dates from the 12th century and is one of the best preserved of Glendalough's various High Crosses. Made of granite, the cross may once have marked the boundary of the monastic cemetery. Below, nestled in the lush valley, a minuscule oratory with a steeply pitched stone roof is a charming sight. Erected in the 11th century or even earlier, it is popularly known as **St Kevin's Kitchen**; this is perhaps because its belfry, thought to be a later addition, resembles a chimney. One of the earliest churches at Glendalough, **St Mary's**, lies across a field to the west.

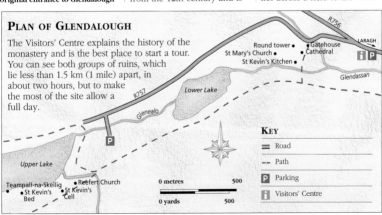

## PLAN OF GLENDALOUGH

The Visitors' Centre explains the history of the monastery and is the best place to start a tour. You can see both groups of ruins, which lie less than 1.5 km (1 mile) apart, in about two hours, but to make the most of the site allow a full day.

R756   LARAGH

Round tower ●   ●Gatehouse
St Mary's Church ●   ●Cathedral
St Kevin's Kitchen ●

Glendassan

R757   Lower Lake

Glenealo

Upper Lake

Teampall-na-Skellig   ●Reefert Church
●  ●St Kevin's  ●St Kevin's
St Kevin's   Cell
Bed

0 metres      500

0 yards      500

**KEY**

| | |
|---|---|
| ▭ | Road |
| -- | Path |
| 🅿 | Parking |
| 🛈 | Visitors' Centre |

**Round tower at Glendalough**

Some traces of Romanesque moulding are visible outside the east window. Following the path along the south bank of the river, you reach the Upper Lake. This is the site of more monastic ruins and is also the chief starting point for walks through the valley and to a number of abandoned lead and zinc mines.

Situated in a grove not far from the Poulanass waterfall are the ruins of the **Reefert Church**, a simple Romanesque building. Its unusual name is a corruption of *Righ Fearta*, meaning "burial place of the kings"; the church may mark the site of an ancient cemetery. Near here, on a rocky spur overlooking the Upper Lake, stands **St Kevin's Cell**, the ruins of a beehive-shaped structure which is thought to have been the hermit's home.

There are two sites on the south side of the lake which cannot be reached on foot but are visible from the opposite shore. **Teampall-na-Skellig**, or the "church on the rock", was supposedly built on the site of the first church that St Kevin founded at Glendalough. To the east of it, carved into the cliff, is **St Kevin's Bed**. This small cave, in reality little more than a rocky ledge, may have been used as a tomb in the Bronze Age, but it is more famous as St Kevin's favourite retreat. It was from here that the saint allegedly rejected the advances of a naked woman by tossing her into the lake.

## St Kevin at Glendalough

St Kevin was born in 498, a descendant of the royal house of Leinster. He rejected his life of privilege, however, choosing to live instead as a hermit in a cave at Glendalough. He later founded a monastery here, and went on to create a notable centre of learning devoted to the care of the sick and the copying and illumination of manuscripts. St Kevin attracted many disciples to Glendalough during his life-time, but the monastery became more celebrated as a place of pilgrimage after his death in around 618.

Colourful legends about the saint make up for the dearth of facts about him. That he lived to the age of 120 is just one of the stories told about him. Another tale claims that one day, when St Kevin was at prayer, a blackbird laid an egg in one of his outstretched hands. The saint remained in the same position until it was hatched.

## Avondale House ⓮

**Road map** D4. Co Wicklow. 📞 *0404 46111*. 🚌 🚆 *to Rathdrum*. **House** 🕐 *Mar–Oct: 11am–6pm (Nov–Feb 5pm) daily.* ● *Good Fri & 23–28 Dec.* 🎥 ⛺ 🏠 ♿ *Limited.* **Grounds** 🕐 *daily.*

L YING JUST south of Rathdrum, Avondale House is the birthplace of the 19th-century politician and patriot, Charles Stewart Parnell *(see p41)*. The Georgian mansion is now a museum dedicated to Parnell and the fight for Home Rule.

The house is now a forestry school, but the grounds are open to the public. Known as **Avondale Forest Park**, they include an impressive arboretum first planted in the 18th century and much added to since 1900. There are some lovely walks through the woods, with pleasant views along the River Avonmore.

## Browne's Hill Dolmen ⓯

**Road map** D4. Co Carlow. 🚌 🚆 *to Carlow.* 🕐 *daily.*

I N A FIELD 3 km (2 miles) east of Carlow, along the R726, stands a dolmen boasting the biggest capstone in Ireland. Weighing a reputed 100 tonnes, this massive stone is embedded in the earth at one end and supported at the other by three much smaller stones. Dating back to 2000 BC, Browne's Hill Dolmen is thought to mark the tomb of a local chieftain. A path leads to it from the road.

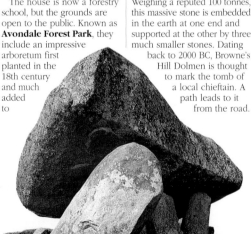

**Browne's Hill Dolmen, famous for its enormous capstone**

# Street-by-Street: Kilkenny ⑯

**Kilkenny coat of arms**

**K**ILKENNY is undoubtedly Ireland's loveliest inland city. It rose to prominence in the 13th century and became the medieval capital of Ireland. The Anglo-Norman Butler family came to power in the 1390s and held sway over the city for 500 years. Their power has gone but their legacy is visible in the city's historic buildings, many of which have been restored. Kilkenny is proud of its heritage and every August hosts the Republic's top arts festival.

**To Irishtown, St Canice's Cathedral**

**Grace's Castle** was built in 1210 and later converted into a jail. Remodelled in the 18th century, it has functioned as a courthouse ever since.

PARLIAMENT STREET

ST KIERAN'S STREET

HIGH STREET

**Narrow alleyways**, known locally as "slips", are part of Kilkenny's medieval heritage. Several slips survive, and these are currently undergoing restoration.

**Marble City Bar**

**Tholsel (City Hall)**

**★ Rothe House**
*This fine Tudor merchant's house, built around two court-yards, is fronted by arcades once typical of Kilkenny's main streets. A small museum inside the house contains a display of local archaeological artifacts and a costume collection.*

**Butter Slip**
*The alley is named after the butter stalls that once lined this small market place.*

**View of the High Street**
*The 18th-century Tholsel, with its distinctive clock tower and arcade, is the main landmark on the High Street. Its elegant Georgian chamber is used by city councillors to this day.*

**STAR SIGHTS**

★ **Kilkenny Castle**

★ **Rothe House**

## Kyteler's Inn

*This medieval coaching inn (see p318) is named after Dame Alice Kyteler, a 14th-century witch who once lived in the building. Like most of the pubs in the city, Kyteler's Inn sells Smithwick's beer, which has been brewed in Kilkenny since 1710.*

### VISITORS' CHECKLIST

**Road map** C4. Co Kilkenny. 20,000. Dublin Road (056 22024). Dublin Road (056 64933). Shee Almshouse, Rose Inn St (056 51500). **Rothe House** 056 22893. Mar–Oct: 10:30am–5pm Mon–Sat, 3pm–5pm Sun; Nov–Feb: 1pm–5pm daily.

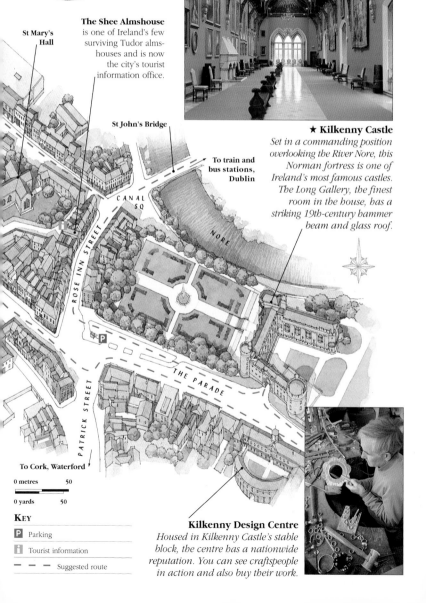

**The Shee Almshouse** is one of Ireland's few surviving Tudor almshouses and is now the city's tourist information office.

St Mary's Hall

St John's Bridge

To train and bus stations, Dublin

CANAL SQ

NORE

ROSE INN STREET

THE PARADE

PATRICK STREET

To Cork, Waterford

0 metres 50

0 yards 50

### KEY

P Parking

i Tourist information

– – – Suggested route

### ★ Kilkenny Castle

*Set in a commanding position overlooking the River Nore, this Norman fortress is one of Ireland's most famous castles. The Long Gallery, the finest room in the house, has a striking 19th-century hammer beam and glass roof.*

### Kilkenny Design Centre

*Housed in Kilkenny Castle's stable block, the centre has a nationwide reputation. You can see craftspeople in action and also buy their work.*

## Exploring Kilkenny

In a lovely spot beside a kink in the River Nore, Kilkenny is of great architectural interest, with much use made of the distinctive local black limestone, known as Kilkenny marble. A tour of the town also reveals many unexpected treasures: a Georgian façade often seems to conceal a Tudor chimney, a Classical interior or some other surprise.

The survival of the Irishtown district, now dominated by St Canice's Cathedral, recalls past segregation in Kilkenny. The area once known as Englishtown still boasts the city's grandest public buildings.

As a brewery city, Kilkenny is a paradise for keen drinkers. Not counting the popular private drinking clubs, there are about 80 official pubs.

North side of Kilkenny Castle showing Victorian crenellations

Sign of the Marble City Bar on Kilkenny's High Street

### ♣ Kilkenny Castle

The Parade. 【 056 21450.
◯ Apr–Sep: daily; Oct–Mar: Tue–Sun. ● Good Fri & 10 days at Christmas. 🎫 🖪 🎫 obligatory.
🚻 limited. Queues are likely during the summer.

Built in the 1190s, Kilkenny Castle was occupied right up until 1935. The powerful Butler family (see p134) lived in it from the late 14th century, but because of the exorbitant running costs, their descendants eventually donated Kilkenny Castle to the nation in 1967.

With its drum towers and solid walls, the castle retains its medieval form, but has undergone many alterations. The Victorian changes made in Gothic Revival style have had the most enduring impact, and are even more impressive since recent restoration work.

High spots of a tour include the library, the wood-panelled dining room and the Chinese bedroom. Best of all, however, is the Long Gallery, built in the 1820s to house the Butler art collection. Its elaborate painted ceiling has a strong Pre-Raphaelite feel, with many of the motifs inspired by the *Book of Kells (see p62)*.

The castle grounds have shrunk over the centuries, but the French Classical gardens remain, with terraces opening onto a woodland walk and pleasant rolling parkland.

### ♙ St Canice's Cathedral

Irishtown. 【 056 64971 ◯ daily.
**Donation.** 🚻 🚻
The hilltop cathedral, flanked by a round tower, was built in the 13th century in an Early English Gothic style. It was

sacked by Cromwell's forces in 1650, but has survived as one of Ireland's medieval treasures. Walls of the local Kilkenny limestone and pillars of pale sandstone combine to create an interior of simple grandeur. An array of splendid 16th-century tombs includes the beautiful effigies of the Butler family in the south transept. It is worth climbing the round tower for a fine view over Kilkenny.

### ♙ Black Abbey

Abbey St. 【 056 21279. ◯ daily. 🚻
Lying just west of Parliament Street, this Dominican abbey was founded in 1225. Part of the abbey was turned into a courthouse in the 16th century, but is once again a working monastery. The church boasts a fine vaulted undercroft and distinctive stonework. There are also some beautiful stained-glass windows, several of which date back to the 14th century.

**Environs:** Just north of the town lies **Dunmore Cave**, a limestone cavern with an impressive series of chambers, noted for its steep descent and curious rock formations.

**Bennettsbridge**, on the Nore 8 km (5 miles) south of Kilkenny, is famous for its ceramics. The Nicholas Mosse Pottery *(see p327)* specializes in colourful earthenware made from the local clay.

### 🐾 Dunmore Cave

Ballyfoyle. 【 056 67726.
◯ Mar–Oct: daily; Nov–Feb: Sat, Sun & public hols. 🎫

Tomb of 2nd Marquess of Ormonde in St Canice's Cathedral

# Jerpoint Abbey ⑰

**Road map** D5. Thomastown, Co
Kilkenny. ☎ 056 24623. 🚌 🚋 to
Thomastown. ⏺ Mar–May & mid-
Sep–Oct: 10am–5pm (Nov 4pm) daily;
Jun–mid–Sep: 9:30am–6:30pm daily;
Dec: by appt only. 🖼 ✔ ♿

O N THE BANKS of the Little
Arrigle just south of
Thomastown, Jerpoint Abbey
is one of the finest Cistercian
ruins in Ireland. Founded in
1160, the fortified medieval
complex rivalled Duiske
Abbey (see p141) in prestige.
Jerpoint flourished until the
Dissolution of the Monasteries
(see pp34–5), when it passed
to the Earl of Ormonde.

The 15th-century cloisters
have not survived as well as
some earlier parts of the
abbey. Despite this,
they are the highlight
of Jerpoint, with their
amusing sculptures of
knights, courtly ladies,
bishops and dragons.
The church itself is
well preserved. The
Irish-Romanesque
transepts date back to
the earliest period of
the Abbey's develop-
ment and contain
several 16th-century
tombs decorated with
exquisite stylized
carvings. The north
side of the nave has a
rich array of decorated
Romanesque capitals
and throughout the
abbey are tombs and
effigies of early
bishops and patrons. The
battlemented crossing tower
was added during the 1400s.

**Stylized carving of saints on 16th-century tomb in Jerpoint Abbey**

# Lismore ⑱

**Road map** C5. Co Waterford.
🏘 1,100. 🚌 ℹ Lismore Heritage
Centre (058 54975).

T HIS GENTEEL riverside town
is dwarfed by **Lismore
Castle**, perched romantically
above the River Blackwater.
Built in 1185 but re-
modelled in the 19th
century, the castle is the
Irish seat of the Duke
of Devonshire and is
closed to the public.
However, you can visit
the sumptuous gardens,
which include a lovely
riverside walk. **Lismore
Heritage Centre** tells
the story of St Carthage,
who founded a monas-
tic centre here in the
7th century. The town
has two cathedrals
dedicated to him. The
Protestant **Cathedral
of St Carthage** is the
more interesting. It
dates from 1633
but incorporates
older elements and
was later altered to suit the
Neo-Gothic tastes of the
Victorians. There is some fine
Gothic vaulting, and two
stained-glass windows in the
south transept are by the Pre-
Raphaelite artist, Sir Edward
Burne-Jones.

**Burne-Jones window
in St Carthage's
Cathedral, Lismore**

♠ **Lismore Castle
Gardens** ☎ 058 54424. ⏺ Apr–
mid-Oct: daily (pm only). 🖼

**ENVIRONS:** From Lismore you
can follow a picturesque
route through the **Blackwater
Valley** (see p169). This runs
from Cappoquin, in an idyllic
woodland setting just east of
Lismore, down to the estuary
at Youghal (see p171).

# Ardmore ⑲

**Road map** C5. Co Waterford. 🏘 450.
🚌 ℹ Jun–Sep: Beach Car Park (024
94444).

A RDMORE is a popular seaside
resort with a splendid
beach, lively pubs, good cliff
walks and some interesting
architecture. The hill beside
the village is the site of a
monastery established in the
5th century by St Declan, the
first missionary to bring
Christianity to this area.

Most of the buildings, including the ruined **St Declan's
Cathedral**, date from the
12th century. The cathedral's
west wall has fine Romanesque
sculptures, arranged in a
series of arcades. The scenes
include The *Archangel
Michael Weighing Souls* in the
upper row, and below this
*The Adoration of the Magi* and
*The Judgment of Solomon.*

The adjacent round tower is
one of the best preserved
examples in Ireland, and rises
to a height of 30 m (95 ft). An
oratory nearby is said to mark
the site of St Declan's grave.

**St Declan's Cathedral at Ardmore, with its near-perfect round tower**

# Waterford ⑳

**Waterford city coat of arms**

WATERFORD, IRELAND'S oldest city, was founded by Vikings in 914. Set in a commanding position by the estuary of the River Suir, it became southeast Ireland's main seaport. From the 18th century, the city's prosperity was consolidated by local industries, including the glassworks for which Waterford is famous. The strong commercial tradition persists today and Waterford's port is still one of Ireland's busiest. In the last few years, following extensive archaeological excavations in the city centre, a new heart and atmosphere has been put into the old city with the creation of pedestrian precincts in the historic quarter and along the quays.

**Reginald's Tower on the quayside**

**Cathedral Close, looking towards Lady Lane in the heart of the city**

## Exploring Waterford

The extensive remains of the city walls clearly define the area originally fortified by the Vikings. The best-preserved section runs northwest from the **Watch Tower** on Castle Street, although Reginald's Tower, overlooking the river, is the largest structure in the old defences. In the Reginald Bar (*see p318*) you can see the arches through which boats sallied forth down the river; these sallyports are one of several Viking sections of the largely Norman fortifications.

Although Waterford retains its medieval layout, most of the city's finest buildings are Georgian. Some of the best examples can be seen on the Mall, which runs southwest from Reginald's Tower, and in the lovely Cathedral Square. The latter takes its name from **Christchurch Cathedral**,

which was built in the 1770s to a design by John Roberts, a local architect who contributed much to the city's Georgian heritage. It is fronted by a fine Corinthian colonnade. A grim 15th-century effigy of a rotting corpse is an unexpected sight inside. Heading down towards the river, you pass the 13th-century ruins of **Grey Friars**, often known as the French Church after it became a Huguenot chapel in 1693.

West along the waterfront, a Victorian clock tower stands at the top of Barronstrand Street. Rising above the busy shops is the **Holy Trinity Cathedral**, which has a rich Neo-Classical interior. George's Street, which runs west from here, is dotted with period houses and cosy pubs. It leads to O'Connell Street, whose partially restored warehouses contrast with the shabbier buildings on the quay. In the summer, you can enjoy another view of the waterfront by taking a cruise on the river.

### ♣ Reginald's Tower

The Quay. 📞 051 304220.
🕐 Apr–Oct: daily.
The Vikings built a fort on this site in 914 but it was the Anglo Normans who, in 1185, built the stone structure seen today. With impregnable walls 3 m (10 ft) thick, the tower is said to be the first Irish building to use mortar, a primitive concoction of blood, lime, fur and mud. It is the oldest civic urban building in Ireland.

### 🏛 Waterford Museum of Treasures

Merchants Quay. 📞 051 304500.
🕐 Apr–May, Sep: 9:30am–6pm daily;
Jun–Aug: 9:30am–9pm daily; Oct–Mar:
10am–5pm daily. 🌑 25 & 26 Dec. 🗓
♿ 🚻 🛍
This multi award-winning interactive museum featuring an important collection, tells the story of Waterford from its Viking foundations to the late 19th century.

**View of the city of Waterford across the River Suir**

## Waterford Crystal Factory

Kilbarry. 051 332500. Mar–Dec: 8:30am–6pm daily; Jan–Feb: 9am–5pm Mon–Fri. Last tour 2 hrs before close.

A visit to the Waterford Crystal Factory, just 2.5 km (1.5 miles) south of the city, is highly recommended to observe the process of crystal-making.

The original glass factory was founded in 1783 by two brothers, George and William Penrose, who chose Waterford

**Craftsman engraving a vase at the Waterford Crystal Factory**

because of its port. For many decades their crystal enjoyed an unrivalled reputation, but draconian taxes caused the firm to close in 1851. A new factory was opened in 1947, however, and master blowers and engravers were brought from the Continent to train local apprentices. Competition from Tipperary and Galway Crystal had an effect in the early 1990s, but sales have revived in recent years.

Visitors can follow all stages of production, observing the process by which sand, lead and potash are transformed by fire into sparkling crystal. The main difference between ordinary glass and crystal is the latter's high lead content, 30 per cent in Waterford's case. The glass-blowers require great skill to create walls of the right thickness to take the heavy incisions typical of Waterford Crystal. The factory's other main hallmark is the Waterford signature, which is engraved on the base of each piece.

In the gallery showroom, a crystal chandelier lights up a dining table laden with Wedgwood pottery and Waterford glass, tempting visitors to buy.

**Ballyhack port, across Waterford Harbour from Passage East**

**ENVIRONS:** The small port of **Passage East**, 12 km (7 miles) east of Waterford, witnessed the landing of the Normans in 1170 (see p34), but little has happened since. A car ferry links the village to Ballyhack in County Wexford, providing a scenic shortcut across Waterford Harbour as well as an excellent entry point to the Hook Peninsula (see p140).

**WATERFORD CITY CENTRE**

Christchurch Cathedral ④
Clock Tower ①
Holy Trinity Cathedral ②
Reginald's Tower ⑥
Watch Tower ③
Waterford Museum of Treasures ⑤

**KEY**

River boat service
Parking
Tourist information
Church
City walls

## Dunmore East ㉑

**Road map** D5. Co Waterford.
🚶 *1,500*. 🚌

THE APPEAL of Dunmore East, Waterford's most charming fishing village, lies chiefly in its red sandstone cliffs and bustling harbour. Paths run along the foot of the cliffs, but for the best views take the road that winds uphill from the beach, past tidy cottages and the ivy-clad Ship Inn to the Haven Hotel. A gate nearby leads to delightful gardens overlooking the fishing boats below. Climbing further, up steps cut into the rock, you are rewarded by views of the cliffs and noisy kittiwake colonies.

**Busy fishing harbour at Dunmore East**

## Hook Peninsula ㉒

**Road map** D5. Co. Wexford. 🚌 *to Duncannon.* ⛴ *from Passage East to Ballyhack (051 382480).* ℹ️ *Fethard-on-Sea (051 397502).*

THIS TAPERING HEADLAND of gentle landscapes scattered with ancient ruins and quiet villages is perfect for a circular tour. The "Ring of Hook" route begins south of New Ross at **Dunbrody Abbey**, the ruins of a 12th-century Cistercian church, but **Ballyhack** is another good place to start. Once a fortified crossing point into County Waterford, the town still has a ferry service to neighbouring Passage East (*see p139*). **Ballyhack Castle**, built by the Knights Templar in about 1450, contains a small museum. About 4 km (2.5 miles) beyond is the small

resort of **Duncannon**, with a broad sandy beach and a star-shaped fort, which was built in 1588 in expectation of an attack by the Spanish Armada.

The coast road continues south to **Hook Head**. Here, perched on red sandstone, is Europe's oldest working lighthouse, dating from 1172 and now with its own visitor centre. Paths skirt the coast famous for its fossils, seals and a variety of seabirds.

Just 2 km (1.5 miles) east is the picturesque village of **Slade**. A ruined 15th-century tower house, **Slade Castle**, presides over the tiny harbour where fishing boats cluster around the slipways. The road proceeds along the rugged coastline, past the resort of Fethard-on-Sea and Saltmills to the dramatic ruin of **Tintern Abbey**. This 13th-century Cistercian foundation was built by William Marshall, Earl of Pembroke, in fulfilment of a vow made when his boat was caught in a storm off the coast nearby. The west end has been restored, but excavation work

continues. Fields lead to an old stone bridge and views over **Bannow Bay**, where it is thought the Normans made their first landing in 1169.

🏛 **Dunbrody Abbey**
Campile. 📞 *051 388603.*
🕐 *Apr–Sep: daily.* 🅿️ ♿ 🚻 🍴
🏰 **Ballyhack Castle**
Ballyhack. 📞 *051 389468.*
🕐 *Jun–Sep: daily.*

**Norman lighthouse at Hook Head, on the tip of the Hook Peninsula**

## New Ross ㉓

**Road map** D5. Co Wexford. 🚶 *6,000.* 🚌 ℹ️ *mid-Jun–Aug: The Quay (051 421857).* 🛒 *Tue.* **Galley Cruising Restaurants** *The Quay (051 421723).*

LYING ON the banks of the River Barrow, New Ross is one of the oldest towns in the county. Its importance, now as in the past, stems from its status as a port. In summer there is much activity on the river. Cruises run by Galley Cruising Restaurants ply the Barrow, Nore and Suir rivers. Traditional shopfronts line the streets, which rise steeply

**Castle ruins and harbour at Slade on the Hook Peninsula**

from the quayside. The **Tholsel**, now the town hall but originally a tollhouse, was occupied by the British during the 1798 rebellion *(see pp38–9)*. Opposite, a monument to a Wexford pikeman commemorates the bravery of the Irish rebels who faced the British cannons.

Nearby is **St Mary's** which, when founded in the 13th century, was the largest parish church in Ireland. A modern church occupies the site, but the original (now roofless) south transept remains, as do many medieval tombstones.

View over Enniscorthy and St Aidan's cathedral from Vinegar Hill

**ENVIRONS:** A popular trip up the meandering Barrow goes 16 km (10 miles) north to **Graiguenamanagh**. The main attraction of this market town is **Duiske Abbey**, the largest Cistercian church in Ireland. Founded in 1207, it has been extensively restored and now acts as the parish church. The most striking features include a Romanesque door in the south transept, the great oak roof and traces of a medieval pavement below floor level. There is also a cross-legged statue of the Knight of Duiske, which is one of the finest medieval effigies in Ireland. Outside are two 9th-century granite High Crosses.

Trips along the Nore take you to **Inistioge**. Lying in a deep, wooded valley, this is an idyllic village, with neat 18th-century houses, a square planted with lime trees and a ten-arched bridge spanning the Nore. On a rock above the river stands a ruined Norman fort, a popular place for picnics. From Inistioge you can walk along the river or up to **Woodstock House Demesne**, a national park. Among the

beech woods stands an 18th-century mansion, currently undergoing restoration.

On a hill 12 km (7.5 miles) south of New Ross, a large area of woodland is enclosed within the **John F Kennedy Park and Arboretum**. Founded in 1968, near the late president's ancestral home in Dunganstown (now **The Kennedy Homestead**), the park boasts more than 4,500 types of tree and provides splendid panoramic views. There are marked paths and nature trails.

🔒 **Duiske Abbey**
Graiguenamanagh, Co Kilkenny.
📞 *0503 24238.* ⏰ *daily.* ♿

🌿 **John F Kennedy Park and Arboretum**
New Ross, Co Wexford. 📞 *051 388171.* ⏰ *daily.* ⛔ *Good Fri & 25 Dec.* 📷 ♿ 🅿 *May–Dec.*

## Enniscorthy ㉔

**Road map** D5. Co Wexford.
👥 *5,000.* 🚌 🚆 ℹ️ *The Castle (054 34699).*

THE STREETS of Enniscorthy, on the banks of the River Slaney, are full of character and redolent of the town's turbulent

past. In 1798, Enniscorthy witnessed the last stand of the Wexford pikemen, when a fierce battle was fought against a British force of 20,000 on nearby **Vinegar Hill**. The events of that year are told both at the County Museum inside the imposing **Enniscorthy Castle**, and at the multimedia **National 1798 Visitor Centre**. Enniscorthy's other main sight is the Neo-Gothic **St Aidan's Cathedral**, designed in the 1840s by AWN Pugin (1812–52), better known for his work on London's Houses of Parliament.

Granaries mills and potteries overlook the Slaney, including Carley's Bridge, founded in 1654 and still operational. Enniscorthy's historic pubs are another attraction. They include the Antique Tavern *(see p318)*, which is hung with pikes used during the Battle of Vinegar Hill in 1798.

⚓ **Enniscorthy Castle**
Castle Hill. 📞 *054 35926.*
⏰ *daily (Oct–Dec: pm only).*
📷 ♿ *limited.*
🏛 **National 1798 Visitor Centre**
Millpark Road. 📞 *054 37596.*
⏰ *daily.* 📷 🅿🅿

The inland port of New Ross seen from the west bank of the River Barrow

**View across the harbour to Wexford town**

# Irish National Heritage Park ㉕

**Road map** D5. Ferrycarrig, Co Wexford.
🚌 *from Wexford in summer.*
📞 *053 20733.* ⏰ *9:30am–6:30pm
daily (last adm 5pm).* ⚫ *week at
Christmas.* 🅿️ 🎥 🛍 🍴 ♿

**B**UILT ON former
marshland near
Ferrycarrig, just north
of Wexford, the Irish
National Heritage
Park is a bold open-
air museum. Trails
lead visitors through
woods to replicas of
homesteads, places
of worship and burial
sites. These provide a
fascinating
introduction to the
country's ancient
history *(see pp30–31)*.
Other highlights
include the Viking
boatyard, complete with
raiding ship, and a 7th-
century horizontal watermill.

# Wexford ㉖

**Road map** D5. Co Wexford.
👥 *17,000.* 🚉 🚌 ℹ️ *Crescent Quay
(053 23111).*

**W**EXFORD'S name derives
from *Waesfjord*, a Norse
word meaning "estuary of the
mud flats". It thrived as a port
for centuries but the silting of
the harbour in the Victorian era
put an end to most sea traffic.
Wexford's quays, from where
ships once sailed to Bristol,
Tenby and Liverpool, are now
used mainly by a fleet of
humble mussel dredgers.
Wexford is a vibrant place,
packed with fine pubs and

**Sign of a popular
Wexford pub**

boasting a varied arts scene.
The town's singular style is
often linked to its linguistic
heritage. The *yola* dialect,
which was spoken by early
settlers, survives in the local
pronunciation of certain words.
Wexford retains few traces
of its past, but the Viking fish-
bone street pattern still exists,
with narrow alleys fanning off
the meandering Main
Street. Keyser's Lane,
linking South Main
Street with the lively
Commodore pub on
Paul Quay, is a tiny
tunnel-like Viking
alley which once led
to the Norse water-
front. The Normans
were responsible for
Wexford's town walls,
remnants of which
include one of the
original gateways.
Behind it lies
**Selskar Abbey**, the
ruin of a 12th-century
Augustinian monastery. King
Henry II is said to have done
penance here for the murder
of Thomas à Becket in 1170.
Wexford also has several
handsome buildings dating
from a later period, including
the 18th-century market house,
known as the **Cornmarket**,
on Main Street. The nearby
square, the **Bull Ring**, is
notable only for its history: it
was used for bull-baiting in
Norman times and was the
scene of a cruel massacre by
Cromwell's men in 1649.
Wexford Opera Festival,
held in October, is the leading
operatic event in the country.
Aficionados praise it for its
intimate atmosphere – both
during performances and
afterwards, when artists and
audience mingle together in

the pubs: the Centenary
Stores off Main Street is a
favourite, though the Wren's
Nest, on Custom House Quay,
is better for traditional music.

**ENVIRONS:** Skirting the shore
just east of the town is the
**Wexford Wildfowl Reserve**.
It covers 100 ha (250 acres) of
reclaimed land and is noted in
particular for its geese: over a
third of the world's entire
population of Greenland white-
fronted geese winter here
between October and April.
The mudflats also attract
large numbers of swans and
waders, and provide a rich
hunting ground for birds of
prey. The birds can be viewed
from a number of hides and
an observation tower.
Another way to enjoy the
wildlife in the region is to
take a boat trip up the Slaney
River to Raven Point.

## 🦆 Wexford Wildfowl Reserve

Wexford. 📞 *053 23129.* ⏰ *daily.*
🎥 *at weekends.*

### Boat Trips

Wexford Harbour. 📞 *053 40564 or
086 8608328.* 🎥

# Johnstown Castle ㉗

**Road map** D5. Co Wexford. 📞 *053
42888.* 🅿️ 🚌 *to Wexford.* **Gardens**
⏰ *daily.* ⚫ *24 & 25 Dec.* 🎥

**Façade of Johnstown Castle**

**J**OHNSTOWN CASTLE, a splendid
Gothic Revival mansion, lies
amid ornamental gardens
and mature woodland 6 km
(4 miles) southwest of Wexford.
In state hands since 1945, the
castle is currently closed for

**Vast crescent of sand and shingle beach at Rosslare**

refurbishment. However, it is possible to visit the **Irish Agriculture Museum**, housed in the castle's farm buildings. Reconstructions illustrate traditional trades and there is an exhibition on the Famine.

The real glory of Johnstown Castle are the grounds, from the sunken Italian garden to the ornamental lakes. Azaleas and camellias flourish alongside an array of trees including Japanese cedars and redwoods.

Hidden among the dense woods west of the house lurk the ruins of **Rathlannon Castle**, a medieval tower house.

### 🏛 Irish Agriculture Museum
Johnstown Castle. ☎ 053 42888 ◌ Apr, May & Sep–Nov: 9am–5pm Mon–Fri, 2–5pm Sat, Sun & bank hols; Jun–Aug: 9am–5pm Mon–Fri, 11am–5pm Sat, Sun & bank hols. 🎫 🚻 🛍 🔶 limited.

## Saltee Islands ㉘

**Road map** D5. Co Wexford. 🚌 from Wexford to Kilmore Quay: Wed & Sat. 🚢 from Kilmore Quay: Apr–Sep (weather permitting). ☎ 053 29684.

THESE ISLANDS off the south coast of Wexford are a haven for sea birds. Great and Little Saltee together form Ireland's largest bird sanctuary, nurturing an impressive array of birds, from gannets and gulls to puffins and Manx shearwaters. Great Saltee particularly is famous for its colonies of cormorants. It also

has more than 1,000 pairs of guillemots and is a popular stopping-off place for spring and autumn migrations. A bird-monitoring and research programme is in progress, and a close watch is also kept on the colony of grey seals.

The two uninhabited islands are privately owned, but visitors are welcome. Boat trips are run in fine weather from **Kilmore Quay**. These leave in late morning and return mid-afternoon.

Kilmore Quay is a fishing village built on Precambrian gneiss rock – the oldest rock in Ireland. Pretty thatched cottages nestle above a fine sandy beach and the harbour, where a moored lightship houses a **Maritime Museum**. The boat's original fittings are just as interesting as the exhibits.

### 🏛 Guillemot Maritime Museum
Kilmore Quay. ☎ 053 21572. ◌ Apr–Sep: daily. 🎫

## Rosslare ㉙

**Road map** D5. Co Wexford. 🚶 1,200. 🚌 🚆 🛈 Kilrane, Rosslare Harbour (053 33232).

ROSSLARE REPLACED Wexford as the area's main port after the decline of the original Viking city harbour. The port is so active today that people tend to associate the name Rosslare more with the ferry terminal for France and Wales than with the town lying 8 km (5 miles) further north.

Rosslare town is one of the sunniest spots in Ireland and draws many holidaymakers. It boasts a fine beach stretching for 9.5 km (6 miles), lively pubs and an excellent golf course fringed by sand dunes. There are good walks north to Rosslare Point.

**ENVIRONS:** At Tagoat, 6 km (4 miles) south of Rosslare, **Yola Farmstead** displays traditional crafts such as thatching, glass-blowing and bread-and-butter-making.

### 🏛 Yola Farmstead
Tagoat. ☎ 053 32611. ◌ Mar, Apr & Nov: Mon–Fri; May–Oct: daily. 🎫 🛍 🔶 🚻

**Colony of gannets nesting on the cliffs of Great Saltee Island**

# CORK AND KERRY

### CORK · KERRY

**M**AGNIFICENT SCENERY *has attracted visitors to this region since Victorian times. Rocky headlands jut out into the Atlantic and colourful fishing villages nestle in the shelter of the bays. County Kerry offers dramatic landscapes and a wealth of pre-historic and early Christian sites, whereas County Cork's gentle charm has enticed many a casual visitor into becoming a permanent resident.*

Killarney and its romantic lakes are a powerful magnet for tourists, and so are Cork's attractive coastal towns and villages. Yet the region remains remarkably unspoilt, with a friendly atmosphere and authentic culture still alive in Irish-speaking pockets. There is also a long tradition of arts and crafts in the area.

This corner of Ireland used to be the main point of contact with the Continent. In the 17th century, in response to the threat of invasions from France and Spain, the English built a line of forts along the Cork coast, including the massive Charles Fort at Kinsale.

In the 19th century, the city of Cork was an important departure point for people fleeing from the Famine *(see p211)*, with Cobh the main port for emigrants to the New World. Cork's importance as a port has diminished, but it is still the Republic's second city with a lively cultural scene.

Poverty and temperament helped foster a powerful Republican spirit in the southwest. The region saw much guerrilla action in the War of Independence and the subsequent Civil War. In 1920, the centre of Cork city was burned in an uncontrolled act of reprisal by the notorious Black and Tans *(see pp42–3)*.

Kerry is known as "the Kingdom" on account of its tradition of independence and disregard for Dublin rule. The Irish recognize a distinctive Kerry character, with a boisterous sense of living life to the full. They also make Kerrymen the butt of countless jokes.

As well as the friendliest people in Ireland, the region has some of the finest scenery. Cork has lush valleys and a beautiful coast while Kerry is wilder and more mountainous. The islands off the Kerry coast appear bleak and inhospitable, but many were once inhabited. Remote, rocky Skellig Michael, for example, was the site of a 6th-century Christian monastery.

Puffins on the island of Skellig Michael off the coast of Kerry

◁ Beach at Barley Cove near Mizen Head, County Cork

# Exploring Cork and Kerry

KILLARNEY IS A POPULAR BASE with tourists for exploring Cork and Kerry, especially for touring the Ring of Kerry and the archaeological remains of the Dingle Peninsula. Despite the changeable weather, the region attracts many visitors who come to see its dramatic scenery and lush vegetation. As you pass through quiet fishing villages and genteel towns, such as Kenmare, you will always encounter a friendly welcome from the locals. For the adventurous there are plenty of opportunities to go riding, hiking or cycling. Cork city offers a more cosmopolitan atmosphere, with its art galleries and craft shops.

TARBERT ①
CARRIGAFOYLE CASTLE
Limerick
R551
R553
LISTOWEL
N69
R551
R556
② ARDFERT CATHEDRAL
TRALEE ③
N86
N21
N22
N23
DINGLE PENINSULA ⑥
GALLARUS ORATORY ⑤
④
SLIEVE MISH MOUNTAINS
R561
N70
N72
DINGLE
BLASKET ISLANDS
KILLORGLIN
⑦ KILLARNEY
MACGILLICUDDY'S REEKS
⑧ LAKES OF KILLARNEY
DINGLE BAY
CAHERCIVEEN
VALENTIA ISLAND ⑨
R568
N71
R562
N70
⑫ KENMARE
WATERVILLE
⑪
SNEEM
RING OF KERRY
N70
CAHA MOUNTAINS
⑩ THE SKELLIGS
GLENGARIFF
R571
GARINISH ISLAND ⑭
R572
⑮
CASTLETOWNBERE ⑯
BEARA PENINSULA ⑬
BANTRY BAY
R591
BANTRY HOUSE
BALLYDEHOB
N71
SCHULL    R592
MIZEN HEAD
⑰
BALTIMORE ⑱

**KEY**

| | |
|---|---|
| | Motorway |
| | Major road |
| | Minor road |
| | Scenic route |
| | River |
| ☀ | Viewpoint |

0 kilometres 10
0 miles        10

**Newman's Mall in the quaint village of Kinsale**

Cattle grazing near Ardfert Cathedral

## SIGHTS AT A GLANCE

Ardfert Cathedral **2**
Baltimore **18**
Bantry Bay **16**
*Bantry House pp160–61* **15**
Beara Peninsula **13**
Blarney Castle **23**
Carrigafoyle Castle **1**
Clonakilty **20**
Cobh **27**
*Cork pp166–9* **25**
Dingle **4**
Drombeg Stone Circle **19**
Gallarus Oratory **5**

Garinish Island **14**
Old Midleton Distillery **28**
Kenmare **12**
Killarney **7**
*Kinsale pp164–5* **24**
*Lakes of Killarney pp154–5* **8**
Mizen Head **17**
River Blackwater **26**
River Lee **22**
The Skelligs **10**
Timoleague Abbey **21**
Tralee **3**
Valentia Island **9**
Youghal **29**

### Tours

Dingle Peninsula **6**
Ring of Kerry **11**

Limerick

R579

KANTURK

MITCHELSTOWN

Cahir

N20

N73

N8

N72

RIVER BLACKWATER **26**

MALLOW

Blackwater

N72

FERMOY

N72

Waterford →

MILLSTREET

R582

N20

BLARNEY CASTLE **23**

N8

YOUGHAL **29**

N22

R618

RIVER LEE **22**

OLD MIDLETON DISTILLERY **28**

R584

N22

N71

CORK **25**

COBH **27**

Lee

BANDON

R600

BANDON

KINSALE **24**

Bandon

CLONAKILTY **20**

TIMOLEAGUE ABBEY **21**

N71

DROMBERG STONE CIRCLE **19**

## GETTING AROUND

To explore the region a car is essential. The N22 connects Cork, Killarney and Tralee while the N71 follows the coastline via Clonakilty, Bantry and on to Killarney. In the more remote parts the road signs may only be written in Irish. Killarney is the base for organized coach tours of the area. The train service from Cork to Dublin is efficient, and trains also connect Killarney with Dublin and Cork, but you may have to change trains en route. Buses run throughout the region, but services to the smaller sights may be infrequent.

### SEE ALSO

- *Where to Stay* pp291–3

- *Restaurants, Cafés and Pubs* pp310–12 & p319

Kissing the Blarney Stone at
Blarney Castle near Cork

**Ardfert Cathedral and the ruins of Teampall na Hoe and Teampall na Griffin**

# Carrigafoyle Castle ❶

**Road map** B5. Co Kerry.
🚌 *to Listowel.*

**Ruined keep of Carrigafoyle Castle**

H IGH ABOVE the Shannon estuary, just west of Ballylongford, this 15th-century castle belonged to the O'Connor clan, who ruled much of northern Kerry. The English besieged or sacked it repeatedly but the body blow was delivered in 1649 by Cromwellian forces *(see p37)*. The ruins include a keep and walled bawn, with romantic views of the estuary from the top of the tower.

# Ardfert Cathedral ❷

**Road map** A5. Co Kerry. 🚌 *to Ardfert.*
📞 *066 7134711.* ⭕ *Easter–Sep:
daily; rest of year on request.* 🖼 ♿

T HIS COMPLEX of churches is linked to the cult of St Brendan the Navigator *(see p205)*, who was born nearby

in 484 and founded a monastery here. The ruined cathedral dates back to the 12th century and retains a delicate Romanesque doorway and blind arcading. The south transept is now restored and houses an exhibition of the history of the site. In the graveyard stand the remains of a Romanesque nave-and-chancel church, Teampall na Hoe, and a late Gothic chapel, Teampall na Griffin. The latter is named after the curious griffins carved beside an interior window.

A short walk away are the ruins of a Franciscan friary. It was founded by Thomas Fitzmaurice in 1253, but the cloisters and south chapel date from the 15th century.

**ENVIRONS:** Just northwest of Ardfert is **Banna Strand**. Irish patriot Roger Casement landed here in 1916 on a German U-boat, bringing in rifles for the Easter Rising *(see pp42–3)*. He was arrested as soon as he landed and a memorial stands

on the site of his capture. This beach was also used for the filming of David Lean's *Ryan's Daughter* (1970).

# Tralee ❸

**Road map** B5. Co Kerry. 🚶 *22,000.*
🚉 🚌 ℹ *Ashe Memorial Hall, Denny St (066 7121288).* 🕑 *Thu.*

H OST TO the renowned Rose of Tralee International Festival *(see p47)*, Tralee has made great strides in promoting its cultural and leisure facilities. The town's main attraction is **Kerry County Museum** with its theme park, "Kerry the Kingdom". It offers three exhibitions: an audiovisual show on Kerry scenery; a display of archaeological finds and interactive models; and a "time travel experience" through Anglo-Norman Tralee, complete with medieval smells.

Also based in Tralee is the **Siamsa Tíre** National Folk Theatre of Ireland, a great

**Steam train on the narrow gauge railway between Tralee and Blennerville, with Blennerville Windmill in the background**

ambassador for Irish culture. Traditional song and dance performances take place here throughout the summer.

Just outside Tralee is the authentic **Blennerville Windmill**. Built in 1800, it is Ireland's largest working mill and one of Tralee's most popular attractions. The **Steam Railway** connects Blennerville with Tralee along a narrow gauge track. The train also runs from Ballyard Station to the windmill.

🏛 **Kerry County Museum**
Ashe Memorial Hall, Denny St.
📞 06671 27777. ⏱ mid-Mar–Dec: daily. ● 25 & 26 Dec. 🈴 ♿
🎭 **Siamsa Tire**
Town Park. 📞 06671 23055. ⏱ for performances only May–Oct. 🈴 ♿
🏛 **Blennerville Windmill**
📞 06671 21064.
⏱ Apr–Oct: daily. 🈴 🍴 🅿
🚂 **Steam Railway**
Ballyard Station. 📞 06671 21064.
⏱ May–Sep: daily. 🈴 ♿

# Dingle ④

**Road map** A5. Co Kerry. 🚶 1,500.
🚌 Mar–Oct. ℹ Main St (06691 51188). 🚌 Sat.

THIS ONCE REMOTE Irish-speaking town is today a thriving fishing port and an increasingly popular tourist

centre. Brightly painted craft shops and cafés abound, often with slightly hippy overtones.

Dingle Bay is attractive with a somewhat ramshackle harbour lined with fishing trawlers. Along the quayside are lively bars offering music and seafood. The harbour is home to Dingle's biggest star: Fungie, the dolphin, who has been a permanent resident since 1983 and can be visited by boat or on swimming trips.

Although Dingle has few architectural attractions, it makes an engaging base for exploring the archaeological remains on the Dingle Peninsula *(see pp150–51)*.

**Gallarus Oratory, a dry-stone early Christian church**

# Gallarus Oratory ⑤

**Road map** A5. Co Kerry.
🚌 to Dingle.

SHAPED LIKE an upturned boat, this miniature church overlooks Smerwick harbour. Gallarus was built some time between the 6th and 9th centuries and is the best preserved early Christian church in Ireland. It represents the apogee of dry-stone corbelling, using techniques first developed by Neolithic tomb-makers. The stones were laid at a slight angle, lower on the outside than the inside, allowing water to run off.

**Fishing trawlers moored alongside the quay at Dingle**

# A Tour of the Dingle Peninsula ❻

**GUINNESS**
**Mar is gnách**

Pub sign,
Ballyferriter

T HE DINGLE PENINSULA offers some of
Ireland's most beautiful scenery. To
the north rises the towering Brandon
Mountain, while the west coast has
some spectacular seascapes. A drive
around the area, which takes at least
half a day, reveals fascinating antiquities
ranging from Iron Age stone forts to
inscribed stones, early Christian oratories
and beehive huts. These are sometimes
found on private land, so you may be
asked for a small fee by the farmer to
see them. Some parts of the peninsula – especially
the more remote areas – are still Gaelic speaking,
so many road signs are written only in Irish.

View from Clogher Head

**Riasc (An Riasc)** ⑦
This excavated monastic
settlement dates from the 7th
century. The enclosure contains
the remains of an oratory,
several crosses and an inscribed
pillar stone *(see p235).*

**Ballyferriter**
**(Baile an Fheirtéaraigh)** ⑥
The attractions of this friendly
village include the pastel-coloured
cottages, Louis Mulcahy's pottery
and a museum featuring the
cultural heritage of the area.

R559

**Blasket Centre**
**(Ionad an Bhlascaoid)** ⑤
Overlooking Blasket Sound, the
centre explains the literature,
language and way of life of the
inhabitants of the Blasket
Islands. The islanders moved to
the mainland in 1953.

*Dunquin*
*(Dún Chaoin)*

Ve
(Ceann

R559

*Mount*
*Eagle*

Ven

BLASKET ISLANDS

Blasket Sound

Clogher Head

**Dunmore Head**
**(Ceann an Dúin Mhoir)** ④
Mainland Ireland's most westerly point
offers dramatic views of the Blaskets.

**Slea Head**
**(Ceann Sléibe)** ③
As you round the Slea
Head promontory, the
Blasket Islands come
into full view. The
sculpture of the
Crucifixion beside the
road is known locally
as the Cross *(An Cros).*

DINGLE BA

**KEY**

▬ Tour route

── Other roads

🔆 Viewpoint

0 kilometres 2

0 miles 1

**Jaunting cars waiting to take visitors to sights around Killarney**

**Kilmalkedar (Cill Maolchéadair)** ⑨
Once a pagan centre of worship, Kilmalkedar is home to a ruined Irish Romanesque church with stone carvings. The graveyard still contains primitive pagan stones, a cross and a sundial.

**Gallarus Oratory (Séipéilín Ghallrois)** ⑧
This tiny, dry-stone church *(see p149)* is a relic of early Irish Christianity.

**Dingle (An Daingean)** ①
Dingle, famous for local resident Fungie the dolphin, is a good place to eat, drink or stay the night *(see p149)*.

**Dunbeg Fort (An Dún Beag)** ②
Dating from the Iron Age, this is one of the best preserved promontory forts in Ireland. Just beyond are the Fahan bee-hive huts, early Christian huts thought to have been built for pilgrims visiting the area.

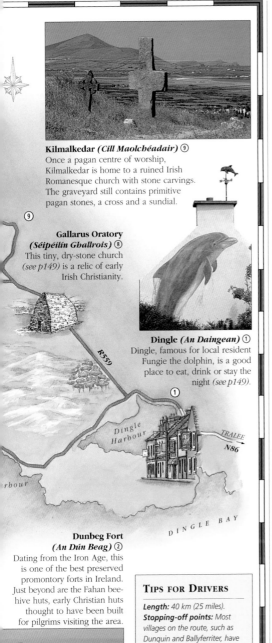

## Killarney ⑦

**Road map** B5. Co Kerry. 🚶 *9,500.*
🚌 🚆 🛈 *Beech Road (064 31633).*

KILLARNEY is commonly derided as "a tourist town" but this has not dented the town's open, cheerful atmosphere. The infectious Kerry humour is personified by the wise-cracking jarveys whose families have run jaunting cars (pony and trap rides) here for generations. The town does get crowded in summer but has much to offer, with shops open until 10pm in summer, several excellent restaurants, and a sprinkling of prestigious hotels around the lake and the heights. From the town visitors can explore the sights around the Lakes of Killarney *(see pp154–5)* and the surrounding heather-covered hills.

**ENVIRONS:** Overlooking the lakes and a short drive from Killarney is **Muckross House**. This imposing Victorian mansion was built in 1843 in Elizabethan style. Inside, the elegant rooms are decorated with period furnishings. There is also a museum of Kerry Life, with displays on the history of southwest Ireland, and a craft centre and workshops. The landscaped gardens are especially beautiful in spring when the rhododendrons and azaleas are in bloom. A short walk away is Muckross Farm, which still uses traditional farming techniques.

**🏛 Muckross House**
4 km (2.5 miles) S of Killarney.
📞 *064 31440.* 🕐 *July– Aug: 9am– 7pm daily; Sep–Jun: 9am–6pm daily.*
🌑 *7 days at Christmas.* 🅿 🍴 ⑀ 🔕

### TIPS FOR DRIVERS

**Length:** *40 km (25 miles).*
**Stopping-off points:** *Most villages on the route, such as Dunquin and Ballyferriter, have friendly bars offering pub meals. There are also many opportunities to stop for a picnic. On the winding coast road around Slea Head stop only at the safe and clearly marked coastal viewing points. (See also pp355–7.)*

**Stunning mountain scenery near Moll's Gap on the Ring of Kerry** ▷

# Lakes of Killarney ❽

**Fruit of the strawberry tree**

Rᴇɴᴏᴡɴᴇᴅ ꜰᴏʀ ɪᴛs splendid scenery, the area is one of Ireland's most popular tourist attractions. The three lakes are contained within Killarney National Park. Although the landscape is dotted with ruined castles and abbeys, the lakes are the focus of attention: the moody watery scenery is subject to subtle shifts of light and colour. The area has entranced many artists and writers including Thackeray, who praised "a precipice covered with a thousand trees ... and other mountains rising as far as we could see". In autumn, the bright red fruits of the strawberry tree colour the shores of the lakes.

**Meeting of the Waters**
*This beauty spot, best seen from Dinis Island, is where the waters from the Upper Lake meet Muckross Lake and Lough Leane. At the Old Weir Bridge, boats shoot the rapids.*

**Long Range River**

**Torc Waterfall**
*The Owengarriff River cascades through the wooded Friars' Glen into Muckross Lake. A pretty path winds up to the top of this 18-m (60-ft) high waterfall, revealing views of Torc Mountain.*

**Muckross Abbey** was founded by the Franciscans in 1448, but was burnt down by Cromwellian forces in 1653.

**Killarney** *(see p151)* is the main town from which tourists visit the sights around the lakes.

**N22 to Tralee** *(see pp148–9)*

**Muckross Lake**

**Dinis Island**

**Lough Leane**

**Innisfallen Island**

**Ross Castle**, built around 1420, was the last stronghold under Irish control to be taken by Cromwellian forces in 1653.

**★ Muckross House**
*The 19th-century manor* (see p151) *enjoys a lovely location overlooking the lakes. Visit the wildlife centre for an introduction to the flora and fauna of the National Park.*

**Upper Lake**
*This narrow lake is the smallest of the three lakes. It flows into the Long Range River to the Meeting of the Waters.*

**VISITORS' CHECKLIST**

**Road map** B5. Killarney, Co Kerry.
✈ *Kerry (066 64644).* 🚌 🚂
**National Park** ⏰ *9am–6pm
(6:30pm Jun–Aug) daily (for access
by car).* ℹ️ *Killarney (064 31633).*
**Muckross House** 📞 *064 31440.*
⏰ *9am–6pm (5:30pm Nov–Mar)
daily.* ⏺ *25 Dec–1 Jan.* 🏛 📷 🏠
🏰 **Ross Castle** 📞 *064 35851.*
⏰ *Mar–Apr: 11am–6pm Tue–
Sun; May–Sep: 9am–6pm daily;
Oct: 9am–5pm daily.* 🏛 📷
*obligatory.* 🚢 *from Ross Castle:
**Destination Killarney** (064
32638): daily (weather permit-
ting); The Lily of Killarney (064
31068): Mar–Oct.* **Kate Kearney's
Cottage** 📞 *064 44146.* ⏰
*Easter–Sep: 9am–midnight daily;
Oct–Easter: 9:30am–6pm.* 🏠 🚻

**Ladies' View** gets its name from the delight it gave Queen Victoria's ladies-in-waiting when they visited the spot in 1861.

**N71 to Moll's Gap and Kenmare** *(see pp156–8)*

**Upper Lake**

**Purple Mountain, 832 m (2,730 ft)**

**Tomies Mountain, 735 m (2,411 ft)**

**★ Gap of Dunloe**
*Glaciers carved this dramatic mountain pass which is popular with walkers, cyclists and horse riders. The route through the gap offers fabulous views of the boulder-strewn gorge and three small lakes.*

**Kate Kearney's Cottage** was home to a local beauty who ran an illegal drinking house for passing travellers in the mid-19th century.

**R562 to Killorglin** *(see pp156–7)*

0 kilometres            2

0 miles            1

**STAR SIGHTS**

★ **Muckross House**

★ **Gap of Dunloe**

**Lough Leane**
*The largest lake is dotted with un-inhabited islands and fringed with wooded slopes. Boat trips run between Ross Castle and Innisfallen.*

## Valentia Island ⑨

**Road map** A5. Co Kerry. 🚌 *to Caherciveen.* 🛈 *Caherciveen (06694 72589).*

ALTHOUGH it feels like the mainland, Valentia is an island, albeit linked by a causeway to Portmagee. It is 11 km (7 miles) long and noted for its water sports, seascapes and views from Geokaun Mountain. Valentia is also popular for its proximity to the Skellig Islands which lie around 15 km (10 miles) southwest of the Iveragh Peninsula.

The **Skellig Experience Centre**, near the causeway linking Valentia to the mainland, houses an audiovisual display about the construction and history of the monastery on Skellig Michael, the largest of the Skellig Islands. Other subjects covered include sea birds and the marine life around the islands, a reminder that the Skellig cliffs lie underwater for a depth of 50 m (165 ft), providing a habitat for giant basking sharks, dolphins and turtles. The centre also operates cruises around the islands.

**Stairway leading to Skellig Michael monastery**

The main village on Valentia is **Knightstown**, which offers accommodation and lively pubs with music and dancing.

The first transatlantic cable was laid from the southwest point of the island to Newfoundland, Canada, in 1866.

🏛 **Skellig Experience Centre**
Valentia Island. 📞 *06694 76306.* 🕐 *late-Mar–Sep: daily.* 🧡 ♿

## The Skelligs ⑩

**Road map** A6. Co Kerry. 🚢 *mid-Mar–Oct: from Valentia Island.* 📞 *06694 77156 (ring a few days ahead).*

SKELLIG MICHAEL, also known as Great Skellig, is an inhospitable pinnacle of rock rising out of the Atlantic and covering an area of 17 ha (44 acres). Perched on a ledge almost 218 m (714 ft) above sea level and reached by an amazing 1,000-year-old

# A Tour of the Ring of Kerry ⑪

THIS LONG-ESTABLISHED ROUTE around the Iveragh Peninsula, which can be taken in either direction, is always referred to as the Ring of Kerry. Allow a day to see its captivating mountain and coastal scenery, dotted with slate-roofed fishing villages. Set out early to avoid the mass of coach tours which converge on the towns for lunch and tea. There are interesting detours across the spine of the peninsula.

**Glenbeigh ③**
Stop here to visit the Kerry Bog Village, a cluster of reconstructed cottages dating from the 1800s.

**Caherciveen ④**
The main town on the peninsula is home to a local heritage centre.

**Beach at Ballinskelligs**

*VALENTIA ISLAND*
Skellig Experience Centre

*Little Skellig*
*Skellig Michael*

**KEY**

▬▬ Tour route
═══ Other roads
🚢 Boats to the Skelligs
🌿 Viewpoint

**Derrynane House ⑤**
Dating from the 17th century, the former home of Daniel O'Connell *(see p40)* now houses a museum featuring his memorabilia.

*Ballinskelligs*
*Ballinskelligs Bay*
*Waterville*
*Coomakista Pass*

**Staigue Fort ⑥**
Set on a hill up a narrow track, the Iron Age, dry-stone fort *(caher)* the best preserved in Ireland

stairway is an isolated early Christian monastery. Monks settled for solitude on Skellig Michael during the 6th century, building a cluster of six corbelled beehive cells and two boat-shaped oratories. These dry-stone structures are still standing, despite being raked by storms over the centuries. The monks were totally self-sufficient, trading eggs, feathers and seal meat with passing boats in return for cereals, tools and animal skins. The skins were needed to produce the vellum on which the monks copied their religious manuscripts. They remained on this bleak island until the 12th century, when they retreated to the Augustinian priory at Ballinskelligs on the mainland.

Today the only residents on Skellig Michael are the thousands of sea birds which nest

**Gannets flying around the precipitous cliffs of Little Skellig**

and breed on the high cliffs, including storm petrels, puffins and Manx shearwaters. The huge breeding colonies are protected from predators by the sea and rocky shores.

Slightly closer to the mainland is Little Skellig. Covering an area of 7 ha (17 acres), the island has steep cliffs. Home to a variety of sea birds, it has one of the largest colonies of gannets (about 22,000 breeding pairs) in the British Isles.

A cruiser from Valentia Island circles the Skelligs but does not dock. Except for a pier on Skellig Michael, there are no proper landing stages on the islands. This is to discourage visitors from disturbing the birdlife, fragile plant cover and archaeological remains.

Atlantic gales permitting, local fishermen may run unofficial trips around the islands from Portmagee or Ballinskelligs, during the summer.

**Killorglin ② ** This pretty village, sitting on the slopes above a river, is famous for its Puck Fair (see p47).

**Killarney ①**
Visitors touring the Ring of Kerry usually start and finish here. The route passes lovely views of the Lakes of Killarney (see pp154–5).

**Moll's Gap ⑧**
Cutting through bleak bogland and high mountainous terrain, Moll's Gap offers some stunning views.

**Sneem ⑦**
Brightly painted cottages line the streets of this charming town which also has a quaint village green.

0 kilometres          10

0 miles          5

**TIPS FOR DRIVERS**

*Length:* 180 km (112 miles).
*Stopping off points:* Many towns such as Killorglin or Caherciveen offer pub snacks. Finish the day in one of the excellent gourmet restaurants in Kenmare (see also pp355–7).

**Lace making at Kenmare**

# Kenmare **⑫**

**Road map** B5. Co Kerry. 🏃 *1,400.*
🚌 🛈 *May–Sep: Main St (064
41233).* 🛒 *Wed.*

T HIS TOWN, on the mouth of
the River Sheen, was
founded in 1670 by William
Petty, Cromwell's surveyor
general. However, Kenmare's
appearance owes more to his
descendant, the first Marquess
of Lansdowne who, in 1775,
made it a model landlord's
town of neat stone façades
with decorative plasterwork.

Today Kenmare is renowned
for its traditional lace. During
the famine years, nuns from
the local convent, St Clare's,
introduced lace making to
create work for the women
and girls. Other attractions
include the fine hotels *(see
p292)* and gourmet restaurants
*(p311).* The town is also an

excellent base for exploring
the Beara Peninsula and the
Ring of Kerry *(see pp156–7).*
Set in a riverside glade off
Market Street is the **Druid's
Circle**, a prehistoric ring of
15 stones associated with
human sacrifice.

# Beara Peninsula **⑬**

**Road map** A6. Co Cork & Co Kerry.
🚌 *to Glengarriff (daily) &
Castletownbere (Mon, Wed, Fri & Sun).*
🛈 *Castletownbere (027 70344).*

D OTTED WITH sparsely
populated fishing villages
surrounded by bleak moor-
land, this peninsula is remote.
It used to be a refuge for
smugglers, with the Irish
getting the better deal in their
exchange of pilchards for
contraband French brandy.

The peninsula offers some
spectacular scenery and
wonderful walking country.
From the **Healy Pass**, which
cuts a jagged path across the
spine of the Caha Mountains,
there are some fine views of
Bantry Bay and the rugged
landscape of West Cork. To
the west of the pass is
**Hungry Hill**, the highest
mountain in the Caha range
and popular with hill walkers.

Encircled by the Caha and
Slieve Miskish Mountains is
**Castletownbere**, the main
town on the peninsula. This
sheltered port was once a
haven for smugglers, but is
now awash with foreign
fishing trawlers. McCarthey's

Bar on Town Square features
an authentic matchmaking
booth, where Cork families
used to agree marriage terms
until a generation ago.

West of Castletownbere
stands the shell of **Puxley
Mansion**, home of the Puxley
family who owned the mines
at nearby **Allihies**. Centre of
the copper-mining district until
the 1930s, it is now a desolate
place, with tall Cornish-style
chimneys and piles of ochre-
coloured spoil; beware of
unguarded mine shafts.

From the tip of the peninsula
a cable car travels across to
**Dursey Island**, with its
ruined castle and colonies of
sea birds. Licensed to carry
three passengers and one cow,
the cable car swings across
the strait, offering views of
Bull, Cow and Calf islands.

From the headland the R757
road back to Kenmare passes
through the pretty villages of
**Eyeries**, noted for its brightly
painted cottages and crafts,
and **Ardgroom**, a centre for
mussel farming and a base for
exploring the scenic glacial
valley around **Glenbeg Lough**.

# Garinish Island **⑭**

**Road map** B6. Co Cork. 🚤 *from
Glengarriff.* **Gardens** 🄲 *027 63040.*
⭘ *Mar–Oct: daily.* 📷 🚻 ♿ *limited.*

A LSO KNOWN as Ilnacullin, this
small island was turned
into an exotic garden in 1910
by Harold Peto for Annan
Bryce, a Belfast businessman.

**View of Caha Mountains from the Healy Pass, Beara Peninsula**

Italianate garden with lily pool and folly on Garinish Island

Framed by views of Bantry Bay, the gardens are landscaped with Neo-Classical follies and planted with rich subtropical flora. The microclimate and peaty soil provide the damp, warm conditions needed for these ornamental plants to flourish.

Exotic shrubberies abound especially during the summer months. Throughout May and June, visitors can admire the beautiful camellia beds, azaleas and rhododendrons. There is also a New Zealand fernery and a Japanese rockery, as well as a rare collection of Bonsai trees. A Martello tower crowns the island and among the follies are a clock tower and a Grecian temple.

The centrepiece is a colonnaded Italianate garden, with a Classical folly and ornamental lily pool. Much of its charm resides in the contrast between the cultivated lushness of the garden and the glimpses of wild seascape and barren mountains beyond. An added attraction of the boat trip across to this Gulf Stream paradise is the chance to see cavorting seals in Bantry Bay.

## Bantry House **⑮**

*See pp160–61.*

## Bantry Bay **⑯**

Road map A6. Co Cork. 🚌 *to Bantry and Glengarriff.* ℹ️ *Mar–Oct: The Square, Bantry (027 50229).*

BANTRY BAY ENCOMPASSES the resorts of **Bantry** and **Glengarriff**. It is also a springboard for trips to Mizen Head and the Beara Peninsula.

Bantry nestles beneath the hills which run down to the bay. Just offshore you can see **Whiddy Island**, the original home of the White family, who moved to Bantry House in the early 18th century. Further along is **Bere Island**, a British base until World War II which still boasts Martello towers on its southern side.

Glengarriff at the head the bay, exudes an air of Victorian gentility with its neatly painted shopfronts and craft shops. On the coast is the Eccles Hotel, a haunt of Queen Victoria and where George Bernard Shaw supposedly wrote *Saint Joan*.

The wooded hinterland to the north of Glengarriff is set in a bowl of the Caha Mountains. There are some pleasant walks leading to waterfalls.

## Mizen Head **⑰**

Road map A6. Co Cork.
🚌 *to Goleen.* ℹ️ *Town Hall, North St, Skibbereen (028 21766).*

MIZEN HEAD, the most southwesterly tip of Ireland, has steep cliffs, which are often lashed by storms. Here, a lighthouse and visitors' centre, **Mizen Vision**, are reached by a bridge across a rocky chasm. From the car park, a fine headland walk takes in views of vertiginous cliffs and Atlantic breakers. The sandy beaches of nearby **Barley Cove** attract bathers and walkers alike, and to the east is **Crookhaven**, a pretty yachting harbour. From here, a walk to Brow Head offers views of the lighthouse.

Mizen Head can be reached either from Bantry via Durrus or from the market town of **Skibbereen**, on the R592, via the charming crafts centre of **Ballydehob** and the village of **Schull**. Trips to Clear Island *(see p162)* leave from Schull.

### 🏛 Mizen Vision
Mizen Head. 📞 *028 35115.* ⏰ *Apr–Oct: daily; Nov–Mar: Sat & Sun.* 🅿️

Rocky cliffs at Mizen Head

# Bantry House ⓯

**B**ANTRY HOUSE has been the home of the White family, formerly Earls of Bantry, since 1739. The original Queen Anne house was built around 1700, but the north façade overlooking the bay was a later addition. Inside there is an eclectic collection of art and furnishings brought from all over Europe by the 2nd Earl of Bantry. In the carriage house and stable block is the French Armada Centre, which explains the events surrounding Wolfe Tone's attempted invasion in 1796.

**William and Mary clock in anteroom**

**North façade**

**The anteroom** contains family mementoes, china and a collection of 18th-century prints.

**Loggia**

**To car park**

**Gobelins Room**
*The subject of this 18th-century Gobelins tapestry is* The Bath of Cupid and Psyche. *The room also contains an early 19th-century piano.*

**The Rose Garden**, laid out in the early 18th century, is, in the words of the 1st Earl of Bantry, "a parterre after the English manner".

**Tearoom and shop**

## 1ST EARL OF BANTRY (1767–1851)

Richard White, 1st Earl of Bantry, played a leading role in defending Ireland against an attempted invasion by Wolfe Tone and the United Irishmen *(see pp38–9)*. On 16 December 1796, Tone sailed from Brest in Brittany with a fleet of 43 French ships bound for Ireland. White chose strategic spots around Bantry Bay and mustered volunteers to fight. His efforts proved unnecessary as the French fleet was forced back by bad weather. Nonetheless, White was rewarded with a peerage by George III for his "spirited conduct and important services". In 1801 he was made Viscount Bantry, becoming Earl of Bantry in 1816.

★ **Dining Room**
*This room is dominated by portraits of King George III and Queen Charlotte by court painter, Allan Ramsay. The Spanish chandelier is decorated with Meissen china flowers.*

★ **Rose Room**
*The rose-coloured tapestries (c. 1770) hanging in this room are thought to have been made for Marie Antoinette on her marriage to the Dauphin of France.*

Entrance hall

Statue of Diana (1840)

South façade

To 1796 French Armada Centre

Library

**VISITORS' CHECKLIST**

**Road map** B6. Bantry, Co Cork.
027 50047. from Cork to Bantry (Mon–Sat).
mid-Mar–Oct: 9am–6pm daily.
25 Dec.
limited. Concerts (summer only).
See also *Hotels* p291.
**1796 French Armada Centre**
027 50047. Apr–Sep: 10am–6pm daily (last adm: 5:40pm). limited. Joint tickets for House and Armada Centre available.

★ **View of House and Bantry Bay**
*Bantry House enjoys a magnificent location overlooking Bantry Bay. This lovely view, from the terraces above the house, shows the harbour with Whiddy Island and the Caha Mountains beyond.*

**STAR FEATURES**

★ **View of House and Bantry Bay**

★ **Rose Room**

★ **Dining Room**

**The steps,** known as the "Staircase to the Sky", lead to a series of terraces with fabulous views over the house and across the bay.

**Italian Garden**
*Inspired by the Boboli Gardens in Florence, this garden encircles a pool decorated in Classical Grotesque style. It was designed in the early 1850s by the 2nd Earl.*

## Baltimore ⑱

**Road map** B6. Co Cork. 🚶 220.
🚌 ⛴ *to Sherkin Island (028 20218); to Clear Island (028 39119).*

**B**ALTIMORE'S most bizarre claim to fame dates back to 1631 when more than 100 citizens were carried off as slaves by Algerian pirates. Now that the threat of being kidnapped has gone, this village appeals to the yachting fraternity and island-hoppers. Like neighbouring Schull and Castletownshend, the town bustles with summer festivals.

Overlooking the harbour is a ruined 15th-century castle, once the stronghold of the O'Driscoll clan. Also worth a visit are the seafood pubs, including Bushe's Bar, an atmospheric inn hung with nautical memorabilia. Behind the village, cliff walks lead to splendid views of Carbery's Hundred Isles – mere specks on Roaringwater Bay. Baltimore Beacon is an important marker for boats in the bay.

A short ferry ride away is **Sherkin Island** with its sandy beaches in the west, a ruined 15th-century abbey, marine station and pubs. The ferry ride to **Clear Island** is more dramatic, as the boat weaves between sharp black rocks to this remote, Irish-speaking island, noted for its bird observatory in the North Harbour. There are some spectacular views of the mainland from Clear Island.

**Distinctive white beacon for boats approaching Baltimore**

**Drombeg Stone Circle, erected around the 2nd century BC**

## Drombeg Stone Circle ⑲

**Road map** B6. Co Cork. 🚌 *to Skibbereen or Clonakilty.*

**S**ITUATED ON the Glandore road 16 km (10 miles) west of Clonakilty, Drombeg is the finest of the many stone circles in County Cork. Dating back to about 150 BC, this circle of 17 standing stones is 9 m (30 ft) in diameter. At the winter solstice, the rays of the setting sun fall on the flat altar stone which faces the entrance to the circle, marked by two upright stones.

**Sign for Clonakilty black pudding**

Nearby is a small stream with a Stone Age cooking pit *(fulacht fiadh)*, similar to one at Craggaunowen *(see p182)*. A fire was made in the hearth and hot stones from the fire were dropped into the cooking pit to heat the water. Once the water boiled, the meat, usually venison, was added.

## Clonakilty ⑳

**Road map** B6. Co Cork. 🚶 3,000.
🚌 ℹ️ *Mar–Dec: Ashe Street (023 33226) .*

**F**OUNDED as an English outpost around 1588, this market town has a typically hearty West Cork atmosphere. The **West Cork Regional Museum**, housed in an old schoolhouse, remembers the town's industrial heritage. A number of quayside buildings, linked to the town's industrial past, have been restored. Particularly pleasant is the Georgian nucleus of Emmet Square.

Until the 19th century Clonakilty was a noted linen producer. Today, however, it is renowned for its rich black puddings, handpainted Irish signs and traditional music pubs. A short walk from the town centre is a model village exhibition, depicting Clonakilty as it was during the 1940s. Just east of town is the reconstructed **Lisnagun Ring Fort**, with earthworks, huts and souterrains *(see p18)*. A causeway links Clonakilty to **Inchydoney** beach.

🏛 **West Cork Regional Museum**
Western Road. ⭕ *May–Oct: daily.*
📷 ♿

## Timoleague Abbey ㉑

**Road map** B6. Co Cork.
🚌 *to Clonakilty or Courtmacsherry.*
⭕ *daily.*

**T**IMOLEAGUE ABBEY enjoys a waterside setting overlooking an inlet where the Argideen estuary opens into Courtmacsherry Bay. Founded around the late 13th century, the abbey is a ruined Franciscan friary. The buildings have been extended at various times. The earliest section is the chancel of the Gothic church. The most recent addition, the 16th-century tower, was added by the Franciscan Bishop of Ross. The friary was ransacked by the English in 1642 but much of significance remains, including the church, infirmary, fine lancet windows, refectory and a walled courtyard in the west. There are also sections of cloisters and wine cellars. In keeping with Franciscan tradition, the complex is plain to the point of austerity. Yet

**Lancet window in ruined church at Timoleague Abbey**

such restraint belied the friars' penchant for high living: the friary prospered on trade in Spanish wines, easily delivered thanks to its position on the then navigable creek.

## River Lee ㉒

**Road map** B6. Co Cork. 🚃 🚃 to Cork. 🚌 Cork (021 4273251).

CARVING A COURSE through farm- and woodland to Cork city (*see pp166–9*), the River Lee begins its journey in the lake of the enchanting **Gougane Barra Park**. The shores of the lake are linked by a causeway to **Holy Island**, where St Finbarr, the patron saint of Cork, founded a monastery. The Feast of St Finbarr, on 25 September,

signals celebrations that climax in a pilgrimage to the island on the following Sunday.

The Lee flows through several Irish-speaking market towns and villages. Some, such as **Ballingeary**, with its fine lakeside views, have good angling. The town is also noted for its Irish language college. Further east, near the town of Inchigeela, stand the ruins of **Carrignacurra Castle**. Further downstream lies the Gearagh, an alluvial stretch of marsh and woods which has been designated a wildlife sanctuary.

The river then passes through the Sullane valley, home of the thriving market town of **Macroom**. The hulk of a medieval castle, with its restored entrance, lies just off the main square. In 1654, Cromwell granted the castle to Sir William Penn. His son, who was to found the American state of Pennsylvania, lived there for a time.

Between Macroom and Cork, the Lee Valley passes through a hydroelectric power scheme surrounded by artificial lakes, water meadows and wooded banks. Just outside Cork, on the south bank of the river is **Ballincollig**, home to the fascinating Royal Gunpowder Mills museum (*see p169*).

## Blarney Castle ㉓

**Road map** B5. Blarney, Co Cork. 📞 *021 4385252.* 🚃 *to Cork.* 🚌 *to Blarney.* ⭘ *daily.* ⬤ *24 & 25 Dec.* ♿ ♿ *Grounds only.*

VISITORS from all over the world flock to this ruined castle to see the legendary Blarney Stone. Kissing the stone is a long-standing tradition, intended to confer a magical eloquence. It is set in the wall below the castle battlements and, in order to kiss it, the visitor is grasped by the feet and suspended backwards under the parapet.

Little remains of the castle today except the keep, built in 1446 by Dermot McCarthy. Its design is typical of a 15th-century tower house (*see p18*). The vaulted first floor was once the Great Hall. To reach the battlements you need to climb the 127 steps to the top of the keep.

The castle grounds offer some attractive walks, including a grove of ancient yew trees and limestone rock formations at Rock Close. **Blarney House**, a Scottish baronial mansion and the residence of the Colthurst family since the 18th century, is not open to the public.

Just a short walk from the castle, Blarney also has a pretty village green with welcoming pubs and a number of craft shops. The **Blarney Woollen Mills,** selling quality garments and souvenirs, is well worth a visit.

**Battlemented keep and ruined towers of Blarney Castle**

# Street-by-Street: Kinsale ㉔

**Old office sign in Kinsale**

FOR MANY VISITORS to Ireland, Kinsale heads the list of places to see. One of the prettiest small towns in Ireland, it has had a long and chequered history. The defeat of the Irish forces and their Spanish allies in the Battle of Kinsale in 1601 signified the end of the old Gaelic order. An important naval base in the 17th and 18th centuries, Kinsale today is a popular yachting centre. It is also famous for the quality of its cuisine – the town's annual Gourmet Festival attracts food lovers from far and wide. As well as its many wonderful restaurants, the town has pubs and wine bars to cater for all tastes.

**Desmond Castle** was built around 1500. It is known locally as the "French Prison".

★ **Old Market House**
*Incorporating the old courthouse, this museum includes a toll board listing local taxes for 1788.*

Market Square

## CHARLES FORT

The star-shaped fort is 3 km (2 miles) east of town in Summercove, but can be reached by taking the signposted coastal walk from the quayside, past the village of Scilly. The fort was built in the 1670s by the English to protect Kinsale harbour against foreign naval forces but, because of its vulnerability to land attack, was taken during the siege of 1690 by William of Orange's army. Nonetheless, it remained in service until 1922 when the British forces left the town and handed it over to the Irish Government. Charles Fort remains one of the finest remaining examples of a star-shaped bastion fort in Europe.

Kieran's Fo House Inn

★ **St Multose Church**
*This much-altered Norman church is named after an obscure 6th-century saint and marks the centre of the medieval town.*

**Walls and bastions of Charles Fort**

| 0 metres | | 50 |
| 0 yards | | 50 |

### KEY

| P | Parking |
| i | Tourist information |
| – – – | Suggested route |

**VISITORS' CHECKLIST**

**Road map** B6. Co Cork. 👥
3,413. 🚌 🛈 *Pier Road (021
4772234).* 🎉 *Annual Regatta
(Aug); Kinsale Fringe Jazz Festival
(Oct); Gourmet Festival (Oct).* **Old
Court House** ▌ *021 4772044.*
◯ *Apr–Oct: daily; Nov–Mar: by
appt.* ⛪ **St Multose Church** ▌
*021 4772220.* ◯ *variable.* ♿
**Desmond Castle and
International Museum of
Wine** ▌ *021 4774855.* ◯
*May–Oct: daily.* 🏛 **Charles Fort**
▌ *021 4772263.* ◯ *Mar–Oct:
daily; Nov–Feb: Sat & Sun.* 🏛

**Kinsale Harbour**
*Situated on the estuary of the Bandon
River, this is one of Ireland's most
scenic harbours. Kinsale is host to a
number of international sailing
events throughout the year.*

**Mother Hubbard's**, one
of Kinsale's most popular
cafés, is situated in the heart
of town on Market Street.

**To Charles Fort**

🅿

**The Blue Haven**,
easily identified by
the ornate clock
above the entrance,
is one of Kinsale's
finest seafood
restaurants.

**To Kinsale Harbour, Denis
Quay and Compass Hill**

**To Bandon**

**STAR SIGHTS**

★ **Old Market House**

★ **Main Street**

★ **St Multose Church**

★ **Main Street**
*Many of Kinsale's
best eating and
drinking places can
be found on this
picturesque street.*

# Cork ㉕

Cork city derives its name from the marshy land on the banks of the River Lee – its Irish name *Corcaigh* means marsh – on which St Finbarr founded a monastery around AD 650. The narrow alleys, waterways and Georgian architecture give the city a Continental feel. Since the 19th century, when Cork was a base for the National Fenian movement *(see p41)*, the city has had a reputation

**Sign outside a Cork pub**

for political rebelliousness. Today this mood is reflected in the city's attitude to the arts and its bohemian spirit, much in evidence at the lively October jazz festival.

### St Ann's Shandon

Church St. **(** *021 4505906.* **○** *daily.* **●** *25 Dec.* 🎫 🚻
This famous Cork landmark stands on the hilly slopes of the city, north of the River Lee. Built in 1722, the church has a façade made of limestone on two sides, and of red sandstone on the other two. The steeple is topped with a weather vane in the shape of a salmon. The clock face is known by the locals as the "four-faced liar" because, up until 1986 when it was repaired, each face showed slightly different times. Visitors can climb the tower and, for a small fee, ring the famous Shandon bells.

### Butter Exchange Shandon Craft Centre

John Redman St. **○** *daily.* 🎫 🚻
The Butter Exchange opened in 1770 and was where butter was graded before it was exported to the rest of the world. It also supplied butter to the British navy. By 1892 the exchange was exporting around 500,000 casks of butter a year, bringing prosperity to the city. The exchange shut in 1924.

Part of the building was re-opened in the 1980s to house the Shandon Craft Centre. Here visitors can watch artists and craft workers, such as crystal cutters and weavers, at work.

### Crawford Municipal Art Gallery

Emmet Place. **(** *021 4273377.* **○** *Mon–Sat.* **●** *public hols.* 🚻
The red brick and limestone building that houses Cork's major art gallery dates back to 1724. Built as the city's original custom house, it became a school of design in 1850. In 1884, a well known art patron, William Horatio Crawford, extended the building to accommodate studios and sculpture and picture galleries.

The gallery houses some fine examples of late 19th- and early 20th-century Irish art including paintings by

**Clock tower and weather vane of St Ann's Shandon**

**Detail of stained-glass window** *The Meeting of St Brendan and the Unhappy Judas* **(1911) by Harry Clarke, Crawford Art Gallery**

## SIGHTS AT A GLANCE

Butter Exchange ②
Crawford Art Gallery ④
Elizabeth Fort ⑩
English Market ⑥
Father Mathew Statue ⑤
National Monument ⑦
Parliament Bridge ⑧
Red Abbey ⑨
St Ann's Shandon ①
St Finbarr's Cathedral ⑪
St Mary's Dominican Church ③

Jack Yeats. There are also three fine windows by Ireland's foremost stained-glass artist, Harry Clarke (1889–1931).

Another attraction is the small collection by British artists and international works by artists such as Joan Miró and Georges Rouault.

The gallery is well known for its excellent restaurant which is run by the Ballymaloe cookery school (see p331), the exponents of authentic Irish cooking with a modern twist.

**Richly decorated apse ceiling of St Finbarr's Cathedral**

### 🔒 St Finbarr's Cathedral

Bishop Street. 【 021 4963387. ○ daily. **Donation.** ㅂ

Situated in a quiet part of town south of the Lee, St Finbarr's Cathedral is dedicated to the founder and patron saint of the city. Completed in 1878 to the design of William Burges, it is an exuberant

### VISITORS' CHECKLIST

**Road map** C5. Co Cork.
🏘 136,000. ✈ 6 km (4 miles) S of Cork (021 4313131).
🚉 Kent Station (021 4506766).
🚌 Parnell Place (021 4508188).
ℹ Tourist House, Grand Parade (021 4255100). 🎷 Cork Jazz Festival (Oct); Cork Film Festival (Oct). 🅦 www.corkkerry.ie

triple-spired edifice built in Gothic Revival style, and decorated with stone tracery. Inside, the painted and gilded apse ceiling shows Christ in Glory surrounded by angels. The stained-glass windows below tell the story of Christ's life.

### 🏛 Cork City Gaol

Convent Avenue, Sunday's Well. 【 021 4305022. ○ daily. 🎫 🎦 ㅂ

A pretty, 20-minute walk west of the city centre leads to the restored City Gaol, complete with its furnished cells. The exhibition and audiovisual display trace the lives of individual inmates imprisoned here during the 19th and 20th centuries. Conditions were miserable and, for punishment, prisoners were made to run on a human treadmill that was used to grind grain. The gaol cafe is worth a visit.

The Radio Musuem Experience is also housed in this building and chronicles the development of radio in Ireland and across the world.

### KEY

| 🚌 | Coach station |
|---|---|
| 🅿 | Parking |
| ℹ | Tourist information |
| ✝ | Church |

0 metres 250

0 yards 250

**South Channel of the River Lee, looking towards Parliament Bridge**

## Exploring Cork

ONE OF CORK'S great attractions is that it is a city built on water. Its heart lies on an island between two arms of the River Lee, and many of today's streets were in fact once waterways lined with warehouses and merchants' residences. Although the Dutch canalside appearance has faded, picturesque quays and bridges remain. Steep lanes rise to the north and south of the central island to the city's 19th-century suburbs, offering wonderful views of the city and its fine buildings.

### The Quays

Although the river now plays only a minor part in the city's economy, much of Cork's commercial activity still takes place around the Quays (pronounced "kays" in the Cork accent). The South Mall, which covers an arm of the River Lee, was a waterway until the late 18th century. Boats were once moored at the foot of a series of stone steps, some of which are still intact today. These led to merchants' domestic quarters above. The arches below led to warehouses where goods were unloaded.

Near South Mall is **Parliament Bridge**, built in 1806 to commemorate the Act of Union (*see p40*). Walk across the bridge to George's Quay to see Fitzpatrick's second-hand shop, with its bizarre display of bicycles, cartwheels, farm implements and other assorted bric-a-brac on its façade. A short walk away, on Sullivan's Quay, is the Quay Co-Op, a popular restaurant and meeting place. From Sullivan's Quay an elegant footbridge, built in 1985, crosses the river to the south end of Grand Parade.

### Grand Parade and St Patrick's Street

On Grand Parade, also once a waterway, stands the grandiose **National Monument**, recalling the Irish patriots who died between 1798 and 1867. Bishop Lucey Park, off Grand Parade, has a section of city walls and a fine gateway from the old cornmarket. Between St Patrick's Street and Grand Parade is the well-restored **English Market**, a covered fruit and vegetable market established in 1610. Bustling St Patrick's Street, the backbone of the city, was a waterway until 1800 when boats were moored under the steps of gracious houses such as the Chateau Bar (*see p319*). A landmark at the top of the street, near Patrick Bridge, is the **Father Mathew Statue**, a monument to the founder the Temperance Movement.

**National Monument, Grand Parade**

Fitzpatrick's second-hand shop on George's Quay

### Paul Street

Noted for its ethnic restaurants, chic bars, bookshops and trendy boutiques, Paul Street is the hub of the liveliest district in town. Just off Paul Street are the busy backstreets of Carey's Lane and French Church Street. In the early 18th century, Huguenots (French Protestants) settled in these streets and set themselves up as butter exporters, brewers and wholesale merchants. This area is Cork's equivalent to Dublin's Temple Bar (*see p76*).

### Shandon Quarter

Crossing the Christy Ring Bridge to Pope's Quay, you will see on your left **St Mary's Dominican Church**, with its portico of Ionic columns topped by a huge pediment. John Redmond Street leads to the northern slopes of Cork, dominated by the spire of St Ann's Shandon (*see p166*) with its fine views of the city. To the northeast lies the lofty Montenotte district, once the epitome of Victorian gentility.

### St Finbarr's Quarter

South of the river, rising above the city, this area's distinctive landmark is St Finbarr's Cathedral (*see p167*). Nearby is the ivy-clad **Elizabeth Fort**, a 16th-century structure which was converted into a prison in 1835 and later a *Garda* (police) station. A short walk to the east lies the **Red Abbey**, a 13th-century relic from an Augustinian abbey – the oldest building in Cork.

Selling fruit and vegetables at the English Market

**ENVIRONS:** Some beautiful countryside surrounds the city of Cork, especially along the lush valley of the River Lee *(see p163)*. The landscape of East Cork is much gentler than the wild, rocky coastline of West Cork and County Kerry, and the land is much more fertile. Many local attractions make good day trips and there are also plenty of opportunities for outdoor activities such as walking, riding and fishing.

### ♣ Blackrock Castle
Blackrock. ● *to the public.*
On the banks of the River Lee 1.5 km (1 mile) downstream from the city centre stands Blackrock Castle. Originally built in 1582 by Lord Mountjoy as a harbour fortification, the castle was destroyed by fire in 1827. It was rebuilt in 1830 to the design of architects J and GR Pain. The castle was recently bought by a private company and is no longer open to the public. A little further south at Carrigtuohill, near Fota Wildlife Park *(see pp170–71)*, is the 13th-century Barryscourt Castle, with its two intact towers.

**Blackrock Castle standing on the banks of the River Lee**

### ⊞ Dunkathel House
Glanmire. ( *021 4821014.*
○ *May–mid-Oct: Wed–Sun (pm only or by appt).* ▨ & *ground floor.*
Standing just outside the village of Glanmire, 6 km (3.5 miles) northeast of Cork, is this gracious Neo-Classical country house. The building was totally remodelled around 1785 for Abraham Morris, a wealthy Cork merchant, but retains a few features from an earlier

**Copy of *The Three Graces* by Antonio Canova, Dunkathel House**

house, including some Italianate stuccowork. The interior is decorated with Adam fireplaces and a fine collection of Irish furniture. In the spacious entrance hall is an elegant Bath stone staircase with an iron balustrade. On the half landing stands a plaster copy of Canova's *The Three Graces*, thought to have been cast in the early 19th century. The drawing room, hung with Victorian watercolours, offers lovely views of the wooded banks of the River Glanmire. Charming parkland surrounds the house.

### �ⅲ Royal Gunpowder Mills
Ballincollig. ( *021 4874430.*
○ *mid-Mar–mid-Apr: Sat & Sun; mid-Apr–Sep: daily.* ▨ ☑ &
This unusual museum is 10 km (6 miles) west of Cork. Covering 320 ha (130 acres) of landscaped grounds, it is an impressive heritage project featuring canals, weirs, sluice gates, mills and workers' cottages. The mills were established in 1794 and flourished during the Napoleonic Wars, when they were also used as a British military base. By the 1850s, gunpowder production had become one of Cork's foremost industries. The mills finally closed in 1903, at the end of the Boer War. A guided tour covers the production of gunpowder in the main mills, and visitors are free to explore the rest of the complex.

## River Blackwater ㉖

**Road map** B5. Co Cork. ▯ *to Mallow.* ▯ *to Fermoy, Mallow or Kanturk.*

THE SECOND LONGEST RIVER in Ireland after the Shannon *(see p177)*, the Blackwater rises in high bogland in County Kerry. It then flows eastwards through County Cork until it reaches Cappoquin, County Waterford, where it changes course south through wooded sandstone gorges to the sea at Youghal *(see p171)*. Much of the valley is wooded, a reminder that the entire area was forested until the 17th century. The river passes some magnificent country houses and pastoral views. However, the region is best known for its fishing – the Blackwater's tributaries are filled with fine brown trout.

The best way to see the valley is to take the scenic Blackwater Valley Drive from Youghal to Mallow. The route passes through **Fermoy**, a town founded by Scottish merchant John Anderson in 1789. Angling is the town's main appeal, especially for roach, rudd, perch and pike. Further west is **Mallow**, a prosperous town noted for its fishing, golf and horse racing, and a good base for tours of the area. Detours along the tributaries include **Kanturk**, a pleasant market town with a castle, on the River Allow.

**Weirs and bridge at Fermoy on the River Blackwater**

# Cobh ㉗

**Road map** C6. Co Cork. 🚶 *12,000.*
🚉 ℹ️ *Old Yacht Club (021 4813301).*

COBH (pronounced "cove")
lies on Great Island, one
of the three islands in Cork
harbour which are now linked
by causeways. The Victorian
seafront has rows of steeply
terraced houses overlooked
by **St Colman's**, an imposing
Gothic Revival cathedral.

Following a visit by Queen
Victoria in 1849, Cobh was
renamed Queenstown but
reverted to its original name
in 1921. The town commands
one of the world's largest
natural harbours – the reason
for its rise to prominence as a
naval base in the 18th century.
It was also a major port for
merchant shipping and the
main port from which Irish
emigrants left for America.

Cobh was also a port of call
for luxury passenger liners. In
1838, the *Sirius* made the first
transatlantic crossing under
steam power from here. Cobh
was also the last stop for the
*Titanic*, before its doomed
Atlantic crossing in 1912.
Three years later,
the *Lusitania* was
torpedoed and
sunk by a German
submarine just
off Kinsale *(see
pp164–5)*, south-
west of Cobh. A
memorial on the
promenade is
dedicated to all
those who died
in the attack.

## IRISH EMIGRATION

Between 1848 and 1950 almost six million people emigrated
from Ireland – two and a half million of them leaving from
Cobh. The famine years of 1844–8 *(see p211)* triggered mass
emigration as the impoverished made horrific transatlantic
journeys in cramped, insanitary conditions. Many headed
for the United States and Canada, and a few risked the
long journey to Australia. Up until the early 20th century,
emigrants waiting to board the ships were a familiar sight
in Cobh. However, by the 1930s world recession and
immigration restrictions in the United States and Canada
led to a fall in the numbers leaving Ireland.

**19th-century engraving of emigrants gathering in Cobh harbour**

### 🏛 The Queenstown Story

Cobh Heritage Centre. 📞 *021
4813591.* ⭕ *daily.* ♿ 🍴 ⚑
Housed in a Victorian railway
station, *The Queenstown Story*
is an exhibition detailing the
town's marine history. Exhibits
and audiovisual displays recall
the part Cobh played in Irish
emigration and the transportation of convicts. Between 1791
and 1853, 40,000 convicts
were sent to Australian penal
colonies in notorious "coffin
ships"; many prisoners were
also kept in floating jails
in Cork Harbour.

On a happier note, the exhibition also documents Cobh's
role as a port of call for
glamorous transatlantic liners.

**ENVIRONS:** North of Cobh is the
280-ha (700-acre) Fota Estate.
Surrounding the Regency
mansion is the **Fota Wildlife
Park and Arboretum**, which
concentrates on breeding and
reintroducing animals to their
natural habitat. The white-
tailed sea eagle is one native
species that has been saved
from extinction in Ireland.
The landscaped park boasts

**Cobh harbour with the steeple of St Colman's rising above the town**

over 70 species of animal, including giraffes, flamingoes, and zebras. Only the cheetahs, subject to a long-term breeding programme, are restricted in enclosures. A train links the various sections of the park.

The arboretum has rare trees and shrubs from Japan, China, South America, the Himalayas and North America.

**✗ Fota Wildlife Park and Arboretum**
Carrigtuohill. ☏ 021 4812678.
◯ daily. 🎦 ♿

## Old Midleton Distillery ㉘

**Road map** C5. Distillery Walk, Midleton, Co Cork.
☏ 021 4613594. 🚌 to Midleton.
◯ daily. ● 24 Dec–2 Jan. 🎦 ♿
🛈 🛒 🍴 in summer only.

A SENSITIVELY RESTORED 18th-century distillery, Old Midleton Distillery is part of the vast Irish Distillers group at Midleton. Bushmills (see p258) is the oldest distillery in Ireland but Midleton is the largest, with a series of distilleries each producing a different whiskey, including Jameson and Tullamore Dew.

The story of Irish whiskey is presented through audiovisual displays, working models and authentic machinery. A tour of the old distillery takes in the mills, maltings, still-houses, kilns, granaries and ware-houses. Visitors can take part in whiskey tasting and try to distinguish between various brands of Irish whiskey and Scotch. Highlights of the visit include the world's largest pot still, with a capacity of over 30,000 gallons, and the working water wheel.

Clock tower on the main street of Youghal

## Youghal ㉙

**Road map** C5. Co Cork.
👥 7,500. 🚌 🛈 Market House, Market Square (024 20170).

YOUGHAL (pronounced "yawl") is a historic walled town and thriving fishing port. The town was granted to Sir Walter Raleigh by Queen Elizabeth I but later sold to the Earl of Cork. In Cromwellian times, Youghal became a closed borough – an English Protestant garrison town.

The picturesque, four-storey **Clock tower** was originally the city gate, but was recast as a prison. Steep steps beside the tower lead up to a well-preserved section of the medieval town wall and fine views across the Blackwater estuary. Through the tower, in the sombre North Main Street, is the **Red House**. This authentic Dutch mansion was built in 1710. Virtually next door are some forbidding Elizabethan almshouses and, on the far side of the road, a 15th-century tower, known as **Tynte's Castle**.

Nestling in the town walls opposite is **Myrtle Grove**, one of the few unfortified Tudor manor houses to survive in Ireland. It has a triple-gabled façade and exquisite interior oak panelling. Just uphill is the Gothic **Church of St Mary**. Inside are tomb effigies and stained-glass windows depicting the coats of arms of local families.

Grain truck (c. 1940) at the Jameson Heritage Centre

# THE LOWER SHANNON

·········································

## CLARE · LIMERICK · TIPPERARY

I N THE THREE COUNTIES *which flank the lower reaches of the Shannon, Ireland's longest river, the scenery ranges from the rolling farmland of Tipperary to the eerie limestone plateau of the Burren. The Shannon's bustling riverside resorts draw many visitors, and there are medieval strongholds and atmospheric towns of great historic interest. The region also boasts a vibrant music scene.*

The River Shannon has long made this area an attractive prospect for settlers. There are several important Stone Age sites, including a major settlement by Lough Gur. From the 5th century, the region lay at the heart of Munster, one of Ireland's four Celtic provinces. The Rock of Cashel, a remarkable fortified abbey in county Tipperary, was the seat of the Kings of Munster for more than 700 years.

The Vikings penetrated the Shannon in the 10th century, but Gaelic clans put up stern resistance. During the Norman period, the chieftains of these clans built Bunratty Castle and other fortresses that were impressive enough to rival the strongholds erected by the Anglo-Irish dynasties. Foremost among the latter families were the Butlers, the Earls of Ormonde, who held much land in Tipperary, and the Fitzgeralds, the main landowners in the Limerick area. From the Middle Ages, Limerick was often at the centre of events in the Lower Shannon. In 1691, the army of William of Orange laid siege to the town, heralding the Treaty of Limerick that triggered the Catholic nobility's departure for Europe – the so-called "Flight of the Wild Geese".

Lush grassland, which has turned the Lower Shannon into prime dairy country, is typical of the region. In places this gives way to picturesque glens and mountains, such as the Galty range in southern Tipperary. The region's most dramatic scenery, however, is found along the coast of Clare, a county otherwise best known for its thriving traditional music scene.

Ruins of Dysert O'Dea monastery in County Clare with an outstanding 12th-century High Cross

◁ Traditional musicians playing at Feakle in County Clare

# Exploring the Lower Shannon

THE CENTRAL LOCATION of Limerick city makes it a natural focus for visitors to the region. However, there are many charming towns that make pleasanter bases, such as Adare, Cashel and also Killaloe, which is well placed for exploring the River Shannon. Most places of interest in Tipperary lie in the southern part of the county, where historic towns such as Clonmel and Cahir overlook the River Suir. By contrast, County Clare has few towns of any size, though it boasts the major attraction of Bunratty Castle. Beyond Ennis, the landscape becomes steadily bleaker until you reach the Burren.

**Looking up at the Cliffs of Moher**

*Map labels:*

N67

R477

DOOLIN

THE BURREN ①

CLIFFS OF MOHER ②

KILFENORA

ENNISTIMON

R460

N18

Galway

R462

R461

FEAI

DYSERT O'DEA ⑦

N67

ENNIS ⑧

CRAGGAUNOWI ⑩

KNAPPOGUE CASTLE ⑨

N68

SHANNON ⑥

⑬ BUNR CASTL

LIMERIC

KILRUSH ③

R487

FOYNES ⑤

N69

GLIN ④

R521

ADARE ⑮

NEWCASTLE WEST

N21

N522

MULLAGHAREIRK MOUNTAINS

Tralee

N20

Cork

## GETTING AROUND

Roads extend from Limerick into every corner of the region, providing good access for motorists; the car ferry from Tarbert in Kerry to Killimer, near Kilrush in Clare, is a convenient route across the Shannon. Trains from Limerick serve Cahir, Clonmel and Carrick, but in other areas you must rely on the bus network. This is rather limited, especially in County Clare, although buses to the Burren from Limerick pass the Cliffs of Moher. Some of the most popular sights, such as Bunratty Castle and the Burren, can be reached on bus tours from Limerick.

0 kilometres    25

0 miles    25

## KEY

Major road

Minor road

Scenic route

River

Viewpoint

**Boats sailing on Lough Derg near Mountshannon**

## SIGHTS AT A GLANCE

Adare **15**
Athassel Priory **20**
*Bunratty Castle pp184–5* **13**
*The Burren pp178–80* **1**
Cahir **22**
Carrick-on-Suir **24**
*Cashel pp187–9* **19**
Cliffs of Moher **2**
Clonmel **23**
Craggaunowen **10**
Dysert O'Dea **7**
Ennis **8**
Foynes **5**
Glen of Aherlow **21**
Glin **4**
Holy Cross Abbey **18**
Killaloe **12**
Kilrush **3**
Knappogue Castle **9**
Limerick **14**
Lough Gur **16**
Mountshannon **11**
River Shannon **6**
Roscrea **17**

Tullamore

*Shannon*

**BORRISOKANE**
**MOUNTSHANNON** **11**
*Lough Derg*
**ROSCREA** **17**
N52
N65
N7
N52

**NENAGH**
N7
**ILLALOE**
*SILVERMINE MOUNTAINS*
R497
R503

*SLIEVEFELIM MOUNTAINS*
N24
N62

**THURLES**
N8
Portlaoise

**HOLY CROSS ABBEY** **18**
R497
R660
*Suir*

**CASHEL** **19**

**LOUGH GUR**
R516
**TIPPERARY**
N74
N8
R688
N76  Kilkenny

**ATHASSEL PRORY** **20**
R513

**GLEN OF AHERLOW** **21**
*GALTY MOUNTAINS*
**CAHIR** **22**
N24
**CLONMEL** **23**
**CARRICK-ON-SUIR** **24**
Waterford

N8
Cork

### SEE ALSO

• *Where to Stay* pp294–5

• *Restaurants, Cafés and Pubs*
  pp312–13 & 319–20

**Feehan's BAR**

**Painted pub sign in Cashel**

Looking south along the Cliffs of Moher, one of the most dramatic stretches of Ireland's west coast

# The Burren ❶

*See pp178–9.*

# Cliffs of Moher ❷

**Road map** B4. Co Clare. 🚌 *from Ennis & Limerick.* **Visitors' Centre** 🕿 *061 360788.* ⃝ *daily.* ● *25, 26 Dec.* **O'Brien's Tower** 🕿 *061 360788.* ⃝ *Mar–Oct: daily.* 📷 ▢ 🏪

**E**VEN WHEN SHROUDED in mist or buffeted by Atlantic gales, the Cliffs of Moher are breathtaking, rising to a height of 200 m (650 ft) out of the sea and extending for 8 km (5 miles). The sheer rock face, with its layers of black shale and sandstone, provides sheltered ledges where guillemots and other sea birds nest.

Well-worn paths lead along the cliffs. From the **Visitors' Centre**, 5 km (3 miles) northwest of Liscannor, you can walk south to **Hag's Head** in an hour. To the north, a good alternative is the three-hour walk along the coast between **O'Brien's Tower** – a viewing point built for the benefit of Victorian tourists – and Fisherstreet near **Doolin** *(see p180).*

# Kilrush ❸

**Road map** B4. Co Clare. 🏠 *2,800.* 🚌 ℹ️ *Heritage Centre, Market House (065 9051577).* ⃝ *May–Sep.*

**W**ITH A NEW MARINA and the promotion of Kilrush as a heritage town, the fortunes of this 18th-century estate town have been greatly revived. It now has a **Heritage Centre**, where an exhibition covers the Great Famine *(see p211)* and the landlord evictions of 1888

*(see pp40–41).* A well-marked walking trail around the town's historic sights also starts here.

**ENVIRONS:** From Kilrush, boats take visitors dolphin-spotting or to nearby **Scattery Island**, site of a medieval monastery. The ruins include five churches and one of the tallest round towers in the country.

The **Loop Head Drive** is a 27-km (17-mile) route which begins at the resort of Kilkee, west of Kilrush. It winds south past dramatic coastal scenery to Loop Head, from where you can enjoy superb views.

# Glin ❹

**Road map** B5. Co Limerick. 🏠 *600.* 🚌 *from Limerick.*

**T**HIS CHARMING village on the banks of the Shannon is the seat of the Knights of Glin, a branch of the Fitzgeralds who have lived in the district for seven centuries. Their first medieval castle is a ruin, but west of the village you can see

Rare 18th-century double "flying" staircase in Glin Castle

their newer ancestral home, **Glin Castle**. Originally built in 1780, the Georgian manor succumbed to the vogue for Gothic romance in the 1820s, when it acquired battlements and gingerbread lodges. There is some fine stuccowork and 18th-century furniture inside.

♣ **Glin Castle**
🕿 *068 34173.* ⃝ *by appointment only.* 📷 🎥 *obligatory.*

# Foynes ❺

**Road map** B5. Co Limerick. 🏠 *650.* 🚌 *from Limerick.*

**F**OYNES ENJOYED short-lived fame in the 1930s and 1940s as the eastern terminus of the first airline passenger route across the Atlantic. **Foynes Flying Boat Museum** presents a detailed history of the seaplane service. The original Radio and Weather Room and a 1940s-style tea room are particularly evocative of the era.

🏛 **Foynes Flying Boat Museum**
Aras Ide, Foynes. 🕿 *069 65416.* ⃝ *Apr–Oct: daily.* 📷 ▢ 🏪 ♿

**ENVIRONS:** The historic town of **Askeaton**, 11 km (7 miles) east of Foynes, has a castle and Franciscan friary founded by the Fitzgeralds. The friary is particularly interesting, with a 15th-century cloister of black marble. In Rathkeale, 8 km (5 miles) south, **Castle Matrix** is a restored 15th-century tower house renowned for the fine library in the Great Hall.

♣ **Castle Matrix**
Rathkeale. 🕿 *069 64284.* ⃝ *May–Sep: Sat–Thu.* 📷

**Fishing on Lough Derg, the largest of the lakes on the Shannon**

# River Shannon ❻

**Road map** B4, C4, C3. 🚉 *to Limerick or Athlone.* 🚌 *to Carrick-on-Shannon, Athlone or Limerick.* 🛈 *Arthur's Quay, Limerick (061 317522).* ⓦ *www.shannon-dev.ie*

THE SHANNON IS the longest river in Ireland, rising in County Cavan and meandering down to the Atlantic. Flowing through the heart of the island, it has traditionally marked the border between the provinces of Leinster and Connaught. In medieval times, castles guarded the major fords from Limerick to Portumna, and numerous monasteries were built along the riverbanks, including the celebrated Clonmacnoise *(see pp242–3)*. Work began on the Shannon navigation system in the 1750s, but it fell into disuse with the advent of the railways. It has since been revived with the Shannon–Erne Waterway the latest stretch to be restored *(see p227)*.

There are subtle changes of landscape along the length of the river. South of **Lough Allen**, the countryside is covered with the drumlins or low hills typical of the northern Midlands. Towards **Lough Ree**, islands stud the river in an area of ecological importance which is home to otters, geese, grey herons and whooper swans. Continuing south beyond **Athlone** *(see p241)*, the river flows through flood plains and bog before reaching **Lough**

## EXPLORING THE SHANNON

Carrick-on-Shannon is the main centre for boating on the upper reaches of the river, while Portumna and the atmospheric ports of Mountshannon and Killaloe are the principal bases for exploring Lough Derg.

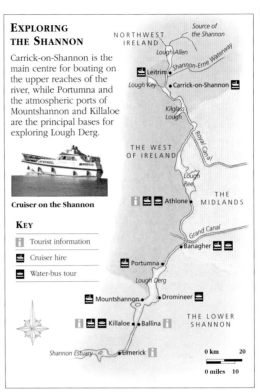

**Cruiser on the Shannon**

**KEY**

🛈 Tourist information

⚓ Cruiser hire

⚓ Water-bus tour

**Derg**, the biggest of the lakes on the Shannon. The scenery is more dramatic here, with the lough's southern end edged by wooded mountains. From **Killaloe** *(see p182)*, the river gains speed on its rush towards **Limerick** *(see p183)* and the sea. The mudflats of the Shannon estuary attract a great variety of birdlife. The port of **Carrick-on-Shannon** *(see p227)* is the cruising centre of Ireland, but there are bases all along the river – especially

**Grey heron on the Shannon**

around Lough Derg, which is the lake most geared to boating. Water-buses connect most ports south of Athlone. If you hire a cruiser, enquire about the weather conditions before setting out, particularly on Loughs Ree and Derg, which are very exposed. The calm stretch from **Portumna** *(see p205)* to Athlone is easier for inexperienced sailors.

Walkers can enjoy the Lough Derg Way, a signposted route around the lake. The woods by **Lough Key** *(see p211)* also provide good walking territory.

**Athlone and the southern reaches of Lough Ree**

# The Burren ●

Tʜᴇ ᴡᴏʀᴅ ʙᴜʀʀᴇɴ derives from *boireann*, which means "rocky land" in Gaelic – an apt name for this vast limestone plateau in northwest County Clare. In the 1640s, Cromwell's surveyor described it as "a savage land, yielding neither water enough to drown a man, nor tree to hang him, nor soil enough to bury". Few trees manage to grow in this desolate place, yet other plants thrive. The Burren is a unique botanical environment in which Mediterranean and alpine plants rare to Ireland grow side by side. From May to August, an astonishing array of flowers adds splashes of colour to the austere landscape. These plants grow most abundantly around the region's shallow lakes and pastures, but they also take root in the crevices of the limestone pavements which are the most striking geological feature of the rocky plateau. In the southern part of the Burren, limestone gives way to the black shale and sandstone that form the dramatic Cliffs of Moher *(see p176)*.

**Dark red helleborine**

**Grazing in the Burren**
*A quirk in the local climate means that, in winter, the hills are warmer than the valleys – hence the unusual practice in the Burren of letting cattle graze on high ground in winter.*

## Fᴀᴜɴᴀ ᴏꜰ ᴛʜᴇ Bᴜʀʀᴇɴ

The Burren is one of the best places in Ireland for butterflies, with 28 species found in the area. The birdlife is also varied. Skylarks and cuckoos are common on the hills and in the meadows, while the coast is a good place for razorbills, guillemots, puffins and other sea birds. Mammals are harder to spot. Badgers, foxes and stoats live here, but you are much more likely to see a herd of shaggy-coated wild goats or an Irish hare.

**The pearl-bordered fritillary**, *one of a number of fritillaries found in the Burren, can be seen in no other part of Ireland.*

**An Irish hare's** *white and brown winter coat turns to reddish-brown in the summer.*

**Whooper swans** *from Iceland flock to the wetlands of the Burren in winter.*

**The hooded crow** *is easily identified by its grey and black plumage.*

**Turloughs** are shallow lakes which are dry in summer but flood in winter, when they attract wildfowl and waders.

**Spring gentian**

**Bloody Cranesbill**
*This striking plant, common in the Burren, is a member of the geranium family. It flowers in June.*

**Limestone Pavement**
*Glaciation and wind and rain erosion have formed limestone pavements with deep crevices known as "grykes". The porous rock is easily penetrated by rainwater, which has gouged out an extensive cave system beneath the rocky plateau.*

**Hawthorn** is one of the few trees which manages to grow in the Burren, although the plants are usually twisted and stunted.

**Exposed layers of limestone**

**Stone-built Burren cottage**

**Dry-stone wall**

**Limestone slabs, or "clints"**

**The hoary rock rose** is one of several rare plants to grow abundantly in the Burren.

**Holly trees** can gain a foothold in the pavement, but grazing and wind restrict their growth.

**Maidenhair fern** thrives in the damp crevices of the Burren.

**Mountain Avens**
*Normally a mountain plant, this flower grows here at sea level.*

## Exploring the Burren

If you are interested in the unique geology and natural history of the Burren, head for **Mullaghmore**, to the south-east of the area. This is one of the wildest parts of the plateau and reaches a height of 191 m (626 ft), with some of the best limestone pavements in the area.

A good place to begin a tour of the more accessible parts of the Burren is at the **Cliffs of Moher** (see p176). From here it is a short drive north to **Doolin**, near the port for the Aran Islands (see pp206–7). This rather spread-out village is renowned for its traditional music; Gus O'Connor's pub (see p320) acts as a focus for music-lovers in the area. The coastal road runs north from Doolin to a desolate limestone outcrop at **Black Head**, while turning inland you will reach **Lisdoonvarna**. The Victorians developed the town as a spa, but it is now most renowned for its colourful pubs and its matchmaking festival (see p48).

**Music shop in Doolin**

To the north along the N67 lies **Ballyvaughan**, a fishing village dotted with slate-roofed cottages and busy with tourists in summer. It is well placed for reaching a number of sights. Nearby **Bishop's Quarter** has a sheltered beach with glorious views across a lagoon towards Galway Bay. **Aillwee Cave**, to the south, is just one of thousands of caves in the Burren, but is the only one open to the public. It consists of a tunnel which opens into a series of caverns. In the first, known as Bear Haven, the remains of hibernation pits used by bears are still visible.

Ruined forts and castles and numerous prehistoric sites dot the landscape. Just west of Aillwee Cave is **Cahermore Stone Fort**, with a lintelled doorway, and to the south

**Poulnabrone Dolmen in the heart of the Burren's limestone plateau**

**Gleninsheen Wedge Tomb**, a style of grave which marks the transition between Stone and Bronze Age cultures. The more famous **Poulnabrone Dolmen** nearby is a striking portal tomb dating back to 2500–2000 BC. Continuing south you reach the ghostly shell of **Leamaneagh Castle**, a 17th-century mansion that incorporates an earlier tower house built by the O'Briens.

On the southern fringe of the Burren lies **Kilfenora**, a Catholic diocese which, by a curious historical quirk, has the Pope for its bishop. The village's modest cathedral, one of many 12th-century churches in the Burren, has a roofless chancel with finely sculpted capitals. Kilfenora, however, is more famous for its High Crosses, of which there are several in the graveyard. Best preserved is the Doorty Cross, with a carving of a bishop and two other clerics on the east face. Next door, the refurbished **Burren Centre** offers an excellent multi-dimensional exhibition giving information on the geology and fauna of the area and man's impact on the landscape.

**Carved capital in Kilfenora Cathedral**

🐾 **Aillwee Cave**
Ballyvaughan. 📞 06570 77036.
🕐 daily. 🦽 💷 🎫 🚻 🛗
🏛 **Burren Centre**
Kilfenora. 📞 06570 88030. 🕐
Mar–Oct: daily. 🦽 ♿

---

## THE BURREN REGION

**KEY**

| | |
|---|---|
| ☐ | Exposed limestone |
| ═ | Minor roads |
| ▭ | Major roads |
| 🛈 | Tourist information |
| 🔆 | Viewpoint |

0 kilometres        10
0 miles        5

Black Head
Bishop's Quarter Beach
Ballyvaughan
Cahermore Stone Fort
SLIEVECARRAN
Aillwee Cave
SLIEVE ELVA
Gleninsheen Wedge Tomb
Poulnabrone Dolmen
Lisdoonvarna
Doolin
Leamaneagh Castle
MULLAGHMORE
Kilfenora
Cliffs of Moher
N67
R477
R479
R481
R476
R480
R67
R478
R460

## Dysert O'Dea ⓴

**Road map** 4B. Corrofin, Co Clare.
🚍 *from Ennis.* **Archaeology Centre**
☎ 06568 37722. ⏰ *May–Sep: daily.*

DYSERT O'DEA CASTLE stands on a rocky outcrop 9 km (6 miles) north of Ennis. This tower house, erected in the 15th century, is home to the **Archaeology Centre**, which includes a small museum and also marks the start of a trail around nearby historic sights. A map of the path, designed for both walkers and cyclists, is available from the tea room.

Across a field from the castle is a monastic site said to have been founded by the obscure St Tola in the 8th century. The ruins are overgrown and rather worn, but the Romanesque carving above one doorway is still clear, and there is also an impressive 12th-century High Cross, with a bishop sculpted on the east side *(see p235)*.

Further south, the trail leads past the remains of two stone forts, a ruined castle and the site of a 14th-century battle.

## Ennis ⓳

**Road map** 4B. Co Clare. 👥 *25,000.*
🚍 🛈 *Clare Rd (06568 28366).*

CLARE'S COUNTY TOWN, on the banks of the River Fergus, is a charming place. Narrow, winding lanes are particularly characteristic and recall Ennis's medieval beginnings. The town is also renowned for its painted shopfronts and folk music festivals (known as *fleadh* in Gaelic). It abounds in "singing" pubs and traditional music shops.

*Colourful exterior of Michael Kerins pub in Ennis*

Ennis can trace its origins to the 13th century and to the O'Briens, Kings of Thomond, who were the area's feudal overlords in the Middle Ages. The Franciscan friary that they founded here in the 1240s is now the town's main attraction. Dating from the 14th and 15th centuries, the ruined **Ennis Friary** is famous for its rich carvings and decorated tombs in the chancel – above all the 15th-century MacMahon tomb with its finely carved alabaster panels. Extensive conservation work is ongoing here.

Next door to the friary is a delightful 17th-century house, now Cruise's restaurant *(see p312)*, and on the corner of nearby Francis Street stands the Queen's Hotel – featured in James Joyce's *Ulysses*. To the south, O'Connell Square has a monument to Daniel O'Connell *(see p40)*, who was elected MP for Clare in 1828. He also gave his name to the town's main street, where, among the pubs and shops, you can spot a medieval tower, a Jacobean chimney stack and an 18th-century arch.

*Finely carved Romanesque doorway at Dysert O'Dea*

### 🏛 Ennis Friary
Abbey St. ☎ 06568 29100. ⏰ *May–Sep: daily.* 📷 ♿

**ENVIRONS:** The area around Ennis is rich in monastic ruins. Just 3 km (2 miles) south of the town is **Clare Abbey**, an Augustinian foundation set up by the O'Briens in 1189 but dating mainly from the 1400s.

**Quin Franciscan Friary**, set in meadows 13 km (8 miles) southeast of Ennis, was also built in the 15th century, and incorporates the romantic ruins of a Norman castle. The well-preserved cloister is one of the finest of its kind in Ireland.

## Knappogue Castle ⓴

**Road map** 4B. Quin, Co Clare.
☎ 061 360788. 🚍 *to Ennis.*
⏰ *Apr–Oct: daily.* 📷 🏛 ♿ *limited.*

A POWERFUL LOCAL CLAN called the MacNamaras erected Knappogue Castle in 1467. Apart from a ten-year spell in Cromwellian times, it stayed in their hands until 1815. During the War of Independence *(see pp42–3)*, the castle was used by the revolutionary forces.

Knappogue, now owned by Shannon Development, has been well restored and is one of Ireland's most charmingly furnished castles. The central tower house is original, but the rest is Neo-Gothic. Inside are fine Elizabethan fireplaces and linenfold wood panelling.

Medieval banquets are staged in the castle *(see p330)*, with storytelling and singing forming part of the entertainment.

# Craggaunowen ⑩

**Road map** B4. Kilmurry, Co Clare.
🚌 🚉 to Ennis. 📞 061 360788.
🕐 mid-Apr–Sep: daily. 🈂️ ♿

THE CRAGGAUNOWEN PROJECT, known as "Craggaunowen: the Living Past" and designed to bring Bronze Age and Celtic culture to life, is a shining example of a recreated pre-historic site. The centre was created in the grounds of Craggaunowen Castle in the 1960s by John Hunt, a noted archaeologist who had been inspired by his excavations at Lough Gur *(see p186)*. The castle's tower house contains bronzes and other objects from Hunt's archaeological collection, the rest of which can be seen in Limerick.

Occasionally, people in costume act out particular trades, such as spinning or potting, or serve as guides. A French slave describes how communities lived in the ring fort, a typical early Christian homestead. You can also see meat being prepared in the *fulacht fiadh*, a traditional hunter's cooking hole.

The complex includes part of a *togher*, an original Iron Age timber road that was discovered in Longford. The most eye-catching sight, however, is the crannog *(see p31)*, a man-made island enclosing wattle and daub houses – a style of defensive homestead that survived until around 1600.

Another interesting exhibit is a leather-hulled boat built in the 1970s by the explorer, Tim Severin. He used it to retrace

**A woman in peasant costume spinning wool at Craggaunowen**

the route which legend says St Brendan took in a similar vessel across the Atlantic in the 6th century *(see p25)*.

# Mountshannon ⑪

**Road map** C4. Co Clare. 🚶 240.
⛴️ to Holy Island. 📞 061 921531.

THIS PRETTY VILLAGE on the banks of Lough Derg *(see p177)* seems to have its back turned to the lake but is nevertheless a major angling centre. Solid 18th-century stone houses and churches cluster around the harbour, together with some good pubs.

Mountshannon is well placed for exploring the lake's western shores, with plenty of scope for walks and bicycle rides. Fishing boats are available for hire, and in summer you can go by boat to **Holy Island**, the site of a monastery founded in the 7th century. The ruins include four chapels and a graveyard of medieval tombs.

# Killaloe ⑫

**Road map** C4. Co Clare. 🚶 950.
🚌 ℹ️ May–Sep: Heritage Centre, The Bridge (061 376866).

KILLALOE, birthplace of Brian Boru (940–1014), High King of Ireland *(see p32)*, lies close to where the Shannon emerges from Lough Derg, and is the lake's most prosperous pleasure port. A 17th-century stone bridge separates Killaloe from its twin town of Ballina on the opposite bank. Ballina has better pubs, such as Goosers on the waterfront *(see p320)*, but Killaloe is the main boating centre *(see p335)* and also offers more of historical interest.

Killaloe's grandest building is **St Flannan's Cathedral**, built around 1182. Its richly carved Romanesque doorway was once part of an earlier chapel. The church also has an ancient Ogham Stone *(see p32)*, unusual because the inscription is carved in both Nordic runes and Ogham. Outside stands St Flannan's Oratory, built around the same time as the cathedral.

**The Heritage Centre**, in a converted boathouse on the bridge, contains an exhibition about the Shannon and Lough Derg, and is the starting point for a marked walk along sections of the old Killaloe Canal. It is also possible to arrange for local fishermen to take you out on the lake.

# Bunratty Castle ⑬

See pp184–5.

**Bicycle hire and boat trips at Mountshannon**

# Limerick ⑭

**Road map** B4. Co Limerick. 🚶 90,000.
🚂 *Shannon.* 🚌 🚍 ℹ️ *Arthur's
Quay (061 317522).* 🚏 *Sat.*

THE THIRD LARGEST CITY in the
Republic, Limerick was
founded by the Vikings. Given
its strategic point on the River
Shannon, it thrived under the
Normans, but later bore the
brunt of English oppression.
After the Battle of the Boyne
(see p236), the rump of the
defeated Jacobite army with-
drew here. The siege which
followed has entered Irish
folklore as a heroic defeat,
sealed by the Treaty
of Limerick in 1691.
English treachery
in reneging on
most of the terms
of the treaty still
rankles. It is no
coincidence that
Catholicism and
nationalism are
strong in the city.
Limerick has a
reputation for high
unemployment,
crime and general
neglect. However, it is fast
acquiring a new image as a
commercial city, revitalized by
new industries and laudable
restoration projects. Even so,
visitors may still have to dig a
little to appreciate its charm.
The city centre consists of
three historic districts. King's
Island was the first area to be
settled by the Vikings and was
later the heart of the medieval
city, when it was known as
Englishtown. The island boasts
Limerick's two main landmarks,
King John's Castle and St Mary's
Cathedral. The old Irishtown,
south of the Abbey River, has
its fair share of drab houses
and shops, but also has its own
historic buildings and a pocket

**Carved misericord in
St Mary's Cathedral**

of Georgian elegance in St
John's Square. Near here is
Limerick's most conspicuous
sight, St John's Cathedral, built
in 1861. Its 85-m (280-ft) spire
is the tallest in the country.
The most pleasant part of
Limerick in which to stroll is
Newtown Pery – a grid of
gracious Georgian terraces
focused on O'Connell Street.

## ♟ King John's Castle

Nicholas St. 📞 *061 411201.*
🕐 *Apr–Oct: 9:30am–5:30pm daily
(last adm. 4:30pm).* 🚫 🔢 🍴 ⏰ 🚻
Supposedly founded by King
John in 1200, not long after the
Normans arrived, this castle is
an imposing sight
with five drum
towers and solid
curtain walls.
Inside, the
castle is less
interesting
architecturally,
but it houses a
good audio
visual exhibition
on the history of
the city. Ongoing
excavations have
unearthed pots
and jewellery, and you can
also see Viking houses and
later fortifications. One of the
most dramatic artifacts on
display is a soldier's diary
recording the horrors of the
Siege of Limerick.
Across the nearby Thomond
Bridge, the Treaty Stone marks
the spot where the Treaty of
Limerick was signed in 1691.

## ✝ St Mary's Cathedral

Bridge Street. 📞 *061 416238.*
🕐 *9am–5pm daily.*
Built in 1172, this is the oldest
structure in the city. Except for
a fine Romanesque doorway
and the nave, however, little
remains of the early church.
The 15th-century misericords

**Characteristic Georgian doorway
in St John's Square**

in the choir stalls are the pride
of St Mary's, with superb
carvings in black oak of angels,
griffins and other creatures
both real and imaginary.
Nearby, George's Quay is a
pleasant street with restaurants
and outdoor cafés and good
views across the river.

## 🏛 Hunt Museum

Rutland St. 📞 *061 312833.*
🕐 *10am–5pm Mon–Sat, 2pm–5pm
Sun.* 🚫 🍴 ⏰ 🚻
Located in the Old Customs
House, this fine museum has
one of the greatest collections
of antiquities in Ireland,
gathered by the archaeologist,
John Hunt. The best exhibits,
dating from the Bronze Age,
include gold jewellery and a
magnificent shield. Among the
other artifacts are Celtic
brooches and the Antrim
Cross, a masterpiece of 9th-
century metalwork.

## 🏛 Limerick Museum

Nicholas St. 📞 *061 417826.* 🕐
*10am–5pm Tue–Sat.* ⏰ *7 days at
Christmas.* ⏰
The city museum is in a fine
19th-century granary building.
Limerick's history and traditions from lace-making to
rugby are on display.

**View of Limerick showing Thomond Bridge across the Shannon and King John's Castle**

# Bunratty Castle & Folk Park ⓭

THIS FORMIDABLE CASTLE, built in the 15th century, is one of Ireland's major tourist attractions. Its most important residents were the O'Briens, Earls of Thomond, who lived here from around 1500 until the 1640s. The present interior looks much as it did under the so-called "Great Earl", who died in 1624. Abandoned last century, the castle was derelict when Lord Gort bought it in the 1950s, but it has been beautifully restored to its original state. The adjacent Folk Park includes Hazelbrook House, a recent addition showing the evolution of ice-cream making. Bunratty is also famous for its splendid medieval banquets.

**The chimney** is a replica in wood of the stone original. It provided a vent for the smoke given off by the fire in the centre of the Great Hall.

**★ North Solar**
*This 17th-century German chandelier is the most curious feature in the Great Earl's private apartments. The term "solar" was used during the Middle Ages to describe an upper chamber.*

**The Murder Hole** was designed for pouring boiling water or pitch on to the heads of attackers.

**Entrance**

**The basement**, with walls 3 m (10 ft) thick, was probably used for storage or as a stable.

**North Front**
*Bunratty Castle is unusual for the high arches on both the north and south sides of the keep. However, the first-floor entrance, designed to deter invaders, was typical of castles of the period.*

---

**STAR FEATURES**

★ **Great Hall**

★ **Main Guard**

★ **North Solar**

**VISITORS' CHECKLIST**

**Road map** B4. Bunratty, Co Clare.
061 360788. Shannon.
from Ennis, Limerick, Shannon.
**Castle & Folk Park** 9:30am–
5:30pm (Jun–Aug: 9am–
6:30pm) daily. Good Friday,
23–26 Dec. to
Folk Park. **Banquets** see p330.
www.shannonheritage.com

★ **Main Guard**
*Now used for medieval-style
banquets, this was the room where
Bunratty's soldiers ate, slept
and relaxed. Music
was played to them
from the Minstrels'
Gallery, and a gate
in one corner gave
instant access to
the dungeons.*

**Anteroom**

**The Robing Room**
was where the earls
put on their gowns
before an audience
in the Great Hall.
They also used it for
private interviews.

**South Solar**
*These guest apartments have
fine linenfold wood panelling,
a form of decoration popular
during the Tudor period. The
elaborate fan-vaulted ceiling
is partly a reconstruction.*

**A spiral
staircase** is
found in each
of the four
towers.

★ **Great Hall**
*This Tudor standard
was among the many
furnishings that Lord
Gort brought to the
castle. It stands in the
Great Hall, once the
banqueting hall and
audience chamber,
and still Bunratty's
grandest room.*

**BUNRATTY FOLK PARK**

A meticulous recreation of rural life in Ireland at the
turn of the century, this Folk Park began with the
reconstruction of a farmhouse which was saved during
the building of nearby Shannon Airport. It now consists
of a complete village, incorporating shops and a whole
range of domestic architecture from a labourer's cottage
to an elegant Georgian house. Other buildings include
a farmhouse typical of the Moher region in the Burren
(see p176) and a working corn mill. During the main
summer season, people in authentic costume wander
through the streets and demonstrate traditional crafts
and trades such as weaving and butter-making.

**Main street of Bunratty Folk Park village**

Typical thatched cottage in the village of Adare

# Adare ⑮

**Road map** B5. Co Limerick. 🚶 *1,000.*
🚉 ℹ️ *Heritage Centre, Main St
(061 396255).* ⭕ *Mar–Dec: daily.*

ADARE IS BILLED as Ireland's prettiest village. Cynics call it the prettiest "English" village since its manicured perfection is at odds with normal notions of national beauty. Originally a fief of the Fitzgeralds, the Earls of Kildare, Adare owes its present appearance more to the Earls of Dunraven, who restored the estate village in the 1820s and 1830s. The long, thin village is a picture of neat stonework and thatched roofs punctuated by picturesque ruins, all in a woodland setting.

The tourist office is at the new Heritage Centre, which includes a good exhibition on Adare's monastic history. Next

door is the **Trinitarian Priory**, founded by the Fitzgeralds in 1230 and over-restored by the first Earl of Dunraven; it is now a Catholic church and convent. Opposite, by a stone-arched bridge, is the Washing Pool, a restored wash-house site.

By the main bridge, on the Limerick road, is the **Augustinian Priory** which was founded by the Fitzgeralds in 1315. Also known as Black Abbey, this well-restored priory has a central tower, subtle carvings, delightful cloisters and a graceful sedilia – a carved triple seat. Just over the bridge, from where it is best viewed, is **Desmond Castle**, a 13th-century feudal castle set on the banks of the River Maigue.

Nearby stands the main gate to **Adare Manor**, a luxury hotel and golf course *(see p294)*. Within its 900 ha (365 acres) of parkland lie two evocative

ruins. The **St Nicholas Church** and **Chantry Chapel** date back to the 12th century; both are accessible by path. The graceful 15th-century **Franciscan Friary**, however, is surrounded by the golf course, though it can be seen clearly from the pathway.

In the heart of the village is the elegant Dunraven Arms Hotel *(see p294)* from where the local hunt rides to hounds. Some of the nearby cottages, originally built by the Earl of Dunraven in 1828 for his estate workers, have been converted into restaurants, including the cosy Inn-Between *(see p312)*.

# Lough Gur ⑯

**Road map** B5. Co Limerick. 🚉
**Visitors' Centre** 📞 *061 360788.*
⭕ *May–Sep: 10am–6pm daily.* 🎫 ♿

THIS STONE AGE settlement, 26 km (16 miles) south of Limerick, was extensively inhabited in 3000 BC. Today the horseshoe-shaped lough and surrounding hills enclose an intriguing if rather inscrutable archaeological park. All around Lough Gur are standing stones and burial mounds, including megalithic tombs. One of the most impressive sights is the 4,000-year-old **Great Stone Circle**, just outside the park, by the Limerick–Kilmallock road. Excavations in the 1970s unearthed rectangular, oval and rounded Stone Age huts with stone foundations. The

Colourfully painted shopfronts on Main Street in Adare

**Façade of Cashel Palace Hotel**

interpretive centre, which is housed in mock Stone Age huts on the site of the original settlement, offers a range of audiovisual displays, models of stone circles, burial chambers and tools and weapons.

As well as the various pre-historic sights scattered all over the Knockadoon Peninsula, there are two castle ruins from more recent times beside the lough – the 15th-century **Bourchier's Castle** and **Black Castle**, a 13th-century seat of the Earls of Desmond.

## Roscrea ⓱

**Road map** C4. Co Tipperary.
🚶 5,500. 🚌 🚆 ℹ️ *Heritage Centre, Castle St (0505 21850).*
🕐 *mid-Apr–Oct: daily.*

This monastic town on the banks of the River Bun-now has an interesting historic centre. The 13th-century Anglo-Norman **Roscrea Castle**, recently fully restored, consists of a gate tower, curtain walls and two corner towers. In the courtyard stands Damer House, a Queen Anne-style residence with a magnificent staircase and Georgian garden. Just over the river lies **St Cronan's Monastery** with a High Cross, Romanesque church gable and a truncated round tower. There are remains of a 15th-century **Franciscan Friary** on Abbey Street and nearby in St Cronan's churchyard is **Roscrea Pillar**, an enigmatic early Christian stone.

⚜️ **Roscrea Castle & Gardens**
Castle Street. 📞 *0505 21850.*
🕐 *mid-Apr–Oct: daily.* 📷

## Holy Cross Abbey ⓲

**Road map** C5. Thurles, Co Tipperary.
📞 *0504 43241.* 🚌 🚆 *to Thurles.*
🕐 *9am–8pm daily.*
📷 🅿️ ♿

Founded in 1169 by the Benedictines, Holy Cross was supposedly endowed with a splinter from the True Cross, hence its name. Now it has been completely re-stored, and the church is once again a popular place of worship and pilgrimage. Most of the present structure dates from the 15th century. It was built by the Cistercians, who took over the abbey in 1180. This gracious cruciform church, embellished with mullioned win-dows and sculpted pillars, is one of the finest examples of late Gothic architecture in Ireland.

The chancel has fine ribbed vaulting and, in the south wall, an exquisitely carved sedilia, which is rather oddly called "the tomb of the Good Woman's son". The abbey complex, set in charming gardens, also houses an old-fashioned pub.

**Crucifixion carving at Holy Cross Abbey**

## Cashel ⓳

**Road map** C5. Co Tipperary.
🚶 2,500. 🚌 ℹ️ *Heritage Centre, Main St (062 62511).*

The great attraction of the town is the magnificent medieval **Rock of Cashel** *(see pp188–9)*. Many people stay overnight to enjoy eerie floodlit views of the Rock. A private path leads to it from **Cashel Palace Hotel** *(see p294)*, an opulent Queen Anne residence that was once the Bishop's Palace. Nearby, the remnant of a 12th-century castle has been turned into Kearney Castle Hotel. In the evening you can sample traditional Irish culture at the **Brú Ború Heritage Centre**. Named after Brian Boru, the 10th-century king of Munster *(see pp32–3)*, the centre offers folk theatre, traditional music, banquets, and a craft shop.

At the foot of the Rock is the 13th-century **Dominican Friary**. This austere sandstone church has a fine west door, a 15th-century tower and lancet windows. On farmland outside Cashel lie the scant remains of **Hore Abbey**, a 13th-century Cistercian foundation. The abbey was largely remod-elled and a tower added in the 15th century, but the barrel-vaulted sacristy, the nave, choir and chapter house are all original.

🏛️ **Brú Ború Heritage Centre**
Cashel. 📞 *062 61122.* 🕐 *Jun–Sep: daily; Oct–May: Mon–Fri.* ♿
⛪ **Dominican Friary**
Dominic Street. ♿ *limited.*

**Ruins of Hore Abbey (1272) with the Rock of Cashel in the background**

# Rock of Cashel

THIS ROCKY STRONGHOLD, which rises dramatically out of the Tipperary plain, was a symbol of royal and priestly power for more than a millennium. From the 5th century it was the seat of the Kings of Munster, whose kingdom extended over much of southern Ireland. In 1101, they handed Cashel over to the Church, and it flourished as a religious centre until a siege by a Cromwellian army in 1647 culminated in the massacre of its 3,000 occupants. The cathedral was finally abandoned in the late 18th century. Two hundred years on, the Rock of Cashel is besieged by visitors. A good proportion of the medieval complex is still standing, and Cormac's Chapel is one of the most outstanding examples of Romanesque architecture in the country.

**★ St Patrick's Cross**
*The carving on the east face of this cross is said to be of St Patrick, who visited Cashel in 450. The cross is a copy of the original which stood here until 1982 and is now in the museum.*

**Hall of the Vicars' Choral**
*This hall was built in the 15th century for Cashel's most privileged choristers. The ceiling, a modern reconstruction based on medieval designs, features several decorative corbels including this painted angel.*

**Dormitory block**

**Entrance**

**The Museum**
in the undercroft contains a display of stone carvings, including the original St Patrick's Cross.

**Outer wall**

**Limestone rock**

**★ Cormac's Chapel**
*Superb Romanesque carving adorns this chapel – the jewel of Cashel. The tympanum over the north door shows a centaur in a helmet aiming his bow and arrow at a lion.*

## STAR FEATURES

★ Cormac's Chapel

★ St Patrick's Cross

★ Cathedral

**KEY**

☐ **12th Century**
  4 St Patrick's Cross (replica)
 12 Cormac's Chapel
 13 Round tower

☐ **13th Century**
  6 Cathedral porch
  7 Nave
  8 Crossing
  9 South transept
 10 Choir
 11 North transept

☐ **15th Century**
  1 Ticket office
  2 Hall of the Vicars' Choral (museum)
  3 Dormitory
  5 Castle

0 metres      50
0 yards       50

**VISITORS' CHECKLIST**

Road map C5. Cashel. 062 61437. to Thurles. to Cashel. mid-Jun–mid-Sep: 9am–7:30pm: daily; mid-Sep–mid-Mar: 9am–4:30pm; mid-Mar–mid-Jun: 9am–5:30pm. 24–28 Dec.

Round tower

Crossing

**The Rock**
*The 28-m (92-ft) round tower, the oldest and tallest building on the rock, enabled Cashel's inhabitants to scour the surrounding plain for potential attackers.*

**The Choir** contains the 17th-century tomb of Miler Magrath, who caused a scandal by being both a Protestant and Catholic archbishop at the same time.

Graveyard

**The O'Scully Monument**, an ornate memorial erected in 1870 by a local landowning family, was damaged during a storm in 1976.

**North Transept**
*Panels from three 16th-century tombs in the north transept are decorated with remarkably fresh and intricate carvings. This one, against the north wall, features a vine-leaf design and strange stylized beasts.*

★ **Cathedral**
*The roofless Gothic cathedral has thick walls riddled with hidden passages; in the north transept these are seen emerging at the base of the windows.*

## Athassel Priory ⑳

**Road map** C5. 8 km (5 miles) W of Cashel, Co Tipperary. 🚌 *to Tipperary.* 🕐 *daily.*

T HIS RUINED Augustinian priory is situated on the west bank of the River Suir. The tomb of William de Burgh, the Norman founder of the priory, lies in the church. Established in 1192, Athassel is believed to have been the largest medieval priory in Ireland until it burned down in 1447. The scattered monastic site conveys a tranquil atmosphere, from the gatehouse and church to the remains of the cloisters and chapter house. The church has a fine west doorway, nave and chancel walls, as well as a 15th-century central tower.

## Glen of Aherlow ㉑

**Road map** C5. Co Tipperary. 🚌 *to Bansha or Tipperary.* 🛈 *Coach Road Inn, on R663 8 km (5 miles) E of Galbally (062 56331).*

T HE LUSH VALLEY of the River Aherlow runs between the Galty Mountains and the wooded ridge of Slievenamuck. Bounded by the villages of **Galbally** and **Bansha**, the glen was historically an important pass between Limerick and Tipperary and a notorious hideout for outlaws.

Today there are opportunities for riding, cycling, rambling and fishing. Lowland walks

The ruins of Athassel Priory, on the banks of the River Suir

follow the trout-filled river along the valley floor. More adventurous walkers will be tempted by the Galty range, which offers more rugged hill-walking, past wooded foothills, mountain streams, tiny corrie lakes and splendid sandstone peaks.

## Cahir ㉒

**Road map** C5. Co Tipperary. 👥 2,100. 🚌 🚉 🛈 *May–Sep: Castle Street (052 41453).* 🚢 *Fri.*

O NCE A GARRISON and mill town, Cahir is today a busy market town. The publined Castle Street is the most appealing area. It leads to the Suir River, Cahir Castle and the well-signposted rural walk to the Swiss Cottage.

On the edge of town lies the ruined **Cahir Abbey**, a 13th-century Augustinian priory. Its fine windows are decorated with carved heads.

### ♣ Cahir Castle

Castle Street. 📞 *052 41011.* 🕐 *daily.* ● *24–30 Dec.* 🎦 🛝 🛗 *limited.*

Built on a rocky island in the River Suir, Cahir is one of the most formidable castles in Ireland and a popular film set. This well-preserved fortress dates from the 13th century but is inextricably linked to its later owners, the Butlers. A powerful family in Ireland since the Anglo-Norman invasion, they were considered trusty lieges of the English crown and were granted the Cahir barony in 1375. Under their command, the castle was renovated and extended throughout the 15th and 16th centuries. It remained in the Butler family until 1964.

The castle is divided into outer, middle and inner wards, with a barbican at the outer entrance. The inner ward is on the site of the original Norman castle; the foundations are 13th century, as are the curtain walls and keep. The restored interior includes the striking great hall, which dates largely from the 1840s, though two of the walls are original and the windows are 15th century. From the ramparts there are views over the river and millrace.

### ⚏ Swiss Cottage

Ardfinnan Road, Cahir. 📞 *052 41144.* 🕐 *May–Sep: daily; Mar–Apr & Oct– Nov: Tue–Sun.* 🎦 *obligatory.* 🛗
The Swiss Cottage is a superb example of a *cottage orné,* a rustic folly. It was designed for the Butlers by the Regency architect John Nash in 1810. Here, Lord and Lady Cahir played at bucolic bliss, enjoying picnics dressed as peasants. Fashion dictated a *cottage*

View across the unspoilt Glen of Aherlow

*orné* should blend in with the countryside and all designs should be drawn from nature with nothing matching, so the windows and sloping eaves are all of different sizes and design. The beautifully restored cottage contains a tea room, gracious music room and two bedrooms.

## Clonmel ㉓

**Road map** C5. Co Tipperary.
🏃 *17,000.* 🚉 🚌 🛈 *8 Sarsfield St (052 22960).*

SET ON THE RIVER SUIR and framed by the Comeragh Mountains, Clonmel is Tipperary's main town. This Anglo-Norman stronghold was a fief of the Desmonds and eventually of the Butlers. Its prosperity was founded on milling and brewing; attractive mills still line the quays. Today, Clonmel is a bustling, brash town with quirky architecture and lively nightlife.

The **Franciscan Friary** by the quays was remodelled in Early English style in Victorian times but retains a 15th-century tower and houses 16th-century Butler tomb effigies. Nearby is O'Connell Street, Clonmel's main shopping street, which is straddled by the West Gate, built in 1831. Visitors to **Hearn's**

**Clonmel's mock Tudor West Gate, spanning O'Connell Street**

**The Swiss Cottage at Cahir, beautifully restored to its original state**

**Hotel** on Parnell Street can see memorabilia of Charles Bianconi (1786–1875), including pictures of the horse-drawn coach service he established between Clonmel and Cahir. Eventually this developed into a nationwide passenger service.

## Carrick-on-Suir ㉔

**Road map** C5. Co Tipperary.
🏃 *5,500.* 🚉 🛈 *Heritage Centre (051 640200).*

THIS SLEEPY MARKET TOWN has a distinctly old-fashioned air. In the 15th century, it was a strategic site commanding access west to Clonmel and southeast to Waterford, but after Tudor times the town sank into oblivion. Apart from Ormond Castle, there are few specific sights. However, you can stroll by the old waterside warehouses or shop for Tipperary Crystal *(see p323).*

### ♠ Ormond Castle

Castle Park. 📞 *051 640787.* 🔾 *May–Oct: daily.* 🚫 ✅ 🛈 ♿ *limited.*

Although once a fortress, Ormond Castle is the finest surviving Tudor manor house in Ireland. It was built by the powerful Butler family, the Earls of Ormonde, who were given their title by the English crown in 1328. The castle has a gracious Elizabethan façade overlaying the medieval original; the battlemented towers on the south side sit oddly with the gabled façade and its mullioned and oriel windows.

The finest room is the Long Gallery, which has a stuccoed ceiling studded with heraldic crests, and two ornately carved fireplaces. The Elizabethan section was added by

Black Tom Butler, the 10th Earl of Ormonde, a loyal subject to Elizabeth Tudor. On his death, the Ormondes abandoned Carrick for Kilkenny *(see pp134–6).*

**Intricate wood carving on a four-poster bed at Ormond Castle**

**ENVIRONS:** In the churchyard at **Ahenny**, about 10 km (6 miles) north of Carrick, stand two magnificent High Crosses *(see p235).* Both are crowned by "caps" or "bishops' mitres" and have intricate cable, spiral and fret patterns.

At **Kilkieran**, 5 km (3 miles) north of Carrick, are three other interesting High Crosses, dating from the 9th century. The Plain Cross is unadorned but capped; the West Cross is profusely ornamented though weathered; the Long Shaft Cross has an odd design of stumpy arms on a long shaft.

# THE WEST OF IRELAND

MAYO · GALWAY · ROSCOMMON

THIS IS THE HEART OF CONNAUGHT, *Ireland's historic western province. The West lives up to its image as a traditional, rural, sparsely populated land, with windswept mountains and countryside speckled with low stone walls and peat bogs. Yet it also encompasses Galway, a fast-growing university town whose youthful population brings life to the medieval streets and snug pubs.*

The rugged Atlantic coastline of the West has been occupied for over 5,000 years. It is rich in prehistoric sites such as the land enclosures of Céide Fields and the ring forts on the Aran Islands. Evidence of the monastic period can be seen in the mysterious and beautiful remains at Kilmacduagh and Clonfert; and the region's religious associations still exert an influence, apparent in the pilgrimages to Knock and Croagh Patrick in County Mayo.

In medieval times, the city of Galway was an Anglo-Norman stronghold, surrounded by warring Gaelic clans. After the Cromwellian victories of the 1640s, many Irish were dispossessed of their fertile lands and dispatched "to hell or Connacht". Landlords made their mark in the 17th and 18th centuries, building impressive country houses at Clonalis, Strokestown Park and Westport. During the Great Famine, the West – especially County Mayo – suffered most from emigration, a trend that continues to this day. In spite of this, strong Gaelic traditions have survived in County Galway, the country's largest Gaeltacht *(see p221)*, where almost half the population speaks Irish as a first language.

The bracken browns and soft violets of Connemara in the west of Galway and the fertile farmland, extensive bogs and placid lakes of County Roscommon are in striking contrast to the magnificent cliff scenery of the remote islands off the coast. This region is often shrouded in a misty drizzle or else battered by Atlantic winds and accompanying heavy downpours.

Summer is a time for festivities: the Galway Races in July, traditional sailing ship races off Kinvarra in August and the Galway Oyster Festival in September are all lively events that attract a stream of visitors.

Swans by the quayside of the Claddagh area of Galway

◁ Typical Connemara landscape dominated by the peaks of the Twelve Bens

# Exploring the West of Ireland

GALWAY CITY, CLIFDEN AND WESTPORT make the best bases for exploring the region, with cosy pubs, good walks and access to the scenic islands. Connemara and the wilds of County Mayo attract nature lovers, while the islands of Achill, Aran, Clare and Inishbofin appeal to water-sports enthusiasts and ramblers. The lakes of County Roscommon are popular with anglers, and Lough Corrib and Lough Key offer relaxing cruises.

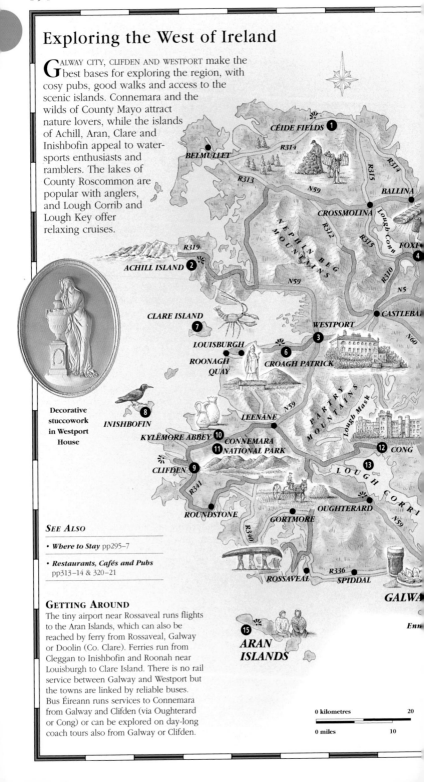

Decorative stuccowork in Westport House

## SEE ALSO

- *Where to Stay* pp295–7

- *Restaurants, Cafés and Pubs* pp313–14 & 320–21

## GETTING AROUND

The tiny airport near Rossaveal runs flights to the Aran Islands, which can also be reached by ferry from Rossaveal, Galway or Doolin (Co. Clare). Ferries run from Cleggan to Inishbofin and Roonah near Louisburgh to Clare Island. There is no rail service between Galway and Westport but the towns are linked by reliable buses. Bus Éireann runs services to Connemara from Galway and Clifden (via Oughterard or Cong) or can be explored on day-long coach tours also from Galway or Clifden.

0 kilometres      20

0 miles      10

**River valley at Delphi in northern Connemara**

## SIGHTS AT A GLANCE

Achill Island ❷
*Aran Islands pp206–7* ⓯
Boyle ㉕
Céide Fields ❶
Clare Island ❼
Clifden ❾
Clonalis House ㉓
Clonfert Cathedral ⓴
Cong ⓬
Connemara National Park ⓫
Croagh Patrick ❻
Foxford ❹
*Galway pp202–3* ⓮
Inishbofin ❽
Kilmacduagh ⓱
Kinvarra ⓰
Knock ❺
Kylemore Abbey ❿
Lough Corrib ⓭
Portumna ⓳
Roscommon ㉒
Strokestown Park House ㉔
Thoor Ballylee ⓲
Turoe Stone ㉑
Westport ❸

**Colourful shopfronts lining
Quay Street, Galway**

## KEY

| | |
|---|---|
| ▦ | Major road |
| ▦ | Minor road |
| ▦ | Scenic route |
| ～ | River |
| ☆ | Viewpoint |

**Bogwood centrepiece in Céide Fields interpretative centre**

## Céide Fields ❶

**Road map** B2. 8 km (5 miles) W of Ballycastle, Co Mayo. 📞 *096 43325.* 🚌 *from Ballycastle.* ⏰ *mid-Mar–Nov: daily.* 🅿️ 🎥 🍽 ♿ *ground floor.*

Surrounded by heather-clad moorlands and mountains along a bleak, dramatic stretch of north Mayo coastline is Europe's largest Stone Age land enclosure. Over 10 sq km (4 sq miles) were enclosed by walls to make fields suitable for growing wheat and barley, and grazing cattle. Remains of farm buildings indicate that it was an extensive community. The fields were slowly buried below the creeping bog formation, where they have been preserved for 5,000 years.

Part of the bog has been cut away to reveal the collapsed stone walls of the ancient fields. The remains are simple rather than spectacular, but excellent guides help visitors to find and recognize key features. Stone Age pottery and a primitive plough have been found in recent excavations. The striking, pyramid-shaped interpretative centre has a viewing platform overlooking the site, audiovisual presentations and displays on local geology and botany.

**ENVIRONS:** Scattered around the wilderness of the spectacular north Mayo coast from Ballina to the end of the Mullet peninsula is a series of sculptures forming the **North Mayo Sculpture Trail**. Created by 12 sculptors from three continents, the 15 works, often on a huge scale, are made from earth, stone and other natural materials; additional sculptures are planned. They aim to highlight the coast's grandeur and enduring nature.

## Achill Island ❷

**Road map** A3. Co Mayo. 🚌 *from Westport.* 🛈 *098 47353.* 🌐 *www.achilltourism.com*

Ireland's largest island, 22 km (13.5 miles) long and 19 km (12 miles) wide, is reached by a road bridge that can be raised for boats to pass through. Achill offers moorland, mountains, rugged cliffs and long beaches, and is a popular spot for angling and water sports.

For motorists, the best introduction is the **Atlantic Coast Drive**, a circular, signposted route from Achill Sound, by the bridge. The road goes to the island's southern tip, then north around the rest of Achill. Between Doeega and Keel in the southwest, run the dramatic Minaun Cliffs and Cathedral Rocks. In the north is Slievemore, a mountain overlooking the village of Slievemore, which was abandoned during the Great Famine (*see p211*). Sharks can be spotted off Keem Bay in the west.

## Westport ❸

**Road map** B3. Co Mayo. 🏠 *4,700.* 🚉 🚌 🛈 *James Street (098 25711).* 🗓 *Thu.* 🌐 *www.visitmayo.com*

**The *Angel of Welcome* above the marble staircase at Westport House**

Westport is a neat landlord town and has a bustling, prosperous air. In the 1770s, architect James Wyatt laid out the wide, tree-lined streets, including the North and South Mall on either side of Carrowbeg River. The town traded in yarn, cloth, beer and slate, but industrialization and the Great Famine (*see p211*) brought decline until the 1950s when new industry and visitors were attracted to the area.

Beyond the South Mall is Bridge Street, lined with cafés and pubs; the most appealing is Matt Molloy's (*see p320*), named after and owned by the flautist from The Chieftains.

### 🏛 Westport House
Off Louisburgh Rd. 📞 *098 27766.* ⏰ *Easter weekend; May: Sun only; Jun–Sep: daily.* 🅿️ 🎥 🍽

Just west of the town is the Carrowbeg estuary and Clew Bay. At the head of the bay

**The deserted village of Slievemore on Achill Island**

**Statue of St Patrick at the foot of Croagh Patrick, looking out to Clew Bay**

stands Westport House, the seat of the Earls of Altamont, descendants of the Browne family, who were Tudor settlers. The town of Westport itself was started in the 1750s by John Browne, first Lord Altamont, to complement the house. Designed in 1732 by Richard Castle, and completed by James Wyatt in 1778, the limestone mansion stands on the site of an O'Malley castle. Its imposing interior includes a sweeping marble staircase and an elegant James Wyatt dining room and is adorned with family portraits, antique Waterford chandeliers and 18th-century Chinese wallpaper. The estate includes a boating lake, miniature railway, small zoo, museum, amusement arcade and several shops.

**Bog oak and silver bowl from Westport House**

## Foxford ❹

Road map B3. Co Mayo. 1,000. from Galway. Westport (098 25711).

THIS TRANQUIL market town is known for good angling in nearby Lough Conn and for its woven rugs and tweeds. In the town centre is **Foxford Woollen Mills**, founded in 1892 by an Irish nun, Mother Arsenius (originally named Agnes). The thriving mill now supplies top fashion houses. An audiovisual tour traces the mill's history, and visitors can see craftspeople at work.

### Foxford Woollen Mills and Visitor Centre
St Joseph's Place. 094 56756. daily. Good Fri, 24–26 Dec. Exhibition Centre.

## Knock ❺

Road map B3. Co Mayo. 575. 15 km (9 miles) N of Knock. May–Sep: Knock (094 88193).

IN 1879, two local women saw an apparition of the Virgin, St Joseph and St John the Evangelist by the gable of the Church of St John the Baptist. It was witnessed by 13 more onlookers and validated by the Catholic Church amid claims of miracle cures. Every year, a million and a half believers make the pilgrimage to the shrine, including Pope John Paul II in 1979 and Mother Teresa in 1993. Its focal point is the gable where the apparition was seen, which is now covered over to form a chapel. Nearby is the Basilica of Our Lady, a modern basilica and Marian

**Bottles of holy water for sale at the shrine in Knock**

shrine. **Knock Folk Museum**, beside the basilica, portrays life in 19th-century rural Ireland with reconstructions of a cottage and schoolroom. An Apparition section covers the background to the miracle.

### Knock Shrine and Folk Museum
094 88100. May–Oct: daily; Nov–Apr: by appt.

## Croagh Patrick ❻

Road map B3. Murrisk, Co Mayo. from Westport. Murrisk (098 45384).

IRELAND'S holy mountain, named after the national saint (see p273), is one of Mayo's best-known landmarks. From the bottom it seems cone-shaped, an impression dispelled by climbing to its flat peak. This quartzite, scree-clad mountain has a history of pagan worship from 3000 BC. However, in AD 441, St Patrick is said to have spent 40 days on the mountain fasting and praying for the Irish.

Since then, penitents, often barefoot, have made the pilgrimage to the summit in his honour, especially on Reek or Garland Sunday, the last in July. From the start of the trail at Campbell's Pub in Murrisk, where there is huge statue of the saint, it is a two-hour climb to the top, at 765 m (2,510 ft). Mass is celebrated on the peak in a modern chapel. There are panoramic views over Clew Bay and a visitor centre with amenities for exhausted hikers.

# Clare Island 7

**Road map** A3. Co Mayo. 👥 *165.* 🚤
*from Roonagh Quay, 6.5 km (4 miles)*
*W of Louisburgh* ☎ *098 25045 &*
*28288.* ☎ *098 25711.* ℹ *Westport.*

C LARE ISLAND, set in Clew
Bay, is dominated by two
hills, and a square 15th-
century castle commands the
headland and harbour. In the
16th century the island was
the stronghold of Grace
O'Malley, pirate queen and
patriot, who held sway over
the western coast. Although,
according to Tudor state
papers, she was received at
Queen Elizabeth I's court, she
stood out against English rule
until her death in her seventies
in 1603. She is buried here in
a tiny Cistercian abbey decorated with medieval murals
and inscribed with her motto:
"Invincible on land and sea."
The island is dotted with Iron
Age huts and field systems as
well as promontory forts and
Bronze Age cooking sites *(see
p162)*. Clare is rich in bog
flora and fauna, making it
popular with walkers. Animal
lovers come to see the seals,
dolphins, falcons and otters.

**ENVIRONS:** The mainland coastal
village of **Louisburgh** offers
rugged Atlantic landscape,

**The ferry to Inishbofin leaving Cleggan Harbour**

sheltered coves and sea
angling. The **Granuaile
Centre** tells the story of Grace
O'Malley (*Granuaile* in Gaelic)
and has displays on Mayo
folklore and archaeology.

🏛 **Granuaile Centre**
St Catherine's Church, Louisburgh.
☎ *098 66195.* ◯ *May–Sep: daily.*
📷 ♿

# Inishbofin 8

**Road map** A3. Co Galway. 👥 *200.*
🚤 *from Cleggan.* ℹ *Clifden.*

T HE NAME Inishbofin means
"island of the white cow".
This mysterious, often mist-
swathed island was chosen
for its remoteness by the
exiled 7th-century St Colman,
English Abbot of Lindisfarne.
On the site of his original
monastery is a late medieval
church, graveyard and holy
well. At the sheltered harbour

entrance lies a ruined castle,
occupied in the 16th century
by Spanish pirate Don Bosco
in alliance with Grace O'Malley.
In 1653 it was captured by
Cromwellian forces and used
as a prison for Catholic priests.
Inishbofin was later owned
by a succession of absentee
landlords and now survives
on farming and lobster-fishing.
Surrounded by reefs and
islets, the island's landscape is
characterized by stone walls,
small abandoned cottages,
reed-fringed lakes and hay
meadows, where the corn-
crake *(see p16)* can be seen,
or heard. Inishbofin's beaches
offer bracing walks.

# Clifden 9

**Road map** A3. Co Galway. 👥 *920.*
🚌 ℹ *Mar–Nov: Galway Road (095
21163).* 🛒 *Tue & Fri.*

F RAMED by the grandeur of
the Twelve Bens mountain
range and with a striking
skyline dominated by two
church spires, this early 19th-
century market town passes
for the capital of the Connemara region and is a good
base for exploring. Clifden
was founded in 1812 by John
d'Arcy, a local landowner and
High Sheriff of Galway, to
create a pocket of respect-
ability within the lawlessness
of Connemara. The family
eventually went bankrupt
trying to bring prosperity and
order to the town. The Protestant church contains a copy
of the Cross of Cong *(see p65)*.
Today craft shops have
taken over much of the town.
In the centre is the Square, a
place for lively pubs such as
EJ Kings *(see p320)*. Nearby is
O'Grady's Seafood Restaurant
*(see p313)*, one of the finest
in Galway. Connemara is
noted for its *sean-nos*

**Clifden against a backdrop of the Twelve Bens mountains**

## CONNEMARA

This wild region in the west of Galway encompasses bogs, mountains and a rugged coastline. Major sights include the Connemara National Park and Kylemore Abbey *(see p200)*. For those without a car, coach tours are available from Galway and Clifden *(see p360)*.

**Cottage in Connemara**

### KEY

| | |
|---|---|
| ▬▬ | Major road |
| ═══ | Regional road |
| ══ | Minor road |
| ── | National Park boundary |
| ⛴ | Ferry to Inishbofin |
| ℹ | Tourist information |
| ☼ | Viewpoint |

0 kilometres     10
0 miles     5

(unaccompanied singing), but in Clifden, general traditional music is more common.

Jutting out into **Clifden Bay** is a sand spit and beach, signposted from Clifden Square. South of Clifden, at the start of the Roundstone Road, is Owenglen Cascade where, in May, salmon leap on their way to spawn upstream.

**ENVIRONS:** The **Sky Road** is an 11-km (7-mile) circular route with stunning ocean views. The road goes northwest from Clifden and passes desolate scenery and the narrow inlet of Clifden Bay. Clifden Castle, John d'Arcy's Gothic Revival ruin, lies just off the Sky Road, as do several beaches.

The coastal road north from Clifden to **Cleggan**, via Claddaghduff, is spectacular, passing former smuggling coves. Cleggan, an attractive fishing village, nestles into the head of Cleggan Bay. From here boats leave for Inishbofin and Inishturk. **Cleggan Hill** has a ruined Napoleonic Martello tower at the top and a megalithic tomb at the foot.

To the south of Clifden, the coastal route to Roundstone skirts a mass of bogland pitted with tiny lakes. The **Alcock and Brown Memorial** overlooks the bog landing site of the first transatlantic flight made by Alcock and Brown in 1919. Nearby is Marconi's wireless station, which exchanged the first transatlantic radio messages with Nova Scotia in 1907. The **Ballyconneely** area has craggy islands and the beautiful **Coral Strand Beach**. The village of **Roundstone** is best seen during the summer regatta of traditional Galway hookers *(see p203)*.

A short drive to the east of Clifden is **Dan O'Hara's Homestead**. In a wild, rocky setting, this organic farm recreates the tough conditions of life in Connemara before the 1840s. There is an audio visual display on the history of Connemara.

🏛 **Dan O'Hara's Homestead**
Heritage Centre, Lettershea, off N59.
📞 *095 21246.* ⏰ *Apr–end Oct: daily.*
♿ 🅿 📷 ♿
🆆 www.connemaraheritage.com

**View of the coast from the Sky Road**

**The imposing Kylemore Abbey on the shores of Kylemore Lough**

# Kylemore Abbey ⑩

**Road map** A3. Connemara, Co Galway. 🕿 095 41146. 🚌 from Galway and Clifden. 🔘 daily. ⚫ Christmas & Good Fri. **Walled garden** 🔘 Easter–Oct. 🎫 🍴 🎁 ♿ limited.

SHELTERED BY THE SLOPES of the Twelve Bens, this lakeside castle is a romantic, battlemented Gothic Revival fantasy. It was built as a present for his wife by Mitchell Henry (1826–1911), who was a Manchester tycoon and later Galway MP. The Henrys also purchased a huge area of moorland, drained the boggy hillside and planted thousands of trees as a windbreak for their new orchards and exotic walled gardens. After the sudden deaths of his wife and daughter, Henry left Kylemore and the castle was sold.

It became an abbey when Benedictine nuns, fleeing from Ypres in Belgium during World War I, sought refuge here. The nuns now run the abbey as a select girls' boarding school. Visitors are restricted to the grounds, restaurant and craft shop. The cream earthenware pottery is painted with a fuchsia motif.

There is also a 2.5 ha (6-acre) restored Victorian walled garden in the abbey grounds, featuring the longest double herbaceous borders in Ireland, a nuttery and a meandering stream-side walk.

# Connemara National Park ⑪

**Road map** A3. Letterfrack, Connemara, Co Galway. 🕿 095 41054. **Visitors' Centre** 🔘 Mar–Oct: daily. 🎫 ♿ ▢

A COMBINATION of bogland, lakes and mountains makes up this National Park in the heart of Connemara. Within its more than 2,000 ha (5,000 acres) are four of the Twelve Bens, including Benbaun, the highest mountain in the range at 730 m (2,400 ft), and the peak of Diamond Hill. At the centre is the valley of Glanmore with the Polladirk River flowing through it.

Visitors come for some of the most spectacular landscape in the region and to glimpse the famous Connemara ponies.

Part of the land originally belonged to the Kylemore Abbey estate. In 1980 it became a National Park. There are traces of the land's previous uses all over the park: megalithic tombs, up to 4,000 years old, can be seen as well as old ridges marking former grazing areas and arable fields.

The park is open all year, while the Visitors' Centre near the entrance, just outside Letterfrack, is open only from March to October. It features displays on how the landscape developed and was used and on local flora and fauna. There is also an audiovisual theatre and an indoor picnic area. Two signposted walks start from the Visitors' Centre. In summer there are guided walks, some led by botanists, and various children's activities. Climbing the Twelve Bens should be attempted only by experienced walkers equipped for all weather conditions.

## CONNEMARA WILDLIFE

The blanket bogs and moorlands of Connemara are a botanist's paradise, especially for unusual bog and heathland plants. Birdlife is also varied with hooded crows, which can be recognized by their grey and black plumage, stonechats, peregrines and merlins – the smallest falcons in the British Isles. Red deer have been successfully reintroduced into the area and a herd can be seen in the National Park. Badgers, foxes, stoats and otters may also be spotted, as well as grey seals along the rocky coast.

*The merlin nests in old clumps of heather and feeds mainly on small birds.*

*St Dabeoc's heath, a pretty heather, grows nowhere else in Ireland or Great Britain.*

# Cong

**Road map** B3. Co Mayo. 🏨 *350.*
🚌 🛈 *Mar–Oct (092 46542).*

THIS PICTURESQUE VILLAGE lies on the shores of Lough Corrib, just within County Mayo. Cong means isthmus – the village lies on the strip of land between Lough Corrib and Lough Mask. During the 1840s, as a famine relief project, a canal was built linking the two lakes, but the water drained through the porous limestone bed. Stone bridges and stone-clad locks are still in place along the dry canal.

**Cong Abbey** lies close to the main street. The Augustinian abbey was founded in the early 12th century by Turlough O'Connor, King of Connaught and High King of Ireland, on the site of a 6th-century monastery established by St Fechin. The abbey has doorways in a style transitional between Romanesque and Gothic, stone carvings and restored cloisters. The Cross of Cong, an ornate processional cross intended for the abbey, is now in Dublin's National Museum *(see pp64–5).* The most fascinating remains are the Gothic chapter house, stone bridges and the monks' fishing-house overhanging the river – the monks devised a system so that a bell rang in the kitchen when a fish took the bait.

**Carved 12th-century doorway of Cong Abbey**

Just south of Cong is **Ashford Castle**, rebuilt in Gothic Revival style in 1870 by Lord Ardilaun of the Guinness family. One of Ireland's best hotels *(see p284),* its grounds can be visited by boat from Galway and Oughterard. Cong was the setting for *The Quiet Man,* the 1950s' film starring John Wayne. "Quiet Man" tours cover locations near the castle.

## Lough Corrib ⑬

**Road map** B3. Co Galway. 🚌 *from Galway and Cong.* 🚢 *from Oughterard and Wood Quay, Galway.* 🛈 *Oughterard (091 552808).*

AN ANGLER'S PARADISE, Lough Corrib offers the chance to fish with local fishermen for brown trout, salmon, pike, perch and eels. Despite its proximity to Galway, the lake is a haven of tranquillity, dotted with uninhabited islands and framed by meadows, reedbeds and wooded shores. The waterside is home to swans and coots. On **Inchagoill**, one of the largest islands, stand the ruins of an early Christian monastic settlement and a Romanesque church.

The lake's atmosphere is best appreciated on a cruise. From Galway, the standard short cruise winds through the marshes to the site of an Iron Age fort, limestone quarries and the battlemented Menlo Castle. Longer cruises continue to Cong or include picnics on the islands.

**ENVIRONS:** On the banks of Lough Corrib, **Oughterard** is known as "the gateway to Connemara". The village has craft shops, thatched cottages and friendly pubs. It is also an important centre for golf, angling, hiking and pony trekking. Other country pursuits include riverside walks, a stroll to a waterfall west of the village and cycle rides.

About 4 km (2.5 miles) southeast of Oughterard (off the N59) is **Aughnanure Castle**. This well-restored six-storey tower house clings to a rocky island on the River Drimneen. The present castle, built by the O'Flaherty clan, is on the site of one dating from 1256. The clan controlled West Connaught from Lough Corrib to Galway and the coast in the 13th to 16th centuries. From this castle the feuding O'Flaherty chieftains held out against the British in the 16th century. In 1545 Donal O'Flaherty married the pirate Grace O'Malley *(see p198).* The tower house has an unusual double bawn *(see p18)* and a murder hole from which missiles could be dropped on invaders.

**View over Lough Corrib from the shore northwest of Oughterard**

⚓ **Aughnanure Castle**
Oughterard. 📞 *091 552214.*
🕑 *mid-Jun–mid-Sep: daily.* 🚫
🚻 *limited.*

***Connemara ponies** roam semi-wild and are fabled to be from Arab stock that came ashore from Spanish Armada wrecks.*

***Fuchsias** grow profusely in the hedgerows of Connemara, thriving in the mild climate.*

# Galway ⑭

Sign with Claddagh ring design

GALWAY IS BOTH THE CENTRE for the Irish-speaking regions in the West and a lively university city. Under the Anglo-Normans, it flourished as a trading post. In 1396 it gained a Royal Charter and, for the next two centuries, was controlled by 14 merchant families, or "tribes". The city prospered under English influence, but this allegiance to the Crown cost Galway dear when, in 1652, Cromwell's forces wreaked havoc. After the Battle of the Boyne *(see p236)*, Galway fell into decline, unable to compete with east-coast trade. In recent years, as a developing centre for high-tech industry, the city's profile has been revived.

Inside The Quays seafood restaurant and pub

Houses on the banks of the Corrib

## Exploring Galway

The centre of the city lies on the banks of the River Corrib, which flows down from Lough Corrib *(see p201)* widening out as it reaches Galway Bay. Urban renewal since the 1970s has led to extensive restoration of the narrow, winding streets of this once-walled city. Due to its compact size, Galway is easy to explore on

foot, and a leisurely pace provides plenty of opportunity to stop off at its shops, pubs and historic sights.

## Eyre Square

The square encloses a pleasant park lined with imposing, mainly 19th-century, buildings. On the northwest of the square is the **Browne Doorway**, a 17th-century entrance from a mansion in Abbeygate Street Lower. Beside it are two cannons from the Crimean War and a fountain adorned with a sculpture of a Galway hooker boat. The **Eyre Square Centre**, overlooking the park, is a modern shopping mall built to incorporate sections of the historic city walls. Walkways link Shoemakers and Penrice towers, two of the wall towers that used to ring the city in the 17th century.

Lynch family crest on Lynch's Castle

## Latin Quarter

From Eyre Square, William Street and Shop Street are the main routes into the bustling "Latin Quarter". On the corner of Abbeygate Street Upper and Shop Street stands **Lynch's Castle**, now a bank, but still the grandest 16th-century town house in Galway. It was owned by the Lynch family, one of the 14 "tribes".

A side street leads to the **Collegiate Church of St Nicholas**, Galway's finest medieval building. The church, founded in 1320, was extended in the 15th and 16th centuries, but then damaged by the Cromwellians, who used it to stable horses. The west porch is from the 15th century and there are some finely carved gargoyles under the parapet.

Quay Street is lined with restaurants and pubs, including **The Quays** *(see p320)*. Ti Neachtain is a town house which belonged to "Humanity Dick", an 18th-century MP who promoted laws against cruelty to animals. Today, it too is a restaurant and pub *(see p320)*. Nearby are the Taibhdhearc and Druid theatres *(see p328)*.

## North Galway

The **Cathedral of St Nicholas** (1965), made from local limestone and Connemara marble, stands on the west bank. From here you can see Wood Quay, where Lough Corrib cruises start *(see p201)*. **University College Galway**, further west,

Outside dining at one of the cosmopolitan cafés in Shop Street

## GALWAY HOOKERS

Galway's traditional wooden sailing boats, featured on the city's coat of arms, were known as *pucans* and *gleotogs* – hookers in English. They have broad black hulls, thick masts and white or rust-coloured sails. Once common in the Claddagh district, they were also used along the Atlantic coast to ferry peat, cattle and beer. Hookers can be seen in action at the Cruinniú na mBád festival in Kinvarra *(see p204)*.

**Small Galway hooker sailing by the old quays and Spanish Arch**

is a sprawling campus with a 1849 Gothic Revival quad. Salmon Weir Bridge links the two banks. Shoals of salmon rest under the bridge on their way upstream to spawn.

### The Old Quays

The **Spanish Arch**, where the river opens out, was built in 1584 to protect the harbour, which was then outside the city walls. Here, Spanish traders unloaded their ships. The old quays are a tranquil spot for a stroll down the Long Walk to the docks.

### The Claddagh

Beyond the Spanish Arch, on the west bank of the Corrib, lies the Claddagh. The name comes from *An Cladach*, meaning "flat, stony shore". From medieval times, this fiercely independent fishing community beyond the city walls was governed by a "king" or "mayor", the last of whom died in 1954. The only remnants of this once close-knit, Gaelic-speaking community

are friendly pubs and Claddagh rings, betrothal rings traditionally handed down from mother to daughter *(see p326)*.

**ENVIRONS:** Just west of the city is **Salthill**, Galway's seaside resort. The beaches at Palmer's Rock and Grattan Road are particularly popular with families in summer. A bracing walk along the promenade is still a Galway tradition.

**Spanish Arch on the site of the former docks**

## GALWAY CITY CENTRE

Browne Doorway ④
Cathedral of
  St Nicholas ①
The Claddagh ⑦
Collegiate Church of
  St Nicholas ②
Lynch's Castle ③
The Quays ⑤
Spanish Arch ⑥

### KEY

🚆 Railway station

🚌 Coach station

P Parking

⊔⊔ Weir

0 metres          200

0 yards          200

**Mural in the centre of Kinvarra depicting a shopfront**

# Aran Islands 🕔

*See pp206–7.*

# Kinvarra 🕖

**Road map** B4. Co Galway. 🏠 *550.*
🚌 ℹ️ *Galway (091 563081).*

O NE of the most charming
fishing villages on Galway
Bay, Kinvarra's appeal lies in
its sheltered, seaweed-clad
harbour and traditional seafaring atmosphere. From medieval times, its fortunes were
closely linked to Kilmacduagh,
the powerful monastery and
bishopric upon which the
village depended.

The pier is bordered by a
row of fishermen's cottages.
Kinvarra remains a popular
port of call for sailors
of traditional Galway
hookers *(see p203)*
and is known for
the Cruinniú na
mBád (gathering
of the boats)
festival in August.
Rambles include
historical and
nature trails.
Bird-watchers
may spot teal,
curlews and
oystercatchers
by the shore.

**ENVIRONS:** North of Kinvarra,
on a promontory on the shore
of Galway Bay, lies **Dunguaire
Castle**. It is perched just
beyond some quaint thatched
cottages and a stone bridge.
The castle is named after the
7th-century King Guaire of
Connaught, whose court here
was renowned as the haunt
of bards and balladeers. Although the medieval earthworks survive, the present
castle was built in the 16th
century, a quintessential
tower house *(see p18)* with
sophisticated machicolations.
The banqueting hall is still
used for "medieval banquets"
with Celtic harp music and
the recital of Irish poetry.

⚓ **Dunguaire Castle**
📞 *061 360788.* 🕐 *May–Oct: daily.* 📷
📁 💻 🌐 www.shannonheritage.com

# Kilmacduagh 🕗

**Road map** B4. Outside Gort on
Corofin Rd, Co Galway. 🚌 *to Gort.*
🕐 *daily.*

T HIS MONASTIC SETTLEMENT is
in a remote location on
the borders of Counties Clare
and Galway, roughly 5 km
(3 miles) southwest of Gort.
The sense of isolation is
accentuated by the stony

moonscape of the Burren to
the west *(see pp178–80)*. Reputedly founded by St Colman
MacDuagh in the early 7th
century, Kilmacduagh owes
more to the monastic revival
which led to rebuilding from
the 11th century onwards.

The centrepiece of the extensive site is a large, slightly
leaning 11th- or 12th-century
round tower and a roofless
church, known as the cathedral
or Teampall. The cathedral is
a pre-Norman structure, which
was later remodelled in Gothic
style, with flamboyant tracery
and fine tomb carvings. In the
surrounding fields lie the
remains of several other
churches that once depended
on the monastery. To the
northeast of the Teampall is
the late medieval Glebe or
Abbot's House, a variant of a
14th- or 15th-century tower
house *(see p18)*.

# Thoor Ballylee 🕘

**Road map** B4. Gort, Co Galway.
📞 *091 631436.* 🚌 *to Gort.* 🕐
*May–Sep: daily.* 📷 📁 ♿ *limited.*

F OR MUCH of the 1920s, this
beguiling tower house was
a summer home to the poet
WB Yeats *(see pp20–21)*. Yeats
was a regular visitor to nearby
Coole Park, the home of his
friend Lady Gregory (1852–
1932), who was a cofounder
of the Abbey Theatre *(see p86)*.

On one visit Yeats came
upon Ballylee Castle, a 14th-
century de Burgo tower
adjoining a cosy cottage with
a walled garden and stream.
In 1902, both the tower and
the cottage became part of
the Gregory estate and Yeats
bought them in 1916. From
1919 onwards, his family
divided their time between

**Round tower and cathedral, the most impressive monastic remains at Kilmacduagh**

Dublin and their Galway tower. Yeats used the name Thoor Ballylee as the address, using the Irish word for tower to "keep people from suspecting us of modern gothic and a deer park". His collection, *The Tower* (1928), includes several poems inspired by Thoor Ballylee.

Today, the audiovisual tour includes readings from Yeats's poetry, but the charm of a visit lies in the tower itself, with its spiral stone steps and views over forest and farmland.

**ENVIRONS:** Just to the north of Gort is **Coole Park**, once the home of Lady Gregory. Although the house was demolished in the 1950s, the estate farm has been restored and the fine gardens survive. In particular, there is the "autograph tree", a spreading copper beech carved with the initials of George Bernard Shaw, JM Synge *(see pp20–21)*, Jack Yeats *(see p68)* and other famous visitors. In the farm buildings is an audiovisual display. The emphasis of the visitors' centre is on natural history: it is the start of two signposted walks, one around the gardens and the other through beech, hazel, birch and ash woodland to Coole Lake.

### ⚘ Coole Park
3 km (2 miles) NE of Gort. **☎** 091 631804. **Visitors' centre** ☐ mid-Apr–mid-Jun: Tue–Sun; mid-Jun–Sep: daily; park open all year. ⚹ ▣ ⚹ limited.

**Thoor Ballylee tower house, the summer home of WB Yeats**

**Gentle hills and woodland by Coole Lake in Coole Park**

## Portumna ⑲

**Road map** C4. Co Galway. ⚹ 1,200. ▣ ▮ *Galway (091 563081).* ⚹ *Fri.*

PORTUMNA is a historic market town with scattered sights, many of which are newly restored. Situated on Lough Derg, it is a convenient base for cruising the River Shannon *(see p177)* and has a modern marina. **Portumna Castle**, built in the early 17th century, was the main seat of the de Burgo family. Now partially restored, it has a symmetrical façade and some elaborate interior stonework. The façade surveys formal gardens. Near the castle is **Portumna Priory**. Most of the remains date from around 1414 when the priory was founded by the Dominicans, but traces can also be found of the Cistercian abbey that was previously on the site. The large de Burgo estate to the west of the town now forms **Portumna Forest Park**, with picnic sites and signposted woodland trails leading to Lough Derg.

## Clonfert Cathedral ⑳

**Road map** C4. Clonfert, Co Galway. ☐ *daily.* ⚹

SITUATED near a bleak stretch of the Shannon bordering the boglands of the Midlands, Clonfert is one of the jewels of Irish-Romanesque architecture.

**Human heads carved on the tympanum at Clonfert Cathedral**

The tiny cathedral occupies the site of a monastery, which was founded by St Brendan in AD 563, and is believed to be the burial place of the saint.

Although a great scholar and enthusiastic founder of monasteries, St Brendan is best known as the "great navigator". His journeys are recounted in *Navigatio Sancti Brendani*, written in about 1050, which survives in medieval manuscripts in several languages including Flemish, Norse and French. The account seems to describe a voyage to Wales, the Orkneys, Iceland and conceivably the east coast of North America. His voyage and his boat *(see p182)*, have been recreated by modern explorers in an attempt to prove that St Brendan may have preceded Columbus by about 900 years.

The highlight of Clonfert is its intricately sculpted sandstone doorway. The round arch above the door is decorated with animal and human heads, geometrical shapes, foliage and symbolic motifs. The carvings on the triangular tympanum above the arch are of strange human heads. In the chancel, the 13th-century east windows are fine examples of late Irish-Romanesque art. The 15th-century chancel arch is adorned with sculptures of angels and a mermaid. Although Clonfert was built over several centuries and altered in the 17th century, the church has a profound sense of unity.

# Aran Islands ⑮

**Jaunting car on Inishmore**

INISHMORE, INISHMAAN and Inisheer, the three Aran Islands, are formed from a limestone ridge. The largest, Inishmore, is 13 km (8 miles) long and 3 km (2 miles) wide. The attractions of these islands include the austere landscape crisscrossed with dry-stone walls, stunning coastal views and several large prehistoric stone forts. In the 5th century, St Enda brought Christianity to the islands, starting a long monastic tradition. Protected for centuries by their isolated position, the islands today are a bastion of traditional Irish culture. Farming, fishing and tourism are the main occupations of the islanders.

**Looking over the cliff edge at Dún Aonghasa**

**Clochán na Carraige** is a large, well-preserved beehive hut *(see p19)*, probably built by early Christian settlers on the islands.

The Seven Churches
(Na Seacht dTeampaill)

Clochán na Carraige

Dún Eoghanachta

**Dún Eoghanachta** is a 1st-century BC circular stone fort with a single wall terraced on the inside.

Dun Aengus
(Dún Aonghasa)

KILMURVY
(Cill Mhuirbhig

**Na Seacht dTeampaill**
*The so-called Seven Churches make up a monastic settlement dedicated to St Brecan. Built between the 9th and 15th centuries, some are probably domestic buildings.*

**★ Dún Aonghasa**
*This Iron or Bronze Age promontory fort (see p18), has four concentric stone walls. It is also protected by a chevaux de frise, a ring of razor-sharp, pointed stone stakes.*

## ARAN TRADITIONS

**Colourful Aran costume**

The islands are famous for their distinctive knitwear *(see p324)* and for the traditional Aran costume that is still worn: for women this consists of a red flannel skirt and crocheted shawl; for men it includes a sleeveless tweed jacket and a colourful knitted belt. From time to time you also see a *currach* or low rowing boat, the principal form of transport for centuries. Land-making, the ancient and arduous process of creating soil by covering bare rock with sand and seaweed, continues to this day.

***Currach* made from canvas coated in tar**

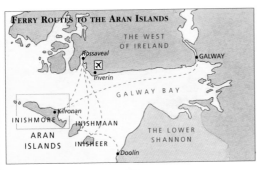

## FERRY ROUTES TO THE ARAN ISLANDS

THE WEST OF IRELAND

Rossaveal

Inverin

GALWAY

GALWAY BAY

Kilronan

INISHMORE

INISHMAAN

ARAN ISLANDS

INISHEER

THE LOWER SHANNON

Doolin

## VISITORS' CHECKLIST

**Road map** A4, B4. Co Galway.
🏠 1,500. ✈ *from Connemara Airport, Inverin (091 593034).*
⛴ *from Rossaveal:* **Island Ferries** (091 561767), **Inis Mor Ferries** (091 566535); *from Galway:* **O'Brien Shipping** (091 567676); *from Doolin:* **Doolin Ferry Company** *(from Easter: 065 74455, 091 567676). Ferries sail throughout the year; some go to all three main islands. Phone for details. Cars cannot be taken to the islands. From Kilronan, you can hire bicylcles and jaunting cars, or go on minibus tours (099 61169).* ℹ️ *Kilronan, Inishmore (099 61263).* **Aran Heritage Centre** *Kilronan.* 📞 *099 61355.* 🕐 *Apr–May, Sep–Oct: 11am–5pm daily; Jun–Aug: 10am–7pm daily.* 🅦 *www.visitaranislands.com*

### Kilmurvey Beach

*The attractive sandy beach east of Kilmurvy offers safe swimming in a sheltered cove. The town itself is a quiet place to stay near a number of the island's most important sights.*

**Teampall Chiaráin**, dedicated to St Ciaran, is a ruined 12th-century church with striking doorways. Nearby are several stones inscribed with crosses.

Teampall Chiaráin

Dún Eochla

KILRONAN (Cill Rónáin)

Dún Duchathair

**Dún Eochla** is a circular Bronze Age fort standing close to the highest point on Inishmore.

Inis Mór

### KEY

| | |
|---|---|
| ▭▭ | Main road |
| ▭▭ | Minor road |
| - - - | Track |
| ▦ | Beach |
| ✕ | Airport |
| ⛴ | Ferry service |
| ℹ️ | Tourist information |
| ☀ | Viewpoint |

0 kilometres                2

0 miles                1

### ★ Kilronan

*The Aran Islands' main port is a busy place, with jaunting cars (ponies and traps) and minibuses waiting by the pier to give island tours; bicycles can also be hired. Nearby, the fascinating Aran Heritage Centre is dedicated to the disappearing Aran way of life.*

### ★ Dún Duchathair

*Built on a headland, this Iron Age construction is known as the Black Fort. It has dry-stone ramparts.*

## STAR SIGHTS

★ **Kilronan**

★ **Dún Aonghasa**

★ **Dún Duchathair**

Farmer on Inishmore, largest of the Aran Islands ▷

East wall and gatehouse at Roscommon Castle

# Turoe Stone ㉑

**Road map** B4. Turoe, Bullaun, Loughrea, Co Galway. ( 091 841580. ☐ May–Sep: daily; Oct–Apr: weekends and public hols. 🖾 🕹 🖵

THE TUROE STONE stands at the centre of a large area of parkland, the Turoe Pet Farm and Leisure Park, near the village of Bullaun (on the R350). The white granite boulder, which stands about 1 m (3 ft) high, dates back to the 3rd or 2nd century BC. Its top half is carved with curvi-linear designs in a graceful Celtic style, known as La Tène, also found in Celtic parts of Europe, particularly Brittany. The lower half has a smooth section and a band of step-pattern carving. The stone was originally found at an Iron Age ring fort nearby, and is thought to have been used there in fertility rituals.

The park around the Turoe Stone is designed mainly for children. The Pet Farm has some small fields containing farm animals and a pond with several varieties of ducks and geese. There is also a wooded

**The Celtic Turoe Stone carved with graceful swirling patterns**

riverside walk (wear heavy shoes or walking boots as it's often muddy), a picnic area, tea rooms and a playground.

# Roscommon ㉒

**Road map** C3. Co Roscommon. 🚶 3,500. 🚉 🚌 🛉 Jun–Sep: Harrison Hall (0903 26342). 🖾 Fri.

THE COUNTY CAPITAL is a busy market town with scattered sights. In Main Street is the former gaol, celebrated for having a woman as its last ex-ecutioner. "Lady Betty", as she came to be known, was sen-tenced to death for the murder of her son in 1780, but nego-tiated a pardon by agreeing to become a hangwoman. She continued for 30 years.

South of the town centre, just off Abbey Street, is the **Dominican Friary**, founded in 1253 by Felim O'Conor, King of Connaught. Set in the north wall of the choir is a late 13th-century effigy of the founder. **Roscommon Castle**, an Anglo-Norman fortress north of the town, was built in 1269 by Robert d'Ufford, Lord Justice of Ireland, and rebuilt 11 years later after being des-troyed by the Irish led by Hugh O'Conor, King of Connaught. The rectangular castle has 16th-century mullioned windows.

# Clonalis House ㉓

**Road map** B3. Castlerea, Co Roscommon. ( 0907 20014. ☐ Jun–mid-Sep: Tue–Sun. 🖾 🕹 ground floor.

THIS VICTORIAN manor just outside Castlerea is the an-cestral home of the O'Conors, the last High Kings of Ireland

and Kings of Connaught. This old Gaelic family can trace its heritage back 1,500 years. The ruins of their gabled 17th-century home are visible in the grounds. On the lawn lies the O'Conor inauguration stone, dating from 90 BC.

The interior includes a Venetian hallway, a library of many books and documents recording Irish history, a tiny private chapel and a gallery of family portraits spanning 500 years. In the billiard room is the harp once played by Turlough O'Carolan (1670–1738), blind harpist and last of the Gaelic bards *(see p22)*.

# Strokestown Park House ㉔

**Road map** C3. Strokestown, Co Roscommon. 🏠 **House, Pleasure Gardens and Museum** ( 078 33013. ☐ mid-Mar–Oct: daily; Nov–mid-Mar: by appt. 🖾 🍴 🛉 🕹

STROKESTOWN PARK HOUSE, the greatest Palladian mansion in County Roscommon, was built in the 1730s for Thomas Mahon, an MP whose family was granted the lands by Charles II after the Restoration. It incorporates an earlier 17th-century tower house *(see p18)*. The design of the new house owes most to Richard Castle, architect of Russborough *(see p124)*. The galleried kitchen, panelled stairwell and groin-vaulted stables are undoubtedly his work, tailoring Palladian principles to the requirements of the Anglo-Irish gentry.

The house stayed in the fam-ily's hands until 1979, when major restoration began. In its heyday, the estate included ornamental parkland, a deer park, folly, mausoleum and the town of Roscommon itself. By 1979, the estate's original 12,000 ha (30,000 acres) had dwindled to 120 ha (300 acres), but recent re-creation of the Pleasure Gardens and the Fruit and Vegetable Garden have greatly increased the area. The original interior of the house is intact.

Set in the stable yards, the **Famine Museum** uses the Strokestown archives to tell the story of tenants and landlords during the 1840s Famine. During the crisis, landlords divided into two camps: the charitable, some of whom started up Famine Relief schemes, and the callous, like the Mahons of Strokestown. Major Denis Mahon was murdered after forcing two-thirds of the starving peasantry off his land by a combination of eviction and passages in "coffin ships" to North America. A section of the exhibition deals with continuing famine and malnutrition worldwide.

## Boyle ㉕

**Road map** C3. Co Roscommon.
🚶 2,200. 🚌 🚪 Apr–Oct: King House (079 63242). 🚌 Fri.

COUNTY ROSCOMMON's most charming town, Boyle is blessed with fine Georgian and medieval architecture. **Boyle Abbey** is a well-preserved Cistercian abbey founded in 1161 as a sister house to Mellifont in County Louth (see p237). It survived raids by Anglo-Norman barons and Irish chieftains, as well as the 1539 suppression of the monasteries. In 1659 it was

### THE GREAT FAMINE

The failure of the Irish potato crop in 1845, 1846 and 1848, due to potato blight, had disastrous consequences for the people of Ireland, many of whom relied on this staple crop. More than a million died of starvation and disease, and by 1856 over two and a half million had been forced to emigrate. The crisis was worsened by unsympathetic landlords who often continued collecting rents. The Famine had far-reaching effects: mass emigration became a way of life (see pp40–41) and many rural communities, particularly in the far west, were decimated.

Peasants queuing for soup during the Famine (1847)

turned into a castle. The abbey is still remarkably intact, with a church, cloisters, cellars, sacristy and even kitchens. The nave of the church has both Romanesque and Gothic arches and there are well-preserved 12th-century capitals. The visitors' centre in the old gatehouse has exhibits on the abbey's history.

**King House**, a Palladian mansion near the centre of town, is the ancestral home of the Anglo-Irish King family, later Earls of Kingston. Inside is a contemporary art gallery, as well as displays covering various subjects, such as Georgian architecture and the mansion's restoration, the history of the surrounding area and the Connaught chieftains.

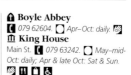

Carved capital in the nave at Boyle Abbey

🛐 **Boyle Abbey**
📞 079 62604. 🕐 Apr–Oct: daily. 🅿️
🏛 **King House**
Main St. 📞 079 63242. 🕐 May–mid-Oct: daily; Apr & late Oct: Sat & Sun.
🅿️ 🍽 🛍 🚻 ♿

**ENVIRONS:** Lough Key is often called the loveliest lake in Ireland. The island-studded lake and surrounding woodland make a glorious setting for the **Lough Key Forest Park**. The 320-ha (790-acre) park formed part of the Rockingham estate until 1957, when Rockingham House, a John Nash design, burnt down. The extensive woods were added by 18th-century landlords. Other features of the park include nature trails, an observation tower, a 17th-century ice house, a deer enclosure and, by the lake, a 17th-century gazebo known as the Temple. The park also has several ring forts (see p18). From the jetty, cruisers ply the Boyle River. A river bus visits Church and Trinity Islands, which both contain medieval ruins, and Castle Island, which has a 19th-century folly.

🏞 **Lough Key Forest Park**
N4 8 km (5 miles) E of Boyle.
🕐 daily. 🅿️ 🛳 Easter–Sep. ♿

The gatehouse and remains of the nave at Boyle Abbey

# NORTHWEST IRELAND

## DONEGAL · SLIGO · LEITRIM

Towering cliffs, *deserted golden beaches and rocky headlands abound along the rugged coast of Donegal, which incorporates some of Ireland's wildest scenery. To the south, Sligo is steeped in prehistory and Celtic myth, with its legacy of ancient monuments and natural beauty enriched by associations with the poet, WB Yeats. By contrast, Leitrim is a quiet county of unruffled lakes and waterways.*

In Celtic mythology Sligo was the power base of the warrior Queen Maeve of Connaught *(see p24)*, and the county's legacy of prehistoric sites shows that the area was heavily populated in Celtic times. Later, however, both County Sligo and neighbouring County Leitrim often seemed to be little affected by events taking place in the rest of Ireland. The Normans, for example, barely disturbed the rule of local Gaelic clans.

Donegal, on the other hand, was part of Ulster until 1921 and played an active role in that province's history. The O'Donnells held sway over most of Donegal in the Middle Ages, but they fled to Europe in 1607 following their ill-fated stand against the English alongside the O'Neills *(see p247)*. Protestant settlers moved on to land confiscated from the two clans, but they left much of Donegal and its poor soil to the native Irish, who lived there in isolation from the rest of Ulster. This remote corner of the province remained largely Catholic and, at the time of Partition in 1921, Donegal was excluded from the new Protestant Northern Ireland.

County Donegal has little in common with its neighbours in the Republic, either geographically or historically. It is one of the most remote parts of Ireland, and it is no coincidence that Donegal boasts the country's largest number of Gaelic speakers.

While the beauty of Donegal lies mainly along the coast, Sligo's finest landscapes are found inland, around Lough Gill and among the sparsely populated Bricklieve Mountains.

The 19th-century interior of Hargadon's bar in Sligo town, with its original counter and stout jars

◁ **View across to Falcarragh from Bloody Foreland in County Donegal**

# Exploring Northwest Ireland

The supreme appeal of Donegal lies in the natural beauty of its coast, with windswept peninsulas, precipitous cliffs and a host of golden beaches. There is a scattering of small seaside resorts which make good bases, and Donegal town is well placed for exploring the southern part of the county. The cultural heartland of the Northwest lies in and around Sligo, the only sizeable town in the region, from where you can reach several prehistoric remains and other historic sights. Further south, lovely scenery surrounds Lough Gill and the more remote Lough Arrow. In Leitrim, a county of lakes and rivers, the main centre of activity is the lively boating resort of Carrick-on-Shannon.

**Procession during the Mary of Dungloe beauty contest in July**

## See Also

- **Where to Stay** pp297–8

- **Restaurants, Cafés and Pubs** pp314–15 & p321

## Key

| | |
|---|---|
| ▬ | Major road |
| ▬ | Minor road |
| ▬ | Scenic route |
| ∼ | River |
| ☀ | Viewpoint |

0 kilometres    20

0 miles    10

TORY ISLAND ①
BLOODY FORELAND    HORN H
② R257    DUNFANA
BUNBEG
ARANMORE ISLAND    THE ROSSES ③
BURTONPORT ⑩    DERRYVEA MOUNTAI
DUNGLOE
N56
R255
ARDARA ⑪    BLUE STA MOUNTAI
GLENCOLUMBKILLE ⑫
SLIEVE LEAGUE ⑬    KILLYBEGS ⑭    DONEG ⑮
ROSSNOWLAGH ⑰
R231    N15
BALLYSHANN ⑱
BUNDORAN    Lough Melvin
LISSADELL HOUSE ⑲    ⑳
DRUMCLIFF
N16    Enniski
SLIGO ㉒    MANORHAMILTON
PARKE'S CASTLE ㉑
N59    N17    N4
Ballina    OX MOUNTAINS
LOUGH ARROW ㉓    Lough Allen
BRICKLIEVE MOUNTAINS    R280
CARRICK-ON-SHANNON ㉔

**GETTING AROUND**

The N56, linking Letterkenny and Donegal, provides access to much of the Northwest's best scenery, with minor roads branching off it around the coast's rocky peninsulas. A few buses serve this route, but travelling around without a car is easier further south, with buses running daily from Donegal along the N15 to Sligo via Ballyshannon. The rail network barely reaches the Northwest, though there are daily trains between Sligo and Carrick-on-Shannon.

Thatched cottage near Malin Head on Inishowen Peninsula

## SIGHTS AT A GLANCE

Ardara ⑪
Ballyshannon ⑱
Bloody Foreland ②
Carrick-on-Shannon ㉔
Derryveagh Mountains ③
Donegal ⑮
Fanad Peninsula ⑥
Glencolumbkille ⑫
Grianán of Aileach ⑧
Horn Head ④
Killybegs ⑭
Letterkenny ⑨
Lissadell House ⑲
Lough Arrow ㉓

Lough Derg ⑯
Lough Rynn Estate ㉕
Parke's Castle ㉑
Rosguill Peninsula ⑤
The Rosses ⑩
Rossnowlagh ⑰
Slieve League ⑬
Sligo ㉒
Tory Island ①

**Tours**
Inishowen Peninsula ⑦
Yeats Country ⑳

View from Carrowkeel Bronze Age cemetery above Lough Arrow

**Quartzite cone of Errigal, the highest of the Derryveagh Mountains**

# Tory Island ❶

**Road map** C1. Co Donegal. 🚶 175.
🚢 *from Magheraroarty Pier near Gortahork (074 35061) and Bunbeg (075 31991): daily in summer, weather permitting in winter.*

THE TURBULENT Tory Sound separates this windswept island from the northwestern corner of mainland Donegal. Given that rough weather can cut off the tiny island for days, it is not surprising that Tory's inhabitants have developed a strong sense of independence. Most of the islanders speak Gaelic and they even have their own monarch: the powers of this non-hereditary position are minimal, but the current incumbent is heavily involved in promoting the interests of his "subjects" and in attracting visitors to the island.

During the 1970s, the Irish government tried to resettle most of the islanders on the mainland, but they refused to move. Their campaign of resistance was led by Tory's school of Primitive artists. This emerged after 1968, inspired by a local man called James Dixon who claimed he could do better than a visiting English painter, Derek Hill. Since then, the school of artists has drawn a growing number of tourists; the **Dixon Gallery** opened in 1992 in the main village of West Town. There are ruins of a monastery founded by St Columba *(see p32)* nearby, or else you can explore the island's dramatic cliffs and seabird rookeries.

**🏛 Dixon Gallery**
West Town. 📞 074 35011.
⬜ *Easter–Sep: daily.*

# Bloody Foreland ❷

**Road map** C1. Co Donegal. 🚌 *to Bunbeg from Letterkenny or Dungloe.*

BLOODY FORELAND, which gets its name from the rubescent glow of the rocks at sunset, boasts magnificent scenery. The R257 road skirts the coast around the headland, providing lovely views. The most scenic viewpoint is on the north coast and looks across to the cliffs of nearby offshore islands, including Tory. A short distance further south, the tiny village of **Bunbeg** has a pretty harbour, but elsewhere the rocky landscape is spoilt by a blanket of holiday bungalows.

# Derryveagh Mountains ❸

**Road map** C1. Co Donegal.

THE WILD BEAUTY of these mountains provides one of the high spots of a visit to Donegal. Errigal Mountain, the range's tallest peak at 751 m (2,466 ft), attracts keen hikers, but the cream of the mountain scenery lies within **Glenveagh National Park**. Covering nearly 16,500 ha (40,000 acres), this takes in the beautiful valley occupied by Lough Veagh, and Poisoned Glen, a marshy valley enclosed by dramatic cliffs. The park also protects the largest herd of red deer in the country.

**Glenveagh Castle** stands on the southern shores of Lough Veagh, near the visitors' centre. This splendid granite building was constructed in 1870 by John Adair, notorious for his eviction of many families from the area after the Famine *(see p211)*. The castle was given to the nation in the 1970s by its last owner, a wealthy art dealer from Pennsylvania.

Minibuses whisk you up the private road to the castle from the visitors' centre. You can go on a guided tour of the sumptuous interior or just stroll

**Glenveagh Castle overlooking Lough Veagh**

Looking across to Dunfanaghy, gateway to the Horn Head peninsula

through the formal gardens and rhododendron woods. Trails weave all around the castle grounds; one path climbs steeply to reward you with a lovely view over Lough Veagh.

**Glebe House and Gallery** overlooks Lough Gartan 6 km (4 miles) south of the visitors' centre. This modest Regency mansion was the home of the painter, Derek Hill, who was also a keen collector. The house reveals his varied tastes, with William Morris wallpapers, Islamic ceramics and paintings by Tory Island artists. The gallery contains works by Picasso, Renoir and Jack B Yeats among others.

**Fountain at Glenveagh**

The **Colmcille Heritage Centre**, a short distance south, uses stained glass and illuminated manuscripts to trace the life of St Columba (Colmcille in Gaelic), who was born in nearby Church Hill in AD 521 (*see p32*). A flagstone in the village is said to mark the site of the saint's birthplace.

🍀 **Glenveagh National Park and Castle**
Off R251, 16 km (10 miles) N of Churchill. ☎ 074 37090. **Park** *and* **Castle** ◯ *Mar–Nov: daily.* 🅿️ 📷 🚻 ♿ *limited.* 🌐 *www.heritageireland.ie*
🏛 **Glebe House and Gallery**
☎ 074 37071. ◯ *Easter & May– Sep: Sat–Thu.* 🅿️ ♿ *limited.*
🏛 **Colmcille Heritage Centre**
☎ 074 37306. ◯ *Easter & May– Sep: daily.* 📷

# Horn Head ❹

**Road map** C1. Co Donegal. 🚌 *to Dunfanaghy from Letterkenny.* ℹ️ *The Workhouse, Dunfanaghy (074 36540) mid-Mar–mid-Oct.*

CARPETED IN HEATHER and rich in birdlife, Horn Head is the most scenic of the northern Donegal headlands. It rises 180 m (600 ft) straight out of the Atlantic and gives lovely views out to sea and inland towards the mountains. The appeal of the area is enhanced by **Dunfanaghy**, a delightful town with an air of affluence and Presbyterianism unusual in this area. The local beach, **Killahoey Strand**, offers excellent swimming.

# Rosguill Peninsula ❺

**Road map** C1. Co Donegal.

ROSGUILL PENINSULA juts out into the Atlantic Ocean between Sheephaven and Mulroy bays. The simplest way to see it is to follow the 11-km (7-mile) Atlantic Drive, a circular route which skirts the clifftops at the tip of the headland.

Doe Castle, 5 km (3 miles) north of Creeslough village, is worth a visit as much for its setting on a promontory overlooking Sheephaven Bay as for its architectural or historical interest. Even so, it is still a substantial ruin – the remains of a castle erected in the 16th century by the MacSweeneys, a family of Scottish mercenaries.

# Fanad Peninsula ❻

**Road map** C1. Co Donegal. 🚌 *to Rathmelton & Portsalon from Letterkenny.*

A PANORAMIC ROUTE winds between the hilly spine and rugged coast of this tranquil peninsula. The eastern side is by far the most enjoyable and begins at **Rathmelton,** a charming Plantation town founded in the 17th century. Elegant Georgian homes and handsome old warehouses flank its tree-lined Main Street.

Further north, **Portsalon** offers safe bathing and great views from nearby Saldanha Head. Near **Doaghbeg**, on the way to Fanad Head in the far north, the cliffs have been eroded into arches and other dramatic shapes.

Doe Castle on Rosguill Peninsula, with its 16th-century battlements

# A Tour of the Inishowen Peninsula ⓐ

INISHOWEN, THE LARGEST of Donegal's northern peninsulas, is an area laden with history, from early Christian relics to strategically positioned castles and forts. The most rugged scenery lies in the west and north, around the the steep rock-strewn landscape of the Gap of Mamore and the spectacular cape of Malin Head, the northern-most point in Ireland. Numerous beaches dot the coastline and cater for all tastes, from the remote Isle of Doagh to the busy family resort of Buncrana. From the shores, there are views to Donegal's Derryveagh Mountains in the west and the Northern Ireland coast in the east. The Inishowen Peninsula can be explored by car as a leisurely day trip.

**Tower on Banba's Crown, Malin Head**

**Carndonagh Cross** ④
This 7th-century early Christian cross is carved with human figures and inter-lacing lines.

**Gap of Mamore** ③
The road between Mamore Hill and the Urris Hills is 250 m (820 ft) above sea level and offers panoramic views.

**Dunree Head** ②
On the headland, Dunree Fort overlooks Lough Swilly. It was built in 1798 to counter the threat of French invasion. Since 1986, it has been a military museum.

**Buncrana** ①
Buncrana has 5 km (3 miles) of sandy beaches and two castles. Buncrana Castle was rebuilt in 1718 and the intact keep of O'Doherty Castle dates from Norman times.

**Shores of Lough Swilly near Dunree Fort**

**KEY**

| | |
|---|---|
| ▬▬ | Tour route |
| ═══ | Other roads |
| ☀ | Viewpoint |

**Grianán of Ailigh** ⑦
At the neck of the Inishowen Peninsula, perched on a hilltop, stands this formidable circular stone fort. The solid structure that can be seen today is the result of extensive restoration in the 1870s.

Enjoying the views from the ramparts of the Grianán of Ailigh

## TIPS FOR DRIVERS

**Tour length:** *157 km (98 miles).*
**Stopping-off points:** *Malin, Greencastle and Carndonagh all have pubs and eating places; picnic sites are dotted around the coast. The Guns of Dunree Military Museum has a café. There is a 3 km (1.5 mile) scenic walk between Moville and Greencastle. (See also pp355–7.)*

**Malin Head ⑤**
This traditional cottage makes a good stop for tea after enjoying the superb Atlantic views from Malin Head. At the highest point, Banba's Crown, stands a tower built in 1805 to monitor shipping.

**Greencastle ⑥**
A resort and fishing port, Greencastle is named after the overgrown castle ruins just outside town. Built in 1305 by Richard de Burgo, Earl of Ulster, the castle guarded the entrance to Lough Foyle.

0 kilometres 5
0 miles 5

# Grianán of Ailigh ⑧

**Road map** C1. Co Donegal. ☐ *from Letterkenny or Londonderry.* ℹ Burt (077 68512).

DONEGAL'S most impressive and intriguing ancient monument stands just 10 km (6 miles) west of Londonderry *(see pp250–51)* at the entrance to the Inishowen Peninsula. Overlooking Lough Swilly and Lough Foyle, the circular stone structure, measuring 23 m (77 ft) in diameter, is believed to have been built as a pagan temple around the 5th century BC, although the site was probably a place of worship before this date. Later, Christians adopted the fort: St Patrick is said to have baptized Owen, founder of the O'Neill dynasty, here in AD 450. The fort became the royal residence of the O'Neills, but was damaged in the 12th century by the army of Murtagh O'Brien, King of Munster.

The fort was restored in the 1870s. Two doorways lead from the outside through 4-m (13-ft) thick defences into a grassy arena ringed by three terraces. The most memorable feature of the fort, however, is its magnificent vantage point, which affords stunning views in every direction.

At the foot of the hill stands an attractive church, dedicated to St Aengus and built in 1967. Its circular design echoes that of the Grianán.

# Letterkenny ⑨

**Road map** C1. Co Donegal. 🚌 7,100. ☐ ℹ *Derry Rd (074 21160).* �🌐 www.donegal.ie.

STRADDLING the river Swilly, with the Sperrin Mountains to the east and the Derryveagh Mountains *(see pp216–17)*

to the west, Letterkenny is Donegal's largest town. It is also the region's main business centre, a role it took over from Londonderry after partition in 1921. The likeable town makes a good base from which to explore the northern coast of Donegal and, for anglers, is well placed for access to the waters of Lough Swilly.

Letterkenny has one of the longest main streets in Ireland, which is dominated by the 65-m (215-ft) steeple of **St Eunan's Cathedral**. A Neo-Gothic creation built in the late 19th century, it looks particularly impressive when floodlit at night. It contains Celtic-style stonework, a rich marble altar and vivid stained-glass windows. The **County Museum** has increased in size over the last couple of years and offers informative displays on local history from the Stone Age to the 20th century. It also has a collection of archaeological artifacts found in Donegal, some of them dating from the Iron Age.

🏛 **County Museum**
High Rd. ☏ *074 24613.* ◯ *Mon–Sat.* ● *10 days at Christmas and public hols.* ♿

The imposing spire of St Eunan's Cathedral in Letterkenny

**Isolated cottage near Burtonport in the Rosses**

# The Rosses 🔟

**Road map** C1. Co Donegal. 🚌 *to Dungloe or Burtonport from Letterkenny.* 🛈 *Jun–Sep: Main St, Dungloe (075 21297).* ⛴ *to Aranmore from Burtonport (075 20532).*

A ROCKY HEADLAND dotted with more than 100 lakes, the Rosses is one of the most picturesque and unspoilt corners of Donegal. It is also a strong Gaeltacht area, with many people speaking Gaelic.

The hub of the Rosses, at the southern end of the headland, is **Dungloe**, a bustling market town and major angling centre.

**ENVIRONS:** There is a glorious sheltered beach 8 km (5 miles) west of Dungloe at **Maghery Bay**. From here you can also walk to nearby **Crohy Head**, known for its caves, arches and unusual cliff formations. From Burtonport, 8 km (5 miles)

north of Dungloe, car ferries sail daily to Donegal's largest island, **Aranmore**. The rugged northwest coast is ideal for clifftop walks, and from the south coast you can enjoy fine views across to the Rosses. Most of Aranmore's population of 700 lives in Leabgarrow. The village's thriving pub culture is due partly to the granting of 24-hour licences, for the benefit of fishermen returning from sea.

# Ardara 11

**Road map** C2. Co Donegal. 👥 700. 🚌 *from Killybegs or Donegal.* 🛈 *Easter–Sep: Heritage Centre, The Diamond (075 41704).*

T HE TOWN of Ardara is the weaving capital of Donegal and proliferates in shops selling locally made tweeds and hand-knitted sweaters.

Some larger stores put on displays of hand-loom weaving. Ardara is also worth a stop for its pubs, which are much loved for their fiddle sessions.

**ENVIRONS:** There is superb scenery between Ardara and **Loughros Point**, 10 km (6 miles) west of the town: the drive along the narrow peninsula provides dramatic coastal views. Another picturesque route runs southwest from Ardara to Glencolumbkille, going over **Glengesh Pass**, a series of bends through a wild, deserted landscape.

**Hand-loom worker in Ardara**

# Glencolumbkille 12

**Road map** B2. Co Donegal. 👥 260. 🚌 *from Killybegs.* 🛈 *Cashel St (073 30116) or Donegal (073 21148).*

G LENCOLUMBKILLE, a quiet, grassy valley scattered with brightly coloured cottages, feels very much like a backwater, in spite of the sizeable number of visitors who come here.

The "Glen of St Colmcille" is a popular place of pilgrimage due to its associations with the saint more commonly known as St Columba. Just north of the valley's main village of Cashel, on the way to Glen Head, there is a tiny church where St Columba worshipped: it is said that between prayers the saint slept on the two stone slabs still visible in one corner.

Another attraction here is the **Folk Village Museum**, which depicts rural Donegal lifestyles through the ages. It was started in the 1950s by a local priest called Father James

**Old irons at the Folk Village Museum in Glencolumbkille**

**Slieve League, the highest sea cliffs in Europe**

## Killybegs ⓮

Road map C2. Co Donegal. 🏠 1,700.
🚌 from Donegal. 🚊 Donegal
(073 21148).

NARROW WINDING streets give
Killybegs a timeless feel,
which contrasts sharply with
the industriousness of this small
town. The sense of prosperity
stems in part from the manufacture of the Donegal carpets
for which the town is famous,
and which adorn Dublin
Castle (see pp74–5) and other
palaces around the world.
Killybegs is one of Ireland's
busiest fishing ports and the
quays are well worth seeing
when the trawlers arrive to off-
load their catch: gulls squawk
overhead and the smell of fish
fills the air. Trawlermen come
from far and wide – so do
not be surprised if you hear
Eastern European voices as
you wander around the town.

**Trawler crew in Killybegs relaxing
after unloading their catch**

MacDyer. Concerned about
the high rate of emigration
from this poor region, he
sought to provide jobs and a
sense of regional pride, partly
by encouraging people to set
up craft cooperatives. The
Folk Village shop sells local
wares, and has a good stock of
wine – made of anything
from seaweed to fuchsias.
There is plenty to explore
in the valley, which is littered
with cairns, dolmens and other
ancient monuments. The
nearby coast is lovely too, the
best walks taking you west
across the grassy foreland of
**Malinbeg**. Beyond the small
resort of Malin More, steps
drop down to an idyllic sandy
cove hemmed in by cliffs.

🏛 **Folk Village Museum**
Cashel. 📞 073 30017. ⬜ Easter–
Sep: daily. 🌐 ✔ ▣ 🅿 ♿

## Slieve League ⓭

Road map B2. Co Donegal. 🚌 to
Carrick from Glencolumbkille or
Killybegs.

THE HIGHEST cliff face in
Europe, Slieve League is
spectacular not just for its sheer
elevation but also for its colour:
at sunset the rock is streaked
with changing shades of red,
amber and ochre. The 8-km
(5-mile) drive to the eastern
end of Slieve League from
**Carrick** is bumpy but well
worth enduring. Beyond
Teelin, the road becomes a

series of alarming switchbacks
before reaching **Bunglass
Point** and Amharc Mor, the
"good view". From here, you
can see the whole of Slieve
League, its sheer cliffs rising
dramatically out of the ocean.
Only experienced hikers
should attempt the treacherous
ledges of **One Man's Pass**.
This is part of a trail which
climbs westwards out of
Teelin and up to the highest
point of Slieve League – from
where you can admire the
Atlantic Ocean shimmering
598 m (1,972 ft) below. The
path then continues on to
Malinbeg, 16 km (10 miles)
west. During the summer, for
a less strenuous but safer and
equally rewarding excursion,
pay a boat-owner from Teelin
to take you out to see Slieve
League from the sea.

### THE IRISH GAELTACHTS

The term "Gaeltacht" refers to Gaelic-speaking areas of
Ireland. Up to the 16th century, virtually the entire population
spoke the native tongue. British rule,
however, undermined Irish culture,
and the Famine (see p211) drained the
country of many of its Gaelic-speakers.
The use of the local language has fallen
steadily since. Even so, in the Gaeltachts
75 per cent of the people still speak it,
and road signs are exclusively in Irish –
unlike in most other parts of Ireland.
The Donegal Gaeltacht stretches
almost unbroken along the coast from
Fanad Head to Slieve League and boasts
the largest number of Irish-speakers in
the country. Ireland's other principal
Gaeltachts are in Galway and Kerry.

**Gaelic pub sign in
Gaeltacht region**

**Donegal town, overlooked by the ruins of its 15th-century castle**

# Donegal ⓯

**Road map** C2. Co Donegal. 🚶 2,300.
🚌 ℹ️ Quay St (073 21148).

DONEGAL MEANS "Fort of the Foreigners", after the Vikings who built a garrison here. However, it was under the O'Donnells that the town began to take shape. The ruins of **Donegal Castle** in the town centre incorporate the gabled tower of a fortified house built by the family in the 15th century. The adjoining house and most other features are Jacobean – added by Sir Basil Brooke, who moved in after the O'Donnells were ousted by the English in 1607 *(see pp36–7)*. The castle has recently been partly restored.

Brooke was also responsible for laying out the market square, which is known as the **Diamond**. An obelisk in the centre commemorates four Franciscan monks who wrote the *Annals of the Four Masters* in the 1630s, tracing the history of the Gaelic people from 40 days before the Great Flood up until the end of the 16th century. Part of it was written at **Donegal Abbey**, south of the market square along the River Eske. Built in 1474, little now remains of the abbey but a few Gothic

windows and cloister arches. About 1.5 km (1 mile) further on is **Donegal Craft Village**, a showcase for the work of local craftspeople.

Donegal town has some pleasant hotels *(see p298)* and makes a good base for exploring the southern part of the county.

⚓ **Donegal Castle**
Tirchonaill St. 📞 073 22405. 🕐 Easter–Jun: Sat & Sun; Jun–Aug: daily. 🎫 🎥 ♿ limited.
🏛️ **Donegal Craft Village**
Ballyshannon Rd. 📞 073 22015. 🕐 May–Sep: Mon–Sat; Jun–Aug: daily. 🚻 ♿ limited.

# Lough Derg ⓰

**Road map** C2. Co Donegal. 🚤 Jun–mid-Aug (pilgrims only). 🚌 to Pettigo from Donegal.

PILGRIMS HAVE made their way to Lough Derg ever since St Patrick spent 40 days praying on one of the lake's islands in an attempt to rid Ireland of all evil spirits. The Pilgrimage of St Patrick's Purgatory began in around 1150 and still attracts thousands of Catholics every summer. Their destination is the tiny **Station Island**, close to Lough Derg's southern shore and reached by boat from a jetty

8 km (5 miles) north of the border village of Pettigo. The island is completely covered by a religious complex, which includes a basilica, built in 1921, and hostels for pilgrims.

The pilgrimage season runs from June to mid-August. People spend three days on the island, eating just one meal of dry bread and black tea per day. Although only pilgrims can visit Station Island, it is interesting to go to the jetty to savour the atmosphere and get a good view of the basilica near the shore.

# Rossnowlagh ⓱

**Road map** C2. Co Donegal. 🚶 55.
🚌 from Bundoran & Donegal.
ℹ️ Apr–Oct: Main St, Bundoran (072 41350).

**Holiday-makers enjoying the fine sandy beach at Rossnowlagh**

AT ROSSNOWLAGH, Atlantic waves break on to one of Ireland's finest beaches, drawing crowds of both bathers and surfers to this tiny place. Even so, the village remains far more peaceful than the resort of Bundoran, 14 km (9 miles) south. In addition, the cliffs at Rossnowlagh provide scope for exhilarating coastal walks. Away from the sea, you can visit the **Donegal Historical Society Museum**, housed in a striking Franciscan friary

**Basilica on Station Island viewed from the shores of Lough Derg**

**Lissadell House dining room with Gore-Booth family portraits**

built in the 1950s. The tiny but fascinating collection includes displays of Stone Age flints, Irish musical instruments and other local artifacts.

Rossnowlagh never fails to make the news on 12 July, when it hosts the only parade to take place in the Republic by the Protestant organization, the Orange Order *(see p47)*.

🏛 **Donegal Historical Society Museum**
📞 *072 51267.* 🔵 *daily.* ⚫ *25 Dec.*

## Ballyshannon ⑱

**Road map** C2. Co Donegal. 🔠 *2,600.*
🚌 *from Bundoran & Donegal.*

IN BALLYSHANNON, well-kept Georgian homes jostle for space along hilly streets on the banks of the River Erne, near where it flows into Donegal Bay. This is a bustling town, full of character and off the main tourist track – though it gets packed during August's festival of traditional music, which is one of the best of its kind in the country.

The festival apart, Ballyshannon is most famous as the birthplace of poet William Allingham (1824–89), who recalled his home town in the lines "Adieu to Ballyshanny and the winding banks of the

Erne". He lies buried in the graveyard of St Anne's Church, off Main Street. There is a fine view over the river from here: you can see the small island of **Inis Saimer** where, according to legend, Greeks founded the first colony in Ireland after the Great Flood. Beyond, you can glimpse a large Irish Army base: Ballyshannon's position on a steeply rising bluff overlooking the River Erne has always made the town a strategic military site.

**Mural of the family dog in Lissadell's dining room**

About 1.5 km (1 mile) northwest of town lie the scant ruins of **Assaroe Abbey**, founded by Cistercians in 1184. A graveyard with some ancient burial slabs and headstones is all that remains. Nearby, two water wheels installed by the monks have been restored. **Water Wheels** has a small heritage centre as well as a café.

🏛 **Water Wheels**
Assaroe Abbey. 📞 *072 51580.*
🔵 *Apr–Aug: daily.* ▫ ▫ ♿
**Heritage centre** 🔵 *Apr–Aug:daily.*

## Lissadell House ⑲

**Road map** B2. Carney, Co Sligo.
📞 *071 63150.* 🚌 *or* 🚆 *to Sligo.*
🔵 *Jun–Sep: Mon–Sat.* ▫ ♿

A LATE GEORGIAN mansion built in the 1830s, Lissadell is famous more for its occupants than its architecture. It was once the home of the Gore-Booths who, unlike some of the Anglo-Irish gentry, contributed much to the region. During the Famine *(see p211)*, Sir Robert mortgaged the house to help feed his employees.

The most famous member of the Gore-Booth family was Sir Robert's granddaughter, Constance Markievicz (1868–1927). She was a leading revolutionary who took part in the 1916 Rising *(see pp42–3)* and was the first woman to be elected to the British House of Commons. WB Yeats, a regular visitor to the house, immortalized Constance and her sister, Eva, in one of his poems, describing them as "Two girls in silk kimonos, both beautiful, one a gazelle". The house is still in the hands of the Gore-Booth family.

Built in grey limestone, the exterior of Lissadell House is rather austere. The interior, on the other hand, has an appealing atmosphere of faded grandeur, with peeling paintwork and copious memorabilia of the building's former occupants. The finest rooms are the gallery (previously the music room) and the dining room, which is decorated with extraordinary full-length murals of the Gore-Booth family, their servants and their dog. Painted directly on to the wall, they were the work of Constance's husband, Count Casimir Markievicz.

Both the house and the overgrown estate are slowly being restored. There are plans, for example, to open up the woodland vistas to recreate the sweeping views down to the sea. You can already explore along paths skirting the lakeshore, and there is also a wildlife reserve which is a popular winter refuge for barnacle geese.

# A Tour of Yeats Country ⑳

**Yeats tour sign**

EVEN FOR PEOPLE unfamiliar with the poetry of WB Yeats, Sligo's engaging landscapes are reason enough to make a pilgrimage. This tour follows a route through varied scenery, taking you past sandy bays and dramatic limestone ridges, through forest and alongside rivers and lakes. The delightful Lough Gill lies at the heart of Yeats country, enclosed by wooded hills crisscrossed by walking trails. In summer, boats ply the length of the lough, or you can head to one of the northwest's best beaches, at Rosses Point.

**Ben Bulben** ⑤
The eerie silhouette of Ben Bulben rises abruptly out of the plain. You can climb to the top, but go with great care.

**Lissadell House** ④
Yeats was a close friend of the Gore-Booth sisters who lived at Lissadell. You can see the room where the poet slept as a guest *(see p223)*.

**Drumcliff** ③
Although he died in France, in 1948 Yeats's body was laid to rest in Drumcliff churchyard. The ruins of an old monastic site include a fine High Cross.

DONEGAL
N15
⑤
Carney
④
Drumcliff Bay
③
Sligo Harbour
R291
N15
N16
Drum
①
Garavogue
R287
⑨
N4
R284
GALWAY

## TIPS FOR DRIVERS

**Length:** 88 km (55 miles).
**Stopping-off points:** Outside Sligo, the best choice of eating places is at Rosses Point, although there are good pubs in Drumcliff and Dromahair, and Parke's Castle has a café. Lough Gill provides most choice in terms of picnic spots.
**Boat trips:** Wild Rose Water Bus (071 64266 or 087 2598869). (See also pp355–7.)

## KEY

▭▭▭ Tour route
⚌⚌⚌ Other roads
🚤 Boat trips
✹ Viewpoint

**Rosses Point** ②
Yeats and his brother used to spend their summers at this pretty resort. It stands at the entrance to Sligo Bay, and a steady flow of boats passes by.

**Sligo** ①
This town is a good place to begin a tour of Yeats country. It has many connections with the poet and his family, whose literary and artistic legacy has helped to inspire Sligo's thriving arts scene *(see p226)*.

Parke's Castle viewed from across the calm waters of Lough Gill

## Parke's Castle ㉑

**Road map** C2. 6 km (4 miles) N of Dromahair, Co Leitrim. ☎ 071 64149. ▢ or ▢ to Sligo. ◯ *mid-Mar–Oct: 10am–6pm daily.* ▨ ♿ *ground floor only.* ▨ ▣

THIS FORTIFIED manor house dominates the eastern end of Lough Gill. It was built in 1609 by Captain Robert Parke, an English settler who later became MP for Leitrim. It has been beautifully restored by the Office of Public Works using 17th-century building methods and native Irish oak.

Parke's Castle was erected on the site of a 16th-century tower house belonging to the O'Rourkes, a powerful local clan, and stones from this earlier structure were used in the new building. The original foundations and part of the moat were incorporated, but otherwise Parke's Castle is the epitome of a Plantation manor house *(see p37)*. It is protected by a large enclosure or bawn, whose sturdy wall includes a gatehouse and two turrets as well as the house itself.

Among the most distinctive architectural features of Parke's Castle are the diamond-shaped chimneys, mullioned windows and the parapets. There is also a curious stone hut, known as the "sweathouse", which was an early Irish sauna. Inside, an exhibition and audiovisual display cover Parke's Castle and various historic and prehistoric sites in the area, with photos and archaeological finds. There is also a working forge.

Boat trips around sights on Lough Gill that are associated with the poet, WB Yeats, leave from outside the castle walls.

**Glencar Lough** ⑥
"There is a waterfall ... that all my childhood counted dear", wrote Yeats of the cataract which tumbles into Glencar Lough. A path leads down to it from the road.

**Parke's Castle** ⑦
This 17th-century fortified manor house commands a splendid view over the tranquil waters of Lough Gill. It is a starting point for boat trips around the lough.

**Isle of Innisfree** ⑧
"There midnight's all a glimmer, and noon a purple glow", is how Yeats once described Innisfree. There is not much to see on this tiny island but it is a romantic spot. In summer, a boatman ferries visitors here.

**Dooney Rock** ⑨
A steep path leads from the road to Dooney Rock, from where glorious views extend over the lough to Ben Bulben. Trails weave through the surrounding woods and by the lake.

N16
ENNISKILLEN

LOUGH GILL

R288
Dromahair

R289
CARRICK-ON-SHANNON

R287

0 kilometres 3
0 miles 2

Hargadon's bar, one of Sligo town's most famous watering holes

# Sligo ㉒

**Road map** C2. Co Sligo. 🏘 20,000.
🚂 🚌 🚕 ℹ️ *Aras Reddan, Temple St (071 61201).* ⛴ *Fri.*
🌐 *www.ireland-northwest.travel.ie*

THE PORT of Sligo sits at the mouth of the River Garavogue, sandwiched between the Atlantic and Lough Gill. The largest town in the north-west, it rose to prominence under the Normans, being well placed as a gateway between the provinces of Ulster and Connaught. The appearance of Sligo today is mainly the result of growth during the late 18th and 19th centuries.

Sligo is perfectly situated for touring the ravishing countryside nearby, and it is also a good centre for traditional music. While at first sight it can seem a bit sombre, the town is thriving as the arts capital of northwest Ireland.

Sligo's link with the Yeats family is the main source of the town's appeal. WB Yeats (*see pp224–5*), Ireland's best-known poet, was born into a prominent local family. The Pollexfen warehouse, at the western end of Wine Street, has a rooftop turret from which the poet's grandfather would observe his merchant fleet moored in the docks.

The town's sole surviving medieval building is **Sligo Abbey**, founded in 1253. Some original features remain, such as the delicate lancet windows in the choir, but this ruined Dominican friary dates mainly from the 15th century. The best features are a beautifully carved altar and the cloisters.

A short distance west from the abbey is O'Connell Street, with the town's main shops and Hargadon's bar – an old Sligo institution complete with a dark, wooden interior, snugs and a grocery counter. Near the junction with Wine Street, overlooking Hyde Bridge, is the Yeats Memorial Building. This houses the Yeats Society and the **Sligo Art Gallery**, which puts on shows by foreign and Irish artists. The Yeats International Summer School is held here too: a renowned annual festival of readings and lectures on the poet's life and work.

**Bronze statue of WB Yeats**

Just the other side of Hyde Bridge is a statue of the poet, engraved with lines from his own verse. **Sligo County Museum** has a collection of Yeatsian memorabilia and local artifacts but the entire Niland Collection including the paintings by Jack B. Yeats have been moved to the **Model Arts & Niland Gallery** in the Mall. This outstanding new centre also puts on temporary exhibitions of major Irish and International Contemporary Art.

**🔒 Sligo Abbey**
Abbey St. 📞 071 46406. 🕐 *daily.*
🚫 *Easter–Oct.*

**🏛 Sligo Art Gallery**
Hyde Bridge. 📞 071 45847.
🕐 *Mon–Sat.*

**🏛 Sligo County Museum**
Stephen St. 📞 071 47190.
🕐 *Tue–Sat daily (Oct–May: pm only).*

**🏛 Model Arts & Niland Gallery** The Mall. 📞 071 41405.
🕐 *Mon–Sat.*

**ENVIRONS:** Improbably set in the suburbs of Sligo, **Carrowmore Megalithic Cemetery** once held the country's largest collection of Stone Age tombs. Quarrying destroyed much, but about 40 passage tombs (*see pp238–9*) and dolmens (*see p30*) survive among the abandoned gravel pits, with some in private gardens and even protruding from cottages.

The huge unexcavated cairn atop **Knocknarea** mountain dates back about 5,000 years and is said to contain the tomb of the legendary Queen Maeve of Connaught (*see p24*). It is about an hour's climb and the path starts 4 km (2.5 miles) west of Carrowmore.

**Tobernalt**, by Lough Gill 5 km (3 miles) south of Sligo, means "cliff well", after a nearby spring with alleged curative powers. It was a holy site in Celtic times and later became a Christian shrine. Priests came here to celebrate Mass in secret during the 18th century, when Catholic worship was illegal. The Mass rock, next to an altar erected around 1900, remains a place of pilgrimage.

**🔒 Carrowmore Cemetery**
📞 071 61534. 🕐 *May–Sep: daily.* 🖼

Altar by the holy well at Tobernalt, overlooking Lough Gill in Sligo

## Lough Arrow ㉓

**Road map** C3. Co Sligo. 🚌 *to Ballinafad.* ℹ️ *May–Oct: Boyle (079 62145).*

PEOPLE GO to Lough Arrow to sail and fish for the local trout, and also simply to enjoy the glorious countryside. You can explore the lake by boat, but the views from the shore are the real joy of Lough Arrow. A full circuit of the lake is recommended, but for the most breathtaking views head for the southern end around **Ballinafad**. This small town lies in a gorgeous spot, enclosed by land to the north and south by the Bricklieve and Curlew Mountains.

The **Carrowkeel Passage Tomb Cemetery** occupies a remote and eerie spot in the Bricklieve Mountains to the north of Ballinafad. The best approach is up the single track road from Castlebaldwin, 5 km (3 miles) northeast of the site.

The 14 Neolithic passage graves, which are scattered around a hilltop overlooking Lough Arrow, are elaborate corbelled structures. One is comparable with Newgrange (*see pp238–9*), except that the burial chamber inside this cairn is lit by the sun on the day of the summer solstice (21 June) as opposed to the winter solstice. On a nearby ridge are the remains of Stone Age huts, presumably those occupied by the farmers who buried their dead in the Carrowkeel passage graves.

Passage tomb in Carrowkeel cemetery above Lough Arrow

## Carrick-on-Shannon ㉔

**Road map** C3. Co Leitrim. 🚶 *1,900.* 🚌 🚆 ℹ️ *Apr–Sep: The Marina (078 20170).* 🌐 www.leitrimtourism.com

THE TINY CAPITAL of Leitrim, one of the least populated counties in Ireland, stands in a lovely spot on a tight bend of the River Shannon.

The town's location by the river and its proximity to the Grand Canal were crucial to Carrick's development. They are also the main reasons for its thriving tourist industry. There is a colourful, modern marina, which in summer fills up with private launches and boats available for hire.

Already a major boating centre, Carrick has benefited from the reopening of the Shannon-Erne Waterway, one end of which begins 6 km (4 miles) north at Leitrim. The channel was restored in a cross-border joint venture billed as a symbol of peaceful cooperation between Northern Ireland and the Republic.

Away from the bustle of the marina, Carrick-on-Shannon is an old-fashioned place, with 19th-century churches and convents mixed in with more refined Georgian houses and shopfronts. The town's most curious building is the quaint **Costello Chapel** on Bridge Street. One of the smallest of its kind anywhere in the world, the chapel was built in 1877 by local businessman, Edward Costello, to house the tombs of himself and his wife.

## Lough Rynn Estate ㉕

**Road map** C3. Mohill, Co Leitrim. 🚌 *or* 🚆 *to Carrick-on-Shannon.* 🅾️ *April–mid-Sep: daily.*

THIS VAST ESTATE, lying 3 km (2 miles) south of Mohill, was the ancestral seat of the Clements family, Earls of Leitrim. The baronial-style house, constructed in 1832, is currently closed and at the centre of a development dispute. However, it is still possible to visit the grounds, which extend across 40 ha (100 acres) of land and more than 240 ha (600 acres) of lakes. There is a lot to explore, including ornamental gardens, water meadows, lush wood-land and an arboretum with California redwoods and other exotic trees. The ruins of a 16th-century castle overlook one of the lakes, and you can also walk up to the remains of a Neolithic burial site.

---

### SHANNON-ERNE WATERWAY

This labyrinthine system of rivers and lakes passes through unspoilt border country, linking Leitrim on the Shannon and Upper Lough Erne in Fermanagh. It follows the course of a canal which was completed and then abandoned in the 1860s. The channel was reopened in 1993, enabling the public to enjoy both the Victorian stonework (including 34 bridges) and the state-of-the-art technology used to operate the 16 locks.

Cruiser negotiating a lock on the Shannon-Erne Waterway

# THE MIDLANDS

CAVAN · MONAGHAN · LOUTH · LONGFORD · WESTMEATH
MEATH · OFFALY · LAOIS

T HE CRADLE *of Irish civilization and the Celts' spiritual home,
the Midlands encompass some of Ireland's most sacred and
symbolic sites. Much of the region is ignored, but the ragged
landscapes of lush pastures, lakes and bogland reveal ancient Celtic
crosses, gracious Norman abbeys and Gothic Revival castles.*

The fertile Boyne Valley in County Meath was settled during the Stone Age and became the most important centre of habitation in the country. The remains of ancient sites from this early civilization fill the area and include Newgrange, the finest Neolithic tomb in the country. In Celtic times, the focus shifted south to the Hill of Tara, the seat of the High Kings of Ireland and the Celts' spiritual and political capital. Tara's heyday came in the 3rd century AD, but it retained its importance until the Normans invaded in the 1100s.

Norman castles, such as the immense fortress at Trim in County Meath, attest to the shifting frontiers around the region of English influence known as the Pale *(see p124)*. By the end of the 16th century, this area incorporated nearly all the counties in the Midlands.

The Boyne Valley returned to prominence in 1690, when the Battle of the Boyne ended in a landmark Protestant victory over the Catholics *(see pp36–7)*.

Although part of the Republic since 1921, historically Monaghan and Cavan belong to Ulster, and the former retains strong links with the province. The rounded hills called drumlins, found in both counties, are typical of the border region between the Republic and Northern Ireland.

Grassland and bog dotted with lakes are most characteristic of the Midlands, but the Slieve Bloom Mountains and the Cooley Peninsula provide good walking country. In addition to Meath's ancient sites, the historical highlights of the region are monasteries like Fore Abbey and Clonmacnoise, this last ranking among Europe's greatest early Christian centres.

Carlingford village and harbour, with the hills of the Cooley Peninsula rising behind

◁ Temple Finghin round tower at Clonmacnoise monastery on the banks of the River Shannon

# Exploring the Midlands

DROGHEDA IS THE OBVIOUS BASE from which to explore the Boyne Valley and neighbouring monastic sites, such as Monasterboice. Trim and Mullingar, to the southwest, are less convenient but make pleasanter places in which to stay. The northern counties of Monaghan, Cavan and Longford are quiet backwaters with a patchwork of lakes that attract many anglers. To the south, Offaly and Laois are dominated by dark expanses of bog, though there is a cluster of sights around the attractive Georgian town of Birr. For a break by the sea, head for the picturesque village of Carlingford on the Cooley Peninsula.

**West doorway of Nuns' Church at Clonmacnoise**

## KEY

| | |
|---|---|
| | Motorway |
| | Major road |
| | Minor road |
| | Scenic route |
| | River |
| ❀ | Viewpoint |

## SEE ALSO

- *Where to Stay* p299

- *Restaurants, Cafés and Pubs* pp315–16 & p321

## GETTING AROUND

In the Midlands, there is an extensive network of roads and rail lines fanning out across the country from Dublin. As a result, getting around on public transport is easier than in most other areas. The Dublin–Belfast railway serves Dundalk and Drogheda, while Mullingar and Longford town lie on the Dublin–Sligo route. The railway and N7 road between Dublin and Limerick give good access to Laois and Offaly. For motorists, roads in the Midlands are often flat and straight but also potholed.

Statue in Birr Castle's
formal gardens

## SIGHTS AT A GLANCE

Athlone **18**
Birr **21**
Carlingford **8**
Carrigglas Manor **3**
*Clonmacnoise pp242–3* **19**
Drogheda **10**
Drumlane **2**
Dundalk **7**
Emo Court **23**
Fore Abbey **5**
Hill of Tara **14**
Kells **6**
Kilbeggan **17**
Mellifont Abbey **12**
Monaghan **1**
Monasterboice **9**
Mullingar **16**
*Newgrange and the Boyne
    Valley pp236–9* **11**
Rock of Dunamase **24**
Shannonbridge Bog Railway **20**
Slane **13**
Slieve Bloom Mountains **22**
Trim **15**
Tullynally Castle **4**

View of Trim across the River Boyne

0 kilometres                    20

0 miles              10

Rossmore Memorial drinking fountain in Monaghan

## Monaghan ❶

**Road map** D2. Co Monaghan.
🏠 6,000. 🚌 🛈 *Market House,
Market Square (047 81122).*

THE SPRUCE AND THRIVING town
of Monaghan is the urban
highlight of the northern Midlands. Planted by James I in
1613 *(see p37)*, it developed
into a prosperous industrial
centre, thanks mainly to the
local manufacture of linen. A
crannog *(see p31)* off Glen
Road is the sole trace of the
town's Celtic beginnings.

Monaghan centres on three
almost contiguous squares.
The main attraction in Market
Square is the 18th-century
**Market House**, a squat but
charming building with the
original oak beams still visible.
It is now home to the tourist
office. To the east lies Church
Square, very much the heart of
modern Monaghan and lined
with dignified 19th-century
buildings, such as the Classical-
style courthouse. The third
square, which is known as the
Diamond, was the original
marketplace. It contains the
**Rossmore Memorial**, a large
Victorian drinking fountain
with an ornate stone canopy
supported by marble columns.

Do not miss the excellent
**County Museum**, just off
Market Square, which tells the
story of Monaghan's linen and
lace-making industries. The
pride of its historical collection
is the Cross of Clogher, an
ornate bronze altar cross which
dates from around 1400.

The Gothic Revival Cathedral
of St Macartan perches on a
hilltop south of the town, from
where you can enjoy a fine
view over Monaghan.

### 🏛 County Museum
Hill St. 📞 047 82928. ◯ *Tue–Sat.*
● *public hols.* ♿ *limited.*

## Drumlane ❷

**Road map** C3. 1 km (0.5 miles) S of
Milltown, Co Cavan. 🚌 *to Belturbet.*

STANDING ALONE by the River
Erne, the medieval church
and round tower of Drumlane
merit a visit as much for their
delightful setting as for the
ruins themselves. The abbey
church, founded in the early
13th century but significantly
altered about 200 years later,
features fine Romanesque
carvings. The nearby round
tower has lost its cap but is
unusual for the well-finished
stonework, with carvings of
birds on the north side.

## Carrigglas Manor ❸

**Road map** C3. Co Longford. 📞 043
45165. 🚌 *to Longford.* ◯ *May–Sep:
11am–3pm Mon, Tue, Fri & Sat.* 🎫 ◯
🚻 🛈 ♿ *limited.*

CARRIGGLAS MANOR has been
the seat of the Lefroys, a
family of Huguenot descent,
ever since its construction in
1837. It has changed little in
the intervening years and is a
fine example of the Tudor
Revival style. The Victorian
atmosphere is still very much
alive inside, where the rooms
are decorated with pseudo-

Drawing room in Carrigglas Manor with original 19th-century features

**Authentic Victorian kitchen in Tullynally Castle**

Gothic panelling and ornate plasterwork ceilings. The stable block, by contrast, is a grand Neo-Classical building by James Gandon, the architect of Dublin's Custom House *(see p86)*. The manor grounds are primarily woodland but include a wild flower garden.

**ENVIRONS:** Just 14 km (9 miles) south of Carrigglas Manor, **Ardagh** is considered the most attractive village in Longford, with pretty stone cottages gathered around a green.

## Tullynally Castle ❹

Road map C3. Castle Pollard, Co Westmeath. 📞 044 61159. 🚌 to Mullingar. **Castle** 🕒 mid-Jun–Jul: daily (pm only). 🎟 🔲 obligatory. 🔲 **Gardens** 🕒 May–Aug: daily (pm only). 🎟 🔲 limited.

THIS HUGE STRUCTURE, adorned with numerous turrets and battlements, is one of Ireland's largest castles. The original 17th-century tower house was given a Georgian gloss, but this was all but submerged under later Gothic Revival changes. The Pakenham family have lived at Tullynally since 1655. Thomas Pakenham, son of the present Earl of Longford, now manages the estate.

The imposing great hall leads to a fine panelled dining room hung with family portraits. Of equal interest are the Victorian kitchen, laundry room and the adjacent drying room, complete with its immense boiler.

The 8,000-volume library looks out on to rolling wooded parkland, much of which was landscaped in the 1760s. The grounds include Victorian terraces, walled kitchen and flower gardens, and two small lakes where black swans have recently been introduced.

## Fore Abbey ❺

Road map C3. Fore, Castle Pollard, Co Westmeath. 🚌 to Castle Pollard. 🕒 daily.

THE RUINS of Fore Abbey lie in glorious rolling country-side about 8 km (5 miles) east of Tullynally Castle. St Fechin set up a monastery here in 630, but what you see now are the remains of a large Benedictine priory founded around 1200. Located on the northern border of the Pale *(see p124)*, Fore Abbey was heavily fortified in the 15th century as protection against the native Irish.

The ruined church was part of the original Norman priory, but the cloister and refectory date from the 1400s. On the hill opposite lies St Fechin's Church, a Norman building said to mark the site of the first monastery. The tiny church nearby incorporates a 15th-century anchorite's cell.

## Kells ❻

Road map D3. Co Meath. 🏠 5,500. 🚌 🚂 Kells Heritage Centre, Navan Road (046 47840).

SIGNPOSTED by its Irish name, Ceanannus Mór, this modest town provides an unlikely backdrop to the monastery for which it is so famous.

**Kells Monastery** was set up by St Columba in the 6th century, but its heyday came after 806, when monks fled here from Iona. They may have been the scribes who illuminated the superb *Book of Kells,* now kept at Trinity College, Dublin *(see p62)*.

Lying in the west of town, the monastery centres on a rather gloomy 18th-century church beside which stands a decapitated round tower. There are several 9th-century High Crosses; the South Cross is in the best condition.

Just north of the enclosure is **St Columba's House**, a tiny steep-roofed stone oratory, similar to St Kevin's Kitchen at Glendalough *(see p132)*.

The Market Cross, a High Cross that once marked the entrance to the monastery, now stands outside the Heritage Centre in the Old Courthouse. It was used as a gallows during the uprising in 1798 *(see p39)*. The battle scene on the base is a subject rarely used in High Cross art.

**Ruins of Fore Abbey, a medieval Benedictine priory**

Thatched cottage in Carlingford on the mountainous Cooley Peninsula

## Dundalk ❼

**Road map** D3. Co Louth. 👥 32,000.
🚉 🚌 🛈 Jocelyn Street
(042 9335484). ⛴ Fri.

DUNDALK once marked the northernmost point of the Pale, the area controlled by the English during the Middle Ages (see p124). Now it is the last major town before the Northern Irish border.

Dundalk is also a gateway to the magnificent countryside of the Cooley Peninsula. The **County Museum**, which is housed in an 18th-century distillery in the town, gives an imaginative history of the county, including a section on some of Louth's traditional industries such as beer-making.

🏛 **County Museum**
Jocelyn St. 📞 042 9327056.
⬜ Mar–Sep: daily; Oct–Feb: Tue–Sat.
⬛ 25 & 26 Dec, 1 Jan. 📷 ♿

## Carlingford ❽

**Road map** D3. Co Louth. 👥 650. 🚌
🛈 Holy Trinity Heritage Centre
Churchyard Rd (042 9373454).
**Carlingford Adventure Centre**
Tholsel St (042 9373100).

THIS IS A PICTURESQUE fishing village, beautifully located between the mountains of the Cooley Peninsula and the waters of Carlingford Lough. The border with Northern Ireland runs right through the centre of this drowned river valley, and from the village you can look across to the Mountains of Mourne on the Ulster side (see pp276–7). Carlingford is an interesting place to explore, with its

pretty whitewashed cottages and ancient buildings clustered along medieval alleyways. The ruins of **King John's Castle**, built by the Normans to protect the entrance to the lough, still dominate the village, and there are other impressive fortified buildings, including the Mint. The **Holy Trinity Heritage Centre**, which is housed in a medieval church, traces the history of the port from Anglo-Norman times.

Carlingford is the country's oyster capital, and its oyster festival in August draws a large crowd. The lough is a popular watersports centre too, and in summer you can go on cruises around the lough from the village quayside where there is a smart new international marina.

The **Carlingford Adventure Centre** provides information for walkers and also organizes its own tours.

**ENVIRONS:** A scenic route weaves around the **Cooley Peninsula**, skirting the coast and then cutting right through the mountains. The section along the north coast is the most dramatic: just 3 km (1.5 miles) northwest of Carlingford, in the **Slieve Foye Forest Park**, a corkscrew road climbs to give a gorgeous panoramic view over the hills and lough.

The Tain Trail, which you can join at Carlingford, is a 30-km (19-mile) circuit through some of the peninsula's most rugged scenery, with cairns and other prehistoric sites scattered over the moorland. Keen hikers will be able to walk it in a day.

## Monasterboice ❾

**Road map** D3. Co Louth. 🚌 to
Drogheda. ⬜ daily.

FOUNDED in the 5th century by an obscure disciple of St Patrick called St Buite, this monastic settlement is one of the most famous religious sites in the country. The ruins of the medieval monastery are enclosed within a graveyard in a lovely secluded spot north of Drogheda. The site includes a roofless round tower and two churches, but Monasterboice's greatest treasures are its 10th-century High Crosses.

Muiredach's High Cross is the finest of its kind in Ireland, and its sculpted biblical scenes are still remarkably fresh. They depict the life of Christ on the west face, while the east face, described in detail opposite, features mainly Old Testament scenes. The cross is named after an inscription on the base – "A prayer for Muiredach by whom this cross was made" – which is perhaps a reference to the abbot of Monasterboice. The 6.5-m (21ft) West Cross, also known as the Tall Cross, is one of the largest in Ireland. The carving has not lasted as well as on Muiredach's Cross, but you can make out scenes from the Death of Christ. The North Cross, which is the least notable of the three, features a Crucifixion and a carved spiral pattern.

**Detail from a tomb in
Monasterboice graveyard**

**Round tower and West High
Cross at Monasterboice**

# Ireland's High Crosses

HIGH CROSSES exist in Celtic parts of both Britain and Ireland. Yet in their profusion and craftsmanship, Irish High Crosses are exceptional. The distinctive ringed cross has become a symbol of Irish Christianity and is still imitated today. The beautiful High Crosses associated with medieval monasteries were carved between the 8th and 12th centuries. The early crosses bore only geometric motifs, but in the 9th to 10th centuries a new style emerged when sculpted scenes from the Bible were introduced. Referred to as "sermons in stone", these later versions may have been used to educate the masses. In essence, though, the High Cross was a status symbol for the monastery or a local patron.

*Pillar stones* inscribed with crosses, like this 6th-century example at Riasc (see p150), were precursors of the High Cross.

Capstone, showing St Anthony and St Paul meeting in the desert

Tenon

*The High Cross at Abenny* (see p191) is typical of 8th-century "ornamental" crosses. These were carved with interlacing patterns and spirals similar to those used in Celtic metalwork and jewellery.

## MUIREDACH'S CROSS

Each face of this 10th-century cross at Monasterboice features scenes from the Bible, including the east face seen here. The 5.5-m (18-ft) cross consists of three blocks of sandstone fitted together by means of tenons and sockets.

**The Last Judgment** shows Christ in Glory surrounded by a crowd of resurrected souls. The devil stands on his right clutching a pitchfork, ready to chase the damned souls into Hell.

Angle moulding

Adoration of the Magi

David struggling with Goliath

**The ring** served a functional as well as a decorative purpose, providing support for the head and arms of the stone cross.

**Moses** smites the rock to obtain water for the Israelites.

*The Dysert O'Dea Cross* (see p181) dates from the 1100s and represents the late phase of High Cross art. It features the figures of Christ and a bishop carved in high relief.

Socket

Base

Tenon

*The Fall of Man* shows Adam and Eve beneath an apple-laden tree, with Cain slaying Abel alongside. Both scenes are frequently depicted on Irish High Crosses.

## Drogheda ⑩

**Road map** D3. Co Louth. 🚗 30,000.
🚌 🚆 🛈 Donore Rd (041 9837070).
📅 Sat.

IN THE 14TH CENTURY, this historic Norman port near the mouth of the River Boyne was one of Ireland's most important towns. However, the place seems never to have recovered from the trauma of a vicious attack by Cromwell in 1649 *(see p37)*, in which 2,000 citizens were killed. Although it now looks rather dilapidated, the town has retained its original street plan and has a rich medieval heritage.

Little remains of Drogheda's medieval defences but **St Lawrence Gate**, a fine 13th-century barbican, has survived. Nearby, there are two churches called **St Peter's**. The one belonging to the Church of Ireland, built in 1753, is the more striking and has some splendid grave slabs. The Catholic church is worth visiting to see the embalmed head of Oliver Plunkett, an archbishop martyred in 1681.

South of the river you can climb Millmount, a Norman motte topped by a Martello tower. As well as providing a good view, this is the site of the **Millmount Museum**,

**Drogheda viewed from Millmount across the River Boyne**

which contains an interesting display of historical artifacts, as well as craft workshops.

### 🏛 Millmount Museum
Millmount Square. 📞 041 9833097. ⭕ daily (Sun pm only). ● 7 days at Christmas. 📷 ♿ limited.

## Newgrange and the Boyne Valley ⑪

**Road map** D3. Co Meath. 🚌 to Drogheda. 🚌 to Slane or Drogheda. 🛈 Brú na Bóinne Interpretive Centre (041 9880300). ⭕ daily.

KNOWN AS Brú na Bóinne, the "Palace of the Boyne", this river valley was the cradle of Irish civilization. The fertile soil supported a sophisticated society in Neolithic times. Much evidence survives, in the form of ring forts, passage graves and sacred enclosures. The most important Neolithic monuments in the valley are three passage graves: supreme among these is **Newgrange** *(see pp238–9)*, but **Dowth** and **Knowth** are significant too. The Boyne Valley also encompasses the Hill of Slane and the Hill of Tara *(see p240)*, both of which are major sites in Celtic mythology. Indeed, this whole region is rich in

**River Boyne near the site of the Battle of the Boyne**

---

### THE BATTLE OF THE BOYNE

In 1688, the Catholic King of England, James II, was deposed from his throne, to be re-placed by his Protestant daughter, Mary, and her husband, William of Orange. Determined to win back the crown, James sought the support of Irish Catholics, and challenged William at Oldbridge by the River Boyne west of Drogheda. The Battle of the Boyne took place on 1 July 1690, with James's poorly trained force of 25,000 French and Irish Catholics facing William's hardened army of 36,000 French Huguenots, Dutch, English and Scots. The Protestants triumphed and James fled to France, after a battle that signalled the beginning of total Protestant power over Ireland. It ushered in the confiscation of Catholic lands and the suppression of Catholic interests, sealing the country's fate for the next 300 years.

**William of Orange leading his troops at the Battle of the Boyne, 1 July 1690**

associations with Ireland's prehistory. With monuments predating Egypt's pyramids, the Boyne Valley is marketed as the Irish "Valley of the Kings".

Newgrange and Knowth can only be seen on a tour run by **Brú na Bóinne Interpretive Centre** near Newgrange. The centre also has displays on the area's Stone Age heritage and a reconstruction of Newgrange.

### Dowth

Off N51, 3 km (2 miles) E of Newgrange. ● *to the public.*

The passage grave at Dowth was plundered by Victorian souvenir hunters and has not been fully excavated. You cannot approach the tomb, but it can be seen from the road.

### Knowth

1.5 km (1 mile) NW of Newgrange. ○ *as Newgrange (see pp238–9).*

Knowth outdoes Newgrange in several respects, above all in the quantity of its treasures, which form the greatest concentration of megalithic art in Europe. Also, the site was occupied for a much longer period – from Neolithic times right up until about 1400.

Unusually, Knowth has two passage tombs rather than one. The excavations begun in 1962 are now complete and the site is open. The tombs can only be viewed externally to prevent further decay. Keep a look out for the finely carved kerbstones. Visitors sign up for tours via Brú na Bóinne.

**Ruined lavabo at Mellifont Abbey**

**Slane Castle in grounds landscaped by Capability Brown**

## Mellifont Abbey 🄲

**Road map** D3. Cullen, Co Louth.
**☏** 041 9826459. **🚌** *to Drogheda.*
**🚆** *to Drogheda or Slane.* ○ *May–Oct: daily; Nov–Apr: by appt.* 🔖

ON THE BANKS of the River Mattock, 10 km (6 miles) west of Drogheda, lies the first Cistercian monastery to have been built in Ireland. Mellifont was founded in 1142 on the orders of St Malachy, the Archbishop of Armagh. He was greatly influenced

**Glazed medieval tiles at Mellifont Abbey**

by St Bernard who, based at his monastery at Clairvaux in France, was behind the success of the Cistercian Order in Europe. The archbishop introduced not only Cistercian rigour to Mellifont, but also the formal style of monastic architecture used on the continent. His new monastery became a model for other Cistercian centres built in Ireland, retaining its supremacy over them until 1539, when the abbey was closed and turned into a fortified house. William of Orange used Mellifont as his headquarters during the Battle of the Boyne in 1690. The abbey is now a ruin, but it is still possible to appreciate the scale and ground

plan of the original complex. Not much survives of the abbey church, but to the south of it, enclosed by what remains of the Romanesque cloister, is the most interesting building at Mellifont: a unique 13th-century lavabo where monks came to wash their hands in a fountain before meals. Four of the building's original eight sides survive, each with a graceful Romanesque arch. On the eastern side of the cloister stands the 14th-century chapter house. It has an impressive vaulted ceiling and a floor laid with glazed medieval tiles taken from the abbey church.

## Slane 🄳

**Road map** D3. Co Meath. 🚶 *950.* 🚆

SLANE IS AN ATTRACTIVE estate village, centred on a quartet of Georgian houses. The Boyne flows through it and skirts **Slane Castle Demesne**, set in glorious grounds laid out in the 18th century by Capability Brown. The castle was damaged by fire in 1991 but reopened in 2001 after a decade of restoration.

Just to the north rises the **Hill of Slane** where, in 433, St Patrick is said to have lit a Paschal (Easter) fire as a challenge to the pagan High King of Tara *(see p240)*. The event symbolised the triumph of Christianity over paganism.

# Newgrange

**Tri-spiral carving on stone in chamber**

THE ORIGINS of Newgrange, one of the most important passage graves in Europe, are steeped in mystery. According to Celtic lore, the legendary kings of Tara *(see p240)* were buried here, but Newgrange predates them. Built in around 3200 BC, the grave was left untouched by all invaders until it was rediscovered in 1699. When it was excavated in the 1960s, archaeologists discovered that on the winter solstice (21 December), rays of sun enter the tomb and light up the burial chamber – making it the world's oldest solar observatory. All visitors to Newgrange and Knowth *(see pp236–7)* are admitted through the visitors' centre from where tours of the historic sight are taken. Early arrival is advised in summer to avoid long queues.

**Basin Stone**
*The chiselled stones, found in each recess, would have once contained funerary offerings and the bones of the dead.*

**The chamber** has three recesses or side chambers: the north recess is the one struck by sunlight on the winter solstice.

**Chamber Ceiling**
*The burial chamber's intricate corbelled ceiling, which reaches a height of 6 m (20 ft) above the floor, has survived intact. The overlapping slabs form a conical hollow, topped by a single capstone.*

## CONSTRUCTION OF NEWGRANGE

The tomb at Newgrange was designed by people with clearly exceptional artistic and engineering skills, who had use of neither the wheel nor metal tools. About 200,000 tonnes of loose stones were transported to build the mound, or cairn, which protects the passage grave. Larger slabs were used to make the circle around the cairn (12 out of a probable 35 stones have survived), the kerb and the tomb itself. Many of the kerbstones and the slabs lining the passage, the chamber and its recesses are decorated with zigzags, spirals and other geometric motifs. The grave's corbelled ceiling consists of smaller, unadorned slabs and has proved completely waterproof for the last 5,000 years.

Mound
Entrance

Stone circle (existing stones shaded)

100 m
328 ft

Decorated stones (shaded)

Recesses    Passage    Entrance

25 m
82 ft

**Plan of passage and burial chamber**

## Restoration of Newgrange

*Located on a low ridge north of the Boyne, Newgrange
took more than 70 years to build. Between 1962
and 1975 the passage grave and mound were
restored as closely as possible to their original state.*

**The standing stones** in
the passage are slabs of
slate which would have
been collected locally.

### Passage

*At dawn on 21
December, a beam of
sunlight shines through
the roof box (a feature
unique to Newgrange),
travels along the 19-m
(62-ft) passage and hits
the central recess in the
burial chamber.*

**The retaining
wall** around the
front of the cairn
was rebuilt using
the white quartz
and granite
stones found
scattered around
the site during
excavations.

### Entrance

*The opening was originally
blocked by the stone standing
to its right. Newgrange's most
elaborately carved kerbstone
is in front, part of the kerb of
huge slabs around the cairn.*

**Roof box**

Trim Castle set in water meadows beside the River Boyne

## Hill of Tara

**Road map** D3. Nr Killmessan Village, Co Meath. 𝄞 046 25903 (May–Oct), 041 9880300 (Nov–Apr). 🚌 to Navan. ◯ May–Oct: daily; Nov–Apr: by appt. 🏛 for Interpretative Centre. 🔧

A SITE of mythical importance, Tara was the political and spiritual centre of Celtic Ireland and the seat of the High Kings until the 11th century. The spread of Christianity, which eroded the importance of Tara, is marked by a statue of St Patrick. The symbolism of the site was not lost on Daniel O'Connell *(see p40)*, who chose Tara for a rally in 1843, attended by over one million people.

Tours from the Interpretative Centre take in a Stone Age passage grave and Iron Age hill forts, which, to the untutored eye, look like mere hollows and grassy mounds. Clearest is the Royal Enclosure, an oval fort, in the centre of which is Cormac's House containing the "stone of destiny" *(Lialh Fail)*, fertility symbol and inauguration stone of the High Kings. Most moving, however, is the poignant atmosphere and views over the Boyne Valley.

## Trim

**Road map** D3. Co Meath. 🏠 6,500. 🚌 ℹ Mill St (046 37111). 🛍 Fri.

T RIM IS ONE of the most pleasing Midlands market towns. A Norman stronghold on the River Boyne, it marked a boundary of the Pale *(see p124)*. Trim runs efficient heritage and genealogy centres

while the **Duchas Trim Folk Theatre** provides rousing summer entertainment. (This popular company is at present in search of new premises.) Equally engrossing is the Nun Run, a bizarre summer horse race with nuns as jockeys, which takes place near **Trim Castle**. The castle was founded in 1173 by Hugh de Lacy, a Norman knight, and is one of the largest medieval castles in Europe. It makes a spectacular backdrop for films and was used, among others, in Mel Gibson's film *Braveheart* in 1995. Over the river is **Talbot Castle**, an Augustinian abbey converted to a manor house in the 15th century. Just north of the abbey, **St Patrick's Cathedral** incorporates part of a medieval church with a 15th-century tower and sections of the original chancel.

**Butterstream Gardens**, on the edge of town, are the best in the county. A luxuriant herbaceous bed is the centrepiece, but equally pleasing are the exotic woodland, rose and white gardens. The design is enhanced by pergolas, pools and bridges.

🏰 **Trim Castle**
𝄞 046 38619. ◯ ring for details.
🌹 **Butterstream Gardens**
Kildalkey Rd. 𝄞 046 36017.
◯ May–Sep: daily. 🏛

## Mullingar

**Road map** C3. Co Westmeath. 🏠 14,000. 🚌 🚏 ℹ Market Square (044 48650). 🛍 Sat.

T HE COUNTY TOWN of Westmeath is a prosperous but unremarkable market town encircled by the Royal Canal

Aerial view of Iron Age forts on the Hill of Tara

*(see p99),* which with its 46 'locks links Dublin with the River Shannon. The cost of building the canal bankrupted its investors and it was never profitable. Although Mullingar's main appeal is as a base to explore the surrounding area, pubs such as Con's and the cheery Canton Casey's can make a pleasant interlude.

**ENVIRONS:** The Dublin to Mullingar stretch of the Royal Canal has attractive towpaths for walkers, and fishing.

Just off the Kilbeggan road from Mullingar stands **Belvedere House**, a romantic Palladian villa overlooking Lough Ennel. The house, built in 1740 by Richard Castle, is decorated with Rococo plasterwork and set in beautiful grounds.

Shortly after the house was built, the first Earl of Belvedere accused his young wife of having an affair with his brother, and imprisoned her for 31 years in a neighbouring house. In 1760, the Earl built a Gothic folly – the Jealous Wall – to block the view of his second brother's more opulent mansion across the lake. The Jealous Wall remains as does an octagonal gazebo and other follies.

Charming terraces descend to the lake. On the other side of the house is a picturesque walled garden, enclosed by an arboretum and parkland.

### ⚜ Belvedere House
6.5 km (4 miles) S of Mullingar. **(** 044 49060. **◯** May–Aug: 10:30am–7pm daily; Sep–Oct: 10:30am–6pm daily; Nov–Apr: 10:30–4:30pm daily (last adm 1hr before closing). **🎫 🖼 📷** **♿** gallery & theatre.

**The Jealous Wall at Belvedere House, near Mullingar**

**Athlone Castle below the towers of the church of St Peter and St Paul**

## Kilbeggan ⓱

**Road map** C4. Co Westmeath. **🚶** 600. **🚌**

SITUATED BETWEEN Mullingar and Tullamore, this pleasant village has a small harbour on the Grand Canal. However the main point of interest is **Locke's Distillery**. Founded in 1757, it claims to be the oldest licensed pot still distillery in the world. Unable to compete with Scotch whisky manufacturers, the company went bankrupt in 1954, but the aroma hung in the warehouses for years and was known as "the angel's share". The distillery was reopened as a museum in 1987. The building is authentic, a solid structure complete with water wheel and inside steam engine. A tour traces the process of Irish whiskey-making, from the mash tuns to the vast fermentation vats and creation of wash (rough beer) to the distillation and maturation stages. At the tasting stage, workers would sample the whiskey in the can pit room. Visitors can still taste whiskeys in the bar but, unlike the original workers, cannot bathe in the whiskey vats.

**Miniature whiskey bottles at Locke's Distillery in Kilbeggan**

## 🏛 Locke's Distillery
Main Street. **(** 0506 32134. **◯** Apr–Oct: 9am–6pm daily; Nov–Mar: 10am–4pm daily. **🎫 ❚❚**

## Athlone ⓲

**Road map** C3. Co Westmeath. **🚶** 16,000. **🚌 🚉 ℹ** Market Square (0902 94630). **🚌** Fri.

THE TOWN owes its historical importance to its position by a natural ford on the River Shannon. **Athlone Castle** is a much altered 13th-century fortress, which was badly damaged in the Jacobite Wars *(see pp36–7).* It lies in the shadow of the 19th-century church of St Peter and St Paul. The neighbouring streets offer several good pubs. Across the river from the castle, boats depart for Clonmacnoise *(see pp242–3)* or Lough Ree.

## ♜ Athlone Castle
**Visitors' Centre (** 0902 92912. **◯** May–Oct: daily; Nov–Apr: by appt. **🎫 ♿** limited.

**ENVIRONS:** The **Lough Ree Trail** starts 8 km (5 miles) northeast of Athlone, at Glasson. The route passes picturesque views and unspoilt countryside. The trail is a popular cycling tour.

# Clonmacnoise ⑲

THIS MEDIEVAL MONASTERY, in a remote spot by the River Shannon, was founded by St Ciaran in 545–548. Clonmacnoise lay at a crossroads of medieval routes, linking all parts of Ireland. Known for its scholarship and piety, it thrived from the 7th to the 12th century. Many kings of Tara and of Connaught were buried here. Plundered by the Vikings and Anglo-Normans, it fell to the English in 1552. Today, a group of stone churches (temples), a cathedral, two round towers and three High Crosses remain.

**Detail on a grave slab**

**Last Circuit of Pilgrims at Clonmacnoise**
*This painting (1838), by George Petrie, shows pilgrims walking the traditional route three times around the site. Pilgrims still do this every year on 9 September, St Ciaran's Day.*

**Cross of the Scriptures**
*This copy of the original 9th-century cross (now in the museum) is decorated with biblical scenes, but the identity of most of the figures is uncertain.*

**The Pope's Shelter** was where John Paul II conducted Mass during his visit in 1979.

## VISITING CLONMACNOISE

The Visitors' Centre is housed in three buildings modelled on beehive huts *(see p19)*. The museum section contains early grave slabs and the three remaining High Crosses, replicas of which now stand in their original locations. The Nuns' Church, northeast of the main site, has a Romanesque doorway and chancel arch.

### KEY

| | |
|---|---|
| 1 South Cross | 7 Cathedral |
| 2 Temple Dowling | 8 North Cross |
| 3 Temple Hurpan | 9 Cross of the Scriptures |
| 4 Temple Melaghlin | 10 Round Tower |
| 5 Temple Ciaran | 11 Temple Connor |
| 6 Temple Kelly | 12 Temple Finghin |

0 metres        50

0 yards         50

Pilgrim path to Nuns' Church

Entrance

Pope's Shelter

To Visitors' Centre

### Whispering Door

*Above the cathedral's 15th-century north doorway are carvings of saints Francis, Patrick and Dominic. The acoustics of the doorway are such that even a whisper is carried inside the building.*

The Shannonbridge Bog Railway passing an area of cut bog

# Shannonbridge Bog Railway �20

**Road map** C4. 5 km (3 miles) E of Shannonbridge, Co Offaly. ☎ 0905 74114. 🚃 to Athlone. ⏰ Apr–Oct: daily; Nov–Mar: groups by appt. 🅿 🚻 🔗 www.bnm.ie

STARTING near Shannonbridge, this guided tour by train is run by the Irish Peat Board (Bord na Móna). The 45-minute tour covers 9 km (6 miles) of bogland and gives a fascinating insight into the history and development of the Blackwater raised bogs – an area of great ecological importance, parts of which are protected.

Tour guides describe the transformation from lake to marshy fen and thence to bog *(see p244)*, and explain that in several hundred years the bog will become fields and woodland. They also point out the area's distinctive flora and fauna, from dragonflies to bog cotton, bog asphodel and sphagnum moss. The small lakes and pools that punctuate the bog provide excellent habitats for wetland birds.

Bog oaks – old trees which have been preserved in the bog – are visible in the places where the peat has been harvested. For centuries, peat has been the main source of fuel in rural Ireland, and visitors can watch peat being cut by hand using the traditional tool known as a "slane". Modern peat-harvesting machines in use nearby supply the power station at Shannonbridge. There is a craft shop and also a machinery museum here.

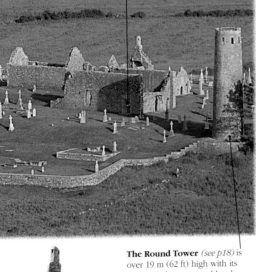

The Round Tower *(see p18)* is over 19 m (62 ft) high with its doorway above ground level.

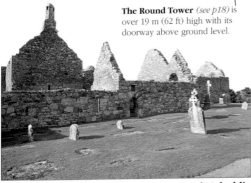

### Temples Dowling, Hurpan and Melaghlin

*Built as a family crypt, Temple Hurpan was a 17th-century addition to the early Romanesque Temple Dowling. The 13th-century Temple Melaghlin has two fine round-headed windows.*

# The Raised Bogs of the Midlands

**Four-spotted chaser dragonfly**

Peatland or bog, which covers about 15 per cent of the Irish landscape, exists in two principal forms. Most extensive is the thin blanket bog found chiefly in the west, while the dome-shaped raised bogs are more characteristic of the Midlands – notably in an area known as the Bog of Allen.

Although Irish boglands are some of the largest in Europe, the use of peat for domestic fuel and fertilizer has greatly reduced their extent. This has threatened not only the shape of the Irish landscape but also the survival of a unique habitat and the unusual plants and insects it supports.

**Unspoilt expanse of the Bog of Allen**

***Peat cutters*** *still gather turf (as peat is known locally) by hand in parts of Ireland. It is then set in stacks to dry. Peat makes a good fuel, because it is rich in partially decayed vegetation, laid down over thousands of years.*

Fen plants

Birch and willow scrub

Moraine (glacial deposits)

***8000 BC:*** *Shallow meltwater lakes that formed after the Ice Age gradually filled with mud. Reeds, sedges and other fen plants began to dominate in the marshy conditions which resulted.*

Fen plants (reeds and sedges)

Fen peat

Mud

***6000 BC:*** *As the fen vegetation died, it sank to the lake bed but did not decompose fully in the waterlogged conditions, forming a layer of peat. This slowly built up and also spread outwards.*

Fen peat

Fresh sphagnum peat

Buried tree stumps

***3000 BC:*** *As the peat built up and the lake slowly disappeared, plant life in the developing bog had to rely almost exclusively on rainwater, which is acid. Fen plants could not survive in these acidic conditions and gave way to bog mosses, mainly species of sphagnum. As these mosses died, they formed a layer of sphagnum peat on the surface of the bog which, over the centuries, attained a distinctive domed shape.*

Pine and alder trees

Raised bog

Tree stumps

***Present day:*** *Few raised bogs are actively growing today. Those that remain contain a fascinating historical record of the landscape. The survival of ancient tree stumps shows how well plants are preserved in peat.*

**Sphagnum moss**

# Birr ㉑

**Road map** 4C. Co Offaly. 🏃 *4,100.*
🚌 ℹ️ *May–Sep: Rosse Row (0509 20110).*

Birr, a gentrified estate town, grew up in the shadow of the castle where the Earls of Rosse have resided for almost four centuries. It is famous for its authentic Georgian layout, with houses displaying original fanlights, door panelling and iron railings. Two particularly elegant streets are Oxmantown Mall, designed by the 2nd Earl of Rosse, and John's Mall. Emmet Square may have sold its Georgian soul to commerce, but Dooly's Hotel is still a fine example of an old coaching inn. Foster's bar, in nearby Connaught Street, is one of many traditional shopfronts to have been restored in Birr.

### ⚘ Birr Castle Demesne

Rosse Row. 📞 *0509 20336.*
**Gardens** ⬜ *daily.* 🏞️ 🚹 🛍️ 🚻
Birr Castle was founded in 1620 by the Parsons, later Earls of Rosse, and is still the family seat. They are most noted for their contribution to astronomy – a telescope, built by the 3rd Earl in 1845, was the largest in the world at the time. The 17-m (56-ft) wooden tube, supported by two walls, can be seen in the grounds fully restored to its original working condition. The Historic Science Centre traces the family's pioneering work.

The castle is closed to the public, but the glory of Birr lies in its grounds. First landscaped in the 18th century, these are famous for their 9-m (30-ft) box hedges and for the exotic trees and shrubs that were gathered during foreign expeditions sponsored by the 6th Earl. The magnolias and maples are particularly striking. The gardens overlook the meeting of two rivers, and water greatly influenced the planning of the grounds.

# Slieve Bloom Mountains ㉒

**Road map** D4. Co Offaly and Co Laois.
🚌 *to Mountmellick.* ℹ️ *May–Sep: Rosse Row, Birr (0509 20110).*

This low range of mountains rises unexpectedly from the bogs and plains of Offaly and Laois, providing a welcome change in the predominantly flat Midlands. You can walk along the **Slieve Bloom Way**, a 30-km (19-mile) circular trail through an unspoilt landscape of open vistas, deep wooded glens and mountain streams. There are other marked paths too. Good starting points are **Cadamstown**, with an attractive old mill, and the pretty village of **Kinnitty** – both in the northern foothills.

An alcove in the front hall of Emo Court with a *trompe l'oeil* ceiling

# Emo Court ㉓

**Road map** D4. 13 km (8 miles) NE of Portlaoise, Co Laois. 📞 *0502 26573.*
🚌 *to Monasterevin or Portlaoise.*
**House** ⬜ *mid-Jun–mid-Sep: Tue–Sun.*
**Gardens** ⬜ *daily.* 🏞️ 🚹 *limited.*

Emo court, commissioned by the Earl of Portarlington in 1790, represents the only foray into domestic architecture by James Gandon, designer of the Custom House in Dublin *(see p86)*. The monumental Neo-Classical mansion has a splendid façade featuring an Ionic portico. Inside are a magnificent gilded rotunda and fine stuccowork ceilings.

Emo Court became the property of the Office of Public Works in 1994 but the previous owner, who restored the house, is still resident and is now working on the grounds. These are adorned with fine statuary and include a lakeside walk.

# Rock of Dunamase ㉔

**Road map** D4. 5 km (3 miles) E of Portlaoise, Co Laois. 🚌 *to Portlaoise.*

The Rock of Dunamase, which looms dramatically above the plains east of Portlaoise, has long been a military site. Originally crowned by an Iron Age ring fort, the 13th-century castle which succeeded it is now more prominent – though it was virtually destroyed by Cromwellian forces in 1650. You can reach the battered keep by climbing up banks and ditches through two gateways and a fortified courtyard.

**Rock of Dunamase viewed from Stradbally to the east**

# NORTHERN IRELAND

LONDONDERRY · ANTRIM · TYRONE · FERMANAGH
ARMAGH · DOWN

NORTHERN IRELAND *has sights from every era of Ireland's history as well as magnificently varied coastal and lakeland scenery. In the past, it has received fewer visitors than the Republic as a result of the "Troubles". Following recent moves towards peace, there seems every chance that it will at last attract the attention it deserves.*

The province of Northern Ireland was created after partition of the island in 1921. Its six counties (plus Donegal, Monaghan and Cavan) were part of Ulster, one of Ireland's four traditional kingdoms. It was most probably in Ulster that Christianity first ousted the old Celtic pagan beliefs. In 432 St Patrick landed at Saul in County Down, later founding a church at Armagh, which is still the spiritual capital of Ireland.

The dominant political force in early Christian times was the Uí Néill clan. Their descendants, the O'Neills, put up fierce resistance to English conquest in the late 16th century. Hugh O'Neill, Earl of Tyrone, had some notable successes against the armies of Elizabeth I, but was defeated and in 1607 fled to Europe with other Irish lords from Ulster, in what became known as the "Flight of the Earls". Vacant estates were granted to individuals and companies, who planted them with English and Scottish Protestants *(see p37)*. Many Plantation towns, such as Londonderry, preserve their 17th-century layout around a central square or "diamond". The arrival of new settlers meant that Irish Catholics were increasingly marginalized, thereby sowing the seeds of 400 years of conflict.

In the relative tranquillity of the 18th century, the Anglo-Irish nobility built stately homes, such as Mount Stewart House on the Ards Peninsula and Castle Coole near Enniskillen. Ulster also enjoyed prosperity in the 19th century through its ship-building, linen and rope-making industries.

Though densely populated and industrialized around Belfast, away from the capital the region is primarily agricultural. It also has areas of outstanding natural beauty, notably the rugged Antrim coastline around the Giant's Causeway, the Mountains of Mourne in County Down and the Erne lakeland in the west of the region.

**Belfast's City Hall (1906), symbol of the city's civic pride**

◁ **Carrick-a-rede Rope Bridge, an unusual tourist attraction on the Causeway Coast**

# Exploring Northern Ireland

THE STARTING POINT for most visitors to the province is Belfast. The capital has grand Victorian buildings, good pubs and the excellent Ulster Museum. However, Northern Ireland's greatest attractions lie along its coast. These range from the extraordinary volcanic landscape of the Giant's Causeway to Carrickfergus, Ireland's best preserved Norman castle. There are also Victorian resorts, like Portstewart, tiny fishing villages and unspoilt sandy beaches, such as Benone Strand. Ramblers are drawn to the Mountains of Mourne, while anglers and boating enthusiasts can enjoy the lakeland of Lower Lough Erne.

**Harbour and promenade at the seaside resort of Portstewart**

0 kilometres    10

0 miles    5

BENONE STRAND

CAUSEWAY COA

PORTSTEW

MUSSENDEN TEMPLE

COLE

Lough Foyle

Letterkenny

LONDONDERRY

Foyle

Roe

A2

A6

STRABANE

B48

SPERRIN MOUNTAINS

Derg

ULSTER HISTORY PARK

BEAGHMORE STONE CIRCLES

A505

COOKSTOWN

ULSTER-AMERICAN FOLK PARK

OMAGH

A32

A5

A29

DUNGANNON

A47

Sligo

LOWER LOUGH ERNE

A4

BELLEEK POTTERY

DEVENISH ISLAND

ENNISKILLEN

ARMAGH

A509

A4

MARBLE ARCH CAVES

FLORENCE COURT

Upper Lough Erne

A34

Monaghan

## GETTING AROUND

Belfast is the transport hub of Northern Ireland. From here the very limited train network runs northwest to Londonderry and south to Dublin. In most parts of the province you have to rely on buses, but fortunately, even in rural areas, these are fairly frequent and punctual. However, a car is essential if you want to go off the beaten track in search of ancient monuments or tour the coast at leisure. Depending on the security situation, you may still encounter temporary checkpoints set up by the army and police (see p343).

## KEY

| | |
|---|---|
| | Motorway |
| | Major road |
| | Minor road |
| | Scenic route |
| | River |
| | Viewpoint |

## SIGHTS AT A GLANCE

Ards Peninsula **29**
Armagh **23**
Ballycastle **9**
Beaghmore Stone Circles **13**
*Belfast pp268–71* **27**
Belleek Pottery **16**
Benone Strand **2**
Carrickfergus **26**
Castlewellan Forest Park **34**
Causeway Coast **5**
Cookstown **12**
Cushendall **10**
Devenish Island **18**
Downpatrick **32**
Dungannon **22**
Enniskillen **19**

Florence Court **21**
*Giant's Causeway pp254–5* **6**
Glenariff Forest Park **11**
Hillsborough **31**
Larne **25**
Lecale Peninsula **33**
*Londonderry pp250–51* **1**
Lough Neagh **24**
Marble Arch Caves **20**
Mountains of Mourne **35**
*Mount Stewart House pp274–5* **30**
Mussenden Temple **3**
Old Bushmills Distillery **7**
Portstewart **4**
Rathlin Island **8**
Ulster-American Folk Park **15**
Ulster Folk and Transport
 Museum **28**
Ulster History Park **14**

### Tours
Lower Lough Erne **17**
Mourne Coast **36**

Gold Salamander from
Armada wreck at the
Ulster Museum, Belfast

### SEE ALSO

- *Where to Stay* pp300–301

- *Restaurants, Cafés and Pubs* pp316–17 & p321

Dry-stone walls on slopes of the Mountains of Mourne

# Londonderry ①

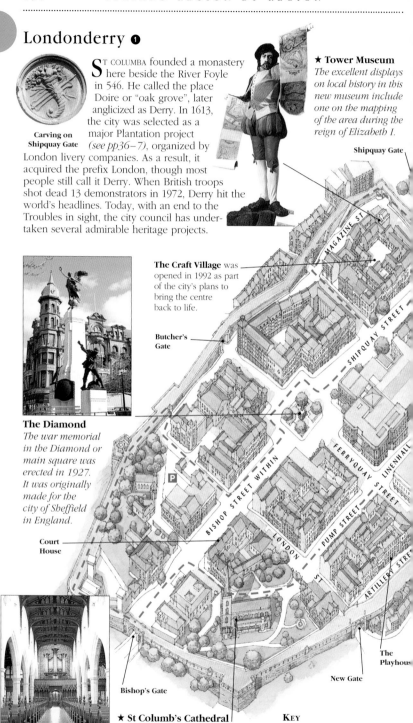

**Carving on Shipquay Gate**

St columba founded a monastery here beside the River Foyle in 546. He called the place Doire or "oak grove", later anglicized as Derry. In 1613, the city was selected as a major Plantation project *(see pp36–7)*, organized by London livery companies. As a result, it acquired the prefix London, though most people still call it Derry. When British troops shot dead 13 demonstrators in 1972, Derry hit the world's headlines. Today, with an end to the Troubles in sight, the city council has undertaken several admirable heritage projects.

★ **Tower Museum**
*The excellent displays on local history in this new museum include one on the mapping of the area during the reign of Elizabeth I.*

**Shipquay Gate**

**The Craft Village** was opened in 1992 as part of the city's plans to bring the centre back to life.

**Butcher's Gate**

MAGAZINE ST

SHIPQUAY STREET

FERRYQUAY STREET

LINENHALL

**The Diamond**
*The war memorial in the Diamond or main square was erected in 1927. It was originally made for the city of Sheffield in England.*

BISHOP STREET WITHIN

LONDON ST

PUMP STREET

ARTILLERY STRE

**Court House**

**The Playhouse**

**New Gate**

**Bishop's Gate**

★ **St Columb's Cathedral**
*The nave's wooden ceiling dates from 1862. The corbels are carved with the heads of former bishops and deans.*

**KEY**

| P | Parking |
|---|---------|
| — | Suggested route |

★ **Guildhall**
*This stained-glass
window shows
St Columba.
Others feature
incidents from
the siege of Derry,
including the
apprentice boys
shutting the city
gates in 1688.*

Ferryquay
Gate

**To Craigavon Bridge
and River Foyle**

0 metres        100

0 yards          100

## 🔓 St Columb's Cathedral

St Columb's Court. 📞 028 7126
7313. 🕐 Mon–Sat. 🎟 📷 👣 ♿
Built between 1628 and 1633,
in "Planters' Gothic" style, St
Columb's was the first cathedral to be founded in
the British Isles after
the Reformation.
The interior was
extensively restored
in the 19th century.
A small museum in
the Chapter House
contains relics from the
siege of 1689 (*see
pp36–7*), including
the 17th-century
locks and keys of the city. In
the vestibule is a hollow mortar
cannonball that was fired into
the city by James II's army. It
carried terms for capitulation,
but the reply of the Protestants
within the walls was a defiant
"No surrender", a phrase used
by Loyalists to this day.

**Lock of city gate in
St Columb's Cathedral**

## 🏛 Tower Museum

Union Hall Place. 📞 028 7137 2411.
🕐 Jul & Aug: daily; Sep–Jun: Tue–Sat;
bank hols. 🎟 ♿
Housed in O'Doherty Tower
(a replica of the original 16th-
century building on this site),
the museum traces the history
of the city from its foundation
to the recent Troubles using
multimedia displays. Upstairs,
an exhibition about the 1688
Spanish Armada includes
artifacts from ships wrecked
in nearby Kinnagoe Bay.

## ⚓ Walls of Derry

Access from Magazine Street.
Among the best preserved city
fortifications in Europe, the
city walls rise to a height of
8 m (26 ft) and in places are
9 m (30 ft) wide. Completed
in 1618 to defend the new
merchant city from Gaelic

chieftains in Donegal, the
walls have never been
breached, not even during
the siege of 1689, when 7,000
out of a population of 20,000
perished from disease or
starvation. Extensive
restoration work
means that it should
soon be possible to
walk right around
the walls for the first
time in decades. Just
outside the old fortifications, beyond Butcher's
Gate, is the Bogside,
a Catholic area with
a famous mural that
announces "You are now
entering Free Derry".

## 🏛 Guildhall

Guildhall Square. 📞 028 7137 7335.
🕐 Mon–Fri.
Standing between the walled
city and the River Foyle, this
Neo-Gothic building was constructed in 1890, but a fire in
1908 and a bomb in 1972 both
necessitated substantial repairs.
Stained-glass windows – copies
of the originals – recount the
history of Derry. To the rear
of the Guildhall is Derry Quay,
from where Irish emigrants
sailed to America in the 18th
and 19th centuries.

**ENVIRONS:** Just off the B194,
on the way to Muff, stands a
memorial to American aviator
Amelia Earhart, the first woman
to complete a transatlantic solo
flight. She had intended to fly
to Paris, but in May 1932
landed in a field outside Derry.
A sculpture marks the spot and
the nearby **Earhart Centre**
contains a small exhibition.

## 🏛 Earhart Centre

Ballyarnet. 📞 028 7135 4040.
🕐 Mon–Fri.

**The old walled city viewed across the River Foyle**

Terraced houses behind the promenade at Portstewart

# Benone Strand ❷

**Road map** D1. Co Londonderry.
🚹 Benone Tourist Complex, 53
Benone Ave, Seacoast Rd, Magilligan
(028 7775 0555). ⬭ daily.

THE WIDE, golden sands of
Ireland's longest beach,
also known as Magilligan
Strand, sweep along the Londonderry coastline for more
than 10 km (6 miles). The
magnificent beach has been
granted EU Blue Flag status
for its cleanliness. Marking the
western extremity of the beach
is **Magilligan Point** where a
Martello tower, built during
the Napoleonic wars, stands
guard over the bottleneck
entrance to Lough Foyle. To
get to the point, renowned
for its rare shellfish and sea
birds, you have to drive over
ramps below the watchtowers
and listening devices of a
huge army base. The ex-
perience is rather unsettling,
but well worth the trouble.

# Mussenden Temple ❸

**Road map** D1. Co Londonderry.
🅒 028 7084 8728. ⬭ Jul–Aug: daily
(pm only); Apr–Jun & Sep: Sat, Sun &
public hols (pm only). 🅖 limited.

THE ODDEST SIGHT along the
Londonderry coast is this
small, domed rotunda perched
precariously on a windswept
headland outside the family resort of Castlerock. The temple
was built in 1785 by Frederick

Augustus Hervey, the eccentric
Earl of Bristol and Protestant
Bishop of Derry, as a memorial
to his cousin Mrs Frideswide
Mussenden. The design was
based on the Temple of Vesta
at Tivoli outside Rome.

The walls, made of basalt
faced with sandstone, open
out at the four points of the
compass to three windows
and an entrance. Originally
designed for use as a library
(or, as some stories go, an
elaborate boudoir for the
bishop's mistress), the structure is now maintained by the
National Trust and remains in
excellent condition.

The bishop allowed the local
priest to say Mass for his
Roman Catholic tenants in the
basement. Today, this contains
artifacts from the bishop's
former residence, the nearby
Downhill Castle, which was
gutted by fire and is now little
more than an impressive shell.

The surrounding area offers
some good glen and cliff walks
and there are some magnificent views of the Londonderry
and Antrim coastline. Below
the temple is Downhill
Strand, where the
bishop sponsored
horseback
races be-
tween his
clergy.

# Portstewart ❹

**Road map** D1. Co Londonderry.
🚶 6,000. 🚉 to Coleraine or Portrush.
🚌 🚹 Jul & Aug: Town Hall, The
Crescent (028 7083 2286).

A POPULAR HOLIDAY destination
for Victorian middle-class
families, Portstewart is still a
family favourite today. Its
long, crescent-shaped seafront
promenade is sheltered by
rocky headlands. Just west of
town, and accessible by road
or by a cliffside walk, stretches
**Portstewart Strand**, a magnificent, long, sandy beach,
protected by the National Trust.

On Ramore Head, just to the
east, lies **Portrush**, a brasher
resort with an abundance of
souvenir shops and amusement
arcades. The East Strand is
backed by sand dunes and runs
parallel with the world-class
**Royal Portrush Golf Links**.
You can stroll along the beach
to White Rocks – limestone
cliffs carved by the wind and
waves into caves and arches.

To the south is the university
town of **Coleraine**. The North
West 200 (see p26), the world's
fastest motorcycle road race, is
run between Portstewart,
Coleraine and Portrush. The
race is held in May in front of
100,000
people.

Mussenden Temple set on a cliff top on the Londonderry coast

# Causeway Coast ⑤

**Road map** D1. Co Antrim. ℹ️ *Giant's Causeway (028 2073 1855).* **Carrick-a-rede Rope Bridge** ☎ *028 2073 1582.* ⭕ *Mar–early Sep: daily.* 💷 *for car park.* 🖥️ 🚻 ♿

THE RENOWN of the **Giant's Causeway** *(see pp254–5)*, Ireland's only World Heritage Site, overshadows the other attractions of this stretch of North Antrim coast. When visiting the Causeway, it is well worth investigating the sandy bays, craggy headlands and dramatic ruins that punctuate the rest of this inspirational coastline.

Approaching the Causeway from the west, you pass the eerie ruins of **Dunluce Castle** perched vulnerably on a steep crag – a storm once blew its kitchen into the sea. Dating back to the 13th century, it was the main fortress of the MacDonnells, chiefs of Antrim. Although the roof has gone, it is still well preserved, with its twin towers, gateway and some original cobbling intact.

**Dunseverick Castle** can be reached by road or a lengthy hike from the Causeway. It is a much earlier fortification than Dunluce and only one massive

The roofless ruins of 13th-century Dunluce Castle

wall remains. Once the capital of the kingdom of Dalriada, it was linked to Tara *(see p240)* by a great road and was the departure point for 5th-century Irish raids on Scotland.

Just past the attractive, sandy **White Park Bay**, a tight switchback road leads down to the picturesque harbour of **Ballintoy**, reminiscent – on a good day – of an Aegean fishing village. **Sheep Island**, a rocky outcrop just offshore, is a cormorant colony. Boat trips run past it in the summer.

Just east of Ballintoy is one of the most unusual and scary tourist attractions in Ireland, the **Carrick-a-rede Rope Bridge**. The bridge hangs 25 m (80 ft) above the sea and wobbles and twists as soon as you stand on it. Made of planks strung between wires, it provides access to the salmon

fishery on the tiny island across the 20-m (65-ft) chasm. There are strong handrails and safety nets, but it's definitely not for those with vertigo. Further east along the coast lies **Kinbane Castle**, a 16th-century ruin with spectacular views.

♖ **Dunluce Castle**
☎ *028 2073 1938.* ⭕ *Apr–Sep: daily; Oct–Mar: Tue–Sun.* 💷 🗎

Fishing boats moored in the shelter of Ballintoy harbour

Carrick-a-rede Rope Bridge

## THE NORTH ANTRIM COASTLINE

### KEY

═ Minor road

▬ Major road

🅿 Parking

ℹ️ Tourist information

*Map showing the North Antrim coastline with locations including Giant's Causeway, B146, Dunseverick Castle, White Park Bay, Sheep Island, Carrick-a-rede Rope Bridge, Ballintoy, Kinbane Castle, B15, Portballintrae, Bushmills, Dunluce Castle, A2, B17, B147, B17, Ballycastle, Portrush, B62, B17, B66, B67, Portstewart.*

0 kilometres 5

0 miles 3

# Giant's Causeway

Chimney
stacks

THE SHEER STRANGENESS of this place and the bizarre regularity of its basalt columns has made the Giant's Causeway the subject of numerous legends. The most popular tells how the giant, Finn MacCool *(see pp24–5)*, laid the causeway to provide a path across the sea to his lady love, who lived on the island of Staffa in Scotland – where similar columns are found. The Giant's Causeway attracts many tourists, who are taken by the busload from the visitors' centre down to the shore. Nothing, however, can destroy the magic of this place, with its looming grey cliffs and shrieking gulls; paths along the coast allow you to escape the crowds.

**Aird's Snout**
*This nose-shaped promontory juts out from the 120-m (395-ft) basalt cliffs that soar above the Giant's Causeway.*

## THE FORMATION OF THE CAUSEWAY

Wooded
landscape

Hot lava

Valley

Lower
basalts

Limestone

**61 million years ago:** In a series of massive volcanic eruptions molten lava poured from narrow fissures in the ground, filling in the valleys and burning the vegetation that grew there.

Tholeiitic
basalt
lava

Non-eroded
surface

Inter-
basaltic
layer

**60 million years ago:** This layer of tholeiitic basalt lava cooled rapidly. In the process it shrank and cracked evenly into polygonal-shaped blocks, forming columnar jointing beneath the surface.

Steam and
gas clouds

New
lava
flows

**58 million years ago:** New volcanic eruptions produced further lava flows. These had a slightly different chemical composition from earlier flows and, once cool, did not form such well defined columns.

Snow

Scree

Ice

Sea water

**15,000 years ago:** At the end of the Ice Age, when the land was still frozen, sea ice ground its way slowly past the high basalt cliffs, eroding the foreshore and helping to form the Giant's Causeway.

Inter-basaltic
layer

**Shape of the Columns**
*Most columns are hexagonal, but some have four, five, eight or even ten sides. They generally measure about 30 cm (12 in) across.*

### VISITORS' CHECKLIST

**Road Map** D1. Co Antrim. ☐ to Portrush. ☐ from Portrush, Bushmills or Coleraine. **Visitors' Centre** Causeway Head, 3 km (2 miles) N of Bushmills (028 2073 1855). ☐ Mar–May: 10am–5pm daily; Jun–Oct: 10am–6pm (Jul & Aug: 7pm); Nov–Feb: 10am–4:30pm. ☐ limited. ☐ on request. ☐

**Giant's Causeway and the North Antrim Coast**
*Millions of years of geological activity can be witnessed in the eroded cliffs flanking the Causeway. The striking band of reddish rock is the inter-basaltic layer, which formed during a long period of temperate climatic conditions. The high iron content explains the rock's rich ochre colour.*

Road

Little Causeway

**Middle Causeway**
*This section of the Middle Causeway is known as the Honeycomb. Like other unusual rock formations along the coast, it was christened by local guides during Victorian times.*

## GIANT'S CAUSEWAY TODAY

It has been estimated that 37,000 basalt columns extend from the cliffs down into the sea. Close to the shore, they have been eroded to form the Grand, Middle and Little Causeways.

**Plant debris**
is trapped between the lava flows.

**Wishing Chair**
*Myth has it that this rocky seat was made for Finn MacCool when he was a boy, and that wishes made here will come true.*

Lower basalts

Grand Causeway

**Visitors exploring the Giant's Causeway at low tide** ▷

# Old Bushmills Distillery **❼**

**Road map** D1. Bushmills, Co Antrim.
**📞** 028 2073 1521. **🚌** from Giant's
Causeway & Coleraine. **🕐** Apr–Oct:
daily; Nov–Mar: Mon–Fri. **●** 2 weeks
at Christmas. **📷 🎫** obligatory.
**🏠 🍴 ♿** limited.

THE SMALL TOWN of Bushmills has an attractive square and a great river for salmon and trout fishing, but its main claim to fame is whiskey. The Old Bushmills plant on the edge of town prides itself on being the world's oldest distillery. Its Grant to Distil dates from 1608, but the spirit was probably made here at least 200 years before that.

In 1974 Bushmills joined the Irish Distillers Group based at the Jameson plant *(see p171)* in Midleton, but its products have retained their own character. Most are a blend of different whiskeys; Old Bushmills, in contrast, is made from a blend of a single malt and a single grain.

The tour of the distillery ends with a whiskey sampling session in the 1608 Bar in the former malt kilns, which are also home to a small museum with old distilling equipment on display.

**Whiskey barrel at Bushmills Distillery**

**Murlough Bay, on the coast facing Scotland to the east of Ballycastle**

# Rathlin Island **❽**

**Road map** D1. Co Antrim. **🚶** 120.
**⛴** daily from Ballycastle (028 2076
9299). **ℹ** Ballycastle (028 2076 2024).

RATHLIN IS SHAPED rather like a boomerang – 11 km (7 miles) in length and at no point more than 1.6 km (1 mile) wide. The island is just a 50-minute boat ride from Ballycastle. About 30 families remain on Rathlin Island, making a living from fishing, farming and a little tourism. Facilities are limited to a café, a pub, a guesthouse, a hostel and a campground. The fierce, salty Atlantic winds ensure that the landscape on Rathlin is virtually treeless.

High white cliffs encircle much of the island, and at craggy **Bull Point** on the westerly tip, tens of thousands of seabirds, including kittiwakes, puffins and razorbills, make their home. A local minibus service will take visitors to view the birds. At the opposite end of the island is **Bruce's Cave**, where, in 1306, Robert Bruce, King of Scotland, supposedly watched a spider climbing a thread. The spider's perseverance inspired the dejected Bruce to return and win back his kingdom.

# Ballycastle **❾**

**Road map** D1. Co Antrim. **🚶** 4,500.
**🚌 ⛴** to Campbeltown (Scotland)
**ℹ** Sheskburn House, 7 Mary St (028
2076 2024). **🎪** Apple Fair (end Oct).

A MEDIUM-SIZED resort town, Ballycastle boasts an attractive harbour and a central sandy beach. Near the harbour is a memorial to Guglielmo Marconi, whose assistant sent the first wireless message across water from here to Rathlin Island in 1898.

Ballycastle's annual Oul' Lammas Fair, held in late August, is one of the oldest traditional fairs in Ireland. It features noisy livestock sales and stalls selling yellowman (honeycomb toffee) and dulce (dried, heavily salted seaweed).

On the outskirts of town, the ruined 15th-century **Bonamargy Friary** houses the remains of Sorley Boy MacDonnell, former chieftain of this part of Antrim. Sections of the church, gatehouse and cloisters are well preserved.

## IRISH WHISKEY

The word whiskey comes from the Gaelic *uisce beatha*, meaning water of life. Distillation was probably introduced to Ireland by monks from Asia over 1,000 years ago. Small-scale production became part of the Irish way of life, but in the 17th century, the English introduced a licensing system and started to close down stills. In the 19th century, post-famine poverty and the Temperance movement combined to lower demand. The result was that Scotch whisky (with no "e") stole an export march on the Irish, but in recent years, thanks to lower production costs, improved marketing and the rise in popularity of Irish coffee, sales have been increasing.

**Poster showing the Old Bushmills Distillery beside the River Bush**

**ENVIRONS:** Off the A2, 5 km (3 miles) east of town, a narrow scenic road starts to wind its way along the coast to Cushendall. First stop is **Fair Head**, where a poorly marked path meanders across heathery marshland to towering cliffs 200 m (650 ft) above the sea. From here there are stunning views of Rathlin and the islands off the Scottish coast.

To the lee side of the headland lies **Murlough Bay**, the prettiest inlet along the coast. This can be reached by road. Further to the southeast stands **Torr Head**, a peninsula that reaches to within 21 km (13 miles) of the Mull of Kintyre making it the closest point in Ireland to Scotland.

Carnlough harbour, a popular stop south of Cushendall

## Cushendall ⑩

Road map D1. Co Antrim. 🚶 2,400.
🚍 ℹ️ 4b Mill St (028 2177 1180).
🕐 all year; Oct–June: mornings only.

THREE OF THE NINE Glens of Antrim converge towards Cushendall, earning it the unofficial title of "Capital of the Glens". This attractive village has brightly painted houses and a distinctive edifice known as Curfew Tower,

built of local red sandstone in the early 19th century as a lock-up for thieves and idlers.

**ENVIRONS:** About 1.5 km (1 mile) north of the village stands **Layde Old Church**. It can be reached by a pretty walk along the cliffs. Founded by the Franciscans, it was a parish church from 1306 to 1790 and contains many monuments to the local chieftains, the MacDonnells.

Just over 3 km (2 miles) west of Cushendall, on the slopes of Tievebulliagh mountain, lies **Ossian's Grave**, named after the legendary warrior-poet and son of the giant Finn MacCool (see pp24–5). It is in fact a Neolithic court

tomb: the area was a major centre of Stone Age tool-making and axeheads made of Tievebulliagh's hard porcellanite rock have been found at a wide range of sites all over the British Isles.

Other attractive villages further south along the coast road include **Carnlough**, which has a fine sandy beach and a delightful harbour, and **Ballygally**, whose supposedly haunted 1625 castle is now a hotel (see p300).

## Glenariff Forest Park ⑪

Road map D1. Co Antrim.
📞 028 2175 8232. 🕐 daily. 🅿️ for car park. ♿ limited.

NINE RIVERS have carved deep valleys through the Antrim Mountains to the sea. Celebrated in song and verse, the Glens of Antrim used to be the wildest and most remote part of Ulster. This region was not "planted" with English and Scots settlers in the 17th century and was the last place in Northern Ireland where Gaelic was spoken.

Today the Antrim coast road brings all the glens within easy reach of the tourist. Glenariff Forest Park contains some of the most spectacular scenery. The main scenic path runs through thick woodland and wildflower meadows and round the sheer sides of a gorge, past three waterfalls. There are also optional trails to distant mountain viewpoints. William Makepeace Thackeray, the 19th-century English novelist, called the landscape "Switzerland in miniature".

Glenariff Forest Park

Stone circle and stone rows at Beaghmore

## Cookstown ⑫

**Road map** D2. Co Tyrone. 🚍 *11,000.*
🚌 ℹ️ *Burnavon, Burn Road (028 8676 6727).* 🐄 *Cattle Market: Mon, Wed, Fri.* 🌐 *www.cookstowngov.uk*

COOKSTOWN STICKS in the memory for its grand central thoroughfare – 2 km (1.25 miles) long and perfectly straight. The road is about 40 m (130 ft) wide and, as you look to the north, it frames the bulky outline of Slieve Gallion, the highest of the Sperrin Mountains. A 17th-century Plantation town *(see pp36–7)*, Cookstown takes its name from its founder Alan Cook.

**ENVIRONS:** The countryside around Cookstown is rich in Neolithic and early Christian monuments. To the east, on a desolate stretch of Lough

Ardboe Cross

Neagh shoreline, the **Ardboe Cross** stands on the site of a 6th-century monastery. Although eroded, the 10th-century cross is one of the best examples of a High Cross *(see p235)* in Ulster: its 22 sculpted panels depict Old Testament scenes on the east side and New Testament ones on the west. The **Wellbrook Beetling Mill**, west of Cookstown, is a relic of Ulster's old linen industry. "Beetling" was the process of hammering the cloth to give it a sheen. Set amid trees beside the Ballinderry River, the mill dates from 1768 and is now a popular tourist attraction. The National Trust has restored the whitewashed two-storey building and its water wheel. Inside, working displays demonstrate just how loud "beetling" could be. From the mill, there are pleasant walks along the river banks.

🏛️ **Ardboe Cross**
Off B73, 16 km (10 miles) E of Cookstown.
🏭 **Wellbrook Beetling Mill**
Off A505, 6.5 km (4 miles) W of Cookstown. 📞 *028 8675 1735.* 🕐 *(pm only) Jul & Aug: Wed–Mon; Apr–Jun & Sep: Sat, Sun & public hols.* ♿

## Beaghmore Stone Circles ⑬

**Road map** D2. Co Tyrone. Off A505, 14 km (9 miles) NW of Cookstown.

ON A STRETCH of open moorland in the foothills of the Sperrin Mountains lies a vast collection of stone monuments, dating from between 2000 and 1200 BC. There are seven stone circles, several stone rows and a number of less prominent features, possibly collapsed field walls of an earlier period. Their exact purpose remains unknown, though in some cases their alignment correlates with movements of the sun, moon and stars. Three of the rows, for example, are clearly aligned with the point where the sun rises at the summer solstice.

The individual circle stones are small – none is more than 1.20 m (4 ft) in height – but their sheer numbers make them a truly impressive sight. As well as the circles and rows, there are a dozen round cairns (burial mounds). Up until 1945, the whole complex, one of Ulster's major archaeological finds, had lain buried beneath a thick layer of peat.

---

### ULSTER'S HISTORIC LINEN INDUSTRY

The rise in Ulster's importance as a linen producer was spurred on by the arrival from France of refugee Huguenot weavers at the end of the 17th century. Linen remained a flourishing industry for a further two centuries, but today it is produced only in small quantities for the luxury goods market. Hundreds of abandoned mills dot the former "Linen Triangle" bounded by Belfast, Armagh and Dungannon. One of the reasons why the

**18th-century print, showing flax being prepared for spinning**

material diminished in popularity was the expensive production process: after cutting, the flax had to be retted, or soaked, in large artificial ponds so that scutching – the separation of the fibres – could begin. After combing, the linen was spun and woven before being bleached in the sun, typically in fields along river banks. The final stage was "beetling", the process whereby the cloth was hammered to give it a sheen.

**Copy of Iron Age Celtic stone head at the Ulster History Park**

# Ulster History Park ⑭

**Road map** C2. Co Tyrone. 📞 028 8164 8188. 🚌 from Omagh. ◯ Apr–Sep: daily; Oct–Mar: Mon–Fri. ● 1 Jan, 23–29 Dec. 📷 🎫 👤 🛒 🏪

NESTLING AT THE EDGE of the Sperrin Mountains, the Ulster History Park is filled with full-scale models of structures built by successive waves of settlers in Ireland. They range from a Mesolithic hunter/gatherer's hut covered with animal pelts, dating from 7000 BC, to a 17th-century Plantation village (see pp36–7). There are also megalithic burial tombs, a crannog (see p31) from the early Christian period and a Norman motte and bailey (a wooden fortress built on a high mound). An exhibition centre helps put the exhibits in perspective.

# Ulster-American Folk Park ⑮

**Road map** C2. Co Tyrone. 📞 028 8224 3292. 🚌 from Omagh. ◯ Easter–Sep: daily; Oct–Easter: Mon–Fri. 📷 🍴 👤 🛒 [W] www.folkpark.com

ONE OF THE BEST open-air museums of its kind, the Folk Park grew up around the restored boyhood home of Judge Thomas Mellon (founder of the Pittsburgh banking dynasty). The Park's permanent exhibition, called "Emigrants", examines why two million people left Ulster for America during the 18th and 19th centuries. It also shows what became of them, following stories of both fortune and failure, including the grim lives of indentured servants and the 15,000 Irish vagrants and convicts transported to North America in the mid-18th century.

The park has more than 30 historic buildings, some of them original, some replicas. There are settler homesteads (including that of John Joseph Hughes, the first Catholic Archbishop of New York), churches, a schoolhouse and a forge, some with craft displays, all with costumed interpretative guides. There's also an Ulster streetscape, a reconstructed emigrant ship and a Pennsylvania farmstead, complete with log barn, corn crib and smokehouse. The six-roomed farmhouse is based on one built by Thomas Mellon and his father in the early years of their new life in America.

A fully stocked library and database allow visitors to trace their family roots. Popular American festivals such as Independence Day and Hallowe'en are celebrated at the park and there is an Appalachian-Bluegrass music festival in early September.

# Belleek Pottery ⑯

**Road map** C2. Belleek, Co Fermanagh. 📞 028 6865 8501. 🚌 ◯ Apr–Sep: daily; Oct–Mar: Mon–Fri. ● 17 Mar & 10 days at Christmas. 📷 👤 🛒 🏪 [W] www.belleek.ie

**Worker at the Belleek factory making a Parian ware figurine**

THE LITTLE BORDER VILLAGE of Belleek would attract few visitors other than anglers were it not for the world-famous Belleek Pottery, founded in 1857. The company's pearly coloured china is known as Parian ware. Developed in the 19th century, it was supposed to resemble the famous Parian marble of Ancient Greece.

Belleek is now best known for its ornamental pieces of fragile lattice work decorated with pastel-coloured flowers. These are especially popular in the USA. Several elaborate showpieces stand on display in the visitors' centre and small museum. There's also a 20-minute video presentation on the company's history, a gift shop and ample parking space for tour buses.

Pennsylvania farmhouse

**Pennsylvania log farmhouse at the Ulster-American Folk Park**

# A Tour of Lower Lough Erne ⑰

THE AREA AROUND Lower Lough Erne boasts a rich combination of both natural and historic sights. From pre-Christian times, settlers sought the security offered by the lough's forests and inlets. Monasteries were founded on several of its many islands in the Middle Ages, and a ring of castles recalls the Plantation era *(see p37)*. The lake is a haven for water birds such as ducks, grebes and kingfishers, and the trout-rich waters attract many anglers. Lough Erne is a delight to explore by land or by boat. In summer, ferries serve several islands, and cruisers are available for hire.

**Kingfisher**

**View across Lower Lough Erne**

### Boa Island ⑤
Two curious double-faced figures stand in Caldragh cemetery, a Christian graveyard on Boa Island. While little is known about the stone idols, they are certainly pre-Christian.

### Belleek ⑦
Northern Ireland's most westerly village, Belleek is famous for its pottery *(see p261)*. There is also a new museum, ExplorErne, which covers most aspects of the region.

### Castle Caldwell Forest Park ⑥
The park's wooded peninsulas are a sanctuary for birds, and you can watch waterfowl from hides on the shore. You may see great crested grebes, the common scoter duck and perhaps even otters.

← BALLYSHANNON

R230
A47
Erne
A46
B52
SLIGO

LOWER LOUG

Cliffs of Magho

B136

Lusty Beg

### Lough Navar Forest Drive ⑧
An 11-km (7-mile) drive through pine forest leads to a viewpoint atop the Cliffs of Magho, with a magnificent panorama over Lough Erne and beyond. Trails weave through the woods.

### Tully Castle ⑨
A delightful 17th-century-styl herb garden has recently been planted and is maturing well alongside thi fortified Plantation house.

## TIPS FOR DRIVERS

**Length:** 110 km (68 miles).
**Stopping-off points:** Outside Enniskillen, the best places to eat are the pubs in Kesh and Belleek; in summer, a café opens in Castle Archdale Country Park. There are good picnic places all along the route of this tour, including at the Cliffs of Magho viewpoint. (See also pp355–7.)

### KEY

▬▬▬ Tour route

═══ Other roads

🚢 Boats to islands

🗾 Viewpoint

**White Island** ④

The Romanesque church on White Island has bizarre pagan-looking figures set into one wall. Of uncertain origin, they probably adorned an earlier monastery on this site. Ferries to the island leave from Castle Archdale Marina in summer.

**Boats moored at Castle Archdale Marina**

**Castle Archdale Country Park** ③
With a marina and caravan site, the park is busy in summer. Trails through the woods enable you to escape the crowds, and you may see red deer and other animals.

**Devenish Island** ②
Site of Lower Lough Erne's most important monastery, this island can be reached in summer by ferry or water-bus from Enniskillen.

**Enniskillen** ①
Dominated by its famous castle, Enniskillen (*see p264*) is the main cruiser base on the Erne. It overlooks the river flowing between the upper and lower loughs.

**Monea Castle** ⑩
Occupying a rocky bank in a remote spot away from the lake, this is the best-preserved Plantation castle in Fermanagh. Built around 1618, it has striking barrel towers.

0 kilometres    4

0 miles    2

**Beautifully constructed round tower on Devenish Island**

# Devenish Island ⑱

**Road map** C2. Co Fermanagh.
🚢 *Devenish Ferry (028 686 21588 & 077 020 52873) from Trory Point, 5 km (3 miles) N of Enniskillen: Easter–Sep: daily.* 🎫 *for museum and tower.*

ST MOLAISE, who had 1,500 scholars under his tutelage, founded a monastery on this tiny windswept island in the 6th century. Although raided by Vikings in the 9th century and burnt in 1157, it remained an important religious centre up to the early 17th century.

Several fine buildings from the medieval monastery have survived, including **Teampall Mor** near the jetty. Built in 1225, this church displays the transition between Romanesque and Gothic styles. On the highest ground stands **St Mary's Priory**, an Augustinian church that was erected in the 15th century. An intricately carved stone cross close by dates from the same period.

The most spectacular sight on Devenish Island, however, is the 12th-century round tower, which stands some 25 m (82 ft) tall. From the high windows the monks could spot approaching strangers. It is perfectly preserved, and the five floors can be reached by internal ladders. Supporting the roof is an elaborate cornice with a human face carved above each of the four windows; this is a unique feature in an Irish round tower. A small museum covers both the history and architecture of the island, and contains a collection of antiquities discovered at the site.

# Enniskillen ⑲

**Road map** C2. Co Fermanagh.
🏃 14,000. 🚌 🚆 *Wellington Road*
*(028 6632 3110).* 🛒 *Thu.*

T HE BUSY tourist centre of
Enniskillen occupies an
island between Upper and
Lower Lough Erne. The town
gained fame for the wrong
reason in 1987, when 11
people died in an IRA bomb
attack, but it deserves a visit
for its setting and sights.

At the west end of town
stands **Enniskillen Castle**,
which dates back to the 15th
century. It houses a heritage
centre and the Inniskilling
Regimental Museum. Its most
stunning feature, however, is
the Watergate, a fairy-tale twin-
turreted tower, best admired
from the far bank of the river.
Further west, **Portora Royal
School**, founded in 1618,
counts among its old boys the
playwrights Oscar Wilde and
Samuel Beckett *(see pp20–21).*

The **Cole Monument**
stands on a little hill in a
pretty Victorian park on the
east side of town. It is a tall
Doric column with an internal

Enniskillen Castle seen from across the River Erne

spiral staircase that can be
climbed for magnificent views
of the lake country.

### ⚓ Enniskillen Castle
📞 *028 6632 5000.* ⬜ *Jul & Aug:
10am–5pm Tue–Fri, 2–5pm Sat–Mon;
May–Jun & Sep: 10am–5pm Tue–Fri,
2–5pm Mon & Sat; Oct–Apr: 10am–
5pm Tue–Fri, 2–5pm Mon.* 🗓
⬛ *1 Jan, 25 & 26 Dec.* 🚪 ♿ *limited.*

**ENVIRONS:** Just outside town,
set in a park with mature oak
woodland overlooking a lake,
is **Castle Coole**, one of the

finest Neo-Classical homes in
Ireland. It has a long Portland
stone façade, with a central
portico and small pavilions at
each end. The stone was
shipped from Dorset to
Ballyshannon in Co Donegal.
The first Earl of Belmore, who
commissioned the house in
the 1790s, was almost bankrupted by the cost of it. The
original design was by Irish
architect Richard Johnston, but
the Earl then commissioned a
second set of drawings by the
fashionable English architect
James Wyatt. The extravagant
Earl died, deep in debt, in 1802
and it was left to his son to
complete the decorating and
furnishing during the 1820s.

The glory of Castle Coole is
that almost all the house's
original furniture is still in
place. Family portraits from
the 18th century line the walls
of the dining room. In the
lavish State Bedroom there is
a bed made specially for King
George IV on the occasion of
his visit to Ireland in 1821,
though in the end he never
came here to sleep in it. One
of the finest rooms is the oval
saloon (or ballroom) at the
back of the house. The heavy
curtains and richly gilded
Regency furniture may not be
to everyone's taste, but the
spacious oak-floored room
produces a magnificent effect
of unostentatious luxury.

### ♨ Castle Coole
Off A4, 1.6 km (1 mile) SE of Enniskillen.
📞 *028 6632 2690.* **House** ⬜ *Jun–
Aug: Fri–Wed (pm only); Apr, May &
Sep: Sat, Sun & public hols (pm only)*
🗓 ♿ 🚪 🛒 **Park** ⬜ *daily.*

The saloon at Castle Coole, with original Regency furnishings

## Marble Arch Caves 🔟

**Road map** C2. Marlbank Scenic Loop, Florence Court, Co Fermanagh. 📞 028 6634 8855. ⏱ *Apr–Sep: daily (phone first as bad weather can cause closure).* 📷 ✓ *obligatory.* 🍴 🎁

THE CAVES are cut by three streams which flow down the slopes of Cuilcagh Mountain, unite underground and emerge as the Cladagh River. Tours lasting 75 minutes consist of a boat ride into the depths of the cave complex and a guided walk that leads past stalagmites, calcite cascades and other curious limestone formations. The 9-m (30-ft) "Marble Arch" itself stands outside the cave system in the glen where the river gushes out from below ground.

The caves are very popular, so it's best to book ahead. It is also advisable to ring to check the local weather conditions before setting out; the caves may be closed because of rain. Whatever the weather, bring a sweater and sensible walking shoes.

## Florence Court 🔟

**Road map** C2. Co Fermanagh. 📞 028 6634 8249. 🚌 from Enniskillen (Jul & Aug). **House** ⏱ Apr–May & Sep: Sat, Sun & public hols (pm only); Jun–Aug: (pm only) daily. 📷 ♿ 🍴 🎁 **Grounds** ⏱ daily. 📷 for car park.

THIS THREE-STOREY Palladian mansion was built for the Cole family in the mid-18th century. The arcades and pavilions, which are of a later date than the main house, were probably added around 1770 by William Cole, first Earl of Enniskillen. The house

**Boat trip through Marble Arch Caves**

features flamboyant Rococo plasterwork said to be by the Dublin stuccodore Robert West. Sadly, however, not much of what you see today is original as most of the central block was seriously damaged by fire in 1955. Much of the furniture was lost, but the plasterwork was painstakingly recreated from photographs. The finest examples are in the dining room, the staircase and the small Venetian room.

Perhaps more spectacular are the grounds, which occupy a natural mountain-ringed amphitheatre. The area is fairly wild and there are many enjoyable walks around the house. One woodland trail leads to the famous Florence Court yew tree, whose descendants are to be found all over Ireland. Closer to the house is a walled garden where pink and white roses make an attractive sight in summer.

## Dungannon 🔟

**Road map** D2. Co Tyrone. 👥 10,000. 🅿 ℹ *Killymaddy Tourist Centre, Ballygawly Rd, 8 km (5 miles) W of town (028 8776 7259).* 🛒 Thu.

DUNGANNON'S HILLY location made an ideal site for the seat of government of the O'Neill dynasty from the 14th century until Plantation (*see pp36–7*), when their castle was razed. The town's **Royal School** claims to be the oldest school in Northern Ireland. Opened in 1614, it moved to its present site on Northland Row in 1789.

Once a major linen centre, this busy market town's best-known factory is now **Tyrone Crystal**, the largest concern of its kind in Northern Ireland. Tours of its modern complex cover all stages of production, including glass-blowing.

🏭 **Tyrone Crystal**
Coalisland Road. 📞 028 8772 5335. ⏱ 9am–6pm Mon–Sat; 1–5 pm Sun. ⏱ 10 days Christmas. 📷 ✓ ♿

**Florence Court, the former seat of the Earls of Enniskillen**

**View of Armagh dominated by St Patrick's Roman Catholic Cathedral**

# Armagh ㉓

**Road map** D2. Co Armagh.
🚶 15,720. 🚌 ℹ️ 40 English St
(028 3752 1800). 🗓️ Tue & Fri.

O NE OF IRELAND's oldest cities, Armagh dates back to the age of St Patrick (see p273) and the advent of Christianity. The narrow streets in the city centre follow the ditches that once ringed the church, founded by the saint in 455. Two cathedrals, both called **St Patrick's**, sit on opposing hills. The more visually striking is the huge Roman Catholic one, a twin-spired Neo-Gothic building with seemingly every inch of wall covered in mosaic. The older Protestant Cathedral dates back to medieval times. It boasts the bones of Brian Boru, the King of Ireland who defeated the Vikings in 1014 (see pp32–3), and an 11th-century High Cross.

**Skull of Barbary ape from Navan Fort**

Armagh's gorgeous oval, tree-lined Mall, where cricket is played in summer, is surrounded by dignified Georgian buildings. One of these houses the small **Armagh County Museum**, which has a good exhibition on local history. Off the Mall, **St Patrick's Trian** is a heritage centre telling the story of the city. It also has a "Land of Lilliput" fantasy centre for children, based on *Gulliver's Travels* by Jonathan Swift (see p80). Ireland's only planetarium is on College Hill in the **Observatory Grounds**, from where there are splendid views over the city.

🏛 **Armagh County Museum**
The Mall East. ☎ 028 3752 3070.
⭘ Mon–Sat. ⬤ some public hols.
✔️ by arrangement.
🏛 **St Patrick's Trian**
40 English St. ☎ 028 3752 1801.
⭘ daily. ⬤ 25, 26 Dec. 🍴 🚻 ♿
🌺 **Observatory Grounds**
College Hill. ☎ 028 3752 2928.
⭘ daily. **Planetarium** ☎ 028 3752
3689. ⬤ closed for renovation work.
Phone for up-to-date information.

**ENVIRONS:** To the west of Armagh stands **Navan Fort**, a large earthwork on the summit of a hill. In legend, Navan was Emain Macha, ceremonial and spiritual capital of ancient Ulster, associated with tales of the warrior Cuchulainn (see p24). The site may have been in use as much as 4,000 years ago, but seems to have been most active around 100 BC when a huge timber building, 40 m (130 ft) across, was erected over a giant cairn. The whole thing was then burnt and the remains covered with soil. Archaeological

evidence indicates that this was not an act of war, but a solemn ritual performed by the inhabitants of Emain Macha themselves.

Below the fort, the grass-roofed **Navan Centre** interprets the archaeology and mythology of the site through interactive displays and a 25-minute film. One unexpected exhibit is the skull of a Barbary ape, found in the remains of a Bronze Age house. The animal must come from Spain or North Africa, evidence that by 500 BC Emain Macha was already a place with far-flung trading links.

🏛 **Navan Centre**
On A28 4 km (2.5 miles) W of Armagh.
☎ 028 3752 5550. ⭘ daily.
⬤ 5 days at Christmas. 🌐 ♿

# Lough Neagh ㉔

**Road map** D2. Co Armagh, Co Tyrone, Co Londonderry, Co Antrim.

L EGEND HAS IT that the giant Finn MacCool (see pp24–5) created Lough Neagh by picking up a piece of turf and hurling it into the Irish Sea, thus forming the Isle of Man in the process. At 400 sq km (153 sq miles), the lake is the largest in Britain. Bordered by sedgy marshland, it has few roads along its shore. The best recreational areas lie in the south: Oxford Island, actually a peninsula, has walking trails, bird lookouts and the informative **Lough Neagh Discovery Centre**. In the southwest corner, a narrow-gauge railway runs through the bogs of **Peatlands Park**. Salmon and trout swim in the

**Navan Fort, the site of Emain Macha, legendary capital of Ulster**

Hide for birdwatchers at Oxford Island on the southern shore of Lough Neagh

rivers that flow from Lough Neagh. The lake is famous for its eels, with one of the world's largest eel fisheries at **Toome** on the north shore.

### 🏛 Lough Neagh Discovery Centre
Oxford Island. Exit 10 off M1. 📞 028 3832 2205. ⬜ Apr–Sep: daily; Oct–Mar: Wed–Sun. ⬤ 25, 26 Dec. ♿ 📷 🚻 🎁

### 🌿 Peatlands Park
Exit 13 off M1. 📞 028 3885 1102. **Park** ⬜ daily. ⬤ 25 Dec. **Visitors' centre** ⬜ Jun–Aug: daily (pm only); Easter–May & Sep: Sat, Sun & public hols (pm only). ♿ 📷 🎁
W www.peatlandspark.co.uk

## Larne ㉕

**Road map** D1. Co Antrim. 👥 18,000. 🚆 🚌 ℹ️ Narrow Gauge Rd (028 2826 0088).

INDUSTRIAL LARNE is the arrival point for ferries from Scotland (see pp352–4). The town is not the finest introduction to Ulster scenery, but it lies on the threshold of the magnificent Antrim coastline (see p259).

The sheltered waters of Larne Lough have been a landing point since Mesolithic times – flint flakes found here provide some of the earliest evidence of human presence on the island – nearly 9,000 years ago. Since then, Norsemen used the lough as a base in the 10th century, Edward Bruce landed his Scottish troops in the area in 1315, and in 1914 the Ulster Volunteer Force landed a huge cache of German arms here during its campaign against Home Rule (see pp42–3).

## Carrickfergus ㉖

**Road map** E2. Co Antrim. 👥 37,700. 🚆 🚌 ℹ️ Antrim St (028 9336 6455). ⬤ Thu.

CARRICKFERGUS grew up around the massive castle begun in 1180 by John de Courcy to guard the entrance to Belfast Lough. De Courcy was the leader of the Anglo-Norman force which invaded Ulster following Strongbow's conquest of Leinster in the south (see pp34–5).

**Carrickfergus Castle** was shaped to fit the crag on which it stands overlooking the harbour. The finest and best-preserved Norman castle in Ireland, it even has its original portcullis (see pp34–5). Naturally, many changes and adaptations have been made since the 12th century, including wide ramparts to accommodate the castle's cannons. Arms and armour are on display in the large rectangular keep, while life-size model soldiers are posed along the ramparts.

In continuous use up to 1928, the castle has changed hands several times over the years. The Scots, under Edward Bruce, took it in 1315, holding it for three years. In the 17th century James II's army was in control of the castle from 1688 until General Schomberg took it for William III in 1690. William himself stayed at the castle before the Battle of the Boyne (see p236) in July 1690.

The history of the town is recreated in a series of audio-visual displays at **Knight Ride**. The exhibition is literally a ride through history as you are transported from scene to scene in small cable cars. This appeals principally to children, who also enjoy the gorier episodes from the history of Carrickfergus.

### ⚓ Carrickfergus Castle
📞 028 9335 1273. ⬜ daily (Sun pm). ⬤ 25 Dec. 📷 ♿ 🚻 🎁
### 🏛 Knight Ride
Antrim St. 📞 028 9336 6455. ⬜ daily (Sun pm). ⬤ 25 Dec. 📷 ♿

The massive Norman keep of Carrickfergus Castle

# Belfast ㉗

**B**ELFAST WAS THE ONLY CITY in Ireland to experience the full force of the Industrial Revolution. Its ship-building, linen, rope-making and tobacco industries caused the population to rise to almost 400,000 by the end of World War I. The Troubles and the decline of traditional industries have since damaged economic life, but regeneration projects, such as the Odyssey complex at Queen's Quay, are breathing new life into run down areas. Belfast remains a handsome city and visitors are agreeably surprised by the friendliness of the "Big Smoke".

**Red Hand of Ulster, Linen Hall Library**

**Mosaic in St Anne's Cathedral, showing St Patrick's journey to Ireland**

**Interior of the Grand Opera House**

### ⌂ City Hall
Donegall Square. ☎ 028 9032 0202 ext 2346. ⏰ 2.30pm daily; all other times by appointment.
Most of Belfast's main streets (and many major bus routes) radiate out from the hub of Donegall Square. In the centre of the square stands the vast rectangular Portland stone bulk of the 1906 City Hall. It has an elaborate tower at each corner and a central copper dome that rises to a height of 53 m (173 ft). Highlight of the tour of the interior is the sumptuous oak-panelled council chamber.

Statues around the building include a glum-looking Queen Victoria outside the main entrance and, on the east side, Sir Edward Harland, founder of the Harland and Wolff shipyard, which built the *Titanic*. A memorial to those who died when the *Titanic* sank in 1912 stands close by.

**Detail of *Titanic* Memorial outside City Hall**

### ▣ Grand Opera House
Great Victoria St. ☎ 028 9024 0411.
Designed by Frank Matcham, the renowned theatre-architect, this exuberant late-Victorian building opened its doors in 1894. The sumptuous interior, with its gilt, red plush and intricate plasterwork, was restored to its full glory in 1980. On occasions, bombings of the adjacent Europa Hotel disrupted business at the theatre, but it survives as a major venue for plays and concerts. In 1984, Belfast-born singer Van Morrison recorded a famous live album here.

### ✝ St Anne's Cathedral
Donegall St. ☎ 028 9032 8332.
The Neo-Romanesque façade of this Protestant cathedral, consecrated in 1904, fails to make much of an impression. The interior is far more attractive, especially the vast, colourful mosaics executed by the two Misses Martin in the 1920s. The one covering the baptistry ceiling contains over 150,000 pieces. The wide nave is paved with Canadian maple and the aisles with Irish marble. Lord Carson (1854–1935), implacable leader of the campaign against Home Rule (*see p42*), is buried in in the south aisle.

## SIGHTS AT A GLANCE

Albert Memorial Clock Tower ⑩
Botanical Gardens ⑨
City Hall ③
Crown Liquor Saloon ②
The Entries ⑤
Grand Opera House ①
Lagan Weir Lookout ⑪
Linen Hall Library ④
Queen's University ⑦
St Anne's Cathedral ⑥
Ulster Museum ⑧

0 metres          500

0 yards          500

### VISITORS' CHECKLIST

**Road map** D2. Co Antrim.
🚶 305,000. ✈ Belfast City
Airport, 6.5 km (4 miles) E; Belfast
International, 29 km (18 miles)
NW. 🚊 Central Station, East
Bridge St (028 9089 9411); Great
Victoria St Station. 🚌 Europa
Buscentre, Great Victoria St &
Oxford St (028 9033 3000). 🛈
47 Donegall Pl (028 9024 6609).
🎪 Royal Ulster Agricultural
Show & Lord Mayor's Show (May);
Belfast Festival at Queen's (Nov).

if only for the delightful coffee shop and the vast selection of newspapers and periodicals. Above the library door you will see the Red Hand of Ulster, the emblem of the province. It is the subject of a gory legend about two Celtic heroes racing to see who would touch the land of Ulster first. In his determination to win, one cut off his own hand and threw it to the shore.

#### 🍺 The Entries

The Entries are a series of narrow alleys between Ann Street and High Street. They feature some of the best pubs in the city, including White's Tavern (*see p321*), reputedly the oldest bar in Belfast. The Globe in Joy's Entry and the

Morning Star on Pottinger's Entry both serve excellent lunches. In 1791, the United Irishmen, a radical movement inspired by the new ideas of the French Revolution, was founded in a tavern on Crown Entry. Its most famous member was Wolfe Tone (*see pp38–9*).

#### 🍺 Crown Liquor Saloon

Great Victoria St. 📞 028 9024 9476. 🕐 daily.
Even teetotallers should make a detour to the tiled façade of this flamboyant Victorian drinking palace. The Crown, which dates back to the 1880s, is the only pub owned by the National Trust. The lovingly restored interior features stained glass, marbling, mosaics and a splendid ceiling with scrolled plasterwork. The wooden snugs facing the long bar have their original gas lamps: the perfect place for a pint of Guinness or Bass and some Strangford Lough oysters.

#### 🍺 Linen Hall Library

17 Donegall Square North.
📞 028 9032 1707. 🕐 Mon–Sat.
Founded as the Belfast Society for Promoting Knowledge in 1788, the library has thousands of rare, old books in its dark wooden stacks. There is also extensive documentation of political events in Ireland since 1968 and a vast database of genealogical information. Even if you have no special reason for visiting the library, it is still well worth going inside,

#### KEY

| | |
|---|---|
| 🚊 | Railway station |
| 🚌 | Coach station |
| ⛴ | Ferry port |
| P | Parking |
| 🛈 | Tourist information |
| ✝ | Church |

**The ornate Victorian interior of the Crown Liquor Saloon**

# Exploring Belfast

AWAY FROM THE CITY CENTRE, Belfast has many pleasant suburbs unaffected by the civil strife of recent times. The area around Queen's University to the south of the city has two major attractions in the Ulster Museum and the Botanic Gardens. To the north, there are splendid views to be enjoyed from the heights of Cave Hill, while visitors interested in Belfast's industrial heritage will be keen to see both the old docks and the Harland and Wolff working shipyards.

## 🏛 Ulster Museum

Botanic Gardens. ☎ 028 9038 3000.
○ daily (Sat & Sun: pm only).
● public hols. 🎫 🚻 📷 🚹
This four-floor bunker of a museum covers all aspects of Ulster, from local history, archaeology, antiquities and art to geology, natural history and technology. Especially prized treasures include gold and silver jewellery recovered from the *Girona*, a Spanish Armada ship that sank off the Giant's Causeway in 1588 (*see p249*). One of the most interesting exhibits is of Belfast industry, featuring some crude turn-of-the-century textile machinery.

In the top-floor gallery is a collection of paintings mostly by British and Irish artists, including a large number by Belfast-born Sir John Lavery (1856–1941).

In addition to the Irish collections, there are exhibits ranging from ancient Egyptian mummies to dinosaurs. The museum also mounts frequent temporary exhibitions on a wide variety of themes.

**Interior of the Victorian Palm House at the Botanic Gardens**

## 🌸 Botanic Gardens

Stranmillis Rd. ☎ 028 9032 4902.
○ daily.
Backing on to the university, the Botanic Gardens provide a quiet refuge from the bustle of campus. The 1839 Palm House is a superb example of curvilinear glass and cast-iron work. The Tropical Ravine, or Fernery, is another fine piece of Victorian garden architecture. Visitors can look down from the balcony to a sunken glen of exotic plants.

## 🎓 Queen's University

University Rd. ☎ 028 9024 5133.
A 15-minute stroll south from Donegall Square, through the lively entertainment district known as the Golden Mile, leads to Northern Ireland's most prestigious university. The main building, designed in Tudor-style red and yellow brick by Charles Lanyon in 1849, bears similarities to Magdalene College, Oxford. A towered gateway leads to a colonnaded quadrangle.

*Weighing Room, Hurst Park* (1924) by Sir John Lavery, Ulster Museum

---

## THE POLITICAL MURALS OF WEST BELFAST

**Republican mural in the Falls Road**

Ever since the onset of the "Troubles" in 1968, popular art has played a conspicuous role in proclaiming the loyalties of Belfast's two most intransigent working-class communities, on the Protestant Shankill Road and the Catholic Falls Road. The gable walls of dozens of houses in these areas have been decorated with vivid murals expressing local political and paramilitary affiliations. Likewise, kerbstones on certain streets are painted either in the red, white and blue of the United Kingdom or the green, white and gold of Ireland. Even with the successes of the current peace process, many are likely to remain. Some tourists make the journey out to West Belfast just to see the murals. The simplest way to do this is to take a taxi from the centre; cabs that go to the Falls Road leave from Castle Street, while those for the Shankill Road leave from North Street.

**Protestant Loyalist mural**

## ⚜ Albert Memorial Clock Tower

Queen's Square.

One of Belfast's best-known monuments, the clock tower, was designed by WJ Barre. Prince Albert, Queen Victoria's consort, had no personal connection with Belfast, but memorials to him were built in many British cities in the decade following his death in 1861. Today, the tower arouses most interest for the fact that it leans slightly as a result of subsidence. Beyond it, facing the river, stands the Custom House (1854) by Charles Lanyon, architect of Queen's University.

**Belfast cityscape showing the giant cranes, Samson and Goliath**

## 🏛 Lagan Weir Lookout

Donegall Quay. 🕿 028 9031 5444. ☐ daily (Sat & Sun: pm only). 🌐

Belfast's once thriving harbour area, five minutes' walk from Donegall Square, can best be viewed from the footbridge alongside the new Lagan Weir development. Five computer-controlled steel gates, unveiled in 1994, maintain a fixed water level, getting rid of the smelly mudbanks produced by varying tide levels and creating possibilities for angling and watersports along the river. The Visitors' Centre, on the footbridge, explains how it all works and tells some good tales of modern Belfast folklore. At night, the weir is lit by gas-filter blue light that shimmers across the water.

Unfortunately, the new Cross-Harbour Road and Rail Link bridge partly obscures the view across to the giant yellow cranes – appropriately named Samson and Goliath – of the once-mighty Harland and Wolff shipyards.

**The unmistakeable profile of Cave Hill above the roofs of Belfast**

**ENVIRONS:** The best place for an overall view of Belfast and Belfast Lough is the 360-m (1,118-ft) summit of Cave Hill, the most distinctively shaped of the hills encircling the city.

## 🏞 Cave Hill

Antrim Rd, 6.5 km (4 miles) N of city centre. **Heritage Centre** 🕿 028 9077 6925. ☐ daily. 🌑 25 Dec. ♿ 🍴 🏠 **Zoo** 🕿 028 9077 4625. ☐ daily. 🌑 25 Dec. 🌐 ♿ 🍴 🏠

It was on Cave Hill, next to the remains of MacArt's Fort (named after an Iron Age chieftain), that Wolfe Tone (see p39) and the northern leaders of the United Irishmen met in 1795 to pledge themselves to rebellion. The five artificial caves near the fort were carved out during the Neolithic period.

On the thickly wooded, eastern slopes of the hill stands the baronial pile of Belfast Castle, built in 1870. Previously home to the Earl of Shaftesbury, the castle now belongs to the city and houses two restaurants and a new heritage centre that interprets the area's history. A little further along the road past the castle is Belfast Zoo, which makes the most of its steep woodland setting.

## ⋔ Giant's Ring

Off B23, 5 km (3 miles) S of city centre.

Little is known about this awe-inspiring prehistoric enclosure almost 200 m (660 ft) in diameter. It is surrounded by a grassy bank averaging almost 6 m (20 ft) in width and 4.5 m (15 ft) in height. Bones from a Stone Age burial were found under the dolmen in the centre. During the 18th century the ring was a popular venue for horse races.

## ⚜ Stormont

Newtownards Rd, 8 km (5 miles) SE of city centre. 🌑 to the public. 🔒 by arrangement only.

Built between 1928 and 1932, at a cost of £1,250,000, Stormont was designed to house the Northern Ireland Parliament. The huge Anglo-Palladian mass of Portland stone and Mourne granite stands at the end of a majestic avenue, 1.6 km (1 mile) long, bordered by parkland. A statue of Lord Carson (see p42) stands near the front entrance.

Since the parliament was disbanded in 1972, the building has been used as government offices. Its future depends very much on the outcome of the ongoing peace process. The debating chamber was badly damaged in a fire in 1994.

**Stormont in its parkland setting outside Belfast**

# Ulster Folk and Transport Museum ❷❽

**Road map** E2. Cultra, near Holywood, Co Down. **(** 028 9042 8428. ⬛ ⬛ ◯ *daily.* ● *24–26 Dec.* ⬛ *(free for the disabled).* ♿ ⬛ ⬛

DOZENS of old buildings, including flax-, corn- and sawmills, have been plucked from the Ulster countryside and re-erected in this absorbing folk park. Demonstrations of traditional crafts, industries and farming methods are given all year round.

The A2 road splits the folk museum from the transport section. This is dominated by a hangar that houses the Irish Railway Collection. The smaller Transport Gallery exhibits machinery made in Ulster, including a saloon carriage from the tram service that ran from Portrush to Giant's Causeway *(see pp254–5)*. Of particular note is a test model of the spectacularly unsuccessful De Lorean car, made in the early 1980s with a huge government subsidy. There's also a popular exhibit on another ill-fated construction – the *Titanic*. It's best to allow half a day to take in most of the attractions.

Scrabo Tower, a prominent landmark of the Ards Peninsula

**1883 tram carriage at the Ulster Folk and Transport Museum**

# Ards Peninsula ❷❾

**Road map** E2. Co Down. ⬛ ⬛ *to Bangor.* 🚉 *34 Quay St, Bangor (028 9127 0069).* **Heritage Centre (** 028 9127 1200.

THE PENINSULA – and some of Northern Ireland's finest scenery – begins east of Belfast at **Bangor**. This resort town has a modern marina and some well-known yacht clubs. A little way south is **Donaghadee**, from where boats sail to the three **Copeland Islands**,

inhabited only by seabirds since the departure of the last human residents in the 1940s. The **Ballycopeland Windmill** (1784) is Northern Ireland's only working windmill and stands on the top of a small hill a little further south, near the town of Millisle.

Just across the peninsula is **Newtownards**. On a hill above the town is the pleasant and shady **Scrabo Country Park**. In the park stands the **Scrabo Tower**, built in 1857 as a memorial to the third Marquess of Londonderry.

Past the grounds of **Mount Stewart House** *(see pp274–5)* is the hamlet of Greyabbey, with its antique shops and Cistercian abbey ruins. Founded in 1193, **Grey Abbey** was used as a parish church until the 17th century. It is idyllically set in lush meadows by a stream and some of its features, particularly the finely carved west doorway, are well preserved.

On the tip of the peninsula, **Portaferry** overlooks the Strangford Narrows across from the Lecale Peninsula *(see p276)*. Portaferry's large aquarium, **Exploris**, displays the surprising diversity of marine life in the Irish Sea and Strangford Lough.

### 🏭 Ballycopeland Windmill
On B172 1.6 km (1 mile) W of Millisle.
**(** 028 9054 3033. ◯ *Easter–Sep: Tue–Sun & public hols.* ⬛

### 🏭 Scrabo Country Park
Near Newtownards. **(** 028 9181 1491. ◯ *daily.* **Tower** ◯ *Easter–Sep: Sat–Thu or by appt.*

### 🏛 Grey Abbey
Greyabbey **(** 028 4278 8585. ◯ *Apr–Sep: Tue–Sun; Oct–Mar: Sat and Sun only.* ⬛ ♿

### 🐟 Exploris
Castle Street, Portaferry. **(** 028 4272 8062. ◯ *daily.* ● *25 Dec.* ⬛ ♿ ⬛

**Ballycopeland Windmill, which dates back to 1784**

# Mount Stewart House ⓷⓪

See pp274–5.

# Hillsborough ⓷①

**Road map** D2. Co Down. 🏚 2,600.
🚌 ℹ *The Square (028 9268 9717).*

**Terraced houses in the town of Hillsborough**

Dⓞ OTTED WITH antique shops and restaurants, this Georgian town lies less than 16 km (10 miles) from Belfast. Its most impressive building is **Hillsborough Castle**, where visiting dignitaries to Northern Ireland stay. The elaborate wrought-iron gates and coat of arms are worth seeing.

Across from the 18th-century Market House in the town square, and next to the pleasant Forest Park, is **Hillsborough Fort**. An artillery fort dating from 1650, it was remodelled in the 18th century for feasts held by the descendants of Arthur Hill, founder of the town.

♠ **Hillsborough Castle**
📞 028 9268 1309. ⬜ *Sat only.*
♠ **Hillsborough Fort**
Access from town square or car park at Forest Park. 📞 028 9268 3285.
⬜ *Tue–Sun (pm).*

# Downpatrick ⓷②

**Road map** E2. Co Down. 🏚 10,300.
🚌 ℹ *53a Market St (028 4461 2233).* ⬛ *Sat.*

Wⓔ ERE IT NOT for its strong links with St Patrick, Downpatrick would attract few visitors. The Protestant **Down Cathedral**, high on the Hill of Down, dates in its present form from the early 19th century – many previous incarnations have been razed to the ground. In the churchyard is a well-worn 10th-century cross and the reputed burial place of St Patrick, marked by a granite slab (placed here this century) with the inscription "Patric".
**Down County Museum**, which is housed in the 18th-century Old County Gaol, features refurbished cells and exhibits relating to St Patrick, while close by is the **Mound of Down**, a large Norman motte and bailey.

🏛 **Down County Museum**
English Street, The Mall.
📞 028 4461 5218. ⬜ *daily.*
⬛ *25 & 26 Dec.* ♿ *limited.* 🖥 📷

**ENVIRONS:** There are several sights associated with St Patrick on the outskirts of Downpatrick. **Struell Wells**, believed to be a former pagan place of worship that the saint blessed, has a ruined church, 17th-century bath houses and good potential for a picnic. Further out and to the north at **Saul**, where St Patrick landed and began his Irish mission in 432, is a small memorial church.

The nearby hill of **Slieve Patrick** is an important place of pilgrimage and has a granite figure of the saint at its summit. An open-air mass is celebrated here every June.

Not far from the banks of the River Quoile is the Cistercian **Inch Abbey**, founded by John de Courcy in about 1180. Its attractive marshland setting is probably more memorable than its scant remains, but it's worth a visit nonetheless.

♠ **Inch Abbey**
5 km (3 miles) NW of Downpatrick.
⬜ *Apr–Sep: Tue–Sun.* 🅿

## THE LIFE OF ST PATRICK

Little hard information is known about St Patrick, the patron saint of Ireland, but he was probably not the first missionary to visit the country – a certain Palladius was sent by Pope Celestine in 431. Most stories tell that Patrick was kidnapped from Britain by pirates and brought to Ireland to tend sheep. From here he escaped to France to study Christianity. In 432, he sailed to Saul in County Down, where he quickly converted the local chieftain. He then travelled throughout the island convincing many other Celtic tribes of the truth of the new religion. The fact that Ireland has no snakes is explained by a legend that St Patrick drove them all into the sea.

**19th-century engraving showing St Patrick banishing all snakes from Ireland**

# Mount Stewart House ③

**Lord Castlereagh
(1769–1822)**

THIS GRAND 19TH-CENTURY HOUSE has a splendid interior, but it is the magnificent gardens which are the main attraction. These were planted only in the 1920s, but the exotic plants and trees have thrived in the area's subtropical microclimate. Now owned by the National Trust, Mount Stewart used to belong to the London-derry family, the most famous of whom was Lord Castlereagh, British Foreign Secretary from 1812 until his death in 1822.

**The Sunk Garden** comprises symmetrical beds which in summer are full of rich blue, yellow and orange flowers, complemented by purple foliage.

**Stone pergola**

★ **Shamrock Garden**
*A yew hedge in the shape of a shamrock encloses this topiary Irish harp and a striking flower-bed designed in the form of a red hand, emblem of Ulster.*

**The Music Room** has a beautiful inlaid floor of mahogany and oak.

**Italian Garden**
*The flowers in the Italian Garden, the largest of the formal gardens, are planted so that strong oranges and reds on the east side contrast with the softer pinks, whites and blues on the west.*

**Fountain**

## THE TEMPLE OF THE WINDS

This banqueting pavilion looks over Strangford Lough to the east of the house. It was built in 1785 by James "Athenian" Stuart, a renowned pioneer of Neo-Classical architecture, who took his inspiration from the Tower of the Winds in Athens. Restored in the 1960s and now being worked on once more, the building's finest features are the spiral staircase and the upper room's plasterwork ceiling and exquisite inlaid floor.

**The Spanish Garden** is framed by a neat arcade of clipped cypress trees.

★ **Hambletonian by George Stubbs**
*This picture of the celebrated racehorse at Newmarket, painted in 1799, hangs halfway up the main staircase.*

**Entrance**

**The Dining Room** contains 22 chairs used at the Congress of Vienna (1815) and given to Lord Castlereagh in recognition of his role in the talks.

**Entrance Hall**
*The most austere room in the house, this hall features Ionic stone pillars which have been painted to resemble green marble. It is lit by an impressive glass dome.*

**The Chapel,** converted from a sitting room in 1884, is still used by the Londonderry family.

**STAR FEATURES**

★ **Dodo Terrace**

★ **Shamrock Garden**

★ **Hambletonian by George Stubbs**

★ **Dodo Terrace**
*The stone dodos and ark on this terrace relate to the Ark Club, a social circle set up by Lady Londonderry in London during World War I. Each member was given an animal nickname.*

Lady Bangor's Gothic boudoir in Castle Ward on the Lecale Peninsula

## Lecale Peninsula ㉝

**Road map** E2. Co Down. 🚌 to Ardglass. 🚶 Downpatrick (028 4461 2233).

A GOOD WAY to get to this part of County Down is to take the short but scenic car ferry from Portaferry on the Ards Peninsula to Strangford. Just outside this tiny port is **Castle Ward**, the intriguing estate of Lord and Lady Bangor, who seemed to argue about everything – including the design of their mansion, built in the 1760s. His choice, Palladian, can be seen at the front, while her favourite Gothic style influences the garden façade. Likewise, the interior is a mix of Classical and Gothic fantasy. Look out for Lady Bangor's cluttered boudoir, with its extravagant fan-vaulted ceiling based on Henry VIII's chapel in Westminster Abbey. Around the grounds are fine gardens, walking trails, children's play areas and a lakeside farmyard with a working corn mill.

About 4 km (2.5 miles) south of Strangford, the A2 passes **Kilclief Castle**, which dates from the 15th century and is one of the oldest tower houses *(see p18)* in Ireland. The road continues to **Ardglass**, now a small fishing village but once Ulster's busiest harbour. A cluster of castles was erected between the 14th and 16th centuries to protect the port, of which six remain. Only one of these is open to the public,

**Jordan's Castle**. The finest view in the area is from **St John's Point**, 6 km (3.5 miles) southwest of Ardglass, which provides a sweeping panorama over Dundrum Bay.

### 🏰 Castle Ward
On A25, 2.5 km (1.5 miles) W of Strangford. 🕿 028 4488 1204.
**House** 🕐 Jun–Aug: Fri–Wed (pm only); Apr–May, Sep–Oct: Sat, Sun & public hols (pm only). 🍽 ♿ 📷 🛍
**Grounds** 🕐 daily. 🅿 for car park.
⚓ **Jordan's Castle**
Ardglass. 🕐 Apr–Sep: Tue–Sun. 🍽

## Castlewellan Forest Park ㉞

**Road map** D2. Main St, Castlewellan, Co Down. 🕿 028 4377 8664.
🕐 daily. 🅿 for car park.

T HE OUTSTANDING FEATURE of Castlewellan Forest Park, in the foothills of the Mourne Mountains, is its magnificent arboretum. This has grown far beyond the

original walled garden, begun in 1740, and now comprises hothouses, dwarf conifer beds and a rhododendron wood.

Elsewhere in the park are a 19th-century Scottish baronial-style castle (now a conference centre), a lake and pleasant woodlands; these are at their most colourful in autumn.

## Mountains of Mourne ㉟

**Road map** D2. Co Down. 🚌 to Newry. 🚌 to Newcastle. 🚶 10–14 Central Promenade, Newcastle (028 4372 2222). 🌐 www.newcastletic.org

T HESE MOUNTAINS occupy just a small corner of County Down, with no more than a dozen peaks surpassing 600 m (2,000 ft), and yet they attract thousands of visitors each year.

Only one road of any size, the B27 between Kilkeel and Hilltown, crosses the Mournes, making this ideal territory for walkers. A popular but tough trail runs from **Newcastle**, the main gateway to the area, up to the peak of **Slieve Donard**: at 848 m (2,796 ft), this is the highest mountain in the range. Part of the route follows the **Mourne Wall**, which was erected in 1904–22 to enclose the catchment area of the two reservoirs in the **Silent Valley**.

Over 20 other short hikes are described in the *St Patrick's Vale Walks* booklet, available from local tourist offices. These range from easy strolls around Rostrevor Forest to rather more arduous treks up Slieve Muck and other Mourne peaks.

Some 35 km (22 miles) north of Newcastle, the **Legananny Dolmen** *(see p30)* is one of the finest and most photographed ancient sights in the country.

Rounded peaks of the Mountains of Mourne

# A Tour of the Mourne Coast ㊱

N EWCASTLE, where, in the words of the 19th-century songwriter Percy French, "the Mountains of Mourne sweep down to the sea", makes a good base from which to explore this area. Driving up and down the dipping roads of the Mournes is one of the highlights of a trip to Northern Ireland. Along the coast, the road skirts between the foothills and the Irish Sea, providing lovely views and linking a variety of fishing villages and historic castles. Heading inland, you pass through an emptier landscape of moorland, purple with heather. The Silent Valley, with a visitors' centre and well-marked paths, is the only area to have been developed especially for tourists.

**Dundrum ②**
The town is overlooked by the ruins of a Norman castle, and from the nearby bay you can see the mountains rising in the distance.

**Tollymore Forest Park ③**
This attractive park is dotted with follies like the Gothic Gate that formed part of the original 18th-century estate.

**Spelga Dam ④**
There are stunning views north from the Spelga Dam over the Mourne foothills.

**Newcastle ①**
A popular resort since the early 19th century, Newcastle has a promenade overlooking a sweeping, sandy beach.

**Rostrevor with Slieve Martin behind**

**Silent Valley ⑦**
The valley is closed to traffic, but you can walk to the top of Ben Crom Mountain from the car park, or in summer go by bus.

**Rostrevor ⑤**
This tranquil and leafy Victorian resort nestles below the peak of Slieve Martin, on the shores of Carlingford Lough.

**Green Castle ⑥**
Erected in the 13th century, Green Castle lies at the end of a single track road on a rocky outcrop at the entrance to Carlingford Lough.

## TIPS FOR DRIVERS

**Length:** 85 km (53 miles).
**Stopping-off points:** Newcastle has the biggest choice of pubs and restaurants. Dundrum, Annalong, Kilkeel and Rostrevor all have pubs, and a café opens in the Silent Valley in summer. The Spelga Dam and Tollymore Forest Park are good picnic spots.
(See also pp355–7.)

0 kilometres      5

0 miles      3

**KEY**

▬▬ Tour route

═ ═ Other roads

☀ Viewpoint

# TRAVELLERS' NEEDS

WHERE TO STAY 280-301

RESTAURANTS, CAFÉS AND PUBS 302-321

SHOPPING IN IRELAND 322-327

ENTERTAINMENT IN IRELAND 328-335

# WHERE TO STAY

WHETHER YOU ARE STAYING in exclusive luxury or modest self-catering accommodation, one thing you can be certain of in Ireland is that you'll receive a warm welcome. The Irish are renowned for their friendliness. Even in big corporate hotels, where you might expect the reception to be more impersonal, the staff go out of their way to be hospitable. The choice is enormous: you can stay in an elegant 18th-century country house, a luxurious (or slightly run-down) castle, a Victorian town house, an old-fashioned commercial hotel, a cosy village inn, or on a working farm. For the hardier visitor there are good hostels, plenty of caravan and camping sites, or even your own horse-drawn caravan. We give details here on the various types of accommodation available, tourist board gradings and the choices for self-catering. Our listings on pages 286–301 recommend over 200 hotels around the country – all places of quality, ranging from simple bed-and-breakfast to unashamed luxury accommodation. Bord Fáilte (the Irish Tourist Board) and the Northern Ireland Tourist Board both publish comprehensive guides.

**Waterford Castle doorman**

Entrance hall of the Delphi Lodge *(see p296)* in Connemara

## HOTELS

AT THE TOP of the price range there are a handful of expensive, luxury hotels in castles and stately country houses. Magnificently furnished and run, they offer maximum comfort, delicious food and a wide range of sports facilities – either owned by the hotel or available close by. Salmon-fishing, foxhunting and shooting can be arranged as well as riding, golf, sailing and cycling.

If your priority is a full range of indoor facilities, such as a gym, sauna and swimming pool, the modern hotel chains will best cater to your needs. **Jury's**, **Great Southern Hotels** and **Irish Welcome** offer this standard of accommodation in the Republic, as do **Hastings Hotels** and Irish Welcome in Northern Ireland. However, these establishments can lack the charm and individuality of privately run hotels.

Coastal resort hotels usually offer a range of sports activities or can advise you on the best places to go. In smaller towns, the main hotel is often the social centre of the area with a lively public bar, popular with locals and guests alike.

The shamrock symbols of both the Northern Ireland Tourist Board and Bord Fáilte are displayed by hotels (and other forms of accommodation) that have been inspected and officially approved.

### COUNTRY HOUSE ACCOMMODATION

VISITORS WISHING to stay in a period country home and sample authentic Irish country life can contact a specialist organization called **Hidden Ireland**. However, this type of accommodation may not suit everybody, as the houses are not guesthouses, hotels or bed-and-breakfast establishments, but something quite different. You should therefore not expect the same facilities and service usually found in a hotel, such as a swimming pool, lifts, televisions, porters or room service. Instead, the experience is a very intimate one; guests dine together with their host and hostess as if at a private dinner party. Many of the houses have been in the same family for hundreds of years and the history attached to them can be fascinating. Prices reflect the type of house and the standard of accommodation, but all offer excellent value for money and

The entrance to the Shelbourne Hotel in Dublin *(see p287)*

Bar at the Hunter's Hotel *(see p290)* in Rathnew, County Wicklow

a first-hand experience of an aspect of the Irish way of life.

There are many other private residences that also take paying guests. Two useful publications, *Friendly Homes of Ireland* and *Ireland's Blue Book*, provide listings and information and are available from tourist offices and bookshops. Tourist boards throughout Ireland also supply listings and make reservations.

## GUESTHOUSES

M OST GUESTHOUSES are found in cities and large towns. They are usually converted family homes and have an atmosphere all of their own. Most offer a good-value evening meal and all give you a delicious full Irish breakfast *(see p304)*. Top-of-the-range guesthouses can be just as good, and sometimes even better, than hotels. You will see a much more personal side of a town or city while staying at a guesthouse. If you are looking for anonymity, however, a guesthouse may not suit you – both the proprietor and your fellow guests are likely to try and draw you into conversation.

There are plenty of good guesthouses to choose from in the Dublin area and the prices are usually extremely reasonable. The **Irish Hotel Federation** publishes a useful booklet with guesthouse listings that cover the whole of Ireland including Dublin. The Northern Ireland Tourist Board publishes its own

similar booklet, called *Where to Stay in Northern Ireland*. This includes a comprehensive list of approved guesthouses which is updated annually. However, it is hard to beat personal recommendations you might receive from fellow guests.

Bedroom at Enniscoe House *(see p295)*, Crossmolina in County Mayo

## PRICES

R OOM RATES advertised in both Northern Ireland and the Republic are inclusive of tax and service. In general, prices in the Republic are marginally cheaper than

in the North. Hotel rates can vary by as much as 40 per cent depending on the time of year; country house rates also vary a great deal according to the season. Guesthouse prices are influenced more by their location in relation to tourist sights and public transport.

For those on a tight budget, farmhouse accommodation represents excellent value for money, though the cheapest option is self-catering in a rented cottage *(see p282)*.

## TIPPING

T IPPING IN IRELAND is a matter of personal discretion but is not common practice, even at the larger hotels. Tasks performed by staff are considered part of the service. Tipping is not expected, for example, for carrying bags to your room or for serving drinks. However, it is usual to tip the waiting staff in hotel restaurants: the standard tip is around 10 per cent and anything over 15 per cent of the bill would be considered generous.

## BOOKING

I T IS WISE to reserve your accommodation during the peak season and public holidays *(see p49)*, particularly if your visit coincides with a local festival or major sporting event *(see pp26–7)*. Bord Fáilte can offer advice and make reservations through its nationwide accommodation service; the Northern Ireland Tourist Board runs a similar service. Central reservation facilities are available at the hotel chains that have been listed here.

Façade of the Londonderry Arms *(see p300)* in Carnlough, County Antrim

A bed-and-breakfast on the River Corrib in Galway

## BED-AND-BREAKFAST ACCOMMODATION

IRELAND has the reputation for the best B&Bs in Europe. You will never be far from a place to stay, even in the remotest spots. Your welcome will always be friendly and the food and company excellent. Even if the house is no architectural beauty, the comfort and atmosphere will more than compensate. Not all bedrooms have bathrooms *en suite*. When one is available, you may have to pay a little extra, but considering the generally cheap rates, the surcharge is negligible.

The Irish swear by their B&Bs and many stay in them by choice rather than suffer the impersonality and prices of the mainstream hotels; frequent visitors to Ireland agree. The **Town and Seaside House Association** will provide details of bed-and-breakfast accommodation in Northern Ireland, while the **Town and Country Homes Association** covers the Republic.

## FARMHOUSE ACCOMMODATION

FARMHOUSE HOLIDAYS are a popular tradition in Ireland. **Irish Farmhouse Holidays Ltd** has a list of farmhouses in the Republic that take paying guests. You can stay for

one night or longer and they make an excellent base for touring the countryside. As with most things in Ireland, it is the hospitality and friendliness of the people that makes staying on a farm so memorable. You get a feel of rural Ireland with its rich agricultural heritage, and the families are determined you will enjoy every moment of your stay.

## SELF-CATERING

SELF-CATERING HOLIDAYS are an increasingly popular option in Ireland and there are properties to rent all over the country. You are likely to have more choice in the south and west as these areas have traditionally attracted the majority of tourists. Bord Fáilte has a small self-catering section in its general accommodation guide, but local tourist offices have

lists of apartments and houses to let in their area. It is also worth looking for adverts in the newspapers, both local and international. Accommodation can range from quaint, stone cottages, converted barns and stable yards to more modern, purpose-built bungalows. All will generally have adequate facilities, with simple but comfortable furnishings, modern kitchen equipment and televisions.

An organization called **Rent an Irish Cottage** runs a popular form of self-catering. Its cottages are built in traditional style with whitewashed walls inside and out, and painted roofs and windows; the decor is also traditional – simple and attractive. Locations are generally superb; the only possible criticism is, if you wanted to be "away from it all", they are built in clusters of about ten, so there isn't a great deal of privacy.

At the other end of the scale, you could rent a castle or country house, furnished with paintings and antiques. In some cases, the properties are fully staffed. A company called **Elegant Ireland** has a selection of such properties.

## CAMPING AND CARAVANNING

A LIST of fully inspected caravan and camping parks is given in the Bord Fáilte accommodation guide. Many of the camping sites and caravan parks offer additional facilities – these might include a shop, restaurant or café/snack bar, an indoor games room, laundry, tennis court and pitch-and-putt course. The standard

A farmhouse in Clonakilty, County Cork

**Traditional painted horse-drawn caravan from Slattery's in Tralee**

and condition of these facilities will vary but you can be reliably guided by the tourist board's star ratings: four-star parks have an extensive range of facilities with a high standard of management; three-star parks have good facilities and management; two-star parks offer limited facilities and good management and the one-star parks have the minimum facilities required for registration with Bord Fáilte. A complete list of approved camping sites in the North is produced by the Northern Ireland Tourist Board.

If you want to experience the Irish countryside at a more leisurely pace, it is possible to hire a traditional horse-drawn caravan. Two of the best companies specializing in this type of holiday are **Kilvahan Caravans**, based at Portlaoise in the Midlands, and **Slattery's Travel Agency** in Tralee, County Kerry.

## YOUTH HOSTELS

THERE ARE 40 youth hostels registered with **An Óige** (the Irish Youth Hostel Association), set in some wonderfully scenic areas of Ireland in buildings ranging from castles to military barracks. Accommodation is generally provided in simple dormitories with comfortable beds and basic cooking facilities. You can only use these hostels if you are a member of An Óige or

another youth organization affiliated to the International Youth Hostel Federation. Charges vary according to standard, location and season. Northern Ireland is covered by the **Youth Hostel Association of Northern Ireland**, which has 8 registered hostels.

**Independent Holiday Hostels of Ireland** publish a guide to 151 independent hostels, and there are places such as universities offering similar inexpensive accommodation. Tourist boards have listings of those they recommend.

## DISABLED TRAVELLERS

A FACT SHEET for disabled visitors is produced by Bord Fáilte and in their main accommodation guide there is a symbol for wheelchair accessibility. A similar symbol is used in the accommodation listings in this book *(see pp286–301)*. The National Rehabilitation Board *(see p340)* publishes two free guides *Accommodation for Disabled Persons* and *Dublin: A Guide for Disabled Persons*, both in conjunction with the tourist board. The annual publication *Holidays in the British Isles* caters specifically for the disabled traveller and covers Northern Ireland. There is also a guide, with comprehensive listings, available from the Northern Ireland Tourist Board entitled *Accessible Accommodation*.

**Bord Fáilte sign for approved accommodation**

**Typical bed-and-breakfast sign in Pettigo, County Donegal**

### USEFUL ADDRESSES

**An Óige (Irish YHA)**
61 Mountjoy St, Dublin 7.
☎ 01 8304555. FAX 01 8305808.

**Elegant Ireland**
15 Harcourt St, Dublin 2.
☎ 01 4751665. FAX 01 4751012.

**Great Southern Hotels**
6 Charlemont Terrace, Crofton Rd,
Dun Laoghaire, Co Dublin.
☎ 1850 383848. FAX 01 2144805.

**Hastings Hotels**
Midland Building, Whitla St,
Belfast. ☎ 028 9075 1066.
FAX 028 9074 8152.

**Hidden Ireland**
P.O. Box 31, Westport, Co Mayo.
☎ 01 6627166. FAX 01 6627144.

**Independent Holiday Hostels of Ireland**
57 Lower Gardiner St, Dublin 1.
☎ 01 8364700. FAX 01 8364710.

**Irish Farmhouse Holidays Ltd**
2 Michael St, Limerick.
☎ 061 400700. FAX 061 400771.

**Irish Hotels Federation**
13 Northbrook Rd, Dublin 6.
☎ 01 4976459. FAX 01 4974613.

**Irish Welcome**
4 Whitefriars, Aungier St, Dublin 2.
☎ 01 4757017. FAX 01 4750222.

**Jury's**
Pembroke Rd, Dublin 4.
☎ 01 6070000. FAX 01 6675471.

**Kilvahan Caravans**
Cullenagh, Portlaoise, Co Laois.
☎ 0502 27048. FAX 0502 27225.

**Rent an Irish Cottage**
51 O'Connell St, Limerick.
☎ 061 411109. FAX 061 314821.

**Slattery's Travel Agency**
1 Russell St, Tralee, Co Kerry.
☎ 066 7121722.
FAX 066 7186222.

**Town and Country Homes Association**
Belleek Rd, Ballyshannon,
Co Donegal. ☎ 072 51377.
FAX 072 51207 / 22207.

**Town and Seaside House Association**
Mr Barney Devenny, Ashling
House B&B, Taunton Avenue,
Belfast. ☎ 028 90771529.

**Youth Hostel Association of Northern Ireland**
22–32 Donegall Rd, Belfast.
☎ 028 9032 4733.
FAX 028 9043 9699.

# Ireland's Best: Hotels

THE HOTELS featured here are a selection from our lists of recommended places to stay on pages 286–301. They give an indication of the very best that Ireland has to offer, ranging from private establishments which are members of the Hidden Ireland group *(see p280)* to the efficiency and luxury of five-star hotels or the romance of historic castles. All are impressive places, both for their setting and the buildings themselves.

**St Ernan's House**
*This elegant, pink Regency country house is situated on its own private island not far from Donegal.* (See p298.)

NORTHWEST IRELAND

**Delphi Lodge**
*The atmosphere at this comfortable, well-run fishing lodge is extremely relaxing. The River Delphi and nearby loughs provide plenty of sport.* (See p296.)

THE WEST OF IRELAND

**Ashford Castle**
*This huge Gothic-style edifice is set on the shores of Lough Corrib. The standard of service is impeccable and the food is excellent.* (See p296.)

THE LOWER SHANNON

**Adare Manor**
*Set in a large estate beside one of the prettiest villages in the country, this luxurious hotel occupies a magnificent Victorian Gothic mansion.* (See p294.)

CORK AND KERRY

**Bantry House**
*The spacious library in this 18th-century house looks out on to the gardens. Many of the bedrooms enjoy superb views of Bantry Bay.* (See pp160–61 and p291.)

**Streeve House**
*This 18th-century dower house is a member of the Hidden Ireland group. A stay here gives access to the stunning gardens of Drenagh House, which include the hidden Moon Garden. (See p301.)*

**Hunter's Hotel**
*Cobbled courtyards, paddocks and a magnificent garden are only a few of the attractions of this friendly and comfortable inn. The building dates back to 1720, and is owned and run by the fourth generation of the Hunter family. (See p290.)*

NORTHERN IRELAND

THE MIDLANDS

SOUTHEAST IRELAND

**Roundwood House**
*This fine, small Palladian house is set in chestnut and beech woods. The Slieve Bloom Mountains are close by and you can fish and play golf locally. The lovely rooms are filled with antiques, books and pictures and the atmosphere is one of relaxed informality. (See p299.)*

0 kilometres 50

0 miles 25

**Waterford Castle**
*The ultimate in "getting away from it all", this 15th-century castle sits on a beautifully located island in the estuary of the River Suir. The hotel is reachable only by its own private ferry. (See p291.)*

# Choosing a Hotel

THESE HOTELS have been selected across a wide price range for their good value, facilities and location; they are listed by region, starting with Dublin. Use the colour-coded thumb tabs, which indicate the regions covered on each page, to guide you to the relevant section of the chart. For Dublin map references see pages 110–11; for road map references see the inside back cover.

| | CREDIT CARDS | CHILDREN'S FACILITIES | PARKING FACILITIES | RESTAURANT | PUBLIC BAR |
|---|---|---|---|---|---|

## DUBLIN

| | | | | | |
|---|---|---|---|---|---|
| **SOUTHEAST DUBLIN:** *Fitzwilliam Guest House* €€<br>41 Fitzwilliam St Upper, Dublin 2. **Map** E5. **(** *01 6600448.* **FAX** *01 6767488.*<br>A friendly, unpretentious guesthouse in an attractive Georgian street, with simple, elegant decor and comfortable bedrooms. 🛏 TV *Rooms: 13* | MC V AE DC | ● | ■ | ● | |
| **SOUTHEAST DUBLIN:** *Kilronan House* W www.dublinn.com €€<br>70 Adelaide Rd, Dublin 2. **(** *01 4755266.* **FAX** *01 4782841.*<br>A reasonably priced, small guesthouse in a quiet street in the centre. Charming owners and delicious breakfasts. 🛏 TV *Rooms: 15* | MC V AE | ● | ■ | | |
| **SOUTHEAST DUBLIN:** *Leeson Court* €€<br>26 Leeson St Lower, Dublin 2. **Map** E5. **(** *01 6763380.* **FAX** *01 6618273.*<br>Spread across two Georgian houses, this cheerfully decorated hotel has a relaxed, informal atmosphere and the service is good. St Stephen's Green is only a few minutes' walk away. 🛏 TV *Rooms: 20* | MC V AE DC | ● | ■ | | ■ |
| **SOUTHEAST DUBLIN:** *Russell Court* €€<br>21–25 Harcourt St, Dublin 2. **Map** D5. **(** *01 4784066.* **FAX** *01 4781576.*<br>Jolly, welcoming hotel with young staff and a lively atmosphere in the evenings. There's a choice of bars and a more formal restaurant. Bedrooms are neat and well-equipped. 🛏 TV *Rooms: 46* | MC V AE DC | ● | ■ | ● | ■ |
| **SOUTHEAST DUBLIN:** *Georgian Hotel* €€€<br>18 Baggot St Lower, Dublin 2. **Map** F5. **(** *01 6345000.* **FAX** *01 6345100.*<br>A short walk from St Stephen's Green, this small hotel is a good base for exploring Dublin. The bedrooms are large and comfortable and there's a good traditional restaurant in the basement. 🛏 TV *Rooms: 47* | MC V AE DC | ● | ■ | ● | ■ |
| **SOUTHEAST DUBLIN:** *Harcourt* €€€<br>60 Harcourt St, Dublin 2. **Map** D5. **(** *01 4783677.* **FAX** *01 4752013.*<br>Just off St Stephen's Green, this hotel is close to many of the city's main sights. The bedrooms are modern and well-equipped, there is a popular bar, a restaurant for evening meals and a nightclub. 🛏 TV *Rooms: 98* | MC V AE DC | ● | | ● | ■ |
| **SOUTHEAST DUBLIN:** *Buswells* €€€<br>25 Molesworth St, Dublin 2. **Map** E4. **(** *01 6764013.* **FAX** *01 6762090.*<br>A short walk from Grafton Street, this smart, newly refurbished hotel is a listed Georgian building with a fine interior. 🛏 TV & *Rooms: 69* | MC V AE DC | ● | ■ | ● | ■ |
| **SOUTHEAST DUBLIN:** *Clarion Stephen's Hall* €€€<br>14–17 Leeson St Lower, Dublin 2. **Map** E5. **(** *01 6381111.* **FAX** *01 6381122.*<br>All the rooms are suites and represent good value for families who want smart, comfortable accommodation in the centre of the city near St Stephen's Green. Cooking facilities are available. 🛏 TV & *Rooms: 38* | MC V AE DC | ● | ■ | ● | |
| **SOUTHEAST DUBLIN:** *Temple Bar Hotel* €€€<br>Fleet St, Temple Bar, Dublin 2. **Map** D3. **(** *01 6773333.* **FAX** *01 6773088.*<br>This hotel, situated in a trendy area of Dublin, is a popular meeting place with its theme bar "Buskers" attracting a lively crowd. Bedrooms are comfortable but lack character. 🛏 TV & *Rooms: 129* | MC V AE DC | ● | | ● | ■ |
| **SOUTHEAST DUBLIN:** *Conrad Hotel* W www.conraddublin.com €€€€<br>Earlsfort Terrace, Dublin 2. **Map** D5. **(** *01 6765555.* **FAX** *01 6765424.*<br>This international-style hotel by St Stephen's Green is geared to business people, but has a jolly pub with a large terrace. 🛏 TV 🍴 🎿 & *Rooms: 191* | MC V AE DC | ● | ■ | ● | ■ |
| **SOUTHEAST DUBLIN:** *Longfields* €€€€<br>10 Fitzwilliam St Lower, Dublin 2. **Map** F5. **(** *01 6761367.* **FAX** *01 6761542.*<br>Two Georgian town houses have been knocked together to create this stylish hotel with an attractive sitting room and smart, pretty bedrooms. There is a very good restaurant in the basement. 🛏 TV *Rooms: 26* | MC V AE DC | ● | | ● | ■ |

**Price categories** are for a standard double room (not per person) for one night, including tax, service charges and breakfast.
€ under 65 euros
€€ 65–130 euros
€€€ 130–190 euros
€€€€ 190–260 euros
€€€€€ over 260 euros

**CHILDREN'S FACILITIES**
Cots and high chairs are available and some hotels will also provide a baby-sitting service.

**PARKING FACILITIES**
Parking provided by the hotel in either a private car park or a private garage close by.

**RESTAURANT**
The hotel has a restaurant for residents which also welcomes non-residents – usually only for evening meals.

**PUBLIC BAR**
The hotel has a bar that is open to non-residents and residents alike.

| | CREDIT CARDS | CHILDREN'S FACILITIES | PARKING FACILITIES | RESTAURANT | PUBLIC BAR |
|---|---|---|---|---|---|
| **SOUTHEAST DUBLIN:** *Mont Clare* W www.ocallaghanhotels.ie €€€€<br>Merrion Square, Dublin 2. **Map** F4. ( 01 6073800. FAX 01 6615663.<br>Not as grand as the Davenport opposite, but with the same club-like feel. A busy, traditional pub takes up most of the ground floor. 🔧 TV *Rooms: 80* | MC V AE DC | ● | ▪ | ● | ▪ |
| **SOUTHEAST DUBLIN:** *Davenport* W www.ocallaghanhotels.ie €€€€€<br>Merrion Square, Dublin 2. **Map** F4. ( 01 6073500. FAX 01 6615663.<br>The grand proportions of the Neo-Classical façade are carried through into the lobby – a vast, marble-floored atrium. Opened in 1993, it is elegant but rather like a gentleman's club. 🔧 TV 🍴 🛁 🔧 *Rooms: 118* | MC V AE DC | ● | ▪ | ● | |
| **SOUTHEAST DUBLIN:** *The Merrion* W www.merrionhotel.com €€€€€<br>Merrion Street Upper, Dublin 2. **Map** E4. ( 01 6030600. FAX 01 6030700.<br>This top-class hotel was created from four Georgian townhouses. Its elegant interior is full of antiques and it has an outstanding art collection. It is highly civilised but relaxing. 🔧 TV 🍴 🛁 🏊 🔧 *Rooms: 145* | MC V AE DC | ● | | ● | ▪ |
| **SOUTHEAST DUBLIN:** *Shelbourne Hotel* W www.shelbourne.ie €€€€€<br>27 St Stephen's Green, Dublin 2. **Map** D4. ( 01 6766471. FAX 01 6616006.<br>The Shelbourne has been the city's most distinguished hotel since it opened in the 19th century. Although it has every facility for the business traveller, it retains a personal atmosphere. 🔧 TV🍴 🛁 🔧 *Rooms: 190* | MC V AE DC | ● | ▪ | ● | ▪ |
| **SOUTHEAST DUBLIN:** *Westbury Hotel* €€€€€<br>Grafton St, Dublin 2. **Map** D4. ( 01 6791122. FAX 01 6797078.<br>You couldn't get much closer to the centre of things than here, only seconds from Dublin's major shopping street. It is a smart, ritzy hotel decorated in traditional style. 🔧 TV 🔧 *Rooms: 203* | MC V AE DC | ● | ▪ | ● | ▪ |
| **SOUTHWEST DUBLIN:** *Avalon House* €<br>55 Aungier St, Dublin 2. **Map** C4. ( 01 4750001. FAX 01 4750303.<br>This cheap and cheerful accommodation has over 300 beds. It is centrally located and has clean bedrooms and a communal kitchen. *Rooms: 60* | MC V AE | | | | |
| **SOUTHWEST DUBLIN:** *Jury's Christchurch Inn* €€<br>Christchurch Place, Dublin 8. **Map** B4. ( 01 4540000. FAX 01 4540012.<br>The Jury's group "inns" offer spruce modern facilities. This "inn", 15 minutes from St Stephen's Green, has a good bar and restaurant, and neat, well-equipped rooms at reasonable prices. 🔧 TV 🔧 *Rooms: 182* | MC V AE DC | ● | | ● | ▪ |
| **SOUTHWEST DUBLIN:** *Blooms Hotel* €€€<br>Anglesea St, Temple Bar, Dublin 2. **Map** D3. ( 01 6715622. FAX 01 6715997.<br>Situated near Trinity College, this modern hotel is very convenient for exploring, but its reception areas are slightly limited. 🔧 TV *Rooms: 86* | MC V AE DC | ● | | ● | ▪ |
| **SOUTHWEST DUBLIN:** *Central Hotel* €€€<br>1–5 Exchequer St, Dublin 2. **Map** D5. ( 01 6797302. FAX 01 6797303.<br>As its name suggests, one of the great advantages of this hotel is its position. The Exchequer Bar has live music at the weekends, so choose your neat, functional bedroom carefully. 🔧 TV *Rooms: 70* | MC V AE DC | ● | | ● | ▪ |
| **SOUTHWEST DUBLIN:** *Grafton Capital Hotel* W www.capital-hotels.com €€€<br>Lower Stephen's Street, Dublin 2. **Map** D4. ( 01 4750888. FAX 01 6481122.<br>This neat hotel, with a Georgian façade is neat and tastefully decorated throughout. Only a few minutes' walk from Grafton Street, it makes an excellent city base. 🔧 TV 🔧 *Rooms: 75* | MC V AE DC | ● | | ● | ▪ |
| **SOUTHWEST DUBLIN:** *Clarence* €€€€€<br>6–8 Wellington Quay, Dublin 2. **Map** C3. ( 01 6709000. FAX 01 6707800.<br>The hotel is owned by the rock band U2 and has been completely refurbished. A stylish restaurant sets the standard for the rest of the hotel – one of the trendiest places to stay in town. 🔧 TV 🔧 *Rooms: 50* | MC V AE DC | ● | | ● | ▪ |

**Price categories** are for a standard double room (not per person) for one night, including tax, service charges and breakfast.
€ under 65 euros
€€ 65–130 euros
€€€ 130–190 euros
€€€€ 190–260 euros
€€€€€ over 260 euros

**CHILDREN'S FACILITIES**
Cots and high chairs are available and some hotels will also provide a baby-sitting service.

**PARKING FACILITIES**
Parking provided by the hotel in either a private car park or a private garage close by.

**RESTAURANT**
The hotel has a restaurant for residents which also welcomes non-residents – usually only for evening meals.

**PUBLIC BAR**
The hotel has a bar that is open to non-residents and residents alike.

| | Price | CREDIT CARDS | CHILDREN'S FACILITIES | PARKING FACILITIES | RESTAURANT | PUBLIC BAR |
|---|---|---|---|---|---|---|
| **NORTH OF THE LIFFEY:** *Isaacs Hotel* W www.isaacs.ie<br>Store St, Dublin 1. **Map** E2. ( 01 855 0067. **FAX** 01 836 5390.<br>Recently developed alongside an older hostel of the same name, the hotel is reasonably priced, well-run and centrally located. **Rooms: 58** | €€ | MC V | ● | ▪ | ● | ▪ |
| **NORTH OF THE LIFFEY:** *Royal Dublin* W www.royaldublin.com<br>40–42 O'Connell St Upper, Dublin 1. **Map** D1. ( 01 8733666. **FAX** 01 8733120.<br>Modern hotel in one of Dublin's most famous streets. It has well-equipped rooms and is smart, though lacking in atmosphere. **Rooms: 117** | €€€ | MC V AE DC | ● | ▪ | ● | ▪ |
| **NORTH OF THE LIFFEY:** *Gresham Hotel* W www.thegresham.com<br>23 O'Connell St Upper, Dublin 1. **Map** D1. ( 01 8746881. **FAX** 01 8787175.<br>One of Dublin's oldest and best known hotels. It is a popular rendezvous spot so the public areas are always busy. The bedrooms are comfortable and there is ample safe parking. **Rooms: 288** | €€€€€ | MC V AE DC | ● | ▪ | ● | ▪ |
| **NORTH OF THE LIFFEY:** *The Morrison* W www.morrisonhotel.ie<br>Ormond Quay, Dublin 1. **Map** C3. ( 01 878 2999. **FAX** 01 878 3185.<br>Built in 1999 with John Rocha as design consultant, this is the ultimate cool but comfortable hotel. **Rooms: 95** | €€€€€ | MC V AE DC | ● | ▪ | ● | ▪ |
| **BALGRIFFIN:** *Belcamp Hutchinson* W www.belcamphutchinson.com<br>Carrs Lane, Malahide Rd, Balgriffin, Dublin 17. ( 01 8460843. **FAX** 01 8485703.<br>Poorly located for central Dublin but only ten minutes from the airport, a comfortable, pleasant place to stay with good food. **Rooms: 6** | €€ | MC V | | ▪ | | |
| **BALLSBRIDGE:** *Anglesea Town House*<br>63 Anglesea Rd, Dublin 4. ( 01 6683877. **FAX** 01 6683461.<br>This Edwardian house is beautifully decorated and furnished. It has a lovely drawing room, very comfortable bedrooms and offers a superb breakfast – all within ten minutes' drive of the centre. **Rooms: 6** | €€ | MC V AE | ● | ▪ | | |
| **BALLSBRIDGE:** *Bewleys Hotel* W www.bewleyshotels.com<br>Merrion Road, Ballsbridge, Dublin 4. ( 01 6681111. **FAX** 01 6681999.<br>This magnificent building used to be a school but is now part of the reliable Bewleys chain. It offers very good value for families. **Rooms: 200** | €€ | MC V AE DC | ● | ▪ | ● | ▪ |
| **BALLSBRIDGE:** *Glenogra Guesthouse*<br>64 Merrion Rd, Ballsbridge, Dublin 4. ( 01 6683661. **FAX** 01 6683698.<br>Attractive, stylish guesthouse convenient for both Dun Laoghaire and the centre. The bedrooms are charming and very comfortable. **Rooms: 13** | €€ | MCV AE DC | ● | | | |
| **BALLSBRIDGE:** *Mount Herbert Hotel* W www.mountherberthotel.ie<br>7 Herbert Rd, Landsdowne Rd, Ballsbridge, Dublin 4. ( 01 6684321. **FAX** 01 6607077.<br>A Victorian hotel close to Lansdowne Road stadium. The rooms are light with modern furnishings and it is reasonably priced. **Rooms: 185** | €€€ | MC V AE DC | ● | ●▪ | ▪ | ▪ |
| **BALLSBRIDGE:** *Herbert Park Hotel* W www.herbertparkhotel.ie<br>Ballsbridge, Dublin 4. ( 01 6672200. **FAX** 01 6672595.<br>This hotel adjoins Herbert Park, close to the Royal Dublin Showground. Public areas are light and spacious. **Rooms: 153** | €€€€ | MC V AE DC | ● | ▪ | ● | ▪ |
| **BALLSBRIDGE:** *Hibernian*<br>Eastmoreland Place, Ballsbridge, Dublin 4. ( 01 6687666. **FAX** 01 6602655.<br>Tucked away in a quiet street but close to the centre, this smart, comfortable hotel offers elegant, luxurious rooms. **Rooms: 42** | €€€€ | MC V AE DC | ● | ▪ | ● | ▪ |
| **BALLSBRIDGE:** *Berkeley Court Hotel* W www.jurysdoyle.com<br>Lansdowne Rd, Dublin 4. ( 01 6601711. **FAX** 01 6617238.<br>The very smart lobby area sets the standard for this luxury hotel, which is well located for Lansdowne Road stadium. **Rooms: 187** | €€€€€ | MC V AE DC | ● | ▪ | ● | ▪ |

**BALLSBRIDGE:** *Jury's Hotel & The Towers at Jury's*   €€€€€   MC V AE DC
Pembroke Rd, Ballsbridge, Dublin 4. [C] *01 6605000.* [W] *www.jurysdoyle.com*
A modern hotel, popular with business people and tourists, a short distance
from the centre with all the facilities you'd expect from a five-star hotel. The
adjacent Towers is the hotel's luxury wing. **Rooms: 400**

**BOOTERSTOWN:** *Doyle Tara* [W] *www.jurysdoyle.com*   €€€   MC V AE DC
Merrion Rd, Dublin 4. [C] *01 2694666.* [FAX] *01 2691027.*
Conveniently situated for Dun Laoghaire, the hotel has recently undergone
refurbishment with a number of new rooms added. **Rooms: 113**

**RATHMINES:** *Clara House*   €€   MC V
23 Leinster Rd, Rathmines, Dublin 6. [C] *01 4975904.* [FAX] *01 4975904.*
In an attractive area, ten minutes' walk from the centre, this Georgian
house is a comfortable B&B with a friendly atmosphere. **Rooms: 13**

## SOUTHEAST IRELAND

**BAGENALSTOWN:** *Lorum Old Rectory*   €€   MC V AE
Co Carlow. **Road map** D4. [C] *0503 75282.* [FAX] *0503 75455.*
Set beneath the Blackstairs Mountains with a cosy atmosphere and log fires
and an inspired six-course dinner. Member of Hidden Ireland. **Rooms: 5**

**BALLYMACARBRY:** *Clonanav Farm Guesthouse*   €€   MC V AE DC
Clonmel, Co Waterford. **Road map** C5. [C] *052 36141.* [FAX] *052 36294.*
A friendly welcome and lots of outdoor activities at this bungalow
farmhouse. A delicious full Irish breakfast is provided.
**Rooms: 14**

**BALLYMURN:** *Ballinkeele House*   €€   MC V AE
Enniscorthy, Co Wexford. **Road map** D5. [C] *053 38105.* [FAX] *053 38468.*
The comfortable rooms overlook its parkland setting. Delicious dinners are
served in the original dining room. Member of Hidden Ireland. **Rooms: 5**

**BLESSINGTON:** *Tulfarris Hotel and Golf Resort*   €€€   MC V AE DC
Blessington Lakes, Co Wicklow. **Road map** D4. [C] *045 867555.* [FAX] *045 867561.*
In a lovely position overlooking Blessington Lake, the hotel offers stylish
comfort and lots of facilities. **Rooms: 80**

**CAPPOQUIN:** *Richmond House* [W] *www.richmondhouse.net*   €€   MC V AE DC
Co Waterford. **Road map** C5. [C] *058 54278.* [FAX] *058 54988.*
A delightful 18th-century, Georgian country house, charmingly decorated
and furnished with antiques, set in peaceful parkland. **Rooms: 9**

**CASTLEDERMOT:** *Kilkea Lodge*   €€   MC V AE
Co Kildare. **Road map** D4. [C] *0503 45112.* [FAX] *0503 45112.*
A member of Hidden Ireland, this attractive house is popular with racegoers
as the Curragh, Punchestown and Naas are within easy reach. **Rooms: 5**

**CLONEA:** *Clonea Strand Hotel* [W] *www.clonea.com*   €€   MC V AE DC
Dungarvan, Co Waterford. **Road map** C5. [C] *058 42416.* [FAX] *058 42880.*
A large, modern resort hotel without huge charm but located next to a lovely
beach and with lots of facilities – great for families. **Rooms: 59**

**DUNLAVIN:** *Rathsallagh House*   €€€   MC V AE DC
Dunlavin, Nr. Naas, Co. Wicklow. **Road map** D4 [C] *045 403112.* [FAX] *045 403343.*
Open fires, comfortable furnishings, an excellent restaurant and a relaxed
atmosphere, make this large country house 15 miles outside Naas a great
place to stay. Closed Christmas and January. **Rooms: 29**

**DUNMORE EAST:** *Church Villa*   €
Co Waterford. **Road map** D5. [C] *051 383390.* [FAX] *051 383023.*
Situated in the village, this attractive house offers excellent-value, simple
B&B. Very friendly owners and neat, comfortable bedrooms. **Rooms: 6**

**ENNISCORTHY:** *Salville House*   €
Enniscorthy, Co Wexford. **Road map** D5. [C] *054 35252.* [FAX] *054 35252.*
Spacious rooms with huge windows give views over wooded countryside.
Delicious breakfasts. Dinner available if pre-booked. **Rooms: 5**

**INISTIOGE:** *Cullintra House* [W] *indigo.ie/~culhse*   €
The Rower, Inistioge, Co Kilkenny. **Road map** D5. [C] & [FAX] *051 423614.*
An attractive farmhouse set in beautiful scenery with woods and farmland all
around. It is a very cosy place with log fires. **Rooms: 6**

| | | | CREDIT CARDS | CHILDREN'S FACILITIES | PARKING FACILITIES | RESTAURANT | PUBLIC BAR |
|---|---|---|---|---|---|---|---|

**Price categories** are for a standard double room (not per person) for one night, including tax, service charges and breakfast.
€ under 65 euros
€€ 65–130 euros
€€€ 130–190 euros
€€€€ 190–260 euros
€€€€€ over 260 euros

**CHILDREN'S FACILITIES**
Cots and high chairs are available and some hotels will also provide a baby-sitting service.

**PARKING FACILITIES**
Parking provided by the hotel in either a private car park or a private garage close by.

**RESTAURANT**
The hotel has a restaurant for residents which also welcomes non-residents – usually only for evening meals.

**PUBLIC BAR**
The hotel has a bar that is open to non-residents and residents alike.

| | CREDIT CARDS | CHILDREN'S FACILITIES | PARKING FACILITIES | RESTAURANT | PUBLIC BAR |
|---|---|---|---|---|---|
| **KILKENNY:** *Lacken House* w www.lackenhouse.ie €€€ <br> Dublin Rd, Kilkenny, Co Kilkenny. **Road map** C4. ( 056 61085. FAX 056 62435. <br> Only five minutes walk from the city centre, this Victorian house is a very comfortable place to stay with a highly regarded restaurant. 📺 TV 🔧 <br> **Rooms:** 11 | MC V AE | ● | ■ | ● | ■ |
| **KILKENNY:** *Butler House* w www.butler.ie €€€ <br> 16 Patrick St, Kilkenny, Co Kilkenny. **Road map** C4. ( 056 65707. FAX 056 65626. <br> The former dower house of Kilkenny Castle right in the heart of town, it has been restored by the Civic Trust. The 18th-century building has fine proportions and is stylishly decorated throughout. 📺 TV **Rooms:** 13 | MC V AE DC | ● | ■ | | |
| **MACREDDIN VILLAGE:** *The BrookLodge* w www.brooklodge.com €€€ <br> Macreddin Village, Co. Wicklow. **Road map** D4. ( 0402 36444. FAX 0402 36580. <br> This is a new hotel in a new village in the middle of the Wicklow countryside. Evan Doyle of The Strawberry Tree restaurant in Killarney has masterminded the project and the restaurant has relocated here. <br> 📺 TV 🔧 🔧 **Rooms:** 40 | MC V AE DC | ● | ■ | ● | ■ |
| **RATHASPECK:** *Rathaspeck Manor* w www.iol.ie/ecuddiny € <br> Co Wexford. **Road map** D5. ( 053 42661/45148. <br> This 300-year-old Georgian manor has an 18-hole, par three golf course and a tennis court. Offering B&B only, the bedrooms are large and comfortable and the breakfast excellent. 📺 TV **Rooms:** 6 | | | ■ | | |
| **RATHNEW:** *Hunter's Hotel* w www.hunters.ie €€€ <br> Co Wicklow. **Road map** D4. ( 0404 40106. FAX 0404 40338. <br> This inn on the old Dublin coaching road dates from 1720 and is run by the fifth generation of the Hunter family. It is a very relaxing place to stay with delicious food and a lovely garden. 📺 TV 🔧 **Rooms:** 16 | MC V AE DC | ● | ■ | ● | ■ |
| **RATHNEW:** *Tinakilly House, Hotel and Restaurant* €€€€ <br> Co Wicklow. **Road map** D4. ( 0404 69274. FAX 0404 67806. w www.tinakilly.ie <br> The many outstanding features of this Victorian house include lovely views over the coast and large, attractive gardens. Comfort is assured with a mix of antiques and modern facilities. 📺 TV 🔧 **Rooms:** 51 | MC V AE DC | ● | ■ | ● | |
| **ROSSLARE:** *Kelly's Resort Hotel* w www.kellys.ie €€€ <br> Co Wexford. **Road map** D5. ( 053 32114. FAX 053 32222. <br> This hotel on the beach is ideal for families who don't mind any lack of character but want lots of leisure and sports facilities. 📺 TV 🔧 🔧 🔧 <br> **Rooms:** 99 | MC V AE | ● | ■ | ● | |
| **STRAFFAN:** *Kildare Hotel & Country Club* w www.kclub.ie €€€€€ <br> Co Kildare. **Road map** D4. ( 01 6273333. FAX 01 6017299. <br> Parts of this exclusive hotel building date back to the 17th century. As well as luxurious bedrooms and a grand drawing room, it boasts a one-star Michelin restaurant, The Byerley Turk. Facilities include a championship golf course and extensive fishing. 📺 TV 🔧 🔧 🔧 🔧 **Rooms:** 79 | MC V AE DC | ● | ■ | ● | ■ |
| **THOMASTOWN:** *Mount Juliet Conrad* €€€€€ <br> Co Kilkenny. **Road map** D5. ( 056 24455. w www.mountjulietconrad.com <br> One of Ireland's luxury hotels but retaining the character and style of a grand family house. Set in an estate of over 450 ha (1500 acres) with lots of sports facilities including an 18-hole golf course. 📺 TV 🔧 🔧 🔧 🔧 <br> **Rooms:** 59 | MC V AE DC | ● | ■ | ● | ■ |
| **WATERFORD:** *Foxmount Country House* €€ <br> Passage East Rd, off Dunmore Rd, Waterford, Co Waterford. **Road map** D5. <br> ( 051 874308. FAX 051 854906. w www.iol.ie/tipp/foxmount.htm <br> An attractive, 17th-century house, full of antiques and personality. The atmosphere is homely and you can bring your own wine to dinner. 📺 **Rooms:** 5 | | | ■ | | |

**WATERFORD:** *Waterford Castle Hotel*   €€€€€   MC V AE DC
The Island, Ballinakill, Waterford, Co Waterford. **Road map** D5.
[ 051 878203. FAX 051 879316. W www.waterfordcastle.com
Guests are ferried across the river to this romantically sited, 15th-century castle. Log fires blaze in lofty rooms and both the large suites and the smaller cosy bedrooms are truly luxurious. TV **Rooms:** 19

**WEXFORD:** *Newbay Country House Hotel*   €€   MC V AE DC
Newbay, Wexford, Co Wexford. **Road map** D5. [ 053 42779. FAX 053 46318.
Part Georgian and part early Victorian, the house feels very much like a private home and guests are given a great welcome. It is a very comfortable and relaxing hotel with peat fires and interesting antiques.
TV **Rooms:** 15

**WEXFORD:** *White's Hotel* W www.whiteshotel.ie   €€   MC V AE DC
George St, Wexford, Co Wexford. **Road map** D5. [ 053 22311. FAX 053 45000.
Centrally located, this former coaching inn is neat and reasonably comfortable with a gothic-style restaurant. There is also a fitness and leisure centre with gym and solarium. TV **Rooms:** 82

## CORK AND KERRY

**BALLINADEE:** *Glebe Country House*   €   MC V
Bandon, Co Cork. **Road map** B6. [ 021 4778294. FAX 021 4778456.
Only ten minutes from Kinsale with lots of sports opportunities close by, this attractive Georgian rectory is beautifully furnished and makes a great base for the area. Book by noon if you want dinner. **Rooms:** 4

**BALLYLICKEY:** *Ballylickey Manor House*   €€€€€   MC V AE DC
Bantry Bay, Co Cork. **Road map** B6. [ 027 50071. W www.ballylickeymanorhouse.com
A 17th-century shooting lodge which has been completely refurbished over recent years. It's an attractive place to stay with lovely, comfortable rooms and delicious food. TV **Rooms:** 14

**BANTRY:** *Bantry House*   €€   MC V AE DC
Co Cork. **Road map** B6. [ 027 50047. FAX 027 50795.
An outstanding, 18th-century, stately home *(see pp160–61)*, open to the public since 1946 and a Member of the Hidden Ireland Group. It has a fine collection of pictures, furniture and works of art. The comfortable bedrooms have *en suite* bathrooms. Open March to October. **Rooms:** 8

**CARAGH LAKE:** *Caragh Lodge* W www.caraghlodge.com   €€   MC V AE DC
Co Kerry. **Road map** A5. [ 066 9769115. FAX 066 9769316.
Colonial-style fishing lodge in magnificent, award-winning gardens bordering the lake. All rooms are neatly decorated and furnished with antique furniture. Open mid-April to mid-October. **Rooms:** 15

**CARAGH LAKE:** *Ard-na-Sidhe*   €€€€   MC V AE DC
Co Kerry. **Road map** A5. [ 066 9769105. FAX 066 9769282.
This attractive Victorian mansion enjoys a wonderfully peaceful setting beside the lake. The ambience is somewhat old-fashioned, reinforced by the neat period furnishings. Open May to September. **Rooms:** 20

**CASTLELYONS:** *Ballyvolane House*   €€   MC V AE DC
Co Cork. **Road map** C5. [ 025 36349. FAX 025 36781.
A lovely 18th & 19th-century house surrounded by very attractive gardens and parkland. All of the large rooms have a view and are very comfortable, furnished with the family antiques. Fishing available. **Rooms:** 6

**CLONAKILTY:** *O'Donovan's Hotel* W www.odonovanhotel.com   €€   MC V AE
Co Cork. **Road map** B6. [ 023 33250. FAX 023 33250.
A traditional, centrally located, family-run hotel in the old commercial mould with unremarkable decor but a very friendly welcome. TV **Rooms:** 20

**CORK:** *Jury's Cork Inn* W www.jurysdoyle.com   €€   MC V AE DC
Anderson's Quay, Cork, Co Cork. **Road map** C5. [ 021 4276444. FAX 021 4276144.
A fixed room-rate hotel with modern, attractive furnishings and good facilities at reasonable prices – ideal for families. TV **Rooms:** 133

**CORK:** *Lotamore House*   €€   MC V AE
Tivoli, Cork, Co Cork. **Road map** C5. [ 021 4822344. FAX 021 4822219.
This Georgian Manor converted into a guesthouse is surrounded by lovely grounds with good views of the harbour and Blackrock Castle. Five minutes' drive from the city centre. TV **Rooms:** 20

For key to symbols see back flap

**Price categories** are for a standard double room (not per person) for one night, including tax, service charges and breakfast.

€ under 65 euros
€€ 65–130 euros
€€€ 130–190 euros
€€€€ 190–260 euros
€€€€€ over 260 euros

**CHILDREN'S FACILITIES**
Cots and high chairs are available and some hotels will also provide a baby-sitting service.

**PARKING FACILITIES**
Parking provided by the hotel in either a private car park or a private garage close by.

**RESTAURANT**
The hotel has a restaurant for residents which also welcomes non-residents – usually only for evening meals.

**PUBLIC BAR**
The hotel has a bar that is open to non-residents and residents alike.

| | Credit Cards | Children's Facilities | Parking Facilities | Restaurant | Public Bar |
|---|---|---|---|---|---|
| **CORK:** *Seven North Mall* €€<br>7 North Mall, Cork, Co Cork. **Road map** C5. ☎ 021 4397191. ℻ 021 4300811.<br>This smart 18th-century house overlooks the River Lee and is a convenient base for exploring the city and surrounding areas. ⊞ TV ♿ **Rooms:** 7 | MC V | | ▪ | | |
| **COURTMACSHERRY:** *Travara Lodge* €<br>Courtmacsherry, Co Cork. **Road map** C5. ☎ 023 46493.<br>Sea views from some of the rooms in this comfortable, house. Simple and extremely tasty food served in the small restaurant. ⊞ ♿ **Rooms:** 6 | MC V | ● | ▪ | ● | |
| **DINGLE:** *Doyle's Seafood Bar and Townhouse* Ⓦ www.doylesofdingle.com €€<br>John St, Dingle, Co Kerry. **Road map** A5. ☎ 066 9151174. ℻ 066 9151816.<br>Famous for its delicious seafood, Doyle's also provides first-class accommodation. Smart and stylish bedrooms with luxurious bathrooms and an attractive sitting room. Informal, relaxed atmosphere. ⊞ TV **Rooms:** 8 | MC V AE | | | ● | |
| **DINGLE:** *Benners Hotel* €€€<br>Main St, Dingle, Co Kerry. **Road map** A5. ☎ 066 9151638. ℻ 066 9151412.<br>American-owned hotel right in the centre of town. The old building has been converted to provide an efficient hotel with a choice of bars, a restaurant and comfortable bedrooms. ⊞ TV **Rooms:** 52 | MC V AE DC | ● | ▪ | ● | ▪ |
| **INISHANNON:** *Inishannon House Hotel* Ⓦ www.inishannonhouse.ie €€€<br>Co Cork. **Road map** B6. ☎ 021 4775121. ℻ 021 4775609.<br>This 18th-century house is very romantic with lovely gardens and parkland leading down to the River Bandon. The bedrooms are individual both in shape and decor. ⊞ TV **Rooms:** 17 | MC V AE DC | ● | ▪ | ● | |
| **KANTURK:** *Assolas Country House* €€€<br>Co Cork. **Road map** B5. ☎ 029 50015. ℻ 029 50795.<br>An elegant, 17th-century house, with cosy decor and an excellent restaurant. Open mid-March to November. ⊞ **Rooms:** 9 | MC V AE | ● | ▪ | | |
| **KENMARE:** *Park Hotel* Ⓦ www.parkkenmare.com €€€€€<br>Co Kerry. **Road map** B5. ☎ 064 41200. ℻ 064 41402.<br>Built in 1897 in a stunning setting by Kenmare Bay, the Park is rated one of Ireland's finest hotels, luxurious with an individual style and lots of original touches. The facilities include an 18-hole golf course. Open mid-April to November, Christmas and New Year. ⊞ TV ♿ **Rooms:** 46 | MC V AE DC | ● | ▪ | ● | ▪ |
| **KENMARE:** *Sheen Falls Lodge* Ⓦ www.sheenfallslodge.ie €€€€€<br>Co Kerry. **Road map** B5. ☎ 064 41600. ℻ 064 41386.<br>The new hotel blends in well with the original 17th-century house. Luxurious, spacious bedrooms with great views over the falls or the huge grounds. Closed January. ⊞ TV ♨ ♿ **Rooms:** 61 | MC V AE DC | ● | ▪ | ● | ▪ |
| **KILLARNEY:** *Dunloe Castle Hotel* €€€<br>Co Kerry. **Road map** B5. ☎ 064 44111. ℻ 064 44583.<br>A member of the Historic Castles and Gardens Association. The modern buildings are in lovely grounds by the ruins of the 13th-century castle. Excellent facilities. Open April to September. ⊞ TV ⊞ ♿ **Rooms:** 102 | MC V AE DC | ● | ▪ | ● | ▪ |
| **KILLARNEY:** *Killarney Royal Hotel* Ⓦ www.killarneyroyal.ie €€€<br>College St, Killarney, Co Kerry. **Road map** B5. ☎ 064 31853. ℻ 064 34001.<br>A short walk from the centre of town, this traditional hotel is a smart, comfortable place to stay. ⊞ TV ♿ **Rooms:** 29 | MC V AE DC | ● | | ● | ▪ |
| **KILLARNEY:** *Hotel Europe* Ⓦ www.iol.ie/khl €€€€<br>Co Kerry. **Road map** B5. ☎ 064 31900. ℻ 064 32118.<br>Huge five-star resort hotel with stunning views of the Lakes of Killarney and the mountains, with every facility from beauty salon to 25 metres pool and lots of outdoor sports. Open April to October. ⊞ TV ⊞ ♿ **Rooms:** 206 | MC V AE DC | ● | ▪ | ● | ▪ |

**KILLARNEY:** *Killarney Park Hotel* w www.killarneyparkhotel.ie €€€€€
Kenmare Place, Killarney, Co Kerry. **Road map** B5. 064 35555. FAX 064 35266.
This tasteful, modern hotel is conveniently located in the centre of town.
It also has a fully equipped leisure centre. *Rooms: 75*
*MC V AE*

**KILLEAGH:** *Ballymakeigh House* €€
Youghal, Co Cork. **Road map** C5. 024 95184. FAX 024 95370.
This attractive 18th-century farmhouse is a comfortable, reasonably priced
base to explore the area. It offers cosy bedrooms and good, home-
cooked food. *Rooms: 7*
*MC V*

**KINSALE:** *Old Presbytery* w www.oldpres.com €€
43 Cork St, Kinsale, Co Cork. **Road map** B6. 021 4772027. FAX 021 4772166.
A comfortable, relaxing place to stay in a quiet street in the town centre.
Bedrooms are simple but stylish, furnished mainly with Victorian pieces.
*Rooms: 6*
*MC V AE*

**KINSALE:** *The Blue Haven* w www.bluehavenkinsale.com €€€
3–4 Pearse St, Kinsale, Co Cork. **Road map** B6. 021 4772209. FAX 021 4774268.
Attractive, small hotel right in the centre of Kinsale, built on the site of
the old fish market. It is smart throughout and has a very popular
restaurant. *Rooms: 17*
*MC V AE DC*

**KINSALE:** *Scilly House* €€€
Co Cork. **Road map** B6. 021 4772413. FAX 021 4774629.
Very attractive old house overlooking Kinsale Bay and the harbour. The
charming bedrooms and reception rooms are full of interesting and
original furniture. Open May to September. *Rooms: 7*
*MC V AE*

**KINSALE:** *Old Bank House* w www.oldbankhousekinsale.com €€€€
11 Pearse St, Kinsale, Co Cork. **Road map** B6. 021 4774075. FAX 021 4774296.
Right in the centre of town, the Old Bank House used to be a branch of
the Munster and Leinster Bank. A listed Georgian building, it has finely
proportioned, comfortable rooms and excellent staff. *Rooms: 17*
*MC V AE*

**MALLOW:** *Longueville House* €€€€€
Co Cork. **Road map** B5. 022 47156. FAX 022 47459. w www.longuevillehouse.ie
The main part of the house is Georgian; the rooms are elegant and
individually decorated, many with huge old-style beds. The hotel's
Presidents' Restaurant has won a number of awards. *Rooms: 20*
*MC V AE DC*

**PARKNASILLA:** *Great Southern Hotel* w www.greatsouthernhotel.com €€€
Sneem, Co Kerry. **Road map** A6. 064 45122. FAX 064 45323.
Sitting in acres of sub-tropical gardens, the main building is Victorian.
Leisure and conference facilities have been added, including a 9-hole golf
course. All the rooms are smartly co-ordinated. *Rooms: 83*
*MC V AE DC*

**SHANAGARRY:** *Ballymaloe House* w www.ballymaloe.com €€€€
Midleton, Co Cork. **Road map** C6. 021 4652531. FAX 021 4652021.
This has become one of the most famous country house hotels in
Ireland. It is not only a charming farmhouse with plenty of places to
relax, but is also the home of the famous Tim and Darina Allen cookery
school, and one of Ireland's best restaurants. *Rooms: 32*
*MC V AE DC*

**TAHILLA:** *Tahilla Cove Country House* w www.tahillacove.com €
Nr Sneem Co Kerry. **Road map** A6. 064 45204. FAX 064 45104.
A friendly guesthouse spread over two houses and set in lovely gardens.
Views from the rooms are either of the sea or mountains. The bar is open
to non-residents and is a great focus of hospitality. *Rooms: 9*
*MC V AE*

**WATERVILLE:** *The Smugglers' Inn* €
Cliff Rd, Waterville, Co Kerry. **Road map** A6. 066 9474330. FAX 066 9474422.
A 100-year-old, modernized, whitewashed inn on the Ring of Kerry right
next door to Waterville championship golf course and overlooking a fine
sandy beach. It is an unpretentious, jolly place with comfortable
bedrooms, friendly bar and good restaurant. *Rooms: 15*
*MC V AE DC*

**YOUGHAL:** *Aherne's Seafood Restaurant* w www.ahernes.com €€€
163 North Main St, Youghal, Co Cork. **Road map** C5. 024 92424. FAX 024 93633.
Aherne's is run by the third generation of the Fitzgibbon family. The
outstanding reputation of this place is due as much to the family's
incredible hospitality and friendliness as it is to the delicious food and
luxuriously appointed bedrooms. *Rooms: 13*
*MC V AE DC*

For key to symbols see back flap

**Price categories** are for a standard double room (not per person) for one night, including tax, service charges and breakfast.
€ under 65 euros
€€ 65–130 euros
€€€ 130–190 euros
€€€€ 190–260 euros
€€€€€ over 260 euros

**CHILDREN'S FACILITIES**
Cots and high chairs are available and some hotels will also provide a baby-sitting service.

**PARKING FACILITIES**
Parking provided by the hotel in either a private car park or a private garage close by.

**RESTAURANT**
The hotel has a restaurant for residents which also welcomes non-residents – usually only for evening meals.

**PUBLIC BAR**
The hotel has a bar that is open to non-residents and residents alike.

## THE LOWER SHANNON

| | Price | Credit Cards | Children's Facilities | Parking Facilities | Restaurant | Public Bar |
|---|---|---|---|---|---|---|
| **ADARE:** *Adare Manor* W www.adaremanor.com<br>Co Limerick. **Road map** B5. 061 396566. FAX 061 396124.<br>This huge, Victorian-Gothic mansion was the former seat of the Earls of Dunraven. Built in 1720, it was elaborated and enlarged in the 19th century. It's both tasteful and luxurious throughout. **Rooms:** 138 | €€€€€ | MC V AE DC | ● | ■ | ● | ■ |
| **ADARE:** *Dunraven Arms* W www.dunravenhotel.com<br>Co Limerick. **Road map** B5. 061 396633. FAX 061 396541.<br>Set in the extremely pretty village of Adare, this inn was established in 1792 and is a great touring base for the southwest. The bedrooms are luxurious and the restaurant is outstanding. **Rooms:** 76 | €€€€ | MC V AE DC | ● | ■ | ● | ■ |
| **AGLISH:** *Ballycormac House*<br>Borrisokane, Co Tipperary. **Road map** C4. 067 21129. FAX 067 21200.<br>Located in a quiet rural setting this cosy, 300-year-old house has a relaxed, informal atmosphere with lots of activities on offer, including riding and golf. Dinner is by reservation only. **Rooms:** 5 | €€ | MC V | ● | ■ | | |
| **AHERLOW:** *Aherlow House* W www.dunravenhotel.com<br>Glen of Aherlow, Co Tipperary. **Road map** C5. 062 56153. FAX 062 56212.<br>Set in the middle of a pine forest with a view of the mountains, this is a comfortable and welcoming hunting lodge. **Rooms:** 29 | €€ | MC V AE DC | ● | ■ | ● | ■ |
| **BALLYVAUGHAN:** *Hylands*<br>Co Clare. **Road map** B4. 065 7077037. FAX 065 7077131.<br>Dating back to the 18th century, this family run hotel is traditional in style, with simple but pretty bedrooms. Irish music in the bar. **Rooms:** 30 | €€ | MC V AE DC | ● | ■ | ● | ■ |
| **BALLYVAUGHAN:** *Gregans Castle Hotel* W www.gregans.ie<br>Co Clare. **Road map** B4. 065 7077005. FAX 065 7077111.<br>This is a marvellous hotel in the middle of the Burren, with views towards Galway Bay. Open Apr to Oct & winter weekends. **Rooms:** 22 | €€€ | MC V AE | ● | ■ | | |
| **CASHEL:** *Legends Townhouse & Restaurant*<br>Co Tipperary. **Road map** C5. 062 61292. W www.legendsguesthouse.com<br>This small townhouse and restaurant is just beside the great Rock of Cashel and has great views from both the bedrooms and the dining room. Bedrooms are simply furnished with good bathrooms. Open all year except two weeks in February and November. **Rooms:** 7 | € | MC | | ■ | ● | |
| **CASHEL:** *Cashel Palace Hotel* W www.cashel-palace.ie<br>Main St, Cashel, Co Tipperary. **Road map** C5. 062 62707. FAX 062 61521.<br>Beautiful Palladian house originally built as an archbishop's palace in the 1730s. Right in the centre of town but surrounded by a peaceful garden, it is an extremely civilized place to stay. **Rooms:** 23 | €€€€ | MC V AE DC | ● | ■ | ● | ■ |
| **CLARECASTLE:** *Carnelly House* W www.carnellyhouse.com<br>Co Clare. **Road map** B4. 065 6828442. FAX 065 6829222.<br>A lovely Queen Anne house designed by Francis Bindon and set in delightful grounds. A member of Hidden Ireland, it is elegantly and tastefully furnished and has a relaxed atmosphere. **Rooms:** 5 | €€€€ | MC V AE | ● | ■ | | |
| **CLONMEL:** *Clonmel Arms Hotel* W www.clonmelarmshotel.com<br>Sarsfield St, Clonmel, Co Tipperary. **Road map** C5. 052 21233. FAX 052 21526.<br>A predictable but comfortable central hotel. The bars and restaurants are popular with the locals. Particularly helpful staff. **Rooms:** 30 | €€ | MC V AE DC | ● | ■ | ● | ■ |
| **FEAKLE:** *Smyths Country Lodge Hotel*<br>Co Clare. **Road map** B4. 061 924002. FAX 061 924244.<br>A complex made up of modern cottages and a restaurant. Set in lovely countryside, it is a comfortable and jolly place to stay. **Rooms:** 35 | €€€ | MC V AE DC | ● | ■ | ● | ■ |

**GLIN:** *Glin Castle* w www.glincastle.com — €€€€€ | MC V AE DC
Co Limerick. **Road map** B5. 068 34173. FAX 068 34364.
You can stay in this historic Irish house either as an individual or in a group. Built in the 1780s, this magnificent building is owned by the Knight of Glin. It is also a member of Ireland's Blue Book. TV **Rooms:** 15

**KILNABOY:** *Fergus View* — €€
Corrofin, Co Clare. **Road map** B4. 065 6837606. FAX 065 6837192.
Very good-value, friendly guesthouse and a useful base for exploring the Burren. Recently refurbished, it is pristine and comfortable. Dinner is available Monday to Thursday, but only if pre-booked. **Rooms:** 6

**LIMERICK:** *Woodfield House* w www.woodfieldhousehotel.com — €€ | MC V AE DC
Ennis Rd, Limerick, Co Limerick. **Road map** B4. 061 453022. FAX 061 326755.
Located just out of town, this traditional hotel has a friendly, informal family atmosphere. The bedrooms are smartly co-ordinated and well-equipped. TV **Rooms:** 26

**LIMERICK:** *Jury's Hotel* — €€€ | MC V AE DC
Ennis Rd, Limerick, Co Limerick. **Road map** B4. 061 327777. FAX 061 326400.
Reliable part of the Jury's chain with good quality furnishings and dependable service. Lovely location in 2 ha (5 acres) of garden on the banks of the River Shannon. TV **Rooms:** 98

**LISDOONVARNA:** *Sheedy's Country House Hotel* — €€ | MC V AE
Co Clare. **Road map** B4. 065 7074026. w www.sheedyscountryhouse.com
This house has been in the Sheedy family for five generations and has now been converted into a very comfortable, efficient hotel by the present owners. TV **Rooms:** 11

**LISMACUE:** *Lismacue House* w www.limascue.com — €€€ | MC V AE
Bansha, Co Tipperary. **Road map** C5. 062 54106. FAX 062 54126.
The house is part of the Hidden Ireland group. It is a classically beautiful, Irish country house built at the beginning of the 19th century; it has particularly fine reception rooms and comfortable bedrooms. **Rooms:** 5

**NEWMARKET-ON-FERGUS:** *Dromoland Castle* — €€€€€ | MC V AE DC
Co Clare. **Road map** B4. 061 368144. FAX 061 363355. w www.dromoland.ie
Sister hotel to Ashford Castle in Cong, you can expect a high standard of luxury here, too. The castle dates back to the 16th century and has a fascinating history and acres of grounds. TV **Rooms:** 100

## THE WEST OF IRELAND

**BALINA:** *Teach Iorrais* w www.teachiorrais.com — €€€ | MC V AE
Geesala, Ballina, Co. Mayo. **Road map** B2. 097 86888. FAX 097 86855.
This small and functional modern hotel (opened 1999) in the Gaeltacht has good value rooms and excellent facilities that include conference and banqueting. The hotel has its own garden and offers good fishing and walking nearby. TV **Rooms:** 31

**BALLYNAHINCH:** *Ballynahinch Castle Hotel* — €€€ | MC V AE DC
Recess, Connemara, Co Galway. **Road map** A3. 095 31006. FAX 095 31085.
A magnificent castle, once owned by a maharajah, in a superb location. The hotel is well-run, and friendly. There is an excellent restaurant and lots of sporting possibilities. Closed Christmas and February. TV **Rooms:** 40

**CASHEL BAY:** *Cashel House* w www.cashel-house-hotel.com — €€€ | MC V AE DC
Connemara, Co Galway. **Road map** A3. 095 31001. FAX 095 31077.
In a stunning position at the head of Cashel Bay, this is a hotel with comfortable, relaxing rooms, full of interesting antiques. It is also very popular with families. Closed January. TV **Rooms:** 32

**CASHEL BAY:** *Zetland House* w www.zetland.com — €€€ | MC V AE DC
Connemara, Co Galway. **Road map** A3. 095 31111. FAX 095 31117.
A stylishly decorated, 19th-century shooting lodge. Set on the edge of Cashel Bay in lovely gardens, most of the bedrooms and the dining room share the superb views. Open Easter to end-October. TV **Rooms:** 19

**CLIFDEN:** *Erriseask House* — €€ | MC V AE DC
Ballyconneely, Connemara, Co Galway. **Road map** A3. 095 23553. FAX 095 23639.
This modern farmhouse is stylishly decorated, with light, comfortable bedrooms. It's set in a beautiful spot, only a short walk away from the sea and the food is superb. TV **Rooms:** 12

For key to symbols see back flap

<table>
<tr><td colspan="2">

**Price categories** are for a standard double room (not per person) for one night, including tax, service charges and breakfast.

€ under 65 euros
€€ 65–130 euros
€€€ 130–190 euros
€€€€ 190–260 euros
€€€€€ over 260 euros

</td><td colspan="2">

**CHILDREN'S FACILITIES**
Cots and high chairs are available and some hotels will also provide a baby-sitting service.
**PARKING FACILITIES**
Parking provided by the hotel in either a private car park or a private garage close by.
**RESTAURANT**
The hotel has a restaurant for residents which also welcomes non-residents – usually only for evening meals.
**PUBLIC BAR**
The hotel has a bar that is open to non-residents and residents alike.

</td></tr>
</table>

| | CREDIT CARDS | CHILDREN'S FACILITIES | PARKING FACILITIES | RESTAURANT | PUBLIC BAR |
|---|---|---|---|---|---|
| **CLIFDEN:** *Ardagh Hotel & Restaurant* W www.commerce.ie/ardaghhotel €€€<br>Connemara, Co Galway. **Road map** A3. **(** 095 21384. **FAX** 095 21314.<br>Many rooms at this modern, chalet-style hotel look out onto Ardbear Bay.<br>The gardens are beautiful. Open April to October. **TV** *Rooms: 21* | MC<br>V<br>AE<br>DC | ● | ▨ | ● | ▨ |
| **CLIFDEN:** *Rock Glen Country House Hotel* €€€€<br>Connemara, Co Galway. **Road map** A3. **(** 095 21035. **FAX** 095 21737.<br>This traditional hotel used to be a shooting lodge for Clifden Castle.<br>Comfortable rooms and reliable, friendly service. Open mid-February to<br>October. **TV** *Rooms: 26* | MC<br>V<br>AE | ● | ▨ | ● | ▨ |
| **CONG:** *Ashford Castle* W www.ashford.ie €€€€€<br>Co Mayo. **Road map** B3. **(** 092 46003. **FAX** 092 46260.<br>A mixture of 13th-century and Gothic Revival, this magnificent castle is set<br>on the shore of Lough Corrib. Rich wall-to-wall carpeting kills a lot of the<br>historical atmosphere, but it is undoubtedly luxurious. **TV** **&** *Rooms: 83* | MC<br>V<br>AE<br>DC | ● | ▨ | ● | |
| **CROSSMOLINA:** *Enniscoe House* W www.enniscoe.com €€€<br>Castlehill, Nr Crossmolina, Ballina, Co Mayo. **Road map** B2. **(** 096 31112. **FAX** 096 31773.<br>This fine Georgian house, set in magnificent grounds which lead down to<br>Lough Conn, is full of beautiful antiques and has a relaxed, lived-in feel with<br>attractive bedrooms and good food. Member of Hidden Ireland. *Rooms: 6* | MC<br>V<br>AE | ● | ▨ | | |
| **GALWAY:** *Brennan's Yard Hotel* €€€<br>Lower Merchant's Rd, Galway, Co Galway. **Road map** B4.<br>**(** 091 568166. **FAX** 091 568262. W www.brennansyardhotel.com<br>Converted from a stone warehouse, and now decked with designer fabrics<br>and Irish art, it offers comfortable rooms with city views. **TV** **&** *Rooms: 45* | MC<br>V<br>AE<br>DC | ● | ▨ | ● | ▨ |
| **GALWAY:** *Ardilaun House* W www.ardilaunhousehotel.ie €€€€<br>Taylor's Hill, Galway, Co Galway. **Road map** B4. **(** 091 521433. **FAX** 091 521546.<br>A short distance from the city centre and quite close to Salthill, this hotel<br>is popular with business people and tourists. Smart decor, friendly,<br>efficient service and comfortable rooms. **TV** **&** *Rooms: 89* | MC<br>V<br>AE<br>DC | ● | ▨ | ● | ▨ |
| **GALWAY:** *Great Southern Hotel* €€€€€<br>Eyre Sq, Galway, Co Galway. **Road map** B4. **(** 091 564041. **FAX** 091 566704.<br>The rooftop swimming pool is an unusual feature of this large and<br>rambling Victorian hotel in the heart of the city. The rooms are<br>comfortable and there are plenty of facilities. **TV** 🏊 **&** *Rooms: 108* | MC<br>V<br>AE<br>DC | ● | ▨ | ● | ▨ |
| **KNOCKFERRY:** *Knockferry Lodge* W www.knockferrylodge.com €<br>Roscahill, Co Galway. **Road map** B3. **(** 091 550122. **FAX** 091 550328.<br>Situated in a tranquil spot on the western shore of Lough Corrib, the<br>prices reflect the simple accommodation with plain decor and furnishings.<br>The atmosphere is very friendly and the food good. *Rooms: 10* | MC<br>V<br>AE<br>DC | ● | ▨ | ● | |
| **LEENANE:** *Delphi Lodge* W www.delphilodge.ie €€€<br>Co Galway. **Road map** B3. **(** 095 42222. **FAX** 095 42296.<br>A sporting lodge in a lovely setting by a lough surrounded by mountains.<br>Informal atmosphere with plenty of fishing on the loughs and River Delphi.<br>A member of Hidden Ireland. Open Feb to mid-Dec. *Rooms: 12* | MC<br>V<br>AE | ● | ▨ | ● | |
| **LETTERFRACK:** *Rosleague Manor House* €€€<br>Connemara, Co Galway. **Road map** A3. **(** 095 41101. **FAX** 095 41168.<br>A substantial Georgian house overlooking Ballinakill Bay and well placed<br>for the Connemara National Park. Confotatble and relaxed with an<br>excellent restaurant. Open Easter to end-October. **TV** *Rooms: 20* | MC<br>V<br>AE | ● | ▨ | ● | ▨ |
| **MOYARD:** *Crocnaraw Country House* W www.crocnaraw.itgo.com €€€<br>Connemara, Co Galway. **Road map** A3. **(** 095 41068. **FAX** 095 41068.<br>Beautifully furnished Georgian house on Ballinakill Bay with award-winning<br>gardens. Relaxed atmosphere and comfortable bedrooms. *Rooms: 6* | MC<br>V<br>AE | ● | ▨ | | |

**NEWPORT:** *Newport House* €€€€ MC V AE DC ● ● ● ■
Co Mayo. **Road map** B3. [ 098 41222. FAX 098 41613.
A stay at this historic, creeper-covered Georgian house is extremely
comfortable and civilized. It stands beside the River Newport, renowned
as a great fishing centre. Open 19-March to end-September. ⬛ **Rooms:** 18

**OUGHTERARD:** *Currarevagh House* €€€ ■ ●
Connemara, Co Galway. **Road map** B3. [ 091 552312. FAX 091 552731.
In an isolated, peaceful spot on the shores of Lough Corrib and surrounded
by woods, parkland and gardens, this Victorian country house is traditionally run with a cosy, slightly old-fashioned atmosphere. ⬛ **Rooms:** 15

**OUGHTERARD:** *Ross Lake House* €€€ MC V AE DC ■ ● ■
Rosscahill, Oughterard, Co Galway. **Road map** B3.
[ 091 550109. FAX 091 550184. W www.rosslakehotel.com
This 19th-century house feels spruce and efficient. Fishing is available in
nearby loughs and you can play tennis in the hotel grounds. Open mid-
March to end-October. ⬛ TV ♿ **Rooms:** 13

**PONTOON:** *Healy's* W www.irelandmayohotel.com €€ MC V AE DC ● ● ■ ●
Foxford, Co Mayo. **Road map** B3. [ 094 56443. FAX 094 56572.
In a stunning position on the shores of Lough Conn and Lough Cullen,
this traditional old stone hotel is a great spot for bird-watchers. Simple,
neat bedrooms and good Irish cooking. ⬛ TV **Rooms:** 14

**RENVYLE:** *Renvyle House* W www.renvyle.com €€€€ MC V AE DC ● ● ■ ●
Connemara, Co Galway. **Road map** A3. [ 095 43511. FAX 095 43515.
A very relaxed, family hotel on the edge of the Atlantic, it offers lots of
sporting activities as well as comfort and good food. Beams and polished
wooden floors with rugs give atmosphere and style. ⬛ ≋ TV ♿ **Rooms:** 65

**ROSTURK:** *Rosturk Woods* W www.rosturk-woods.com €€ ● ■
Mulrany, Westport, Co Mayo. **Road map** B3. [ 098 36264. FAX 098 36264.
In a wonderfully quiet spot by the sea, 11 km (7 miles) from Newport,
this stylishly furnished guesthouse is an extremely attractive and
comfortable place to stay. ⬛ ♿ **Rooms:** 3

**WESTPORT:** *Olde Railway* W www.anu.ie/railwayhotel €€€ MC V AE DC ● ■ ● ■
The Mall, Westport, Co Mayo. **Road map** B3. [ 098 25166. FAX 098 25090.
Situated in the centre of town, this traditional hotel is comfortable and
reliable and has recently been attractively refurbished. It makes an
excellent base for the area. ⬛ TV **Rooms:** 26

## NORTHWEST IRELAND

**ARDARA:** *The Green Gate* € ●
Ardvally, Co Donegal. **Road map** C2. [ 075 41546.
This highly original bed and breakfast can be found at the end of a steep,
winding lane. The accommodation is spread over three cottages and the
place is run in unique style by Paul Chatenoud. ⬛ **Rooms:** 5

**BALLYMOTE:** *Temple House* €€ MC V AE ● ■
Co Sligo. **Road map** B3. [ 071 83329. FAX 071 83808.
This lovely Georgian house is set in extensive parkland. A member of
Hidden Ireland, the house is open April to end-November. Guests are
asked not to use scented products, due to allergy in host. ⬛ **Rooms:** 6

**BRUCKLESS:** *Bruckless House* W www.iol.ie/~bruck/bruckless €€ MC V AE ■
Co Donegal. **Road map** C2. [ 073 37071. FAX 073 37070.
Set in 7 ha (17 acres) of attractive grounds on the shores of Bruckless
Bay, this 18th-century farmhouse is a comfortable and relaxing place to
stay with friendly hosts and good food. Two rooms are *en suite*. **Rooms:** 4

**CASTLEBALDWIN:** *Cromleach Lodge Country House* €€€€ MC V AE DC ● ■ ● ■
Boyle, Co Sligo. **Road map** C3. [ 071 65155. FAX 071 65455. W www.cromleach.com
Superbly positioned in the hills above Lough Arrow, the hotel has
spacious bedrooms, an excellent restaurant and a high standard of
comfort. ⬛ TV **Rooms:** 10

**COLLOONEY:** *Markree Castle* W www.markreecastle.ie €€€ MC V AE DC ● ■ ● ■
Co Sligo. **Road map** C2. [ 071 67800. FAX 071 67840.
In the Cooper family since 1640, the castle has recently been restored and
turned into a hotel. Stately rooms and lovely grounds make this a
civilized and relaxing experience. ⬛ TV ♿ **Rooms:** 30

<table>
<tr><td colspan="5">
Price categories are for a standard double room (not per person) for one night, including tax, service charges and breakfast.

€ under 65 euros
€€ 65–130 euros
€€€ 130–190 euros
€€€€ 190–260 euros
€€€€€ over 260 euros
</td></tr>
</table>

**CHILDREN'S FACILITIES**
Cots and high chairs are available and some hotels will also provide a baby-sitting service.

**PARKING FACILITIES**
Parking provided by the hotel in either a private car park or a private garage close by.

**RESTAURANT**
The hotel has a restaurant for residents which also welcomes non-residents – usually only for evening meals.

**PUBLIC BAR**
The hotel has a bar that is open to non-residents and residents alike.

| | CREDIT CARDS | CHILDREN'S FACILITIES | PARKING FACILITIES | RESTAURANT | PUBLIC BAR |
|---|---|---|---|---|---|
| **DONEGAL:** *St Ernan's House* W www.sainternans.com  €€€€<br>Co Donegal. **Road map** C2. 📞 073 21065. FAX 073 22098.<br>Set on a small island, linked to the mainland by a causeway, this pink-painted, 19th-century house is elegantly furnished but retains an informal atmosphere. Open mid-April–end-October. 🚗 TV **Rooms: 10** | MC V | | ▪ | ● | |
| **DRUMCLIFF:** *Urlar House*  €<br>Co Sligo. **Road map** C2. 📞 071 63110. @ urlarhouse@eircom.net<br>In a peaceful, secluded position in the shadow of Ben Bulben, this attractive farmhouse offers good, simple *en suite* accommodation and makes a perfect base for exploring Yeats Country. 🚗 TV **Rooms: 5** | AE | | ▪ | | |
| **DUNKINEELY:** *Castle Murray House* W www.castlemurray.com  €€<br>St John's Point, Co Donegal. **Road map** C2. 📞 073 37022. FAX 073 37330.<br>Stunningly located with views of McSweeney Bay, this small hotel is a wonderful place to stay. The decor is simple but smart and the restaurant offers a delicious menu. 🚗 TV **Rooms: 10** | MC V | ● | ▪ | ● | |
| **LETTERKENNY:** *Castle Grove Country House Hotel*  €€€<br>Co Donegal. **Road map** C1. 📞 074 51118. FAX 074 51384. W www.castlegrove.com<br>Approached down a long avenue through lovely parkland, this 17th-century house looks out on to Lough Swilly and is a peaceful and relaxing place to stay. 🚗 TV ♿ **Rooms: 15** | MC V AE DC | | ▪ | ● | |
| **LOUGH ESKE:** *Ardnamona House*  €€€<br>Co Donegal. **Road map** C2. 📞 073 22650. FAX 073 22819.<br>A member of Hidden Ireland, this Edwardian house is in a beautiful spot, surrounded by famous gardens and backed by the Blue Stack Mountains. Comfortable rooms and a hospitable, informal atmosphere. 🚗 **Rooms: 6** | MC V AE DC | ● | ▪ | | |
| **LOUGH ESKE:** *Harvey's Point* W www.harveyspoint.com  €€€<br>Donegal Town, Co Donegal. **Road map** C2. 📞 073 22208. FAX 073 22352.<br>Swiss-style hotel on the banks of Lough Eske. Neat, modern furnishings, excellent restaurant and lots of sports facilities. Most rooms overlook the lough. 🚗 TV ♿ **Rooms: 33** | MC V AE DC | | ▪ | ● | ▪ |
| **MOHILL:** *Glebe House* W www.glebehouse.com  €€<br>Ballinamore Rd, Mohill, Co Leitrim. **Road map** C3. 📞 078 31086. FAX 078 31886.<br>This early 19th-century former rectory is set in 20 ha (50 acres) of parkland, woods and farmland, and is peaceful and attractive. 🚗 TV **Rooms: 10** | MC V AE | ● | ▪ | | |
| **RIVERSTOWN:** *Coopershill House*  €€€<br>Co Sligo. **Road map** C2. 📞 071 65108. FAX 071 65466.<br>Very civilized, elegant 17th-century house surrounded by a vast estate. Fine rooms with lovely antiques, huge bedrooms and excellent food. 🚗 **Rooms: 8** | MC V AE DC | ● | ▪ | | |
| **ROSSNOWLAGH:** *Smuggler's Creek*  €€<br>Co Donegal. **Road map** C2. 📞 072 52366. FAX 072 32000<br>This is a very cosy place in a wonderful position on top of the cliff looking down over the Rossnowlagh beach. There's a choice of bar food or the restaurant, and three of the bedrooms have sea views. 🚗 **Rooms: 5** | MC V | | ▪ | ● | ▪ |
| **ROSSNOWLAGH:** *Sand House Hotel* W www.sandhouse-hotel.ie  €€€<br>Co Donegal. **Road map** C2. 📞 072 51777. FAX 072 52100.<br>An imposing, white castellated building right on a sandy beach overlooking Donegal Bay, this long-established hotel is very comfortable and well decorated and has a relaxed atmosphere. 🚗 TV ♿ **Rooms: 60** | MC V AE DC | ● | ▪ | ● | ▪ |
| **STRANORLAR:** *Kee's Hotel and Leisure Club* W www.keeshotel.ie  €€€<br>Ballybofey, Co Donegal. **Road map** C2. 📞 074 31018. FAX 074 31917.<br>A coaching inn and mail staging post in the 19th century, the hotel maintains a tradition of generous hospitality. It has an excellent leisure centre and is well located for exploring Donegal. 🚗 TV ♿ 🍴 **Rooms: 53** | MC V AE DC | ● | ▪ | ● | ▪ |

## THE MIDLANDS

**ARDEE:** *Red House* [w] homepage.eircom.net/~redhouse   €€€
Co Louth. **Road map** D3. 📞 041 6853523. **FAX** 041 6853523.
This very attractive Georgian manor house is a member of Hidden Ireland.
The rooms are comfortable and there is a floodlit tennis court. *Rooms: 3*

**CARLINGFORD:** *Viewpoint*   €   V
Omeath Rd, Carlingford, Co Louth. **Road map** D3. 📞 042 9373149. **FAX** 042 9373149.
Motel-style, modern accommodation. Well-equipped bedrooms with
wonderful views across Carlingford Lough. B & B only. [TV] *Rooms: 8*

**CARLINGFORD:** *McKevitt's Village Hotel* [w] www.mckevittshotel.com   €€
Market Sq, Carlingford, Co Louth. **Road map** D3. 📞 042 9373116. **FAX** 042 9373144.   MC V AE DC
Popular village inn at the heart of the local scene. Rooms have real fires
and a great atmosphere, bedrooms are pristine and pretty. [TV] *Rooms: 13*

**CARRICK-ON-SHANNON:** *Hollywell Country House*   €€
Co Leitrim. **Road map** C3. 📞 078 21124. **FAX** 078 21124.   MC V
Set on the hillside close to the town, there are great views across the
Shannon and surrounding countryside from the house. It is a very
welcoming and relaxing place to stay. *Rooms: 4*

**CLONES:** *Hilton Park* [w] www.hiltonpark.ie   €€€
Co Monaghan. **Road map** C2. 📞 047 56007. **FAX** 047 56033.   MC V
Superb mansion in magnificent parkland. A member of Hidden Ireland
and extremely civilized. The rooms have a relaxed grandeur. *Rooms: 6*

**CROSSDONEY:** *Lisnamandra Farmhouse*   €
Lisnamandra, Crossdoney, Co Cavan. **Road map** C3. 📞 049 4337196.   MC V
Simple but comfortable accommodation in hospitable 17th-century
farmhouse. *Rooms: 4*

**DROGHEDA:** *Boyne Valley Hotel & Country Club*   €€
Co Louth. **Road map** D3. 📞 041 9837737. [w] www.boyne-valley-hotel.ie   MC V AE DC
A much extended and refurbished 18th-century manor house. Although
most of the decor and furnishings are modern, the hotel preserves much
of the house's traditional feel. [TV] *Rooms: 37*

**DULEEK:** *Annesbrook* [w] www.annesbrook.com   €€
Co Meath. **Road map** D3. 📞 041 9823293. **FAX** 041 9823024.   MC V
This fine 17th-century house is a lovely, welcoming place to stay with
spacious bedrooms. Open April to end September. *Rooms: 5.*

**KILMESSAN:** *Station House Hotel and Restaurant*   €€
Co Meath. **Road map** D3. 📞 046 25239 **FAX** 046 25588.   MC V AE DC
The railway used to run through Kilmessan, but now this Victorian station
building is a comfortable hotel with a good restaurant. [TV] *Rooms: 20*

**MOUNTRATH:** *Roundwood House*   €€€
Co Laois. **Road map** C4. 📞 0502 32120. **FAX** 0502 32711.   MC V AE DC
A beautiful, 18th-century Palladian villa set in lovely grounds close to the
Slieve Bloom Mountains. Civilized but informal atmosphere. *Rooms: 10*

**MULLINGAR:** *Bloomfield House Hotel* [w] www.bloomfieldhouse.com   €€€
Co Westmeath. **Road map** C3. 📞 044 40894. **FAX** 044 43767.   MC V AE DC
A manor house on Lough Ennell with great views. Traditional in atmosphere
but recently refurbished, it's comfortable and friendly. [TV] *Rooms: 65*

**MULLINGAR:** *Crookedwood House*   €€€
Crookedwood, Co Westmeath. **Road map** C3. 📞 044 72165. **FAX** 044 72166.   MC V AE DC
This handsome house started life as an 18th-century rectory and is now a
leading hotel and restaurant. There are some lovely views over Lough
Derravaragh. Smoking is not allowed in the restaurant. [TV] *Rooms: 8*

**MULLINGAR:** *Greville Arms* [w] www.grevillearms.com   €€€
Pearse Street, Co Westmeath. **Road map** C3. 📞 044 48563. **FAX** 044 48052.   MC V AE DC
Centrally located, this traditional hotel caters for both locals and tourists. It
has two large and very welcoming bars. [TV] *Rooms: 39*

**SLANE:** *Conyngham Arms* [w] www.conynghamarms.com   €€
Co Meath. **Road map** D3. 📞 041 9824155. **FAX** 041 9824205.   MC V AE DC
In the heart of the estate village, this traditional family hotel is welcoming
and comfortable. Good base for touring the Boyne Valley. [TV] *Rooms: 15*

**Price categories** are for a standard double room (not per person) for one night, including tax, service charges and breakfast.
£ under £50
££ £50–100
£££ £100–150
££££ £150–200
£££££ over £200

**CHILDREN'S FACILITIES**
Cots and high chairs are available and some hotels will also provide a baby-sitting service.
**PARKING FACILITIES**
Parking provided by the hotel in either a private car park or a private garage close by.
**RESTAURANT**
The hotel has a restaurant for residents which also welcomes non-residents – usually only for evening meals.
**PUBLIC BAR**
The hotel has a bar that is open to non-residents and residents alike.

# NORTHERN IRELAND

| | CREDIT CARDS | CHILDREN'S FACILITIES | PARKING FACILITIES | RESTAURANT | PUBLIC BAR |
|---|---|---|---|---|---|
| **ANNALONG:** *Glassdrumman Lodge* W www.glassdrummanlodge.co.uk £££<br>Mill Rd, Annalong, Co Down. **Road map** D2. ( 028 4376 8451. FAX 028 4376 7041.<br>Set deep in the "Kingdom of Mourne", the hotel looks out on the region's famous dry-stone walls. Excellent reputation for food. ■ TV & **Rooms:** 10 | MC V AE DC | ● | ■ | ● | |
| **ARMAGH:** *Charlemont Arms* W www.charlemontarmshotel.com ££<br>57–65 English St. Co Armagh. **Road map** D2. ( 028 3752 2028. FAX 028 3752 6979.<br>A country-style hotel perfectly located for the major attractions. What it lacks in luxury it makes up for in the warmth of its welcome. ■ TV & **Rooms:** 30 | MC V | ● | ■ | ● | ■ |
| **BALLYGALLY:** *Hastings Ballygally Castle* ££<br>274 Coast Rd, Ballygally, Co Antrim. **Road map** D1.<br>( 028 2858 3212. FAX 028 2858 3681. W www.hastings.com<br>Reputedly haunted, the castle showpiece is the Ghost Room, a tiny old tower bedroom with a macabre legend. The hotel bar provides a jolly atmosphere in a modern setting. ■ TV **Rooms:** 44 | MC V AE DC | ● | ■ | ● | ■ |
| **BALLYMENA:** *Galgorm Manor* W www.galgorm.com £££<br>Co Antrim. **Road map** D1. ( 028 2588 1001. FAX 028 2588 0080.<br>The River Maine sweeps past the hotel, enhancing the view from many of the rooms. Fishing is available on the magnificent estate. There is a first-rate restaurant and a traditional, Irish-style bar. ■ TV & **Room:** 24 | MC V AE DC | ● | ■ | ● | ■ |
| **BANGOR:** *Clandeboye Lodge* ££<br>10 Estate Rd, Bangor, Co Down. **Road map** E2. ( 028 9185 3777. FAX 028 9185 2772.<br>Resembling a Victorian church school, the hotel has reasonably priced rooms and a stylish dining room with a great menu. ■ TV & **Rooms:** 43 | MC V AE DC | ● | ■ | ● | ■ |
| **BELFAST:** *Duke's Hotel* W www.dukeshotel.com £££<br>65 University St, Belfast BT7 1HL. **Road map** D2. ( 028 9023 6666. FAX 028 9023 7177.<br>A modern hotel offering comfort, style and international cuisine in the heart of the city. It has a good public bar. ■ TV & **Rooms:** 20 | MC V AE DC | ● | | ● | ■ |
| **BELFAST:** *The Europa Hotel* W www.hastingshotels.com £££<br>Great Victoria St, Belfast BT2 7AP. **Road map** D2. ( 028 9032 7000. FAX 028 9032 7800.<br>An imposing building in the heart of the Golden Mile, ideal for business people and tourists, with very good restaurants. ■ TV & **Rooms:** 240 | MC V AE DC | | | ● | ■ |
| **BELFAST:** *Hastings Stormont Hotel* £££<br>587 Upper Newtownards Rd, Belfast BT4 3LP. **Road map** D2.<br>( 028 9065 1066. FAX 028 9048 0240. W www.hastingshotels.com<br>Close to Stormont and the airport, it's excellent for business people. Modern and functional with an award-winning restaurant. ■ TV & **Rooms:** 109 | MC V AE DC | ● | ■ | ● | ■ |
| **BELFAST:** *Malone Lodge Hotel* W www.malonelodgehotel.com £££<br>60 Eglantine Ave, Belfast BT9 6DY. **Road map** D2. ( 028 9038 8000. FAX 028 9038 8088.<br>Centrally located, it's ideal for business people and tourists and offers comfortable, modern facilities. ■ TV & **Rooms:** 51 | MC V AE | ● | ■ | ● | |
| **CARNLOUGH:** *Londonderry Arms Hotel* ££<br>20 Harbour Rd, Carnlough, Co Antrim. **Road map** D1.<br>( 028 2888 5255. FAX 028 2888 5263. W www.glensofantrim.com<br>Winston Churchill once owned this ivy-covered inn next to the harbour of Carnlough in a breathtaking setting at the foot of Glencloy. Family owned, it has a genuine warmth of welcome. ■ TV & **Rooms:** 35 | MC V AE DC | ● | ■ | ● | ■ |
| **CRAWFORDSBURN:** *The Old Inn at Crawfordsburn* W www.theoldinn.com ££<br>Co Down. **Road map** E2. ( 028 9185 3255. FAX 028 9185 2775.<br>One of Ireland's oldest hostelries, this thatched 16th-century inn offers quality and comfort with roaring log fires and four-poster beds in some rooms. A good Irish menu and an excellent wine list. ■ TV & **Rooms:** 32 | MC V AE DC | ● | ■ | ● | ■ |

**DUNGANNON:** *Grange Lodge*  ££  MC V
Grange Rd, Dungannon, Co Tyrone. **Road map** D2.
028 8778 4212. **FAX** 028 8778 4313. @ grangelodge@nireland.com
The hotel is set in pleasant surroundings and offers good Ulster home-
style cooking and a hospitable family welcome. TV **Rooms:** 5

**ENNISKILLEN:** *Killyhevlin Hotel*  £££  MC V AE DC
Dublin Rd, Enniskillen, Co Fermanagh. **Road map** C2.
028 6632 3481. **FAX** 028 6632 4726. W www.killyhevlin.com
The grounds sweep down to Lower Lough Erne and many bedrooms look
out on the lough, but you must pay extra for the view. TV **Rooms:** 42

**ENNISKILLEN:** *Manor House Country Hotel*  £££  MC V AE
Killadeas, Enniskillen, Co Fermanagh. **Road map** C2.
028 6862 1561. **FAX** 028 6862 1545. W www.manor-house-hotels.com
Situated on the shores of Lough Erne, this country hotel has a rich interior,
with antiques and paintings, a warm atmosphere and friendly staff. The emphasis is on healthy eating using local seasonal produce. TV **Rooms:** 81

**IRVINESTOWN:** *Mahon's Hotel*  ££  MC V AE
Hill Street, Co Fermanagh. **Road map** C2. 028 6862 1656. **FAX** 028 6862 8344.
A family-run hotel offering very pleasant service and accommodation in
well-maintained surroundings. An eclectic collection of bric-a-brac adorns
the bar and restaurants. TV **Rooms:** 30

**HOLYWOOD:** *Hastings Culloden Hotel*  £££  MC V AE DC
142 Bangor Rd, Holywood, Co Down. **Road map** E2.
028 9042 5223. **FAX** 028 9042 6777. W www.hastingshotels.com
A very fine hotel, set in gardens and woodlands by Belfast Lough. Originally the palace of the Bishops of Down, it retains its opulence with many
fine antiques and valuable paintings. TV **Rooms:** 79

**KILKEEL:** *The Kilmorey Arms Hotel*  £  MC V
41 Greencastle St, Kilkeel, Co Down. **Road map** D3.
028 4176 2220. **FAX** 028 4176 5399. W www.kilmoreyarmshotel.co.uk
An excellent base for the Mourne area. The rooms are well furnished and
the Smugglers' Bar's ambience fits well with the area. TV **Rooms:** 30

**LIMAVADY:** *Streeve Hill*  ££  MC V AE
Co Londonderry. **Road map** D1. 028 7776 6563. **FAX** 028 7776 8285.
This 18th-century dower house on the Drenagh estate is a good base for
the area. The gardens at Drenagh House are exquisite. Plenty of golf,
riding and fishing nearby. Member of Hidden Ireland. **Rooms:** 3

**LONDONDERRY:** *Beechill Country House Hotel*  ££  MC V AE
32 Ardmore Rd, Londonderry, Co Londonderry. **Road map** C1.
028 7134 9279. **FAX** 028 7134 5366. W www.beech-hill.com
Good service and food and a real "home from home" atmosphere. The
bedrooms, some with beautiful pieces of Victorian furniture, give the feel
of a grand old country home. TV **Rooms:** 27

**NEWCASTLE:** *Burrendale Hotel and Country Club*  £££  MC V AE DC
51 Castlewellan Rd, Co Down. **Road map** E2.
028 4372 2599. **FAX** 028 4372 2328. W www.burrendale.com
An excellent base for climbing, horse riding and golf. Good facilities for
the disabled with a comfortable bar and restaurant. TV **Rooms:** 69

**NEWCASTLE:** *Hastings Slieve Donard Hotel*  £££  MC V AE DC
Downs Rd, Newcastle, Co Down. **Road map** E2.
028 4372 3681. **FAX** 028 4372 4830. W www.hastingshotels.com
A stunning red-brick building overlooking the beach and the famous Royal
County Down Golf Course. Good efficient service. TV **Rooms:** 124

**NEWTOWNARDS:** *Edenvale Country House*  £  MC V
130 Portaferry Road, Newtownards, Co Down. **Road map** E2.
028 9181 4881. **FAX** 028 9182 6192.
Set in extensive grounds next to a wildfowl reserve, this Georgian house is a
haven for nature lovers, and provides croquet on the lawns. **Rooms:** 4

**PORTAFERRY:** *Portaferry Hotel*  ££  MC V AE DC
The Strand, Portaferry, Co Down. **Road map** E2.
028 4272 8231. **FAX** 028 4272 8999. W www.portaferryhotel.com
This waterside inn on the Ards Peninsula overlooks Strangford Lough.
A pleasant atmosphere and an award-winning restaurant. TV **Rooms:** 14

For key to symbols see back flap

# RESTAURANTS, CAFÉS AND PUBS

ALTHOUGH the highest concentration of top gourmet restaurants is in Ireland's main cities, equally fine cuisine can be found in some very unlikely, remote locations around the country. Good, plain cooking is on offer at moderately priced, family-style restaurants all over Ireland. The restaurants listed on pages 306–17 are recommended for their high standards of service, quality of food and value

Restaurant sign
in Kinsale

for money. To supplement these listings, look out for the *Dining in Ireland* booklet published by Bord Fáilte, the Irish Tourist Board. Pub lunches are one of Ireland's top travel bargains, offering generous portions of fresh vegetables and prime meats, and can often serve as the main meal of the day for a very reasonable price. Light meals, bar food and a variety of takeaways are also widely available.

## IRISH EATING PATTERNS

TRADITIONALLY, the Irish have started the day with a huge breakfast: bacon, sausages, black pudding, eggs, tomatoes and brown bread. In Northern Ireland this, plus potato cakes and soda farls *(see p304)*, is known as an "Ulster Fry". The main meal, dinner, was served at midday, with a lighter "tea" in the early evening.

Although continental breakfasts are now available, you will be hard-pressed to escape the traditional breakfast, which is included in most hotel and bed-and-breakfast rates. Increasingly, however, even the Irish settle for a light salad or soup and sandwiches at midday and save their main meal for the evening. Vestiges of the old eating patterns remain in the huge midday platefuls still served in pubs.

**Enjoying breakfast at Adare Manor Hotel** *(see p294)*

Arriving at a café in Kinvarra *(see p204)*

## TIPS ON EATING OUT

ELEGANT DINING becomes considerably more affordable when you make lunch your main meal of the day. In many of the top restaurants, the fixed-price lunch and dinner menus offer much the same, but lunch will usually come to about half the price. House wines are quite drinkable in most restaurants and can reduce the total cost of your meal. If you are travelling with children, shop around for one of the many restaurants that provide a less expensive children's menu.

Lunch is usually served between noon and 2:30pm, with dinner between 6:30 and 10pm, although many ethnic and city-centre restaurants stay open later, particularly in Temple Bar. Bed-and-breakfast hosts will often provide an ample home-cooked evening meal, and many will serve tea and scones in the late evening at no extra charge.

In top restaurants, men are expected to wear a jacket, though not necessarily a tie, and women to wear a dress or trouser suit. Elsewhere, the dress code is pretty informal, stopping short of bare chests and too-brief shorts.

Visa (V) and Mastercard/Access (MC) are the most commonly accepted credit cards, with Diners Club (DC) and American Express (AE) also in use. The abbreviations in brackets are used in the restaurant listings to indicate which cards are accepted.

## GOURMET AND ETHNIC DINING

THIS ONCE gourmet-poor land now sports restaurants that rank among Europe's very best, with chefs trained in outstanding domestic and continental institutions. There is a choice of Irish, French, Italian, Chinese, Indonesian and even Russian and Cuban cuisines, with styles ranging from traditional to regional to *nouvelle cuisine*. Locations vary as widely as the cuisine, from hotel dining rooms, town house basements and city mansions to castle hotels and tiny village cafés. The small County Cork town of Kinsale has established itself as the "Gourmet Capital of Ireland". Outstanding chefs also reign over the gracious houses listed in *Ireland's Blue Book of Country Houses and Restaurants*, available from tourist offices.

Selection of cakes served at Bantry House café *(see pp160–61)*

## BUDGET DINING

IT IS QUITE POSSIBLE to eat well on a small budget wherever you are in Ireland. In both city and rural locations, there are small cafés, tea rooms and family-style restaurants with value-for-money meals. Even if a café or tea room is at a main tourist attraction, such as Bantry House, you can still expect good, home-made food and freshly baked bread and cakes. Sandwiches are usually made with thick, tasty slices of fresh, rather than processed, cheese or meat; salad plates feature smoked salmon, chicken, ham, pork and beef; and hot meals usually come with large helpings of vegetables, with the beloved potato often showing up roast, boiled and mashed, all on one plate.

## PUB FOOD

IRELAND'S PUBS have moved into the food field with a vengeance. In addition to bar snacks (soup, sandwiches and

so on), available from noon until late, salads and hot meals are served from midday to 2:30pm. At rock-bottom prices, hot plates all come heaped with mounds of fresh vegetables, potatoes in one or more versions, and good portions of local fish or meat. Particularly good value are the pub carveries that offer a choice of joints, sliced to your preference. In recent years, the international staples of spaghetti, lasagne and quiche have also appeared on pub menus. For a list of recommended pubs, see pages 318–21.

**Café sign at Baltimore**

## FISH AND CHIPS AND OTHER FAST FOODS

THE IRISH, from peasant to parliamentarian, love their "chippers", immortalized in Roddy Doyle's novel *The Van*, and any good pub night will end with a visit to the nearest

fish-and-chip shop. At virtually any time of day, however, if you pass by Leo Burdock's in Dublin, there will be a long queue for this international institution *(see p307)*. With Ireland's long coastline, wherever you choose, the fish will usually be the freshest catch of the day – plaice, cod, haddock, whiting or ray (a delicacy). The many other fast-food outlets include a host of familiar international names, such as McDonald's and Kentucky Fried Chicken, as well as a wide variety of burger and kebab shops. Relatively new arrivals on the scene are several quite good pasta and pizza chains, such as Pizza Express and Milano.

## PICNICS

IRELAND IS GLORIOUS picnic country. Farmhouse cheeses and flavoursome tomatoes are picnic treats, or stop by one of the many small shops that offer sandwiches made with fresh local ingredients. As for where to picnic, the long, indented coast is ringed with wide, sandy beaches; with over 400 forest areas, many with picnic tables; great views add to the pleasure of mountainside picnics; and there are often lay-bys in scenic spots. Turn off a main road onto almost any country lane and you will soon find a picnic spot by a lakeside, riverbank or the shady edge of a field.

The 1601 pub in Kinsale *(see p319)*

# What to Eat in Ireland

*Irish coffee*

IRELAND's rich pastureland, unpolluted rivers and extensive coastline provide tender lamb, beef and pork, an array of fish and seafood and fresh fruit and vegetables. From hearty rural fare that makes the most of the ingredients available, Irish cooking has evolved into the gourmet cuisine created by internationally trained chefs. Often you will find the best of both worlds, with Irish stew or ham and cabbage on the same menu as more exotic dishes. The ideal end to a meal is an Irish coffee – coffee, cream and whiskey.

Wheaten bread　Soda bread　Soda farl　Potato cake

***Bread***, *invariably baked daily, comes in different guises. Soda bread may be brown or white. In Northern Ireland, brown soda bread is called wheaten bread.*

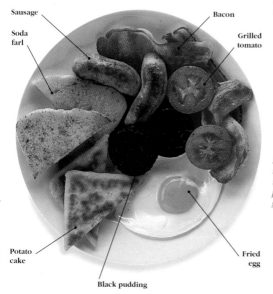

Sausage　Bacon　Soda farl　Grilled tomato　Potato cake　Fried egg　Black pudding

***An Ulster fry*** *consists of home-baked soda farls (soft bread cakes leavened with soda and buttermilk) and potato cakes (bread made from mashed potato, butter and flour), as well as the basic ingredients of a fry-up. The ultimate Irish break-fast, the "fry" is a perfect way to set yourself up for the day. Without the soda farls and potato cakes, meals like this are consumed with relish all over Ireland at any time of day.*

***Mushroom soup*** *makes a wholesome starter or snack. It is normally made with freshly picked local mushrooms and a generous amount of cream.*

***Smoked salmon***, *is very popular all over Ireland and is generally served as simply as possible. Eat wild salmon, rather than farmed, for a truly wonderful flavour.*

***Mussel soup*** *is a substantial dish made with fresh local mussels in a creamy fish stock flavoured with vegetables and herbs. Try it with wheaten bread.*

***Fresh oysters***, *here served on a bed of seaweed and cracked ice, make a light but delicious lunch – especially when accom-panied by a glass of Guinness.*

***Dublin coddle***, *a traditional Saturday night supper dish, consists of chopped sausages and ham or bacon cooked in stock with potatoes and onions.*

***Irish stew***, originally a peasant dish, is a thick casserole made with lamb or mutton, onions, and parsley, topped with potatoes.

***Fresh salmon*** is often poached in fish stock or wine and herbs. Galway salmon is particularly sought after for its fine taste.

***Lamb cutlets*** are usually served with mint sauce or jelly. Lamb from Kerry and Wicklow is renowned for its tenderness.

Mashed potato     Roast potatoes

***Vegetables*** are served in generous portions, usually as an accompaniment to the main course. It is not uncommon to be given potatoes in a number of different forms – roast, boiled, mashed, baked or chipped – together with whichever vegetables happen to be fresh and in season.

Broccoli

Boiled potatoes     Carrots

***Baked ham***, coated with cloves and brown sugar, is commonly served with boiled cabbage in butter and eaten at Christmas or on other festive occasions.

***Strawberries and cream*** are the archetypal summer dessert. They are sometimes sweetened with honey rather than sugar.

***Porter cake***, a classic Irish cake made with dried fruit, is most famous for the inclusion of stout, usually in the form of Guinness.

***Apple tart***, or "cake" as the Irish often call it, is eaten all year round but is traditionally associated with Hallowe'en.

## CHEESES

For centuries, cheese has been made in farms and monasteries throughout Ireland. Cheese-making has expanded in the last 25 years and Ireland now produces cheeses with a worldwide reputation, from semi-soft ones such as Cashel Blue and St Killian, which is similar to Camembert, to Gouda-like Carrigaline and smoked Durrus.

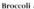

**St Killian**

**Carrigaline**

**Cashel Blue**     **Durrus**

***Tea-time*** favourites include sponges, fruit cakes and white or brown scones, made with or without fruit. Barm brack, a doughy, fruity bread, is traditionally eaten at Hallowe'en and on All Saint's Day, when a ring is hidden in the cake. According to tradition, the finder of the ring will marry by the following Easter.

Brown scone     Fruit scone

Plain scone     Barm brack

# Choosing a Restaurant

THIS CHART LISTS restaurants, selected for their good value, food and location, by region, starting with Dublin. Use the colour-coded thumb tabs, which indicate the regions covered on each page, to guide you to the relevant section of the chart. For Dublin map references, see the map on pages 110–11; for road map references, see the inside back cover.

| | | CREDIT CARDS | OPEN LUNCH TIME | OPEN LATE | FIXED-PRICE MENU | GOOD WINE LIST |
|---|---|---|---|---|---|---|
| **DUBLIN** | | | | | | |
| **SOUTHEAST DUBLIN:** *Bewley's Oriental Café*<br>78–79 Grafton St, Dublin 2. **Map** D4. ( *01 6776761.*<br>This Dublin institution is open from breakfast time onwards. Its<br>breads, pastries and home-made soups are superb. 🔧 ♿ 🍴 **V** | €€ | MC<br>V<br>AE<br>DC | ● | ■ | ● | |
| **SOUTHEAST DUBLIN:** *Kilkenny Shop Restaurant*<br>The Kilkenny Shop, 6–10 Nassau St, Dublin 2. **Map** E4. ( *01 6777066.*<br>A busy restaurant, overlooking Trinity College playing fields, offering<br>traditional Irish cooking, homemade quiches and salads. ♿ 🍴 **V** | €€ | MC<br>V<br>AE<br>DC | ● | | | ■ |
| **SOUTHEAST DUBLIN:** *Gotham Café*<br>8 Anne St South, Dublin 2. **Map** D4. ( *01 6795266.*<br>The American-style menu at this bright, funky café includes "Bowery",<br>"Upper East Side" and "Central Park" gourmet pizzas. 🔧 ♿ 🍴 **V** | €€€ | MC<br>V<br>AE | ● | ■ | | ■ |
| **SOUTHEAST DUBLIN:** *Pearl Brasserie*<br>20 Upper Merrion St, Dublin 2. **Map** D4. ( *01 661 3627.*<br>A classical French brasserie serving traditional French cuisine and<br>combining charm, friendly service and affordable prices. 🍴 **V** | €€€ | MC<br>V<br>AE | ● | ■ | | ■ |
| **SOUTHEAST DUBLIN:** *Rajdoot Tandoori*<br>26–28 Clarendon St, Dublin 2. **Map** D4. ( *01 6794274.*<br>This authentically decorated North Indian restaurant serves mildly<br>spiced curries and, from the clay oven, tandoori barbecued dishes. 🍴 **V** | €€€ | MC<br>V<br>AE<br>DC | ● | ■ | ● | ■ |
| **SOUTHEAST DUBLIN:** *Celts Banquet*<br>20 Baggot St Lower, Dublin 2. **Map** F5. ( *01 6618832.*<br>As the name suggests, traditional Irish food is served<br>in this cosy basement restaurant in the Georgian House Hotel. ♿ 🍴 | €€€€ | MC<br>V<br>AE<br>DC | ● | ■ | ● | ■ |
| **SOUTHEAST DUBLIN:** *The Commons*<br>85–6 Newman House, St Stephen's Green South, Dublin 2. **Map** D5. ( *01 4780530.*<br>Specially commissioned paintings by Irish artists share the honours<br>in this tasteful restaurant with gourmet specialities. On sunny days,<br>aperitifs can be taken in the pretty courtyard. 🍴 **V** | €€€€ | MC<br>V<br>AE<br>DC | ● | ■ | ● | ■ |
| **SOUTHEAST DUBLIN:** *Dobbin's Wine Bistro*<br>15 Stephen's Lane, Mount St, Dublin 2. **Map** F5. ( *01 6764679.*<br>An intimate, friendly bistro with an innovative monthly menu and<br>one of Dublin's best wine lists. ♿ 🍴 **V** | €€€€ | MC<br>V<br>AE<br>DC | ● | ■ | ● | ■ |
| **SOUTHEAST DUBLIN:** *L'Ecrivain*<br>109 Baggot St Lower, Dublin 2. **Map** F5. ( *01 6611919.*<br>In the heart of Georgian Dublin, French classics here have an Irish<br>touch, such as breast of guinea fowl with a black pudding mousse. 🍴 **V** | €€€€ | MC<br>V<br>AE<br>DC | ● | ■ | | ■ |
| **SOUTHEAST DUBLIN:** *The Fado*<br>Mansion House, Dawson Street, Dublin 2. **Map** D4. ( *01 676 7200.*<br>Part of the Mansion House, the stunning dining room is in the Belle<br>Epoque Style. The cuisine is Irish with French influence. 🍴 **V** | €€€€ | MC<br>V<br>AE<br>DC | ● | ■ | | ■ |
| **SOUTHEAST DUBLIN:** *Pier 32*<br>22–23 Pembroke St Upper, Dublin 2. **Map** D4 . ( *01 6761494.*<br>Open fires and a great atmosphere are the hallmark of this warm and<br>friendly place. Their specialities are seafood and regional dishes. 🍴 **V** | €€€€ | MC<br>V<br>AE<br>DC | | ■ | | ■ |
| **SOUTHEAST DUBLIN:** *La Stampa*<br>35 Dawson St, Dublin 2. **Map** D4. ( *01 6778611.*<br>This up-market restaurant in the heart of Dublin is noted<br>for its sumptuous, highly ornate Georgian decor. Service is<br>efficient and there is a lively atmosphere. Book at weekends. 🍴 **V** | €€€€ | MC<br>V<br>AE<br>DC | | ■ | | ■ |

**Average prices** for a three-course meal for one, half a bottle of house wine and all extra service and cover charges:
€ under 14 euros
€€ 14–20 euros
€€€ 20–32 euros
€€€€ 32–66 euros
€€€€€ over 66 euros

**OPEN LUNCH TIME**
Many restaurants open only in the evening, but those in large towns and attached to pubs often open at lunch time.

**OPEN LATE**
Restaurant remains open with the full menu available after 10pm.

**FIXED-PRICE MENU**
A good-value fixed-price menu on offer at lunch, dinner or both, usually with three courses.

**GOOD WINE LIST**
Denotes a wide range of good wines, or a more specialized selection of wines.

| | Credit Cards | Open Lunch Time | Open Late | Fixed-Price Menu | Good Wine List |
|---|---|---|---|---|---|
| **SOUTHEAST DUBLIN:** *Sandbank Bistro Cafe* €€€€ <br> Westbury Hotel, Grafton St, Dublin 2. **Map** D4. ☎ 01 6791122. <br> Completely refurbished, this smart but simple bistro has beech tables and a minimalist feel to the decor. ⚒ ⚡ V | MC V AE DC | ● | ■ | | ■ |
| **SOUTHWEST DUBLIN:** *Leo Burdock's* € <br> 2 Werburgh St, Dublin 8. **Map** C4. ☎ 01 4540306. <br> Dublin's oldest fish-and-chip takeaway attracts a mix of patrons. The fish is fresh, and the chips made from top-grade Irish potatoes. ⚒ | | ● | ■ | | |
| **SOUTHWEST DUBLIN:** *Elephant and Castle* €€€ <br> 18 Temple Bar, Dublin 2. **Map** D3. ☎ 01 6793121. <br> This boisterous American-style restaurant serves up-market fast food from tortillas to hamburgers. It is popular for brunch on Sunday. ⚒ ⚡ V | MC V AE DC | ● | ■ | ● | ■ |
| **SOUTHWEST DUBLIN:** *Les Frères Jacques* €€€€ <br> 74 Dame St, Dublin 2. **Map** C3. ☎ 01 6794555. <br> This French restaurant next to the Olympia Theatre adds Irish flair to many of its classical French dishes. Live piano music at weekends. ⚡ | MC V AE DC | | ■ | ● | ■ |
| **SOUTHWEST DUBLIN:** *Lord Edward* €€€€ <br> 23 Christchurch Place, Dublin 8. **Map** B4. ☎ 01 4542420. <br> Dublin's oldest seafood restaurant serves lunch in the ground-floor pub and evening meals in the upstairs restaurant. Service is courteous. ⚒ ⚡ V | MC V AE DC | ● | ■ | ● | ■ |
| **SOUTHWEST DUBLIN:** *Mermaid Cafe* €€€€ <br> 69-70 Dame Street, Dublin 2. **Map** C3. ☎ 01 670 8236. <br> This popular café serves delicious, trendy, european dishes. Decor is simple but smart with wooden polished tables. ⚡ ⚒ V | MC V | ● | ■ | | |
| **NORTH OF THE LIFFEY:** *Flanagan's Restaurant* €€ <br> 61 O'Connell St Upper, Dublin 1. **Map** D2. ☎ 01 8731388. <br> Popular Flanagan's is great value for money with an extensive menu ranging from burgers and salads to vegetarian and pasta choices. ⚒ ⚡ V | MC V | ● | ■ | ● | ■ |
| **NORTH OF THE LIFFEY:** *101 Talbot* €€€ <br> 100–102 Talbot St, Dublin 1. **Map** E2. ☎ 01 8745011. <br> A cheerful and relaxed restaurant close to the Abbey Theatre – good for pre-theatre meals. Excellent choice of vegetarian dishes. ⚡ V | MC V AE DC | | ■ | | ■ |
| **NORTH OF THE LIFFEY:** *Chapter One Restaurant* €€€€ <br> Below Dublin Writers Museum, Parnell Square, Dublin 1. **Map** C1. ☎ 01 8732266. <br> Across the square from the Gate Theatre, this excellent restaurant does pre–theatre dinners. Cuisine is modern European. ⚒ ⚡ V | MC V AE DC | ● | ■ | ● | ■ |
| **NORTH OF THE LIFFEY:** *The Halo* €€€€ <br> The Morrison Hotel, Ormond Quay, Dublin 1. **Map** C3. ☎ 01 887 2421. <br> The Morrison is a chic, minimalist designed hotel and The Halo is its excellent restaurant. The style of cooking is modern European with Asian influence and the ingredients are predominantly organic. ⚒ ⚡ V | | ● | ■ | ● | |
| **BALLSBRIDGE:** *Palmcourt Cafe* €€€€ <br> Berkeley Court Hotel, Lansdowne Rd, Dublin 4. ☎ 01 6601711. <br> In this bright, conservatory-style room in one of the city's most luxu- rious hotels, meals from the extensive menu are excellent value for money. Very popular with Dubliners. ⚒ ⚡ V | MC V AE DC | ● | | ● | ■ |
| **BALLSBRIDGE:** *Roly's Bistro* €€€€ <br> 7 Ballsbridge Terrace, Dublin 4. ☎ 01 6682611. <br> Lively bistro with Irish cuisine, including seasonal delights such as venison pie with juniper berries and wood mushrooms. Book ahead. ⚒ ⚡ V | MC V AE DC | ● | | ● | ■ |

For key to symbols see back flap

**Average prices** for a three-course meal for one, half a bottle of house wine and all extra service and cover charges:
- € under 14 euros
- €€ 14–20 euros
- €€€ 20–32 euros
- €€€€ 32–66 euros
- €€€€€ over 66 euros

**OPEN LUNCH TIME**
Many restaurants open only in the evening, but those in large towns and attached to pubs often open at lunch time.

**OPEN LATE**
Restaurant remains open with the full menu available after 10pm.

**FIXED-PRICE MENU**
A good-value fixed-price menu on offer at lunch, dinner or both, usually with three courses.

**GOOD WINE LIST**
Denotes a wide range of good wines, or a more specialized selection of wines.

| Restaurant | Price | Credit Cards | Open Lunch Time | Open Late | Fixed-Price Menu | Good Wine List |
|---|---|---|---|---|---|---|
| **DUN LAOGHAIRE:** *Brasserie Na Mara*<br>1 Harbour Rd. 01 2806767.<br>This restaurant, overlooking the harbour, serves the best just-caught seafood in the area. Non-fish dishes are also available. | €€€ | MC V AE DC | ● |  | ● | ■ |
| **HOWTH:** *Abbey Tavern*<br>Abbey St. 01 8390307.<br>A 16th-century tavern just off Howth Harbour and specializing in seafood. Its Irish music session is an institution. Book ahead. | €€€€ | MC V AE DC | ● |  |  | ■ |
| **HOWTH:** *King Sitric Fish Restaurant*<br>East Pier. 01 8325235.<br>Howth crab and lobster star on the menu of this well-known restaurant. In summer, a seafood bar serves lunch. Reserve for dinner. | €€€€ | MC V AE DC | ● | ■ | ● |  |
| **SANDYCOVE:** *Caviston's*<br>58 Glasthule Road. 01 280 9120.<br>This excellent fish restaurant serves the freshest mouthwatering dishes. Open noon to 3pm only. Booking recommended. | €€€ | MC V AE DC | ● |  | ● |  |

## SOUTHEAST IRELAND

| Restaurant | Price | Credit Cards | Open Lunch Time | Open Late | Fixed-Price Menu | Good Wine List |
|---|---|---|---|---|---|---|
| **BRAY:** *The Tree of Idleness*<br>Seafront. Road map D4. 01 286 3498.<br>This attractive and very welcoming restaurant serves outstanding Greek-Cypriot cooking such as their delicious roast suckling pig. | €€€ | MC V AE DC |  | ■ |  | ■ |
| **CAPPOQUIN:** *Richmond House*<br>Cappoquin. Road map C5. 058 54278.<br>On the banks of the Blackwater River, this 18th-century country home serves French dishes and local salmon and trout. | €€€€ | MC V AE DC |  |  | ● | ■ |
| **CARLOW:** *The Beams Restaurant*<br>59 Dublin St. Road map D4. 0503 31824.<br>A family-run restaurant with beamed ceilings and an old wall oven. Dishes include wild Atlantic salmon with white wine sauce, plus a huge choice of Irish cheeses. | €€€€ | MC V |  |  |  | ■ |
| **DUNGARVAN:** *Merry's Restaurant*<br>Main St. Road map C5. 058 41974.<br>Set in an atmospheric 19th-century wine merchant's shop, Merry's menu features shellfish and other seafoods, plus game in season. | €€€ | MC V | ● |  | ● | ■ |
| **FERRYCARRIG BRIDGE:** *Tides Restaurant*<br>Ferrycarrig Hotel. Road map D5. 053 20999.<br>One of the best restaurants in County Wexford, this relaxed room filled with greenery overlooks the Slaney estuary. Book ahead. | €€€€ | MC V AE DC |  |  |  | ■ |
| **GOREY:** *Marlfield House*<br>Courtown Rd. Road map D4. 055 21124.<br>This Regency mansion houses one of the Southeast's premier dining rooms. Only organically grown vegetables are used. | €€€€ | MC V AE DC | ● |  | ● | ■ |
| **GREYSTONES:** *The Hungry Monk*<br>Greystones. Road map D4. 01287 5759.<br>This attractive monk-themed restaurant has a very welcoming atmosphere. Excellent wine list and seafood specials. | €€€ | MC V AE | ● | ■ | ● | ■ |
| **KILDARE:** *Silken Thomas*<br>The Square. Road map D4. 0455 22232.<br>Located near the Norman castle keep in the town centre, this restaurant includes beef stroganoff and Gaelic steak on its menu. | €€€ | MC V AE | ● |  |  | ■ |

**KILKENNY:** *Kilkenny Design Centre Restaurant*  €€
Castle Yard. **Road map** C4. 📞 *056 22118.*
A bright, self-service restaurant with home-cooked casseroles and
other hot dishes, plus salads, quiches, soups and patés. 🚻 ⭐ 🅅 ♿
MC V AE DC

**KILKENNY:** *Langtons Restaurant and Bar*  €€€
69 John St. **Road map** C4. 📞 *056 65133.*
At Langton's, each of several small rooms has its own distinctive
decor. Stuffed mussels are among local favourites. ♿ 🚻 ⭐ 🅅
MC V AE DC

**LEIGHLINBRIDGE:** *Lord Bagenal Inn*  €€€
Main St. **Road map** D4. 📞 *0503 21668.*
This riverside restaurant has an old-world air and award-winning wine
list. Wild Irish salmon and game dishes appear in season. ♿ 🚻 ⭐ 🅅
MC V DC AE

**LISMORE:** *Eamonn's Place*  €€€
Main St. **Road map** C5. 📞 *058 54025.*
In summer, meals in the stone-walled beer garden here are delightful,
while a cheerful turf fire adds a glow to winter meals inside. ♿ 🚻 🅅

**NAAS:** *Manor Inn*  €€€€
Main St. **Road map** D4. 📞 *045 897471.*
A haunt of punters en route to and from the nearby Curragh
racecourse. Fish, steaks, pasta and grills feature on the menu. ♿ 🚻 ⭐ 🅅
MC V AE DC

**RATHNEW:** *Hunter's Hotel*  €€€€
Rathnew. **Road map** D4. 📞 *0404 40106.*
Cheerful hotel dining room attracting patrons from Dublin and nearby,
with its friendly ambience and superb meat and fish dishes. ♿ 🚻 ⭐ 🅅
MC V AE DC

**ROSSLARE:** *The Lobster Pot*  €€€€
Carne, Sore Point. **Road map** D5. 📞 *053 31110.*
Lobster and oysters come straight from sea tanks in this tradi-
tional pub and restaurant near Rosslare ferry harbour. ♿ 🚻 ⭐ 🅅
MC V AE

**THOMASTOWN:** *Kendals Restaurant*  €€€€
Mount Juliet Conrad Hotel. **Road map** D5. 📞 *056 73073.*
Bright and spacious, this modern restaurant offers delicious dishes that
are a fusion of Modern Irish and International cuisine. 🚻 ⭐ 🅅 ♿
MC V AE DC

**THOMASTOWN:** *Lady Helen Restaurant*  €€€€€
Mount Juliet Conrad Hotel. **Road map** D5. 📞 *056 73000.*
The menu, as elegant as the decor, includes chicken breast with fennel
stuffing in a tomato and red pepper sauce. Book ahead. ♿ ⭐ 🅅
MC V AE DC

**WATERFORD:** *The Munster Bar*  €€
Bailey's New St. **Road map** D5. 📞 *051 874656.*
Open at lunch time only, one popular speciality at The Munster Bar is a
"blaa" (meat, onion, tomato and lettuce on a roll), found only in Waterford
City. Other traditional dishes feature on the extensive menu. ♿ 🚻 🅅
MC V

**WATERFORD:** *The Olde Stand Pub and Restaurant*  €€€
45 Michael St. **Road map** D5. 📞 *051 879488.*
A glowing fireplace adds to the ambience upstairs in this Victorian-style
restaurant. More casual meals are served downstairs. Skip dessert and
indulge in one of their connoisseur coffees. 🚻 ⭐ 🅅
MC V AE

**WATERFORD:** *O'Grady's*  €€€€
Cork Rd. **Road map** D5. 📞 *051 378851.*
Innovative use of fresh local ingredients characterizes the delectable fare
at this bright restaurant near the Waterford Crystal factory. ⭐ 🅅
MC V AE DC

**WATERFORD:** *Waterford Castle Hotel*  €€€€€
The Island, Ballinakill. **Road map** D5. 📞 *051 878203.*
A small car ferry crosses to Waterford Castle on its River
Suir estuary island. Fish and seafood are the specialities in
the magnificent wood-panelled dining room. ♿ 🚻 ⭐ 🅅
MC V AE DC

**WEXFORD:** *La Dolce Vita*  €€€€
Westgate. **Road map** D5. 📞 *053 23935.*
Originally a grain store, this attractive building now houses
an inviting restaurant specializing in modern Italian dishes
and fresh seafood. 🚻 ⭐ 🅅
MC V

*For key to symbols see back flap*

**Average prices** for a three-course meal for one, half a bottle of house wine and all extra service and cover charges:
€ under 14 euros
€€ 14–20 euros
€€€ 20–32 euros
€€€€ 32–66 euros
€€€€€ over 66 euros

**OPEN LUNCH TIME**
Many restaurants open only in the evening, but those in large towns and attached to pubs often open at lunch time.

**OPEN LATE**
Restaurant remains open with the full menu available after 10pm.

**FIXED-PRICE MENU**
A good-value fixed-price menu on offer at lunch, dinner or both, usually with three courses.

**GOOD WINE LIST**
Denotes a wide range of good wines, or a more specialized selection of wines.

# CORK AND KERRY

| | | Credit Cards | Open Lunch Time | Open Late | Fixed-Price Menu | Good Wine List |
|---|---|---|---|---|---|---|
| **BALLYFERRITER:** *Tigh an Tobair* <br> Ballyferriter. **Road map** A5. ☎ 066 9156404. <br> A glassed-over wishing-well is the centrepiece of the small "House of the Well" restaurant. The chef always uses local fish. | €€€€ | MC V | ● | | | ■ |
| **BALLYLICKEY:** *Sea View House Hotel* <br> Bantry Bay. **Road map** B6. ☎ 027 50073. <br> The award-winning cuisine at this charming spot centres on local produce and fish from Bantry Bay. Open Sunday lunch only, Mar–Nov. | €€€€ | MC V AE DC | | | ● | ■ |
| **BANTRY:** *O'Connor's Seafood Restaurant* <br> The Square. **Road map** B6. ☎ 027 50221. <br> Right in the centre of town, Bantry Bay's famed mussels and live lobsters take pride of place in this established restaurant. | €€€€ | MC V | ● | | | |
| **BLARNEY:** *Phelan's Woodview House* <br> Tweedmount. **Road map** B5. ☎ 021 4385197. <br> This intimate restaurant often draws diners from nearby Cork. Make sure you sample chef Billy Phelan's hot seafood parcel. | €€€€ | MC V DC | | ■ | ● | |
| **CASTLETOWNSHEND:** *Mary Ann's Bar* <br> Skibbereen. **Road map** B6. ☎ 028 36146. <br> Local seafood features prominently on the menu of this 150-year-old bar and restaurant. Try the baked brill with prawns. | €€€€ | MC V | | | ● | ■ |
| **CORK:** *Beechers* <br> 3 Faulkner's Lane. **Road map** C5. ☎ 021 4273144. <br> A little hard to find, Beechers is in a lane between St Patrick's Street and Emmet Place. Home-made lunches and seafood specialities. | €€€ | | ● | | | |
| **CORK:** *Arbutus Lodge Hotel* <br> Montenotte. **Road map** C5. ☎ 021 4501237. <br> This informal bar provides some of the best-value lunch-time food in Cork. The more formal restaurant in the same hotel offers gourmet dinners mixing Irish, French and other international cuisine. | €€€€ | MC V AE DC | ● | | ● | ■ |
| **CORK:** *Isaac's Restaurant* <br> 48a MacCurtain St. **Road map** C5. ☎ 021 4503805. <br> The menu in this converted warehouse in the centre of Cork is extensive, offering both traditional Irish and Mediterranean dishes. | €€€€ | MC V AE DC | ● | | | ■ |
| **CORK:** *The Ivory Tower* <br> The Exchange Buildings, 35 Princes St. **Road map** C5. ☎ 021 4274665. <br> Unusual and delicious combinations grace the menu of this attractive and rather trendy restaurant. by arrangement | €€€€€ | MC V | | ■ | ● | ■ |
| **DINGLE:** *Beginish* <br> Green St. **Road map** A5. ☎ 066 9151321. <br> This award-winning restaurant offers mainly seafood specialities but there is always a meat dish, too. Efficient and friendly service. | €€€€ | MC V AE DC | | | ● | ■ |
| **DINGLE:** *Half Door Restaurant* <br> 3 John St. **Road map** A5. ☎ 066 9151600. <br> A combination of stone and light woods creates a relaxed ambience at the Half Door. The day's catch determines the menu. | €€€€ | MC V AE | ● | | | ■ |
| **DURRUS:** *Blair's Cove House Restaurant* <br> Blair's Cove. **Road map** B6. ☎ 027 61127. <br> In this romantic waterside restaurant on the shores of Dunmanus Bay, both wine list and cheeseboard are exceptional. | €€€€ | MC V | | | ● | ■ |

**INNISHANNON:** *Innishannon Hotel & Restaurant*          €€€€   MC
Innishannon. **Road map** B6. [ 021 4775121.                         V
The setting of this lovely 18th-century house beside the river makes   AE
it a very romantic spot. The owners' son, Pearse, is the excellent chef
producing modern Irish and classical French dishes. 🔥 🔥 V

**KENMARE:** *The Purple Heather*          €€
Henry St. **Road map** B5. [ 064 41016.
This town-centre pub and restaurant serves up tasty, hearty food.
Dishes include chicken liver terrine and Cumberland sauce. 🔥 V

**KENMARE:** *Lime Tree Restaurant*          €€€€   MC
Shelburne St. **Road map** B5. [ 064 41225.                         V
Housed in a charming 1830s school, the Lime Tree offers imaginative
dishes like goats' cheese potato cakes. Open April to October. 🔥 🔥 🔥

**KENMARE:** *Packie's*          €€€€   MC
35 Henry St. **Road map** B5. [ 064 41508.                         V
On the eclectic menu here, you're likely to find touches of Californian
or Mediterranean cuisine along with traditional Irish dishes, such as
a delicious Irish lamb stew with fresh herbs. 🔥 🔥 V

**KILLARNEY:** *The Cooperage Restaurant*          €€€   MC
Old Market Lane. **Road map** B5. [ 064 37716.                         V
A very attractive modern restaurant in the centre of town. The menu is
simple but delicious making the most of seasonal produce. 🔥 V

**KILLARNEY:** *Dingle's Restaurant*          €€€€   MC
40 New St. **Road map** B5. [ 064 31079.                         V
Glowing open fires, oak and leather panelling and exposed           AE
stone create an inviting decor at Dingle's. Irish stew is a         DC
speciality, and there's a terrific vegetarian casserole. Closed Tuesday. 🔥 V

**KILLARNEY:** *Gaby's*          €€€€€   MC
27 High St. **Road map** B5. [ 064 32519.                         V
Gaby's is undoubtedly the best seafood restaurant in town. Its interior   AE
incorporates seafaring memorabilia. Specialities include lobster,      DC
shellfish, oysters and Atlantic salmon. Closed Sunday. 🔥 🔥 🔥 V

**KILLORGLIN:** *Nick's Restaurant*          €€€€   MC
Lower Bridge St. **Road map** A5. [ 066 9761219.                         V
Chef Nick Foley's background as a butcher ensures that only the      AE
best cuts of meat reach the table. The same care goes into seafood   DC
offerings. There are open fires and a pianist plays regularly. 🔥 🔥 🔥 V

**KINSALE:** *The Blue Haven*          €€€€   MC
3–4 Pearse St. **Road map** B6. [ 021 4772209.                         V
A pleasant family restaurant, the Blue Haven offers a wide variety   AE
of food, from bar lunches to substantial meals. There's always a     DC
good selection of farmhouse cheeses. 🔥 🔥 🔥 V

**KINSALE:** *Max's Wine Bar*          €€€€   MC
Main St. **Road map** B6. [ 021 4772443.                         V
For more than 20 years, Max's has been in the forefront of Kinsale's   AE
gourmet restaurants. The emphasis here is on fresh, locally sourced
ingredients. Open March to October. 🔥 V

**KINSALE:** *Man Friday*          €€€€€   MC
Scilly. **Road map** B6. [ 021 4772260.                         V
Overlooking Kinsale Harbour, this restaurant has won culinary awards   AE
galore. No wonder, with specialities such as grilled turbot with crab   DC
peppercorn sauce and hot seafood platter. 🔥 🔥 🔥 V

**LEAP:** *Friskey's Restaurant*          €€€   MC
The Leap Inn. **Road map** B6. [ 028 33307.                         V
Traditional Irish dishes (Irish stew, bacon and cabbage, roast
stuffed chicken) feature on lunch-time menus in this delightful
country inn. Locally caught seafoods are also a speciality. 🔥 🔥 🔥 V

**MALLOW:** *Presidents' Restaurant*          €€€€   MC
Longueville House. **Road map** B5. [ 022 47156.                         V
Portraits of Irish presidents line the walls in this Georgian mansion.   AE
The modern cuisine uses local farm produce. 🔥 🔥 🔥 V         DC

| | CREDIT CARDS | OPEN LUNCH TIME | OPEN LATE | FIXED-PRICE MENU | GOOD WINE LIST |
|---|---|---|---|---|---|

**Average prices** for a three-course meal for one, half a bottle of house wine and all extra service and cover charges:
€ under 14 euros
€€ 14–20 euros
€€€ 20–32 euros
€€€€ 32–66 euros
€€€€€ over 66 euros

**OPEN LUNCH TIME**
Many restaurants open only in the evening, but those in large towns and attached to pubs often open at lunch time.

**OPEN LATE**
Restaurant remains open with the full menu available after 10pm.

**FIXED-PRICE MENU**
A good-value fixed-price menu on offer at lunch, dinner or both, usually with three courses.

**GOOD WINE LIST**
Denotes a wide range of good wines, or a more specialized selection of wines.

| | | | | | |
|---|---|---|---|---|---|
| **PARKNASILLA:** *Pygmalion Restaurant* €€€€<br>Great Southern Hotel. **Road map** A6. ( 064 45122.<br>Overlooking Kenmare Bay on the Ring of Kerry, the Pygmalion's elegant decor and polished service set off a gourmet cuisine. 🚻 ⚡ V | MC V AE DC | | | ● | ■ |
| **SHANAGARRY:** *Ballymaloe House* €€€€€<br>Shanagarry, Midleton. **Road map** C6. ( 021 4652531.<br>At Ballymaloe House, acclaimed for its Irish and French classics, vegetables and meats come from their own farm, and seafood is local. 🚹 ⚡ V | MC V AE DC | ● | | ● | ■ |
| **YOUGHAL:** *Aherne's Seafood Restaurant* €€€€€<br>163 North Main St. **Road map** C5. ( 024 92424.<br>Chef David Fitzgibbon's seafood chowder is positively addictive. His sumptuous platter of six fish and four shellfish won Aherne's the prestigious Seafood Dish of the Year Award. 🚻 🚹 ⚡ V | MC V AE DC | ● | | ● | ■ |

## THE LOWER SHANNON

| | | | | | |
|---|---|---|---|---|---|
| **ADARE:** *The Mustard Seed at Echo Lodge* €€€€<br>Ballingarry. **Road map** B5. ( 069 68508.<br>In a Victorian style building the Mustard Seed has wonderful views over a vast expanse of countryside. The modern Irish cuisine includes seasonal dishes prepared with the freshest of ingredients. 🚻 🚹 ⚡ V | MC V AE | | | ● | ■ |
| **ADARE:** *The Inn-Between* €€€€€<br>Dunraven Arms Hotel, Main St. **Road map** B5. ( 061 396633.<br>A charming restaurant in a thatched cottage, with informal service and a cosy atmosphere. The cooking is modern cuisine. 🚻 🚹 ⚡ V | MC V AE DC | | | | ■ |
| **BUNRATTY:** *Mews Restaurant* €€€€<br>Bunratty House Mews. **Road map** B4. ( 061 364082.<br>Downstairs in this 1846 mansion, the original kitchen, staff quarters and wine cellars form one of the best restaurants in the country. 🚹 ⚡ V | MC V AE DC | | | ● | ■ |
| **CAHIR:** *Malone's* €€€<br>The Galtee Inn, The Square. **Road map** C5. ( 052 41247.<br>The all-day menu in this family-run restaurant offers prime beef with rich sauces, roasts and seafood dishes as well as light meals. 🚻 🚹 ⚡ V | MC V | ● | | | ■ |
| **CASHEL:** *Chez Hans* €€€€<br>Rockside. **Road map** C5. ( 062 61177.<br>At the foot of the Rock of Cashel, Chez Hans occupies a former Wesleyan chapel. For several years, Hans-Peter Matthiä has created wonderfully innovative versions of traditional dishes. 🚻 🚹 ⚡ V | MC V | | | | ■ |
| **CLONMEL:** *The Old Bank Restaurant* €€€<br>Clonmel Arms Hotel, Sarsfield St. **Road map** C5. ( 052 21233.<br>The Old Bank is a bright, airy hotel dining room, decorated with strong colours, lots of brass and some interesting art. The European-influenced menu changes with the seasons. 🚻 🚹 V | MC V AE DC | | | ● | ■ |
| **DOOLIN:** *Bruach na hAille* €€<br>Roadford. **Road map** B4. ( 065 7074120.<br>This charming, cottage-style restaurant (its name means "banks of the river") uses local produce in unexpected ways, such as fillets of sole in cider served with shellfish in a cream sauce. 🚻 🚹 ⚡ V | MC V AE | | | ● | ■ |
| **ENNIS:** *Cruise's Pub and Restaurant* €€€€<br>Abbey St. **Road map** B4. ( 065 6841800.<br>The 17th-century building's low, beamed ceilings and the open fires in winter create a cosy ambience. There is traditional music in the bar every night which filters through into the restaurant. 🚻 🚹 ⚡ V | MC V AE DC | | | ● | ■ |

**ENNISTIMON:** *Byrnes Restaurant*   €€€   MC V AE DC
Main St. **Road map** B4. 065 7071080.
This smart restaurant is housed in a fine 18th-century building
on the town's main street. Food and drinks are served on
terraces overlooking the river, waterfall and a stone-arched bridge. ⚡ V

**LIMERICK:** *Chez O'Shea*   €€€€   MC V DC
74 O'Connell St. **Road map** B4. 061 316311.
In a Georgian building with roaring open fires, this city-centre restaurant
serves modern Irish dishes with Mediterranean influences. ⚡ V

**LIMERICK:** *Soral's Restaurant*   €€€€   MC V AE DC
Jury's Hotel, Ennis Rd. **Road map** B4. 061 327777.
All-day service makes this bright hotel restaurant one of the most convenient in Limerick. Light snacks share the menu with full meals. The more
formal Copper Room serves gourmet and traditional Irish dishes. ⚡ V

**NEWMARKET-ON-FERGUS:** *Earl of Thomond Room*   €€€€   MC V AE DC
Dromoland Castle. **Road map** B4. 061 368144.
A traditional Irish harper accompanies evening meals in this elegant
dining room. The "Taste of Ireland" set menu has no less than six courses.
Try the hot brown-bread soufflé and the creamy lamb ravioli. ⚡ V

**THURLES:** *Inch House*   €€€€   MC V AE
Thurles. **Road map** B4. 0504 51261.
A mixture of traditional and more adventurous dishes in a fine
country house setting. limited ⚡ V by arrangement.

## THE WEST OF IRELAND

**ACHILL ISLAND:** *The Boley House Restaurant*   €€€   MC V
Keel. **Road map** A3. 098 43147.
Owner Tom McNamara uses only the freshest ingredients, with seafood
from local waters. Roasted free-range duckling is a favourite. ⚡ V

**ARAN ISLANDS:** *Dún Aonghasa & Aran Fisherman Restaurant*   €€€€   MC V
Kilronan, Inishmore. **Road map** B4. 099 61104.
Overlooking the harbour, in a setting of stone, wood and open fires,
owner Grace Flaherty bases her menu on fish fresh from Galway Bay.
Choices include creamy seafood chowder and grilled shark. ⚡ V

**BARNA:** *Donnelly's Seafood Restaurant and Bar*   €€€€   MC V AE DC
Freeport. **Road map** B4. 091 592487.
Fresh seafood is a speciality in this rustic-style restaurant. Among
non-seafood dishes is chicken supreme. ⚡ V

**CLARINBRIDGE:** *Moran's Oyster Cottage*   €€€€   MC V AE
The Weir. **Road map** B4. 091 796113.
Known as "Moran's of the Weir", this 200-year-old restaurant
in a thatched cottage is loved by both locals and celebrities,
especially during the annual Clarinbridge Oyster Festival. ⚡ V

**CLIFDEN:** *O'Grady's Seafood Restaurant*   €€€€€   MC V
Market St. **Road map** A3. 095 21450.
Award-winning O'Grady's offers wonderful seafood, plus superb
vegetarian choices. Open late-March to November. ⚡ V

**CLIFDEN:** *Rock Glen Restaurant*   €€€€€   MC V AE
Rock Glen Manor House. **Road map** A3. 095 21035.
A converted Connemara shooting lodge is the setting for gracious dining
here, with friendly service enhancing an excellent cuisine. ⚡ V

**CONG:** *Connaught Room*   €€€€   MC V AE DC
Ashford Castle. **Road map** B3. 092 46003.
Only the best local ingredients come to table in this wood-panelled
dining room. Its menu includes rack of Connemara hill lamb and
fillet of turbot with scallops. Open May to October. ⚡ V

**GALWAY:** *Rabbitt's Bar and Restaurant*   €€   MC V AE DC
23–25 Forster St, Eyre Sq. **Road map** B4. 091 566490.
Dating back to 1872, this atmospheric bar-restaurant has a menu as traditional as its decor. Irish stew with local lamb is excellent. ⚡ V

For key to symbols see back flap

| | | Average prices info | CREDIT CARDS | OPEN LUNCH TIME | OPEN LATE | FIXED-PRICE MENU | GOOD WINE LIST |
|---|---|---|---|---|---|---|---|

**Average prices** for a three-course meal for one, half a bottle of house wine and all extra service and cover charges:
€ under 14 euros
€€ 14–20 euros
€€€ 20–32 euros
€€€€ 32–66 euros
€€€€€ over 66 euros

**OPEN LUNCH TIME**
Many restaurants open only in the evening, but those in large towns and attached to pubs often open at lunch time.

**OPEN LATE**
Restaurant remains open with the full menu available after 10pm.

**FIXED-PRICE MENU**
A good-value fixed-price menu on offer at lunch, dinner or both, usually with three courses.

**GOOD WINE LIST**
Denotes a wide range of good wines, or a more specialized selection of wines.

| Restaurant | Credit Cards | Open Lunch Time | Open Late | Fixed-Price Menu | Good Wine List |
|---|---|---|---|---|---|
| **GALWAY:** *Kirwan's Lane Restaurant* €€€€<br>Kirwan's Lane. **Road map** B4. ☎ 091 568266.<br>Just beside the Hotel Spanish Arch, this smart, sophisticated restaurant is run by Michael O'Grady of Clifden fame. The freshest local ingredients are used in a huge choice of international and New Irish dishes. 🔣 | MC V AE | ● | ■ | | |
| **GALWAY:** *The Park Room* €€€€€<br>Forster St, Eyre Sq. **Road map** B4. ☎ 091 564924.<br>Inside the Park House Hotel, this restaurant offers a well-priced menu of Irish specialities, all prepared with local ingredients. 🔣 | MC V AE DC | ● | | ● | ■ |
| **MOYCULLEN:** *Moycullen House* €€€€<br>Moycullen. **Road map** B4. ☎ 091 555621.<br>This house was built as a sporting lodge and is surrounded by over 30 acres of grounds. The restaurant is well run and the food excellent. 🔣 | MC V AE | | | ● | ■ |
| **ROSCOMMON:** *Abbey Hotel* €€€€<br>Galway Rd. **Road map** C3. ☎ 0903 26250.<br>Set dinners in this 18th-century turreted mansion feature steak prepared in different ways, grilled sea trout and other fish dishes. 🔣 | MC V AE DC | ● | | ● | ■ |
| **WESTPORT:** *The Lemon Peel* €€€€<br>The Octagon. **Road map** B3. ☎ 098 26929.<br>This small modern restaurant has an informal atmosphere but the service is very professional and the food delicious. 🔣 | MC V | ● | | ● | ■ |

## NORTHWEST IRELAND

| Restaurant | Credit Cards | Open Lunch Time | Open Late | Fixed-Price Menu | Good Wine List |
|---|---|---|---|---|---|
| **BALLYSHANNON:** *Sweeney's White Horse Bar* €€€<br>Assaroe Rd. **Road map** C2. ☎ 072 51452.<br>Sweeney's set bar menu offers good food in an inviting atmosphere. There is traditional music in the Cellar Bar on Friday nights. 🔣 | | ● | | | ■ |
| **CASTLEBALDWIN:** *Cromleach Lodge Country House* €€€€€<br>Ballindoon, Boyle. **Road map** C3. ☎ 071 65155.<br>Fabulous views of Lough Arrow and the Bricklieve Mountains form a backdrop for gourmet dining in this hilltop country house. 🔣 | MC V AE DC | | | ● | ■ |
| **COLLOONEY:** *Glebe House Restaurant* €€€€<br>Collooney. **Road map** C2. ☎ 071 67787.<br>At this Georgian house, there's an emphasis on organically grown produce and imaginative use of local fish and meats. Friendly service. 🔣 | MC V AE DC | | | ● | ■ |
| **DUNKINEELY:** *Castlemurray House* €€€€<br>Dunkineely. **Road map** C2. ☎ 073 37022.<br>There are wonderful views across the bay from the relaxed restaurant – perfect surroundings for you to enjoy classic dishes expertly prepared. 🔣 | MC V | | | ● | ■ |
| **INISHOWEN PENINSULA:** *Bree Inn* €<br>Malin Head. **Road map** C1. ☎ 077 70161.<br>At the northernmost point in Ireland, this lively country inn serves home-cooked meals all day in summer. The place is popular with locals. 🔣 | | ● | ■ | | |
| **INISHOWEN PENINSULA:** *Restaurant St John's* €€€€<br>Fahan. **Road map** C1. ☎ 077 60289.<br>An atmospheric restaurant on the shores of Lough Swilly offering five- and six-course set menus, with excellent fish dishes and desserts. 🔣 | MC V AE DC | ● | | ● | ■ |
| **KILLYBEGS:** *Sail Inn* €€€€<br>Main St. **Road map** C2. ☎ 073 31130.<br>Food is served all day at this traditional inn. Bar food is good value, and fish from the town's fleet is served in the restaurant. 🔣 | MC V AE DC | | | | ■ |

**RATHMULLAN:** *Pavilion Restaurant* €€€€ | MC V AE DC
Rathmullan Country House. **Road map** C1. ( 074 58188.
The Pavilion offers gourmet food in a glass-walled setting. Sample the
seaweed-based dessert of carrageen moss with stewed fruits. 🔥 🚹 💱 **V**

**ROSSES POINT:** *The Austies* €€€ | MC V
Rosses Point Road. **Road map** B2. ( 071 77111.
High above Sligo Bay, The Austies offers fresh seafood dishes
such as crab *au gratin*. Hearty pub lunches in the summer. 🚹 💱 **V**

**SLIGO:** *Garavogue* €€€€ | MC V
Rear 15-16 Stephens Street. **Road map** C2. ( 071 40100.
This excitingly-designed restaurant is named after the river flowing past it.
Dishes include Thai and Spanish, with bar-food portions downstairs and full
menu available in the restaurant. 🔥 🚹 💱 **V**

**TOBERCURRY:** *Killoran's Traditional Restaurant* €€€ | MC V AE DC
Teeling St. **Road map** B3. ( 071 85111.
Irish stew, boxty (potato pancakes) and crubeens (pigs' feet) are
on the traditional menu. Snacks and full meals served all day. 🔥 🚹 💱 **V**

## THE MIDLANDS

**ATHLONE:** *Wineport Lakeshore Restaurant* €€€ | MC V AE DC
Glassan. **Road map** D3. ( 0902 85466.
This lakeside restaurant has a very loyal clientele who find the view, the
atmosphere and the food irresistible. 🔥 🚹 💱 **V**

**ATHLONE:** *L'Escale Restaurant* €€€€ | MC V AE DC
The Hodson Bay Hotel. **Road map** C3. ( 0902 92444.
Cuisine is an international mix. A typical dish is Dublin Bay prawns
with shallots, mushrooms and tomato, flamed in whiskey. 🔥 🚹 💱 **V**

**BUTLER'S BRIDGE:** *Derragarra Inn* €€€ | MC V
Butler's Bridge. **Road map** C3. ( 049 4331003.
A thatched cottage inn decorated with relics of rural Ireland by the River
Annalea. The restaurant menu is available in the bar all day. 🔥 🚹 💱 **V**

**CARLINGFORD:** *Jordan's Town House Restaurant* €€€€ | MC V AE
Newry St. **Road map** D3. ( 042 9373223.
A renovated 19th-century warehouse overlooking the harbour is the
setting for culinary gems with organically grown ingredients. 🔥 🚹 💱 **V**

**CARRICKMACROSS:** *Nuremore Hotel* €€€€ | MC V AE DC
Carrickmacross. **Road map** D3. ( 042 9661438.
This beautiful restaurant has an imaginative menu, including French
and Irish cuisine, served in a tranquil setting. 🔥 🚹 💱 **V**

**DUNDALK:** *Quaglino's Restaurant* €€€€ | MC V AE DC
88 Clanbrassil St. **Road map** D3. ( 042 9338567.
This bright, town-centre restaurant features superb Continental and
Modern Irish cuisine using local produce. 🚹 💱 **V**

**KELLS:** *Carrick House* € | MC V
Carrick St. **Road map** D3. ( 046 40100.
Carrick House is a moderately priced family restaurant. Only locally-
farmed meats are used. Children welcome until 9pm. 🔥 🚹 **V**

**MONAGHAN:** *Andy's Restaurant* €€€ | MC V
Market St. **Road map** D2. ( 047 82277.
This restaurant in Monaghan town centre is above an award-winning
pub. The extensive menu includes sirloin steak in whiskey and beer
sauce and French influenced cuisine. 🔥 🚹 💱 **V**

**MOUNTRATH:** *Roundwood House* €€€€ | MC V AE DC
Mountrath. **Road map** C4. ( 0502 32120.
Pre-booking is a must in this gracious Palladian mansion. The compulsory
four-course set menu changes daily. 🚹 💱 **V**

**MULLINGAR:** *Crookedwood House* €€€€ | MC V AE DC
Crookedwood. **Road map** C3. ( 044 72165.
This 200-year-old restaurant changes its menu with the seasons. A summer
speciality is River Moy salmon with hollandaise sauce. 🔥 🚹 💱 **V**

For key to symbols see back flap

| | CREDIT CARDS | OPEN LUNCH TIME | OPEN LATE | FIXED-PRICE MENU | GOOD WINE LIST |
|---|---|---|---|---|---|

**Average prices** for a three-course meal for one, half a bottle of house wine and all extra service and cover charges:
£ under £10
££ £10–£15
£££ £15–£20
££££ £20–£25
£££££ over £25

**OPEN LUNCH TIME**
Many restaurants open only in the evening, but those in large towns and attached to pubs often open at lunch time.

**OPEN LATE**
Restaurant remains open with the full menu available after 10pm.

**FIXED-PRICE MENU**
A good-value fixed-price menu on offer at lunch, dinner or both, usually with three courses.

**GOOD WINE LIST**
Denotes a wide range of good wines, or a more specialized selection of wines.

## NORTHERN IRELAND

| | | CC | OLT | OL | FPM | GWL |
|---|---|---|---|---|---|---|
| **ARMAGH:** *Pilgrim's Table*     ££ <br> 38–40 English St. **Road map** D2. ( *028 3752 1814.* <br> Fine home cooking with fresh local produce. Non-fussy dishes, especially the soups, are tasty, filling and superb value. No wine licence. ⛄ 🚶 🔀 **V** | | | ● | | | |
| **BALLYCASTLE:** *Wysner's Restaurant*     ££ <br> 16 Anne St. **Road map** D1. ( *028 2076 2372.* <br> Downstairs at Wysner's is a French-style café, while upstairs is a restaurant where the Bushmills Malt cheesecake is a must. ⛄ 🚶 🔀 **V** | | MC<br>V | ● | | ● | ■ |
| **BELFAST:** *Crown Liquor Saloon*     £ <br> 46 Great Victoria St. **Road map** D2. ( *028 9024 9476.* <br> This bar's snug-like booths include table space for a bowl of Irish stew and champ – a local speciality of potatoes, spring onions and butter. 🚶 | | MC<br>V<br>AE | ● | | | ■ |
| **BELFAST:** *Duke of York*     ££ <br> 11 Commercial Court. **Road map** D2. ( *028 9024 1062.* <br> This very reasonably priced restaurant offers typical pub grub. Near St Anne's Cathedral, it is Irish in style and cluttered with Belfast memorabilia. 🚶 **V** | | | ● | | | |
| **BELFAST:** *Manor House Restaurant*     ££ <br> 43–47 Donegall Pass. **Road map** D2. ( *028 9023 8755.* <br> Run by the Wong family since 1982, this Cantonese restaurant is a reliable and popular place. The menu is extensive. ⛄ 🚶 **V** | | MC<br>V | ● | ■ | ● | ■ |
| **BELFAST:** *Metro Brasserie*     £££ <br> 13 Lower Crescent. **Road map** D2. ( *028 9032 3349.* <br> This is a trendy modern version of the traditional brasserie. The interior design is striking and unusual and gives the place a sophisticated but relaxed atmosphere. Bar snacks are available on Sunday. 🚶 🔀 **V** | | MC<br>V<br>AE<br>DC | ● | | ● | ■ |
| **BELFAST:** *Cayenne*     ££££ <br> 7 Lesley House, Shaftesbury Sq. **Road map** D2. ( *028 9033 1532.* <br> Celebrity chefs Paul and Jeanne Rankin opened this restaurant in 1999, and serves a delicious mixture of Thai, Japanese and other Asia-influenced dishes. ⛄ 🚶 🔀 **V** | | MC<br>V<br>AE<br>DC | ● | ● | ● | ■ |
| **BELFAST:** *Malone House*     ££££ <br> Barnett Demesne. **Road map** D2. ( *028 9068 1246.* <br> Only the highest quality Ulster produce is used in the Brasserie style menu served at this local favourite (open for lunch only). Vegetarian dishes are often the house speciality. ⛄ 🚶 🔀 **V** | | MC<br>V<br>AE<br>DC | ● | | ● | ■ |
| **BELFAST:** *Restaurant Michael Deane*     ££££ <br> 38–40 Howard St. **Road map** D2. ( *028 9056 0000.* <br> You have a choice here of smart and elegant formal dining on the first floor or the more informal brasserie on the ground floor. The food is excellent in both. ⛄ 🚶 **V** | | MC<br>V<br>AE | ● | ■ | | |
| **BELFAST:** *Nick's Warehouse*     £££££ <br> 35–39 Hill St. **Road map** D2. ( *028 9043 9690.* <br> Nick and Kathy Price's converted warehouse, tucked away in the cobbled backstreets of city-centre Belfast, gets top marks for atmosphere. The menu regularly includes Nick's latest culinary innovations. ⛄ 🚶 **V** | | MC<br>V<br>AE<br>DC | ● | | | ■ |
| **BUSHMILLS:** *Bushmills Inn*     ££££ <br> 9 Dunluce Rd. **Road map** D1. ( *028 2073 2339.* <br> Originally an old coaching inn, this popular hostelry is only a few miles from the Giant's Causeway and close to Bushmills Distillery. ⛄ 🚶 **V** | | | ● | | ● | ■ |

**DUNDRUM:** *The Buck's Head* £££££ MC V AE
77 Main St. **Road map** E2. 028 4375 1868.
Open fires and hospitable, friendly service make this an excellent stop for
lunch or dinner. Cuisine is a mix of traditional and modern. 🔣

**DUNGANNON:** *Viscount's Restaurant* ££££ MC V
10 Northland Row. **Road map** D2. 028 8775 3800.
A Victorian church has been converted into a medieval-style banqueting
hall with the emphasis on fun as much as food. The large menu caters
to all appetites and is popular with families in the daytime. 🔣

**ENNISKILLEN:** *Arch Tullyhona House Restaurant* £££
59 Marble Arch Rd, Florencecourt. **Road map** C2. 028 6634 8452.
Beside Marble Arch caves, this farm restaurant offers great food and
service. Produce fresh from the farm is used, and desserts such as
lemon soufflé and fresh fruit pavlova are a speciality. 🔣

**ENNISKILLEN:** *The Sheelin* ££££ MC V
Bellanaleck. **Road map** C2. 028 6634 8232.
This thatched cottage restaurant on the shores of Lower Lough
Erne is a gourmet experience. The menu is a mixture of French and
continental cuisine presenting an eclectic range of dishes. 🔣

**ENNISKILLEN:** *Franco's Restaurant* £££££ MC V AE
Queen Elizabeth Rd. **Road map** C2. 028 6632 4424.
A warren of nooks and crannies, this hospitable pizzeria often has live
traditional music. The vast menu offers Italian food with an Irish influence. Seafood dishes include fresh lobster and mussels. 🔣

**HILLSBOROUGH:** *Hillside Restaurant and Bar* £££££ MC V AE DC
21 Main St. **Road map** D2. 028 9268 2765.
This attractive country-style pub and restaurant has an
excellent seasonal menu. The bar serves a good selection of
real ales. 🔣

**HOLYWOOD:** *The Bistro* £££ MC V
27 Church Rd. **Road map** E2. 028 9042 5655.
Roughcast walls and tightly packed tables make this restaurant,
homely, welcoming and bright. "Early bird" menus are great
value. There's no wine licence so bring your own bottle. 🔣

**LIMAVADY:** *The Lime Tree* £££ MC V AE
60 Catherine Street. **Road map** D1. 028 7776 4300.
Right on the main street in this attractive town, the restaurant is small
and quite simply decorated. The interesting menu offers unusual and
subtle tasting dishes put together with local ingredients. 🔣

**LONDONDERRY:** *The Metro* £ MC V
3–4 Bank Pl. **Road map** C1. 028 7126 7401.
Shadowed by Derry's city walls, this is a favourite with locals. The food,
from soup and sandwiches to beef stew in Guinness, is first rate. 🔣

**PORTAFERRY:** *The Narrows* £££ MC V AE
8 Shore Rd. **Road map** E2. 028 4272 8148.
A bright, light restaurant with delicious, locally sourced ingredients.
Seafood is a speciality. 🔣

**PORTBALLINTRAE:** *Sweeny's Wine Bar* £££
6b Seaport Ave. **Road map** D1. 028 2073 2404.
Prices here are cheap and cheerful and the food creatively prepared.
Situated on the Causeway Coast, Sweeny's occupies a converted stable
block overlooking Portballintrae Harbour. 🔣

**PORTRUSH:** *The Harbour Bar* £££
The Harbour. **Road map** D1. 028 7082 2430.
The traditional pub area on the ground floor has roaring fires and a
great atmosphere. The restaurant is also informal and offers a good
selection of a la carte dishes. 🔣

**STRANGFORD:** *The Lobster Pot Bar & Restaurant* £££££ MC V AE DC
The Square. **Road map** E2. 028 4488 1288.
Only the finest local catches are served in this predominantly
fish restaurant overlooking Strangford Lough. 🔣

*For key to symbols see back flap*

# Pubs in Ireland

THE ARCHETYPAL IRISH PUB is celebrated for its convivial atmosphere, friendly locals, genial bar staff and the "crack" – the Irish expression for fun. Wit is washed down with whiskey or Guinness, the national drinks. Irish pubs date back to medieval taverns, coaching inns and shebeens, illegal drinking dens which flourished under colonial rule. In Victorian times, brewing and distilling were major industries. The sumptuous Edwardian or Victorian interiors of some city pubs are a testament to these times, furnished with mahogany and marble bar counters. Snugs, partitioned-off booths, are another typical feature of Irish pubs. Traditional pubs can be boldly painted, thatched or "black-and-white" – beamed with a white façade and black trim. Some rural pubs double as grocers' shops.

Good pubs are not evenly distributed throughout the country: in the Southeast, Kilkenny is paradise for pub-lovers, while Cork and Kerry possess some of the most picturesque pubs. The Lower Shannon region is noted for its boisterous pubs, especially in County Clare where spontaneous music sessions are common. The West has an abundance of typical Irish pubs, and the many tourists and students guarantee a profusion of good pubs in Galway. The listings below cover a selection of pubs throughout Ireland; for Dublin pubs, see pages 104–7.

## SOUTHEAST IRELAND

**Dunmore East:** *The Ship Inn*
**Road map** D5. ( 051 383141.
This old, ivy-clad pub lies above the harbour, away from the crowds on the beach. It is noted both for its seafood and its seafaring links. Inside, nautical memorabilia and half-barrel seats abound in the front bar. The small garden is an appealing spot for drinking in the summer. Lemon sole, turbot and brill are on the menu. 🍴 🎵

**Enniscorthy:** *The Antique Tavern*
14 Slaney St. **Road map** D5.
( 054 33428.
This traditional, timbered, black-and-white pub is charming. The dark, intimate bar contains relics such as pikestaffs from Vinegar Hill, the decisive battle in the 1798 uprising that was fought outside town. Pub lunches and local chat are on offer. In good weather, you can sit on the balcony. 🎵

**Enniscorthy:** *The Cotton Tree*
Slaney Place. **Road map** D5.
( 054 33179.
Although this is essentially a workaday pub with few pretensions, its site makes it worth a visit – it is built into the base of an old quarry and a vertical cliff forms part of the back wall of the bar. A recent renovation means that a full menu of bar food is now served all day.

**Kilkenny:** *Kyteler's Inn*
27 St Kieran's St. **Road map** C4.
( 056 21064.
In good weather you can sit in the courtyard of this historic coaching inn and cellar bar. Food is served all day, and meals are served in the restaurant downstairs until 9:45pm (last orders). An effigy of a witch sits in the window frame, a reminder of the story of a former resident, Dame Alice Kyteler. In 1324, Alice and her maid were pronounced guilty of witchcraft after four of Alice's husbands had died in mysterious circumstances; although pardoned, Alice was again accused but escaped, leaving her maid to burn at the stake. 🍴 🎵

**Kilkenny:** *Langton's*
69 John St. **Road map** C4.
( 056 65133.
Langton's is noted for its black-and-white exterior, Edwardian ambience and the stylish glass interior at the back. The front bar is cosy with a low ceiling. Pub food is on offer, and there's music and dancing three or four nights a week; Tuesday, Thursday and Saturday are disco nights. 🍴 🎵

**Kilkenny:** *Maggie Holland's*
St Kieran's St. **Road map** C4.
( 056 62273.
Set in a central spot near the river, this is a dimly lit but welcoming pub. Traditional music on Tuesday evenings draws plenty of locals. 🎵

**Kilkenny:** *Marble City Bar*
66 High St. **Road map** C4.
( 056 61143.
Marble City Bar, the most famous pub in town, is named after the local limestone, which becomes black when polished. This four-storey building has an Art Deco facade and has recently been restored. Bar food till 8:30pm. 🎵

**Kilkenny:** *Tynan's Bridge House Bar*
2 John's Bridge. **Road map** C4.
( 056 21291.
This is the most genuine old-world pub in town, with an intimate interior lit by charming lamps. Quaint relics of the former grocery store and pharmacy are on display, from a set of old scales to the drawers labelled with names of nuts and spices. No food, no music, no TV; as publican Michael puts it, "a chat bar".

**Kilmore Quay:** *The Wooden House Lodge*
**Road map** D5. ( 053 29804.
This traditional – if over-restored – thatched pub is full of nautical memorabilia and quirky sayings while the small terrace is decorated with anchors. Hearty pub fare is served. 🍴 🏠 🎵

**Waterford:** *T and H Doolin*
George's St. **Road map** D5.
( 051 841504.
Set in the city's most charming pedestrianized street, this traditional, 18th-century black-and-white pub offers an intimate atmosphere and good "crack". Traditional folk music sessions are held every night. 🍴 🏠 🎵

**Waterford:** *The Reginald Bar*
The Mall. **Road map** D5.
( 051 855087.
Set beside Reginald's Tower, the pub incorporates part of the Viking city walls and the medieval sallyports (attack exits), which are still visible. The service is rather brusque but the pub offers carvery lunch (noon–3pm), bar snacks (3–7:30pm) and a restaurant menu (5:30–10:30pm). There is also an adjoining nightclub. 🍴 🎵

**Wexford:** *Centenary Stores*
Charlotte St. **Road map** D5.
( 053 24424.
Tucked away in a converted warehouse, this cosy, dimly lit pub is the most charming in Wexford. The friendly bar staff and a mixed local and bohemian crowd chat in the wood-panelled bar. Drinkers are often entertained with sessions of traditional music. 🍴 🏠 🎵

**Wexford:** *Westgate Tavern*
Westgate. **Road map** D5.
[ 053 22086.
Licensed since 1761, this distinctive tavern faces the path leading to
the famous Selskar Abbey and
Westgate Heritage Centre. Lunch
menu and bar snacks are available
in the welcoming bar and there
are music sessions on Sunday and
Monday evenings. 🎵

## CORK AND KERRY

**Clonakilty:** *De Barra's*
**Road map** B6. [ 023 33381.
This is one of the best-known pubs
in West Cork, with a traditional
folk club open most nights; many
musicians come from the Gaeltacht
*(see p221)*. The bar is lovingly
restored, with hand-painted signs
and traditional whiskey jars. Simple
snacks and full lunches are served
from noon to 3pm. 🍴🎵

**Cork:** *Chateau Bar*
St Patrick's St. **Road map** C5.
[ 021 4270370.
This bar in the heart of the city
occupies a striking building that
was once on the quayside. Founded
in 1793, this elegant pub has a
stylish Victorian interior and offers
good quality bar fare. 🍴

**Cork:** *Chimes*
27 Church St. **Road map** C5.
[ 021 4304136.
Set in the hilly, old-world Shandon
district, this convivial working-
class pub attracts a mixed, friendly
crowd, from local pensioners to
sports fans and students. Simple
bar food is sometimes on offer,
and on Thursday, Saturday and Sunday nights there's music, usually in
the form of accordion or keyboard
soloists. 🎵

**Cork:** *Henchy's*
40 St Luke's Cross. **Road map** C5.
[ 021 4507833.
This traditional pub, situated close
to Chimes *(see above)*, dates from
1884 and has retained much of its
Victorian ambience, enhanced by
the mahogany bar, stained glass and
a snug (a private room, in this case,
with a separate entrance). It has
long been associated with poets
and is where young hopefuls come
to recite their work to a largely
sympathetic audience. A varied
bar menu is on offer at lunch time.

**Cork:** *The Oyster Tavern*
Market Lane, off St Patrick's St.
**Road map** C5. [ 021 4272716.
Founded in the 18th century, this
tavern was sympathetically refurbished by the new management in
1994. Lunches are served between
noon and 3pm. Occasional music.

**Dingle:** *Dick Mack's*
Green St. **Road map** A5.
[ 066 9151960.
This individualistic spot is part
shoe shop, part pub, and retains
the original shop and drinking
counters. The pub is a haunt of
local artists, eccentrics and extro-
verts. In the evening, regulars often
congregate around the piano. 🎵

**Dingle:** *Doyle's Townhouse*
John St. **Road map** A5.
[ 066 9151174.
This charming bar and restaurant is
celebrated for its delicious freshly
caught seafood, and the bar's
rustic, yet cosy, stone interior is an
appealing place for dinner. Doyle's
is open mid-March to mid-
November. 🍴

**Dunquin:** *Krugers*
**Road map** A5. [ 066 9156127.
Situated close to the quays for the
Blasket Islands, this well-known
family pub is also a guesthouse.
The pub serves bar food and is
decorated with family memorabilia
and stills from films made in the
area, such as *Ryan's Daughter.* 🎵

**Killarney:** *Buckley's Bar*
College St. **Road map** B5.
[ 064 31037.
This oak-panelled bar is noted for
its regular traditional music sessions
and its filling meals. The pub was
opened in 1926 when Tom
Buckley, a homesick emigrant,
returned from New York. Bar food
is served until 2:30pm. 🍴🎵

**Killarney:** *The Laurels*
Main St. **Road map** B5.
[ 064 31149.
This claims to be Killarney's
liveliest pub and is popular with
the young locals as well as Irish-
Americans who enjoy listening to
the ballads and singing along. The
pub provides excellent bar snacks
or good meals (steak, mussels,
oysters, fish) in a separate restaurant area. Ballads are performed
nightly from 9:15pm between April
and October, and more sporadi-
cally over the winter. 🍴🎵

**Killorglin:** *The Old Forge*
**Road map** A5. [ 066 9761231.
Set on the popular Ring of Kerry,
this thatched pub and restaurant is
delightfully old-fashioned and
authentic. Expect it to be packed
during the Puck Fair in August
*(see p47)*. 🎵

**Kinsale:** *Kieran's Folk
House Inn*
Guardwell. **Road map** B6.
[ 021 4772382.
This convivial corner of old
Kinsale draws locals and visitors

alike. The interior is snug and
welcoming, with live music every
night during the season. The inn
also houses a pleasant guesthouse
and a noted restaurant, the
Shrimps Seafood Bistro, open for
lunch and dinner all year. 🍴🎵

**Kinsale:** *The Lord Kingsale*
Main St. **Road map** B6.
[ 021 4772371.
This beamed, old-fashioned pub
attracts a quiet, genteel crowd. The
pub is several hundred years
old but the interior is, in part, a
clever fake. In summer, live music
is often performed at weekends.
Bar food: noon to 3pm 🎵

**Kinsale:** *The 1601*
Pearse St. **Road map** B6.
[ 021 4772529.
The front bar is bedecked as a
tribute to the Battle of Kinsale
*(see p164)* while the back bar
incorporates an ever-changing art
gallery. Bar food is served at lunch
time in summer only and the pub
tends to get rather crowded. On
summer evenings you might find
live modern or traditional music
performed in the pub. 🍴🎵

**Kinsale:** *The Spaniard Inn*
Scilly. **Road map** B6. [ 021 4772436.
Set on a hairpin bend above the
village of Scilly, this popular
fishermen's pub has the air of a
smugglers' inn. There is often live
traditional music in one of the bars
every night during the
summer and it is particularly
popular at weekends. The restaurant and bar offer simple, but
excellent fare. 🍴🍴🎵

## THE LOWER SHANNON

**Ballyvaughan:** *Monk's Pub*
The Pier. **Road map** B4.
[ 065 7077059.
This quaint, cosy pub is situated
on the quay. Inside, country furniture and peat fires are matched
by local seafood including
chowder, served until 7pm in the
winter, 8pm in the summer.
There's live music every Saturday
– ring for details. 🍴🍴🎵

**Bunratty:** *Durty Nelly's*
**Road map** B4. [ 061 364072.
Set beside Bunratty Castle, this
touristy, extremely commercialized
pub appeals to locals as well as
tourists. The 17th-century atmosphere is sustained by the warren
of rooms, inglenook fireplaces and
historical portraits. Traditional music
is performed most evenings, and
wholesome food is available both
from the bar and from the two
restaurants. 🍴🍴🎵

**Doolin:** *O'Connor's*
**Road map** B4. **(** *065 7074168.*
This famous pub is known to lovers
of traditional music the world
over. The pub has been in the
O'Connor family for over 150 years
and combines an authentic grocery
store with a lively pub. This is the
place for spontaneous music,
simple bar food, young company
and great "crack".

**Ennis:** *The Cloister*
Abbey St. **Road map** B4.
**(** *065 6829521.*
This historic pub is situated by the
famous Ennis Friary. The pub's
cosy, atmospheric interior is complemented by a patio for summer
dining. Bar food is available as well
as more refined dishes in the restaurant, from Ballyvaughan mussels
to fresh fish from Donegal.

**Killaloe:** *Goosers*
Ballina. **Road map** C4.
**(** *061 376791.*
This delightfully picturesque waterfront pub on the Ballina side of
the river has a thatched roof, traditional interior and a welcoming
atmosphere. Noted for its cuisine,
Goosers serves fairly pricey seafood
in the restaurant and more
reasonably priced but satisfying
"pub grub" in the rustic bar.

**Kilrush:** *Crotty's Pub*
Market Square. **Road map** B4.
**(** *065 9052470.*
This popular pub is named after
the concertina player Lizzie Crotty,
and hosts live traditional music
every night of the week exept
Monday and Friday. Tasty bar food
is available 12pm–3pm.

**Limerick:** *The Locke*
3 George's Quay. **Road map** B4. **(**
*061 413733.*
Set on a quay on the Shannon,
this is a typical black-and-white
pub. In summer, it is a favourite
port of call for riverside strollers.
In winter, blazing fires and snugs
make it a cosy spot. Traditional
music is played on Monday,
Tuesday and Sunday nights.

**Limerick:** *Nancy Blake's*
Upper Denmark St. **Road map** B4.
**(** *061 416443.*
As Limerick's best-known bar,
Nancy Blake's has much to offer
in the way of good "crack" and
traditional music. If you prefer
rhythm and blues, try the adjoining
Outback Bar. The cosy main bar
serves soup and sandwiches at
lunch time. Music is played from
Monday to Wednesday.

## THE WEST OF IRELAND

**Aran Islands:** *Joe Watty's Pub*
Kilronan, Inishmore. **Road map** B4.
**(** *099 61155.*
Set along the road between
Kilronan and Kilmurvy Bay, this
island pub is noted for its informality and huge, hearty portions
of food. Passers by appreciate the
lamb stews, soups, sandwiches
and stout.

**Clarinbridge:** *Moran's Oyster
Cottage*
The Weir, Kilcolgan. **Road map** B4.
**(** *091 796113.*
Set in a thatched cottage, this bar
was a regular port of call for crews
from passing "hookers" (traditional
ships). Nowadays, you can sample
all kinds of seafood here, though
Moran's is best known as an oyster
bar – the owner holds the local
speed record for shelling oysters.
You can watch fishermen at work
from the terrace tables.

**Clarinbridge:** *Paddy Burke's
Oyster Inn*
**Road map** B4. **(** *091 796226.*
Founded in 1835, this authentic
thatched pub has leaded window-
panes and a charming beamed
interior. Apart from the renowned
Clarinbridge oysters and buffet
lunches, gourmet menus are also
available at lunch and dinner.

**Clifden:** *EJ Kings*
The Square. **Road map** A3.
**(** *095 21330.*
This spacious, bustling pub is
situated on several floors, with the
ground floor the most appealing.
Seafood platters or varied pub fare
can be enjoyed by the peat fire.
In summer, live music is often on
offer, especially folk and ballads.
The staff, mainly students, are
exceptionally friendly.

**Galway:** *Cooke's Thatch Bar*
Cooke's Corner, 2 Newcastle Rd.
**Road map** B4. **(** *091 521749.*
Situated on the outskirts of Galway,
this traditional thatched bar has
been in the same family for seven
generations and is renowned for
its friendliness. Recently
refurbished, the pub now includes
an off-licence with over 20 wines
on sale as well as beer and spirits.

**Galway:** *The King's Head*
15 High St. **Road map** B4.
**(** *091 566630.*
Founded in 1649, this historic pub
is adorned with a bow-fronted
façade. The homely interior
contains authentic 17th-century

fireplaces. Simple lunch snacks
are served in the main bar. In the
back bar there are jazz sessions on
Sunday lunch times, and various
live bands playing in the evenings
attract a youthful crowd.

**Galway:** *O'Flaherty's*
Great Southern Hotel, 15 Eyre Sq.
**Road map** B4. **(** *091 564041.*
This solid cellar bar began as wine
cellars but now offers cosy snugs
and railway memorabilia. The
popular pub provides a contrast to
the more sophisticated hotel
cocktail bar on the floor above.
A carvery lunch is on offer daily
in the bar, while at weekends live
popular music sessions (from
traditional music to jazz) draw
large audiences of locals and
visitors.

**Galway:** *The Quays*
11 Quay St. **Road map** B4.
**(** *091 568347.*
This cavernous pub is the
highlight of a Galway pub crawl.
Set in an old stone mansion in
Galway's "Latin Quarter", the
sprawling pub is noted for its old-
world charm, choice of bars and
live music in summer. The quaint
front bar retains its authenticity
while the rest of the pub has been
sensitively converted, using old
materials. The tasty and filling
cooked pub meals are popular
with locals.

**Galway:** *The Slate House*
Cross St Upper. **Road map** B4.
**(** *091 563377.*
This barn-like city pub occupies
several storeys, including the shell
of a 16th-century convent on the
top floor. Busker Brown's, the pub
next door, is under the same management, and both are popular
with local students. There are jazz
sessions on Sundays.

**Galway:** *Tí Neachtain*
Quay St. **Road map** B4.
**(** *091 568820.*
Set in the "Latin Quarter", this
18th-century town house boasts a
distinctive oriel window. Inside, a
musty wood interior is home to
old-world snugs and friendly
service. Traditional music can
often be heard. Upstairs is one of
Galway's best French restaurants.

**Maam Cross:** *Peacocks Hotel*
**Road map** B3. **(** *091 552306.*
Next to a replica of the traditional
cottage used in the 1950s John
Wayne film *The Quiet Man*, is a
brand new Hotel complex with a
modern pub. It is highly popular
with locals and a good choice of
pub food is available daily. Music
every weekend.

**Westport:** *The Asgard Tavern*
The Quay. **Road map** B3.
[ 098 25319.
This old inn facing the pier and
Clew Bay is decorated with a
nautical theme. Both the main
downstairs back bar and the upstairs restaurant provide excellent
seafood and salads. The small
downstairs front bar is the most
atmospheric. 🍴 🎵

**Westport:** *Matt Molloy's*
Bridge St. **Road map** B3.
[ 098 26655.
Founded by the flautist from the
traditional Irish folk band The
Chieftains, this deceptively
spacious pub is designed along
equally traditional lines. There is
live music in the back room every
evening, when the pub is packed.
No children after 9pm. 🍴 🎵

## NORTHWEST IRELAND

**Crolly:** *Leo's Tavern*
Menaleck. **Road map** C1.
[ 075 48143.
Owned by the father of modern
folk musicians Clannad and of the
singer Enya, this friendly pub
attracts locals and tourists for its
sing-songs round the accordion,
and traditional music nights. 🍴 🎵

**Dromahair:** *Stanford's Inn*
Main St. **Road map** C2.
[ 071 64140.
Set in a picturesque village, this
traditional pub has been in the
same family for generations. The
tiny, quaint Biddy's Bar remains
unchanged, adorned with family
portraits and old grocery jars. The
main bar contains mellow brick-
work and flagstones from a ruined
castle, the rustic effect reinforced
by tweed lampshades. Delicious
food is on offer all day, and in
summer there are often impromptu
evening music sessions. 🍴 🎵

**Rossnowlagh:** *Smugglers'
Creek Inn*
**Road map** C2. [ 072 52366.
On a clifftop overlooking Donegal
Bay, this pub is popular with surfers
and other water sports enthusiasts.
There is traditional music at
weekends and the beer garden
offers panoramic views. 🍴 🍴 🎵

**Sligo:** *Beezie's*
Tobbergal Lane. **Road map** C2.
[ 071 43031.
The pub is dedicated to Beezie
Gallagher, a hospitable and much-
loved Sligo character who regularly
rowed from her home on Cottage
Island to Sligo until her death in
1951. A Victorian mood is recreated
by the old-fashioned stained glass,
skylights and fireplaces.

**Sligo:** *Hargadon's*
4–5 O'Connell St. **Road map** C2.
[ 071 70933.
A scruffy, rather ramshackle
exterior reveals the most traditional pub in town. The timeless
atmosphere is enhanced by the
old-fashioned stove, uneven floors
and wooden grocery drawers.
The pub is lined with cosy snugs,
all individually designed. During
the summer, dinner is served in
the beer garden. 🍴 🍴

## THE MIDLANDS

**Abbeyleix:** *Morrissey's*
Main St. **Road map** C4.
[ 0502 31233.
If driving through County Laois, it
is worth stopping at this genuinely
traditional pub. The 18th-century
inn was remodelled in the Victorian
era and has stayed the same ever
since. The grocery section survives
while the plain but unpretentious
bar serves simple bar snacks.

**Carlingford:** *PJ O'Hare's
Anchor Bar*
Tholsel St. **Road map** D3.
[ 042 9373106.
Known locally as PJ's, this atmospheric pub and grocery store is
popular with sailors and locals alike.
A friendly and often eccentric welcome is matched by bar food such
as oysters and sandwiches. 🍴 🎵

**Kilbeggan:** *Locke's Distillery
Museum*
Mullingar. **Road map** C3.
[ 0506 32307.
As well as being the oldest licensed
pot still distillery in the world
(established in 1757), this historic
complex has a tiny whiskey bar –
the ideal place to sample a few
brands of whiskey before buying
*(see p241).* There is an adjoining
restaurant. 🍴

**Portlaoise:** *Tracey's Pub and
Restaurant*
The Heath. **Road map** C4.
[ 0502 46539.
This charming thatched cottage
pub and restaurant is 5 km (3 miles)
outside of the town, but is well
worth the drive. It is the oldest
family-run pub in these parts, and
there is a good range of pub grub
(roasts, fish, salads) as well as
prime steak at amazingly
reasonable prices. 🍴 🍴

## NORTHERN IRELAND

**Bangor:** *Jenny Watt's*
41 High St. **Road map** E2.
[ 028 9146 0682.
Likeable and very popular, this bar
with Victoriana trimmings is found
in the centre of town. The walls

are adorned with local photos and
memorabilia. There's live jazz at
Sunday lunch times, and folk
music on Thursday nights. Bar
food is served until 7pm, and
there's a beer garden. 🍴 🎵

**Belfast:** *Crown Liquor Saloon*
46 Great Victoria St. **Road map** D2.
[ 028 9024 9476.
This Victorian gin palace ranks as
one of the most gorgeous bars in
Ireland *(see p269).* Lunch includes
several local specialities including
Strangford Lough oysters which
are almost too good to believe.
The recently renovated Robinson's
pub next door is particularly lively
in the evening. 🍴

**Belfast:** *Lavery's Gin Palace*
12–14 Bradbury Place. **Road map** D2.
[ 028 9087 1106.
Yet another of Belfast's fine old
gin palaces. Bar food served at
lunch and discos in the evenings.
It is popular with students from
Queen's University. 🎵

**Belfast:** *White's Tavern*
Winecellar Entry. **Road map** D2.
[ 028 9024 3080.
Just one of several daylight-free
pubs tucked away in the Entries
*(see p269)* sector of Belfast city
centre, that are best at lunch time
when decent, reasonably priced
pub food is served. White's lays
claim to be the oldest bar in the
city. Other pubs in this series of
alleys that are worth a look include
the Morning Star and the Globe. 🎵

**Bushmills:** *Bushmills Inn*
9 Dunluce Rd. **Road map** D1.
[ 028 2073 2339.
Set in an old coaching inn, this
cosy bar is lit by gaslights. There
is also an excellent restaurant on
the premises, with patio tables for
summer dining. 🍴 🍴

**Enniskillen:** *Blake's of the
Hollow*
6 Church St. **Road map** C2.
[ 028 6632 2143.
One of a number of popular town-
centre pubs, Blake's dates back to
Victorian days and has many of its
original fittings. 🍴 🎵

**Hillsborough:** *Plough Inn*
The Square. **Road map** D2.
[ 028 9268 2985.
Dating back to the 1750s, this
quintessential village pub has
wooden ceiling beams and a
selection of crockery, china and
other ornaments on the walls.
There's a bistro upstairs open
during the day, serving oysters,
and a good beer garden. The
Hillside, just down the main street,
is also worth a visit. 🍴 🍴

# SHOPPING IN IRELAND

IRELAND OFFERS a wide range of handmade goods, usually regionally based and highly individual. Its most renowned products include chunky Aran sweaters, Waterford crystal, demure Irish linen, hand-loomed Donegal tweed and tasty farmhouse cheeses. The thriving crafts industry is based on traditional products with an innovative twist. Typical of contemporary Irish crafts are good design, quality craftsmanship and a range spanning

Linen shirt and tweed waistcoat

Celtic brooches and bone china, knitwear and designer fashion, carved bogwood and books of Irish poetry. Kitsch souvenirs also abound, from leprechauns and shamrock emblems to Guinness tankards and garish religious memorabilia. In the directory on page 325, a map reference is given for each address. Dublin references are to the map on pages 110–11; road map references are to the towns and cities shown on the inside back cover.

Fruit and vegetable market in Moore Street, Dublin

## WHERE TO SHOP

THE CHOICE of places to shop in Ireland ranges from tiny workshops to large factory outlets, from elegant boutiques to high-street chain stores. Bargains can often be had at bric-a-brac shops and local markets, although the banter is sometimes the best thing on offer. This guide lists market days for every town featured.

## SHOPPING IN DUBLIN

IN DUBLIN there are two major shopping quarters: the north side of the Liffey, centred around O'Connell and Henry Streets, where there are large shopping centres with many of the UK chains and department stores; and the more prestigious south side, around Grafton and Nassau Streets. The Temple Bar area contains a number of trendy craft shops. The two main markets are Mother Redcap's indoor flea market in Christ-church at weekends, and the

fruit and vegetable market in Moore Street from Monday to Saturday. One of Dublin's largest shopping centres is **St Stephen's Green Shopping Centre**, full of clothes and craft shops. Near chic Grafton Street is the Powerscourt Townhouse Shopping Centre (see p76) in its Georgian shell. Traditional department stores in the city include **Brown Thomas** and **Clery's**.

## WHEN TO SHOP

MOST SHOPS are open from Monday to Saturday, 9am to 5:30 or 6pm. In shopping centres and large towns, shops tend to have at least one late-night opening, usually Thursday or Friday (Thursday in Dublin). In tourist areas, craft shops are generally open on Sundays too. Shops are closed at Easter and Christmas and on St Patrick's Day but are open on most other public holidays. In Killarney, Ireland's tourist capital, most shops are open until 10pm in summer.

## HOW TO PAY

MAJOR CREDIT CARDS are generally accepted in department stores and larger retail outlets, but smaller shops prefer cash. Most traveller's cheques are accepted in major stores with a passport as identification. Eurocheques are no longer being issued by Irish banks and so will not be accepted in the shops.

## SALES TAX AND REFUNDS

MOST PURCHASES are subject to VAT (sales tax) at 21 per cent, a sum included in the sales price. However, visitors from outside the European Union (EU) can reclaim VAT prior to departure. If you are shipping goods overseas, refunds can be claimed at the point of purchase. If taking your goods with you, look for the CashBack logo in shops, fill in the special voucher, then visit CashBack offices at Dublin or Shannon Airport.

A traditional fiddle maker in his workshop in Dingle

Colourful bric-a-brac shop in Kilkenny

## BOOKS

READING is a national passion so bookshops are generally good. In larger shops expect solid sections on Irish archaeology and architecture, folklore, history, politics and cuisine. **Eason and Son** is one of the biggest bookshops in Dublin with a wide range of Irish literature and national and international newspapers; seek out the smaller, "Irish interest" shops too. In Galway, **Kennys Bookshop and Art Gallery** is full of both new and second-hand Irish books.

## MUSIC

TRADITIONAL MUSICAL instruments *(see pp22–3)* are made in many regions, especially County Clare, known as "the singing county". Handmade harps are a speciality in Mayo and Dublin. In Dublin, several shops sell musical instruments, such as handcrafted bodhráns (traditional goatskin hand-held drums) and uillean pipes (bagpipes). **Waltons** sells traditional instruments and sheet music, while **Claddagh Records** sells Irish folk and traditional music.

## CRAFTS

CRAFTS are a flourishing way of life in rural Ireland. The **Crafts Council of Ireland**, with branches in Dublin where it is part of **DESIGNYARD**, and in Kilkenny, recommends good small-scale outlets. Tourist offices also provide lists of local workshops, where you can often watch the production process. Many craft shops, such as the **Kilkenny Design Centre** and **Bricín**, sell good examples of several different crafts. Some regions are traditionally associated with specific crafts. In Cork and Kerry there is an abundance of workshops; the *Guide to Craft Outlets* is available from local tourist offices. Distinctive products from this area are traditional tiles based on designs found in Kilkenny Cathedral and nearby medieval abbeys. Further west, Connemara marble, green mottled stone, is made into "worry stones", small charms much like worry beads. Also made in Connemara, particularly Clifden, are wall hangings, hand-knits and woollen rugs.

Other crafts in Ireland include metalwork, leatherwork and carpentry. Local woods are used for ash or beech furniture, blackthorn walking sticks and sculptures made of 1,000-year-old bogwood.

**Kylemore Abbey teapot**

## CERAMICS AND CHINA

ESTABLISHED in 19th-century Ulster, the Belleek Pottery *(see p261)* produces creamy china with a lustrous sheen and subtle decorative motifs, including shamrocks and flowers. **Royal Tara China**, in Galway, is Ireland's leading fine bone china manufacturer, with designs incorporating Celtic themes. Also in County Galway, Kylemore Abbey produces handpainted pottery *(see p200)*. **Louis Mulcahy's Pottery** in Ballyferriter is noted for its fine decorative glazes, while **Nicholas Mosse Pottery** in Bennettsbridge, County Kilkenny, is well known for its colourful handpainted designs. Enniscorthy in County Wexford is another centre for ceramics.

## CRYSTAL AND GLASSWARE

IN THE WAKE of Waterford Crystal *(see p139)*, the brand leader, come countless followers. The price depends on reputation, the quantity of lead used in the glass and the labour-intensiveness of the design. In the North, **Tyrone Crystal** is rated almost as highly as Waterford but is less expensive. Like Waterford, the factory runs an illuminating tour. **Tipperary Crystal** offers a number of lines, including trophies, lamps and gifts. **Galway Irish Crystal** is another elegant brand.

In County Kilkenny, the famous Jerpoint Abbey inspires local designs by **Jerpoint Glass**. Decorated with simple yet stylish motifs, the small vases, candlesticks, jugs and bowls make pleasing gifts. Most stores will pack and send glassware overseas for you.

Pottery display in Kilkenny Design Centre

**Sign for the linen department at Dublin's Brown Thomas store**

## JEWELLERY

IN ITS GOLDEN AGE, Celtic metalwork was the pride of Ireland *(see pp30–33)*, and many contemporary crafts-people are still inspired by traditional Celtic designs. Hand-crafted or factory-made silver, gold, enamel and cera-mic jewellery is produced all over Ireland in a huge variety of designs. The Claddagh ring from Galway is the most famous – the lovers' symbol of two hands cradling a crowned heart. **DESIGN** YARD in Temple Bar sells the best contemporary Irish jewellery. Dublin's Powerscourt Townhouse Shopping Centre *(see p76)* is home to Ceramic Design, a studio producing Celtic-influenced brooches. Gold- and silversmiths can also be seen at work here.

## KNITWEAR AND TWEED

ARAN SWEATERS are sold all over Ireland, but particu-larly in County Galway and on the Aran Islands them-selves. One of Ireland's best

buys, these oiled, off-white sweaters used to be handed down through generations of Aran fishermen. Legend has it that each family used its own motifs so that if a fisherman was lost at sea and his body unidentifiable, his family could recognize him by his sweater.

Given the Irish experience of wet weather, warm and rain-resistant clothes are generally of good quality, from waxed jackets and duffel coats to sheepskin jackets. Knitwear is on sale all over Ireland, with **Avoca Handweavers** and **Blarney Woollen Mills** the best-known outlets. Good buys include embroidered sweaters and waistcoats and hand-woven shawls and scarves.

Donegal tweed is a byword for quality, noted for its texture, tension and subtle colours (originally produced by dyes made from lichens, local plants and minerals). Tweed caps, hats, scarves, ties, jackets and suits are sold in outlets such as **Magee and Co** in Donegal.

**Second-hand furniture shop in Kenmare**

## LINEN

DAMASK LINEN was brought to Armagh by Huguenot refugees fleeing French per-secution. As a result, Belfast became the world linen capi-tal. Ulster is still the place for linen, with sheets and double-damask table linen on sale in Belfast – at **Smyth's Irish**

**Linen**, for example – and in other towns. There are also outlets in the Republic. Hand-embroidered linen is made in County Donegal. Linen-making can be seen at Wellbrook Beetling Mill *(see p260)*.

## FASHION

INSPIRED by a predominantly young population, Ireland is fast acquiring a name for fashion. Conservatively cut tweed and linen suits continue to be models of classic good taste, while younger designers are increasingly experimental, using bold lines and mixing traditional fabrics.

**A-Wear** is a quality boutique that has branches in major cities. Here, and in the **Design Centre** in Powerscourt Town-house Shopping Centre in Dublin, are clothes by the best Irish designers including John Rocha, Paul Costelloe, Louise Kennedy, Quin and Donnelly and Mariad Whisker. Clothing and shoe sizes are identical to British fittings.

## FOOD AND DRINK

SMOKED SALMON, home-cured bacon, farmhouse cheeses, soda bread, preserves and handmade chocolates make perfect last-minute gifts. Several shops will package and send Irish salmon overseas.

Bewley's teas and coffees are sold in **Bewley's Oriental Café** and Bewley shops all over Ireland. Guinness travels less well and is best drunk in Ireland. Irish whiskey is hard to beat as a gift or souvenir. Apart from the cheaper Power and Paddy brands, the big names are Bushmills *(see p258)* and Jameson *(see p171)*. Rich Irish liqueurs include Irish Mist and Baileys Irish Cream.

**Selection of hand-knitted sweaters at a craft shop in Dingle**

## DIRECTORY

### DEPARTMENT STORES AND SHOPPING CENTRES

**Brown Thomas**
88–95 Grafton St, Dublin 2.
**Dublin map** D4.
( 01 605 6666.

**Clery's**
18–27 O'Connell St
Lower, Dublin 1.
**Dublin map** D2.
( 01 8786000.

**St Stephen's Green Shopping Centre**
St Stephen's Green West,
Dublin 2. **Dublin map** D4.

### BOOKS

**Eason and Son**
80 Middle Abbey St,
Dublin 1. **Dublin map** D2.
( 01 8733811.

**Eason Hanna**
27–29 Nassau St, Dublin 2.
**Dublin map** E4.
( 01 6771255.

**Kennys Bookshop and Art Gallery**
High St, Galway.
**Road map** B4.
( 091 562739.

**Waterstone's**
7 Dawson St, Dublin 2.
**Dublin map** D4.
( 01 6791415.

### MUSIC

**Claddagh Records**
2 Cecilia St, Temple Bar,
Dublin 2. **Dublin map** C3.
( 01 6770262.

**J McNeill**
140 Capel St, Dublin 1.
**Dublin map** C2.
( 01 8722159.

**Waltons**
3–5 Frederick St North,
Dublin 1.
( 01 8747805.

### CRAFTS

**Bricín**
26 High Street, Killarney,
Co Kerry. **Road map** B5.
( 064 34902.

**Connemara Marble Factory**
Moycullen, Co Galway.
**Road map** B4.
( 091 555102.

**Crafts Council of Ireland**
Castle Yard, Kilkenny.
**Road map** C4.
( 056 61804.

**DESIGNYARD**
12 Essex Street East,
Dublin 2.
**Dublin map** C3.
( 677 8453.

**Craftworks Shop**
Bedford House, Bedford
Street, Belfast.
**Road map** D2.
( 028 9024 4465.

**Doolin Crafts Gallery**
Ballyvoe, Doolin, Co Clare.
**Road map** B4.
( 065 7074309.

**Kilkenny Design Centre**
Castle Yard, Kilkenny.
**Road map** C4.
( 056 22118.

**The Kilkenny Shop**
6 Nassau St, Dublin 2.
**Dublin map** E4.
( 01 6777066.

**Standuin**
Spiddal, Co Galway.
**Road map** B4.
( 091 553357.

**Tower Enterprise Centre**
Pearse St, Dublin 2.
( 01 6775655.

**The Whichcraft Gallery**
Cow's Lane, Temple Bar,
Dublin 2. **Dublin map** C3.
( 01 474 1011.

### CERAMICS AND CHINA

**Cré Irish Porcelain**
Wellpark, Galway.
**Road map** B4.
( 091 752788.

**Louis Mulcahy's Pottery**
Clogher, Ballyferriter, Tralee,
Co Kerry. **Road map** A5.
( 066 9156229.

**Nicholas Mosse Pottery**
Bennettsbridge, Co
Kilkenny. **Road map** D5.
( 056 27105.

**Royal Tara China**
Tara Hall, Mervue, Galway.
**Road map** B4.
( 091 751301.

**Treasure Chest**
31-33 William St, Galway.
**Road map** B4.
( 091 567237.

### CRYSTAL AND GLASSWARE

**Galway Irish Crystal**
Merlin Park, Galway.
**Road map** B4.
( 091 757311.

**Jerpoint Glass**
Stoneyford, Co Kilkenny.
**Road map** D5.
( 056 24350.

**Sligo Crystal**
2 Hyde Bridge, Sligo,
Co Sligo. **Road map** C2.
( 071 43440.

**Tipperary Crystal**
Ballynoran, Carrick-on-
Suir, Co Tipperary.
**Road map** C5.
( 051 641188.

**Tyrone Crystal**
Killybrackey, Coal Island Rd,
Dungannon, Co Tyrone.
**Road map** D2.
( 028 8772 5335.

**Waterford Crystal**
Kilbarry, Waterford.
**Road map** D5.
( 051 373311.

### JEWELLERY

**Brian de Staic**
18 High St, Killarney,
Co Kerry. **Road map** B5.
( 064 33822.

**Hilser Brothers**
Grand Parade, Cork.
**Road map** C5.
( 021 4270382.

**Saller's Jewellers**
Williamsgate St, Galway.
**Road map** B4.
( 091 561226.

### KNITWEAR AND TWEED

**Avoca Handweavers**
Kilmacanogue, Bray, Co
Wicklow. **Road map** D4.
( 01 2867466.

**Blarney Woollen Mills**
Blarney, Co Cork.
**Road map** B5.
( 021 4385280.

**House of Ireland**
37–38 Nassau Street,
Dublin 2. **Dublin map** D4.
( 01 671 1111.

**Magee and Co**
The Diamond, Donegal.
**Road map** C2.
( 073 22660.

**Quills Woollen Market**
1 High St, Killarney, Co
Kerry. **Road map** B5.
( 064 32277.

**Studio Donegal**
The Glebe Mill, Kilcar,
Co Donegal. **Road map** B2.
( 073 38194.

### LINEN

**Forgotten Cotton**
Savoy Centre, St Patrick's
St, Cork.
**Road map** C5.
( 021 4276098.

**Smyth's Irish Linen**
65 Royal Ave, Belfast.
**Road map** D2.
( 028 9024 2232.

### FASHION

**A-Wear**
26 Grafton St, Dublin 2.
**Dublin map** D4.
( 01 6717200.

### FOOD AND DRINK

**Bewley's Oriental Café**
78 Grafton St, Dublin 2.
**Dublin map** D4.
( 01 6776761.

**Butler's Irish Hand-made Chocolates**
51a Grafton St, Dublin 2.
**Dublin map** D4.
( 01 6710599.

# What to Buy in Ireland

**H**UNDREDS of gift and craft shops scattered throughout Ireland make it easy to find Irish specialities to suit all budgets. The best buys include linen, tweeds and crystal from factory shops which invariably offer an extensive choice of good quality products. Local crafts make unique souvenirs, from hand-made jewellery and ceramics to traditional musical instruments. Religious artifacts are also widely available. Irish food and drink are evocative reminders of your trip.

St Brigid's cross

**Traditional hand-held drum (*bodhrán*) and beater**

**Connemara marble "worry stone"**

**Traditional Claddagh ring**

**Enamel brooch**

*Modern jewellery and metalwork draw on a long and varied tradition. Craftspeople continue to base their designs on sources such as the* Book of Kells *(see p62) and Celtic myths. Local plants and wildlife are also an inspiration. County Galway produces Claddagh rings – traditional betrothal rings – in gold and silver as well as "worry stones".*

**Fuchsia earring from Dingle**

**Celtic-design enamel brooch**

**Bronzed resin Celtic figurine**

**Donegal tweed jacket and waistcoat**

**Tweed skirt and jacket**

*Clothing made in Ireland is usually of excellent quality. Tweed-making still flourishes in Donegal where tweed can be bought ready-made as clothing or hats or as lengths of cloth. Knitwear is widely available all over the country in large factory outlets and local craft shops. The many hand-knitted items on sale, including Aran jumpers, are not cheap but should give years of wear.*

**Tweed cap**

**Aran jumper**

**Tweed fisherman's hat**

*Irish linen* is world-famous and the range unparalleled. There is a huge choice of table and bed linen, including extravagant bedspreads and crisp, formal tablecloths. On a smaller scale, tiny, intricately embroidered handkerchiefs make lovely gifts as do linen table napkins. Tea towels printed with colourful designs are widely available. You can also buy linen goods trimmed with fine lace, which is still hand-made in Ireland, mainly in Limerick and Kenmare.

**Set of linen placemats and napkins**

**Fine linen handkerchiefs**

**Nicholas Mosse plate**

**Belleek teapot**

**Nicholas Mosse cup**

*Irish ceramics* come in traditional and modern designs. You can buy anything from a full dinner service by established factories, such as Royal Tara China or the Belleek Pottery, to a one-off contemporary piece from a local potter's studio.

## IRISH PROVERBS

ILLUSTRATED BY
KAREN BAILEY

**Book of Irish Proverbs**

*Irish crystal*, hand-blown and hand-cut, can be ordered or bought in many shops in Ireland. Visit the outlets of the principal manufacturers, such as Waterford Crystal, Tyrone Crystal and Jerpoint Glass, to see the full range – from glasses and decanters to elaborate chandeliers.

*Books and stationery* are often beautifully illustrated. Museums and bookshops stock a wide range.

**Celtic-design cards**

**Waterford crystal tumbler and decanter**

*Food and drink* will keep the distinctive tastes of Ireland fresh long after you arrive home. Whiskey connoisseurs should visit the Old Bushmills Distillery (see p258) or the Jameson Heritage Centre (see p171) to sample their choice of whiskeys. Good regional food can be found at local shops all over Ireland. Try the dried seaweed, which is eaten raw or added to cooked dishes.

**Jameson whiskey**

**Bushmills whiskey**

**Fruit cake made with Guinness**

**Jar of Irish marmalade**

**Packet of dried seaweed**

# ENTERTAINMENT IN IRELAND

IF THERE IS ONE SPHERE in which Ireland shines, it is entertainment. For details about entertainment in Dublin, see pages 102–7. Elsewhere in Ireland, nightclubs and concerts by international entertainers tend to be concentrated in large cities, but many other events including theatre, arts festivals, traditional music and dance, cultural holidays and even medieval banquets take place all over the country. Most towns and cities also have one or two cinemas showing the latest films on release. Not to be overlooked is the free entertainment (planned or spontaneous) provided by a night in a pub. For more active forms of entertainment, covered on pages 332–5, the list is even longer, from golf to pony trekking and cycling to scuba diving. Those who prefer their sports sitting down can go along as spectators to Ireland's famous horse race meetings, as well as Gaelic football, hurling, soccer and rugby matches. Best of all, a happy mix of these activities can easily be put together with almost any itinerary.

**Morris Minor van advertising the Clonakilty Folk Club**

**Ulster Symphony Orchestra at the Ulster Hall in Belfast**

## INFORMATION SOURCES

THE TOURIST BOARD for the Republic, **Bord Fáilte**, and the **Northern Ireland Tourist Board** both publish a yearly *Calendar of Events* that lists major fixtures around the country, and all the regional tourist offices have information about events in each locality. To supplement these listings, check regional newspapers and enquire locally to find on-the-spot entertainment.

## BOOKING TICKETS

TICKETS can usually be bought at the door on the day or evening of most events. Advance booking is a must, however, for popular concerts and plays. Many cultural and arts festivals require tickets only for the key performances, but for internationally famous festivals, such as the Wexford Opera Festival, you will need to book well in advance through the festival office for all performances.

Credit-card bookings for plays, concerts and other events around Ireland can be made by telephone through **Keith Prowse Travel (IRL) Ltd** and **Ticketmaster** in Dublin.

## MAJOR VENUES

IN MANY IRISH CITIES, the main theatres host a huge variety of events. In Cork, the **Opera House** presents predominantly Irish plays during the summer months, with musical comedy, opera and ballet at other times of year. The city's **Everyman Palace Theatre** stages plays by local and visiting companies interspersed with concerts of both classical and popular music. Sligo's **Hawks Well Theatre** and Limerick's **Belltable Arts Centre** are venues for drama and concerts. In the centre of Belfast, the **Grand Opera House**, **Waterfront Hall** and **Lyric Theatre** present a varied programme, including Irish and international plays, experimental drama, pantomime and opera.

## THEATRE

FROM INTERNATIONAL TOURS to amateur productions, there is excellent theatre to be seen in virtually every location in Ireland. In Galway, the **Druid Theatre** specializes in avant-garde plays, new Irish plays and Anglo-Irish classics, with frequent lunch-time and late-night performances, while Gaelic drama, Irish music, singing and dancing have all thrived at the **Taibhdhearc Theatre** since 1928. Waterford boasts its resident Red Kettle Theatre Company which performs at the **Garter Lane Theatre**, while the **Theatre Royal** brings amateur drama and musicals to the city.

Keep an eye out for small theatre groups performing in local halls around the country. Many of them are superb and they have spawned several of Ireland's leading actors.

**Home of the Druid Theatre Company in Galway** *(see p202)*

The Moscow Ballet at Belfast's Grand Opera House *(see p268)*

## CLASSICAL MUSIC, OPERA AND DANCE

MAJOR VENUES for classical music include the **Crawford Art Gallery**, Opera House and Everyman Palace in Cork; the Theatre Royal in Waterford; the Hawks Well Theatre in Sligo; and the Belltable Arts Centre in Limerick. Belfast's **Ulster Hall** hosts concerts from rock bands to the Ulster Symphony Orchestra.

Opera lovers from around the world come to Ireland for the **Wexford Festival of Opera** in October and November and the **Waterford Festival of Light Opera** in late September and early October. At Wexford, neglected operas are revived, while Waterford selects more mainstream operas and musicals. Elsewhere, opera is performed in Cork's Opera House and in Belfast's Grand Opera House.

Ireland has no resident ballet or avant-garde dance companies, but leading international companies perform occasionally at the major venues around the country.

## ROCK, JAZZ AND COUNTRY

WHEN INTERNATIONAL music stars tour Ireland, concerts outside Dublin are held at large outdoor sites. **Semple Stadium** in County Tipperary and Slane Castle *(see p237)* in County Meath are popular venues. Tickets and information are available from Ticketmaster.

Musical pubs *(see pp318–21)* are your best bet for good rock and jazz performed by Irish groups. Check local tourist offices and newspapers for rock and jazz nights, which usually take place midweek, with country and traditional music at weekends. For some

of Ireland's "big band" jazz music, keep an eye out for Waterford's Brass and Co who play at dances around the country. Jazz lovers have a field day at the **Cork Jazz Festival** in late October, when music pours from every pub and international jazz greats play in the city's theatres.

Pub scene at Feakle Traditional Music Weekend, County Clare

## TRADITIONAL MUSIC AND DANCE

THE COUNTRY PUB has helped keep Irish music alive and provided the setting for the musical revival that began in the 1960s. Today, sessions of informal or impromptu music are still commonplace. In pubs, traditional music embraces ballads and rebel songs, as well as the older *sean-nos* – unaccompanied, understated stories, often sung in Irish.

Nights of Irish music and song are scheduled in many pubs, such as The Laurels and the Danny Mann in Killarney, the Yeats Tavern in Drumcliff, near Sligo, and An Phoenix and The Lobby in Cork. In Derry, the Gweedore Bar, Castle Bar and Dungloe Bar are among the cluster of musical pubs along Waterloo Street. Wherever you are, a query to the locals will send you off to the nearest musical pub. For more pub listings, see pages 318–21.

In Tralee, **Siamsa Tire**, the National Folk Theatre, stages marvellous folk drama incorporating traditional music, singing and dance. The Barn, in Bunratty Folk Park, is the setting for the **Shannon Ceili** – traditional music nights during the summer months.

**Comhaltas Ceoltóirí Éireann**, in Monkstown near Dublin, has branches around the country and organizes traditional music and dance nights all year. Traditional Irish dancing can be stylish step dancing or joyous set dancing. Visitors are usually encouraged to join in the fun.

The **Fleadh Cheoil** (national traditional music festival) is a weekend of music, dance, song and stage shows that spill over into colourful street entertainment. It takes place at the end of August in a different town each year. Earlier in August, the **Feakle Traditional Music Weekend** in County Clare is a more intimate celebration of traditional music, song and dance.

A large audience for open-air music at the Cork Jazz Festival

**Knappogue banquet at Knappogue Castle, County Clare**

## FESTIVALS

THE IRISH are experts at organizing festivals, staging a week of street entertainment, theatre, music and dance to celebrate almost everything under the sun *(see pp46–9)*.

In mid-July the lively town of Galway is host to the **Galway Arts Festival**, one of the largest festivals in Ireland. Here you will find Irish and international theatre and music, street entertainment and events for children. Taking place over two weeks in late July and early August is the **Boyle Arts Festival**. The events here include art exhibitions, poetry and drama performances as well as classical, traditional, folk and jazz concerts. Creative workshops are run for both adults and children.

**Kilkenny Arts Week** in August, another major festival, features poetry, classical music concerts, films and a range of crafts. The **Cork Film Festival** takes place in the first week of October when international feature, documentary and short films are screened at venues all over the city. The **Belfast Festival at Queen's** is held for two weeks in October to late November. The lively and cosmopolitan programme includes a mixture of drama, ballet, comedy, cabaret, music and cinema. These take over the Queen's University campus plus theatres and other venues throughout Belfast.

In May and June, the **County Wicklow Gardens Festival** entices gardening enthusiasts to wander around the county's most beautiful gardens. In mid-June, the **Music Festival in Great Irish Houses** opens the doors to many of Ireland's historic homes to which the public seldom has access, with classical music performed by top-rate musicians. Venues include Strokestown Park House *(see pp210–11)*, Mount Stewart House *(see pp274–5)* and University College, Cork.

**Kilkenny Arts Week street theatre**

## TRADITIONAL BANQUETS WITH ENTERTAINMENT

IRELAND'S BANQUETS have gained international fame and are great fun. Each of the banquets features costumed waiters and performers, as well as traditional food and drink of the chosen period.

Most famous are the medieval banquets – the one at Bunratty Castle *(see pp184–5)* was the first and is the liveliest, with year-round performances. From May to October, there is a glittering pageant at Knappogue Castle *(see p181)*, and at Dunguaire Castle *(see p204)* there is a quieter, more intimate programme of music and poetry. From March until November, the highly enjoyable Killarney Manor Banquet, held at the stately manor on the Loreto road just south of Killarney, creates an early 19th-century atmosphere.

## CULTURAL HOLIDAYS

A HOLIDAY IN IRELAND focused on any one of the cultural aspects of Irish life is enriching as well as fun. Choose from a variety of cultural topics and study courses: Irish music and literature, great houses and gardens, Irish language and folklore, crafts and cookery.

One of the most fascinating possibilities is the exploration of Ireland's 5,000-year history as revealed in the many relics strewn across the landscape. The **Achill Archaeological Summer School** in County Mayo, for example, runs a course that includes the active excavation of ancient relics.

To learn the secret of Irish cooking, there is no better place than the **Ballymaloe School of Cookery** in County Cork; it is run by Darina Allen, Ireland's most famous cook.

For literature enthusiasts, the **Yeats International Summer School** studies the works of Yeats and his contemporaries, while **Listowel Writers' Week** brings together leading writers for lectures and workshops.

**Folk dancers in traditional Irish costume**

## DIRECTORY

### INFORMATION SOURCES

**Bord Fáilte**
Baggot St Bridge,
Dublin 2.
( 01 6024000.

**Northern Ireland Tourist Board**
St Anne's Court, 59 North St, Belfast.
( 028 9023 1221.

### BOOKING TICKETS

**Keith Prowse Travel (IRL) Ltd**
10 St Stephen's Green,
Dublin 2.
( 01 6795333.

**Ticket Master**
Grafton House,
70 Grafton St, Dublin 2.
( 01 4569569.

### MAJOR VENUES

**Belltable Arts Centre**
69 O'Connell St, Limerick.
( 061 319866.

**Everyman Palace Theatre**
MacCurtain St, Cork.
( 021 4501673.

**Grand Opera House**
Great Victoria St, Belfast.
( 028 9024 0411.

**Hawks Well Theatre**
Temple St, Sligo.
( 071 61526.

**Lyric Theatre**
55 Ridgeway St, Belfast.
( 028 9038 1081.

**Opera House**
Emmet Place, Cork.
( 021 4274308.

**Waterfront Hall**
2 Lanyon Place, Belfast.
( 028 9033 4400.

### THEATRE

**Druid Theatre**
Chapel Lane, Galway.
( 091 568617.

**Garter Lane Theatre**
22A O'Connell St,
Waterford.
( 051 877153.

**Taibhdhearc Theatre**
Middle St, Galway.
( 091 562024.

**Theatre Royal**
The Mall, Waterford.
( 051 874402.

### CLASSICAL MUSIC, OPERA AND DANCE

**Crawford Art Gallery**
Emmet Place, Cork.
( 021 4273377.

**Ulster Hall**
Bedford St, Belfast.
( 028 9032 3900.

**Waterford Festival of Light Opera**
60 Morrissons Ave,
Waterford.
( 051 375437.

**Wexford Festival of Opera**
Theatre Royal, High St,
Wexford.
( 053 22144.

### ROCK, JAZZ AND COUNTRY

**Cork Jazz Festival**
20 South Mall, Cork.
( 021 4270463.

**Semple Stadium**
Thurles, Co Tipperary.
( 0504 21308

### TRADITIONAL MUSIC AND DANCE

**Comhaltas Ceoltóirí Éireann**
32 Belgrave Sq,
Monkstown, Co Dublin.
( 01 2800295.

**Feakle Traditional Music Weekend**
Maghera, Caher, Co Clare.
( 061 925125.

**Fleadh Cheoil**
32 Belgrave Sq,
Monkstown, Co Dublin.
( 01 2800295.

**Shannon Ceili**
Bunratty Castle and Folk
Park, Bunratty, Co Clare.
( 061 360788.

**Siamsa Tire**
National Folk Theatre, The
Town Park,Tralee, Co
Kerry. ( 066 7123055.

### FESTIVALS

**Belfast Festival at Queen's**
Festival House, 25 College
Gardens, Belfast.
( 028 9066 7687.

**Boyle Arts Festival**
Festival Office,
Great Meadow, Boyle,
Co Roscommon.
( 079 63085.

**Cork Film Festival**
10 Washington Street,
Cork.
( 021 4271711.

**County Wicklow Gardens Festival**
St Manntan's House,
Kilmantin Hill, Wicklow.
( 0404 66058.

**Galway Arts Festival**
Black Box Theatre, Dyke
Rd, Terryland, Galway.
( 091 509700.

**Kilkenny Arts Week**
92 High St, Kilkenny.
( 056 63663.

**Music Festival in Great Irish Houses**
1st floor Blackrock
Post Office, Blackrock,
Co Dublin.
( 01 2781528.

### CULTURAL HOLIDAYS

#### Archaeology
**Achill Archaeological Summer School**
Folk Life Centre, Dooagh,
Achill Island, Co. Mayo.
( 098 43564.

**Gerard Manley-Hopkins Summer School**
Drogheda Street,
Monasterevin,
Co. Kildare.
( 045 525416.

**Oideas Gael**
Gleanncholmcille,
Co Donegal.
( 073 30248.

#### Cookery
**Ballymaloe School of Cookery**
Shanagarry, Midleton,
Co Cork.
( 021 4646785.

### Crafts
**Ardess Craft Centre**
Ardess House, Kesh,
Co Fermanagh.
( 028 6863 1267.

**Houses, Castles and Gardens of Ireland**
16a Woodlands Park,
Blackrock, Co Dublin.
( 01-454 1786

**National Trust**
Rowallane House,
Saintfield, Ballynahinch,
Co Down.
( 028 9751 0721.

### Irish Language
**Irish Conversation Courses**
Oidhreacht Chorca
Dhuibhne, Ballyferriter,
Co Kerry.
( 066 9156100.

### Literary
**Goldsmith Summer School**
Rathmore, Ballymahon,
Co Longford.
( 0902 32374.

**James Joyce Summer School**
University College Dublin,
Belfield, Dublin 4.
( 01 7068480.

**Listowel Writers' Week**
24 The Square, Listowel,
Co Kerry.
( 068 21074.

**William Carleton Summer School**
Dungannon District
Council, Circular Rd,
Dungannon, Co Tyrone.
( 028 8772 5311.

**Yeats International Summer School**
Yeats Society, Yeats
Memorial Building, Douglas
Hyde Bridge, Sligo.
( 071 42693.

### Music
**South Sligo Summer School of Traditional Music, Song and Dance**
Tubbercurry,
Co Sligo.
( 071 85010.

**Willie Clancy Summer School**
Miltown Malbay, Co Clare.
( 065 7084148.

# Sports and Outdoor Activities

**E**VEN IN THE LARGEST CITIES, the country-side is never far away, and it beckons to all lovers of the outdoors. Topping the list of spectator sports is Ireland's famous horse racing, while hurling, Gaelic football and soccer also make for exciting viewing. Those who want to do more than just watch can choose between fishing, golf, horse riding, cruising, cycling, walking and water sports. Entire holidays can be based

**Horse riding in Killarney**

around any of these activities. In addition to the contacts on page 335, Bord Fáilte in the Republic, the Northern Ireland Tourist Board and all local tourist offices have information on spectator and participant sports. For details of the main events in Ireland's sporting calendar, see pages 26–7.

**Fishing in the canal at Robertstown, County Kildare** *(see p120)*

## SPECTATOR SPORTS

**T**HE IRISH PASSION for horse racing is legendary. Major courses include the Curragh *(see p121)*, where the Irish Derby is held, Fairyhouse, the venue for Ireland's Grand National, Leopardstown and Puncheston. Apart from these major courses, there are smaller ones all over the Republic (and two in Northern Ireland), where the atmosphere is exciting and informal. Galway Race Week in late July is a great social event. A racing calendar for the whole of Ireland, available from the **Irish Horse Racing Authority**, allows you to choose either National Hunt or flat race meets, which take place on 230 days of the year.

**Sign outside a fishing tackle shop in Donegal**

In Dublin, **Croke Park** hosts Gaelic football and hurling matches *(see pp26–7)*, while international rugby and soccer matches are held at Lansdowne Road Stadium. Ticket details for soccer internationals are available from the **Football Association of Ireland**.

For keen golfers, the annual highlight is the Irish Open Golf Championship in July. The venue varies from year to year. For tickets and the latest information, contact the **Irish Open Office**.

## FISHING

**T**HE CLAIM that Ireland is a paradise for anglers is no exaggeration. Coarse, game and sea fishing all enjoy widespread popularity. The lakes and rivers are home to bream, pike, perch

and roach. Coastal rivers yield the famous Irish salmon, and, among other game fish, sea trout and brown trout also offer anglers a real challenge.

Flounder, whiting, mullet, bass and coalfish tempt the sea angler; deep-sea excursions chase abundant supplies of dogfish, shark, skate and ling. You can organize sea-angling trips from many different places – the Cork and Kerry coastline being a particularly popular starting point. Contact the **Irish Federation of Sea Anglers** for information on planning a sea fishing trip or to book organized trips and courses.

Maps and information on fishing locations are provided by the **Central Fisheries Board** and Bord Fáilte in the Republic, and the **Department of Agriculture (Fisheries)** and Northern Ireland Tourist Board. Check permit requirements before you go.

## GOLF

**O**F THE 300 or more golf courses in the whole of Ireland, over 50 are championship class, and many are by spectacular stretches of coast. Mount Juliet's world-class, Jack Nicklaus-designed course in County Kilkenny has won international acclaim, and many others are also kept in top condition. Northern Ireland's best-known courses are Royal Portrush and Royal

**Golfers at Portstewart in Northern Ireland** *(see p252)*

Walking in the Gap of Dunloe, Killarney *(see p155)*

County Down. The **Golfing Union of Ireland**, the **Irish Ladies Golfing Union** and the tourist boards have information on courses, conditions and green fees throughout the Republic and Northern Ireland. Some have clubs for hire, but it is better to bring your own.

**Golfers Abroad** organizes tailor-made golfing holidays for individuals and groups in Northern Ireland.

## CYCLING

CYCLING is one of Ireland's most popular sports. There is an exhilarating range of countryside to be explored and the comparatively traffic-free roads make cycling a pleasure. Limerick, Waterford and Galway make good bases for cycling holidays. Several organizations, such as **Celtic Cycling**, will plan an itinerary and book accommodation.

If you bring your own bike, you can transport it around the country fairly cheaply by train or bus.

Alternatively, try the many **Raleigh Rent-a-Bike** dealers with depots in the Republic and Northern Ireland, or **Cycleways**, based in Parnell Street, Dublin.

## HORSE RIDING AND PONY TREKKING

THE IRISH ARE rightly proud of their fine horses. Many riding centres, both residential and non-residential, offer trail riding and trekking along woodland trails, deserted beaches, country lanes and mountain routes. Dingle, Donegal, Connemara, and Killarney are all renowned areas for trail riding. There are two types of trail riding – post-to-post and based. Post-to-post trails follow a series of routes with accommodation in a different place each night. Based trail rides follow different routes in one area and you stay at the same

place for the whole holiday. Also on offer at many riding centres are lessons for everyone from beginners to more advanced riders to those who want to learn show jumping.

Bord Fáilte and the Northern Ireland Tourist Board publish details of riding centres and courses. **Equestrian Holidays Ireland** organizes holidays for riders of various abilities.

## WALKING AND MOUNTAINEERING

A WALKING HOLIDAY puts you in the very middle of the glorious Irish landscape. The network of waymarked trails all over the country takes you to some of the loveliest areas. Information on long-distance walks is available from Bord Fáilte and the Northern Ireland Tourist Board. Routes include the Wicklow Way *(see p131)*, Dingle Way, Munster Way, Kerry Way and Barrow Towpath. All may be split into shorter sections for less experienced walkers or those short of time. The 800-km (500-mile) Ulster Way encircles Northern Ireland passing through a wide range of locations from the spectacular scenery around the Giant's Causeway *(see pp254–5)* to the peaks of the Mountains of Mourne *(see pp276–7)*. **Irish Ways** offers walking holidays in the Republic. For activities in Northern Ireland, call the **Ulster Federation of Rambling Clubs**.

Hill walking, rock climbing and mountaineering holidays are also available. For information, contact the **Mountaineering Council of Ireland**. Be sure to go well-equipped for the notoriously changeable Irish weather.

**Ulster Way**

**Sign for the Ulster Way, the trail around Northern Ireland**

Cycling through the Muckross House estate near Killarney *(see p151)*

**Surfing at Bundoran** *(see p222)*

## WATER SPORTS

WITH A COASTLINE of over 4,800 km (3,000 miles), small wonder that water sports are among Ireland's favourite recreational activities. Surfing, windsurfing, water-skiing, scuba diving and canoeing are the most popular, and there are facilities for all of these right around the coastline.

Conditions in Sligo are the best in Ireland for surfing, but many other coastal locations offer good conditions. The **British Surfing Association** has information about surfing all over Europe.

Windsurfing centres are mainly found near Dublin, Cork and Westport in County Galway.

There is a wide range of diving conditions off the coast of Ireland – visibility is particularly good on the west coast. The **Irish Underwater Council** will put you in touch with courses and facilities. **DV Diving** organizes scuba diving courses and offers accommodation near Belfast Lough and the Irish Sea where there are a number of historic wrecks to be explored.

Inland, Lower Lough Erne *(see pp262–3)* and Killaloe by Lough Derg *(see p182)* are popular holiday centres. The **Lakeland Canoe Centre**, between Upper and Lower Lough Erne, gives canoeing courses and organizes canoeing holidays (with overnight camping), including one down

the Shannon-Erne Waterway *(see p227)*. **Atlantic Sea Kayaking** organizes daily and two to eight day tours round Castlehaven and Baltimore, amongst others.

## CRUISING AND SAILING

A TRANQUIL CRUISING holiday is an ideal alternative to the stress and strain of driving, and Ireland's 14,500 km (9,000 miles) of rivers and some 800 lakes offer a huge variety of conditions for those who want a waterborne holiday. Stopping over at waterside towns and villages puts you in touch with the Irish on their home ground. Whether you opt for Lough Derg or elsewhere on the Shannon *(see p177)*, or the Grand Canal *(see p99)* from Dublin to the Shannon, a unique view of the Irish countryside opens up all along the way.

Running between Carrick-on-Shannon in County Leitrim and Upper Lough Erne in Fermanagh is the **Shannon-Erne Waterway** *(see p227)*, a disused canal reopened in 1993. From here it is simple to continue through Upper and Lower Lough Erne to Belleek *(see p262)*. **Emerald Star** has a fleet of cruisers for use on the waterway.

A popular sailing area is between Cork and the Dingle Peninsula. The **International Sailing Centre**, near Cork, offers tuition. In Carrickfergus the **Ulster Cruising School** provides lessons at all levels; more experienced sailors can charter a yacht and sail up to the western coast of Scotland.

## HUNTING AND SHOOTING

IRELAND'S HUNTING season runs from October to March, and although fox-hunting predominates, stag and hare hunts also take place. For details, contact the **Irish Master of Foxhounds Association** in the Republic and, in Northern Ireland, the **Countryside Alliance**. Clay-pigeon (year-round) and pheasant (from November to January) shooting are also popular. **Mount Juliet Estate**, in County Kilkenny, offers both with guns and cartridges to hire.

**Yachting off Rosslare** *(see p143)*

## SPORTS FOR THE DISABLED

SPORTS ENTHUSIASTS with a disability can obtain details of facilities for the disabled from the **Irish Wheelchair Association**. Central and local tourist boards and many of the organizations listed in the directory under each sport will also advise on available facilities. The **Share Centre** provides a range of activity holidays for both disabled and able-bodied people.

**Boats moored at Carnlough Harbour on the Antrim coast** *(see p259)*

## DIRECTORY

### SPECTATOR SPORTS

**Croke Park**
Dublin 3. ☎ 01 8363222.

**Football Association of Ireland**
80 Merrion Sq, Dublin 2.
☎ 01 6766864.

**Horse Racing Ireland**
The Curragh, Co Kildare.
☎ 045 445645.

**Irish Open Office**
35 Upper Mount St,
Dublin 2. ☎ 01 6622433.

### FISHING

**Central Fisheries Board**
Mobhi Boreen, Glasnevin,
Dublin 9.
☎ 01 8379206.

**Department of Agriculture (Fisheries)**
Annex 5, Castlegrounds,
Stormont, Belfast.
☎ 028 9052 3434.

**Irish Federation of Sea Anglers**
Mr Hugh O'Rorke,
67 Windsor Drive,
Monkstown, Co Dublin.
☎ 01 2806873.

### GOLF

**Golfers Abroad**
45 Rectory Rd,
Duckmanton,
Chesterfield,
Derbyshire.
☎ 01246 240836.

**Irish Ladies Golfing Union**
1 Clonskeagh Sq., Dublin
14. ☎ 01 2696244.

**Golfing Union of Ireland**
Glencar House, 81
Eglinton Rd, Dublin 4.
☎ 01 2694111.

### CYCLING

**Ardclinis Activity Centre**
High St, Cushendall,
Co Antrim.
☎ 028 2577 1340.

**Cycleways**
185-6 Parnell St, Dublin 1.
☎ 01 873 4748.

**Celtic Cycling**
Lorum Old Rectory,
Bagenalstown, Co Carlow.
☎ 0503 75282.

**Raleigh Rent-a-Bike**
Raleigh House,
Kylemore Rd, Dublin 10.
☎ 01 6261333.

### HORSE RIDING AND PONY TREKKING

**Association of Irish Riding Establishments**
11 Moore Park,
Newbridge, Co Kildare.
☎ 045 431584.

**British Horse Society**
House of Sport, Upper
Malone Rd, Belfast.
☎ 028 9038 1222.

**Equestrian Holidays Ireland**
1 Sandyford Office Park,
Foxrock, Dublin 18.
☎ 01 2958928.

### WALKING AND MOUNTAINEERING

**Mountaineering Council of Ireland**
House of Sport, Longmile
Rd, Dublin 12.
☎ 01 450 7376.

**Irish Ways**
Old Rectory,
Ballycanew, Gorey,
Co Wexford.
☎ 055 27479.

**Ulster Federation of Rambling Clubs**
12B Breda House,
Drumart Drive,
Belfast.
☎ 028 9064 8041.

### WATER SPORTS

**Atlantic Sea Kayaking**
Union Hall, Co Cork.
☎ 028 21058.

**Baltimore Diving & Watersports Centre**
Baltimore, Co. Cork.
☎ 028 20300.

**British Surfing Association**
Champions Yard
Penzance,
Cornwall.
☎ 01736 360250.

**DV Diving**
138 Mountstewart Rd,
Newtownards,
Co Down.
☎ 028 9186 1686.

**Irish Underwater Council**
78a Patrick St, Dun
Laoghaire, Co Dublin.
☎ 01 2844601.

**Lakeland Canoe Centre**
Castle Island, Enniskillen,
Co Fermanagh.
☎ 028 6632 4250.

**Out and Out Activities**
Garrison, Co Fermanagh.
☎ 028 6865 8072.

**Outside World**
Parnell Place, Cork,
Co Cork.
☎ 021 4278833.

**Schull Watersports Centre**
Schull,
Co Cork.
☎ 028 28554.

### CRUISING AND SAILING

**Athlone Cruisers**
Jolly Mariner, Athlone,
Co Westmeath.
☎ 0902 72892.

**Emerald Star**
The Marina, Carrick-on-
Shannon, Co Leitrim.
☎ 078 20234.

**Erne Marine**
Bellanaleck, Enniskillen,
Co Fermanagh.
☎ 028 6634 8267.

**International Sailing Centre**
East Beach, Cobh, Cork.
☎ 021 4811237.

**Ireland Line Cruisers**
Derg Marina, Killaloe,
Co Clare.
☎ 061 375011.

**Lough Melvin Holiday Centre**
Garrison, Co Fermanagh.
☎ 028 6865 8142.

**Shannon-Erne Waterways**
Ballinamore, Co Leitrim.
☎ 078 45185.

**Silver Line Cruisers**
The Marina, Banagher,
Co Offaly.
☎ 0509 51112.

**Ulster Cruising School**
The Marina, Carrickfergus,
Co Antrim.
☎ 028 9336 8818.

### HUNTING AND SHOOTING

**Countryside Alliance**
47 Whiterock Road,
Killinchy, Co Down.
☎ 028 9754 1871.

**Irish Master of Foxhounds Association**
☎ 051 853981.

**Mount Juliet Estate**
Thomastown, Co Kilkenny.
☎ 056 24455.

### SPORTS FOR THE DISABLED

**Irish Wheelchair Association**
Aras Chuchulain,
Blackheath Drive,
Clontarf, Dublin 3.
☎ 01 8338241.

**Share Centre**
Smith's Strand, Lisnaskea,
Co Fermanagh.
☎ 028 6772 2122.

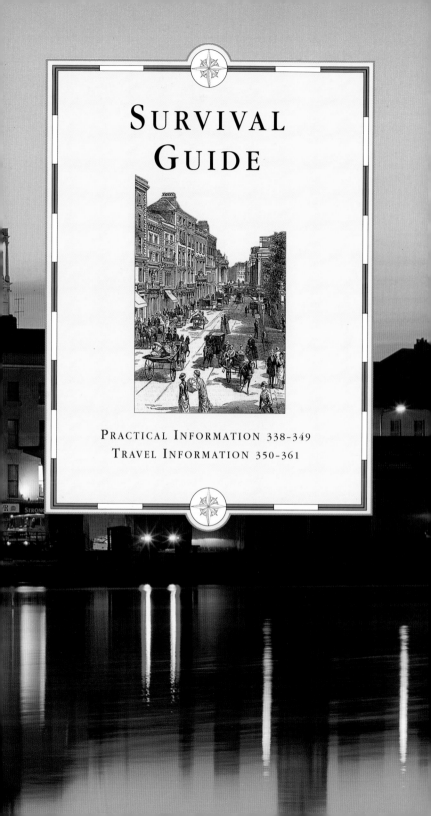

# SURVIVAL
# GUIDE

PRACTICAL INFORMATION 338-349
TRAVEL INFORMATION 350-361

# PRACTICAL INFORMATION

ALTHOUGH IRELAND is quite a small island, visitors should not expect to see everything in a short time, since many of the country's most magnificent attractions are in rural areas. In remote parts of the island the roads are narrow, the pace of life is very slow, banks often open for only one or two days of the week and public transport tends to be infrequent. However, although the Republic of Ireland remains one of

Bord Fáilte logo

Europe's most unspoilt nations, its economy is developing fast. Any decent-sized town in the Republic is likely to have a tourist information centre and offer a full range of facilities for the traveller. Northern Ireland has its own tourist board with offices in most towns. The standard of facilities available to those travelling in the North equals that across the border and, as with the Republic, the level of hospitality is first-rate.

## TOURIST INFORMATION

IN BOTH THE REPUBLIC and Northern Ireland there is an impressive network of tourist information offices. As well as providing lots of free local information, the tourist offices in large towns sell maps and guide books and can reserve accommodation for a nominal charge. There are also tourist information points in some of the smaller towns and villages. The opening hours can be somewhat erratic and many are open only during the summer season. The local museums and libraries often stock a selection of useful tourist literature.

Before leaving for Ireland you can get information from **Bord Fáilte** (Irish Tourist Board) or **Northern Ireland Tourist Board** (NITB) offices, which will supply you with maps and leaflets. Bord Fáilte offices can be found in major cities all over the world – a reflection of the universal appeal of Ireland. It's also worth contacting the regional tourist offices in Dublin, Cork, Limerick and Galway for more information on destinations, including accommodation and car rental. If you call at a tourist office in the Republic and pick up a list of places to stay, you shouldn't expect every local hotel and guesthouse to be included – these lists recommend only those establishments that have been approved by Bord Fáilte.

The Dúchas-run Parke's Castle in County Sligo (see p225)

## ADMISSION CHARGES

MOST OF IRELAND's major sights, including ancient monuments, museums and national parks, have an admission fee. For each place of interest in this guide, we specify whether or not there is a charge. The entrance fees in the Republic of Ireland are normally between 1.50 euro and 6.50 euros, with discounts for students and the elderly.

Heritage card giving access to historic sites

**Dúchas (The Heritage Service)** manages and maintains national parks, museums, monuments and gardens. At most Dúchas sites you can buy a Heritage Card,

Northern Ireland Tourist Board logo

which allows unlimited, free admission to all sites managed by Dúchas for a year. At 19 euros for adults, 13 euros for senior citizens, 7.60 euros for children and students, and 46 euros for a family ticket, the card is a good investment. Popular Dúchas sites include Céide Fields (see p196), Cahir Castle (see p190) and the Blaskett Centre (see p150). Entrance fees in Northern Ireland are about the same as in the Republic, with discounts for students and senior citizens. North of the border the **National Trust** has a scheme similar to the Heritage Card, but membership costs more (£31 per annum per person or £58 for families) and there are fewer sites. It is good value if you are also planning to visit National Trust sites in the UK.

**Interpretative centre at Connemara National Park** *(see p200)*

## OPENING TIMES

THE OPENING DAYS of sights are listed in this guide. Few places are open on a Sunday morning, and some museums are shut on Monday. Opening hours are generally between 10am and 5pm; some sights stay open a little later and others close for lunch.

From June to September all the sights are open but the crowds are at their biggest. In winter many tourist attractions are closed several days per week and keep shorter hours; some close down completely. There are also variations on public holidays – many places open for Easter and then close again until summer.

## INTERPRETATIVE CENTRES

MANY OF IRELAND'S major sights are ruins or Stone Age archaeological sites and can be difficult to appreciate. In recent years, however, money has become available for building interpretative or visitors' centres which explain the historical significance of sites. Entry to the site may be free, but you have to pay to visit the interpretative centre.

In areas of natural beauty, such as Connemara National Park, an interpretative centre acts as a useful focal point. The centre typically provides information leaflets and has reconstructions of sights. Connemara has 3D models and displays, as well as an audiovisual presentation on the development of the local landscape over the last 10,000 years. There is also a shop for postcards, books and posters.

## RELIGIOUS SERVICES

IRELAND is a deeply religious country and for much of the population, churchgoing is a way of life. Because the Republic of Ireland is 95 per cent Roman Catholic, finding a non-Catholic church may sometimes be difficult. In the Republic and Northern Ireland, the tourist offices, hotels and B&Bs all keep a list of local church service times.

### DIRECTORY

**IRISH TOURIST BOARD (BORD FÁILTE) OFFICES**

**Republic of Ireland**
Baggot St Bridge, Dublin 2.
( 01 6024000.

**United Kingdom**
150 New Bond St,
London W1Y 0AQ.
( 020 7518 0800.

**United States**
345 Park Avenue,
New York, NY 10154.
( (212) 418-0800.

**NORTHERN IRELAND TOURIST BOARD OFFICES**

**Northern Ireland Tourist Board**
St Anne's Court, 59 North St,
Belfast BT1 1NB.
( 028 9023 1221.
Belfast Welcome
47 Donegall Pl.
( 028 9024 6609.

**United Kingdom**
24 Haymarket,
London SW1Y 4DG.
( 020 77669920.

**United States**
Tourism Northern Ireland,
345 Park Avenue, 17th Floor, NY.
( (212) 418-0800.

**OTHER ADDRESSES**

**National Trust**
Rowallane House, Saintfield,
Ballynahinch, County Down
BT24 7LH. ( 028 9751 0721.

**Dúchas (Heritage Service)**
6 Upper Ely Place, Dublin 2.
( 01 647 2461/1890 321421.

## LANGUAGE

The Republic of Ireland is officially bilingual – almost all road signs have place names in both English and Irish. English is the spoken language everywhere apart from a few parts of the far west, called Gaeltachts *(see p221)*, but now and then you may find signs written only in Irish. Here are some of the words you are most likely to come across.

## USEFUL WORDS

*an banc* – **bank**
*an lár* – **town centre**
*an trá* – **beach**
*ar aghaidh* – **go**
*bád* – **boat**
*bealach amach* – **exit**
*bealach isteach* – **entrance**
*bus* – **bus**
*dúnta* – **closed**
*fáilte* – **welcome**
*fir* – **men**
*gardaí* – **police**
*leithreas* – **toilet**

**Sign using old form of Gaelic**

*mná* – **women**
*oifig an poist* – **post office**
*oscailte* – **open**
*óstán* – **hotel**
*siopa* – **shop**
*stop/stad* – **stop**
*ticéad* – **ticket**
*traein* – **train**

# Additional Information

**European Youth Card**

Iꜰᴇʟᴀɴᴅ ɪꜱ ᴅɪᴠɪᴅᴇᴅ between the state of the Republic of Ireland, and Northern Ireland – a province of the United Kingdom. Each has a separate currency, postal service and telecommunications system (see pp344–9). However, there are many similarities between them: they are part of the European Union, English is their first language and, both north and south of the border, the tourist industry is well advanced. These two pages describe the regulations that affect the Republic and Northern Ireland, and the special facilities that are available to travellers, including students and the disabled. There is also a general guide to the media in both the North and South as well as a directory of useful names and addresses.

**Students at Trinity College, Dublin**

## VISAS

Vɪꜱɪᴛᴏʀꜱ ꜰʀᴏᴍ the EU, US, Canada, Australia and New Zealand require a valid passport but not a visa for entry into the Republic or Northern Ireland. All others, including those wanting to study or take up work, should check with their local Irish or British Embassy first. UK nationals born in Britain or Northern Ireland do not strictly need a passport to enter the Republic of Ireland but should take one with them for car rental, cashing of traveller's cheques and medical services.

## DUTY-FREE GOODS AND CUSTOMS ALLOWANCES

Iɴ 1999 ᴛʜᴇ duty-free allowances on goods bought between the Republic of Ireland and other countries were abolished. However, a wide range of items may still be purchased at airport shops

and on ferries, including goods that were previously duty-free, such as beers, wines, spirits, perfume and cigarettes. Electrical goods and camera equipment, items which were traditionally considerably cheaper in duty-free, are still on sale at the airport shops but travellers should have some idea of comparative prices for the goods and know the different exchange rates before making an expensive purchase.

## STUDENT INFORMATION

Sᴛᴜᴅᴇɴᴛꜱ ᴡɪᴛʜ a valid ISIC card (International Student Identity Card) benefit from numerous travel discounts as well as reduced admission to museums and concerts. Buy a Travelsave stamp from any branch of **USIT** and affix it to your ISIC card to get a good discount on Irish Rail, NIR train services and Irish Ferries. A Travelsave stamp

will also get you discounts on Bus Éireann routes in the South and special rates on commuter tickets (Sep–Jun only) in Dublin, Limerick, Cork, Galway and Waterford. In the North, an ISIC card gives a 15 per cent discount on Ulsterbus services and 20 per cent on Belfast Citybus "Gold Card" commuter services. ISIC cards can be obtained from branches of USIT travel in Dublin, Belfast and other college towns.

USIT will also supply non-students under 26 with an EYC (European Youth Card) for discounts in restaurants, shops and theatres. The name of the card, which is recognized in over 20 European states, varies from country to country but can be identified by its distinctive logo.

## FACILITIES FOR THE DISABLED

Mᴏꜱᴛ ꜱɪɢʜᴛꜱ in Ireland have access for wheelchairs. This book gives basic information about disabled access for each sight, but it's worth phoning to check details. The Access Department of the **National Disability Authority** provides information for the Republic, publishing county guides to accommodation, restaurants and amenities. In the North, **Disability Action** can advise on accessibility, while the Open Arts organization has a list of entertainment venues and museums providing wheelchair access.

**Shop at Shannon Airport**

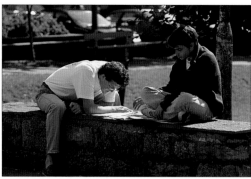
Relaxing with newspapers in Eyre Square, Galway

## RADIO AND TELEVISION

IRELAND has three state-controlled television channels, RTE 1, Network 2 and the Irish-language Teilifís na Gaelige (TG4), and one privately run channel, TV3. There are six national radio stations and many local ones.

The five British TV channels can be picked up in most parts of Ireland on Cable TV, which is commonly available in hotels in the Republic.

A selection of daily newspapers from North and South

## NEWSPAPERS AND MAGAZINES

THE REPUBLIC of Ireland has six national daily papers and five Sunday papers. Quality dailies include the *Irish Independent*, the *Examiner* and the *Irish Times*, the latter being well known for its journalistic excellence. The broadsheets are useful for up-to-date information on theatre and concerts. Ireland's daily tabloid is the *Star*. The North's top local paper is the *Belfast Telegraph*, on sale in the afternoon. The province's morning papers, the *News Letter* and *Irish News*, are less rewarding.

In larger towns throughout Ireland, British tabloids are on sale. Broadsheets such as *The Times* are also available and cost less than the quality Irish press. Most towns have a local or regional paper, which will tell you what's on and where.

*USA Today*, *Newsweek* and *Time* magazine are sold in major cities but are very hard to find in the countryside.

## IRISH TIME

THE WHOLE of Ireland is in the same time zone as Great Britain, i.e. five hours ahead of New York and Toronto, one hour behind Germany and France, and ten hours behind Sydney. In both the North and the South, clocks go forward one hour for summer time.

## CONVERSION CHART

### Imperial to Metric
1 inch = 2.5 centimetres
1 foot = 30 centimetres
1 mile = 1.6 kilometres
1 ounce = 28 grams
1 pound = 454 grams
1 pint = 0.6 litres
1 gallon = 4.6 litres

### Metric to Imperial
1 millimetre = 0.04 inches
1 centimetre = 0.4 inches
1 metre = 3 feet 3 inches
1 kilometre = 0.6 miles
1 gram = 0.04 ounces
1 kilogram = 2.2 pounds
1 litre = 1.8 pints

## METRICATION

THE CHANGE towards metrication is slow in Ireland, particularly the North, where distances are still measured in miles. In the Republic, all new road signs show distances in kilometres, but there are still many old ones left that use miles *(see p356)*. However, throughout Ireland all speed limits are shown in miles. In both Northern Ireland and the Republic, petrol is sold in litres but draught beer is always sold in pints. And just to add to the confusion, food may be weighed out either in imperial or in metric measures.

km **4 Ceann Trá**
**17 Dún Chaoin**

One of the new metric road signs used in the Republic of Ireland

# Personal Security and Health

IRELAND IS PROBABLY one of the safest places to travel in Europe. Petty theft, such as pickpocketing, is seldom a problem outside certain parts of Dublin and a few other large towns. Tourist offices and hoteliers gladly point out the areas to be avoided. In the recent past, the main security risk in Northern Ireland has been the threat of bombings, though this has hardly ever affected tourists. In fact, crimes against the individual tend to be fewer than in other parts of the UK and Europe.

Pharmacy in Dublin showing old-fashioned snake and goblet symbol

Pearse Street Garda Station, Dublin

## PERSONAL SECURITY

THE POLICE, should you ever need them, are called the Gardaí in the Republic of Ireland and the Police Service of Northern Ireland (PSNI) in the North. Violent street crime in Ireland – North or South – is relatively rare but it's still advisable to take suitable precautions, such as avoiding poorly lit streets in the cities and larger towns. Poverty and a degree of heroin addiction

Garda          PSNI policeman

in inner-city Dublin has been known to cause a few problems, and Limerick isn't the most inviting of places after dark. There have also been a number of racial attacks recently in Dublin. But if you take sensible precautions, avoiding back-streets at night and keeping to the popular and busy areas, there should be little cause for concern. In some of the larger southern towns you may be approached in the street by people asking for money. This rarely develops into a troublesome situation, but it is still best to avoid eye contact and leave the scene as quickly as possible.

## PERSONAL SAFETY IN NORTHERN IRELAND

EVEN at the height of the Troubles in Northern Ireland, there was never a significant threat to the tourist, and travelling around the province was deemed to be as safe as in the Republic. As long as peace exists north of the border, no extra precautions need to be taken there, but in the event of the Troubles resurfacing, first-time visitors should be prepared for certain unfamiliar situations. When driving, if you see a sign that indicates you are approaching a checkpoint, slow down and use dipped headlights. To keep fuss down to a minimum in these situations, it is a good idea to keep a passport or some other form of identification close at hand. If you are walking around the city centres of Belfast and

Londonderry, you may notice a strong police or military presence. This is unlikely to inconvenience you. Occasionally, however, you may be asked by shop security to reveal the contents of your bags – don't be alarmed, this is merely a routine procedure.

## PERSONAL PROPERTY

BEFORE YOU LEAVE, make sure that your possessions are insured, as it might be difficult and more expensive to do this in Ireland. Travel insurance for the UK will not cover you for the Republic, so make sure you have an adequate policy. As pickpocketing and bag-snatching can be a problem in some of the larger towns in the Republic, it's best not to carry around your passport or large amounts of cash, or leave them in your room. Most hotels have a safe and it makes sense to take advantage of this facility. Those carrying large amounts of money around should use traveller's cheques (see pp346–7). When out and about, use a bag that can be held securely, and be alert in crowded places and restaurants. A money belt may be a good investment.

If travelling by car, ensure all valuables are locked in the boot and always lock the car, even when leaving it for just a few minutes. If visiting Northern Ireland, do not leave any of your bags or packages unattended, as they are likely to result in a security scare.

Garda station

PSNI badge

## LOST PROPERTY AND LEFT LUGGAGE

REPORT ALL LOST or stolen items at once to the police. In order to make a claim against your insurance company you need to send in a copy of the police report. Most rail and bus stations in the Republic operate a lost-property service but there is no such service in Northern Ireland.

If you wish to do a day's sightseeing unencumbered by luggage most hotels and some main city tourist offices, both in the Republic and Northern Ireland, offer left luggage storage facilities.

## MEDICAL TREATMENT

RESIDENTS OF COUNTRIES in the European Union can claim free medical treatment in the Republic of Ireland by getting form E111 before setting out. In the event of illness, to avoid having to pay for any treatment and pre-scribed medicines, you'll need to show your E111 and a form of identification, such as a driving licence or passport. Also, be sure to let the doctor know that you want treatment under the EU's social security regulations. In Northern Ireland, British citizens need no documentation; visitors from other EU countries should follow the same procedure as for the Republic. Non-EU travellers should either have their own accident and health insurance or be willing to pay for any

Dublin ambulance

Dublin fire engine

Garda patrol car

treatment received. If you have private health insurance this may include a certain level of travel cover.

## PHARMACIES

A WIDE RANGE of medical supplies is available over the counter at pharmacies. However, many medicines are available only with a pre-scription authorized by a local doctor. If you are likely to require specialized drugs during your stay, take your own supplies with a copy of the original prescription. You can also ask your doctor to write a letter with the generic name of the medicine you require. Always obtain a receipt for insurance claims.

Until recently, condoms were not freely available in the Republic but are now relatively easy to obtain in the big cities at least. In some of the small towns you may discover that the pharmacist is opposed to contraception and does not sell condoms, but this is becoming a fairly rare occurrence. There are no such difficulties in Northern Ireland.

Small rural health centre in County Donegal

# Local Currency

T HE REPUBLIC and Northern Ireland have different
currencies. The euro is the currency in the Republic
and the pound sterling is the currency in Northern
Ireland, the same as in the United Kingdom. When
travelling between Northern Ireland and the Republic,
there's no shortage of money-changers in towns on
either side of the border. Look in the daily newspapers
for the standard rate of exchange to give yourself a
guideline. Some tourist attractions offer money changing
facilities but for the best exchange rates use the banks
or *bureaux de change*.

Ulster Bank sub-office in Delvin,
County Westmeath

## CURRENCY IN NORTHERN IRELAND

N ORTHERN IRELAND uses British currency –
the pound sterling (£), which is divided
into 100 pence (p). As there are no exchange
controls in the UK, there is no limit to the
amount of cash you can take into and out of
Northern Ireland. In addition to the British
currency, four provincial banks issue their own
banknotes, worth the same as their
counterparts. To tell them apart, look for the
words "Bank of England" on British notes. It
is best to use the provincial bank notes in
Northern Ireland rather than in the UK –
some shops may be reluctant to accept notes
that are unfamiliar to them.

### Banknotes
*British banknotes are issued in the
denominations £50, £20, £10 and £5.
Their different colours help make them
easily distinguishable.*

£50 note

£20 note

£10 note

£5 note

### Coins
*Coins come in the following
denominations: £2, £1, 50p, 20p, 10p,
5p, 2p and 1p. All have the Queen's
head on one side and are the same as
those elsewhere in the UK, except that
the pound coin has a different detail
- a flax plant - on the reverse side.*

£2        £1        50p

20p      10p      5p      2p      1p

## THE EURO

INTRODUCTION of the single European currency, the euro, is taking place in 12 of the 15 member states of the EU. Austria, Belgium, Finland, France, Germany, Greece, Ireland, Italy, Luxembourg, Netherlands, Portugal and Spain chose to join the new currency; the UK, Denmark and Sweden stayed out, with an option to review their decision. The euro was introduced on 1 January 1999, but only for banking purposes. Notes and coins came into circulation on 1 January 2002. A transition period has allowed euros and the punt (the Irish pound) to be used simultaneously. After July 2002, all currencies of the participating member states are being phased out, although there may be some local variation.

**Bank Notes**
*Euro bank notes have seven denominations. The 5-euro note (grey in colour) is the smallest, followed by the 10-euro (pink), 20-euro (blue), 50-euro (orange), 100-euro (green), 200-euro (yellow) and 500-euro (purple). All notes show the 12 stars of the EU and a specific style of European architecture.*

5 euros

10 euros

20 euros

50 euros

100 euros

200 euros

500 euros

2 euros

1 euro

50 cents

20 cents

10 cents

**Coins**
*The euro has eight coin denominations: 2 euros and 1 euro (gold and silver); 50 cents, 20 cents, 10 cents (gold); 5 cents, 2 cents and 1 cent (bronze). The reverse sides of all coins are the same in all euro-zone countries, while the obverse sides are different in each state.*

5 cents

2 cents

1 cent

# Banks in Ireland

Tᴴᴇ ᴏᴘᴇɴɪɴɢ ᴛɪᴍᴇs of banks in Ireland vary depending on whether the banks are situated in the town or country, in the Republic or Northern Ireland. Both north and south of the border, banks in small towns are often sub-offices where banking services may be provided on only one or two days of the week, so it's advisable to make the most of facilities in the bigger towns whenever you can. Banks throughout Ireland generally provide a very good service and, along with many of the larger post offices, will exchange traveller's cheques, often without charging commission.

**Bank of Ireland sub-office in Sneem, County Kerry**

## Usɪɴɢ Bᴀɴᴋs

Tʜᴇ ꜰɪᴠᴇ ʀᴇᴛᴀɪʟ ʙᴀɴᴋs in the Republic of Ireland are the Bank of Ireland, the Allied Irish Bank (AIB), the Ulster Bank, the National Irish Bank and the TSB Bank. In Northern Ireland there are four retail banks: the Ulster Bank, the Bank of Ireland, the Northern Bank and the First Trust Bank.

**Cash dispenser**

In the Republic of Ireland the usual banking hours are Monday to Friday from 10am to 12:30pm and from 1:30 to 4pm, but most branches now stay open during lunch time. There is extended opening (till 5pm) on one day of the week. In Dublin, Cork and most other cities and towns, late opening is on Thursdays but in rural areas banks often

**First Trust Bank logo**

stay open late on market day instead. Some rural areas are visited once or twice a week by a mobile bank. Check locally for days and times.

Branches of the TSB Bank remain open at lunch time and till 7pm on Thursdays and up to 5pm on other weekdays. Most banks in Northern Ireland open from 10am till 4pm, though a few close for lunch between 12:30 and 1:30pm. In both the Republic and in Northern Ireland, all banks close on public holidays, some of which differ from North to South (see p49). Banks in the cities and most towns are provided with automated teller machines, or cash dispensers, so if you discover the local bank is closed, it isn't necessarily a major catastrophe.

## Cʀᴇᴅɪᴛ Cᴀʀᴅs

Tʜʀᴏᴜɢʜᴏᴜᴛ ɪʀᴇʟᴀɴᴅ you can pay by credit card in most hotels, petrol stations, large shops and supermarkets. VISA or Mastercard (known also as Access) are the most commonly accepted credit cards. Fewer businesses take American Express and Diners Club cards. Cash can be withdrawn from banks displaying the appropriate sign.

## Tʀᴀᴠᴇʟʟᴇʀ's Cʜᴇǫᴜᴇs

Tʀᴀᴠᴇʟʟᴇʀ's ᴄʜᴇǫᴜᴇs are the safest way to carry around large amounts of money. These are best changed at one of the main banks but, failing this, many shops and restaurants accept them – usually for a small charge.

Traveller's cheques can be bought before setting out at American Express, Thomas

Ornate post office and *bureau de change* in Ventry, County Kerry

Cook or your own bank. In Ireland, traveller's cheques can be purchased at banks or from *bureaux de change*, which can be found in the larger cities and at airports.

## THE EURO

THE EURO BECAME legal tender in the Republic of Ireland and 10 other Member States on 1 January 1999 from which time electronic and paper transactions were made. Hard currency came into circulation on 1 January 2002, from which date it has been used for all transactions in all of the 11 Member States.

**Drawing money from an Allied Irish Bank cash dispenser**

## BUREAUX DE CHANGE

IN ADDITION to the foreign exchange counters at the main banks, there are some private *bureaux de change* in Dublin. As with most other exchange facilities, *bureaux de change* open later than banks. However, it's worth checking their rates before undertaking any transactions.

### BUREAUX DE CHANGE

**American Express**
41 Nassau Street, Dublin 2.
( 01 6799000.
Branches also at Dublin Tourism Centre, Suffolk Street & Killarney.

**Thomas Cook**
118 Grafton Street, Dublin 2.
( 01 6771721.
11 Donegall Place, Belfast.
( 028 9088 3900.
Branches also at Belfast International Airport, Ballymena, Bangor, Coleraine, Lisburn, Londonderry, Portadown & Newry.

# Sending a Letter

**Northern Ireland Post Office sign**

MAIN POST OFFICES in the Republic and Northern Ireland are usually open from 9am to 5:30pm during the week and from 9am to around 1pm on Saturdays, although times do vary. Some smaller offices close for lunch on weekdays and do not open on Saturdays. Standard letter and postcard stamps can also be bought from certain newsagents. The Republic of Ireland does not have a first- and second-class system, but sending a postcard is a few cents less expensive than a letter. Though it is

**Republic of Ireland Post Office logo**

improving all the time, the postal service in the Republic is still quite slow – allow three to four days when sending a letter to Great Britain and at least six days for the United States. Swiftpost guarantees delivery within two working days. In Northern Ireland, letters to other parts of the UK can be sent either first- or second-class, with most first-class letters reaching their UK destination the next day. The cost of a letter from Northern Ireland is the same to all EU countries.

## POSTBOXES

POSTBOXES in Ireland come in two colours – green in the Republic and red in the North. Many of Ireland's postboxes are quite historic. Some of those in the Republic even carry Queen Victoria's monogram on the front, a relic from the days of British rule. Even the smallest towns in Ireland have a postbox, from which the mail is collected regularly – anything from once to four times daily.

**Letter stamps used in the Republic of Ireland**

**First-class and second-class stamps used in the North**

First-class and overseas slot — Second-class slot

List of the daily collection times

Insignia of the British monarch

Monogram of Queen Victoria

**Postbox in the Republic**          **Northern Ireland double postbox**

# Using Ireland's Telephones

**eircom phonebox**

THE REPUBLIC's national telephone company, eircom (previously Telecom Eireann), once ran all the telephone services in the country, but changes in the law have meant that other companies can now provide public phones. Eircom's service includes up-to-date coin, card and credit card telephones that provide a modern, efficient service. For those intending to spend more than 5 euros on calls during their stay, it is worth using a phonecard, as these offer discounts. Northern Ireland uses British Telecom public phones. Both BT and eircom phonecards are available from newsagents, post offices, supermarkets and other retail outlets.

**Coffee and computers at the Central Cyber Café in Dublin**

## ACCESSING THE INTERNET

THE MAIN CITIES in the Republic have plenty of public access to computers and the Internet. Public facilities are available free of charge from public libraries, but you may have to book in advance. The easiest and fastest way to access the Internet is at one of the ever-increasing number of Internet cafés found all over Dublin and throughout the country in major towns and cities. The cafés generally charge by the minute for computer use, so costs build up quickly especially when including the cost of printed pages. Internet access is often cheaper during off-peak times so check charges beforehand.

## PHONING FROM THE REPUBLIC OF IRELAND

CHEAP CALL RATES within the Republic and to the UK are from 6pm to 8am on weekdays and all day at weekends. Off-peak times for international calls vary from country to country, but are generally as above.
• To call Northern Ireland: dial 048, then the area code, followed by the number.
• To call the UK: dial 00 44, the area code (minus the

leading 0), then the number.
• To call other countries: dial 00, followed by the country code (for example, 1 for the USA, 61 for Australia), the area code (minus the leading 0), then the number.
• Credit cards issued in certain countries including the USA, Australia and Canada are accepted as payment for calls to the country in which the card was issued.

## USING AN EIRCOM PHONE

1 Lift the receiver and wait for the dial tone.

2 Insert your phone card or credit card into the slot, or deposit any of the following coins: 10c, 20c, 50c, ¤1, ¤2. The minimum amount is 40c. Dial the number and wait to be connected.

3 The display indicates how much credit you have left. A rapid bleeping noise means your credit has run out. Insert more coins or another card.

4 If you want to make a further call and you have credit left, do not replace the receiver, press the follow-on-call button instead.

5 To redial the number you have just called, press the button marked "R".

6 After you have replaced the receiver, retrieve your card or collect your change. Only wholly unused coins are refunded.

**paying by credit card**

Simply talk

€4.00

€7.00

€15.00

**phonecards of varying amounts**

**1 euro**

**50 cents**

**20 cents**

**10 cents**

## PHONING FROM NORTHERN IRELAND

CHEAP CALL RATES within and from the Province are as for the Republic.

• For calls within Great Britain and Northern Ireland: dial the area code and the number required.

• For calls to the Republic of Ireland: dial 00 353, then the area code minus the first 0, then the number.

• For international calls: dial 00, then the country code (for example, 1 for Canada, 64 for New Zealand), then the area code minus the first 0, and finally the number you require.

In addition to using coins and pre-paid phonecards in the BT phone boxes as indicated below, credit card boxes are also available.

In 1999, all phone numbers in Northern Ireland changed from having a prefix of 01 and an area code, to having an area code of 028, followed by an 8-digit local number.

## USING A BT PHONE

1 Lift the receiver and wait for the dial tone.

2 Insert your phone card into the slot or deposit any of the following coins: 10p, 20p, 50p, £1, £2. The minimum amount is 20p.

3 Dial the number and wait to be connected.

4 The display indicates how much credit you have left. A rapid bleeping noise means your money has run out. Deposit more coins or insert another phone card.

5 If you want to make another call and you have money left in credit, do not replace the receiver, press the follow-on-call button.

6 When you have finished speaking, replace the receiver and retrieve your card or collect your change. Only wholly unused coins are refunded.

Phonecard *plus*    BT

| £1 | 50p | 20p | 10p | BT phonecard |

## PHONEBOXES IN NORTHERN IRELAND

*Most of the phone boxes in the Republic are modern. In Northern Ireland there are two different types of BT phone boxes: traditional red phoneboxes and a newer modern style. Both are issued with the same type of telephone. In both Northern Ireland and in the Republic, the wording around the top of each box indicates whether it is a coin, phonecard or credit card phone.*

**Old BT phonebox**     **New BT phonebox**

---

### USEFUL NUMBERS REPUBLIC OF IRELAND

**Emergency Calls**
📞 999.

**Directory Enquiries**
📞 11811 *(Republic and Northern Ireland)*.
📞 11818 *(all other countries)*.

**Operator Assistance**
📞 10 *(Ireland and Great Britain)*.
📞 114 *(international calls)*.

### USEFUL NUMBERS NORTHERN IRELAND

**Emergency Calls**
📞 999.

**Directory Enquiries**
📞 192 *(UK and Republic of Ireland)*.
📞 153 *(all other countries)*.

**Operator Assistance**
📞 100 *(UK)*.
📞 114 *(all other countries)*.

### INTERNET CAFÉS

**Armagh Computer World**
43 Scotch Street, Armagh.
📞 028 3751 0002.

**bean-there.com**
20 The Diamond, Derry.
📞 028 7128 1303.

**Bronco's Web Internet Café**
122 Great Victoria Street, Belfast.
📞 028 9080 8586.

**Central Cyber Café**
6 Grafton Street, Dublin.
📞 878 0295.

**Global Internet Café**
8 Lower O'Connell Street, Dublin.
📞 677 8298.

**Marconi Cyber Café**
Marconi House, Marand Park, Dun Laoghaire.
📞 230 0685.

**Revelations Internet Café**
27 Shaftesbury Square, Belfast.
📞 028 9032 0337.

# TRAVEL INFORMATION

IRELAND'S THREE main airports, Dublin, Shannon and Belfast, are well served by flights from Britain, the United States and an increasing number of countries around the world. If you are travelling by sea from the UK, there is a very good choice of ferry routes from ports in Britain to both the Republic and Northern Ireland. Instead of buying separate tickets, you can purchase combined coach/ferry and rail/ferry tickets from almost all of the towns in mainland Britain. The less-than-comprehensive public transport systems in both the North and South reflect the rural nature of the island. With this in mind, travelling around Ireland is probably best enjoyed if you embrace the Irish way of thinking and just take your time.

Aer Lingus Airbus in flight

The modern exterior of Dublin International Airport

## FLYING TO THE REPUBLIC OF IRELAND

FLIGHTS from most of the major cities in Europe arrive at **Dublin Airport**, which is the country's busiest airport. Regular services to the Republic depart from all five of the London airports (Heathrow, City, Gatwick, Luton and Stansted) and 15 other cities in Britain, plus the Channel Islands and the Isle of Man.

The major airline operating scheduled flights between Britain and the Republic is **Aer Lingus**, although since deregulation rival **Ryanair** has grown fast, with cheap fares from Stansted, Luton, Gatwick and other British airports. Aer Lingus and **Continental Airlines** fly direct from the US to Dublin Airport and **Shannon Airport**, ten miles outside Limerick – gone is the old ruling that all planes flying eastward to Dublin must first touch down at Shannon, but **Delta Airlines** do always stop at both airports. **Aeroflot** has non-stop flights from Moscow to Dublin and Shannon Airports.

**Cork Airport** is served by flights from London (Heathrow and Stansted), Birmingham, Manchester, Bristol, Plymouth, Cardiff, Swansea, Newcastle, Glasgow, Paris, Amsterdam and Dublin. None of the air-lines fly direct to Ireland from Australia and New Zealand, but there are connections from London and Moscow.

The Republic's other airports have fewer flights. There are many charter flights for pilgrims to **Knock International Airport** in Co Mayo, which also has flights from Dublin, London (Stansted) and Manchester. There are flights into Kerry from Dublin and Stansted airports and Waterford Airport has flights from both London and Luton. Galway is well served with five daily flights from Dublin.

## GETTING TO AND FROM THE AIRPORT

THE REPUBLIC'S three main airports are all served by regular bus services, whereas the smaller airports depend mainly on local taxi services. Two express bus services run between Dublin Airport the city's main rail and bus stations and the city centre every 15 to 20 minutes, from early morning to around midnight. The journey takes 30 minutes. At Cork, the Bus Éireann service takes 15 minutes, from the airport into the city. Buses run every 45 minutes on week-days and hourly at the week-ends. At Shannon Airport, Bus Éireann runs a regular service into Limerick which takes 35 minutes to the city centre. In addition, several buses a day go to the town of Ennis, about 30 km (18 miles) away. All airports in the Republic have both long- and short-stay parking facilities.

Information signs in the main concourse of Shannon Airport

One of the Airlink coaches which take passengers from Dublin Airport into the city centre

Passengers checking in at Belfast International Airport

## FLYING TO NORTHERN IRELAND

There are hourly flights, operated by either **British Airways** or **British Midland**, from London Heathrow to **Belfast International Airport** (BIA), 30 km (18 miles) north-west of Belfast city centre. BIA is also served by flights from Luton and some regional airports like Stansted, Bristol and Glasgow. There are also two **Easy Jet** flights every day from Amsterdam to Belfast International Airport.

**Belfast City Airport** is used by smaller aircraft, but is favoured by many because of its location – it is just 6.5 km (4 miles) from the city centre. The airport also has more flights from the UK – around 15 cities plus Gatwick, Stansted and Luton – than BIA. The City of Derry Airport is Northern Ireland's smallest, with one flight daily from Manchester and Glasgow.

## AIRPORT CONNECTIONS IN NORTHERN IRELAND

The arrangements for getting to and from the airports in Northern Ireland are generally good. BIA's Airbus service will take you from the airport to the Europa Bus centre via Oxford Street Bus Station and Central Railway Station. This runs every half hour and takes about 30 minutes from end to end. At Belfast City Airport the number 21 bus passes every half hour, taking around 10 minutes to get to the Belfast City Hall bus depot. There are trains from the airport to Central Station about every 30 minutes. Derry's airport is on a local bus route: the number 143 goes into the city centre once an hour (less frequently at weekends). All airports in Northern Ireland have taxi ranks and both long- and short-term parking facilities.

## AIR FARES

Airlines offer a host of options on air fares to Ireland from Britain. Usually, the amount you pay is determined by how flexible you are prepared to be and how far in advance you book. The best bargains tend to be on flights for which the dates are not changeable. It's not difficult to get a return flight from mainland UK to Dublin for well under £100. However, these tickets often stipulate that your stay must include a Saturday night. The cheapest place to fly from is usually London – in recent years, the air fares from Stansted and Luton to both Dublin Airport and Belfast International have been particularly low.

Ticket prices are generally fairly constant throughout the year except at Christmas, during summer and on bank holidays, when there are comparatively few discounted fares available. During these periods, due to the increased demand by visiting friends and relatives – referred to by airline companies as "VFR" – seats are taken well in advance. Many airlines offer discounts to those under 25, while USIT (see p340), Campus Travel and other specialist travel agents often have cheaper rates for students and under-26s.

Airport sign in English and Gaelic

← Arrivals ↙
↑ Shops    Siopaí
   Bar    Beár
↑ Snacks ✗ Sólaistí

# Arriving by Sea

Travelling by ferry is a popular way of getting to Ireland, especially for groups or families intending to tour the country by car. Nine ports in Great Britain and two in France provide ferry crossings to Ireland's six ports. Nowadays, all ferries are of the modern drive-on/drive-off variety with lounges, restaurants and, if you're sailing to the Republic, duty-free shops. Crossing the Irish Sea is now faster than ever before, thanks to a new generation of high-speed ferries.

Logo of Irish Ferries

Stena HSS on the Dun Laoghaire to Holyhead crossing

## FERRIES TO DUBLIN AND DUN LAOGHAIRE

There is a good choice of ferry services running between Wales and Ireland. **Irish Ferries**, the country's largest shipping company, operates on the Holyhead–Dublin Port route and has up to six crossings a day. The high-speed service takes 1 hour 49 minutes, while the conventional ferry takes about 3½ hours. **Stena Line** also operates two conventional ferry crossings each day on this route. Like most ferry companies, Irish Ferries does not operate on Christmas Day or on Boxing Day.

The service from Holyhead to the Dublin suburb of Dun Laoghaire – traditionally the busiest port in Ireland – is operated by Stena Line. This route is served by the Stena HSS (High-speed Sea Service). As the world's largest fast ferry, the HSS has the same passenger and vehicle capacity as the conventional ferries but its jet-engine propulsion gives it twice the speed.

Vehicle loading and unloading times on the fast ferries are considerably shorter than with other ferries. Passengers requiring special assistance at ports or on board the ship

should contact the company they are booked with at least 24 hours before the departure time. Like most other ferry companies, Irish Ferries and Stena Line take bicycles free of charge, but this should be mentioned when making your reservation. **P&O Irish Sea** operate an 18 hour crossing from Dublin Port to Cherbourg every Saturday between June and September.

## FERRIES TO ROSSLARE

Rosslare, in County Wexford, is the main port for crossings from South Wales to Ireland. Stena Line runs a service from Fishguard using both the conventional ferry and the speedier Sea Lynx

Irish Ferries ship loading up at Rosslare Harbour

catamaran-style ferries. Those intending to take a car on Sea Lynx should make sure the measurements of their vehicle, when fully loaded, are within those specified by Stena Line. The maximum dimensions allowable per vehicle are 3 m (10 ft) high by 6 m (20 ft) long and up to 3 tonnes.

Irish Ferries operates two crossings to Rosslare from Pembroke (4 hours) all year round. They also run a service from Roscoff in France (14 hours) between April and September. Both Irish Ferries and P&O run services to Rosslare from Cherbourg (18 hours). Cabins and berths are available on all crossings to Rosslare and should be booked in advance

## FERRIES TO CORK

The prospect of a 10-hour sea journey could be enough to deter some from taking the ferry to Cork, but for those heading for southwest Ireland, sailing to the small town of Ringaskiddy, near Cork, can help cut out a cross-Ireland car journey of up to 250 miles. During the high season, **Swansea Cork Ferries** has up to six crossings per week between the two cities but the service doesn't operate between the end of January and mid-March. The crossing takes about 10 hours.

There is also one route direct to Cork from Roscoff in France operated by **Brittany Ferries**. The ferry runs once a week leaving from Roscoff on a Saturday and from Cork on a Friday. The service is only available from April to September and the crossing time is 14 hours. Cabins and berths are available on routes to Cork but need to be

**Gallery overlooking the quayside at Rosslare Harbour**

booked well in advance in high season. There is a small charge for taking bicycles on Swansea Cork Ferries and should be mentioned when booking the ticket.

## PORT CONNECTIONS

ALL IRELAND'S PORTS have adequate bus and train connections. At Dublin Port, Bus Eireann buses meet ferry arrivals and take passengers into the city centre for a small charge. From Dun Laoghaire, DART trains run into Dublin every 10 to 15 minutes calling at Pearse Street, Tara Street and Connolly Stations. These go from the railway station near the main passenger concourse. Buses run from Dun Laoghaire to Eden Quay and Fleet Street in the city centre every 10 to 15 minutes. At all ports, taxis are there to meet arrivals. For those interested in car hire, Hertz has a desk at Dun Laoghaire. Passengers arriving at Dublin Port have to hire cars from the city centre.

**Directions for ferry passengers**

## RAIL AND COACH THROUGH-TICKETS

IT IS POSSIBLE TO TRAVEL from any railway station in Great Britain to any specified destination in Ireland on a combined sea/rail ticket. Combined tickets can be bought from most rail stations throughout Britain.

**Eurolines** runs a through-bus service from about 35 towns in Britain to over 100 destinations in the Republic.

**Translink** offers the same service to destinations throughout Northern Ireland. Tickets for both these coach companies can be booked through **National Express**, which has over 2,000 agents in Great Britain. Travellers from North America, Australia, New Zealand and certain countries in Asia can buy a Brit Ireland pass. As well as including the return ferry crossing to Ireland, it allows unlimited rail travel throughout Great Britain and Ireland on any five or ten days during one month.

| FERRY ROUTES TO THE REPUBLIC OF IRELAND | OPERATOR | LENGTH OF JOURNEY |
|---|---|---|
| Fishguard–Rosslare | Stena Line<br>Stena Line | 3hrs 30min (Stena Europe)<br>1hr 50min (Fastcraft) |
| Holyhead–Dublin | Irish Ferries<br>Stena Line | 1hr 49min (Jonathan Swift)<br>3hrs (Stena Forwarder) |
| Holyhead–Dun Laoghaire | Stena Line | 1hr 49min (Stena HSS) |
| Liverpool–Dublin | Norse Merchant Ferries<br>P&O<br>Seacat Dublin Maritime | 8hrs<br>7hrs 30min (Norbay)<br>3hrs 55min (Super Seacat 3) |
| Mostyn–Dublin | P&O<br>P&O | 6hrs (European Ambassador)<br>7hrs 30min (European Envoy) |
| Pembroke–Rosslare | Irish Ferries | 3hrs 45min (Isle of Inishmore) |
| Swansea–Cork | Swansea Cork Ferries | 10hrs |

## FERRIES TO BELFAST AND LARNE

THE FASTEST CROSSING to Belfast is the 90-minute **SeaCat** service from Stranraer in Scotland. This catamaran-style ferry sails up to four times per day, all year round. On the same route, Stena Line has introduced the second of their new HSS ferries. On these the sailing time is only 15 minutes longer than that of the SeaCat.

A Liverpool to Belfast service is run by **Norse Merchant Ferries**, leaving Liverpool every evening and three mornings a week, all year, and taking over 8 hours to reach Belfast. Crossing the Irish Sea with the **Isle of Man Steam Packet Co** lets you visit the Isle of Man en route. Leaving from both Liverpool and Heysham, this service provides the added advantage of allowing you to disembark at Dublin and return from Belfast or vice versa.

There are now three routes to Larne (north of Belfast) from the Scotand ports of Cairnryan (1 hour 45 minutes), Troon (4 hours) and Fleetwood (8 hours). The services are operated by **P&O Irish Sea**, who run both conventional ferries and the new high-speed Jetliner on the Larne–Cairnryan route. This service runs from mid-March to mid-September and takes only an hour. During the week in high season there are a total of eight sailings each day to Cairnryan.

Cars and lorries disembarking at Larne Port

### PORT CONNECTIONS

ALTHOUGH it takes only ten minutes on foot into the city centre from Belfast Port, Flexibus shuttles are on hand to take ferry passengers into the city centre via the Europa Buscentre and Central Railway Station. A regular bus service connects Larne Harbour to the town's bus station, and from here, buses run every hour into Belfast city centre. From Larne Port, there are trains to take ferry passengers to Belfast's Yorkgate and Central railway stations. Taxis are available at both ports.

**Port of Belfast logo**

### FARES AND CONCESSIONS

FARES ON FERRY CROSSINGS to Ireland vary dramatically according to the season – prices on certain days during the peak period of mid-June to mid-September can be double those at other times of the year. Prices increase greatly during the Christmas and New Year period, too. It is advisable to book your journey both ways before setting out. Those travelling to ports without a reservation should always check availability before setting out.

Often, the cheapest way for families or groups of adults to travel is to buy a ticket that allows you to take a car plus a maximum number of passengers. At certain times of the year on particular routes, the return ticket for a car and five adults (two children count as one adult) can cost less than 65 euros. The cheapest crossings are usually those where the passenger must depart and return within a specified period. Fares are normally reduced for mid-week travel and early-morning or late-night crossings. Ferry companies offer discounts for students bearing an ISIC card *(see p340)* and some have cut-price deals for those with InterRail tickets *(see p359)*.

| FERRY ROUTES TO NORTHERN IRELAND | OPERATOR | LENGTH OF JOURNEY |
|---|---|---|
| Cairnryan–Larne | P&O<br>P&O<br>P&O | 1hr 45min (European Causeway)<br>1hr (Superstar Express)<br>1hr 45min (European Highlander) |
| Fleetwood–Larne | P&O<br>P&O | 8hrs (European Pioneer)<br>8hrs (European Leader) |
| Heysham–Belfast | Seacat Scotland | 4hrs (Seacat Rapide) |
| Liverpool–Belfast | Norse Merchant Ferries | 9hrs |
| Stranraer–Belfast | Stena Line | 1hr 45 (Stena HSS)<br>3hrs 15min (Stena Caledonia) |
| Troon–Belfast | Seacat Scotland | 2hrs 30min |
| Troon–Larne | P&O | 4hrs (European Navigator) |

# On the Road

O NE OF THE BEST WAYS to see Ireland's magnificent scenery and ancient sites is by car. Driving on the narrow, twisting country roads can be a pleasure; often you don't see another vehicle for miles. It can also be frustrating, especially if you find yourself stuck behind a slow-moving tractor or a herd of cows. If you don't want to take your own vehicle, car rental in Ireland is no problem. All the international car hire firms operate in the Republic and are also well represented in the North. Touring by bicycle is another enjoyable way of seeing the best parts of the island at your own leisurely pace.

Gaelic road sign instructing motorists to yield or give way

## TAKING YOUR OWN CAR

I F YOU INTEND to take your own car across on the ferry *(see pp352–4)* check your car insurance to find out how well you are covered. To prevent a fully comprehensive policy being downgraded to third-party cover, ask your insurance company for a Green Card. Carry your insurance certificate, Green Card, proof of ownership of the car and, importantly, your driver's licence. If your licence was issued in Great Britain, you should also bring your passport with you for ID.

Membership of a reputable breakdown service like the **AA**, **RAC** or **Green Flag National Breakdown** is advisable unless you are undaunted by the prospect of breaking down in remote parts. Non-members can sign up for just the duration of their holiday. Depending on the type of cover, breakdown organizations may offer only limited services in Ireland.

## RENTING A CAR

C AR RENTAL FIRMS do good business in Ireland, so in summer it's wise to book ahead. Car hire – particularly in the Republic – is quite expensive and the best rates are often obtained by hiring in advance. Broker companies, such as **Holiday Autos**, use the major rental companies and will shop around to get you the best deal. Savings can also be made by choosing a fly-drive or even a rail-sail-drive holiday, but always check for hidden extras. Car rental usually includes unlimited mileage plus passenger

One for the road

indemnity insurance and cover for third party, fire and theft, but not damage to the vehicle. If you plan to cross the border in either direction, however briefly, you must tell the rental company, as there may be a small insurance premium to be paid.

To rent a car, you must show a full driving licence, which you should have held for two years without endorsement. Cars are usually rented only to those aged between 23 and 70, but some companies may make exceptions.

## BUYING PETROL

U NLEADED PETROL and diesel fuel are available just about everywhere in Ireland. Although prices vary from station to station, petrol in the Republic is quite expensive. In Northern Ireland it is slightly cheaper. Almost all the petrol stations accept VISA and Mastercard, although it is worth checking before filling up, particularly in rural areas.

## ROAD MAPS

T HE ROAD MAP on the inside back cover shows all the towns and villages mentioned in this guide. In addition, each chapter starts with a map of the region showing all the major sights and providing tips on getting around. However, if you plan to do much driving or cycling, you should equip yourself with a more detailed map. Ordnance Survey Holiday Maps are among the best road maps. You can usually get town plans free from tourist offices *(see p338)*. The tourist boards of the Republic and Northern Ireland both issue free lists of suggested routes for cyclists.

A busy Hertz car rental desk at Dublin Airport

The familiar sight of a farmer and cattle on an Irish country road

## RULES OF THE ROAD

E VEN FOR THOSE unused to driving on the left, motoring in Ireland is unlikely to pose any great problems. For many, the most difficult aspect of driving on Ireland's roads is getting used to overtaking on the right and giving way to traffic on the right at roundabouts. On both sides of the border, the wearing of safety belts is compulsory for drivers and all front-seat passengers; where fitted, rear safety belts must be worn. All children must have a suitable restraint system. Motorcyclists and passengers must wear crash helmets. Northern Ireland uses the same Highway Code as Great Britain. The Republic of Ireland's Highway Code is very similar – copies of both

Speed limit signs in mph on a country road in County Cork

are available from bookstores. In Northern Ireland, you will notice some cars carrying a red "R" plate. These identify "restricted" drivers who have passed their driving test within the previous 12 months and have to keep to lower speeds.

## SPEED LIMITS

I N THE REPUBLIC and Northern Ireland the maximum speed limits, which are shown in miles, are more or less the same as those in Britain:
• 30 mph (50 km/h) in built-up areas.
• 60 mph (95 km/h) outside built-up areas.
• 70 mph (110 km/h) on motorways.
On certain roads, which are clearly marked, the speed limits are either 40 mph (65 km/h) or 50 mph (80 km/h). Where there is no indication, the speed limit is 60 mph (95 km/h). In the Republic, vehicles towing caravans must not exceed 55 mph (90 km/h) on any road. Speed limits are strictly enforced in both the North and the Republic.

## ROAD SIGNS

M OST ROAD SIGNS in the Republic are in both Gaelic and English. Ireland is striving toward metrication so all the new-style green and white signs are in kilometres. However, nothing's quite that simple in Ireland, so expect to come across some black-on-white signs showing distances in miles. As in Britain, road signs in the North are always

in miles. One road sign that is unique to the Republic is the "Yield" sign – in the UK this is worded "Give Way". Throughout both the Republic and Northern Ireland, brown signs with white lettering indicate places of historic, cultural or leisure interest.

**SIGNS IN THE REPUBLIC**

Unprotected quay or river ahead

Junction ahead

Children or school ahead

Dangerous bends ahead

**SIGNS IN NORTHERN IRELAND**

Motorway direction sign

Primary route sign

## ROAD CONDITIONS

N ORTHERN IRELAND'S roads are well surfaced and generally in better condition than those in the Republic, though there are just as many winding stretches requiring extra caution. The volume of traffic, particularly in the South, is much lower than in Britain. On some of the more rural roads you may not come across another vehicle for miles. Even the major roads can be surprisingly quiet. There are only a few sections of motorway in the whole of Ireland, though recent years have seen extensive construction of dual carriageways in the Republic, including rural areas such as County Donegal.

## PARKING

PREDICTABLY, in a country with so little congestion, finding a parking place is rarely a problem in Ireland but is becoming so in Dublin. Most towns have at least one free car park. Dublin, Belfast and a few other cities have either parking meters or (fairly expensive) car parks. Parking on the street is allowed, though a single yellow line along the edge of the road means there are some restrictions (there should be a sign nearby showing the permitted parking times). Double yellow lines indicates no parking is allowed at any time.

Disc parking and "pay & display" operate in most large towns and cities in the Republic of Ireland. Discs can be purchased from local newsagents, petrol stations, tourist offices and many small shops. In Northern Ireland, almost all towns and villages have Control Zones, which are indicated by large yellow or pink signs. For security reasons, unattended parking in a Control Zone is not permitted at any time of the day.

**Parking disc sign**

**Warning sign in Northern Ireland**

## CYCLING

THE QUIET ROADS of Ireland help to make touring by bicycle a real joy. The **Raleigh** **Rent-a-Bike** network of cycle dealers operates a reasonably priced rental scheme throughout Ireland. Also local shops, such as **Cycle Ways** in Dublin, rent cycles to tourists and are open at least six days a week. You can often hire a bike in one town and drop it off at another for a small charge. Many dealers can also provide safety helmets, but bring your own lightweight waterproof clothing to help cope with the unpredictable weather. Buses and trains will carry bikes for a surcharge.

## SECURITY ROADBLOCKS IN NORTHERN IRELAND

IN THE LATE 1960s, when the Northern Ireland conflicts began, roadblocks were introduced on to the roads of the province. These days if you are travelling by road, whether in the centre of Londonderry or the remote Sperrin Mountains, you may come across several roadblocks or none at all, depending on the political climate at the time. Checkpoints can be staffed by either the army or the police, who will ask for proof of identity. In the unlikely event of being stopped, show your driving licence and insurance certificate or rental agreement when asked and don't make any sudden movements.

---

### DIRECTORY

#### CAR HIRE COMPANIES

**Alamo**
📞 0870 599 6000 (UK).
📞 (800) 327 9633 (US).

**Argus Rent-a-Car**
📞 01 4904444 (Dublin).

**Avis**
📞 1890 40 50 60 (Dublin).
📞 0870 60 60 100 (UK).
📞 028 9024 0404 (Belfast).

**Budget**
📞 01 8445919 (Dublin).
📞 (800) 284 2354 (US).

**Dan Dooley**
📞 01 6772723 (Dublin).
📞 062 53103 (Limerick).

**Hertz**
📞 01 8445466 (Dublin).
📞 0870 599 6699 (UK).

**Holiday Autos**
📞 8705 300454 (UK).

**Murrays/Europcar**
📞 01 6681777 (Dublin).
📞 028 9442 3444 (Belfast).
📞 (877) 940 6900 (US).

**National Car Rental**
📞 021 4318623 (Cork).

**Irish Car Rentals**
📞 061 453049 (Limerick).
📞 00800 47474227 (UK).

#### BREAKDOWN AND RECOVERY SERVICES

**Automobile Association (AA)**
📞 01 617 9977 (to enrol in the Republic of Ireland).
📞 Rescue No. 1800 667788.

**Royal Automobile Club (RAC)**
📞 1800 483483 (to enrol in the Republic of Ireland).
📞 Rescue No. 1800 535005.

**Green Flag National Breakdown**
📞 0800 000111 (to enrol in UK).

#### BICYCLE-HIRE SHOPS

**Cycle Ways**
185-6 Parnell Street,
Dublin 1. 📞 01 873 4748.

**Raleigh Rent-a-Bike**
Unit 1, Finches Park, Longmile Rd,
Dublin 12. 📞 01 456 5280.

**Belfield Bike Shop** (UCD)
Dublin 4. 📞 01 706 1697.

**Cyclists checking their directions in Ballyvaughan, County Clare**

# Travelling by Train

Ｔ HE REPUBLIC OF IRELAND'S RAILWAY NETWORK is run by
**Irish Rail** (Iarnród Éireann) and is state-controlled.
The rail network is far from comprehensive and quite
expensive, but the trains are generally reliable and
comfortable and can be a good way of covering long
distances. The service provided by **Northern Ireland
Railways** (NIR) is more limited but fares are slightly
cheaper. There is an excellent train service between
Dublin and Belfast, with a journey time of just under
two hours. Fares can be as little as 22 euros return.

Train at Killarney station on the
southwest rail network

## TRAIN SERVICES IN THE
## REPUBLIC OF IRELAND

Ａ LTHOUGH the more rural
areas in the Republic of
Ireland are not served by
railways, Irish Rail operates a
satisfactory service to most of
the large cities and towns.
Going by rail is probably the
fastest and most convenient
way of travelling from Dublin
to places like Waterford,
Cork, Limerick and Galway.
However, there are glaring
gaps in the rail network; for
example, Donegal is totally
devoid of train services, so if
you are planning to explore

the west coast of Ireland using
public transport, you will have
to continue westward from
towns such as Galway, Sligo,
Limerick and Westport using
the local bus services.

The two main rail stations
in Dublin are Connolly, for
trains to the north, northwest
and Rosslare, and Heuston,
which serves the west, midlands and southwest. These
two stations are connected by
the No. 90 bus service which
runs every 10 to 15 minutes
and takes a quarter of an
hour – traffic permitting. All
trains in the Republic of
Ireland have standard and

super-standard (first-class)
compartments. Bicycles can
be taken on trains but there is
a supplement of up to 8 euros.

## OUTER DUBLIN RAIL
## SERVICES

Ｔ HE HANDY electric rail
service known as DART
(Dublin Area Rapid Transit)
serves 30 stations between
Malahide and Greystones with
several stops in Dublin city
centre. A Rail/Bus ticket
allows three consecutive days'
travel on DART trains as well
as Dublin Bus services. Tickets
can be purchased at any of the
DART Stations. The Luas light
rail service connects central
Dublin with the suburbs. The
first lines are set for completion
in 2003, and will eventually
intersect with the DART.

## TRAIN SERVICES IN
## NORTHERN IRELAND

Ｏ THER THAN an express
service out to Larne
Harbour and a commuter line
to Bangor, there are only two
main routes out of Belfast: a
line westward to Londonderry
via Coleraine (for the Giant's
Causeway) and Ireland's only
cross-border service, operating
a high-speed link between
Belfast and Dublin eight times
a day. All trains leave from
Central Station except for the
Larne Harbour link, which
departs from Yorkgate. Great
Victoria Street station opened
in 1995 and brings rail travellers right to the heart of the
city's business and shopping
district. Bear in mind that
there are no left-luggage facilities at any of Northern Ireland's
train or bus stations.

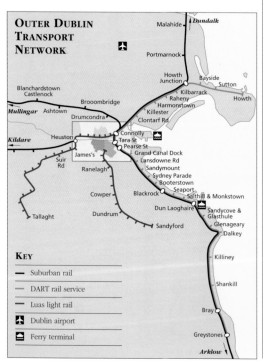

**OUTER DUBLIN
TRANSPORT
NETWORK**

**KEY**

— Suburban rail

– – DART rail service

— Luas light rail

✈ Dublin airport

⛴ Ferry terminal

## TICKETS AND FARES

THROUGHOUT IRELAND, train tickets are generally quite expensive, but there are lots of good value incentive or concessionary passes. Most of these include bus travel, so you can get virtually anywhere in Ireland on one ticket.

The most comprehensive ticket available is the Emerald Card, which can be used on all Irish Rail, Northern Ireland Railways, Dublin Bus and Ulsterbus services. For around 158 euros the Emerald Card gives eight days' unlimited travel in a 15-day period. An 8-day Irish Explorer ticket is slightly cheaper and is valid on all Irish Rail and Bus Éireann transport. For rail travellers, the Irish Rover ticket can be good value. It is valid on all Irish Rail and Northern Ireland Railways journeys for five days within a 15-day period.

**The modern ticket office at Belfast's Central Station**

### CONCESSIONS

STUDENTS CAN BUY a Travel-save Stamp *(see p340)* to affix to their ISIC cards for discounts on train fares. For those under 26, Faircards give good discounts on all Irish Rail single journeys, and can be bought from USIT *(see p340).*

Under-26 InterRail passes allow unlimited rail travel for 15 days or one month in the Republic and 25 other European countries. Older travellers can get InterRail Plus 26 cards costing slightly more. However, InterRail cards allow only a one-third discount on Northern Ireland Railways.

## IRELAND'S RAIL NETWORK

### Irish Rail (Iarnród Éireann)
35 Abbey St Lower, Dublin 1.
**(** *01 8366222.*

### Northern Ireland Railways
Central Station, East Bridge St, Belfast BT1 3PB.
**(** *028 9089 9411.*

# Travelling by Bus and Taxi

THE BUS SERVICES THROUGHOUT IRELAND are quite good, for such a rural island. However, longer journeys often involve changing buses en route so extra travelling time should be allowed for. Touring by coach is also a good way to see Ireland – local tourist offices have details of tours as well as prices and often take bookings. Taxi services are available in all major cities and towns in Ireland. In the Republic, taxis are usually saloon cars and are identified by a yellow light on the roof. In the North, cities like Belfast and Londonderry have both mini-cabs and London-style black cabs.

Boarding a bus at the Europa Buscentre in Belfast

# Bus Éireann

Logo on Bus Éireann local and express buses

## GETTING AROUND BY BUS

THE REPUBLIC OF IRELAND'S national bus company, **Bus Éireann**, operates a countrywide network of buses serving all the cities and most of the towns. In Dublin, the main bus station is the Busáras on Store Street, a short walk from O'Connell Street. There are a number of private bus companies which either compete with the national network or provide services on routes not covered by Bus Éireann. In rural Donegal, for example, there are several private bus services. Some are not fully licensed, so check whether you would be covered in the event of an accident. Local tourist offices should be able to point out the most reputable firms.

**Ulsterbus** runs an excellent service throughout Northern Ireland including express links between all the major towns. Belfast has two main bus stations – the Europa Buscentre off Great Victoria Street and Oxford Street Station. Check before setting out that you are going to the right one. Note that for reasons of security, there are no left-luggage facilities at any of the stations in Northern Ireland.

## FARES AND TICKETS

IN THE REPUBLIC, long-distance buses are about half the price of the equivalent rail journey. If you are making the return trip on the same day, ask for a day-return ticket, which is much cheaper than the normal return fare. Also, between Tuesday and Thursday you can buy a "period" return ticket for the price of a single journey. Under 16s pay half the adult fare. Students with a Travelsave stamp *(see p340)* get a 30 per cent reduction. For those intending to do a lot of travelling it is cheaper to buy a "Rambler" ticket. This allows unlimited bus travel throughout the Republic for a certain number of days in a set period, for example, 15 days' travel out of 30 consecutive days.

A "Freedom of Northern Ireland" ticket gives you unlimited travel on all Ulsterbus routes for either a day or a week. Ulsterbus also offers cheap day-return tickets. Students can get a 15 per cent discount by showing their ISIC card. There are also a number of period passes available that combine bus and rail travel *(see p359)*.

## COACH TOURS

WHILE THE BUS SERVICES in Ireland are generally adequate for getting from town to town, using public transport isn't a very practical way of exploring specific areas or regions in great detail, unless you have a lot of time on your hands. If you find yourself in a remote area like Connemara *(see pp198–201)* but have only a very limited amount of time in which to see its main attractions, a local guided tour of the area is a good idea. For about 13 euros per adult you can do the picturesque "figure of eight" circuit by coach, starting from Galway and taking in Spiddal, Kylemore, Letter-frack, Oughterard and then returning to Galway. The coach sets out at 10am and returns at about 5:30pm, making regular stops at places of interest. The price does not include admission fees or

Express service coach in Northern Ireland

lunch. Bookings are made at Galway Tourist Information Centre and can be arranged in advance or on the day. Four-hour or one-day tours such as this are available in many of Ireland's main tourist areas. Other popular tours of rural Ireland include Glendalough *(see pp132–3)*, Donegal *(see pp216–23)*, and the Ring of Kerry *(see pp156–7)*. In Dublin and other cities in the Republic, Bus Éireann and some local companies run half- and one-day excursions. **Dublin Bus** (Bus Átha Cliath) runs a Dublin City tour, which leaves from O'Connell Street Upper. This guided tour takes in the city's most famous sights.

In Northern Ireland, Ulsterbus operates a number of tours from the Europa Buscentre in Belfast to all the major places of interest. These tours include the Causeway Coast, the Glens of Antrim and the Ulster-American Folk Park near Omagh. Ulsterbus prefers bookings to be made in person at their Belfast office rather than over the phone. During the summer, **Belfast Citybus** operates up to three guided bus tours a week around the city.

## LOCAL TRANSPORT

L OCAL BUS SERVICES throughout the Republic are generally well-run and reasonably priced. **Dublin Bus** runs the bus services in the Greater Dublin area. Buses in the city centre run from about 6am until 11:30pm with an

**Passengers alighting from a Waterford city bus**

extended nitelink service at weekends. One-day passes, costing 5 euros, are good value. The new on-street light rail service, **Luas**, provides an easy way to reach suburban areas previously only accessible by bus. The Luas lines will eventually connect with the DART rail service *(see p358)* and a proposed Metro system. In the rest of the Republic the bus services, including city buses in Galway, Limerick, Waterford and Cork, are operated mainly by Bus Éireann; a comprehensive timetable is available at tourist offices and bus stations. Some bus routes connecting towns and villages are served by private companies as well as Bus Éireann. For bus times (and stops) in more remote areas, try asking the locals.

Except for Belfast, Northern Ireland's bus network is run by **Ulsterbus/Translink**. In the province's capital the local service is operated by **Citybus**. A wide variety of travel passes are available for Citybus and Ulsterbus/Translink lines. Regional timetables are available at bus stations.

## TAXIS IN THE REPUBLIC

E XCEPT in the most rural of places, there is usually a local taxi service – your hotel or B&B will provide details. In Dublin, taxis range from saloon cars to people carriers. Cruising taxis are a rarity: the best places to find taxis are at rail or bus stations, hotels and taxi ranks. Prices are usually based on metered mileage; if not, always ask the fare to your destination.

## TAXIS IN NORTHERN IRELAND

T AXIS IN NORTHERN IRELAND are reasonably priced. Journeys within the centre of Belfast usually cost no more than £4 by mini-cab or black cab. In most decent-sized towns in the North you will find at least one taxi office or rank where you can queue for a cab. Otherwise, ask for the number of a taxi firm at a local hotel or B&B.

---

### DIRECTORY

#### NATIONAL BUS COMPANIES

**Bus Éireann**
( 01 8366111.

**Ulsterbus/Translink**
( 028 9033 3000.
( 028 9033 7004 (day tours).

#### CITY TRANSPORT

**Citybus**
( 028 9024 6485.
( 028 9045 8484 (day tours).

**Dublin Bus**
( 01 8734222.

**Luas**
( 01 7032029.

#### COACH TOUR COMPANIES

**Guide Friday Ireland**
13 South Leinster Street, Dublin 2.
( 01 605 7705.

**McGeehan Coaches**
Fintown PO, Co Donegal.
( 075 46101.

**Taxis lined up outside the arrivals building at Dublin Airport**

# General Index

Page numbers in **bold** type refer to main entries.

## A

A-Wear (Dublin) 325
Abbey Theatre (Dublin) **86**, 105
  Dublin's Best: Entertainment 107
  history 42
  Literary Ireland 20–21
  Street-by-Street map 85
Abbeyleix, pubs 321
Abbeys and priories
  Assaroe Abbey (Ballyshannon) 223
  Athassel Priory **190**
  Augustinian Priory (Adare) 186
  Black Abbey (Kilkenny) 136
  Bonamargy Friary 258
  Boyle Abbey 211
  Cahir Abbey 190
  Clare Abbey (Ennis) 181
  Cong Abbey 201
  Donegal Abbey 222
  Duiske Abbey 141
  Dunbrody Abbey 140
  Ennis Friary 181
  Fore Abbey **233**
  Grey Abbey 272
  Holy Cross Abbey **187**
  Hore Abbey 187
  Inch Abbey 273
  Jerpoint Abbey **137**
  Kylemore Abbey **200**
  Mellifont Abbey 33, **237**
  Moore Abbey (Monasterevin) 120
  Muckross Abbey 154
  Portumna Priory 205
  Quin Franciscan Friary 181
  Red Abbey (Cork) 168
  Rock of Cashel **114**
  St Mary's Abbey (Dublin) **91**
  Selskar Abbey (Waterford) 142
  Sligo Abbey 226
  Timoleague Abbey **162–3**
  Tintern Abbey 140
  *see also* Monasteries
Achill Archaeological Summer
  School 331
Achill Island **196**
  restaurants 313
Act of Union (1800) 38
Adair, John 216
Adams, Gerry 45
Adare 13, **186**
  hotels 294
  restaurants 312
Adare Jazz Festival 46
Adare Manor 284, 302
Admission charges 338
Aer Lingus 350, 351
Aeroflot 351
Aglish, hotels 294
Agricola 31
Ahenny 191
  High Cross 235

Aherlow, Glen of **190**
Aherlow, hotels 294
Aherlow, River 190
Aillwee Cave 180
Air travel 350–51
Aird's Snout 254
Airports
  Belfast City 351
  Belfast International 351
  Cork 351
  Dublin International **350**, 351, 361
  Knock International 351
  Shannon 340, **350**, 351
Albert, Prince Consort 271
Alcock and Brown Memorial 199
Alcohol, duty-free allowances 340
All-Ireland Football Final 27, 48
All-Ireland Hurling Final 27, 48
Allen, Lough 177
Allied Irish Bank (AIB) 346
Allihies 158
Allingham, William 223
Allow, River 169
Altamont, Earls of 197
Altamont, John Browne, 1st Earl 196
Ambulances 342, 343
American Express 347
An Béal Bocht (Dublin restaurant) 105
An Óige 283
*An Taisce* (Irish National Trust) 80
An Tostal 46
Anderson, John 169
Andrews Lane Theatre (Dublin) 105
Anglo-Irish Agreement 45
Anglo-Irish families 117
  The Pale 124
Anglo-Irish Treaty (1921) 42–3
Anglo-Normans **34–5**
  Dublin Castle 71, 74
  invasion of Ireland 29, 117
Animals, wildlife 16–17
Annalong, hotels 300
*The Annals of the Four Masters* 37
Antrim, County 247
  coastline map 253
  map 248–9
Apprentice boys (Londonderry) 37
Aquariums
  Exploris (Portaferry) 272
Aran Islands 20, **206–7**
  pubs 320
  restaurants 313
Aranmore 220
Áras an Uachtaráin (Dublin) 94
Archaeological holidays 330, 331
Architecture **18–19**
  Georgian terraces **67**
Ardagh 233
Ardagh Chalice 53, 64
Ardara **220**
  hotels 297
Ardboe Cross 260
Ardclinis Activity Centre
  (Cushendall) 335

Ardee
  hotels 299
Ardess Crafts Centre (Kesh) 331
Ardfert Cathedral 147, **148**
Ardglass 276
Ardgroom 158
Ardilaun, Lord 58
Ardmore 19, **137**
Ards Peninsula **272**
Argus Rent-a-Car 357
Arkle 121
Armada, French (1796)
  French Armada Centre 160
Armada, Spanish (1588)
  history 36
  treasure 270
  Ulster Museum 270
  wreck 249
Armagh **266**
  Christianity 32
  hotels 300
  restaurants 316
Armagh, County 247
Arrow, Lough 215, **227**
Arsenius, Mother 197
*Asgard* (ship) 95
Ashford Castle 201, 284
Ashtown Castle (Dublin) 94
Askeaton 176
Assaroe Abbey 223
Athassel Priory **190**
Athlone 177, **241**
  restaurants 315
Athlone Castle 241
Athlone Cruisers 335
Atlantic Coast Drive
  (Achill Island) 196
Atlantic Sea Kayaking 334
Aughnanure Castle 201
Augustinian order 190, 201
Auld Dubliner (Dublin pub) 105
Automobile Association (AA) 357
Autumn in Ireland 48
Avis 357
Avoca 131
Avoca Handweavers (Bray) 131, 325
Avondale Forest Park 133
Avondale House **133**
Avonmore River 130, 133

## B

BA Express 351
Bad Bob's Backstage Bar
  (Dublin) 105
Bagenalstown, hotels 289
Baily Lighthouse 100
Balgriffin, hotels 288
Ballina 182
  hotels 295
Ballinadee, hotels 291
Ballinafad 227
Ballinasloe Fair 48
Ballincollig 163
Ballinderry River 260

Ballingeary 163
Ballinskelligs 156, 157
Ballintoy 253
Ballsbridge
  hotels 288
  restaurants 307
Ballycastle **258–9**
  restaurants 316
Ballyconneely 199
Ballycopeland Windmill 272
Ballydehob 159
Ballyferriter
  Dingle Peninsula tour 150
  restaurants 310
Ballygally, hotels 300
Ballyhack 140
Ballyhack Castle 140
Ballylickey
  hotels 291
  restaurants 310
Ballymacarbry, hotels 289
Ballymaloe School of Cookery 331
  Crawford Art Gallery (Cork) 167
Ballymena, hotels 300
Ballymote, hotels 297
Ballymurn, hotels 289
Ballynahinch, hotels 295
Ballyshannon **223**
  restaurants 314
Ballyshannon International Folk
  Festival 47
Ballyvaughan **180**, 357
  hotels 294
  pubs 319
Baltimore **162**
Baltimore Diving & Watersports
  Centre 335
Banba's Crown 219
Bandon River 165
Bangor 272
  hotels 300
  pubs 321
Bangor, Lord and Lady 276
Bank of Ireland (Dublin) **58**, 346
  Street-by-Street map 56
Banknotes 344–5
Banks 346–7
Banna Strand 148
Bannow Bay 140
Banquets **330**, 331
  Bunratty Castle 184–5, 312
  Knappogue Castle 330
Bansha 190
Banshees 24
Banteer, hotels 291
Bantry 159
  hotels 291
  restaurants 310
Bantry, 1st Earl of (Richard White) 160
Bantry, 2nd Earl of 160, 161
Bantry Bay **159**, 161
Bantry House **160–61**, 284, 291
Barley Cove 145, 159
Barna, restaurants 313

Barralet, James 99
Barre, WJ 271
Barrow, River 140, 141
Bars, Dublin 104, 105
Battle of the Boyne Day 47
*Beach Scene* (Degas) 89
Beaghmore Stone Circles **260**
Beaker people 30
Bear Island 159
Beara Peninsula **158**
Becket, Thomas à 142
Beckett, Samuel 21, **60**
  Nobel prize 44
  Portora Royal School 264
  Trinity College, Dublin 60
Bed-and-breakfast
  accommodation 282
Bedell, Bishop 81
Beehive huts 19
Beer
  duty-free allowances 340
  Guinness **96–7**
  Guinness Hop Store (Dublin) **96**
Begging 342
Behan, Brendan 21
  Abbey Theatre 102
  Dublin's pubs 104
  McDaid's (Dublin) 107
Beit, Sir Alfred 124, 125
Beit Art Collection (Russborough
  House) 124–5
Belfast 247, **268–71**
  Albert Memorial Clocktower 271
  Botanic Gardens 270
  buses 360
  Cave Hill 271
  City Hall 268
  Crown Liquor Saloon 269
  The Entries 269
  ferries 354
  Giant's Ring 271
  Grand Opera House 268
  hotels 300
  Lagan Weir Lookout 271
  Linen Hall Library 269
  map 268–9
  personal safety 343
  political murals 270
  pubs 321
  Queen's University 270
  railway station 359
  restaurants 316
  St Anne's Cathedral 268
  Stormont 271
  Ulster Museum 270
  Visitors' Checklist 269
  Waterfront Hall 328, 331
Belfast Castle 271
Belfast City Airport 351
Belfast Civic Festival and Lord
  Mayor's Show 46
Belfast Festival at Queen's 48, 331
Belfast International Airport 351
Belfast Lough 267, 271

Belfast Music Festival 49
*Belfast Newsletter* 38
Belfast Welcome Centre 339
Belfield Bike Shop 357
Bellaghy 37
Belleek 261
  Lower Lough Erne tour 262
  restaurants 316
Belleek Pottery **261**, 323
Belloto, Bernardo 124
Belltable Arts Centre (Limerick) 331
Belmore, 1st Earl of 264
Belvedere, 1st Earl of 241
Belvedere College (Dublin) 88
Belvedere House 241
Ben Bulben 114
  Yeats Country tour 224
Benbaun 200
Benedictine order
  Fore Abbey 233
  Holy Cross Abbey 187
  Kylemore Abbey 200
  St Mary's Abbey (Dublin) 91
Bennettsbridge 136
Benone Strand **252**
Bernard, St 237
Bewley's Oriental Café (Dublin)
  58, 325
  Street-by-Street map 56
Bianconi, Charles 40, 191
Bicycles **357**
  cycling holidays **333**, 335
  on trains 358
  renting 335
Birds
  The Burren 178
  Castle Caldwell Forest Park 262
  Connemara 200
  Saltee Islands 143
  The Skelligs 156–7
  Wexford Wildfowl Reserve 142
Birr **245**
  hotels 299
Birr Castle 231, 245
Bishop's Quarter 180
Black Castle Demesne 187
Black Death 35, 77
Black Head 180
Black, Mary 15, 22
Black and Tans 42
Blackrock Castle 169
Blackwater, River 137, **169**
Blanket bog 17, 244
Blarney Castle 147, **163**
Blarney House 163
Blarney, restaurants 310
Blarney Stone 147, **163**
Blarney Woollen Mills 325
Blasket Centre
  Dingle Peninsula tour 150
Blasket Islands 20, 150, 151
Blennerville Windmill (Tralee)
  148, **149**
Blessing of the Sea 47

Blessington 125, 341
  hotels 289
Bloody Foreland 213, **216**
Bloody Sunday (1972) 44
Bloomsday 21, 46
Blues music, Dublin 103, 105
Boa Island 24
  Lower Lough Erne tour 262
Boats
  cruising and sailing **334**, 335
  *currachs* 206
  ferries 352–4
  Galway hookers 203
*Bodhrán* (drum) 22, 323, 326
Bog of Allen 120, 244
Bogs 17, **244**
  Peatland World 120
  Shannonbridge Bog Railway 243
Bolton, Thomas 64
Bonamargy Friary (Ballycastle) 258
Bonet (gardener) 125
*Book of Durrow* 32, 53, 61
*Book of Kells* **62**, 233
Books
  shops **323**, 325
  What to Buy in Ireland 327
Booterstown, hotels 288
Bord Fáilte 331, **338**, 339
Bosco, Don 198
Bourchier's Castle 187
Boycott, Captain 40
Boyle **211**
Boyle Abbey 211
Boyle family 80
  monument 81
Boyne, Battle of the (1690) 29, **236**
  history 36–7
  Talbot family 100
  tapestry 36
Boyne, River 231, 236, 240
Boyne Valley 229, **236–7**
Brandon Mountain 25, 150
Bray 119, **125**
  restaurants 308
Bray Head 125
Brazen Head (Dublin pub) 105
Break for the Border (Dublin) 105
Breakfast 302
  Ulster fry 304
Brecan, St 206
Brendan, St **25**
  Ardfert Cathedral 148
  Clonfert Cathedral 205
  replica boat 182
  voyages 205
Breweries *see* Beer
Brian Boru 32–3, 77
  grave of 266
Bricin (Killarney) 325
Bricklieve Mountains 227
Brigid, St 120
Bristol, Frederick Augustus Hervey, Earl of 252
British Airways 351

British Commonwealth 44
British Horse Society 335
British Midland 351
British Surfing Association 334, 335
British Telecom 349
Brittany Ferries 353
Broighter gold boat **31**, 64
Bronze Age 30, 64
Brooke, Sir Basil 222
Brown, Capability 237
Brown Thomas (Dublin) 324, 325
Browne family 197
Browne's Cave (Rathlin Island) 258
Browne's Hill Dolmen **133**
Brú Ború *see* Brian Boru
Brú Ború Heritage Centre, Cashel 187
Bruce, Edward 34, 267
Bruce, Robert, King of Scotland 258
Bruce's Cave (Rathlin Island) 258
Bruckless, hotels 297
Bryce, Annan 159
Budget (car hire) 357
Budget restaurants 303
Buite, St 234
Bull Point 258
Bunbeg 216
Buncrana
  Inishowen Peninsula tour 218
Buncrana Castle 218
Bundoran 222, 334
Bunglass Point 221
Bunnow, River 187
Bunratty
  pubs 319
  restaurants 312
Bunratty Castle **184–5**
Bunratty Folk Park 185
*Bureaux de change* 344, **347**
Burges, William 167
Burgh, Thomas 75
Burgh, William de 190
Burke, Éamonn 35
Burke, Edmund 60
  statue of 60
Burne-Jones, Sir Edward 137
The Burren **178–80**
  map 180
Burtonport 220
Bus Éireann 361
Buses **360–61**
  airport 350
  through-tickets 354
Bushmills
  Old Bushmills Distillery **258**
  pubs 321
  What to Buy in Ireland 327
Butler family (Earls of Ormonde) 117, 173
  Cahir Castle 190
  Clonmel 191
  Kilkenny 134
  Kilkenny Castle 115, 136
  Ormond Castle 191
  Swiss Cottage (Cahir) 190–91

Butler family (cont)
  tombs 136
Butler's Bridge, restaurants 315
Butler's Irish Hand-made Chocolates (Dublin) 325

# C

Cadamstown 245
Caha Mountains 158, 161
Caherciveen
  Ring of Kerry tour 156
Cahermore Stone Fort 180
Cahir **190–91**
  restaurants 312
Cahir Abbey 190
Cahir Castle 190
Cahir, Lord and Lady 190
Caldragh cemetery 262
Camcor, River 245
Camogie 27
Camping 282–3
Canals
  Dublin **99**
  Waterways Visitors' Centre (Dublin) 99
Canova, Antonio, *The Three Graces* 169
Cappoquin
  hotels 289
  restaurants 308
Car rental 355
Caragh Lake, hotels 291
Caravaggio, *The Taking of Christ* 53, 69
Caravans 282–3
  horse-drawn 283
Carbery's Hundred Isles 162
Carleton (William) Summer School (Dungannon) 331
Carlingford 229, **234**
  hotels 299
  pubs 321
  restaurants 315
Carlingford Lough 234
Carlow, County 117
Carlow, restaurants 308
Carndonagh Cross
  Inishowen Peninsula tour 218
Carnlough harbour 259, 334
Carnlough, hotels 300
Carrick (Co Donegal) 221
Carrick-a-rede rope bridge 247, 253
Carrickfergus 267
Carrickfergus Castle **34–5**, 267
Carrickmacross, restaurants 315
Carrick-on-Shannon 177, **227**
  Carrick Theatre Festival 48
  hotels 299
Carrick-on-Suir 191
Carrigafoyle Castle **148**
Carrigglas Manor **232–3**
Carrignacurra Castle 163
Carrowkeel Passage Tomb Cemetery 215, 227

Carrowmore Megalithic Cemetery 226
Cars **355–7**
  breakdown and recovery services
  355, 357
  buying petrol 355
  parking 357
  renting **355**, 357
  road conditions 356
  road maps 355
  road signs 356
  rules of the road 356
  security roadblocks 357
  speed limits 356
  taking your own car 355
  see also Tours by car
Carson, Edward (Lord Carson) 42
  statue of 271
  tomb of 268
Casement, Roger 148
Cash dispensers 346
Cashel **187**
  hotels 294
  restaurants 312
  Rock of Cashel 114, 187, **188–9**
Cashel Bay, hotels 295
Cashels (stone forts) 19
Castle Archdale Country Park
  Lower Lough Erne tour 263
Castle Caldwell Forest Park
  Lower Lough Erne tour 262
Castle Clinton 40
Castle Coole 19, 264
Castle Inn (Dublin) 105
Castle Matrix 176
Castle, Richard 19
  Belvedere House 241
  Conolly's Folly, Castletown
  House 123
  Leinster House (Dublin) 63
  Powerscourt 126
  Rotunda Hospital (Dublin) 84, 88
  Russborough House 39, 124
  Strokestown Park House 210
  Westport House 197
Castle Ward 276
Castle Ward Opera 47
Castlebaldwin
  hotels 297
  restaurants 314
Castledermot, hotels 289
Castlelyons
  hotels 291
Castlereagh, Lord 274, 275
Castles
  Anglo-Norman 34–5
  Ashford Castle 201
  Ashtown Castle (Dublin) 94
  Athlone Castle 241
  Aughnanure Castle 201
  Ballyhack Castle 140
  Belfast Castle 271
  Birr Castle 245
  Black Castle 187
  Blackrock Castle 169

Castles (cont)
  Blarney Castle 147, **163**
  Bourchier's Castle 187
  Buncrana Castle 218
  Bunratty Castle **184–5**
  Cahir Castle 190
  Carrickfergus Castle **34–35**, 267
  Carrigafoyle Castle 148
  Carrignacurra Castle 163
  Castle Matrix 176
  Desmond Castle 164
  Doe Castle 217
  Donegal Castle 222
  Dublin Castle 52, **74–5**
  Dunguaire Castle 204
  Dunluce Castle 253
  Dunseverick Castle 253
  Dysert O'Dea 181
  Enniscorthy Castle 141
  Enniskillen Castle 264
  Glenveagh Castle 216
  Green Castle 277
  Hillsborough Castle 273
  Howth Castle 100
  Johnstown Castle **142–3**
  Jordan's Castle 276
  Kilclief Castle 276
  Kilkenny Castle 115, **136**
  Kinbane Castle 253
  King John's Castle
  (Carlingford) 234
  King John's Castle (Limerick) 183
  Knappogue Castle 181
  Kylemore Abbey 200
  Leamaneagh Castle 180
  Lismore Castle 137
  Malahide Castle 100
  Monea Castle 263
  O'Doherty Castle 218
  Ormond Castle 191
  Parke's Castle **225**, 338
  Portumna Castle 205
  Rathlannon Castle 143
  Reginald's Tower (Waterford) 138
  Rock of Dunamase 245
  Roscommon Castle 210
  Roscrea Castle 187
  Ross Castle 154
  Slade Castle 140
  Slane Castle 237
  tower houses 18–19
  Trim Castle 240
  Tully Castle 262
  Tullynally Castle 233
Castletown House **122–3**
  stucco 19, 117
Castletownbere 158
Castletownshend, restaurants 310
Castlewellan Forest Park 276
Cathedrals
  Ardfert 147, **148**
  Christ Church (Dublin) 52, 72, **78–9**
  Christchurch (Waterford) 138
  Clonfert **205**

Cathedrals (cont)
  Down (Downpatrick) 273
  Glendalough 132
  Holy Trinity (Waterford) 138
  Rock of Cashel 189
  St Aidan's (Enniscorthy) 141
  St Anne's (Belfast) 268
  St Brigid's (Kildare) 120–21
  St Canice's (Kilkenny) 136
  St Carthage (Lismore) 137
  St Colman's (Cobh) 170
  St Columb's (Londonderry)
  250, **251**
  St Declan's (Ardmore) 137
  St Eunan's (Letterkenny) 219
  St Finbarr's (Cork) 167
  St Flannan's (Killaloe) 182
  St John's (Limerick) 183
  St Macartan (Monaghan) 232
  St Mary's (Limerick) 183
  St Mary's Pro-Cathedral (Dublin)
  85, **87**
  St Nicholas (Galway) 202
  St Patrick's (Armagh) 266
  St Patrick's (Dublin) 52, **80–81**
  St Patrick's (Trim) 240
  see also Churches in Dublin
Catholic Church 14
  Battle of the Boyne 236
  emancipation 39
  Protestant conquest 36–7
Catholic Emancipation Act 40
Catholic University of Ireland 59
Causeway Coast 247, **253**
Cavan, County 229
Caves
  Aillwee Cave 180
  Bruce's Cave (Rathlin Island) 258
  Dunmore Cave 136
  Marble Arch Caves 265
Céide Fields **196**
Celestine, Pope 273
Celtic Cycling (Bagenalstown) 335
Celts
  Celtic heritage 24–5
  Christianity 32–3
  High Crosses 235
  history 30–31
Central Fisheries Board 335
Ceramics
  Belleek Pottery 261
  shops **323**, 325
  What to Buy in Ireland 327
Chambers, Sir William
  Castletown House 122
  Marino Casino (Dublin) 98
  Trinity College, Dublin 60
Charlemont, 1st Earl of 39, 98
Charles II, King of England 210
Charles Fort 164
Charlotte, Queen 160
Cheeses 305
Chester Beatty, Sir Alfred 99

Chester Beatty Library and Gallery of
   Oriental Art (Dublin) **75**
   Street-by-Street map 72
Chesterfield, Lord 94
The Chieftains 15, 22
Children of Lir 25
*Children of Lir* (Kelly) 89
Children, in restaurants 302
Children's Cultural Centre
   (Dublin) 76
China shops **323**, 325
Christ Church Cathedral
   (Dublin) 52, **78–9**
   Street-by-Street map 72
Christianity
   Celtic 32–3
   St Patrick 29
Churches
   religious services 339
   *see also* Cathedrals
Churches in Dublin
   Church of the Most Holy Trinity
   74, 75
   St Ann's 56, **59**
   St Audoen's **77**
   St Audoen's Roman Catholic
   Church 77
   St Michan's Church **90**
   University Church 59
   Whitefriar Street Carmelite
   Church **81**
Ciaran, St 242
CIE 76
Cigarettes, duty-free allowances 340
Cinema *see* Films
Cistercian order 33
   Assaroe Abbey 223
   Boyle Abbey 211
   Duiske Abbey 141
   Holy Cross Abbey 187
   Hore Abbey 187
   Inch Abbey 273
   Jerpoint Abbey 137
   Mellifont Abbey 237
   Portumna Priory 205
   St Mary's (Dublin) 91
   Tintern Abbey 140
City Art Centre (Dublin theatre) 105
City Hall (Dublin) **75**
   Street-by-Street map 72
Civil War 42, 43
Cladagh River 265
Claddagh Records (Dublin) 325
Clan na Gael 41
Clancy (Willie) Summer School
   (Miltown Malbay) 331
Clannad 15
Clara, Vale of *see* Vale of Clara
Clare Abbey 181
Clare, County 173
Clare Island **198**
Clare, Richard de *see* Strongbow
Clarecastle, hotels 294
Clarendon 81

Clarinbridge
   pubs 320
   restaurants 313
Clarke, Harry, *The Meeting of St
   Brendan and the Unhappy Judas*
   166, 167
Clarke, Tom 43
Clear Island 159, 162
Cleggan 199
Clements family 227
Clery's (Dublin shop) 325
Clew Bay 15, 196, 197
Clifden **198–9**
   hotels 295–6
   pubs 320
   restaurants 313
Cliffs of Magho 262
Cliffs of Moher **176**, 180
Climate 46–9
Clochán na Carraige 206
Clogher Head 150
Clonakilty **162**, 282
   hotels 291
   pubs 319
Clonakilty Folk Club 328
Clonalis House **210**
Clonea, hotels 289
Clones, hotels 299
Clonfert Cathedral **205**
Clonmacnoise **242–3**
   Nuns' Church 33, 230
   Temple Finghin round tower 229
Clonmacnoise Crozier 33
Clonmel **191**
   hotels 294
   restaurants 312
Clontarf, Battle of (1014) 32, 33, 77
Clothes
   in restaurants 302
   shops **324**, 325
   What to Buy in Ireland 326
Coach tours 360–61
Coastguards 342
Coasts 16
Cobblestones 103, 105
Cobh **170–71**
Coins 344–5
Cole family 265
Coleraine 252
Collins Barracks, *see* National
   Museum at Collins Barracks
Collins, Michael 43
Collooney
   hotels 297
   restaurants 314
Colman, St 198, 204
Colmcille Heritage Centre 217
Colmcille, St *see* Columba, St
Colthurst family 163
Columba, St (Colmcille) 32
   Glencolumbkille 220
   Kells Monastery 233
   Londonderry 250, 251
   Tory Island 216

Columbanus, St 32
Columbus, Christopher 205
Comeragh Mountains 191
Comhaltas Ceoltóirí Éireann
   (Monkstown) 331
Comyn, John, Archbishop of
   Dublin 80
Condoms 343
Cong **201**
   hotels 296
   restaurants 313
Cong Abbey 201
Connaught 177, 193
Connemara 193
   map 199
Connemara Marble Factory
   (Moycullen) 325
Connemara National Park 114,
   **200**, 339
Connemara ponies 200, 201
Connolly, James 43, 95
Connolly, Katherine 123
Conolly, William 122
Conolly's Folly, Castletown
   House 123
Continental Airlines 366
Conversion chart 341
Cook, Alan 260
Cook, Thomas 347
Cookery holidays 331
Cookstown 260
Coole Park 205
Cooley Peninsula 229, 234
Cooley, Thomas 75
Copeland Islands 272
Cork **166–9**
   Blackrock Castle 169
   Butter Exchange 166
   Cork City Gaol 167
   Crawford Art Gallery 166–7
   Dunkathel House 169
   ferries 352–3
   hotels 291–2
   map 166–7
   pubs 319
   the Quays 168
   restaurants 310
   Royal Gunpowder Mills 169
   St Ann's Shandon 166
   St Finbarr's Cathedral 167
   Visitors' Checklist 167
Cork Airport 351
Cork Choral Festival 46
Cork, County 145
Cork, Earls of 80, 171
Cork Film Festival 48, 331
Cork Jazz Festival 48, 329, 331
Cork, Katherine Boyle, Countess
   of 80
Cork and Kerry **145–71**
   hotels 291–3
   pubs 319
   restaurants 310–12
Cork Regatta Week 27, 47

Cormac's Chapel (Cashel) 33
Corrib, Lough **201**
Corrib, River 202, 282
Corrigan, Mairead 45
Costello, Edward 227
Costello, John A 44
Cottages 18
Country house accommodation 280–81
Country houses 19
  Avondale House 133
  Bantry House **160–61**, 284, 291
  Belvedere House 241
  Blarney House 163
  Carrigglas Manor **232–3**
  Castle Coole 264
  Castle Ward 276
  Castletown House 117, **122–3**
  Clonalis House **210**
  Derrynane House 156
  Dunkathel House 169
  Emo Court **245**
  Florence Court **265**
  Glin Castle 176
  Johnstown Castle **142–3**
  Killruddery House **125**
  Lissadell House **223**, 224
  Mount Stewart House 115, 272, **274–5**
  Muckross House 151
  Parke's Castle **225**
  Powerscourt 115, **126–7**
  Puxley Mansion 158
  Russborough House **124–5**
  Strokestown Park House **210–11**
  Talbot Castle 240
  Westport House 194, 196–7
Country music **329**, 331
  Dublin 103, 105
Countryside Alliance 334, 335
Countryside Tours (Rathdrum) 335
County Wexford Strawberry Fair 47
County Wicklow Garden Festival 46, 331
Courbet, Gustave 89
Courcy, John de 34, 267, 273
Covered Market (Dublin)
  Street-by-Street map 73
Crafts
  cultural holidays 331
  shops **323**, 325
  What to Buy in Ireland 326–7
Crafts Council of Ireland 323, 325
Craftsworks Gallery (Belfast) 325
Craggaunowen **182**
Cramillion, Bartholomew 88
The Cranberries 15
Crannogs 19, **31**
Crawford Art Gallery (Cork) 331
Crawford, William Horatio 166
Crawfordsburn, hotels 300
Cré Irish Porcelain (Galway) 325
Credit cards 322, 346

Crime 342–3
Croagh Patrick **197**
Crohy Head 220
Croke Park (Dublin) 335
Crolly, pubs 321
Cromwell, Oliver
  destruction of buildings 18
  history 36
  Macroom Castle 163
  sacks Galway 202
  sacks Kilkenny 136
  siege of Drogheda 37, 236
Crookhaven 159
Cross of Cong 65, 201
Crossdoney, hotels 299
Crosses see High Crosses
Crossmolina, hotels 296
Cruinniú na mBad 47
Cruising **334**, 335
Crystal
  shops **323**, 325
  Waterford Crystal **139**, 325
  What to Buy in Ireland 327
Cuchulainn 20, 24, 87
Cuilcagh Mountains 265
Cultural holidays **330**, 331
Culture 15
Cumann na nGaedheal 43
*Currachs* (rowing boats) 206
Curragh racecourse 26, 121
Currency 344–5
Curtain walls 19
Cushendall 259
Custom House (Dublin) 53, 83, **86**
  history 39
  Street-by-Street map 85
Customs allowances 340
Cycling see Bicycles
Cycleways (Dublin) 333, 335

# D

*Dáil Éireann* **63**
  history 42
  Mansion House (Dublin) 59
Dalkey **101**
Dalkey Island 101
Dan Dooley 357
Dan O'Hara's Homestead (Lettershea) 199
Dance **329**, 331
  Dublin 103, 105
  traditional 23, **329**, 331
D'Arcy, John 198, 199
Dargle, River 130
DART rail service 93, 358
Davitt, Michael 41
Davy Byrne's (Dublin pub) 105
Dawson, Joshua 59
De Burgo family 205
De Burgo, Richard 205
De Lorean car factory 45, 272
De Valera, Eamon **43**, 59
  Anglo-Irish Treaty 42
  elected as President 44

De Valera, Eamon (cont)
  imprisonment 95
de Vos, Paul, *The Boar Hunt* 123
Deane, Sir Thomas 63, 64
Declan, St 137
Deerfield (Dublin) 94
Degas, Edgar 69
  *Beach Scene* 89
Delaney, Edward 59
Delphi 195
Delphi Lodge (Connemara) 280, 284
Delta (airline) 351
Department of Agriculture 335
Department stores 325
Derg, Lough 175, 177, 182, **222**
Derg Line Cruisers (Killaloe) 335
Derry see Londonderry
Derrynane House
  Ring of Kerry tour 156
Derryveagh Mountains **216–17**
DESIGNyard (Dublin) 76, 324
Desmond Castle (Kinsale) 164
Desmond, Earls of 187
Desmond family, 191
Desmond rebellion 36
Devenish Island 33, **263**
  Lower Lough Erne tour 263
Devil's Glen 131
Devil's Punchbowl 131
Devonshire, Duke of 137
Dialling codes 348
Diamond Hill 200
Dingle **149**
  Dingle Peninsula tour 151
  hotels 292
  pubs 319
  restaurants 310
Dingle Peninsula
  tour of **150–51**
  wildlife 16
Dinis Island 154
Disability Action 341
Disabled travellers 340
  hotels 283
  sports **334**, 335
Discounts
  students 340
  travel concessions 359
Dixon, James 216
Doaghbeg 217
Doctors 342
Doe Castle 217
Doheny and Nesbitt (Dublin pub) 105
Dolmens 30
  Browne's Hill **133**
  Carrowmore Megalithic Cemetery 226
  Legananny Dolmen 276
  Poulnabrone Dolmen 180
Dominican order 34, 205, 226
Donaghadee 272
Donegal **222**

Donegal (cont)
  hotels 298
Donegal Abbey 222
Donegal Castle 222
Donegal Craft Village 222
Donegal, County 213
Donnybrook, hotels 289
Doolin 176, 180
  pubs 320
  restaurants 312
Doolin Crafts Gallery (Doolin) 325
Dooney Rock
  Yeats Country tour 225
Down, County 247
  map 248–9
Downhill Castle 252
Downpatrick 273
Dowth 236, **237**
Doyle, Roddy 21, 303
Drink *see* Food and drink
Drogheda **236**
  hotels 299
  siege of (1649–52) 37
Drogheda, Earls of 120
Dromahair, pubs 321
Drombeg Stone Circle **162**
Druid Theatre (Galway) 328, 331
Druids 24
Druid's Circle (Kenmare) 158
Drumcliff
  hotels 298
  Yeats Country tour 224
Drumlane **232**
Dublin **51–111**
  *Book of Kells* **62**
  buses 360, 361
  canals 99
  Christ Church Cathedral **78–9**
  DART rail service 93, 358
  Dublin Castle **74–5**
  entertainments 102–7
  ferries 352
  Further Afield 92–101
  Georgian terraces 67
  hotels 286–9
  maps *see Maps*
  millennium 45
  National Gallery **68–9**
  National Museum **64–5**
  North of the Liffey 82–91
  restaurants 306–8
  shops 322
  Southeast Dublin 54–69
  Southwest Dublin 70–81
  train services 358
  Trinity College **60–61**
Dublin Airport 361
Dublin Bus 361
Dublin Castle **52**
  Street-by-Street map 72
Dublin Civic Museum
  Street-by-Street map 73
Dublin Exhibition (1853) 41
Dublin Film Festival 46, 105

Dublin Horse Show 27, 47
Dublin International Airport
  **350**, 351
Dublin Literary Pub Crawl 105
Dublin Marathon 27
Dublin Theatre Festival 48, 105
Dublin Tourism Centre 56
Dublin Writers Museum 19, **89**
The Dubliners 103
Dublinia **77**
  Street-by-Street map 72
Dúchas (The Heritage Service) 339
  Heritage Card 338
Duiske Abbey 141
The Duke (Dublin pub) 105
Duleek, hotels 299
Dún Aonghasa 206
Dún Duchathair 207
Dún Eochla 207
Dún Eoghanachta 206
Dun Laoghaire **100–101**
  ferries 352
  restaurants 308
Dunamase, Rock of *see* Rock of
  Dunamase
Dunbeg Fort
  Dingle Peninsula tour 151
Dunbrody Abbey 140
Duncannon 140
Dundalk **234**
  County Museum 234
  restaurants 315
Dundrum
  Mourne Coast tour 277
  restaurants 317
Dunfanaghy 217
Dungannon **265**
  hotels 301
  restaurants 317
Dungarvan, restaurants 308
Dungloe 220
Dunguaire Castle 204
Dunkathel House 169
Dunkineely, hotels 298
Dunloe, Gap of
  *see* Gap of Dunloe
Dunluce Castle 253
Dunmore Cave 136
Dunmore East 117, **140**
  hotels 289
  pubs 318
Dunmore Head 150, 151
Dunquin, pubs 319
Dunraven, Earls of 186
Dunree Head
  Inishowen Peninsula tour 218
Dunseverick Castle 253
Durrus, restaurants 310
Dursey Island 158
Duty-free goods 340
DV Diving (Newtownards) 335
Dwyer, Michael 131
Dysert O'Dea 173, **181**
  High Cross 235

# E
Earhart, Amelia 251
Eason and Son (Dublin) 325
Easter Rising (1916) **42–3**
  flag 64
  Garden of Remembrance 89
  General Post Office 84, **87**
  O'Connell Street 84
Edgeworth, Maria 20
Edwards, Hilton 88
Eida, Minoru 121
Eida, Tassa 121
Eigse Sliabh Rua 48
Éire 43
Elegant Ireland 283
Elizabeth I, Queen of England
  171, 247
  and Grace O'Malley 198
  Trinity College, Dublin 60
Embassies 341
Emerald Card 359
Emerald Star (Dublin) 335
Emergency numbers 342
Emigration 40–41, **170**
  Ulster-American Folk Park 261
Emmet, Robert 58, **75**
  grave 90
  imprisonment 95
  uprising 40
Emo Court 19, 39, **245**
Enda, St 206
Ennel, Lough 241
Ennis **181**
  pubs 320
  restaurants 312
Enniscoe House (Castle Hill) 281
Enniscorthy **141**
  pubs 318
Enniscorthy Castle 141
Enniskerry 131
  hotels 289
Enniskillen **264**
  hotels 301
  Lower Lough Erne tour 263
  pubs 321
  Remembrance Day bombing 45
  restaurants 317
Enniskillen Castle 264
Enniskillen, William Cole, 1st Earl
  of 265
Ennistimon, restaurants 320
Ensor, John 66, 88
Entertainment **328–35**
  banquets **330**, 331
  booking tickets **328**, 331
  classical music, opera and dance
  **329**, 331
  cultural holidays **330**, 331
  Dublin 102–7
  festivals **330**, 331
  information sources **328**, 331
  major venues **328**, 331
  rock, jazz and country **329**, 331

Entertainment (cont)
theatre **328**, 331
traditional music and dance
**329**, 331
Equestrian Holidays Ireland 335
Erne, Lough 227
Lower Lough Erne tour **262–3**
Erne Marine (Enniskillen) 335
Erne, River 16, 223, 232, 264
Errigal Mountain 216
Ethnic restaurants 302–3
Eurocheques 322, 347
EuroDollar 357
Eurolines 353
Europcar/InterRent 357
European Union 14, 44
European Youth Card (EYC) 340
Everyman Palace Theatre (Cork) 331
Exploris (Portaferry) 272
Eyeries 158

## F

Fair Head 259
Fairies 24
Fairyhouse 26
Falcarragh 213
Famine *see* Great Famine
Fanad Peninsula **217**
Farmhouse accommodation 282
Farrell, Michael 89
Fashion shops **324**, 325
Fast foods 303
Feakle 173
hotels 294
Feakle Traditional Music Weekend
329, 331
*The Feast of St Kevin amid the ruins
of Glendalough* (Peacock) 29
Fechin, St 201, 233
Feis Ceoil 46
Fenian risings 41
Fergus, River 181
Fermanagh, County 247
Fermoy 169
Ferries **352–4**
Ballyhack 119
Killimer 174, 176
Ferrycarrig 142
Ferrycarrig Bridge, restaurants 308
Festivals 15, 46–9, **330**, 331
Fianna 24–5
Fianna Fáil 15, 43
Field, John 75
Fine Gael 15, 43
Finn MacCool **24–5**
Giant's Causeway 115, 254–5
Lough Neagh 266
Fire services 342, 343
First Trust Bank 346
Fish and chips 303

Fishing 49, **332**, 335
The Sporting Year 26
Fitzgerald family 117, 173, 176
Fitzgerald, Lord Edward 75
Fitzgerald, "Silken Thomas" 36, 77, 91
Fitzgibbon, Marjorie
statue of James Joyce 85
Fitzmaurice, Thomas 148
Fitzwilliam Square (Dublin) **66**
Fleadh Cheoil (Monkstown) 331
Fleadh Nua 46
"Flight of the Earls" 247
"Flight of the Wild Geese" 173
Florence Court 265
Flying Boat Museum, Foynes 176
Focus Theatre, Dublin 105
Foley, John
*The Houseless Wanderer* 68
monument to Daniel O'Connell 85
statue of Edmund Burke 60
statue of Henry Grattan 58
Folklore 24–5
Food and drink
fast foods 303
fish and chips 303
Guinness 96–7
picnics 303
pubs and bars 104, 105
shops **324**, 325
What to Buy in Ireland 327
What to Eat in Ireland **304–5**
*see also* Pubs; Restaurants
Football Association of Ireland
26, 335
Football (soccer) 26–7, 332
*For the Road* (J Yeats) 68
Fore Abbey **233**
Forgotton Cotton (Cork) 325
Forts (Iron Age) **18–19**
Cahermore Stone Fort 180
Dún Aonghasa 206
Dún Duchathair 207
Dún Eochla 207
Dunbeg Fort 151
Grianán of Aileach 218, **219**
Hill of Tara 240
Lisnagun Ring Fort 162
Navan Fort 266
Staigue Fort 156
Forts (modern)
Charles Fort 164
Elizabeth Fort (Cork) 168
Hillsborough Fort 273
Fota Wildlife Park and Arboretum
170–71
Four Courts (Dublin) **90–91**
Foxford **197**
Foxford Woollen Mills 197
Foyle, Lough 219
Foyle, River 36, 53, 250, 251
Foynes **176**
Francini, Paolo and Filippo 19
Newman House (Dublin) 59
Russborough House 124

Franciscan order
*Annals of the Four Masters* 222
Ennis Friary 181
Muckross Abbey 154
Quin Franciscan Friary 181
Timoleague Abbey 162–3
French, Percy 277
Friel, Brian 21
Abbey Theatre (Dublin) 86, 107
Fry, Cyril 100
Fry Model Railway 100
Fungie (dolphin) 149
Fusilier's Arch (Dublin)
Street-by-Street map 56

## G

Gaelic Athletic Association **27**, 41
Gaelic football 27
Gaelic language 15, 25, **339**
cultural holidays 331
Gaeltachts **221**, 339
Gaelic literature 20
Gaeltachts **221**, 339
Gaiety Theatre (Dublin) 105
Gainsborough, Thomas 124
Galbally 190
Galilei, Alessandro 122
Gallarus Oratory **149**
Dingle Peninsula tour 151
Galleries *see* Museums and galleries
Galty Mountains 173, 190
Galway 195, **202–3**
hotels 296
map 203
pubs 320
restaurants 313–14
Galway Arts Festival 47, 331
Galway, County 193
Galway hookers 203
Galway Irish Crystal (Galway) 325
Galway Oyster Festival 48
Galway Races 27
Gandon, James
Bank of Ireland (Dublin) 58
Carrigglas Manor 233
Custom House (Dublin) 39, 53,
**86**
Emo Court 39, 245
Four Courts (Dublin) 90–91
King's Inns (Dublin) 90
Gap of Dunloe 155, 333
Gap of Mamore
Inishowen Peninsula tour 218
Garage (Dublin pub) 105
Garavogue, River 226
Gardai 342, 343
Garden of Remembrance
(Dublin) **89**
Gardens *see* Parks and gardens
Gardiner, Luke 86
Garinish Island **158–9**
Garryduff Gold Bird 33
Garter Lane Theatre
(Waterford) 331

Gate Theatre (Dublin) **88**, 105
  Dublin's Best: Entertainment 106
  Street-by-Street map 84
Geese, Wexford Wildfowl
  Reserve 142
Geldof, Bob 45
General Post Office (Dublin) **87**
  Easter Rising 43
  Street-by-Street map 84
General strike (1913) 42
Geokaun Mountain 156
George III, King of England 160
George IV, King of England 264
Georgian country houses **19**
Georgian terraces, Dublin 67
Gerard Manley Hopkins Summer
  School 331
Giant's Causeway 115, **254–5**
  Causeway Coast 253
  legends 25
Giant's Ring 271
Gibson, Mel 240
Gifford, Grace 95
Gill, Lough 225, 226
Giraldus Cambrensis 63
Gladstone, WE 41
Glasnevin Cemetery (Dublin) 98
Glassware
  shops **323**, 325
  Tyrone Crystal 265
  Waterford Crystal 139
  What to Buy in Ireland 327
Glen of Aherlow **190**
Glenariff Forest Park **259**
Glenbeg Lough 158
Glenbeigh
  Ring of Kerry tour 156
Glencar Lough
  Yeats Country tour 225
Glencolumbcille Health Centre 343
Glencolumbkille **220–21**
Glencree
  Military Road tour 130
Glendalough 32, 49, **132–3**
  Military Road tour 130
Glengarriff 159
Glengesh Pass 220
Gleninsheen Gorget **30–31**, 64
Gleninsheen Wedge Tomb 180
Glenmacnass
  Military Road tour 130
Glenveagh Castle 216
Glenveagh National Park 216
Glin **176**
  hotels 295
Glin Castle 176
Glin, Knights of 176
Gobelins tapestries 160
Gogarty, Oliver St John 101
  Dublin pub 105
Goldsmith, Oliver 20, 60
Goldsmith Summer School
  (Ballymahon) 331
Golf 27, **332–3**, 335

Golfers Abroad 333
Golfing Ireland (Dublin) 335
Golfing Union of Ireland 335
Good Friday Agareement 29, 45
Gore-Booth, Eva 223, 224
Gore-Booth family 223
Gore-Booth, Sir Robert 223
Gorey, restaurants 308
Gort, Lord 184, 185
Gougane Barra Park 163
Gourmet restaurants 302–3
Government of Ireland Act (1920)
  29, 42
Goya, Francisco José de 69
Grafton Street (Dublin) **58**
  Street-by-Street map 56
Graham, Patrick 89
Graiguenamanagh 118, **141**
Grand Canal 99, 120, 227
Grand Canal Company 120
Grand Opera House (Belfast) **268**, 329
Granuaile Centre 198
Grattan, Henry 38, 58
Great Charter Roll of Waterford 35
Great Famine (1845–8) 40–41, **211**
  emigration 13, 29
  Famine Museum (Strokestown
  Park House) 211
Great Island 170
Great Saltee Island 143
Great Seal of Ireland 37
Great Stone Circle (Lough Gur) 186
Great Sugar Loaf Mountain 126
  Military Road tour 130
Green Card 355
Green Castle
  Mourne Coast tour 277
Greencastle
  Inishowen Peninsula tour 219
Green Flag National Breakdown 357
Gregory, Lady Augusta 88
  Abbey Theatre (Dublin) 20, 86
  Coole Park 204, 205
Gregory XVI, Pope 81
Grey Abbey 272
Greyhound racing 27
Greystones, restaurants 308
Grianán of Aileach **219**
  Inishowen Peninsula tour 218
Gris, Juan, *Pierrot* 68
Guaire, King of Connacht 204
Guesthouses 281
Guide Friday Ireland 361
Guinness, Arthur 39, 96, **97**
Guinness, Sir Benjamin 80
Guinness Brewery 39, **96–7**
Guinness, Desmond 80
Guinness family
  Iveagh House 59
  memorials 75
Guinness Storehouse (Dublin) 93, **96**
Gundestrup Cauldron 24
Gunpowder Mills (Cork) 169
Gur, Lough **186–7**

# H

Habermel, Erasmus 65
Hag's Head 176
Hallowe'en (Shamhana) 48, 305
Halpin, Robert 101
Hals, Frans 124
*Hambletonian* (Stubbs) 275
Handel, George Frederick 38, 79, 90
Hanly, Daithí 89
Hanna, Fred (Dublin) 325
Ha'penny Bridge (Dublin) **91**
Harland, Sir Edward 268
Harland and Wolff 268, 271
Harp 22–3
Hastings Hotels 283
Hawks Well Theatre (Sligo) 331
Health 342–3
Healy Pass 158
Heaney, Séamus 21
Henry II, King of England 29, 34, 142
Henry VIII, King of England 276
  breaks with Catholic Church 29
  Christ Church Cathedral (Dublin) 79
  Silken Thomas's rebellion 36, 91
Henry, Mitchell 200
Heritage Week 48
Hertz 357
Heuston, Sean J 42
Heuston station (Dublin) 358
Hiberno-Romanesque style 19
Hidden Ireland 283
High Crosses **235**
  Ahenny 191, 235
  Ardboe 260
  Clonmacnoise 242
  Dysert O'Dea 181, 235
  Glendalough 132
  Kells 233
  Kilfenora 180
  Kilkieran 191
  Monasterboice 234, 235
  Rock of Cashel 188
High King 32
Hill, Arthur 273
Hill, Derek 216, 217
Hill of Slane 237
Hill of Tara 32, 238, **240**
Hillsborough **273**
  pubs 321
  restaurants 317
Hillsborough Castle 273
Hillsborough Fort 273
Hilser Brothers (Cork) 325
History **29–45**
HMV (Dublin shop) 105, 331
Hobbema, Meindert 69
Holiday Autos 357
Holidays, public 49
Holy Cross Abbey **187**
Holy Island 163, 182
Holywood
  hotels 301
  restaurants 317

Home Rule 29, 40, 41
Hook Head 140
Hook Peninsula 139, **140**
Hooker Sailing 47
Hookers, Galway 203
Hore Abbey (Cashel) 187
Horn Head **217**
Horse Ploughing Match and Heavy
    Horse Show 46
Horses
    horse-drawn caravans 283
    National Stud 120, 121
    racing 15, 26–7, **121**, 332
    riding and pony trekking **333**, 335
Hotels **280–301**
    booking 281
    chain hotels 283
    Cork and Kerry 291–3
    disabled travellers 283
    Dublin 286–9
    Ireland's Best 284–5
    Lower Shannon 294–5
    Midlands 299
    Northern Ireland 300–301
    Northwest Ireland 297–8
    prices 281
    Southeast Ireland 289–91
    tipping 281
    West of Ireland 295–7
Houghton, Ray 45
House of Ireland 325
*The Houseless Wanderer*
    (Foley) 68
Howth **100**
    restaurants 308
Howth Head 93, 100
Hugh Lane Municipal Gallery of
    Modern Art (Dublin) **89**
    concerts 105
Hughes, John Joseph, Archbishop of
    New York 261
Huguenots
    in Cork 168
    linen industry 39, 260
    St Patrick's Cathedral (Dublin) 80
"Humanity Dick" 202
Hume, John 13
Hungry Hill 158
Hunt, John 182, 183
Hunter's Hotel (Rathnew) 281, 285
Hunting **334**, 335
Hurling 27, 332
Hyde, Douglas 59
    memorial 81

**I**
Iarnród Éireann (Irish Rail) 358, 359
Ilnacullin 158
Inch Abbey 273
Inchagoill 201
Inchydoney 162
Independent Holidays of Ireland 283
Industrial Revolution 268
Inis Saimer 223

Inishannon, hotels 292
    restaurants 311
Inishbofin **198**
Inisheer 206
Inishmaan 206
Inishmore 206
Inish Mor ferries 207
Inishowen Peninsula 215
    restaurants 314
    tour of **218–19**
Inistioge 141
    hotels 289
Innisfallen Island 154
Innisfree, Isle of *see* Isle of Innisfree
Insurance
    cars 355
    travel 342
International Bar (Dublin) 105
International Rally of the Lakes 26
International Sailing Centre
    (Cobh) 335
International Student Identity Card
    (ISIC) 340
Interpretative centres 339
Iona 62
Ireland's Eye 100
Ireland Horse Racing 335
Irish Agriculture Museum (Johnstown
    Castle) 143
Irish Champion Hurdle 26
Irish Citizen Army 87
Irish Conversation Courses
    (Ballyferriter) 331
Irish Derby 26, 121
Irish Distillers Group 171, 258
Irish Explorer tickets 359
Irish Federation of Sea Anglers 335
Irish Ferries 353
Irish Film Centre (Dublin) 76, 105
Irish Football League 26
Irish Free State 13, 29
    Anglo-Irish Treaty (1921) 42
    civil war 43
    Parliament 63
Irish Georgian Society 122
Irish Grand National 26
Irish Heritage Properties (Dalkey) 331
Irish Hotels Federation 283
Irish Ladies Golfing Union 333, 335
*Irish Life* 87
Irish Master of Foxhounds
    Association 335
Irish Museum of Modern Art
    (Kilmainham) **95**
Irish National Heritage Park **142**
Irish National Trust 80
Irish Open Golf Championship 27
Irish Open Office (Dublin) 335
Irish Peat Board 243
Irish Rail 358–9
Irish Republican Army (IRA) 124
    Enniskillen bomb 264
    history 43
    Troubles 44, 45

Irish Republican Brotherhood 41
Irish Revival 20
Irish Rover tickets 359
Irish Tourist Board **338**, 339
Irish Underwater Council 335
Irish Volunteers (18th century) 39
Irish Volunteers (20th century)
    Easter Rising 87
    Garden of Remembrance
        (Dublin) 89
Irish Ways (Ballycanew) 335
Irish Welcome 283
Irish Wheelchair Association 335
Iron Age 30
    *see also* Forts (Iron Age)
Irvinestown, hotels 301
Isle of Innisfree
    Yeats Country Tour 225
Isle of Man Steam Packet Co
    Ltd 353
Iveagh House (Dublin) 59
Iveragh Peninsula 156

**J**
James I, King of England 37, 232
James II, King of England
    Battle of the Boyne 29, 36, 236
    Carrickfergus Castle 267
    siege of Derry 37
Japanese Gardens (Kildare) 121
Jazz **329**, 331
    Dublin 103, 105
    festivals 46, 48
Jerpoint Abbey 35, **137**
Jerpoint Glass (Thomastown) 325
Jewellery
    shops **324**, 325
    What to Buy in Ireland 326
John the Evangelist, St 197
John, King of England 183
John Paul II, Pope 197
    at Clonmacnoise 242
    in Phoenix Park (Dublin) 45, 94
Johnson, Ester (Stella) 80, 81
Johnston, Denis 88
Johnston, Francis 74, 90
Johnston, Richard 264
Johnstown Castle **142–3**
Jordan's Castle 276
Joseph, St 197
Joyce, James 59, **88**
    bust of 58
    and Ennis 181
    James Joyce Cultural Centre
        (Dublin) 84, **88**
    James Joyce Tower (Sandycove,
        Dublin) **101**
    National Library (Dublin) 63
    statues of 83, 85
    Summer School (Dublin) 331
    *Ulysses* 20, 21, 46, 48, 104
*Judith with the Head of Holofernes*
    (Mantegna) 69
Jury's Hotel (Dublin) 105

## K

Kanturk 169
  hotels 292
Kate Kearney's Cottage 155
Kavanagh, Patrick 21, 104
Kearney, Kate 155
Kehoe's (Dublin pub) 105
Kells **233**
  monastery 33, 233
  restaurants 315
  *see also Book of Kells*
Kelly, Oisín, *Children of Lir* 89
Kenmare **158**
  hotels 292
  restaurants 311
  shops 324
Kenmare, Earl of 88
Kennedy, John F 44
  John F Kennedy Park and
    Arboretum 141
Kennys Bookshop and Art Gallery
  (Galway) 325
Kerry *see* Cork and Kerry
Kerry Bog Village 156
Kerry, County 145 .
Kerry, Ring of **156–7**
Kevin, St 132–3
Key, Lough 211
Kilbeggan **241**
  pubs 321
Kilbride, hotels 289
Kilclief Castle 276
Kildare **120–21**
  restaurants 308
Kildare, County 117
Kildare, Earls of 72, 186
Kildare, 8th Earl of 35, 36
  feud with Earl of Ormonde 81
  and Lambert Simnel 35, 79
Kilfenora 180
Kilkeel, hotels 301
Kilkenny 25, **134–6**
  hotels 290
  pubs 318
  restaurants 308–9
  shops 323
  Street-by-Street map 134–5
Kilkenny Arts Week 47, 330, 331
Kilkenny Castle 115, **136**
  Street-by-Street map 135
Kilkenny, County 117
Kilkenny Design Centre 323, 325
Kilkenny Shop (Dublin) 325
Kilkenny, Statute of (1366) 35
Kilkieran 191
Killahoey Strand 217
Killaloe 177, **182**
  pubs 320
Killarney **151**, 332
  hotels 292–3
  pubs 319
  restaurants 311
  Ring of Kerry tour 157

Killarney, Lakes of 114, **154–5**
Killarney National Park 154
Killeagh, hotels 293
Killiney **101**
Killorglin
  pubs 319
  restaurants 311
  Ring of Kerry tour 157
Killruddery House **125**
Killybegs **221**
  restaurants 314
Kilmacduagh **204**
Kilmainham Gaol (Dublin) 43, **95**
Kilmalkedar
  Dingle Peninsula tour 151
Kilmessan, hotels 299
Kilmore Quay 143
  pubs 318
Kilmurvy Beach 207
Kilnaboy, hotels 295
Kilronan 207
Kilrush 176
  pubs 320
Kinbane Castle 253
King family 211
King's Inns (Dublin) **90**
Kinnitty 245
Kinsale **146**
  hotels 293
  pubs 303, 319
  restaurants 302, 311
  Street-by-Street map 164–5
Kinsale Gourmet Festival 48
Kinvarra **204**
  cafés 302
Kitchen (Dublin nightclub) 105
KLM 351
Knappogue Castle **181**
  banquets 330
Knights of St Patrick 52, 74
Knights Templar 140
Knightstown 156
Knitwear shops **324**, 325
Knock **197**
Knock International
  Airport 351
Knockferry, hotels 296
Knocknarea 226
Knowth 236, **237**
Koralek, Paul 61
Koran 99
Kylemore Abbey **200**
Kyteler, Dame Alice 135, 318

## L

La Tène culture 31, 210
Lacy, Hugh de 240
"Lady Betty" 210
Lakeland Canoe Centre
  (Enniskillen) 335
Lakes 16
Lakes of Killarney **154–5**
Land League 41
Land War 41

Lane, Sir Hugh
  Hugh Lane Municipal Gallery of
    Modern Art (Dublin) 89
Language *see* Gaelic language
Lansdowne, 1st Marquess of 158
Lanyon, Sir Charles
  Custom House (Belfast) 271
  Queen's University (Belfast) 270
  Trinity College, Dublin 60
Laois, County 229
Larkin, James, statue of 84, 87
Larne **267**
  ferries 354
*Last Circuit of Pilgrims at
  Clonmacnoise* (Petrie) 242
Lavery, Sir John 270
Lawless, Matthew James
  *The Sick Call* 69
Laytown Beach Races 46
Leamaneagh Castle 180
Lean, David 148
Leane, Lough 155
Leap, restaurants 311
Lecale Peninsula 276
Lee, River **163**, 166, 167
  Cork environs 169
  Exploring Cork 168
Lee, Sir Thomas 36
Leenane, hotels 296
Lefroy family 232
Legananny Dolmen 30, 276
Legends 24–5
Leighlinbridge, restaurants 309
Leinster 177
Leinster Aqueduct 120
Leinster, Duke of 63
Leinster House (Dublin) **63**
  Street-by-Street map 57
Leitrim, County 213, 227
Leitrim, Earls of 227
Leixlip Castle 39
Lennox, Lady Louisa 122–3
Lennox, Tom 122
Leopardstown 26, 49, 121
Leprechauns 24
Letterfrack, hotels 296
Letterkenny **219**
  County Museum 219
  hotels 298
  restaurants 314
Letterkenny Folk Festival 47
Lever Brothers 72
Libraries
  Chester Beatty Library and Gallery
    of Oriental Art (Dublin) 72, **75**
  Linen Hall Library (Belfast) 269
  Marsh's Library (Dublin) 81
  National Library (Dublin) 57, **63**
  Old Library, Trinity College
    (Dublin) 53, 55, 61
Liffey Bridge (Dublin) 91
Liffey, River 125
Lillie's Bordello
  (Dublin nightclub) 105

Limavady, hotels 301
  restaurants 317
Limerick **183**
  history 33
  hotels 295
  pubs 320
  restaurants 313
  River Shannon 177
  siege of 173, 183
Limerick, County 173
Limestone pavement,
  The Burren 179
Linen 39, **260**
  shops **324**, 325
  What to Buy in Ireland 327
Lir, King 25
Lisdoonvarna 180
  hotels 295
Lisdoonvarna Matchmaking Festival 48
Lismacue, hotels 295
Lismore **137**
  restaurants 309
Lismore Castle 137
Lisnagun Ring Fort 162
Lissadell House **223**
  Yeats Country tour 224
Listings magazines, entertainments
  102, 103
Listowel Writers' Week 331
Liszt, Franz 88
Literature **20–21**
  cultural holidays 330, 331
  Literary Pub Crawl (Dublin) 104
Little Arrigle 137
Little Skellig 16, 157
Live Aid 45
Livingstone, Dr David 66
Locke, Josef 22
Locke's Distillery (Kilbeggan) 241
Loftus, Adam 37
Londonderry **250–51**
  hotels 301
  map 250
  personal safety 343
  restaurants 317
  siege of (1689) 37, 251
Londonderry, 3rd Marquess of 272
Londonderry Arms (Carnlough) 281
Londonderry, County 247
Londonderry family 274–5
Londonderry, Lady 274–5
The Long Hall (Dublin pub) 105
  Street-by-Street map 73
Long Range River 154
Longford, County 229
Loop Head 176
Lost property 342
Lough Eske, hotels 298
Lough Key Forest Park 211
Lough Melvin Holiday Centre
  (Garrison) 335
Lough Navar Forest Drive 262
Lough Ree Trail 241
Lough Rynn Estate **227**

Loughros Point 220
Louisburgh 198
Louth, County 229
Lower Shannon **173–91**
  hotels 294–5
  map 174–5
  restaurants 312–13
Luas light rail 358, 361
Lughnasa Fair 47
*Lusitania* (liner) 89, 170
Lynch family 202
Lyric Theatre (Belfast) 331

# M

Maam Cross, pubs 320
Mac Liammóir, Micheál 88
McAleese, Mary 14, 45
McBride, Major John 42
McCarthy, Dermot
  King of Munster 163
McCausland Car Hire 357
McCormack, John F **22**
  Moore Abbey 120
  St Mary's Pro-Cathedral 87
McDaid's (Dublin pub) 105
  Dublin's Best: Entertainment 107
MacDonnell family 253
MacDonnell, Sorley Boy 258
McDonough, Thomas 42
MacDyer, Father James 220–21
McEvoy, Eleanor 22
McGeehan Coaches 361
McGuigan, Barry 45
Mack, Robert 76
Maclise, Daniel
  *Marriage of Strongbow* 34
McMurrough, Art, King of Leinster 35
McMurrough, Dermot, King of
  Leinster 33, 34
MacNamara clan 181
MacNeice, Louis 21
McNeill, J (Dublin) 325
Macreddin Village hotels 290
Macroom 163
MacSweeney family 217
Maeve, Queen of Connaught 213
  and Cuchulainn 24
  Knocknarea 226
Magazines 341
Magee and Co (Donegal) 325
Maghery Bay 220
Magho, Cliffs of *see* Cliffs of Magho
Magilligan Point 252
Magilligan Strand *see* Benone Strand
Mahon, Major Denis 211
Mahon, Derek 21
Mahon, Thomas 210
Mail services 347
Malachy, St 237
Malahide Castle 93, **100**
Malaysia Airlines 351
Malin Head 215
  Inishowen Peninsula tour 219
Malinbeg 221

Mallow 169
  hotels 293
  restaurants 311
Malone, Molly, statue of 56, 58
Mamore, Gap of *see* Gap of Mamore
Mansion House (Dublin) **59**
  Street-by-Street map 56
Mantegna, Andrea, *Judith with the
  Head of Holofernes* 69
Manx Airlines 351
Maps
  Aran Islands 206–7
  Belfast 268–9
  The Burren 180
  Celtic Ireland 32
  Connemara 199
  Cork 166–7
  Cork and Kerry 146–7
  Dingle Peninsula tour 150–51
  Dublin at a Glance 52–3
  Dublin, North of the Liffey 83, 84–5
  Dublin, Southeast 55, 56–7
  Dublin, Southwest 71, 72–3
  Dublin Street Finder 108–11
  Galway 203
  Glendalough 132
  Great Famine 40
  Greater Dublin 11, 93
  Inishowen Peninsula tour 218–19
  Ireland 10–11
  Ireland at a Glance 114–15
  Kilkenny 134–5
  Kinsale 164–5
  Lakes of Killarney 154–5
  Londonderry 250
  Lower Lough Erne tour 262–3
  Lower Shannon 174–5
  Midlands 230–31
  Military Road tour 130
  Mourne Coast tour 277
  North Antrim coastline 253
  Northern Ireland 248–9
  Northwest Ireland 214–15
  Phoenix Park (Dublin) 94
  Ring of Kerry tour 156–7
  Shannon, River 177
  Southeast Ireland 118–19
  Waterford 139
  West of Ireland 194–5
  Yeats Country tour 224–5
Maracycle 46
Marble Arch Caves 265
Marconi, Guglielmo 199, 258
Marie Antoinette, Queen of France 161
Marino Casino (Dublin) 38–9, **98**
Markets in Dublin
  Covered Market 73
  Moore Street Market 84
Markievicz, Count Casimir 223
Markievicz, Countess Constance
  Easter Rising 59
  elected first woman MP 42
  Lissadell House 223
*Marriage of Strongbow* (Maclise) 34

Marsh, Narcissus, Archbishop of
    Dublin 81
Marsh's Library (Dublin) **81**
Martello towers
    Cleggan 199
    Dalkey Island 101
    Drogheda 236
    Howth Head 93
    James Joyce Tower 101
    Magilligan Point 252
Martin, Misses 268
Mary I, Queen of England 36
Mary II, Queen of England 236
Mary from Dungloe International
    Festival 47, 214
Mask, Lough 201
Mason, James 88
Matcham, Frank 268
Mathew, Father Theobald
    statues of 87, 168
    temperance crusade 40
Matisse, Henri 101
Matt Molloy's pub (Westport) 15, 196
Mattock, River 237
Mayo, County 193
Maze Prison (Belfast) 45
Meath, County 229
Meath, Earls of 125
Medical treatment 342
Medieval Trust 77
*The Meeting of St Brendan and the
    Unhappy Judas* (Clarke) 166, 167
Meeting of the Waters 131
Mellifont Abbey 33, **237**
Mellifont, Treaty of (1603) 37
Mellon, Judge Thomas 261
Merrion Square (Dublin) **66**
Metal Bridge (Dublin) 91
Metric system 341
Midlands **229–45**
    hotels 299
    map 230–31
    pubs 321
    restaurants 315
Midleton, hotels 293
Military Road 131
    tour of **130**
Millstreet Indoor International
    showjumping event 27
Milltown, Joseph Leeson, Earl of 124
Minot, Archbishop 80
Miró, Joan 167
Mizen Head 145, **159**
Moher, Cliffs of *see* Cliffs of Moher
Mohill, hotels 298
Molaise, St 263
Molloy, Matt 196
Moll's Gap, Ring of Kerry tour 157
Monaghan **232**
    restaurants 315
Monaghan, County 229
    County Museum 232
Monasterboice **234**
Monasterevin **120**

Monasteries 29
    Celtic 32–3
    Clonmacnoise 229, 230, **242–3**
    Devenish Island 263
    Glendalough 32–3, **132–3**
    Kells 33, 233
    Kilmacduagh 204
    Monasterboice 234
    round towers 18–19
    St Cronan's Monastery
        (Roscrea) 187
    *see also* Abbeys
Monea Castle
    Lower Lough Erne tour 263
Monet, Claude 69, 89
Money 344–5
Monument of Light 84, 87
Monuments
    Alcock and Brown 199
    Daniel O'Connell 85, 87
    O'Scully (Rock of Cashel) 189
    Parnell 84, 87
    Strongbow 78
    Wolfe Tone 59
Moore Abbey 120
Moore, Brian 21
Moore, Henry 58
    *Reclining Connected Forms* 60
Moore Street Market (Dublin)
    shopping 322
    Street-by-Street map 84
Moore, Thomas 131
Morris, Abraham 169
Morris, William 217
Morrison, Van 22, 107, 268
Mosse, Dr Bartholomew 88
Mosse (Nicholas) Pottery
    (Bennettsbridge) 136, 325
    What to Buy in Ireland 327
Mother Redcap's Tavern (Dublin) 105
Motte and bailey 19
Mount Juliet Estate
    (Thomastown) 335
Mount Stewart House 115, 272, **274–5**
Mount Usher Gardens **131**
Mountaineering Council of Ireland
    333, 335
Mountaineering **333**, 335
Mountains of Mourne 249, **276**
Mountains, wildlife 17
Mountjoy, Lord 169
Mountrath
    hotels 299
    restaurants 315
Mountshannon 175, **182**
Mourne, Mountains of *see* Mountains
    of Mourne
Mourne Coast tour 277
Mourne Wall 276
Movies *see* Films
Moyard, hotels 296
Moycullen, restaurants 314
Mr Pussy's Café de Luxe
    (Dublin pub) 105

Muckross Abbey 154
Muckross House 151, 333
Muckross Lake 154
Muiredach's Cross 234, **235**
Mulcahy (Louis) Pottery (Ballyferriter)
    150, 325
Mullaghmore 180
Mulligan's (Dublin pub) 105
Mullingar **240–41**
    hotels 299
    restaurants 315
Munster 173
Munster, Kings of 188
Murals, Belfast 270
Murlough Bay 259
Museums and galleries
    admission charges 338
    Armagh County Museum 266
    Avondale House 133
    Beit Art Collection (Russborough
        House) 124–5
    Blennerville Windmill (Tralee)
        148, 149
    Bunratty Folk Park 185
    Burren Display Centre 180
    Chester Beatty Library and Gallery
        of Oriental Art (Dublin) 72, **75**
    Cobh Heritage Centre 170
    Collins Barracks (Dublin) **99**
    Colmcille Heritage Centre 217
    Cork City Gaol 167
    Crawford Art Gallery (Cork) 166–7
    Dan O'Hara's Homestead
        (Lettershea) 199
    Derrynane House 156
    Dixon Gallery (Tory Island) 216
    Donegal Historical Society Museum
        (Rossnowlagh) 222–3
    Down County Museum
        (Downpatrick) 273
    Dublin Civic Museum 73
    Dublin Writers Museum **89**
    Dublinia 72, **77**
    Dysert O'Dea 181
    Earhart Centre (Londonderry) 251
    Famine Museum (Strokestown Park
        House) 211
    Folk Village Museum
        (Glencolumbkille) 220–21
    Foynes Flying Boat Museum 176
    French Armada Centre (Bantry
        House) 160
    Glebe House and Gallery (Lough
        Gartan) 217
    Granuaile Centre
        (Louisburgh) 198
    Guinness Hop Store (Dublin) **96**
    Heraldic Museum (Dublin) 63
    Holy Trinity Heritage Centre
        (Carlingford) 234
    Horse Museum (National Stud) 121
    Hugh Lane Municipal Gallery of
        Modern Art (Dublin) **89**, 105
    Hunt Museum (Limerick) 183

Museums and galleries (cont)
Irish Agriculture Museum
(Johnstown Castle) 143
Irish Museum of Modern Art
(Kilmainham) **95**
Irish National Heritage Park
(Ferrycarrig) **142**
Jameson Heritage Centre
(Midleton) **171**
Kerry County Museum (Tralee)
148, 149
King House (Boyle) 211
Knight Ride (Carrickfergus) 267
Knock Folk Museum 197
Lagan Weir Lookout (Belfast) 271
Limerick Museum 183
Lough Neagh Discovery
Centre 266, 267
Maritime Museum (Kilmore
Quay) 143
Millmount Museum (Drogheda)
236
Mizen Vision (Mizen Head
Lighthouse) 159
National Gallery (Dublin) 53, **68–9**
National Maritime Museum (Dun
Laoghaire) 101
National Museum (Dublin)
53, **64–5**
Natural History Museum
(Dublin) **66**
Navan Centre (Armagh) 266
Old Jameson's Distillery (Dublin) **90**
Rock of Cashel 188
Royal Gunpowder Mills (Cork) 169
Royal Hibernian Academy
(Dublin) 66
St Patrick's Trian (Armagh) 266
Skellig Experience Centre 156
Sligo Art Gallery 226
Sligo County Museum and Art
Gallery 226
Tower Museum (Londonderry)
250, **251**
Ulster-American Folk Park (Co
Tyrone) **261**
Ulster Folk and Transport Museum
(Cultra) **272**
Ulster History Park (Co Tyrone) **261**
Ulster Museum (Belfast) 270
Water Wheels (Assaroe Abbey) 223
Waterford Heritage Centre 138
West Cork Regional Museum
(Clonakilty) 162
Westgate Heritage Centre
(Wexford) 142
Yola Farmstead (Rosslare) 143
Music 15, **22–3**
classical music, opera and dance
103, 105, 329, 331
cultural holidays 331
festivals 46–9
rock, jazz, blues and country 103,
105, **329**, 331

Music (cont)
shops **323**, 325
traditional music and dance 22–3,
103, 105, **329**, 331
Music in Great Irish Houses 47, 331
Mussenden, Frideswide 252
Mussenden Temple **252**
Myths **24–5**

# N
Naas, restaurants 309
Napoleon I, Emperor 40, 101
Nash, John 190, 211
National 1798 Visitor Centre 375
National Botanic Gardens
(Dublin) **98**
National Breakdown, Green Flag 357
National Concert Hall (Dublin) 105
Dublin's Best: Entertainment 107
National Country Fair, Birr 46
National Express 353
National Gallery (Dublin) 53, **68–9**
National Irish Bank 346
National Library (Dublin) **63**
Street-by-Street map 57
National Monument (Cork) 168
National Museum (Dublin) 53, **64–5**
Street-by-Street map 57
National Museum at
Collins Barracks **99**
National Rehabilitation Board 341
National Stud 120, 121
National Symphony Orchestra 107
National Trust 331, 339
Crown Liquor Saloon (Belfast) 269
Mount Stewart House 274–5
Mussenden Temple 252
Portstewart Strand 252
Wellbrook Beetling Mill 260
Natural History Museum (Dublin) **66**
Navan Fort 266
Neagh, Lough **266–7**
Neary's (Dublin pub) 105
Nelson Pillar (Dublin) 75
Nenagh, restaurants 313
Neo-Classical architecture 19
Neolithic 30
New Ross **140–41**
New York, Irish immigration 41
Newcastle 276
hotels 301
Mourne Coast tour 277
Newgrange 30, 31, 236–7, **238–9**
Newman, John Henry 59
Newmarket-on-Fergus
hotels 295
restaurants 313
Newport, hotels 297
Newspapers 341
Newton, Lord 59
Newtownards 272
Nightclubs, Dublin 103, 105
Nobel prizes 43, 44, 45
Nore, River 136

Norse Merchant Ferries 353
The Norseman (Dublin pub) 105
North Mayo Sculpture Trail 196
North West 200 (motorcycle race)
26, 252
Northern Bank 346
Northern Ireland **247–77**
Anglo-Irish Treaty (1921) 42
Assembly 13, 14, 29, 44
banks 346
buses 360, 361
coach tours 361
currency 345
history 29
hotels 300–301
map 248–9
personal safety 343
pubs 321
restaurants 316–17
taxis 361
telephones 349
terrorism 342
train services 358
Troubles 13, 44–5, 343
Northern Ireland Civil Rights Assoc. 44
Northern Ireland Railways 359
Northern Ireland Tourist Board 331,
338, 339
Northwest Ireland **213–27**
hotels 297–8
pubs 321
restaurants 314–15

# O
O'Brien, Donach 184
O'Brien, Edna 21
O'Brien family
Bunratty Castle 184
Clare Abbey 181
and Ennis 181
Leamaneagh Castle 180
O'Brien, Flann 21
O'Brien, Murtagh, King of Munster 219
O'Brien's Tower (Cliffs of Moher) 176
O'Carolan Harp and Traditional Music
Festival 47
O'Carolan, Turlough **22**
death 38
harp 210
memorial 81
O'Casey, Sean 20, 85
Abbey Theatre (Dublin) 86, 102
O'Connell, Daniel
Catholic emancipation 40
Derrynane House 156
grave 98
Hill of Tara 240
Merrion Square (Dublin) 66
monuments to 85, 87, 181
National Library (Dublin) 63
O'Connell Street (Dublin) 53, **86–7**
Street-by-Street map 84–5
O'Connor, Sinéad 22
O'Conor family 148, 210

O'Conor, Felim, King of
  Connaught 210
O'Conor, Hugh, King of
  Connaught 210
O'Conor, Turlough, King of
  Connaught 201
Octoberfest (Londonderry) 48
O'Doherty Castle 218
O'Donnell family 213, 222
O'Donoghue's (Dublin) 103, 105
O'Driscoll clan 162
Odyssey Complex (Belfast) 268
O'Faolain, Seán 21
Offaly, County 229
O'Flaherty, Donal 201
O'Flaherty clan 201
Ogham Stones 32, 182
Oideas Gael (Glencolumbkille) 331
Old Bushmills Distillery 258
Old Jameson's Distillery
  (Dublin) **90**
Old Midleton Distillery **171**
Oliver St John Gogarty (Dublin pub)
  104, 105
Olympia Theatre (Dublin) 102, 105
O'Malley, Grace
  Achill Island 196
  Clare Island 198
  marriage 201
One Man's Pass 221
O'Neill, Brian 34
O'Neill family 213
  Dungannon 265
  Grianán of Aileach 219
  and Protestant conquest 36, 247
O'Neill, Owen 219
Opening hours
  banks 346
  shops 322
  sights 339
Opera **329**, 331
  Dublin 103, 105
  Wexford Opera Festival 142
Opera House (Cork) 331
*Ór – Ireland's Gold* exhibition 64
Orange Order (Orangemen) 36,
  39, 47
Ormond Castle (Carrick-on-Suir) 191
Ormonde, 2nd Marquess of
  tomb of 136
Ormonde, Black Tom Butler, 10th
  Earl of 191
Ormonde, Earls of 81, 94, 137, 173, 191
O'Rourke family 225
O'Scully Monument 189
Ossian 25
Ossian's Grave 31
O'Toole family 131
O'Toole, St Laurence, Archbishop of
  Dublin 78, 79, 87
Oudry 124
Oughter, Lough 16
Oughterard 201
  hotels 297

Oul' Lammas Fair 47
Out and Out Activities (Garrison) 335
Outside World 335
Oxford Island 267
Oxmanstown 77

# P

P & O 353
Pain, J and GR 169
Paisley, Rev Ian 44
Pakenham family 233
Pakenham, Thomas 233
The Pale 34, **124**
Palestrina Choir 87
Palladian architecture 19
  Castletown House 122
  Florence Court 265
  Marino Casino 39
  Powerscourt 126
  Russborough House 124–5
  Strokestown Park House 210–11
Palladius 32, 273
Pan Celtic Festival 46
Pantomimes 49
Papal Cross (Dublin) 94
Parian ware 261
Parke, Captain Robert 225
Parke's Castle **225**, 338
  Yeats Country tour 225
Parking 357
Parknasilla
  hotels 293
  restaurants 312
Parks and gardens
  cultural holidays 331
  Avondale Forest Park 133
  Bantry House 161
  Birr Castle 245
  Botanic Gardens (Belfast) 270
  Butterstream Gardens (Trim) 240
  Castle Archdale Country Park 263
  Castle Caldwell Forest Park 262
  Castlewellan Forest Park 276
  Connemara National Park 200
  Coole Park 205
  County Wicklow Garden
    Festival 46
  Emo Court 245
  Florence Court 265
  Fota Wildlife Park and Arboretum
    170–71
  Garden of Remembrance
    (Dublin) 89
  Garinish Island 158–9
  Glenariff Forest Park 259
  Glenveagh Castle 217
  Glenveagh National Park 216
  Gougane Barra Park 163
  Irish National Heritage Park 142
  Japanese Gardens (Kildare) 121
  Johnstown Castle 143
  Kennedy (John F) Park and
    Arboretum 141
  Killruddery House 125

Parks and gardens (cont)
  Kylemore Abbey 200
  Lismore Castle 137
  Lissadell House 223
  Lough Key Forest Park 211
  Lough Rynn Estate 227
  Merrion Square (Dublin) 66
  Mount Stewart House 115, **274–5**
  Mount Usher Gardens 131
  Muckross House 151
  National Botanic Gardens
    (Dublin) 98
  Phoenix Park (Dublin) 94
  Portumna Forest Park 205
  Powerscourt 115, **126–7**
  St Stephen's Green (Dublin)
    56, **58–9**
  Slane Castle 237
  Slieve Foye Forest Park 234
  Tollymore Forest Park 277
  Tully Castle 262
  Woodstock House Demesne 141
Parliament **63**
  Bank of Ireland building (Dublin) 58
  history 34, 42
  Leinster House (Dublin) 63
Parnell, Charles Stewart 41
  Avondale House 133
  grave 98
  Home Rule campaign 40, 41
  imprisonment 41, 95
  monument to 87
Parnell Monument (Dublin)
  Street-by-Street map 84
Parsons family 245
Passage East 139
Passage graves
  Carrowkeel Passage Tomb
    Cemetery 227
  Carrowmore Megalithic
    Cemetery 226
  Dowth 236, **237**
  Hill of Tara 240
  Knowth 236, **237**
  Newgrange 236–7, **238–9**
Passports 340, 342
Pastureland 17
Patrick, St 268, **273**
  Armagh 32, 247, 266
  Croagh Patrick 197
  Downpatrick 273
  Grianán of Aileach 219
  Hill of Slane 237
  Hill of Tara 240
  Lough Derg 222
  mission to Ireland 29, 32
  St Patrick's Bell 65
  St Patrick's Cathedral (Dublin) 80
  St Patrick's Cross (Cashel) 188
  *St Patrick* (Smyth) 74
Pavarotti, Luciano 107
Payne-Townsend, Charlotte 98
Peacock, Joseph, *The Feast of St Kevin
  amid the ruins of Glendalough* 29

Peacock Theatre (Dublin) 86
Pearce, Edward Lovett 58
Pearse, Patrick 42, 59, 87
Peat **244**
   Shannonbridge Bog Railway 243
Peatland World **120**
Peatlands Park 266, 267
Pedroza, Eusebio 45
Pembroke, William Marshall, Earl
   of 140
Penn, Sir William 163
Penrose, George 139
Penrose, William 139
People's Garden, Phoenix Park
   (Dublin) 94
Perfume, duty-free allowances 340
Personal security 342–3
Peto, Harold 158–9
Petrie Crown 57
Petrie, George, *Last Circuit of
   Pilgrims at Clonmacnoise* 242
Petrol 355
Pettigo 283
Petty, William 158
Pharmacies 342, **343**
*Phoenix* 36
Phoenix Column (Dublin) 94
Phoenix Park (Dublin) 45, **94**
Phonecards 348–9
Picasso, Pablo 217
Picts 31
*Pierrot* (Gris) 68
Pillar stones 235
Pioneer Total Abstinence
   Movement 87
Place names 25
Planetarium, Observatory Grounds
   (Armagh) 266
Plantation 36, **37**
Plunkett, Joseph 43, 95
Plunkett, Oliver 236
POD (Dublin nightclub) 105
Point Theatre (Dublin) 105
   Dublin's Best: Entertainment 107
Police 342, 343
Political murals, Belfast 270
Pomodoro, *Sphere within Sphere*
   57, 61
Pontoon, hotels 297
Pony trekking **333**, 335
Portaferry 272
   hotels 301
   restaurants 317
Portal tombs 30
Portarlington, Earl of 245
Portballintrae, restaurants 317
Portlaoise, pubs 321
Portrush 252
   restaurants 317
Ports 352–3
Portsalon 217
Portstewart 248, **252**
   golf 332
Portstewart Strand 252

Portumna 177, **205**
Portumna Castle 205
Portumna Forest Park 205
Portumna Priory 205
Post offices 347
Postage stamps 347
Postal services 347
Postboxes 347
Pottery *see* Ceramics
Poulaphouca Reservoir 125
Poulnabrone Dolmen 180
Poussin, Nicolas 69
Powerscourt 115, **126–7**
Powerscourt, Richard Wingfield, 1st
   Viscount 126
Powerscourt, 7th Viscount 126
Powerscourt Townhouse
   (Dublin) **76**
   Street-by-Street map 73
Powerscourt Waterfall
   Military Road tour 130
Poynings, Edward 35
Prehistoric Ireland **30–31**
   interpretative centres 339
   Beaghmore Stone Circles **260**
   Boyne Valley **236–7**
   Browne's Hill 133
   Carrowkeel Passage Tomb
      Cemetery 215, 227
   Carrowmore Megalithic
      Cemetery 226
   Cave Hill (Belfast) 271
   Céide Fields **196**
   Connemara National Park 200
   Craggaunowen **182**
   Drombeg Stone Circle **162**
   Dún Aonghasa 206
   Dún Duchathair 207
   Dún Eochla 207
   Giant's Ring 271
   Gleninsheen Wedge Tomb 180
   Great Stone Circle
      (Lough Gur) 186
   Grianán of Aileach 218, **219**
   Hill of Tara **240**
   Knocknarea 226
   Legananny Dolmen 276
   Lough Gur **186–7**
   Navan Fort 266
   Newgrange 236–7, **238–9**
   Poulnabrone Dolmen 180
   Turoe Stone **210**
   *see also* Forts (Iron Age)
Prime Minister 63
Priories *see* Abbeys and priories
Project Arts Theatre (Dublin theatre)
   76, 105
Promontory forts 18
Prospect Cemetery (Dublin) 98
Protestant Church of Ireland 80
Protestants
   Battle of the Boyne 236
   Protestant Ascendancy 38–9
   Protestant Conquest 36–7

Prowse (Keith) Travel (IRL) Ltd
   (Dublin) 331
Ptolemy 31
Public holidays 49
Public Records Office (Dublin) 91
Pubs **318–21**
   Cork and Kerry 319
   Dublin 104, 105
   Dublin's Best: Entertainment 106–7
   food in 303
   Lower Shannon 319–20
   Midlands 321
   Northern Ireland 321
   Northwest Ireland 321
   Southeast Ireland 318–19
   traditional music 103, 105, 329
   West of Ireland 320–21
Puck Fair 47
Pugin, AWN 141
Punchestown 26, 121
Purple Mountain 155
Puxley Mansion 158

## Q

Qantas 351
Queen's (Dublin pub) 105
Queen's University, Belfast 270
Quills Woollen Market (Killarney) 325
Quin Franciscan Friary 181

## R

Racing, horse 26–7, **121**, 332
Radio 341
Railways *see* Trains
Rainfall 48
Raised bogs 244
Raleigh, Sir Walter 171
Raleigh Rent-a-Bike (Dublin) 335, 357
Ramsay, Allan 160
Rathaspeck, hotels 290
Rathlannon Castle 143
Rathlin Island 258
Rathmelton 217
Rathmines, hotels 289
Rathmullan, restaurants 314
Rathnew
   hotels 290
   restaurants 309
Rathvilly, hotels 290
Carbery 162
Red Abbey (Cork) 168
Ree, Lough 177
Reformation 81
*The Relief of Derry* (Sadler) 37
Religion
   Celtic Christianity 32–3
   religious services 339
   *see also* Abbeys and priories;
      Cathedrals; Churches in Dublin;
      Monasteries
Rembrandt 69
Renoir, Pierre Auguste 217
Rent-a-Bike 357
Rent an Irish Cottage 283

Renting a car 355
Renvyle, hotels 297
Restaurants **302–17**
  budget dining 303
  Cork and Kerry 310–12
  Dublin 306–8
  gourmet and ethnic dining 302–3
  Irish eating patterns 302
  Lower Shannon 312–13
  Midlands 315
  Northern Ireland 316–17
  Northwest Ireland 314–15
  Southeast Ireland 308–9
  West of Ireland 313–14
  What to Eat in Ireland 304–5
Ri-Rá (Dublin nightclub) 105
Riasc
  Dingle Peninsula tour 150
Richard II, King of England 35
Riding **333**, 335
Ring forts 18–19
Ring of Kerry tour **156–7**
River Club (Dublin nightclub) 105
Rivers 16
Riverstown, hotels 298
Road maps 355
Road signs 356
Roberts, John 138
Robertstown **120**, 332
Robinson, Mary 14, 44, 45
Robinson, Sir William
  Dublin Castle 74
  Marsh's Library (Dublin) 81
  Royal Hospital Kilmainham 95
Roche, Steven 45
Rock of Cashel 114, 187, **188–9**
Rock of Dunamase **245**
Rock music **329**, 331
  Dublin 103, 105
Rockingham estate 211
Rodin, Auguste 89
Romans 31
Roonah 194
Roscommon **210**
  restaurants 314
Roscommon Castle 210
Roscommon, County 193
Roscrea **187**
Roscrea Castle 187
Rose of Tralee Festival 47
Rosguill Peninsula **217**
Ross, Bishop of 163
Ross Castle 154
Rosse, 2nd Earl of 245
Rosse, 3rd Earl of 245
Rosse, 6th Earl of 245
The Rosses **220**
Rosses Point
  restaurants 315
  Yeats Country tour 224
Rosslare **143**, 334
  ferries 352
  hotels 290
  restaurants 309

Rossnowlagh **222–3**
  hotels 298
  pubs 321
Rostrevor
  Mourne Coast tour 277
Rosturk, hotels 297
Rotunda Hospital (Dublin) 38, **88**
  Street-by-Street map 84
Rouault, Georges 167
Round Ireland Yacht Race 26
Round towers 18–19
Roundstone 199
Roundwood
  Military Road tour 130
Roundwood House 285
Royal Automobile Club (RAC) 357
Royal Canal 40, 99, 240–41
Royal College of Surgeons
  (Dublin) 59
Royal Cork Yacht Club 27
Royal Dublin Society 38, 63, 105
Royal Gunpowder Mills (Cork) 169
Royal Hibernian Academy
  (Dublin) **66**
Royal Hospital Kilmainham 95
Royal Tara China (Galway) 325
Royal Ulster Agriculture Society
  Show 46
Royal Ulster Constabulary (RUC)
  342
Rubens, Peter Paul 69, 124
Rugby 26, 332
Russborough House 39, **124–5**
  Milltown collection 68
  stucco 19
Rutland Fountain (Dublin) 66
Ryanair 351
Rynhart, Jean, *Molly Malone* 58

**S**
Sadler, William II, *The Relief of Derry* 37
Safety 342–3
Sagas 20
Sailing 26–7, **334**, 335
  regattas 47
St Ann's Church (Dublin) **59**
  Street-by-Street map 56
St Audoen's Church (Dublin) 77
St Audoen's Roman Catholic Church
  (Dublin) 77
St Ernan's House 284
St Fiachra's Garden (Kildare) 121
St James's Gate Brewery (Dublin) 39
St John Ambulance Brigade 79
St John's Point 276
St Mary's Abbey Exhibition
  (Dublin) **91**
St Mary's Pro-Cathedral (Dublin) **87**
  Street-by-Street map 85
St Michael's Tower (Dublin) 77
St Michan's Church (Dublin) 90
St Patrick's Cathedral (Dublin) 52,
  **80–81**

St Patrick's Day 46
St Stephen's Day 49
St Stephen's Green (Dublin) **58–9**
  Street-by-Street map 56
St Stephen's Green Shopping Centre
  (Dublin) 325
Sales tax 322
Saller's Jewellers (Galway) 325
Sally Gap 131
  Military Road tour 130
Salmon fishing 26, 49
Saltee Islands **143**
Salthill 203, 341
Sandel, Mount 30
Sands, Bobbie 45
Sandycove restaurants 308
Saul 273
Saxons 31
Sayers, Peig 20
Scattery Island 176
Schomberg, General 267
Schull 159
Scrabo Country Park 272
Screen (Dublin) 105
Sculpture
  High Crosses 235
  North Mayo Sculpture Trail 196
Scurlogstown Olympiad Celtic
  Festival 47
Sea travel 352–4
Sea trout fishing 49
SeaCat 353
*Seanad Éireann* 63
Self-catering accommodation 282
Selskar Abbey (Wexford) 142
Semple Stadium (Thurles) 331
Seven Churches (Aran Islands) 206
Severin, Tim 182
Shaftesbury, Earl of 271
Shaikh, Ahmad 99
Shanagarry
  hotels 293
  restaurants 312
Shannon Airport 340, **350**, 351
Shannon Ceili (Bunratty) 331
Shannon-Erne Waterway 177,
  **227**, 335
Shannon hydro-electric scheme 43
Shannon, River 16, **177**
  Lower Shannon 173
  map 177
Shannonbridge Bog Railway **243**
Share Centre (Lisnaskea) 335
Shaw, George Bernard 20, 98, 106
  Coole Park 205
  National Gallery (Dublin) 68
  National Library (Dublin) 63
  Nobel prize 43
  *Saint Joan* 159
Shaw's Birthplace (Dublin) **98**
Sheares, Henry and John 90
Sheen, River 158
Sheep Island 253
Shelbourne Bar (Dublin) 105

Shelbourne Hotel (Dublin) 59, 280
    Street-by-Street map 57
Sheridan, Richard Brinsley 20
Sherkin Island 162
Shooting **334**, 335
Shopping **322–7**
    books **323**, 325
    ceramics and china **323**, 325
    crafts **323**, 325
    crystal and glassware **323**, 325
    department stores 325
    Dublin 322
    fashion **324**, 325
    food and drink **324**, 325
    how to pay 322
    jewellery **324**, 325
    knitwear and tweed **324**, 325
    linen **324**, 325
    music **323**, 325
    opening hours 322
    sales tax and refunds 322
    What to Buy in Ireland 326–7
    where to shop 322
Siamsa Tíre folklore theatre 148–9, 331
*The Sick Call* (Lawless) 69
Silent Valley 276
    Mourne Coast tour 277
Silver Line Cruisers (Banagher) 335
Simnel, Lambert 35, 79
Sinn Féin
    cease-fire (1994) 45
    Custom House fire 86
    history 42
*Sirius* (liner) 170
Sirr, Major Henry 75
Sitric Silkenbeard 33
Six Nations Rugby Tournament 26, 49
Skellig Experience Centre 156
Skellig Michael 145, **156–7**
The Skelligs **156–7**
Skibbereen 159
Sky Road 199
Slade 140
Slade Castle 140
Slane **237**
    hotels 299
Slane Castle 237
Slane, Hill of *see* Hill of Slane
Slaney, River 141
Slattery's Travel Agency (Tralee) 283
Slazenger family 126
Slea Head
    Dingle Peninsula tour 150
Slieve Bloom Mountains **245**
Slieve Bloom Way 245
Slieve Donard 276
Slieve Foye Forest Park 234
Slieve Gallion 260
Slieve League **221**
Slieve Patrick 273
Slievemore 196
Sligo 213, 224–5, **226**
    pubs 321
    restaurants 315

Sligo Abbey 226
Sligo Arts Festival 48
Sligo, County 213
    Yeats Country tour 224–5
Sligo Crystal (Grange) 325
Sligo International Choral
    Festival 48
Smith, John Charles 197
Smithfield (Dublin) **90**, 103
Smyth, Edward
    Church of the Most Holy Trinity
        sculptures 74
    Custom House sculpture 85, 86
    King's Inns sculptures 90
    Marino Casino lions 38
    *St Patrick* 74
Smyth's Irish Linen (Belfast) 325
Sneem 346–7
    Ring of Kerry tour 157
Soccer 26–7, 332
South Sligo Summer School of
    Traditional Music, Song and
    Dance 331
Southeast Ireland **117–43**
    hotels 289–91
    map 118–19
    pubs 318–19
    restaurants 308–9
Southern Hotels 283
Spanish Armada 36
Speed limits 356
Spelga Dam
    Mourne Coast tour 277
Sperrin Mountains 260
*Sphere within Sphere* (Pomodoro)
    57, 61
Sports **332–5**
    The Sporting Year **26–7**
Spring in Ireland 46
Stag's Head (Dublin pub) 105
    Dublin's Best: Entertainment 106
Staic, Brian de (Killarney) 325
Staigue Fort
    Ring of Kerry tour 156
Stamps, postage 347
Standuin (Spiddal) 325
Stapleton, Michael 19
    Belvedere College (Dublin) 88
    James Joyce Cultural Centre
        (Dublin) 88
    Powerscourt Townhouse
        (Dublin) 76
    Trinity College, Dublin 60
Station Island 222
Stena Line 353
Stewart, Richard 75
Stoker, Bram 59
Stone Age 173
    interpretative centres 339
    *see also* Prehistoric Ireland
Stone circles
    Beaghmore Stone Circles 260
    Drombeg Stone Circle 162
    Great Stone Circle (Lough Gur) 186

Stormont 271
Stradbally 245
Stradbally Steam-engine Rally 47
Straffan, hotels 290
Strangford, restaurants 317
Stranorlar, hotels 298
Street, George 78
Streeve House 285
Strokestown Park House **210–11**
Strongbow (Richard de Clare)
    Christ Church Cathedral
        (Dublin) 78
    invades Ireland 71, 77
    marriage 34
    monument to 78
Struell Wells 273
Stuart, James "Athenian" 274
Stubbs, George, *Hambletonian* 275
Stucco 19
Student information 340
Students, travel concessions 359
Studio Donegal (Kilcar) 325
Sugar Club, The (Dublin) 103, 105
Suir, River 138, 190, 191
Summer Cabaret (Limerick) 331
Summer in Ireland 46–7
Sunlight Chambers (Dublin)
    Street-by-Street map 72
Sunshine 47
Swans 25
Swansea Cork Ferries 353
Swift, Jonathan 20, **80**
    Dean of St Patrick's Cathedral 38
    *Gulliver's Travels* 266
    marble bust 55
    memorials 52, 81
    *A Modest Proposal* 38
Swilly, Lough 218, 219
Swilly, River 219
Synge, John Millington 20–21, 85
    Abbey Theatre (Dublin) 86, 102

# T

Tahilla, hotels 293
Taibhdhearc Theatre (Galway) 331
Tailors' Hall (Dublin) **80**
Tain Trail 234
*The Taking of Christ* (Caravaggio)
    53, 69
Talbot Castle 240
Talbot family 100
*Tánaiste* 63
*Taoiseach* 63
Tara, Hill of *see* Hill of Tara
Tara Brooch 65
"A Taste of Baltimore" Shellfish
    Festival 46
Tax, sales (VAT) 322
Taxis 360–61
Tay, Lough
    Military Road tour 130
*Teachta Dala* (TDs) 63
Telecom Eireann 348
Telephones 348–9

Television 341
Temperance crusade 40
Temperatures 49
Temple Bar (Dublin) 71, **76**
    Dublin's Best: Entertainment 106
    Street-by-Street map 73
Temple Bar Music Centre (Dublin)
    103, 105
Teresa, Mother 197
Terrorism 342
    see also Troubles
Thackeray, William Makepeace
    154, 259
Theatre **328**, 331
    Dublin 102, 105
    Dublin's Best: Entertainment 106–7
    festivals 48
Theatre Royal (Waterford) 331
Them 22
Thin Lizzy 22, 103
Thomastown
    hotels 290
    restaurants 309
Thomond, Earls of 184
Thoor Ballylee **204–5**
*The Three Graces* (Canova) 169
Thrifty Car Rentals 357
Ticketmaster 105, 328, 331
Ticket Shop (Dublin) 105
Tickets
    air travel 351
    buses 360
    for entertainments 102, 105,
    **328**, 331
    ferries 354
    trains 359
Time zone 341
Timoleague Abbey **162–3**
Tintern Abbey 140
Tipperary, County 173
Tipperary Crystal (Carrick-on-Suir) 325
Tipping, in hotels 281
*Titanic* 42, 170, 272
    Titanic Memorial (Belfast) 268
Tobercurry, restaurants 315
Tobernalt 226
Tola, St 181
Tollymore Forest Park
    Mourne Coast tour 277
Tombs see Passage graves
Tone, Wolfe 269
    Cave Hill (Belfast) 271
    French Armada Centre (Bantry
    House) 160
    marriage 59
    monument 59
    portraits 100
    rebellion 38, 39, 160
    Tailors' Hall rally 80
"Tonehenge" 59
Toner's (Dublin pub) 105
Toome 267
Torc Mountain 154
Torc Waterfall 154

Torr Head 259
Tory Island **216**
Tour de France 45
Tourist information offices 338
Tours by car
    Dingle Peninsula 150–51
    Inishowen Peninsula 218–19
    Lower Lough Erne 262–3
    Military Road 130
    Mourne coast 277
    Ring of Kerry 156–7
    Yeats Country 224–5
Tower Enterprise Centre (Dublin) 325
Tower houses 18–19
Towers, round 18–19
Town and Country Homes
    Association 283
Town and Seaside House
    Association 283
Traditional music and dance **329**, 331
    Dublin 103, 105
Trains **358–9**
    Shannonbridge Bog Railway 243
    Steam Railway (Tralee) 149
    student discounts, 340
    through-tickets, 354
Tralee **148–9**
Translink City Bus (Belfast), 353 361
Travel **350–61**
    air 350–51
    buses 360–61
    cars 355–7
    Cork and Kerry 147
    getting to Ireland 10
    insurance 342
    Lower Shannon 174
    Midlands 230
    Northern Ireland 248
    Northwest Ireland 215
    sea 352–4
    Southeast Ireland 119
    taxis 360–61
    trains 358–9
    Ulster Folk and Transport
    Museum 272
    West of Ireland 194
Traveller's cheques 322, 346–7
Treasure Chest (Galway) 325
Trevor, William 21
Trim 231, **240**
Trim Castle 240
Trimble, David 13
Trinity College, Dublin 13, **60–62**, 340
    *Book of Kells* 62
    history 36
    Old Library 53, 55, 61
    Street-by-Street map 57
The Troubles 13, 44–5
    personal safety 343
    political murals 270
TSB Bank 346
Tully Castle
    Lower Lough Erne tour 262
Tullynally Castle **233**

Turloughs 178
Turner, Richard 98
Turoe Stone **210**
Tweed shops **324**, 325
Twelve Bens 193, 198, 200
Tympanum 19
Tyrone, County 247
Tyrone, Hugh O'Neill,
    Earl of 37, 247
Tyrone Crystal (Dungannon)
    265, 325

**U**

U2 (band) 15, 22, 103
Ufford, Robert d' 210
Uí Néill clan 247
Ulster see also Northern Ireland
Ulster Bank 344
Ulster Cruising School
    (Carrickfergus) 335
Ulster Federation of Rambling Clubs
    (Belfast) 335
Ulster Folk and Transport
    Museum 272
Ulster Hall (Belfast) 331
Ulster History Park 261
Ulster Peace Movement 45
Ulster, Red Hand of 268–9
Ulster, Richard de Burgo,
    Earl of 219
Ulster Volunteer Force 42, 267
Ulster Way 333
Ulster-American Folk Park 261
Ulsterbus 361
Unionist Party 42
United Irishmen
    attempted invasion of Ireland 160
    foundation of 269
    rebellion 38, 39
United Nations 44
United States, Irish immigration
    41, 170
University Church (Dublin) 59
USIT 341

**V**

Valdré, Vincenzo 74
Vale of Avoca 131
Vale of Clara
    Military Road tour 130
Valentia Island **156**
Valentine, St 81
Vanhomrigh, Hester 80
Vartry, River 131
VAT (sales tax) 322
Veagh, Lough 216
Ventry 346–7
Vernet, Joseph 124
Victoria, Queen of England
    Cobh 170
    Glengarriff 159
    Lakes of Killarney 155
    opens Dublin Exhibition 41
    statues of 44, 268

Viking Adventure, Dublin 76
Vikings 32
  Donegal 222
  Dublin 71, **77**
  invasions of Ireland 29, 33, 117
  Limerick 183
  Lower Shannon 173
  National Museum exhibition 65
  Waterford 138
  Wexford 142
  Wood Quay (Dublin) 72, **76**
Vinegar Hill 141
Vintners Company 37
Virgin Atlantic Cityjet 351
Virgin Mary 197
Visas 340

**W**

Walking **333**, 335
Walpole, Edward 131
Waltons (Dublin) 325
Warbeck, Perkin 35
Water sports **334**, 335
Waterfalls
  Glencar Lough 225
  Powerscourt 130
  Torc 154
Waterford 35, **138–9**
  hotels 290–91
  pubs 318
  restaurants 309
Waterford Castle 280, 285
Waterford, County 117
Waterford Crystal 68, 72, **139**, 325
Waterford Festival of Light Opera
  48, 331
Waterford Museum of Treasures 138
Waterstone's (Dublin) 325
Waterville, hotels 293
Waterways Visitors' Centre (Dublin) **99**
Waugh, Samuel 41
Wavertree, Lord 121
Wayne, John 201
Weather 46–9
Wellbrook Beetling Mill 260
Welles, Orson 88
Wellington, Duke of 58, 66
Wellington Testimonial (Dublin) 94
West of Ireland **193–211**
  hotels 295–7
  pubs 320–21
  restaurants 313–14
West, Robert 265
Westmeath, County 229
Westport **196–7**
  hotels 297
  pubs 321
  restaurants 314
Westport House 194, 197
Wetlands 16
Wexford **142**
  hotels 291
  pubs 318–19
  restaurants 309

Wexford, County 117
Wexford Opera Festival 48, 142, 331
Wexford Wildfowl Reserve 142
Wheelchair access *see* Disabled
  travellers
Whelan's (Dublin) 105
Whichcraft Gallery (Dublin) 325
Whiddy Island 159, 161
Whiskey **258**
  Jameson Heritage Centre
    (Midleton) 171
  Locke's Distillery 241
  Old Bushmills Distillery 258
  Old Jameson's Distillery (Dublin) 90
Whitby, Synod of (664) 32
White family 159, 160
White Island
  Lower Lough Erne tour 263
White Park Bay 253
Whitefriar Street Carmelite Church
  (Dublin) **81**
Whyte, Samuel 58
Wicklow, County 117
Wicklow Mountains 17, 117, **131**
  Military Road tour 130
Wicklow Town
  hotels 291
  restaurants 309
Wicklow Way 131
"Wild Geese, Flight of the" 173
Wilde, Oscar 20
  *The Importance of Being Oscar* 88
  Merrion Square (Dublin) 66
  Portora Royal School 264
Wildlife 16–17
Wildlife reserves
  The Burren 178–9
  Castle Caldwell Forest Park 262
  Connemara 200–201
  Fota Wildlife Park and Arboretum
    170–71
  Peatlands Park 266, 267
  Shannonbridge Bog Railway 243
  Wexford Wildfowl Reserve 142
William of Orange
  Battle of the Boyne 29, 36, 236
  Carrickfergus Castle 267
  Mellifont Abbey 237
  siege of Kinsale 164
  siege of Limerick 173
  throne 74
Williams, Betty 45
Wilton, Joseph 98
Windsor, John 91
Wine, duty-free allowances 340
Wingfield family 127
Winter in Ireland 49
Women's Mini Marathon 46
Wood Quay (Dublin) **76**
  Street-by-Street map 72
Woodstock House Demesne 141
World Cup (football) 45
World War I 42
World War II 43

Wyatt, James 19
  Castle Coole 264
  Westport 196
  Westport House 197

**Y**

Yeats, Jack
  Coole Park 205
  Crawford Art Gallery (Cork) 166
  *For the Road* 68
  Glebe House and Gallery 217
  Sligo County Museum and Art
    Gallery 226
Yeats, John 226
Yeats, WB **20**
  Abbey Theatre (Dublin) 86, 102
  *Cathleen ni Houlihan* 13
  Country Tour **224–5**
  and Constance Markievicz 223
  Easter Rising 87
  grave 224–5
  Irish Revival 21
  memorial 58
  Merrion Square (Dublin) 66
  Nobel prize 43
  and Sligo **225**, 226
  statue of 226
  Thoor Ballylee 204–5
  Yeats Country 114, **224–5**
  Yeats International Summer School
    (Sligo) 331
Yola Farmstead (Rosslare) 143
Youghal **171**
  hotels 293
  restaurants 312
Young Ireland Uprising 41
Youth Hostel Association of
  Northern Ireland 283
Youth hostels 283

**Z**

Zoos
  Belfast Zoo 271
  Fota Wildlife Park and Arboretum
    170–71
  Zoological Gardens, Phoenix Park
    (Dublin) 94
Zurbarán, Francisco 69

# Acknowledgments

DORLING KINDERSLEY would like to thank the following people whose contributions and assistance have made the preparation of this book possible.

**MAIN CONTRIBUTORS**
LISA GERARD-SHARP is a writer and broadcaster who has contributed to numerous travel books, including the *Eyewitness Travel Guide to France*. She is of Irish extraction, with roots in County Sligo and County Galway, and a regular visitor to Ireland.

TIM PERRY, from Dungannon, County Tyrone, writes on travel and popular music for various publishers in North America and the British Isles.

**ADDITIONAL CONTRIBUTOR**
Douglas Palmer.

**ADDITIONAL PHOTOGRAPHY**
Peter Anderson, Joe Cornish, Andy Crawford, Michael Diggin, Steve Gorton, Anthony Haughey, Mike Linley, Stephen Oliver, Magnus Rew, Clive Streeter, Matthew Ward.

**ADDITIONAL ILLUSTRATIONS**
Richard Bonson, Brian Craker, John Fox, Paul Guest, Stephan Gyapay, Ian Henderson, Claire Littlejohn, Gillie Newman, Chris Orr, Kevin Robinson, John Woodcock, Martin Woodward.

**ADDITIONAL PICTURE RESEARCH**
Miriam Sharland.

**EDITORIAL AND DESIGN**
MANAGING EDITORS  Vivien Crump, Helen Partington
MANAGING ART EDITOR  Steve Knowlden
DEPUTY EDITORIAL DIRECTOR  Douglas Amrine
DEPUTY ART DIRECTOR  Gaye Allen
PRODUCTION  David Proffit, Hilary Stephens
PICTURE RESEARCH  Sue Mennell, Christine Rista
DTP DESIGNER  Adam Moore
MAPS Gary Bowes, Margaret Slowey, Richard Toomey (ERA-Maptec, Dublin, Ireland)
MAP CO-ORDINATORS  Michael Ellis, David Pugh

Marion Broderick, Margaret Chang, Martin Cropper, Guy Dimond, Fay Franklin, Yael Freudmann, Sally Ann Hibbard, Annette Jacobs, Kathryn Lane, Erika Lang, Maite Lantaron, Oenone Luke, Michael Osborn, Polly Phillimore, Caroline Radula-Scott, Rachel Symons.

**INDEX**
Hilary Bird.

**SPECIAL ASSISTANCE**
Dorling Kindersley would like to thank all the regional and local tourist offices in the Republic and in Northern Ireland for their valuable help. Particular thanks also to: Ralph Doak and Egerton Shelswell-White at Bantry House, Bantry, Co Cork;

Vera Greif at the Chester Beatty Library and Gallery of Oriental Art, Dublin; Alan Figgis at Christ Church Cathedral, Dublin; Labhras Ó Murchu at Comhaltas Ceoltóirí Éireann; Catherine O'Connor at Derry City Council; Patsy O'Connell at Dublin Tourism; Tanya Cathcart at Fermanagh Tourism, Enniskillen; Peter Walsh at the Guinness Hop Store, Dublin; Gerard Collet at the Irish Shop, Covent Garden, London; Dónall P Ó Baoill at ITE, Dublin; Pat Cooke at Kilmainham Gaol, Dublin; Angela Shanahan at the Kinsale Tourist Office; Bill Maxwell, Adrian Le Harivel and Marie McFeely at the National Gallery of Ireland, Dublin; Philip McCann at the National Library of Ireland, Dublin; Willy Cumming at the National Monuments Divison, Office of Public Works, Dublin; Eileen Dunne and Sharon Fogarty at the National Museum of Ireland, Dublin; Joris Minne at the Northern Ireland Tourist Office, Belfast; Dr Tom MacNeil at Queen's University, Belfast; Sheila Crowley at St Mary's Pro-Cathedral, Dublin; Paul Brock at the Shannon Development Centre; Tom Sheedy at Shannon Heritage and Banquets, Bunratty Castle, Co Clare; Angela Sutherland at the Shannon-Erne Waterway, Co Leitrim; Máire Ní Bháin at Trinity College, Dublin; Anne-Marie Diffley at Trinity College Library, Dublin; Pat Maclean at the Ulster Museum, Belfast; Harry Hughes at the Willie Clancy School of Traditional Music, Miltown Malbay, Co Clare.

**ADDITIONAL ASSISTANCE**
Kathleen Crowley, Rory Doyle, Peter Hynes, David O'Grady, Mary O'Grady, Madge Perry, Poppy.

**PHOTOGRAPHY PERMISSIONS**
THE PUBLISHER would like to thank all those who gave permission to photograph at various cathedrals, churches, museums, restaurants, hotels, shops, galleries and other sights too numerous to list individually.

**PICTURE CREDITS**
tl = top left; tc = top centre; tr = top right; cla = centre left above; ca = centre above; cra = centre right above; cl = centre left; c = centre; cr = centre right; clb = centre left below; cb = centre below; crb = centre right below; bl = bottom left; bc = bottom centre; br = bottom right.

The publisher would like to thank the following individuals, companies and picture libraries for permission to reproduce their photographs:

AER LINGUS/AIRBUS INDUSTRIE: 350tc; AKG, LONDON: National Museum, Copenhagen/Erich Lessing 24cl; ALLSPORT: David Rogers 26cb; Steve Powell 45tc; APPLETREE PRESS LTD, BELFAST (*Irish Proverbs* © illustrations Karen Bailey) 327cl.
BORD FÁILTE/IRISH TOURIST BOARD: Brian Lynch 22–23, 23tl, 238tl, 238tr, Pat Odea 330c; © BRISTOL CITY MUSEUMS AND ART GALLERY: 30bl; © BRITISH LIBRARY: *Richard II's Campaigns in Ireland* Ms.Harl.1319, f.18 35tl; © BRITISH MUSEUM: 31bl; BT PAYPHONES: 349cl, 349cr, 349b; BUS ÉIREANN: 360cl; © BUSHMILLS LTD: 258bl.

© CENTRAL BANK OF IRELAND: *Lady Lavery as Cathleen ni Houlihan*, John Lavery 13ca, 344 (all banknotes and coins except for tr), 345; CENTRAL CYBER CAFÉ, DUBLIN: Finbarr Clarkson 348tr; © CHESTER BEATTY LIBRARY, DUBLIN: 75t; © CLASSIC DESIGNS/LJ YOUNG LTD, BLARNEY: 327c; Mark Boulton 17tr; Patrick Clement 16clb, 16bl; Adrian Davies 16br; Rodney Dawson 17cl; Frances Furlong 16tl; David Green 200bl; Pekka Helo 17cr; Jan Van de Kam 178bl; Gordon Langsbury 16cl, 178cr; John Markham 244br; George McCarthy 17tl, 17bl,17br, 130tl, 201bl; MR Phicon 16crb; Eckhart Pott 17cb; Hans Reinhard 17tcb, 154tl, 262tl; Kim Taylor 17tc, 244t; R Wanscheidt 17cbr; Uwe Walz 16cr, 177cb; G Ziesler 201bl; © CORK EXAMINER: 27tl; © CORK PUBLIC MUSEUM: 33cla; JOE CORNISH: 17cla, 204b, 262tr, 336–7; CRAWFORD MUNICIPAL ART GALLERY: *The Meeting of St Brendan and the Unhappy Judas*, Harry Clarke 166bl.

DAVISON & ASSOCIATES, LTD, IRELAND: 79cra; DERRY CITY COUNCIL: 250tr; MICHAEL DIGGIN: 18tl, 145b, 155cr, 156cla, 157tr, 177tl, 198bl, 217t, 218tr, 218cl, 219cra, 332tl, 333tl, 333b, 339br, 341b, 343cl, 346b; BILL DOYLE: 206bl; GA DUNCAN: 44cb, 44bl; © DUNDEE ART GALLERIES AND MUSEUMS: *The Children of Lir*, John Duncan 25tc.

eircom: 348tl, 348bl, 348cr; ET ARCHIVE: 25bl; MARY EVANS PICTURE LIBRARY: 9 (inset), 22tl, 24tr, 24bl, 24br, 25cla, 32bl, 35bc, 36bl; 42bl, 51 (inset), 75cl, 87bl, 113 (inset), 273br, 279 (inset), 337 (inset).

© STEPHEN FALLER LTD, GALWAY: 326cla; © FAMINE MUSEUM CO ROSSCOMMON: 211tr; JIM FITZPATRICK: 77bl.

GILL AND MACMILLAN PUBLISHERS, DUBLIN: 43bl; RONALD GRANT ARCHIVE: *The Commitments*, Twentieth Century Fox 21br; © GUINNESS IRELAND LTD: 96bl, 96br, 97tl, 97tr, 97bl, 97br.

HULTON DEUTSCH COLLECTION: 20clb, 21tr, 37t, 40br, 40cbl, 44crb, Reuter 45crb, 60bl.
IMAGES COLOUR LIBRARY: 46bl, 53tl; 221bc; INPHO, DUBLIN: 26cla, Billy Stickland 26br, Lorraine O'Sullivan 27br; IRISH PICTURE LIBRARY, DUBLIN: 36cla, 39tl, 42tl; IRISH RAIL (IARNRÓD ÉIREANN): 358tr; © IRISH TIMES: 126br; © IRISH TRADITIONAL MUSIC ARCHIVE, DUBLIN: 23bl.

JARROLD COLOUR PUBLICATIONS: JA Brooks 60br; MICHAEL JENNER: 235cr.
TIMOTHY KOVAR: 76bl; 103tl, 106bl.

© LAMBETH PALACE LIBRARY, LONDON: Plan of the London Vintners' Company Township of Bellaghy, Ulster, 1622 (ms. Carew 634 f.34) (detail) 37cra; FRANK LANE PICTURE AGENCY: Roger Wilmshurst 178bc; © LEEDS CITY ART GALLERY: *The Irish House of Commons*, Francis Wheatley 38cla.

HUGH McKNIGHT PHOTOGRAPHY: 99t; MANDER AND MITCHESON THEATRE COLLECTION: 22cl; MANSELL COLLECTION: 38bl, 43cra, 79bl, 260bc; ARCHIE MILES: 200br; JOHN MURRAY: 49bl, 94cl, 120c; © MUSEUM OF THE CITY OF NEW YORK: Gift of Mrs Robert M Littlejohn, *The Bay and Harbor of New York 1855*, Samuel B Waugh 40–41.

NATIONAL CONCERT HALL, DUBLIN: Frank Fennell 107bl; © NATIONAL GALLERY OF IRELAND, DUBLIN: *WB Yeats and the Irish Theatre*, Edmund Dulac 20tr, *George Bernard Shaw*, John Collier 20cr, *Carolan the Harper*, Francis Bindon 22tr, *Leixlip Castle*, Irish School 39cla, *The Custom House, Dublin*, James Malton 39bc, *Queen Victoria and Prince Albert Opening the 1853 Dublin Great Exhibition*, James Mahoney 41bl, *The Houseless Wanderer*, JH Foley 68tl, *Pierrot*, Juan Gris 68tr, *For the Road*, JB Yeats 68cla, *The Taking of Christ*, Caravaggio 69cra, *Judith with the Head of Holofernes*, Andrea Mantegna 69cra, *The Sick Call*, Matthew James Lawless 69crb, *Jonathan Swift, Satirist*, Charles Jerval 80bc, *James Joyce*, Jacques Emile Blanche 88t, *Interior with Members of a Family*, P Hussey 124br, *William Butler Yeats, Poet*, JB Yeats 225tl, *The Last Circuit of Pilgrims at Clonmacnoise*, George Petrie 242tr; © NATIONAL GALLERY, LONDON: *Beach Scene*, Edgar Degas 89br; © NATIONAL LIBRARY OF IRELAND, DUBLIN: 21cla, 21crb, 29b, 32tl, 32clb, 34bl, 36tl, 36clb, 38clb, 40tl, 40cla, 40bl, 41crb, 41tl, 42clb, 43tl, 43crb, *St Stephen's Green*, James Malton 50–51, 133tr, 170cra, 236b; © NATIONAL MUSEUM OF IRELAND, DUBLIN: 3, 30tl, 30clb, 30cb 30crb, 30–31, 31c 31clb, 31br, 32cla, 33cb, 33br, 53bl, 57cr, all 64–5, 99b; THE NATIONAL TRUST, NORTHERN IRELAND: *Lord Castlereagh* after Lawrence 274tl, *Hambletonian*, George Stubbs 275tl, 275cra; THE NATIONAL TRUST PHOTOGRAPHIC

LIBRARY: Mathew Antrobus 265b, John Bethell 276tl, Patrick Pendergast 264bl, Will Webster 269br, 278–9; NATURE PHOTOGRAPHERS: B Burbridge 179bc, Paul Sterry 178clb; NORTHERN IRELAND TOURIST BOARD: 26tr, 250cl, 265tr, 328cl, 329tl; NORTON ASSOCIATES: 72 clb.

KYRAN O'BRIEN 107tr; © THE OFFICE OF PUBLIC WORKS, IRELAND: 164bl, 238cl, 239tl, 239cr, 240br, 242tl; OXFORD SCIENTIFIC FILMS: Frithjof Skibbe 178tl. PACEMAKER PRESS INTERNATIONAL, LTD: 342bc, 342br; WALTER PFEIFFER STUDIOS, DUBLIN: 23t, 23cra, 23c, 23cr, 23crb, 23br; PHOTO FLORA: Andrew N Gagg 178br; PHOTOSTAGE: Donald Cooper 106tr, 107tl; POPPERFOTO: 44cla, 44br, 45tl, Reuter/Crispin Rodwell 45tr; POWERSCOURT ESTATE, ENNISKERRY: 127c.

RANGE PICTURES: 41cra; THE REFORM CLUB, LONDON: 40cla; REPORT/DEREK SPIERS, DUBLIN: 44tl, 44tr, 270bl, 270br; RETNA PICTURES: Chris Taylor 22bl, Jay Blakesberg 22br; RETROGRAPH ARCHIVE, LONDON: © Martin Ranicar-Breese 63br; REX FEATURES: 45ca; Sipa Press 45clb, 45br, 45bl.

SHANNON DEVELOPMENT PHOTO LIBRARY: 330tl; SHANNON-ERNE WATERWAY: 227bc; THE SLIDE FILE, DUBLIN: 14bc, 15t, 15c, 16cla, 16cra, 20cla, 27cra, 27clb, 27bl, 30cla, 46cla, 46bl, 47cb, 48cla, 48cra, 48cb, 48bl, 49cra, 75tr, 75br, 106br, 114cla, 121br, 130cl 130br, 143br, 177br, 203tl, 205tr, 206cb, 206br, 207bc, 216br, 219tr, 222tl, 222b, 224tr, 229b, 232tl, 234tl, 240tl, 242–3, 244cra, 262clb, 329br, 330br; SPORTSFILE, DUBLIN: 27tc; STENA LINE: 352cl; DON SUTTON INTERNATIONAL PHOTO LIBRARY: 282br. © TATE GALLERY PUBLICATIONS: *Captain Thomas Lee,* Marcus Gheeraedts 36br; TOPHAM PICTURE SOURCE: 39br, Tim Graham 94t; TRANSLINK: 360bl; © TRINITY COLLEGE, DUBLIN: Ms.1440 (Book of Burgos) f.20v

35clb; Ms.58 (Book of Kells) f.129v 4tr, *The Marriage of Princess Aoite and the Earl of Pembroke,* Daniel Maclise 34cla, Ms.57 (Book of Durrow) f.84v 53cr, Ms.57 (Book of Durrow) f.85v 61cr, Ms.58 (Book of Kells) f.129v 62cra, Ms.58 (Book of Kells) f.34r 62cl, Ms.58 (Book of Kells) f.28v 62crb, Ms.58 (Book of Kells) f.200r 62b; TRIP: R Drury 15br, 132c.

© ULSTER MUSEUM, BELFAST: *The Festival of St Kevin at the Seven Churches, Glendalough,* Joseph Peacock 28, *The Relief of Derry,* William Sadler II 36–7, 37crb, 42cla, 249crb, 270clb.

VIKING SHIP MUSEUM, STRANDENGEN, DENMARK: watercolour by Flemming Bau 33tl.

© WATERFORD CORPORATION: 33bl, 34tl, 34clb, 35bl; © WRITERS MUSEUM, DUBLIN: 20tl.

PETER ZÖLLER: 12, 14tl, 46tc, 46cr, 47cra, 47bl, 138br, 192, 208–9, 211bl, 212, 228, 241tr, 334tl.

Front endpaper: all commissioned photography with the exception of PETER ZÖLLER: tl, tc, cb.

JACKET
Front - DK PICTURE LIBRARY, Peter Anderson crb; ROBERT HARDING PICTURE LIBRARY bla, Roy Rainford main image; TRINITY COLLEGE, DUBLIN: Courtesy of the Board of Trinity College Dublin bc. Back - COLLECTIONS, Michael St. Maur Sheil t; CORBIS, Richard Cummins b. Spine - ROBERT HARDING PICTURE LIBRARY, Roy Rainford.

All other images © DORLING KINDERSLEY. For further information see www.DKimages.com

---

### DORLING KINDERSLEY SPECIAL EDITIONS

DORLING KINDERSLEY books can be purchased in bulk quantities at discounted prices for use in promotions or as premiums. We are also able to offer special editions and personalized jackets, corporate imprints, and excerpts from all of our books, tailored specifically to meet your own needs.

To find out more, please contact: (in the United Kingdom) SPECIAL SALES, DORLING KINDERSLEY LIMITED, 80 STRAND, LONDON, WC2R 0RL;

(in the United States) SPECIAL MARKETS DEPARTMENT, DK PUBLISHING, INC., 375 HUDSON STREET, NEW YORK, NY 10014.

# Road Map of Ireland

## KEY

- ✈ Airport
- ⚓ Ferry port
- ⚓ Fast ferry port
- ⊠ Main railway station
- Motorway
- Major road
- Minor road
- Railway line

0 kilometres 30

0 miles 30